DESIGN AND ANALYSIS
A Researcher's Handbook

GEOFFREY KEPPEL

Department of Psychology
University of California, Berkeley

PRENTICE-HALL, INC., *Englewood Cliffs, New Jersey*

Library of Congress Cataloging in Publication Data

KEPPEL, GEOFFREY
  Design and analysis: a researcher's handbook.

  Bibliography: p.

  1. Social sciences—Statistical methods.
  2. Factorial experiment designs. 3. Social science research. I. Title.

  H62.K426   300'.1'82   72-6434

  ISBN   0-13-200030-X

To Sheila

PRENTICE-HALL SERIES IN EXPERIMENTAL PSYCHOLOGY
James J. Jenkins, Editor

© 1973 by
Prentice-Hall, Inc., Englewood Cliffs, N.J.

Printed in the United States of America

10   9   8   7   .

PRENTICE-HALL INTERNATIONAL, INC., *London*
PRENTICE-HALL OF AUSTRALIA, PTY. LTD., *Sydney*
PRENTICE-HALL OF CANADA, LTD., *Toronto*
PRENTICE-HALL OF INDIA PRIVATE LIMITED, *New Delhi*
PRENTICE-HALL OF JAPAN, INC., *Tokyo*

CONTENTS

Part VI

DESIGNS INTENDED TO DECREASE ERROR VARIANCE, *475*

PREFACE

This book is designed for the student who is about to engage in research. The analyses and designs covered represent a large portion of the research conducted in the experimental areas of the behavioral sciences. While current statistics texts emphasize the *statistical* side of data analysis, they pay little attention to the problems which beset the researcher. This book remedies this situation by considering the issues and the concerns which confront the investigator in his daily interaction with the design and analysis of his experiments. To this end, mathematical arguments are held to a minimum, and emphasis is placed on an *intuitive* understanding of the mathematical operations involved. The experimental implications of different analyses are stressed. In addition, simple rules for the generation of statistical analyses are presented, freeing the reader of specific formulas that appear in the text. The book provides a *working* knowledge of analysis-of-variance procedures and bridges the gap between an introductory text in statistics and the professional source book, e.g., Winer (1962, 1971).

The book is intended for students who have acquired some degree of sophistication in statistics, such as they would obtain from an undergraduate introductory course. Experience with an earlier draft of the book indicated that first-year graduate students required little or no supervision in working through it. Most important, upon finishing the book, the student should be able to conduct much of the analysis of an experiment on his own, with minimum guidance from his supervisor. The book may even be used in an undergraduate experimental psychology course—probably not the entire book, but certainly through Part III (two-factor analysis of variance) and Chapter 24. Usually I introduce these topics in my undergraduate laboratory courses. Students then are not forced to limit their thinking to the ubiquitous two-group experiment; instead, they can be given examples of trend analyses and other analytical comparisons and of multifactor experiments—experiments which are more challenging in terms of design and interpretation.

In presenting the basic statistical analyses, this book does not stress or even cover statistical theory. In my opinion, these theoretical arguments and proofs, while important for a complete and deep understanding of any given statistical analysis, are not essential for a beginning researcher. If such knowledge is deemed necessary at some later time, the student should benefit considerably from his intuitive and arithmetical familiarity with these analyses.

The book has a number of special features:

(1) It stresses the consistency of computational formulas across all types of designs by presenting a set of rules which allow the generation of analyses for designs of any degree of complexity.

(2) Chapters 6–8 present a comprehensive discussion of additional data analyses, including orthogonal comparisons, trend analyses, and multiple comparisons.

(3) Designs with repeated measures are considered in Part V, and simple computational rules are presented which accommodate designs with any number of repeated factors and any "mixture" of repeated and nonrepeated measures.

(4) The analysis of covariance is presented in Part VI for all of the designs discussed in the earlier chapters. In addition, covariance is contrasted with the "randomized block" or "treatment × level" design.

(5) Part VII brings together discussions of design sensitivity appearing in earlier chapters with a comprehensive consideration of power, determination of sample size, the role of independent replication, and estimates of the magnitude of treatment effects.

(6) A specialized notational system minimizes confusion for the beginning student and ties in directly with the general computational rules.

(7) Exercises appear at the end of most major sections, and answers are given in sufficient detail to enable the student to locate the source of an error.

The book is intended for use in a one-semester or a two-quarter course in experimental design and statistical analysis. For a one-quarter course, Parts V and VI may be omitted, while for an undergraduate course, certain specialized chapters and sections may be deleted in addition. Because students require little supervision in working through the chapters, instructors will not have to duplicate the presentation of the analyses in lecture. Instead, they will be able to supplement the various topics with a development of statistical theory or with an amplification of the problems of experimental design—topics that are often neglected when an instructor must present details of the analyses in class.

I wish to thank the following for their permission to reproduce statistical tables in this book: The Literary Executor of the late Sir. Ronald A. Fisher, F.R.S., Dr. Frank Yates, F.R.S., and Oliver and Boyd, Ltd., Edinburgh, for a table from *Statistical Tables for Biological, Agricultural and Medical Research*; American Statistical Association; *Biometrics*; *Biometrika* Trustees; and *Psychometrika*.

I am indebted to a number of individuals who have criticized earlier versions of this book. The statistical consultant, Raymond O. Collier, Jr., was extremely helpful in pointing out errors of a statistical nature. Albert Erlebacher and Leonard Marascuilo offered useful advice at various points in the writing of the text. I gratefully acknowledge the help of the following professional friends who read and evaluated all or portions of the manuscript: Phebe Cramer, Bruce Ekstrand, Ronald H. Hopkins, Geoffrey Loftus, Peter A. Ornstein, Jack Richardson, William H. Saufley, Jr., Norman E. Spear, Bonnie Z. Strand, and James F. Voss. I also wish to thank graduate students at Berkeley and at Rutgers University for their comments on the book. In particular, I should mention Dennis Bonge, Sheila Burns, Dave Feigley, Ed Gelb, Lynn Hasher, Tony Hutton, Marcia Johnson, Alan King, Steve Klein, Bill McVaugh, Pat Parsons, and Linda Warren; Ruth Hipple and Barbara Shotland also helped to uncover typographical errors in the text and in the numerical examples and exercises. The assistance of others in the production of this book should be mentioned. Don Klose and Jan Majesko helped with the proofreading. In addition, I am indebted to Ed Stanford, the Prentice-Hall representative, for his assistance, to Dr. James J. Jenkins, the editor of this series, for his reading of the entire manuscript and his useful suggestions in the preparation of the manuscript for publication, and to Shirley Stone for her skillful handling of the production details. The art work for the jacket cover was designed by Martha Klose.

The manuscript was completed at the Applied Psychology Research Unit, Medical Research Council, Cambridge, England, during my sabbatical leave from the University of California. I greatly appreciate the support provided me by the director, Dr. Donald E. Broadbent, and by members of the staff.

GEOFFREY KEPPEL

PART I

Introduction

chapter one

AN INTRODUCTION
TO THE DESIGN AND ANALYSIS
OF EXPERIMENTS

This book was written for a relatively diverse audience—one ranging from advanced undergraduates to graduate students and professional researchers. As a result, some sections of the book, especially in the earlier chapters, may safely be omitted by the "seasoned" investigator, just as some sections in the later chapters may not be relevant to the immediate needs of the undergraduate. This first chapter is intended for less experienced investigators. The more advanced readers will find here an unsophisticated rendering of the notion of experimental method, the role of theory, and the philosophy of science; consequently, it is recommended that these latter readers skip to Chapter 2, in which we begin the treatment of the analysis of single-factor experiments.

AN OVERVIEW OF THE RESEARCH ENTERPRISE

Some Basic Definitions

A science is built upon a large body of reliable facts and information. As most of you have discovered, or soon will discover, these facts are not easy to come by.

3

They are established through many hours of patient observation, recording, and analysis of the behavior generated during the observation periods. A common method for establishing facts is the *experimental method*. Although this procedure will be familiar to most of you, a few moments will be taken to describe it in its simplest form.

Basically, the experimental method consists of the contrast between two treatment conditions. The subjects in both of these conditions are treated identically, except for one feature that is different. We will refer to this difference as the *experimental treatment* or more commonly as the *independent variable*. (In this latter designation, *independent* stresses the point that the manipulation is under the control of the experimenter and *variable* indicates that the manipulation may take on two or more values.) Some aspect of the performance of the subjects in the two treatment conditions is measured and recorded after the treatment has been administered. This critical feature of the behavior of the subjects is referred to variously as the *dependent variable*, the *response variable*, or the *criterion variable*. Any difference between these two conditions that we observe on the dependent variable is called the *treatment effect* and is usually assumed to have been *caused* by the experimental treatment.

The experimental method is not the only method with which reliable scientific facts may be discovered. It is possible, for example, to show that two bits of behavior tend to appear together in nature and to use this fact to predict the occurrence of one from a knowledge of the other. Although relationships obtained by this *correlational approach* may be reasonably accurate in their predictions, e.g., the prediction of success in a job by means of scores on an aptitude test, we have not established a *causal* relationship with this procedure. For instance, to establish that cigarette smoking and the incidence of lung cancer tend to be related does not necessarily mean that smoking *caused* the cancer, as the cigarette manufacturers have maintained for years. There is always the possibility that some other factor, a chemical imbalance, say, will account for the smoking and for the occurrence of cancer as well.

The most important feature of the experimental method is that it *is* possible to infer a cause-effect relationship. That is, we can conclude that the difference we observe in the performance of the subjects in our two conditions was caused by the experimental treatment. This book will be concerned exclusively with the analysis of data obtained from such controlled experiments.

The Planning of an Experiment

CONFOUNDING OF VARIABLES   The first step in the chain of events leading to the establishment of a particular fact is, of course, to find a meaningful hypothesis to test. Assuming that this has been accomplished, we can proceed to the next step, which is the evolution of the experimental design. The word "evolution" is used to emphasize the amount of time and energy typically spent in the design of a substantial experiment. The critical requirement is that an experiment be *capable* of answering the question of interest. Although this may seem patently obvious, one is astonished at the number of studies that fail at exactly this point.

Many experiments are rendered useless through a breakdown in the chain of logic between the initial assumptions and the final conclusions. Typically this occurs when factors are introduced which vary systematically with the different experimental treatments. Suppose, for instance, that an investigator is interested in the effects of three drug dosages upon the learning of a maze by rats. He may find it convenient, perhaps, to run the three different dosage groups in the maze at different times of day, with one dosage group run in the morning, another in the afternoon, and the final dosage group in the evening. Or, he might decide to have each of the dosage groups run by a different laboratory assistant.

In the first case, the three dosage groups each learn at a different time of day. If time of day influences performance on the learning task—as it very well might, considering the diurnal cycles of rats—the investigator will be unable to reach an unambiguous conclusion concerning the influence of drug dosage on learning. There will always be the problem of determining how much of this effect is due to the different times of day and how much to the different dosages. In the second case, each assistant runs the rats in only one of the dosage groups. If the assistants treat their animals differently, and if these differences in treatment are related to the rats' performance, then again it will not be possible to attribute any differences in the behavior of the subjects in the three treatment groups to the experimental treatment. Again, how much of the treatment effect is due to the assistants and how much to the drug dosages?

We refer to either state of affairs as a *confounding* of the independent variable (drug dosage) with some other feature of the testing situation (here, time of day or laboratory assistants). There is an extensive discussion of these sorts of problems in Underwood's *Psychological Research* (1957), which you are encouraged to study early in your scientific training.

EFFICIENCY OF THE EXPERIMENT   Another point of concern in the initial planning stages of an experiment is the *efficiency* of the experimental design. Whereas a confounding can render an experiment useless as a device for obtaining scientific information, an inefficient design merely increases the "cost" of uncovering a particular fact. Efficiency may be translated in terms of money, the time needed to gather the data, the total number of subjects required in the experiment, and so on.

The question of efficiency arises in several different ways. Frequently, for instance, the number of treatment conditions in an experiment can be reduced materially without affecting the capability of the design to answer the question being tested. For example, suppose a researcher wants to determine whether or not the removal of a particular area of the brain ("X") will cause the loss of a previously learned habit. Given this interest, how can he establish that any memory loss that he may observe is entirely the result of the removal of Area X?

First, he may want to control for the possibility of *forgetting* during the inevitable delay, necessitated by the operation, between the end of learning and the memory test. To assess this possibility, the investigator might include a control group that receives no operation, but a delay between learning and the test which is identical in length to the one the operated animals receive. Then, too, he might worry that some aspect of the operation, other than the actual removal of Area X, may affect the retention of the original task. That is, any difference in the performance of the operated and the nonoperated animals may have resulted from the anesthesia, the incision, the penetration of the skull, and so on rather than from the removal of Area X. These effects could be assessed by running a group that is treated identically to the experimental group short of removal of brain tissue. Finally, it might occur to him that the sheer removal of brain tissue—any tissue—might cause a memory deficit, a possibility that he could test by introducing a group that has an identical amount of tissue removed as do the experimental animals, but from an area other than Area X.

However, all three alternative explanations of any memory deficit that may be observed for the experimental animals, i.e., forgetting, operation shock, and tissue removal, could have been ruled out simply by including only the *third* control group. This group eliminates the need for the first control group since there is a delay between learning and testing and for the second control group since the animals were also subjected to an operation. In this sense, the experimental group and a group having another portion of the brain removed represent a more efficient design than the one in which the other two control groups are included as well. This does not mean that these latter groups provide only redundant information. On the contrary, the first group could form the basis for a study of forgetting, where different groups of subjects receive different delays between learning and testing. The second group would indicate whether operations without tissue removal have any influence in this type of experiment. They are inefficient with regard to the main question, however, because the factors to which they are presumably sensitive are both "included" in the third group.

Selection of Response Measures

Suppose we have completed the first step in an experimental investigation: the development of a meaningful hypothesis and the choice of a particular experimental design. It is now up to us to work out the specific and minute details of the study and to collect the data. We will have to make a decision concerning the particular aspect of the behavior we will observe and what measures of this behavior we will adopt. Each investigator will select measures that seem to "capture" the phenomenon being studied most accurately. Often these measures will overlap to some degree with those adopted by other investigators who have worked in this research area.

Even the behavior of a subject in an apparently simple experiment may be measured in a number of ways. Suppose we decide to study the effect of different types of food incentives on learning. Hungry rats will be used as the subjects, and their task will be to learn to approach a distinctive goal box which has been consistently associated with food. Different groups of animals are given different types of food in the correct goal box. Since we are interested in learning *efficiency*, we would want to choose a dependent variable that reflects differences in time to learn. For example, we might record the total number of trials required for each animal to reach some predetermined level of performance—10 choices in a row of the correct goal box. We might also want to compare the different groups of subjects at more than one criterion of mastery. For instance, we might want to see if the groups differ early in learning, e.g., a criterion of 5 correct choices in a row, as well as late in learning. By requiring all of our subjects to attain the *highest* level of performance, 10 trials in a row, we are also able to compare the groups at levels of performance that reflect a lower degree of mastery. Alternatively, we might choose to give all animals a constant amount of training, 50 trials say, and to compare the different treatment conditions in the total number of correct choices over the 50 trials. Again, if we want, we can also look at performance at different stages of learning, e.g., the number of correct choices over the first 10 trials or over the second 10 trials. We can use any or all of these measures, just so long as all of the subjects have been tested on all 50 trials.

Up to this point, we have considered only measures which take into consideration the correctness of choice. Other aspects of behavior might be interesting to study. The *speed* with which the rat performs each trial is a commonly used measure. We could record the time for a rat to complete a given trial, from the opening of the start box to his entry into the goal box. More typically, we would probably choose to divide the total time period into subperiods and to record the duration of each subperiod separately. Common subperiods are: (1) starting latency—time to leave the start box after the starting signal is given, (2) speed within different segments of the approach to the discrimination choice point, (3) time spent at the choice point, and (4) time between the initiation of a choice and the entry into the goal box. In addition to speed measures, we could record what the animal is doing during each trial. Does he stay oriented toward the patterns at the choice point at all times? What does he do at the choice point?

It is abundantly clear that any type of behavior which is singled out for study in an experiment may be indexed by a large number of response measures. With each measure, we can ask whether or not the independent variable was effective in producing differences among the treatment conditions. There is no simple rule to govern our actual selection of response measures. Some measures may provide redundant information, i.e., give exactly the same picture of the effect of the independent variable. We would not have to include all of these measures in our experiment, since any one of them would give the same information. Some measures may be explicitly specified by a theory that is being tested in the experiment. Some measures may be easier to record or less subject to error either in measurement or in recording. In any case, it is most economical to attempt to include in any experiment a sufficient variety of response measures to ensure as complete a description as possible of the phenomenon under study.

Statistical Analysis

Finally we come to the part of the research project that will receive our primary attention in this book—the statistical analysis of the data. The statistical analysis provides a way of determining the *repeatability* of any differences observed in an experiment. If the same outcome is found when an experiment is repeated (or replicated) over and over again, we really do not need a statistical analysis to convince us that these differences are "real." A repeatable finding is really what we mean by a *fact* or a *phenomenon*. But rarely do we see replication used as a means for verifying the repeatability of findings, mainly because of the cost of conducting the same experiment more than once. Instead, we usually conduct a *single* experiment, and then we use the statistical analysis to help us to decide whether it is likely that these same differences *would* be found *if* we repeated the experiment.

Whether the repeatability of these findings is established by replication or by statistical analysis (or both), the findings will become a part of the empirical base of the research area. That is, they must eventually be incorporated into any comprehensive theory that is offered to explain the facts in the research area. If the experiment was conducted to test a theory and the outcome of the experiment is favorable to the theory, further tests of the theory (i.e., new experiments) may be proposed. If the outcome is negative, the effect upon the theory is a bit more complicated. At first glance, we might expect the theory either to be discarded, or revised, or perhaps even brought to further test. Actually, theories are much more entrenched than this suggests, and what happens is that the adequacy of the *experiment* is usually questioned instead! For example, its methodology may be reexamined; its supposed relation to the theory is reevaluated; a search for possible contaminating variables may be conducted; and so on. Only after considerable examination of the experiment is there much consideration of changing the theory. When it occurs, however, this complete sequence—hypothesis-experiment-assimilation-hypothesis—corresponds to the familiar *deductive* and *inductive* roles of science, namely, theory testing and theory building.

THE ROLE OF STATISTICS IN THE BEHAVIORAL SCIENCES

We have already discussed how statistical analysis fits into the general framework of an experimental science. The statistical literature offers a wide variety of indispensable and useful tools to aid the researcher in describing his data and in making inferences concerning the reasonableness of the hypotheses that are being tested. No investigator in the behavioral sciences can conduct his research without a thorough working knowledge of statistics. Essentially, we must study statistics with the same seriousness that we study other necessary laboratory skills.

Descriptive Function

The first major use of statistics is in the summary or description of the myriads of discrete observations which constitute the undigested results of an experiment. It is important to note that these observations represent a *coding* of the behavior we have observed. Generally, we do not attempt to obtain a minute and detailed "replay" of that behavior; instead, we accumulate numbers which represent an abstracted description of what took place in the experiment.

Given that we have measured all of the important features of the phenomenon we are studying, what do we do next? Suppose we have just completed an experiment investigating the time required to solve a problem under different motivating instructions and that someone asks us how it came out. We could quite accurately reply, "The 50 subjects in the low group took 79, 45, 81, 53, 57, 105, ..., 77, and 35 seconds to solve the problem, while the ones in the high group took 44, 25, 89, 66, 111, 59, ..., 61, and 33 seconds." Assuming that we still have an audience, just what have we communicated to this person about the outcome of the study other than a very accurate enumeration of the individual scores? It is obvious that these "raw" data must be summarized in such a way as to describe the general features of the results without undue distortion.

A useful summary of an array of data is a measure of "average" performance. By informing our questioner that the group given instructions of low motivation took on the average 55 seconds to solve the problem, while the group given instructions of high motivation took 45 seconds, we have conveyed quite quickly and meaningfully the outcome of our experiment. (We will have more to say about two common summary measures, measures of central tendency and measures of variability, later in this chapter.)

Inferential Function

Generally, we are not *primarily* interested in describing the performance of the subjects in the different treatment conditions. Our main goal is to make inferences about the behavior of subjects who have not been tested in our experiment. Rarely will we choose to test all possible subjects in an experiment, such as all laboratory rats of a particular strain, or all college students enrolled in an introductory psychology class at a particular university. Instead, we select samples from these larger groups, administer the experimental conditions to these samples, and make inferences about the nature of the population on the basis of the experimental outcome. We refer to these large groups as *populations*. Members of any population are identified by a set of rules of membership. A *sample* consists of a smaller set of observations drawn from the population. In order to be able to generalize back to the population in a strict statistical sense, we must select the subjects comprising the sample randomly from the population.

Summary descriptions calculated from the data of a sample are called *statistics*, while measures calculated from all of the observations within the population are called *parameters*. (In most cases, we will use Roman letters to designate statistics and Greek letters to designate parameters.) In order to make inferences from a sample concerning features of the population, we perform two types of operations, *estimation* and *hypothesis testing*. We will consider these two procedures briefly.

ESTIMATION   In the context of an experiment, estimation involves a prediction of what the influence of the experimental treatments would have been if all of the members of the population had been tested instead of just a sample. An estimate of a parameter may be given either as a single value (a *point estimate*) or as a range of values within which the parameter is thought to lie (an *interval estimate*).

A great deal could be said about estimation per se, e.g., the procedures by which estimates are obtained and desirable characteristics of these estimates. [Winer (1962, pp. 4–9; 1971, pp. 4–10) offers a useful summary of these points.] We will not pay much attention to estimation in this book simply because most researchers concentrate their efforts on hypothesis testing instead. Although contemporary experimentation in the behavioral sciences is couched in terms of hypothesis testing, some researchers have argued for a shift of emphasis to include interval estimation. Myers (1966, pp. 33–36) contrasts estimation and hypothesis testing and shows that the principles underlying them are in fact closely related. He also provides a sampling of articles written on this topic (p. 37). In one of these, for example, Grant (1962) argues that estimation procedures provide reasonable and useful assessments of theoretical models.

HYPOTHESIS TESTING   The chain of events which underlies hypothesis testing is summarized in Table 1-1 as a series of steps. The process begins with the formulation of a *research hypothesis* which, in turn, initiates the design of an experiment. Suppose, for example, a theory specifies that learning can occur only when a reward is given for a correct response; an experiment may be designed to test this prediction. The research hypothesis, then, concerns the

TABLE 1-1   *Steps in Hypothesis Testing*

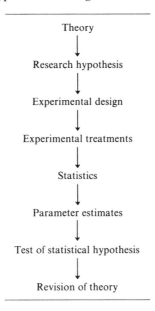

Theory

↓

Research hypothesis

↓

Experimental design

↓

Experimental treatments

↓

Statistics

↓

Parameter estimates

↓

Test of statistical hypothesis

↓

Revision of theory

testing of an implication or an expectation of a theory of behavior. Independent samples of subjects are then drawn from the same population. The different samples are subjected to different treatments and some measure of performance is recorded. At this point, we can view the subjects in the treatment conditions as representing samples drawn from different *treatment populations.* Statistics, calculated on the scores obtained from the different groups of subjects, provide us with estimates of one or more parameters for the different treatment populations.

During the planning of the experiment, the research hypothesis is translated into a *statistical hypothesis,* which is now evaluated in light of the obtained data. This evaluation, or *statistical test* as it is called, consists of the administration of a set of *decision rules,* which are also formed before the start of the experiment. Included in this step is an indication of the accuracy associated with a decision reached by an application of the rules. The results of the statistical test are then incorporated into the theory that spawned the study in the first place.

This, in brief, is hypothesis testing. We have not indicated how statistical hypotheses are arrived at, how estimates of the parameters are obtained, or how the statistical test is performed; these points will be covered in Part II. The present description, however, should give you an appreciation of the difference between estimation per se and hypothesis testing. It would be a mistake to contrast estimation and hypothesis testing too strongly. An estimate usually is obtained in order to be used, and our use, typically, will be in hypothesis testing. We can appropriately think of the two areas of statistical inference as "dovetailing" rather than as distinct alternatives.

MEASURES OF CENTRAL TENDENCY AND VARIABILITY

Most of our attention in the later chapters will be directed toward the testing of hypotheses concerned with a particular population parameter, namely, one that reflects *central tendency* or *average performance*. Fundamental to our evaluation of these hypotheses, however, is the determination of the degree to which a set of observations is *variable*. In this final section, then, we will discuss measures of central tendency and of variability and see how the relevant statistics are calculated from samples and the population parameters are estimated from these values.

Central Tendency

A measure of central tendency provides a number which reflects the average score for a set of observations. It represents the "typical" score. Although several measures of central tendency are available, the *arithmetic mean* or, simply, the *mean* is the one most frequently used. In most applications these different measures tend to produce roughly the same quantitative estimates. In some situations other measures are more appropriate, and introductory statistics texts usually discuss these situations. In this book, however, in the statistical analyses discussed in subsequent chapters, the mean is used exclusively as the measure of average performance.

In order to specify the calculations of the mean, we start with a formal listing of the basic observations. At present we will call these observations X scores, although in subsequent chapters they will take on different designations, depending upon the nature of the design in which they appear. Any score in a set of observations may be designated as X_i. The subscript i is variable, taking on successive integers, beginning with $i = 1$ and' ending with $i = s$. The total set of scores may be specified as follows:

$$X_1, X_2, X_3, \ldots, X_s.$$

The mean is designated as $\overline{X}$ and is calculated by summing the individual scores and dividing by the sample size, s, the number of scores in the array. The basic summing operation may be represented as

$$X_1 + X_2 + X_3 + \cdots + X_s.$$

The computational formula[1] for the mean is specified explicitly as

$$\overline{X} = \frac{\sum\limits_{i=1}^{s} X_i}{s}.$$ (1-1)

The summation sign, $\sum$ (called "sigma" and read as "the sum of"), indicates that the scores to the right of the sign (X_i) are to be summed. The subscript attached to X, i, refers to *any* one of the s observations; X_i is often called the *i*th observation. The notations below and above the summation sign designate, respectively, the lower and upper *limits* of the summation. That is, we are told to begin the summing operation with the first observation in the set of scores, namely, $i = 1$, and to end it with the last observation in the set, $i = s$. We frequently find Eq. (1-1) modified slightly as

$$\overline{X} = \frac{\sum\limits_{i}^{s} X_i}{s},$$ (1-1a)

with the lower limit of summation understood to begin at the value $i = 1$.

Whenever there is no ambiguity in the meaning of the mathematical operations being specified, we will use a simplified version. Consider the following simplification of the computational formula:

$$\overline{X} = \frac{\sum X}{s}.$$ (1-1b)

A summation sign without notation and a score without a subscript will tell us to sum *all* of the scores contained within the set of s such scores. The formula may be read as "the sum of the X scores, divided by s." Additional notation will be introduced only for clarification and for emphasis. This will not be necessary in this chapter.

Several things can be said about the mean. First, every score enters equally into its determination. Second, it does not matter how many cases are involved in its computation; the value always reflects the score obtained per subject or, in other words, the score for the "average" subject. Third, the mean represents the algebraic balancing point of the set of scores, ordered according to the value of X.

Five scores for two hypothetical experiments are listed in the first column of Table 1-2. An application of Eq. (1-1) to the first set of data produces

$$\overline{X}_1 = \frac{7 + 5 + 4 + 10 + 4}{5} = \frac{30}{5} = 6.0.$$

[1] Most of you will be used to seeing n or N in the denominator of Eq. (1-1) and may be surprised to see this "new" formula. Actually, the use of s represents an entire notation, which will be set forth formally in Chapter 3. For the time being, however, it may be beneficial to point out that s will serve as a mnemonic for the number of **subjects** and will be a help in the construction of formulas in subsequent chapters.

TABLE 1-2 *Numerical Example*

Scores (X)	X^2	$(X - \bar{X})$	$(X - \bar{X})^2$
		FIRST EXAMPLE	
7	49	$(7 - 6) = 1$	$(1)^2 = 1$
5	25	$(5 - 6) = -1$	$(-1)^2 = 1$
4	16	$(4 - 6) = -2$	$(-2)^2 = 4$
10	100	$(10 - 6) = 4$	$(4)^2 = 16$
4	16	$(4 - 6) = -2$	$(-2)^2 = 4$
		SECOND EXAMPLE	
10	100	$(10 - 6) = 4$	$(4)^2 = 16$
1	1	$(1 - 6) = -5$	$(-5)^2 = 25$
1	1	$(1 - 6) = -5$	$(-5)^2 = 25$
15	225	$(15 - 6) = 9$	$(9)^2 = 81$
3	9	$(3 - 6) = -3$	$(-3)^2 = 9$

For the second set of scores,

$$\bar{X}_2 = \frac{10 + 1 + 1 + 15 + 3}{5} = \frac{30}{5} = 6.0.$$

The third column of the table illustrates the property of algebraic balance. The numbers in this column represent the amount by which each score deviates from the mean. It can be seen in both cases that the deviations below the mean equal the deviations above the mean so that the total deviations sum to zero. That is,

$$(1) + (-1) + (-2) + (4) + (-2) = 0$$

and

$$(4) + (-5) + (-5) + (9) + (-3) = 0.$$

Finally, the mean of a sample provides an *unbiased* point estimate of the mean of the population from which the sample was drawn.[2] The symbol for a population mean is μ, the Greek letter "mu."

Measures of Variability

The calculations in the last section indicated that the means of the two examples are equal. The same cannot be said for the variability of the scores within each set. An inspection of the scores indicates that they differ considerably in the degree to which they diverge or deviate from the mean. The

[2] Assume that a large number of random samples is drawn from the same population and that a particular statistic, e.g., $\bar{X}$, is calculated for each of the samples. This statistic is said to provide an unbiased estimate of the parameter, μ, if the average of these statistics turns out to be the parameter.

set of numbers in the first example shows little variability, with the scores tending to cluster closely about the mean; the scores in the second example are more variable. A simple index of variability is the *range*, obtained by subtracting the smallest score from the largest score. In the first case the range is $10 - 4 = 6$; in the second it is $15 - 1 = 14$. While easy to compute, the range is not a useful statistic because it does not lend itself to problems of statistical inference. Additionally, the range is not sensitive to the other scores in the set, since only the two extreme scores enter into its determination.

SUM OF SQUARES (*SS*)   An inspection of the entries in the third column of the table indicates that the deviation scores $(X - \bar{X})$ *do* reflect the variability of the two sets of data: the deviations in the first case are smaller than the deviations in the second case. Since the sum of these deviation scores is always zero, however, the sum cannot provide an index of the variability. On the other hand, by *squaring* the deviations we can avoid this difficulty. That is, the *sum of the squared deviations about the mean*, abbreviated *SS*, reflects the variability of a set of scores and equals zero *only* when all of the scores have the same value, i.e., $X_1 = X_2 = \cdots = X_s = \bar{X}$. In all other situations the *SS* is greater than zero.

The defining formula for the *SS* is a direct translation of its verbal description. That is,

$$SS = \sum (X - \bar{X})^2. \tag{1-2}$$

This formula tells us to *subtract* the mean from each observation, to *square* each of these deviations, and then to *sum* all of the squared deviations. In words, the *SS* is defined as the sum of the squared deviations of the X scores about the mean.

Examples of these calculations are given in Table 1-2. The deviation scores are calculated in the third column and are squared in the fourth column. In the first case,

$$SS_1 = (7 - 6)^2 + (5 - 6)^2 + (4 - 6)^2 + (10 - 6)^2 + (4 - 6)^2$$
$$= (1)^2 + (-1)^2 + (-2)^2 + (4)^2 + (-2)^2$$
$$= 1 + 1 + 4 + 16 + 4 = 26,$$

and in the second case,

$$SS_2 = (10 - 6)^2 + (1 - 6)^2 + (1 - 6)^2 + (15 - 6)^2 + (3 - 6)^2$$
$$= (4)^2 + (-5)^2 + (-5)^2 + (9)^2 + (-3)^2$$
$$= 16 + 25 + 25 + 81 + 9 = 156.$$

Although the defining formula for the *SS* makes intuitive sense, it requires a considerable amount of computational work. For the actual calculations we turn to a *computational formula*, which reduces the number of necessary calculations but loses some of the intuitive meaning. Specifically,

$$SS = \sum X^2 - \frac{(\sum X)^2}{s}.$$ (1-3)

The first term on the right tells us to square each of the X scores first and then add them up. [Some students find it clearer initially to place parentheses around X to make the different steps explicit, i.e., $\sum (X)^2$.] The second term tells us to sum the X scores *first*, to square the total next, and finally to divide the squared total by the number of observations (s).

As an illustration of these operations, we will again use the data provided in Table 1-2. For the first example,

$$SS_1 = [(7)^2 + (5)^2 + (4)^2 + (10)^2 + (4)^2] - \frac{(7 + 5 + 4 + 10 + 4)^2}{5}$$

$$= (49 + 25 + 16 + 100 + 16) - \frac{(30)^2}{5}$$

$$= 206 - \frac{900}{5} = 206 - 180 = 26,$$

and for the second example,

$$SS_2 = [(10)^2 + (1)^2 + (1)^2 + (15)^2 + (3)^2] - \frac{(10 + 1 + 1 + 15 + 3)^2}{5}$$

$$= (100 + 1 + 1 + 225 + 9) - \frac{(30)^2}{5}$$

$$= 336 - \frac{900}{5} = 336 - 180 = 156.$$

These two sums of squares are identical to the ones we obtained previously with the defining formula, Eq. (1-2).

Most of you will be convinced by this example of the equivalence of the defining and computational formulas for the SS.[3] One point that may not be obvious, however, is the greater *efficiency* of the computational formula, Eq. (1-3), relative to the defining formula, Eq. (1-2). Both formulas require the sum of the X scores, either for the calculation of the mean in the defining formula or for substitution in the second term of the computational formula. Both equations require the squaring and summing of a set of s numbers; for the defining formula these consist of the deviation scores $(X - \overline{X})$, while for the computational formula they are the individual scores (X). At this point the

---

[3] The algebraic proof of the equivalence of the two formulas is presented in most introductory statistics texts.

computational effort is the same. (Actually, a division and a subtraction remain before the calculations specified by the computational formula are complete.) In addition to these operations, however, the defining formula requires the calculation of the deviation scores. This extra step increases the mathematical operations by approximately one-third and also introduces the possibility of rounding errors. Moreover, with most electric calculators, the computational formula is even more efficient, since the sum of X and of X^2 can be accomplished in the same operation.

VARIANCE   As a measure of variability, the SS has the limitation that it is still a *sum* and as such is not independent of sample size (s). The *variance* overcomes this problem by making an adjustment for the number of scores entering into the calculation of the SS. There are two definitions of the variance. One of these, VAR, is used for purely *descriptive* purposes and is simply the variance of a set of numbers. The formula for this descriptive statistic is reasonable,

$$VAR = \frac{SS}{s},\tag{1-4}$$

since the sum of squares is divided by the number of deviations (s). The VAR can be thought of as the arithmetic mean of the SS—an average sum of squares.

We will find little use for the VAR, simply because our interest extends beyond a mere description of our data. We will be interested instead in the *estimation* of population parameters, and the VAR does not provide an *unbiased* estimate of the population variance (σ^2). (See footnote 2.)

The second definition of a variance serves this inferential function of providing an unbiased point estimate of σ^2. The formula for this estimator is given by

$$\hat{\sigma}^2 = \frac{SS}{s - 1}.\tag{1-5}$$

(The caret above $\hat{\sigma}^2$ indicates that we are dealing with a population estimate.) The only change in the calculations is the division of the SS by a slightly smaller number ($s - 1$). [Hays (1963, pp. 206–208) offers a detailed discussion justifying the substitution of ($s - 1$) for s in the divisor.] It is the definition of the variance given in Eq. (1-5) with which we will be dealing throughout the remainder of the book.

The new divisor has a special name, *degrees of freedom* or *df*. Restated, Eq. (1-5) becomes

$$\hat{\sigma}^2 = \frac{SS}{df},\tag{1-5a}$$

where $df = s - 1$. We can think of $\hat{\sigma}^2$ as an average sum of squares also, but in this case, the average sum of squares *per degree of freedom*. (The concept of *df* will be discussed in Chapter 4.)

Summary

We have discussed important features of the mean and the variance, measures that are used to describe critical characteristics of a set of scores. When these measures are based on the observations taken from different treatment conditions, we can use these statistics to estimate parameters of the corresponding treatment populations. A number of symbols introduced to designate these different quantities are summarized in Table 1-3.

TABLE 1-3   *Symbols for Means and Variances*

	Measure	
Function of Measure	Mean	Variance
Statistic	$\overline{X}$	VAR
Parameter	μ	σ^2
Parameter estimate	$\hat{\mu}$	$\hat{\sigma}^2$

To anticipate subsequent discussions, we will be interested in the effect of different treatments on the *mean* or average performance. As a consequence, our hypotheses will be couched in terms of the equality or inequality of the means of different treatment populations. Occasionally, we will be interested in testing hypotheses about the *variances* of the different treatment populations, asking whether or not the treatments differentially affected the variability of the subjects in the different conditions. We will consider both types of questions in the next section.

PART II

Single-Factor Experiments

A two-group experiment was used in Chapter 1 to illustrate the experimental method. In the not too-distant past, this type of experiment represented the *modal* design in the behavioral sciences. Today, in its place, we see experiments in which a single independent variable is represented by more than two different treatments, and we find many cases in which two or more independent variables are manipulated concurrently in the same experiment.

The major reason for this increase in the complexity of the research is that the basic two-group design can only indicate the presence or the absence of treatment effects, while an experiment with more than two treatment conditions provides for a more *detailed* description of the relationship between variations in the independent variable and changes in behavior. Additionally, as our knowledge increases and more facts are established, our theoretical explanations of this knowledge become increasingly complicated and more elaborate designs

Numerical exercises illustrating arithmetic operations discussed in this section may be found at the end of Part II (pp. 164–166).

are needed to test them. That is, in order to identify the mechanisms and processes that lie behind any given phenomenon, an experimenter frequently must increase the number of treatments and the number of independent variables that he includes in a single experiment.

In Part II we will consider the analysis of experiments in which there is a single classification of the treatment conditions. By this is meant that the different treatments are classified only one way, either on the basis of *qualitative* differences or on the basis of *quantitative* differences among the treatment conditions. Qualitative differences would be involved, for example, in a comparison of the effectiveness of different methods of instruction, or of the learning of different types of material, or of the influence of different types of drugs. Our use of the word "type" emphasizes that it is the *nature* of the different treatments that is being manipulated.

Quantitative variables, on the other hand, vary in *amount*—various amounts of the independent variable are administered to the different groups of subjects. Variations in the dosage levels of a single drug, or in the measured difficulty of prose passages, or in the hours of food deprivation are all examples of quantitative independent variables.

We will refer to either type of manipulation, whether it is qualitative or quantitative, as a *factor*. The terms *independent variable* and *factor* are synonyms. We will often refer to the specific treatment conditions represented in an experiment as the *levels* of a factor. In this book, we will also use the terms *levels, treatments,* and *treatment levels* interchangeably.

The designs considered in this section as well as in Parts III and IV are assumed to be *completely randomized.*[1] This means that subjects are assigned randomly to the treatment conditions and that they provide a single score on the dependent variable for the analysis; i.e., each subject serves in only one treatment condition. (We will discuss the concept of randomization shortly.) Designs in which subjects serve in more than one treatment condition are considered in Part V.

The general purpose of the single-factor experiment may be illustrated by means of a simple example. Suppose we wanted to compare the relative effectiveness of ten different methods of teaching foreign language in elementary school and that we had no particular reason to expect any one method to be better than any other. How might we analyze the results of this experiment? One procedure would be to treat each of the possible two-group comparisons as a different *two-group experiment.* That is, we would compare method 1 versus methods 2, 3, . . . , 9, and 10; method 2 versus methods 3, 4, . . . , 9, and 10; . . . ; method 8 versus methods 9 and 10; and, finally, method 9 versus method 10. There are 45 of these two-group comparisons. Obviously, this sort of analysis would require a considerable amount of calculation. Moreover, we should be concerned with the fact that we are using the same sets of data over and over

---

[1] We will also be assuming the so-called *fixed-effects model,* which is appropriate for most of the research in the behavioral sciences. This and other models are discussed in Chapter 16.

again to make these comparisons. (Actually, we are using each group a total of nine times.) We cannot think of these comparisons as constituting 45 *independent* experiments; if one group is distorted for some reason or other, this distortion will be present in all nine of the comparisons in which it enters.

The single-factor analysis of variance allows us to consider all of the treatments in a *single* comparison. Without going into the details, this analysis sets in *perspective* any interpretations we may want to make concerning the differences we have observed. More specifically, the analysis will tell us whether or not it will be worthwhile to conduct any additional analyses comparing specific treatment groups.

We shall first consider the logic behind the analysis of variance, and then we shall worry about translating these intuitive notions into mathematical expressions and actual numbers.

chapter two

THE LOGIC OF
HYPOTHESIS TESTING

In the ideal experiment, we can treat the subjects in the different conditions exactly alike in every respect except for the necessary variation of the independent variable. Unfortunately, this ideal experiment is never performed in real life. That is, it is virtually impossible to conduct an experiment where the *only* difference among treatment groups is the experimental manipulation. Nonetheless, we are still able to conduct experiments and to draw meaningful conclusions from them.

Let us see how this is accomplished. First, certain features can in fact be held constant across the levels of the experiment. All of the testing can be done in the same experimental room, by the same experimenter, and with the same equipment and testing procedures. Second, control of other features of the experiment, though *not* absolute, is sufficiently close to be considered essentially constant. Consider, for example, the mechanical devices that are used to hold various features of the environment constant. A thermostat, for instance, does not achieve an absolute control of the temperature at some fixed value, but it *reduces* the variation of the room temperature. An uncontrolled room would be subjected to a wider range of temperatures during the course of an experiment than a controlled room, but a variation will still be present. This variation may be sufficiently small to allow us to view the temperature as constant. Even with these features controlled, however, many variables remain uncontrolled that might influence the behavior we are studying.

We have not mentioned yet a major source of uncontrolled variability present in any experiment, namely, the differences in performance among subjects. One obvious way to hold subject differences constant is to use the *same* subject in each treatment condition—a sort of biological analogue of absolute physical control. Unfortunately, even the same subject is not the same person each time he is tested. Moreover, there are potentially serious carry-over effects from one treatment to another, owing to the successive administration of the different treatments to the same subjects. To avoid this problem, we could try to *match* sets of subjects on important characteristics and then assign one member of each matched set to a different treatment, but matching would never be exact. Thus, neither attempt to control for individual differences among subjects guarantees that the treatment groups will contain subjects of the same average ability.

CONTROL BY RANDOMIZATION

This leads us to a third method, one which represents control of a different sort. Specifically, it consists of an elimination of *systematic* differences among the treatment conditions by means of *randomization*. Consider again the control of room temperature. What might we do about controlling the temperature if the room were *not* equipped with a thermostat? We could try to match sets of subjects arriving at different times for the experiment, but for whom the temperature of the room is the same, and then run one of the subjects in one group, one in another group, and so on. But this is an unrealistic and cumbersome procedure. Suppose, instead, that we decide which of the different treatments a subject will receive by some random means at the time of his arrival for the experiment and that we continue to use this method until we have obtained the number of subjects we planned to run in each of the treatment conditions. What happens to the different room temperatures in this case? In a sense, the different temperatures of the experimental room have an equally likely "chance" at the start of each testing session of being assigned to *any one of the treatment levels*. If we follow this procedure with enough subjects, statistical theory tells us that the *average* room temperatures for the treatment groups will be equal. Under these circumstances, then, we will have effected a control of room temperature.

That is fine for temperature, but what about other features of the testing environment which also change from session to session? It may not be immediately apparent, but once we have controlled *one* environmental feature by randomization, we have controlled *all* other environmental differences as well. Suppose we list some of the characteristics of the testing session present during the very first session in the experiment. The room will be at a certain temperature; there will be a certain humidity; the room illumination will be at a particular level; the noise from the outside filtering into the room will be of a certain intensity; the experiment will be given at a particular time of day, on a particular day, and by a particular experimenter; and so on.

When the experimenter is about to begin, he chooses a particular experimental treatment for the first subject in some random fashion. What this means is that at this point each of the treatment conditions has an equally likely chance of being the one chosen for that particular experimental session. The implication is that the total composite of features which happens to be present at that time has an equally likely chance of being "assigned" to each of the experimental treatments. We come next to the second experimental session. The total composite of features present at the second session will be different than the one present at the first. The room will be at a different temperature, the noise level may not be the same, the session will be at a different time of day, and so on. Before the start of the session, the experimenter again chooses randomly which treatment he will present. As with the first session, the composite of features present this time have an equally likely chance of being associated with each of the treatments.

Suppose this argument is continued until all of the subjects have been assigned to treatment conditions in the experiment. Then each and every feature of the experimental situation, which varies from session to session, has been assigned randomly to the different treatment conditions. There was no systematic bias leading to the running of one condition at the same time of day or only in warm rooms or only when the lights were bright, or whatever. The assignment of the testing sessions to the experimental conditions in a random fashion eliminates from the experiment the possibility of systematic biases involving any of these factors.

Subject differences are also "controlled" by randomization. The subjects who are chosen to participate in an experiment will differ widely on a whole host of characteristics. Some of these will affect the behavior being studied and, hence, must be controlled. Suppose we could give each of our subjects a number which represents his general ability to perform on the sort of task being studied. This number will be a composite score, reflecting the influence of his intelligence, his emotionality, his attitude, his background and training, and so on. Now suppose that we assign the subjects to the different treatment conditions randomly. Subjects with high composite scores are just as likely to be assigned to one of the treatments as to any of the others. The same is true for subjects with low and with medium composite scores. Thus, random assignment of subjects to treatments will ensure in the long run that there will be an equivalence of subjects across the different treatments.

Suppose we take one final step in this argument. Somehow we select the first subject who will be run in the experiment; he may be the first subject who shows up as a volunteer for the experiment, or he may be the rat in the first cage that we come to. When we randomly assign this subject to one of the treatment conditions, we are essentially assigning *jointly* the subject *and* the environmental factors. By assigning him randomly to the treatment conditions, then, we are assigning randomly *all* of the ability and environmental factors as well—whatever the combination of ability and environmental factors may be for this subject. Therefore, randomization of subjects in the assignment to conditions is an indispensable method of guaranteeing that in the long run the treatment conditions will be matched on all environmental factors and subject abilities.

A serious problem presented by this argument has undoubtedly occurred to you. Specifically, we *never* run a sufficiently large number of subjects in our experiment to qualify for the statistician's definition of the "long run." In practice, we are operating in the "short run," meaning that we have no guarantee that our groups will be equivalent with regard to differences in environmental features or to differences in the abilities of subjects. We will return to this problem in a moment.

Methods of Randomization

Because of the fundamental importance of randomization to the design and analysis of experiments, we will consider in detail methods by which randomization may be accomplished. Whatever method we use, we must be able to argue that *all* factors not involved in the manipulation of the independent variable have been neutralized by randomization. As an example, suppose we conduct an experiment with three treatment conditions and we plan to run a total of 30 subjects in the experiment. For the first subject who shows up, we will determine which treatment he receives by some random process.[1] The treatment given to the second subject is determined in the same manner. This procedure is followed until all 30 subjects have served in the experiment. Note that *each subject* is randomly assigned to a treatment and *each testing session* is randomly assigned to a treatment. The critical feature of the random assignment, then, is that each subject-session combination is *equally likely* to be

---

[1] If there were only two treatment conditions, the treatment selected could be determined by the flip of a coin. If more than two conditions are included in the experiment, we usually give each condition a different number and then refer to tables of random numbers which provide a source of random sequences of digits. Such tables may be found in many statistics texts and in experimental psychology texts. There are also books of random numbers available, such as Moses and Oakford (1963) and a book published by the RAND Corporation (1955). The tables published in Moses and Oakford are especially useful, since they include random permutations of number sets of different sizes. For example, if there are 30 things that we want to randomize, it is far easier to use a random ordering of the numbers 1–50, say, and to select from that ordering the numbers 1–30, than it is to work through a random sequence of digits, two at a time, searching for the first occurrence of each one of these numbers.

assigned to any one of the three treatments. In other words, each of the treatment conditions is equally likely to be assigned to a given subject and to whatever other uncontrolled factors might be present during that period of testing.

In actual practice, we would probably place a *restriction* on this random procedure of assigning treatments to subjects in order to ensure an *equal number* of subjects at each treatment level. (Reasons for this decision are considered in Chapter 5.) When human subjects are appearing in the laboratory at their own convenience, i.e., at a time that they choose, a typical approach is to make the random assignments so that any given treatment selected is not run again until all of the other treatments are represented *once*. In effect, this is a procedure of *sampling without replacement*. In the example, we would decide randomly which of the three treatments to administer to the first subject. For the second subject, we would randomly select the treatment from the two remaining treatments. For the third subject, we must administer the final remaining treatment, since there are only three treatments in the experiment. This completes a *block* of randomized treatments. The treatment given to the fourth subject is decided by selecting randomly from the *total pool* of treatments, i.e., three; the treatment given to the fifth subject is decided by selecting randomly from the remaining two treatments; and so on.

It is generally advisable to work with the smallest possible block, just as we did in the last paragraph. There is a good reason for following such a procedure. We can think of two general classes of variables which must be controlled in any experiment: those which really do fluctuate randomly from session to session and those which do not. We do not have to worry about the first class of variables—even if we run all the subjects in one treatment first and all the subjects in another treatment second, the particular values of these variables at each testing session by definition occur randomly. Thus, we turn to randomization to control the second class of variables, variables which do not fluctuate haphazardly.

We are usually unable to specify ahead of time exactly what the cycles of fluctuation will be; however, we merely assume that they will be present. For example, subjects volunteering for an experiment do not represent a random flow of participants. There are undoubtedly different reasons why a subject volunteers early in the school term rather than late, and these reasons may reflect differences in abilities. The first subjects may be overly anxious or curious or smarter—who knows? The point is that we cannot assume that the flow of volunteers is random. Nor is the fluctuation of room temperature or of time of day or of noise level outside the testing room random. Randomizing in small blocks "helps" this control by ensuring that a block of three subjects, say, representing each treatment once, will not be placed in a room that is too different in temperature. Or, three subjects appearing one after the other are more likely to have the same reason for volunteering at that time than would three subjects who did not.

It is not sufficient, however, just to introduce some sort of randomization in the testing order. To make the randomization "work," we must choose a method which guarantees that features of the experimental situation and differences in the abilities of the subjects are not allowed to exert a *systematic* influence in the experiment. Any factor which does not vary randomly in its "natural state" must be subjected to a process of *neutralization*, consisting in essence of the superimposition of a random process upon the assignment of testing sessions and subjects to the treatment conditions. That is, variables which fluctuate in a systematic fashion during the course of the experiment are transformed into variables which now fluctuate *unsystematically* with respect to their association with the treatment conditions.

Random Assignment Versus Random Sampling

We should say a few words about the distinction between the *random assignment* of subjects to conditions and the *random sampling* of subjects from a known population.

Random sampling requires the specification of a population of subjects and then the assurance that each member of the population has an equally likely chance of being selected for the experiment. If these conditions are met, we will be able to *generalize* the results of our experiment to the population. It should be noted that even if we are able to obtain our subjects by randomly sampling from a population, we will still have to turn to randomization procedures in the assignment of treatments to subjects and to testing sessions. That is, even randomly selected subjects will come to the experiment one at a time and then be given one of the treatment conditions. Who receives which treatment must be determined by chance; otherwise, a systematic bias may result, and this bias will be damaging to any experiment whether the subjects are selected randomly from a population or not.

What about random sampling? Public opinion polls, voter preference polls, marketing research, and television ratings all depend upon random sampling from a known population. Any findings from the sample are then extended to the population. Only rarely will we see random sampling in an experiment, however. And when we do, the population from which the sample was drawn may be so restricted as to be uninteresting in itself, e.g., the rats in a laboratory animal colony, the students at a university taking a course in introductory psychology, or third-grade children in a particular school system. Almost invariably, our subjects are selected out of *convenience*, rather than at random. The failure to sample randomly from a known population means that we are not justified *statistically* in extending our results beyond the bounds of the experiment itself.

Since most researchers accept this "myopic" view of the results of an experiment, how can we ever discover results that *are* generalizable to a meaningful population of organisms? One answer is that past research in a number of laboratories with subjects chosen from different sources (e.g., different breeding stocks, different suppliers of laboratory animals, and human subjects from different schools in different sections of the country) have shown that these differences are relatively unimportant in the study of various phenomena. Knowing this, an investigator working in this field may feel safe in generalizing his results beyond the single experiment.

The distinction, then, is between a *statistical* generalization, which depends upon random sampling, and a *nonstatistical* generalization, which depends upon knowledge of a particular research area. Cornfield and Tukey (1956) make this point quite clear: "In almost any practical situation where analytical statistics is applied, the inference from the observations to the real conclusion has two parts, only the first of which is statistical. A genetic experiment on *Drosophila* will usually involve flies of a certain race of a certain species. The statistically based conclusions cannot extend beyond this race, yet the geneticist will usually, and often wisely, extend the conclusion to (a) the whole species, (b) all *Drosophila*, or (c) a larger group of insects. This wider extension may be implicit or explicit, but it is almost always present" (pp. 912–913).

In short, the generalizability of a given set of results is influenced by statistical considerations, such as the question of random sampling. For most experimenters, however, the extension of a set of findings to a broader class of subjects (or conditions for that matter) is dictated primarily by subject-matter considerations, i.e., what is known in a particular field of research about the *appropriateness* of certain generalizations and the "length" of these generalizations. The availability of this information will depend upon the state of development of the research area and the extent to which extrapolations beyond the particular subjects tested have been successful in the past.

AN INDEX FOR THE EVALUATION
OF TREATMENT EFFECTS

We now return to our earlier problem: What can we do about the fact that control by randomization will not be perfect when we are assigning relatively small numbers of subjects to our treatment conditions? Expectations from statistical theory are based upon extremely large sample sizes, much larger than those used in any experiment we will ever analyze. Since we are dealing with the "short run," where we have no assurance that our treatment groups are in fact matched on all relevant factors except the experimental treatments, how can we determine whether the differences we observe in the experiment are due either to the experimental treatments or to these chance differences or to both?

Let us consider, in general terms, a statistical solution to this disturbing problem.

Statistical Hypotheses

Hypothesis testing was described briefly in Chapter 1. At that time, we distinguished between a *research* or *scientific hypothesis* and a *statistical hypothesis*. The former is a fairly general statement about the assumed nature of the world which gets translated into an experiment. (Typically, but not always, a research hypothesis asserts that the treatments *will* produce an effect. If it did not, we would probably not have performed the experiment in the first place!) The latter is a set of precise hypotheses about the parameters of the different treatment populations. Two statistical hypotheses are usually stated, and these are mutually exclusive or incompatible statements about the treatment parameters.

The statistical hypothesis which will be *tested* is called the *null hypothesis*, often symbolized as H_0.[2] The function of the null hypothesis is to specify the values of a particular parameter (the mean, for example) in the different treatment populations. The null hypothesis typically chosen gives the *same* value to the different populations—that is,

$$H_0: \mu_1 = \mu_2 = \mu_3 = \cdots = \mu_i.$$

This is tantamount to saying that *no* treatment effects are present in the population. If the parameter estimates obtained from the treatment groups are too deviant from those specified by the null hypothesis, H_0 is rejected in favor of the other statistical hypothesis, called the *alternative hypothesis*, H_1. The alternative hypothesis specifies values for the parameter which are *incompatible* with the null hypothesis. Usually, the alternative hypothesis states simply that the values of the parameter in the different treatment populations are *not* equal. Specifically,

$$H_1: \text{all } \mu_i\text{'s not equal.}$$

Stated even more simply, the alternative hypothesis becomes

$$H_1: \text{not } H_0.$$

A decision to reject H_0 implies an acceptance of H_1, which, in essence, constitutes support of our original *research* hypothesis. On the other hand, if the parameter estimates are reasonably close to those specified by the null hypothesis, H_0 is not rejected. This latter decision can be thought of as a failure of the experiment to support the research hypothesis. We will see in a later discussion that a decision to reject or not reject the null hypothesis is not all that simple. Depending upon the true state of the world, i.e., the equality or inequality of the actual population means, we can make an error of inference with *either* decision, rejection or nonrejection. (More will be said about these errors later.)

---

[2] Authors do not agree in these abbreviations, but the difference is minor and the reader should have no trouble in translating a different designation.

Experimental Error

At the crux of the problem is the fact that we can always attribute some portion of the differences, which we observe among treatment means, to chance factors. All uncontrolled sources of variability in our experiment, which can affect the scores on the response measure, are considered contributors to *experimental error*. As we have noted, the most important uncontrolled source of variability in the behavioral sciences is that due to individual differences. We have also mentioned variations in the various features of the testing environment. Another source of experimental error is what may be called measurement error. A misreading of a dial, a misjudgment that a particular type of behavior had occurred, the variability in reaction time of an experimenter timing a given bit of behavior, and an error in transposing observations recorded in the laboratory to summary worksheets used in performing the statistical analyses are all included in this classification. While not obvious, a given experimental treatment is not exactly the same for each subject serving in that treatment condition; the experimental apparatus cannot be counted on to administer the same treatment for successive subjects. An experimenter cannot construct an identical testing environment (the reading of instructions, the experimenter-subject interaction, and so on) for all subjects in any treatment group. We describe all these different components of experimental error as *unsystematic*, stressing the fact that their influence is *independent* of the treatment effects.

Estimates of Experimental Error

Suppose we were able to estimate the extent to which the differences we observe among the group means are due to experimental error. We would then be in a position to begin to consider the evaluation of the hypothesis that the means of the treatment populations are equal. Consider the scores of subjects in any one of the treatment conditions. We certainly do not expect these scores to be equal. In the *ideal* experiment they would be, with each score reflecting only the effect of the experimental treatment. In an *actual* experiment, of course, all of the sources of uncontrolled variability will also contribute to a subject's score, resulting in a difference in performance for subjects who are administered the same treatment conditions. The variability of subjects treated alike, i.e., within the same treatment level, provides an estimate of experimental error. By the same argument, the variability of subjects within each of the other treatment levels also offers estimates of experimental error. If we assume that experimental error is the same for the different treatment conditions, we can obtain a more stable estimate of this quantity by pooling and averaging these separate estimates.

Assume that we have drawn random samples from a population of subjects, administered the different treatments, recorded the performance of the subjects, and calculated the means of the treatment groups. Further, assume for the moment that the null hypothesis is *true*—that the population means associated with the treatment conditions are *equal.* Would we expect the *sample* means, the means calculated in the experiment, to be equal? Certainly not. From our discussion of the use of randomization to "control" unwanted factors in our experiment, it should be clear that the means will rarely be equal. If the sample means are not equal, the only reasonable explanation that we can offer for these differences is the operation of experimental error. All of the sources of unsystematic variability, which contribute to the differences among subjects within a given treatment condition, will also be operating to produce differences among the sample means.

Take, for instance, error that results from the random assignment of subjects to treatments. If the procedure is truly random, each subject will have an equal chance of being assigned to any one of the different treatments. But this in no way *guarantees* that the average ability of subjects assigned to these groups is equal. Similarly, for the other contributors to experimental error, there is no reason to expect these uncontrolled sources of error to balance out perfectly across the treatment conditions. In short, then, under these circumstances —an experiment conducted when the null hypothesis is true—differences among the sample means will also reflect the operation of experimental error.

Estimate of Treatment Effects

So far in this discussion we have considered only the case in which the null hypothesis is true. Certainly we hope that we will discover at least a few situations in which the null hypothesis is *false!* Under these circumstances, there are real differences among the means of the treatment populations. Assuming that the subjects in each treatment group are drawn randomly from corresponding treatment populations, the means of the different groups in the experiment should reflect the differences in the population means. The mere fact that the null hypothesis is false does *not* imply that experimental error has vanished, however. Not at all. We will still have differences among subjects who were treated alike within each treatment group, which reflects experimental error, and the influence of experimental error will still be reflected in some of the variation among the group means. The only change is that there is now an additional component contributing to the differences among the means, a systematic component as opposed to an unsystematic one, namely, *treatment effects.*

Thus, differences among treatment means may reflect *two different quantities*: When the population means are equal, the differences among the group means will reflect the operation of experimental error alone, but when the population means are not equal, the differences among the group means will reflect the operation of an unsystematic component and a systematic component, i.e., experimental error and treatment effects, respectively.

EVALUATION OF THE NULL HYPOTHESIS

We have seen that when the null hypothesis is true, we will have two estimates of experimental error available from the experiment. If we form a *ratio* of these two estimates, we will find that we have produced a useful statistic. More specifically, consider the following ratio:

$$\frac{\text{differences among treatment means}}{\text{differences among subjects treated alike}}.$$

From our discussion, we can think of this ratio as contrasting an estimate of experimental error, which is based upon between-group differences, with an estimate of experimental error, which is based upon pooled within-group differences. That is, we have

$$\frac{\text{experimental error}}{\text{experimental error}}.$$

If we were to repeat this experiment a large number of times on new samples of subjects drawn from the same population, we would expect to find an average value of this ratio of approximately 1.0.

Consider now the same ratio when the null hypothesis is *false*. Under these circumstances, there is an additional component in the numerator, one which reflects the treatment effects. Explicitly, the ratio becomes

$$\frac{(\text{treatment effects}) + (\text{experimental error})}{\text{experimental error}}.$$

Given this situation, if we were to repeat the experiment a large number of times, we would expect to find an average value of this ratio that is *greater* than 1.0.

You can see, then, that the average value of this ratio, obtained from a large number of replications of the experiment, depends upon the values of the population means. If H_0 is true (i.e., the means are equal), the average value will approximate 1.0; while if H_1 is true (i.e., the means are not equal), the average value will approximate a number greater than 1.0. A problem remains, however, since in any one experiment, it is always possible to obtain a value that is *greater* than 1.0 when H_0 is *true* and one that is *equal* or *less* than 1.0 when H_1 is *true*! Thus, merely checking to see whether or not the ratio is greater than 1.0 does not tell us which statistical hypothesis is correct.

What we will do about this is to make a decision concerning the acceptability of the null hypothesis which is based upon a consideration of the chance probability associated with the ratio we actually found in the experiment. If the probability of obtaining by chance a ratio of this size or larger is reasonably low, we will reject the null hypothesis. On the other hand, if this probability is high, we will not reject, or, in essence, we will accept the null hypothesis. (We will have more to say about the *decision rules* we follow in making this decision in Chapter 4.)

SUMMARY

We have looked at some of the logic underlying the process of hypothesis testing. It is important for you to understand what is going on in general terms, without an elaboration of formulas and calculations—this elaboration will come soon enough! By way of summary, we can describe hypothesis testing in designs where each subject serves in only one treatment condition as consisting of a contrast between two sets of differences. One of these sets is obtained from a comparison involving differences among the treatment means; these differences are often referred to as *external* or *between-group* differences. The other set is obtained from a comparison involving differences among subjects receiving the same treatment within a treatment group; these differences are called *internal* or *within-group* differences. It was argued that the between-group differences are the result of the combined effects of the experimental treatment and of experimental error, while the within-group differences represent the influence of experimental error alone. We saw that the comparison ratio,

$$\frac{\text{between-group differences}}{\text{within-group differences}},$$

provides a numerical index which is "sensitive" to the presence of treatment effects in the population. That is, with no treatment effects, the long-run expectation is that the ratio will approximate 1.0, since the treatment effects will be zero and we will be dividing one estimate of experimental error by the other. On the other hand, whenever there are treatment effects, the expectation is that the ratio will be greater than 1.0.

The statistical hypothesis we test, the null hypothesis, specifies the *absence* of treatment effects in the population. With the help of statistical tables and a set of decision rules, neither of which we have described yet, we can decide whether or not it is reasonable to reject the null hypothesis. If we reject the null hypothesis, we accept the alternative statistical hypothesis, which specifies the presence of treatment effects in the population. If we fail to reject the null hypothesis, essentially we conclude that the independent variable produced no systematic differences in this experiment. In the next chapter we will consider the details of this basic statistical analysis.

chapter three

PARTITIONING THE TOTAL
SUM OF SQUARES

In this chapter and the next, we will see the abstract notions of between-group and within-group variability become concrete arithmetic operations. This chapter will show how information reflecting these two sources of variability can be extracted from scores produced in single-factor experiments. Chapter 4 then indicates how this information is used to provide a test of the null hypothesis.

GEOMETRIC REPRESENTATION OF THE
COMPONENT DEVIATION SCORES

Suppose we have conducted an experiment with school children in which we compared the relative difficulty of three kinds of conceptual tasks. We will refer to our independent variable, types of tasks, as *factor A* and to the three levels of factor A (the three different conceptual tasks) as levels a_1, a_2, and a_3.

Our subjects were drawn from a pool of school children in the fourth and fifth grades of a large school, and we assigned randomly $s = 100$ different subjects to each of the levels of factor A. The response measure was the time required to solve the different conceptual tasks.

Our first step in the analysis would be to compute the means for the three sets of scores and to compare them. As explained previously, we cannot conclude that any differences among the group means represent the "real" effects of the different experimental treatments: the differences may have resulted from experimental error, the short-term siding of uncontrolled sources of variability with one treatment condition or another. We saw that the solution to this problem is to compare the differences among the group means against the differences obtained from subjects within each of the individual groups. Let us see how this is accomplished.

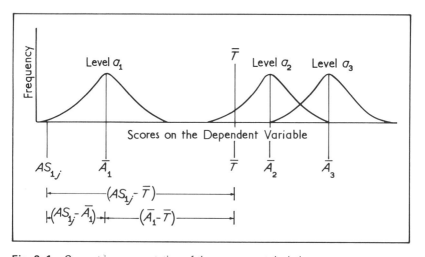

Fig. 3-1   Geometric representation of the component deviation scores.

The frequency distributions of the three sets of scores from this hypothetical experiment are presented in Fig. 3-1. Values of the response measure are indicated on the baseline, and the frequency with which specific scores are observed in each group is listed on the ordinate. (The frequency distributions in Fig. 3-1 have been smoothed; distributions of real scores would be jagged and irregular. The exact shape of these distributions is not important for the exposition which follows.) The means for the different treatment conditions are designated as $\bar{A}_1$, $\bar{A}_2$, and $\bar{A}_3$ and are located in the figure. The *grand mean* of all three conditions, obtained by summing all of the scores in the experiment and dividing by the number of scores involved [$3(100) = 300$, in this example], is also indicated in the plot. The symbol designating the grand mean is $\bar{T}$, where "T" stands for the fact that the mean is based on the *total* sum of the scores.

Consider the score of one of the subjects in the distribution of scores at level a_1. We will represent this score as AS_{1j}, where the first subscript specifies the level of factor A (a_1 in this case) and the second simply refers to any one of the j subjects in this condition. (We will discuss the notational system in the next section.) Consider now the deviation of this score (AS_{1j}) from the grand mean ($\overline{T}$). This deviation ($AS_{1j} - \overline{T}$) is represented geometrically in Fig. 3-1. From the figure, it is obvious that this deviation is made up of *two components*. One consists of the deviation of the score from the mean of the group from which it was drawn, i.e., $AS_{1j} - \overline{A}_1$. The other consists of the deviation of the group mean from the grand mean, i.e., $\overline{A}_1 - \overline{T}$. This relationship may be written as

$$AS_{1j} - \overline{T} = (\overline{A}_1 - \overline{T}) + (AS_{1j} - \overline{A}_1).$$

We can give each of the three deviation scores a name: the deviation on the left ($AS_{1j} - \overline{T}$) is called the *total deviation*; the first deviation on the right ($\overline{A}_1 - \overline{T}$) is called the *between-group deviation*; and the remaining deviation ($AS_{1j} - \overline{A}_1$) is called the *within-group deviation*.

If we can perform this division or *partition*, as it is called, of the total deviation of *one* subject in this group, we can perform the partition on *all* of the 100 subjects in this group. To be more specific, the 100 sets of partitions for the subjects in level a_1 are as follows:

$$AS_{11} - \overline{T} = (\overline{A}_1 - \overline{T}) + (AS_{11} - \overline{A}_1),$$
$$AS_{12} - \overline{T} = (\overline{A}_1 - \overline{T}) + (AS_{12} - \overline{A}_1),$$
$$\cdots \qquad \cdots \qquad \cdots$$
$$AS_{1,99} - \overline{T} = (\overline{A}_1 - \overline{T}) + (AS_{1,99} - \overline{A}_1),$$
$$AS_{1,100} - \overline{T} = (\overline{A}_1 - \overline{T}) + (AS_{1,100} - \overline{A}_1).$$

A similar partition may be accomplished for the 100 subjects in each of the other groups.

If we now sum over all 300 total deviations, all 300 between-group deviations, and all 300 within-group deviations, we can summarize the outcome as follows:

(grand sum of total deviations) = (grand sum of between-group deviations)

+ (grand sum of within-group deviations).

We recall from Chapter 1, however, that the sum of the deviation scores about a mean is *zero*. Thus, for the partition to do us any "good," we must do something else with them. Fortunately, the same additive relationship, which holds for the grand sum of the different deviations, holds for the sums of the *squares* of these deviations as well.[1] This important relationship may be stated as

$$SS_{total} = SS_{between\,groups} + SS_{within\,groups}. \tag{3-1}$$

Translated into our example, Eq. (3-1) reads, "The sum of the squared deviations of all 300 subjects from $\overline{T}$ may be broken down into two components, one obtained by summing all of the squared deviations between individual group means and $\overline{T}$ and the other by summing all of the squared deviations of subjects from their respective group means." (As you will see in the next section, however, we do not calculate these sums of squares by using these deviation scores—there is an easier way.)

SUMS OF SQUARES: DEFINING AND COMPUTATIONAL FORMULAS

While the computational chores required of the analysis of variance may be tedious to do by hand, they are quite simple in conception. In fact, we have already considered the essential logic behind the analysis. There remains only the formal presentation of the defining and computational formulas. It should be noted that these formulas will apply only to the situation in which equal sample sizes (s) are used in the treatment conditions. Although this represents a "special case," it subsumes most of the experiments conducted in the behavioral sciences. The analysis of the "atypical" case, unequal sample sizes, is presented in Chapter 17, although we will discuss in Chapter 5 implications that the presence of unequal sizes may have for our interpretation of a set of results.

Notation

Before presenting the different formulas, we should say a few words about notational systems in general and about the one adopted for this book. The basic job of a notational system is to express unambiguously the arithmetic operations in the most complex of designs as well as in the simplest. Unfortunately, most notational systems produce computational formulas that are quite difficult for students and researchers to comprehend unless they have a strong background in mathematics. The system used in this book attempts to reduce the apparent similarity of different operations by using distinct symbols to denote different sums. This system also emphasizes the consistency of the operations required of the computational formulas differing in complexity. Most important, the present notational system leads to a simple set of general computational rules, which will be introduced in Chapter 10. These rules greatly simplify the construction of computational formulas in most of our

---

[1] The algebraic proof of this statement can be found in most advanced statistics texts, such as Hays (1963, pp. 362–364) and Winer (1962, p. 51; 1971, p. 155).

work. The need for such a set of rules will not be apparent in the single-factor design. On the other hand, the computational rules will be extremely useful when we turn to more complicated designs. Thus, it is important to understand how the notation "works" even in this relatively simple situation.

It is instructive to compare a common notational system with the present one, especially for readers who have been brought up on the former system or some variant of it. The set of scores from a single-factor experiment is written in the two notational systems in the upper portion of Table 3-1. These are the individual scores for all of the subjects in the experiment. The basic score for the typical system is X, while the corresponding score in the present system is AS. The use of the two letters emphasizes the fact that reference is being made to a quantity which is specified by *two* classifications, namely, a classification with respect both to the level of factor A and to an individual subject in that particular treatment condition. Because the scores within the body of the total matrix of scores are each designated as AS, we will refer to the display as an *AS matrix*.

You will note that notational subscripts have been used with both systems. The pair of subscripts is required when it is necessary to designate a *particular* score in the AS matrix. With both systems, i signifies the levels of factor A and j signifies the subjects within a given treatment group. Thus, X_{12} or AS_{12} refers to the second subject at level a_1; X_{21} or AS_{21} refers to the first subject at level a_2, and so on.[2]

We will now compare the two notational systems by specifying the common arithmetic operations we will perform in the analysis of variance. These are listed in the lower portion of Table 3-1. The operation specified in the first row of the table is the sum of all of the scores in the experiment. The typical system denotes this summing operation by means of two summation signs. The first summation sign, the sign closest to X_{ij}, tells us to sum all of the X scores within the ith treatment group, while the second summation sign tells us to combine the p subtotals from the individual groups. The present system uses the letter T to stand for the grand total of all of the scores in the experiment.

The operation specified in row 2 is simply the square of the grand total. This is designated by squaring the totals listed in row 1.

The next quantity in the table is the sum of all of the *squared* basic scores, i.e., either $(X_{ij})^2$ or $(AS_{ij})^2$. Again, the other system uses two summation signs

---

[2] The only difference between the two systems at this point is in the designation of the last subject in any given group and of the final level of factor A. The last subject is n for the common system and is s for the present system. We have used s in order to be consistent in the system throughout the book. The last level of factor A is p for the common system, while it is a for the present system. The reason for this difference is that most authors do not want to use the lower-case a to denote a level of factor A *and* to denote the last level as well. Instead, they use a_i to refer to the ith level of factor A and a_p to refer to the last level. We will be using the letter "a" in both capacities— i.e., a_i as the ith level and a_a as the last level. There is no ambiguity in adopting this convention, however, since an "a" *without* a subscript will *always* refer to the number of levels of factor A, while an "a" *with* a subscript will *always* refer to any one of the levels of factor A; i.e., a_i = the ith level.

TABLE 3-1 *Comparison of Notational Systems*

DENOTATION OF INDIVIDUAL SCORES: THE AS MATRIX

Typical System—Levels of Factor A				Present System—Levels of Factor A			
a_1	a_2	$\ldots$	a_p	a_1	a_2	$\ldots$	a_a
X_{11}	X_{21}	$\ldots$	X_{p1}	AS_{11}	AS_{21}	$\ldots$	AS_{a1}
X_{12}	X_{22}	$\ldots$	X_{p2}	AS_{12}	AS_{22}	$\ldots$	AS_{a2}
$\vdots$				$\vdots$			
X_{1n}	X_{2n}	$\ldots$	X_{pn}	AS_{1s}	AS_{2s}	$\ldots$	AS_{as}

DENOTATION OF COMMON ARITHMETIC OPERATIONS

Operation	Typical System	Present System
(1) Sum of all scores	$\sum\limits_i^p \sum\limits_j^n X_{ij}$	T
(2) Square of (1)	$\left(\sum\limits_i^p \sum\limits_j^n X_{ij} \right)^2$	$(T)^2$
(3) Sum of all squared basic scores	$\sum\limits_i^p \sum\limits_j^n (X_{ij})^2$	$\sum (AS)^2$
(4) Sum of scores at level a_i	$\sum\limits_j^n X_{ij}$	A_i
(5) Square of (4), summed over all groups	$\sum\limits_i^p \left(\sum\limits_j^n X_{ij} \right)^2$	$\sum (A)^2$

and subscripts. The present system uses no subscripts and only a single summation sign without notation. Following the convention adopted for this book, the subscripts and notation are dropped whenever the operation specified is performed on *all* of the scores in a set. Here, we are squaring every individual score and adding them all up; thus, the expression may be simplified.

The operation specified in row 4 is the sum of the individual scores for the ith treatment group, i.e., the group at level a_i. A single summation sign with appropriate limits, namely, $j = 1, 2, \ldots, n$, is required of the other system, while a capital A with a subscript is all that is required of the present system. (The A_i stands for the sum of the scores for *any* A group.)

The quantity in the last row requires the following series of calculations: (1) the sum of the scores in each treatment group, (2) the square of these sums, and (3) the sum of these squares. In the typical system, close attention must be paid to the subscripts and to the limits of summation to make sure that the quantity specified within the parenthesis is understood. In the present system, the operations are clear: the different group totals (A_i) are squared and then summed. The subscripts and notation have been omitted, since the operations are performed on all of the group totals.

Total Sum of Squares (SS_T)

The first step in the analysis of variance is the calculation of the basic sums of squares that we evolved from the deviations specified in Fig. 3-1. The basic relationship was stated in Eq. (3-1), namely, that the total sum of squares could be partitioned into two component sums of squares, one involving between-group deviations and the other involving within-group deviations. We will consider first the computation of the total sum of squares (SS_T).

DEFINING FORMULA   The basic ingredients in the SS_T are the total deviations —i.e., the deviation of each score in the experiment from the grand mean, $\overline{T}$. The SS_T is formed by squaring each one of the total deviations and summing them up for all subjects. These operations are specified in the bottom row of Table 3-2, in the column labeled "defining formulas." The individual deviations are placed within the parenthesis and the other operations, squaring and summing, are indicated outside the parenthesis. (Notational subscripts and summational limits are retained with the defining formulas to emphasize the operations, but they will be dropped from the more useful computational formulas when there is no ambiguity in the operations being specified.) The two summation signs in the defining formula indicate that the summation occurs over all subjects and treatment groups.

COMPUTATIONAL FORMULA   The computational formula is specified in the next column of Table 3-2. The first term tells us to square each AS score and then to add all of them up. (A single summation sign with no notation and an AS score without subscripts are used, since there is no question that the squaring and summing operations are to be performed on all of the AS scores in the experiment.) The second term indicates that the grand total of the AS scores (T) is squared and divided by the total number of subjects in the experiment (as).

Between-Groups Sum of Squares (SS_A)

We saw in Fig. 3-1 that one of the components of a subject's total deviation is the deviation of the subject's group mean from the grand mean ($\overline{A}_i - \overline{T}$). If we square and then sum this component for all of the subjects in the experiment, we will obtain the between-groups SS. (We will refer to this quantity as the SS_A, indicating that this sum of squares is based upon deviations involving the A means.)

DEFINING FORMULA   The defining formula for the SS_A is presented in the first row of Table 3-2. We will work through the "construction" of this formula. You will notice that the quantity specified within the parenthesis is the deviation

TABLE 3-2 *Defining and Computational Formulas*

Source of Variance	Defining Formula	Computational Formula
Between Group (A)	$s\left[\sum\limits_{i}^{a}(\bar{A}_i - \bar{T})^2\right]$	$\dfrac{\sum(A)^2}{s} - \dfrac{(T)^2}{as}$
Within Group (S/A)	$\sum\limits_{i}^{a}\sum\limits_{j}^{s}(AS_{ij} - \bar{A}_i)^2$	$\sum(AS)^2 - \dfrac{\sum(A)^2}{s}$
Total	$\sum\limits_{i}^{a}\sum\limits_{j}^{s}(AS_{ij} - \bar{T})^2$	$\sum(AS)^2 - \dfrac{(T)^2}{as}$

of an individual group mean ($\bar{A}_i$) from the grand mean ($\bar{T}$). This deviation ($\bar{A}_i - \bar{T}$) is obviously the *same* for all of the members of a particular group. Thus, instead of extracting this deviation for each subject separately, it is far more convenient to obtain the deviation, square it, and then to multiply the square by the number of subjects in the group (s). Stated this way, the sum of the squared between-group deviation for a group of subjects at level a_i becomes

$$s(\bar{A}_i - \bar{T})^2.$$

The sample size (s) in this expression is often called the *weighting factor* because it adjusts or weights each between-group deviation for the number of subjects in the group. The final step requires the summing of the separate between-group sums of squares, one for each of the a groups. That is, we will perform the following operation:

$$SS_A = s(\bar{A}_1 - \bar{T})^2 + s(\bar{A}_2 - \bar{T})^2 + \cdots + s(\bar{A}_a - \bar{T})^2.$$

Symbolically, the equation becomes

$$SS_A = \sum_{i}^{a} s(\bar{A}_i - \bar{T})^2,$$

which may be simplified by placing the weighting factor (s) to the left of the summation sign. (This rearrangement indicates that we sum the squared between-group deviations first and *then* multiply by s.) This final form of the defining formula appears in Table 3-2.

COMPUTATIONAL FORMULA   The computational formula is the result of an algebraic expansion of the defining formula.[3] You may be able to see some resemblance between these two formulas. Whether you "see" the resemblance or not, the operations specified by the computational formula are simple: For the first term, we are asked (1) to add up the scores within a treatment group, (2) to square each of these sums, (3) to add up the squares, and (4) to

[3] This algebraic proof can be found in Hays (1963, p. 371), Kirk (1968, p. 49), and Myers (1966, pp. 68–69).

divide this final sum by s; for the second term, we are asked (1) to obtain the grand total, (2) to square this quantity, and (3) to divide by as. (Subscripts and summational limits have been dropped from the computational formula, as there is no ambiguity in the operations.)

Within-Groups Sum of Squares ($SS_{S/A}$)

The final sum of squares is the within-groups sum of squares, denoted by $SS_{S/A}$. This term is read "the sum of squares for subjects within levels (or groups) of factor A" and stresses the fact that we are dealing with the deviation of subjects from their *own* group means. Since we know how to calculate the SS_T and the SS_A, we could obtain the $SS_{S/A}$ by subtraction. We will calculate this sum of squares "directly," however, in order to be consistent with the more complicated designs we will consider later.

DEFINING FORMULA As illustrated in Fig. 3-1, the basic deviation involved in the computation of the $SS_{S/A}$ is $(AS_{ij} - \bar{A}_i)$, the deviation of an AS score from the relevant group mean. As a first step, we can obtain a sum of squares for *each group* using these within-group deviations. That is, for the ith group,

$$SS_{S/A_i} = \sum_j^s (AS_{ij} - \bar{A}_i)^2.$$

The formula tells us to square and then sum the within-group deviations for all of the subjects in the ith group. This sum of squares represents the variability of subjects treated alike.

There is a within-group sum of squares for each of the treatment groups. In the analysis of variance, we will average the different within-group variances to obtain a more stable estimate of experimental error. As a first step, then, we will want to add together the separate within-group sums of squares. This *pooling* of the separate SS's is indicated by the defining formula in Table 3-2. Many students have difficulty in extracting from the defining formula the fact that we are pooling the separate within-group sums of squares. To make the pooling more explicit, we can introduce brackets around the within-group sum of squares:

$$SS_{S/A} = \sum_i^a \sum_j^s (AS_{ij} - \bar{A}_i)^2 = \sum_i^a \left[\sum_j^s (AS_{ij} - \bar{A}_i)^2 \right]. \tag{3-2}$$

The quantity within the brackets is the sum of squares for subjects treated alike; the summation sign to the left of the brackets indicates the pooling of different sets of within-group sums of squares, one for each of the a groups.

COMPUTATIONAL FORMULA The computational formula uses two of the terms we have discussed already. We will develop the computational formula step by step. The basic ingredient is the within-group sum of squares. For the

ith group,

$$SS_{S/A_i} = \sum_j^s (AS_{ij})^2 - \frac{(A_i)^2}{s}.$$

Then, pooling the separate within-group sums of squares, we have

$$SS_{S/A} = \left[\sum_j^s (AS_{1j})^2 - \frac{(A_1)^2}{s}\right] + \left[\sum_j^s (AS_{2j})^2 - \frac{(A_2)^2}{s}\right]$$
$$+ \cdots + \left[\sum_j^s (AS_{aj})^2 - \frac{(A_a)^2}{s}\right].$$

This last step may be represented by

$$SS_{S/A} = \sum_i^a \left[\sum_j^s (AS_{ij})^2 - \frac{(A_i)^2}{s}\right]. \tag{3-3}$$

The quantity within the brackets is the computational formula for any one of the within-group sums of squares; the summation sign to the left of the brackets tells us to sum all of the separate sums of squares.

A form of Eq. (3-3), which is simpler arithmetically, eliminates the brackets and tells us to perform the summation over the a groups separately for each of the two terms inside of the brackets. Specifically,

$$SS_{S/A} = \sum_i^a \sum_j^s (AS_{ij})^2 - \frac{\sum_i^a (A_i)^2}{s}.$$

This formula may be simplified by applying the convention adopted in this book, namely, to use single, unlabeled summation signs and to eliminate subscripts when the summing operations are performed on all of the terms in a set. For the first quantity on the right, all of the AS scores are squared and then summed; for the second quantity on the right, all of the A sums are squared and summed. Thus, the simplification becomes

$$SS_{S/A} = \sum (AS)^2 - \frac{\sum (A)^2}{s}.$$

Computational Rule

One feature of the various computational formulas in Table 3-2 should be pointed out, since it will occur in all of the analyses we will consider in later chapters. Specifically, *computational rule number 1* states that we

always divide by the number of observations contributing to one of the quantities in the numerator.

If we apply this rule to the first term in the computational formula for the SS_A, we see that the basic term in the numerator represents the sum of s observations, and we divide by that number. In the second part of the formula, the basic term is obtained by summing all of the as observations; consequently, we divide by as. Finally, the remaining unique term appearing in the computational formulas, $\sum (AS)^2$, results from a squaring of each *individual* observation. Thus, an application of the rule would require that we divide each square by 1, a division which is implied but not shown in the formulas. (An alternative way of remembering the computational rule is to think of each quantity that is squared as a *mean*, the divisor being a number which reflects the number of observations.) This rule should be memorized, as it will allow the generation of the formulas necessary for the calculation of relatively complex analyses of variance.

NUMERICAL EXAMPLE

Suppose we were interested in the effect on reading comprehension of three different instructions. One group of children is asked to attempt to memorize an essay (level a_1), a second group is asked to concentrate upon the idea units (level a_2), and a third group is given no specific instructions (level a_3). All subjects are allowed to study the essay for 10 minutes; then they are given an objective test to determine their comprehension of the passage. There are $s = 5$ subjects who were randomly assigned to each of the $a = 3$ treatment conditions. Table 3-3 presents an AS matrix containing the data from this hypothetical experiment.

The score for a subject (AS) represents the number of test items correctly answered. Also included at the bottom of the table are the results of basic summing and squaring operations for each group and, in the second to the last row, the group means. For the three groups at levels a_1, a_2, and a_3,

$$A_1 = 16 + 18 + 10 + 12 + 19 = 75,$$

$$A_2 = 4 + 6 + 8 + 10 + 2 = 30,$$

and

$$A_3 = 2 + 10 + 9 + 13 + 11 = 45,$$

respectively. The corresponding sums of the squared AS scores are as follows:

$$\sum (AS_{1j})^2 = (16)^2 + (18)^2 + (10)^2 + (12)^2 + (19)^2 = 1185,$$

$$\sum (AS_{2j})^2 = (4)^2 + (6)^2 + (8)^2 + (10)^2 + (2)^2 = 220,$$

and

$$\sum (AS_{3j})^2 = (2)^2 + (10)^2 + (9)^2 + (13)^2 + (11)^2 = 475,$$

respectively.

TABLE 3-3 *Numerical Example: AS Matrix*

Treatment Levels

	a_1	a_2	a_3
	16	4	2
	18	6	10
	10	8	9
	12	10	13
	19	2	11
A_i:	75	30	45
$\bar{A}_i$:	15.00	6.00	9.00
$\sum\limits_{j}^{s}(AS_{ij})^2$:	1185	220	475

Applying the computational formula in Table 3-2 to the present data, we have

$$SS_A = \frac{\sum(A)^2}{s} - \frac{(T)^2}{as}$$

$$= \frac{(75)^2 + (30)^2 + (45)^2}{5} - \frac{(16 + 18 + \cdots + 13 + 11)^2}{3(5)}.$$

In order to emphasize the application of the computational rule, we can rewrite the first term of the formula by placing each square over s, the number of observations summed to obtain each total. That is,

$$\frac{\sum(A)^2}{s} = \sum\frac{(A)^2}{s}$$

and

$$\frac{(75)^2 + (30)^2 + (45)^2}{5} = \frac{(75)^2}{5} + \frac{(30)^2}{5} + \frac{(45)^2}{5}.$$

Note also that the quantity T, appearing in the numerator of the last term, may be calculated by summing the A_i sums rather than returning to the AS matrix and summing the AS scores individually. This is another way of pointing out that

$$T = \sum AS = \sum A.$$

Completing the calculations,

$$SS_A = \frac{5625 + 900 + 2025}{5} - \frac{(150)^2}{15}$$

$$= \frac{8550}{5} - \frac{22,500}{15}$$

$$= 1710.00 - 1500.00 = 210.00.$$

For the $SS_{S/A}$ we have

$$SS_{S/A} = \sum (AS)^2 - \frac{\sum (A)^2}{s}$$

$$= [(16)^2 + (18)^2 + \cdots + (13)^2 + (11)^2] - \frac{(75)^2 + (30)^2 + (45)^2}{5}$$

$$= 1880 - \frac{8550}{5}$$

$$= 1880 - 1710.00 = 170.00.$$

As we saw in the development of the computational formula, the $SS_{S/A}$ is made up of the separate within-group sums of squares for the treatment groups. To illustrate this point, we will obtain the $SS_{S/A}$ by using Eq. (3-3) and computing the sums of squares separately. For any one group,

$$SS_{S/A_i} = \sum_{j}^{s} (AS_{ij})^2 - \frac{(A_i)^2}{s}.$$

The individual within-group sums for the present example are

$$SS_{S/A_1} = \sum (AS_{1j})^2 - \frac{(A_1)^2}{s} = 1185 - \frac{(75)^2}{5}$$

$$= 1185 - \frac{5625}{5} = 1185 - 1125.00 = 60.00,$$

$$SS_{S/A_2} = \sum (AS_{2j})^2 - \frac{(A_2)^2}{s} = 220 - \frac{(30)^2}{5}$$

$$= 220 - \frac{900}{5} = 220 - 180.00 = 40.00,$$

and

$$SS_{S/A_3} = \sum (AS_{3j})^2 - \frac{(A_3)^2}{s} = 475 - \frac{(45)^2}{5}$$

$$= 475 - \frac{2025}{5} = 475 - 405.00 = 70.00.$$

The total of these sums of squares equals the $SS_{S/A}$, which we found by using the computational formula listed in Table 3-2. That is,

$$SS_{S/A} = \sum SS_{S/A_i} = 60.00 + 40.00 + 70.00 = 170.00.$$

The final computation consists of the calculation of the SS_T. From the computational formula in Table 3-2, we substitute as follows:

$$SS_T = \sum (AS)^2 - \frac{(T)^2}{as}$$

$$= [(16)^2 + (18)^2 + \cdots + (13)^2 + (11)^2] - \frac{(75 + 30 + 45)^2}{3(5)}$$

$$= 1880 - \frac{22{,}500}{15} = 1880 - 1500.00 = 380.00.$$

Several computational checks should be mentioned. First, when we are summing squares with a desk calculator [e.g., $\sum (AS)^2$ or $\sum (A)^2$], we should check to see that the number appearing in the register cumulating the *unsquared* numbers matches the actual total sum (T). If the numbers do not match, then we know we have made a mistake. Second, in the calculation of the sums of squares, we can check our arithmetic by applying Eq. (3-1) and verifying that the two component sums of squares add up to the SS_T. In the present example,

$$SS_T = SS_A + SS_{S/A} = 210.00 + 170.00 = 380.00.$$

Third, a complete check of all of our calculations may be obtained a number of ways. One obvious method is to perform the analysis again, or, perhaps better still, coax another person to go through the calculations independently. An alternative method is to add a constant, say, 1, to each AS score (i.e., $AS_{ij} + 1$) and to repeat the complete analysis. For example, the scores in level a_1 would thus become 17, 19, 11, 13, and 20, respectively. If we have made no error in either set of calculations, we should end up with *identical* sums of squares in the two analyses. The addition of a constant does not change the basic *deviation* scores, upon which the sums of squares are fundamentally based, but it does change the actual numbers entering into the calculations when we use the computational formulas of Table 3-2.

ANALYSIS OF DEVIATION SCORES

In discussing the component sums of squares, we began by considering the deviation of AS scores from $\bar{T}$ and the fact that for each observation this deviation may be divided into a between-group deviation ($\bar{A} - \bar{T}$) and a within-group deviation ($AS - \bar{A}$). We saw that the defining formulas for the corresponding sums of squares were developed directly from these deviations. Our actual calculations, however, were performed with the computational formulas, which are considerably easier to use. Since the intuitive meaning of the sums of squares in general and of the partition of the SS_T into the SS_A and the $SS_{S/A}$ is much clearer with the defining formulas, it is instructive to

TABLE 3-4 *Analysis of Component Deviation Scores*

Deviation Scores

AS_{1j}	Total $(AS_{ij} - \bar{T})$	= Between $= (\bar{A}_i - \bar{T})$	+	Within $+ (AS_{ij} - \bar{A}_i)$
		LEVEL a_1		
16	(6)	= (5)	+	(1)
18	(8)	= (5)	+	(3)
10	(0)	= (5)	+	(−5)
12	(2)	= (5)	+	(−3)
19	(9)	= (5)	+	(4)
		LEVEL a_2		
4	(−6)	= (−4)	+	(−2)
6	(−4)	= (−4)	+	(0)
8	(−2)	= (−4)	+	(2)
10	(0)	= (−4)	+	(4)
2	(−8)	= (−4)	+	(−4)
		LEVEL a_3		
2	(−8)	= (−1)	+	(−7)
10	(0)	= (−1)	+	(1)
9	(−1)	= (−1)	+	(0)
13	(3)	= (−1)	+	(4)
11	(1)	= (−1)	+	(2)
Sum:	(0)	= (0)	+	(0)

work through the numerical example using these formulas and to compare the outcomes with the results obtained with the computational formulas.

The analysis of the deviation scores is presented in Table 3-4. The first column of the table lists the AS scores, grouped according to levels of factor A. The deviation of an AS_{ij} score from $\bar{T}$ is listed in the second column, and the between-group and within-group deviations are entered in the third and fourth columns of the table, respectively. In order to calculate the deviation scores, we need the different means. From Table 3-3, the means for the treatment groups are $\bar{A}_1 = 15$, $\bar{A}_2 = 6$, and $\bar{A}_3 = 9$. The grand mean is

$$\bar{T} = \frac{T}{as} = \frac{150}{3(5)} = 10.00.$$

We are now ready to obtain the deviations. Consider the first subject in level a_1 and his deviation scores:

$$AS_{11} - \bar{T} = (\bar{A}_1 - \bar{T}) + (AS_{11} - \bar{A}),$$
$$16 - 10 = (15 - 10) + (16 - 15).$$

The deviation scores for the last subject in level a_2 are as follows:

$$AS_{25} - \bar{T} = (\bar{A}_2 - \bar{T}) + (AS_{25} - \bar{A}_2),$$
$$2 - 10 = (6 - 10) + (2 - 6).$$

And the deviation scores for the fourth subject in level a_3 are

$$AS_{34} - \bar{T} = (\bar{A}_3 - \bar{T}) + (AS_{34} - \bar{A}_3),$$
$$13 - 10 = (9 - 10) + (13 - 9).$$

The results of the subtractions for these and for the remaining scores are given in the last three columns of the table.

Consider the deviation scores. First, we should note that the between-group deviation is the same for each of the subjects in a given group—namely, 5 for a_1, -4 for a_2, and -1 for a_3. We can also see that the sum of the within-group deviation scores is zero for the subjects in each group. This is as it should be, since the sum of the deviations about a mean is zero. Finally, the sums of the other two sets of deviations are also zero when the summing is taken over all as observations. This, too, makes sense, since the total and between-group deviations represent deviations about the grand mean, and the respective deviations will not balance until all of the deviations are summed.

All that remains now is to square and to sum the deviation scores in the table. For each set,

$$SS_T = (6)^2 + (8)^2 + \cdots + (3)^2 + (1)^2 = 380,$$
$$SS_A = (5)^2 + (5)^2 + \cdots + (-1)^2 + (-1)^2 = 210,$$

and

$$SS_{S/A} = (1)^2 + (3)^2 + \cdots + (4)^2 + (2)^2 = 170.$$

These sums are identical to the ones obtained with the computational formulas in the last section.

This analysis makes explicit the meaning of the component deviation scores. It is clear that the between-group deviation is the same for each observation within a particular group, illustrating why we multiplied the deviation of the group mean from $\bar{T}$ by s in the defining formula listed in Table 3-2. We can also see that the $SS_{S/A}$ represents a pooling of the three within-group sums of squares. From the last column of Table 3-4,

$$SS_{S/A_1} = (1)^2 + (3)^2 + (-5)^2 + (-3)^2 + (4)^2 = 60,$$
$$SS_{S/A_2} = (-2)^2 + (0)^2 + (2)^2 + (4)^2 + (-4)^2 = 40,$$

and

$$SS_{S/A_3} = (-7)^2 + (1)^2 + (0)^2 + (4)^2 + (2)^2 = 70.$$

The sum of these individual sums of squares equals the $SS_{S/A}$. Specifically,

$$SS_{S/A} = \sum SS_{S/A_i} = 60 + 40 + 70 = 170.$$

chapter four

VARIANCE ESTIMATES
AND THE F RATIO

As Winer (1962, p. 59; 1971, p. 163) points out, it is accurate to express the null hypothesis in terms of a between-groups variance, one which is based on deviations of the means of treatment populations from the overall population mean. More specifically,

$$H_0\colon (\mu_1 - \mu) = (\mu_2 - \mu) = \cdots = (\mu_a - \mu) = 0,$$

where the means with subscripts are the population treatment means and μ is the mean of these individual means. An obvious candidate from the data of the experiment to estimate these deviations is the between-group deviation scores $(\bar{A}_i - \bar{T})$. It will be recalled from a previous discussion, however, that differences among the sample means are subject to experimental error, so that the mere presence of sample deviation scores greater than zero is insufficient cause to justify the conclusion that treatment effects are present in the population.

Thus, a variance estimate, which is based on between-group differences, is the sum of two components—a treatment component and an error component.

Recall also that within-group deviation scores $(AS_{ij} - \bar{A}_i)$ can be thought to reflect the influence of the error component alone. It is possible to show that when the null hypothesis is true and there is no population treatment effect, variances based on these two sets of deviations provide independent estimates of the error component. (We will consider this proof subsequently.) Given this fact, then, the ratio

$$F = \frac{\text{between-groups variance}}{\text{within-groups variance}} \qquad (4\text{-}1)$$

provides a useful means for testing the reasonableness of the null hypothesis.

Suppose, for example, that we conducted a particular experiment a large number of times and looked at the *average* value of F resulting from these different experiments. (The distribution of these F values is called the *sampling distribution* of F, and the mean of the sampling distribution is called the *expected value* of F.) When H_0 is true, the expected value of F, which is often designated as $E(F)$, is approximately 1.0; when the alternative hypothesis (H_1)—the hypothesis that the population means are *not* equal—is true, the expected value of F is greater than 1.0. While these expectations are clear, we will *rarely* obtain an F which is equal to the value of F expected under the null hypothesis. The reason is the independence of the two estimates of error variance; sometimes the estimate based on between-group deviations will be larger than the estimate based on within-group deviations, and sometimes the reverse. The problem is to find a way to decide when an F, which is greater than 1, cannot be reasonably accounted for by the fact that the two variances are independent estimates of experimental error.

We will now discuss a solution to this problem. We will consider first the formulas which provide the two estimates needed in Eq. (4-1), and then how we can use the value of F to test the null hypothesis.

VARIANCE ESTIMATES

The remainder of the analysis is outlined in Table 4-1 in an arrangement called a *summary table*. The first two columns list the sources of variability and their respective sums of squares. We indicated in Chapter 1 that a variance to be used to estimate population characteristics is defined differently from one to be used for purely descriptive purposes. In Eq. (1-5a), we expressed the arithmetic operations as

$$\hat{\sigma}^2 = \frac{SS}{df},$$

where SS refers to the basic sum of squares and df represents the *degrees of freedom* associated with the SS.

Degrees of freedom (*df*)

The *df* associated with a sum of squares correspond to the number of scores with *independent information* which enter into the calculation of the sum of squares. Consider, for example, the use of a single sample mean to estimate the population mean. If we want to estimate the population variance as well, we must take account of the fact that we have used up some of the independent information already in estimating the population mean.

Consider a concrete example. Suppose that we have five observations in our experiment and that we determine the mean of the scores to be 7.0. This mean is used to estimate the population mean. With the number of observations set at five and the population mean set at 7.0, how much independent information remains for the estimate of the population variance? The answer is the number of observations which are *free* to vary—i.e., to take on any value whatsoever. The number in this example is *four*, one less than the total number of observations. The reason for this loss of "freedom" is that, while we are free to select any value for the first four scores, the final score is already determined. More specifically, the total sum of all five must equal 35, so that the mean of the sample will equal 7.0; as soon as four scores are selected, the fifth score is fixed and can be obtained by subtraction. In a sense, then, estimating the population mean places a restraint upon the values that the scores are free to take. The general rule for computing the *df* of any sum of squares is

$$df = \begin{pmatrix} \text{number of} \\ \text{independent} \\ \text{observations} \end{pmatrix} - \begin{pmatrix} \text{number of} \\ \text{restraints} \end{pmatrix} \quad (4\text{-}2)$$

or

$$df = \begin{pmatrix} \text{number of} \\ \text{independent} \\ \text{observations} \end{pmatrix} - \begin{pmatrix} \text{number of} \\ \text{population} \\ \text{estimates} \end{pmatrix}. \quad (4\text{-}2a)$$

The *df* associated with each sum of squares in the analysis of variance are presented in the third column of Table 4-1. We can calculate the *df* for each sum of squares by applying Eq. (4-2). For the SS_A, there are *a* basic observations—i.e., *a* different sample means. Since 1 *df* is lost as a result of estimating

TABLE 4-1 *Summary Table for the One-Factor Analysis of Variance*

Source	SS	df	Mean Square (MS)	F Ratio
A	SS_A	$a - 1$	$\dfrac{SS_A}{df_A}$	$\dfrac{MS_A}{MS_{S/A}}$
S/A	$SS_{S/A}$	$a(s - 1)$	$\dfrac{SS_{S/A}}{df_{S/A}}$	
Total	SS_T	$as - 1$		

the overall population mean (μ) from the grand mean of the experiment ($\overline{T}$), $df_A = a - 1$. For the $SS_{S/A}$, the calculation of df is more complicated. This sum of squares represents a pooling of separate estimates of error variance from the different treatment groups. If we consider any one of these groups, there are s basic observations; we will lose 1 df, however, by estimating the mean of the treatment population (μ_i). Thus, there are $df = s - 1$ for each of the treatment groups. The total number of df for the $SS_{S/A}$ is found by pooling the df for each group, just as we pool the corresponding sums of squares. The formula given in Table 4-1,

$$df_{S/A} = a(s - 1),$$

simply has us multiply the df for any one of the groups ($s - 1$) by the number of different groups (a). The df for the SS_T are obtained by subtracting 1 df from the total number of independent observations (as). As a check, we can verify that the df associated with the component sums of squares sum to df_T. That is,

$$df_T = df_A + df_{S/A},$$

$$as - 1 = (a - 1) + a(s - 1) = a - 1 + as - a = as - 1.$$

Mean Squares

The actual variance estimates appear in the next column of Table 4-1. These estimates are called mean squares (MS), a term which refers to an averaging of a set of squared numbers. The mean squares for the two component sources of variance are given by

$$MS = \frac{SS}{df}, \tag{4-3}$$

or, more specifically,

$$MS_A = \frac{SS_A}{df_A} \quad \text{and} \quad MS_{S/A} = \frac{SS_{S/A}}{df_{S/A}}.$$

The first mean square estimates the combined presence of treatment effects plus error variance, while the second mean square independently estimates error variance.

The whole logic of the analysis of variance rests upon the assumption that the MS_A and the $MS_{S/A}$ provide *independent* estimates of error variance when the null hypothesis is true. It is possible to prove the correctness of this assumption mathematically, but this proof is beyond the scope of this book; instead, we will evaluate the assumption in a number of other ways.

First, we use a logical argument. Suppose that we have a sets of s scores each and that we calculate the MS_A and the $MS_{S/A}$. If we change the AS scores by any amount, but hold the treatment means constant, the $MS_{S/A}$ will change but the MS_A will not. On the other hand, if we change the group means by any amount, but do not change the relative standing of the scores within treatment groups, the MS_A will change but the $MS_{S/A}$ will be constant. The two mean squares are independent in the sense that one can be changed without requiring a change in the other.

Another line of argument is empirical. Walker and Lev (1953, p. 210), for example, report the results of a sampling experiment in which the SS_A and the $SS_{S/A}$ were obtained from four sets of random samples of scores, each drawn from the same population of scores. Forty-six such "experiments" were conducted. Since the samples of scores were drawn from the same population, the null hypothesis is true and the pairs of estimates from each experiment should be independent. This is exactly what Walker and Lev report: independence—i.e., an essentially zero correlation ($r = -.05$) between these two component sources of the SS_T.

Finally, Appendix A presents a proof that depends on *orthogonality*, a topic we will consider in Chapter 7.

THE F RATIO

The final step in the calculations consists of the formation of the F ratio. The formula is listed in the last column of Table 4-1. As we have argued previously, the expected value of F is approximately 1.0 when the null hypothesis is true, and is greater than 1.0 when the null hypothesis is false.

Numerical Example

We will continue with the numerical example we used in the last chapter to illustrate the calculation of the sums of squares. The results of these earlier calculations are presented in Table 4-2, an analysis-of-variance summary table. If you recall, there were $a = 3$ treatment conditions and $s = 5$ subjects in this example; the original data may be found in Table 3-3.

The *df* for the three sources of variance are obtained by simple substitution into the formulas listed in Table 4-1. The results of these substitutions are presented in the summary table. Specifically,

$$df_A = a - 1 = 3 - 1 = 2,$$

$$df_{S/A} = a(s - 1) = 3(5 - 1) = 3(4) = 12,$$

and

$$df_T = as - 1 = 3(5) - 1 = 15 - 1 = 14.$$

We can check our separate calculations by verifying that the *df* obtained for the component sums of squares equal the *df* obtained for the SS_T. That is,

$$df_T = df_A + df_{S/A} = 2 + 12 = 14.$$

TABLE 4-2 *Summary Table*

Source	SS	df	MS	F
A	210.00	2	105.00	7.41
S/A	170.00	12	14.17	
Total	380.00	14		

The two variance estimates (mean squares) are found by dividing the SS by the appropriate *df*. In this example,

$$MS_A = \frac{210.00}{2} = 105.00 \quad \text{and} \quad MS_{S/A} = \frac{170.00}{12} = 14.17.$$

These numbers are entered in the MS column of the table. Last, the F ratio becomes

$$F = \frac{MS_A}{MS_{S/A}} = \frac{105.00}{14.17} = 7.41.$$

This value of F is larger than 1.0, bringing into question the correctness of the null hypothesis. On the other hand, we might have obtained a ratio this large (or larger) merely by virtue of the fact that the two mean squares are independent estimates of error variance when H_0 is true.

EVALUATION OF THE F RATIO

Sampling Distribution of F

In view of the minimal mathematical background assumed for the readers of this book, a reasonable approach to this topic is empirical rather than theoretical. Suppose that we had available a large population of scores and that we drew at random three sets of 15 scores each. We can think of the three sets as representing the results of an actual experiment, with $a = 3$ and $s = 15$, for which we *know* the null hypothesis is *true*. That is, the scores placed in each "treatment" condition were in fact drawn from the *same* population. Thus, $\mu_1 = \mu_2 = \mu_3 = \mu$. The two mean squares, MS_A and $MS_{S/A}$, are independent estimates of experimental error: we may estimate the operation of the same chance factors either by looking at the variability among the three sample means or by looking at the pooled variability of the scores within each of the samples.

Assume that we draw a very large number of such "experiments," each consisting of three groups of 15 scores each, and that we compute the value of F for each case. If we group the F's according to size, we can construct a graph relating F and frequency of occurrence. A frequency distribution of a statistic

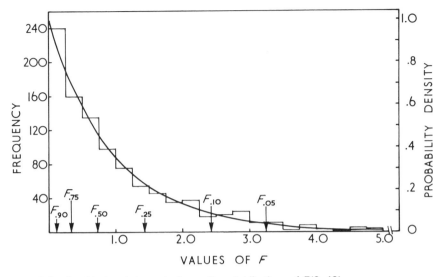

Fig. 4-1   Empirical and theoretical sampling distributions of $F(2, 42)$.

such as *F* is called a *sampling distribution* of the statistic. By obtaining the sampling distribution of *F* *empirically* in this manner, we can see how the theoretical sampling distribution could be developed.

This sort of empirical sampling study is called a "Monte Carlo" experiment. A sampling distribution of *F*, based on 1000 experiments of the sort we have been discussing, is presented in Fig. 4-1. The sampling and calculations were performed on a high-speed computer.[1] The population consisted of 6000 scores with $\mu = 50$ and $\sigma^2 = 225$. The histogram exhibits a regular trend, the frequency of cases tending to drop off rapidly with increasing values of *F*. The smoothed curve represents the theoretical sampling distribution of *F*. The approximation of the theoretical curve to the empirically obtained sampling distribution is extremely close. This correspondence provides a convincing intuitive meaning to the *F* distribution—namely, that it *is* the sampling distribution of *F* obtained when an infinitely large number of experiments, of the sort we have been discussing, are performed.

In evaluating the null hypothesis, we could use information drawn from either the empirical or the theoretical sampling distributions. The great advantage of knowing the mathematical properties of the *F* distribution is that the sampling distribution can be determined for any experiment of any size—i.e., any number of groups and any number of subjects within these groups. Separate Monte Carlo experiments would have to be conducted for each new situation—an inefficient and costly procedure.

[1] The results of this and other sampling experiments which we will discuss were generously made available to me by Drs. Curtis D. Hardyck and Lewis F. Petrinovich.

Let us return to Fig. 4-1 and see what useful information can be obtained from the F distribution. If we know the exact shape of the F distribution for a given experiment, we can make statements concerning how common or how rare an F observed in an actual experiment is. The F distribution is the sampling distribution of F when the population means are equal. If we consider a particular value of F, we can determine (with a working knowledge of the calculus) the probability of obtaining an F that large or larger by finding the percentage of the area under the curve which falls to the right of an ordinate erected at the value of F in question. Several values of F have been indicated in Fig. 4-1. The proportion of the curve falling to the right of F is indicated as a subscript. For example, only 10 percent of the time would we expect to obtain a value of F equal to or greater than 2.44. Stated another way, this probability represents the proportion of F's $\geq$ 2.44 which will occur on the basis of chance factors alone. A comparison of the theoretical probabilities with the empirical probabilities found in the Monte Carlo experiment is presented in Table 4-3. We can see that the correspondence between the two sets of probabilities is quite close.

TABLE 4-3 *Comparison of the Theoretical and Empirical Sampling Distributions of F(2, 42)*

Value of F	Theoretical Probability	Empirical Probability
.11	.900	.950
.29	.750	.754
.70	.500	.518
1.44	.250	.265
2.44	.100	.114
3.23	.050	.050
5.18	.010	.015
8.25	.001	.002

THE F TABLE   The F distribution is actually a family of curves. The exact shape of any one of the curves is determined by the number of df associated with the numerator and denominator mean squares in the F ratio. If we hold numerator df (the number of treatment groups) constant and vary the denominator df (the number of subjects within groups), we will see relatively small changes in the shape of the curves. On the other hand, changing the number of treatment groups produces curves of quite different appearance. [If you are curious about the F distribution and are handy with simple algebra and logarithms, Lewis (1960, pp. 311–312) indicates a method for its determination.] An example of another F distribution, with numerator and denominator df = 4 and 10, respectively, is sketched in Fig. 4-2. [As a shorthand way of referring to a

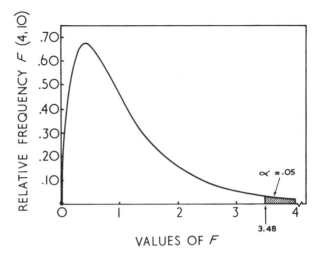

Fig. 4-2   Sampling distribution of $F(4, 10)$.

particular F distribution, we will use the expression, $F(df_{num.}, df_{denom.})$, or in this case, $F(4, 10)$.]

For our experiment, we do not have to know the exact shape of the F distribution. The only information we need is the value of F, to the right of which certain proportions of the area under the curve fall. These values have been tabulated and are readily available. An abridged F table is found in Table C-1 of Appendix C. A particular value of F in this table is specified by three factors: (1) the numerator df (represented by the columns of the table), (2) the denominator df (represented by the main rows of the table), and (3) the value of α (represented by the rows listed for each denominator df), where α refers to the proportion of area to the right of an ordinate drawn at F_α.

For example, the value of $F(4, 10) = 3.48$ at $\alpha = .05$. This F is found by locating the intersection of the column at $df_{num.} = 4$ and the row at $df_{denom.} = 10$. The different values of $F(4, 10)$ in this location represent critical points for a number of different α levels. The one we want is at $\alpha = .05$. What this value of F means is that an ordinate drawn at $F(4, 10) = 3.48$ will divide the sampling distribution of $F(4, 10)$ at a point where the proportion of the area under the curve to the right is .05. Said another way, $\alpha \times 100 = .05 \times 100 = 5$ percent of the area under the curve falls to the right of an ordinate drawn at $F(4, 10) = 3.48$. For $\alpha = .25$, $F(4, 10) = 1.59$ and for $\alpha = .01$, $F(4, 10) = 5.99$; 25 percent and 1 percent of the sampling distribution of $F(4, 10)$ fall to the right of these respective points.

Obviously, not all possible combinations of these three factors are listed in the table. The α levels, $\alpha = .25, .10, .05, .025, .01,$ and $.001$, are ones most commonly encountered. Additional levels of α can be found in the different editions of Fisher and Yates (e.g., 1953) or in the more convenient tables of

Dixon and Massey (1957). The intervals between successive columns and rows increase with the larger numerator and denominator df's. For instance, the $df_{num.}$ include entries for consecutive values of df from 1–10; the next columns are $df_{num.} = 12, 15, 20, 24, 30, 40, 60$, and ∞. The $df_{denom.}$ increase consecutively from 3–20, by two's from 22–30, and then, $df_{denom.} = 40, 60, 120$, and ∞. Fine gradations are not needed for the larger df values, since the numerical values of F do not change greatly from interval to interval.

Sampling Distribution of F'

We have only considered the sampling distribution of F when the null hypothesis is *true*—i.e., when the population means are equal. Obviously, we do not intend to conduct many experiments in which this is the case! We perform an experiment because we expect to find treatment effects. Suppose we assume that H_0 is false. What should happen to the F ratio? From previous discussions, we have argued that the expected value of the ratio should be greater than 1.0. This was because the MS_A contains two components, treatment effects and experimental error, while the $MS_{S/A}$ is the result of experimental error alone. The sampling distribution of the F ratio under these circumstances is no longer the F distribution. Instead, the theoretical distribution is called F' or *noncentral F*. It would be nice to be able to draw the F' distribution and to compare it with a corresponding F distribution. Unfortunately, however, this is difficult to do, since the F' distribution is a function of the *magnitude* of the treatment effects as well as of the numerator and denominator df's. Thus, while there is only one F distribution at any combination of numerator and denominator df's, there is a family of F' distributions, one distribution for each value that the treatment effects may take.

One way to approach this problem is to decide upon treatment effects of a certain size and see what the F' distribution looks like then. It is convenient to turn again to an empirical determination of this distribution. We will consider two such distributions. One was obtained by sampling from populations of 6000 scores each, where the variances are equal, $\sigma^2 = 225$, and the means are different, $\mu_1 = 50$, $\mu_2 = 55$, and $\mu_3 = 60$. The sampling distribution of the different F ratios, which is based on a total of 3036 independent "experiments," is plotted in Fig. 4-3. (The frequencies have been adjusted to a base of 1000 experiments to allow a comparison with other sampling experiments.) The empirical $F(2, 42)$ distribution, which was obtained by an identical procedure except that $\mu_1 = \mu_2 = \mu_3 = \mu = 50$, is replotted for comparison purposes in the same figure. Also plotted is the sampling distribution for a third sampling experiment (unconnected dots), which summarizes the results of drawing 1002 experiments from populations where $\mu_1 = 50$, $\mu_2 = 60$, and $\mu_3 = 70$ and the variances are equal, $\sigma^2 = 225$.

We will compare the sampling distributions labeled "H_0 True" (the F distribution) with the one labeled "H_0 False" (the F' distribution, where the

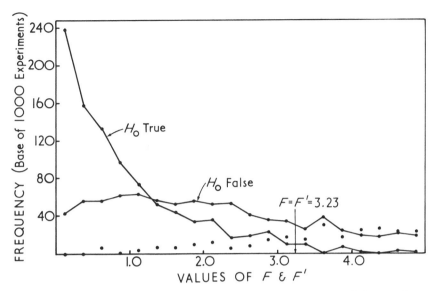

Fig. 4-3 Sampling distributions of F and F' obtained from Monte Carlo experiments. For "H_0 True," $\mu_i = 50$ for all three conditions; for "H_0 False," $\mu_i = 50, 55,$ and 60; and for the curve depicted by unconnected dots, $\mu_i = 50, 60,$ and 70.

population means differ in 5-unit steps). Clearly, the shapes of the two distributions are different. More important, however, is the fact that the F' distribution is shifted to the *right* of the F distribution, centering over numerically larger values of F'. This upward shift is reflected in the means of the sampling distributions. The average value of F is 1.09.[2] In contrast, the average value of F' is 2.90. Looked at another way, the area of the curve to the right of an ordinate drawn from any positive value of F (or F') will always be *greater* for the F' distribution. For example, consider the ordinate drawn at $F = F' = 3.23$: the proportion of the curve to the right of the ordinate is .050 for the F distribution and .333 for the F' distribution. At another point, an ordinate drawn at a value of 2.44 results in proportions of .114 and .463 for the F and F' curves, respectively. [For the other F' distribution, where the means differ in 10-unit steps (the unconnected dots), the two corresponding proportions are .906 and .944.]

Test of the Null Hypothesis

We are now ready to piece together this information concerning the sampling distributions of F and F' to provide a test of the null hypothesis. We start our

[2] The mean of the theoretical distribution is given by

$$E(F) = \bar{F} = \frac{df_{\text{denom.}}}{df_{\text{denom.}} - 2}.$$

testing procedure by specifying H_0 and H_1, the null and alternative statistical hypotheses. To review briefly an earlier discussion, the two hypotheses are

$$H_0: \mu_1 = \mu_2 = \cdots = \mu_a$$

and

$$H_1: \text{all } \mu_i\text{'s not equal.}$$

The hypothesis we will test, the null hypothesis, assumes that the means of the treatment populations are equal. The alternative hypothesis is a mutually exclusive statement which generally asserts simply that the means of the treatment populations are not equal—i.e., that some treatment effects are present. We choose this particular null hypothesis because it is usually the only hypothesis which we can state *exactly*. There is no ambiguity in the assertion that the population means are equal; there is only one way in which this can happen. The alternative hypothesis is an *inexact* statement—an assertion that the population means are not all equal. Nothing is said about the *actual* differences which are present in the population. (If we had that sort of information, we would have no reason for conducting the experiment!) Another advantage of this particular null hypothesis is that the sampling distribution of F is known. Presumably the sampling distribution of F' can be worked out, but we will need a different distribution for treatment effects of different sizes. Just how we use the sampling distribution of F in evaluating the null hypothesis will be considered next.

Assume that we have conducted an experiment and that we have computed the value of F. What we have to decide is whether this value of F came from the F distribution or whether it came from an F' distribution. An inspection of Fig. 4-3 will indicate that we will never be certain, because *any* observed value of F might have come from *either one of the two distributions*. Logically, it could only have come from one, but which one? Since we are evaluating the null hypothesis, we will turn our attention to the F distribution. While some values of F are less likely to occur than are others, it is still possible theoretically to obtain *any* value of F in an experiment when the null hypothesis is true. From one point of view our situation is hopeless: if any value of F may have been the result of chance factors, then we can never be *certain* that the F we observe in an experiment was *not* drawn from the F distribution. Agreed. If we were to take this attitude, however, we would never be able to use the experimental method as a way of finding out about the world. That is, if we maintain that any difference among the sample means may be due to chance, there is no way that we can conclude that our experimental manipulations influenced behavior differentially. As Fisher (1951) puts it, "... an experiment would be useless of which no possible result would satisfy [us]" (p. 13). We will not take this attitude. We must be willing to make mistakes in rejecting the null hypothesis when H_0 is true; otherwise, we can never reject the null hypothesis.

Suppose we could agree upon a dividing line for any F distribution, where values of F falling above the line are considered to be unlikely and values of F falling below the line are considered to be likely. We would then see whether our observed F falls above or below this arbitrary dividing line. If the F falls above the line, we will conclude that the observed F is *incompatible* with the null hypothesis; that is, we will reject H_0 and conclude that the alternative hypothesis is true. If the F falls below the line, we will conclude that the observed F is *compatible* with the null hypothesis. Under these circumstances, then, we will not reject H_0. Following such a set of rules means that we *will* be able to conclude that our independent variable was effective, provided an F ratio is obtained which falls within the region of incompatibility. But it also means that we are willing to make a mistake by rejecting a true null hypothesis a certain proportion of the time.

DECISION RULES   The crux of the problem, of course, is to find a way of objectively defining the regions of "compatibility" and "incompatibility." If the null hypothesis is true, we can determine the sampling distribution of F. Suppose we find a point on this distribution beyond which the probability of occurrence is very, very small. (The probability is represented by the proportion of the total area under the curve that appears beyond this particular point.) We will arbitrarily consider values of F falling within this region as *incompatible* with the *null hypothesis*. We must identify such a region in order to be able to reject the null hypothesis. Our decision rule, then, is to reject the null hypothesis when the observed F falls within the region of incompatibility. We do so, knowing full well that we may be making the wrong decision, which would be the case if the null hypothesis really were true.

Suppose, now, that we begin to enlarge the region of incompatibility, by moving the critical point of transition to the left—toward the larger portion of the curve—and cumulate the probabilities associated with these new portions of the curve. As we increase the size of this region, we also increase the chance of observing values from this region. Said another way, increasing the region of incompatibility results in the inclusion of F's which are becoming increasingly more *compatible* with the null hypothesis. Theoretically, an investigator may pick any cumulative probability he wants, just as long as the decision is made before the start of the experiment. In practice, however, there is fairly common agreement upon a cumulative probability of $\alpha = .05$ to define the region of incompatibility for the F distribution. This probability is called the *significance level*.

We are now in a position to state more formally the decision rules that are followed after the calculation of the F ratio.[3] If the F value falls within the region of incompatibility, the null hypothesis is rejected and the alternative hypothesis is accepted. If the F value falls within the region of compatibility, the null hypothesis is not rejected. (These two regions are often called the regions of

---

[3] Hays (1963, pp. 245–287) provides a detailed discussion of this decision process.

"rejection" and "nonrejection.") The decision to reject or not is made by comparing the observed value of F with the value of F located at the critical point of transition. Symbolically, the rules are stated as

Reject H_0 when $F_{observed} \geq F_{(\alpha)}(m, n)$; otherwise, do not reject H_0. (4-4)

In this statement, α refers to the significance level, and m and n to the df's associated with the numerator and denominator of the F ratio, respectively.

There is often some confusion concerning the exact wording of the decision rules, stemming largely from the fact that we cannot *prove* a hypothesis, only *disprove* it. When we say that a particular hypothesis is "accepted," we do *not* mean that it has been proved—just that it is consistent with the facts. Thus, if we reject H_0, this means that the results of the experiment are consistent with the alternative hypothesis that the treatment means are different; in this sense, then, we accept H_1. By the same token, if we do not reject H_0, this means that we consider the results of the experiment consistent with the hypothesis that the treatment means are equal. It is in this sense, too, that we are accepting the null hypothesis.

We will consider two examples of the use of the rejection rule. The first involves an evaluation of the F we calculated earlier in this chapter (see Table 4-2, p. 56). In this example, $m = 2$ and $n = 12$. If we set $\alpha = .05$, the critical value of F which we find in the tabled values of the F distribution (Table C-1 of Appendix C) is 3.89. The rejection region consists of all values of F equal to or greater than 3.89. Substituting in Eq. (4-4), the decision rule becomes

Reject H_0 when $F_{observed} \geq 3.89$; otherwise, do not reject H_0.

Since the F obtained in this example exceeded this value ($F = 7.41$), we would conclude that treatment effects were present in this experiment.

For the second example, we will return to Fig. 4-3 (p. 61). If we set $\alpha = .05$, the critical value of F at $m = 2$ and $n = 42$ is approximately 3.23. (Table C-1 does not have a value for this combination of df's; the value we have given here is associated with $m = 2$ and $n = 40$.) The rejection region consists of all values of F equal to or greater than 3.23. Since the area under the curve to the right of an ordinate drawn at this value of F consists of 5 percent of the total area under the curve, the probability of obtaining an F at least as deviant as 3.23 is .05. When we substitute in Eq. (4-4), the decision rule becomes

Reject H_0 when $F_{observed} \geq 3.23$; otherwise, do not reject H_0.

The size of the rejection region each of us adopts is a personal choice. What probability we choose is often dictated by our concern for *failing* to reject the null hypothesis when a real difference among treatment means exists. (More about this in a moment.) In presenting the results of a statistical test, however, we should remember that not all researchers who will be reading the report will agree with our choice of significance level. Thus, in order to accommodate most of the researchers adopting different rejection regions, we indicate the *smallest* significance level within which the $F_{observed}$ will fall. For example, suppose we obtained an F of 6.33 in the last experiment we have just considered. An inspection of the F table indicates that the critical value of F at $\alpha = .01$ is approximately 5.18. One way to report the results of this test would be to make the following statement:

$$F(2, 42) = 6.33, p < .01,$$

which means that this value of F falls within a rejection region having an α level that is less than a probability (p) of .01. Such a statement would indicate that the null hypothesis would be rejected by all researchers adopting a significance level at least as small as 1 percent. Since few researchers will be more conservative than this, the smallest rejection region that we would need to report in a scientific journal is one at $\alpha = .01$. We must distinguish in this discussion between the transmission of information concerning the significance level of the $F_{observed}$ from our own decision to reject or not to reject the null hypothesis. In this example, our rejection region was $\alpha = .05$, but we reported the probability associated with the F as $p < .01$. Our decision to reject H_0 depends only upon the presence of $F_{observed}$ in *our* rejection region.

SUMMARY   We have seen that a statistical test begins with the specification of the null and alternative hypotheses. We then conduct our experiment and calculate an F ratio. Next, we judge whether we have obtained an F which is incompatible with the hypothesis that the means of the treatment populations are equal. Incompatibility is defined arbitrarily ahead of time as an F which would occur on the basis of chance, assuming H_0 is true, a small proportion of the time, e.g., 1 time in 20 (5 percent). If the $F_{observed}$ falls within this region of incompatibility, we reject the null hypothesis; it it falls within the region of compatibility, we do not reject the null hypothesis.

Errors in Hypothesis Testing

The procedures we follow in hypothesis testing do *not* guarantee that a correct inference will be drawn when we apply the decision rules enumerated in Eq. (4-4). On the contrary, whether or not we decide to reject the null hypothesis, we will be making either a correct decision or an incorrect decision, depending upon the state of affairs in the real world—i.e., the population. The two types of errors that we can commit are defined in Table 4-4. There are two states that "reality" can take: either the null hypothesis is true or it is false; and there are two decisions that we may make: either reject H_0 or do not. The four possible combinations of states of reality and types of decisions are enumerated in the table. Inspection reveals two situations in which we will make the *correct decision*, i.e., no error of inference: (1) if we reject H_0 when it is *false* and (2) if we accept H_0

when it is *true*. On the other hand, in two complementary situations we will make an *incorrect decision*, i.e., an error of inference : (1) if we reject H_0 when it is *true* and (2) if we accept H_0 when it is *false*. These errors of inference are called type I and type II errors or α or β errors, respectively.

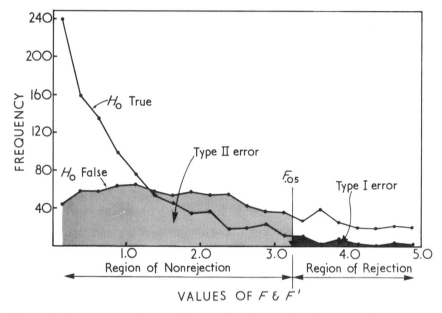

Fig. 4-4   Type I and type II errors illustrated by using empirically determined sampling distributions of F and F'.

To illustrate the two types of errors, we will consider a concrete example. The two sampling distributions from Fig. 4-3 have been reproduced in Fig. 4-4. The curve labeled "H_0 true" is the empirical sampling distribution of $F(2, 42)$

TABLE 4-4   *Errors in Hypothesis Testing*

	Reality	
Decision	H_0 true, H_1 false	H_0 false, H_1 true
Reject H_0 Accept H_1	Incorrect decision : type I error	Correct decision
Accept H_0 Do not accept H_1	Correct decision	Incorrect decision : type II error

when the population means were equal, and the curve labeled "H_0 false" is the empirical sampling distribution of $F'(2, 42)$ when the population means differed in 5-unit steps. These curves indicate the sampling distribution of the *F* ratio when the null hypothesis is true and when the alternative hypothesis is true. (The distribution for F' plotted in the figure is only one of the permissible alternative hypotheses; one is all that we need to make the point.) One thing is clear in comparing these two sampling distributions: any value of $F_{observed}$ is possible under *both* hypotheses. But we have to hazard a guess about $F_{observed}$ and decide whether it is more likely to have come from the *F* distribution or from the F' distribution. Since we are testing the null hypothesis, we will have to make a decision concerning values of *F* that are rare enough—i.e., would occur infrequently enough on the basis of chance—to justify the speculation that $F_{observed}$ came instead from the F' distribution.

Suppose we arbitrarily define rarity in probability terms as $\alpha = .05$. This means that we will consider any $F_{observed}$ that would occur by chance 5 percent of the time or less incompatible with the null hypothesis. The probability is represented by the shaded area under the curve for the *F* distribution to the *right* of an ordinate erected at $F = 3.23$; this area is the rejection region. This probability also represents the calculated risk we are taking in the decision process, namely, that 5 percent of the time when the null hypothesis is true we will be making the wrong decision—a type I error. Of course, when the alternative hypothesis is true, we make the correct decision. The proportion of the time we can expect to enjoy this state of affairs is represented by the area under the F' curve included in the rejection region; in this example, the proportion is .333.

Now, consider what happens when we do not reject the null hypothesis. (The region of nonrejection includes all values of *F* which are less than 3.23.) If the null hypothesis happens to be true, we will have made the correct decision by not rejecting H_0. The probability of such a decision is $1 - \alpha = 1 - .05 = .95$. But if the alternative hypothesis is true, we will be in error by failing to reject H_0, and the probability with which this error will be made (a type II error) is represented by the lightly shaded area under the F' curve to the left of $F_{.05}$. In this example, β is .667.

As long as we are committed to make decisions in the face of incomplete knowledge, as every scientist is, we cannot avoid making these errors. We can, however, try to minimize them. We directly control the size of the type I error in our selection of significance level. By setting a region of rejection, we are taking a calculated risk that a certain proportion of the time (for example, $\alpha = .05$), we will obtain *F*'s which fall into this region when the null hypothesis is true. We accept this fact, recognizing that over our lifetimes we will make the wrong decision 5 percent of the time by falsely rejecting the null hypothesis. The size of the type II error is controlled *indirectly*—a point we will discuss in a moment.

There is an obvious reciprocity between these two types of error: if we make one, we cannot make the other. But there is a less obvious relationship. We have seen that the size of the type I error is under the direct control of the researcher. He sets the α level in the experiment. By decreasing the size of α—i.e., moving to the right the value of F that divides the rejection from the nonrejection region—we will reject *fewer* values of $F_{observed}$ when the null hypothesis is true. However, if the alternative happens to be true, the shaded portion under the F' curve will *increase* and so will our type II error. Consequently, any change in the α level will be accompanied by a change in the opposite direction of the probability of making a type II error. [The relationship between type I and type II errors is developed more fully in Chapter 24.]

How can we control the type II error? In our example, we specified a particular alternative hypothesis, that $\mu_1 = 50$, $\mu_2 = 55$, and $\mu_3 = 60$. We saw that if α is set at .05, we can expect β to equal .667. We could only make this determination by knowing the exact means specified by H_1. In most areas of research in the behavioral sciences, we have no way of offering an *exact* alternative hypothesis such as the one we have been considering. Instead, we settle for the inexact one, namely, that the treatment means are not equal. In some situations it is possible to narrow down the set of reasonable alternative hypotheses, but we will defer a discussion of this possibility to Chapter 24.

There are, however, ways of reducing type II errors. We have already considered an obvious procedure: to *increase* the rejection region. Of course, we do so at the cost of an increase in type I errors! Every researcher must strike a balance between the two types of errors. If it is important to discover *new* facts, then we may be willing to accept more *type I* errors and thus *increase* the rejection region. On the other hand, if it is important not to clog up the literature with *false* facts, then we may be willing to accept more *type II* errors and *decrease* the rejection region. Arguments can be made for both sides of this type I/type II coin; we will discuss these arguments in Chapter 8. Other ways of reducing type II errors will be considered in subsequent chapters (see especially Chapter 24). For the time being, we merely observe that type II errors may be decreased by adding to the number of observations in each treatment condition and by reducing error variance through the design of a more precisely controlled experiment.

ANOTHER NUMERICAL EXAMPLE

Now that we have looked at each step of the one-factor analysis of variance, it is time to work through a numerical example from start to finish. Suppose a researcher is interested in the effect of sleep deprivation on the ability of subjects to perform a vigilance task, such as locating objects moving on a radar screen. He arranged to house the subjects in his laboratory so that he would have control over their sleeping habits. There were $a = 4$ conditions, namely, 4, 12, 20, and 28 hours without sleep. There were $s = 4$ subjects randomly assigned to the different treatments. The subjects were well trained on the vigilance task before the start of the experiment. They were scored on the number of failures to spot objects on a radar screen during a 30-minute test period. The scores for each subject are presented in Table 4-5.

TABLE 4-5 *Numerical Example*

AS MATRIX

Hours Without Sleep (Factor A)

	4 hr. a_1	12 hr. a_2	20 hr. a_3	28 hr. a_4
	37	36	43	76
	22	45	75	66
	22	47	66	43
	25	23	46	62
A_i:	106	151	230	247
$\bar{A}_i$:	26.50	37.75	57.50	61.75
$\sum\limits_{j}^{s}(AS_{ij})^2$:	2962	6059	13,946	15,825

The analysis begins with the basic summing and squaring operation for the scores in each treatment condition. The results of these calculations are also listed in the table. For the subjects in level a_2, for example,

$$A_2 = \sum AS_{2j} = 36 + 45 + 47 + 23 = 151,$$

$$\bar{A}_2 = \frac{A_2}{s} = \frac{151}{4} = 37.75,$$

and

$$\sum (AS_{2j})^2 = (36)^2 + (45)^2 + (47)^2 + (23)^2 = 6059.$$

We will now calculate the three sums of squares. Substituting the values from Table 4-5 into the computational formulas given in Table 3-2,

$$SS_A = \frac{\sum (A)^2}{s} - \frac{(T)^2}{as}$$

$$= \frac{(106)^2 + (151)^2 + (230)^2 + (247)^2}{4} - \frac{(106 + 151 + 230 + 247)^2}{4(4)}$$

$$= \frac{147{,}946}{4} - \frac{538{,}756}{16}$$

$$= 36{,}986.50 - 33{,}672.25 = 3314.25,$$

$$SS_{S/A} = \sum (AS)^2 - \frac{\sum (A)^2}{s}$$

$$= (2962 + 6059 + 13{,}946 + 15{,}825) - \frac{(106)^2 + (151)^2 + (230)^2 + (247)^2}{4}$$

$$= 38{,}792 - \frac{147{,}946}{4}$$

$$= 38{,}792 - 36{,}986.50 = 1805.50,$$

and

$$SS_T = \sum (AS)^2 - \frac{(T)^2}{as}$$

$$= (2962 + 6059 + 13{,}946 + 15{,}825) - \frac{(106 + 151 + 230 + 247)^2}{4(4)}$$

$$= 38{,}792 - \frac{538{,}756}{16}$$

$$= 38{,}792 - 33{,}672.25 = 5119.75.$$

As a check,

$$SS_A + SS_{S/A} = 3314.25 + 1805.50 = 5119.75 = SS_T.$$

The remainder of the analysis is based upon the formulas listed in Table 4-1 (p. 53). The sums of squares we have just calculated are entered in Table 4-6. The df's associated with the different sums of squares are

$$df_A = a - 1 = 4 - 1 = 3,$$
$$df_{S/A} = a(s - 1) = 4(4 - 1) = 12,$$

and

$$df_T = as - 1 = 4(4) - 1 = 15.$$

TABLE 4-6 *Summary of the Analysis*

Source	SS	df	MS	F
A	3314.25	3	1104.75	7.34*
S/A	1805.50	12	150.46	
Total	5119.75	15		

* $p < .01$.

As an arithmetic check,

$$df_A + df_{S/A} = 3 + 12 = 15 = df_T.$$

The between-groups and within-groups mean squares are formed by dividing the relevant sum of squares by the corresponding df. Specifically,

$$MS_A = \frac{SS_A}{a-1} = \frac{3314.25}{3} = 1104.75$$

and

$$MS_{S/A} = \frac{SS_{S/A}}{a(s-1)} = \frac{1805.50}{12} = 150.46.$$

The F ratio is obtained by dividing the first mean square by the second:

$$F = \frac{MS_A}{MS_{S/A}} = \frac{1104.75}{150.46} = 7.34.$$

The results of each of these steps are entered in the summary table. We will assume that the α level has been set at $p = .05$ before the start of the experiment. In order to evaluate the significance of the F, we locate the critical value of F at $\alpha = .05$ and $df_{num.} = 3$ and $df_{denom.} = 12$. From the F table (Table C-1 of Appendix C),

$$F(3, 12) = 3.49.$$

The decision rules given in Eq. (4-4) may be stated as follows:

Reject H_0 if $F_{observed} \geq 3.49$; otherwise, do not reject H_0.

Since $F_{observed}$ exceeds this value, we reject the null hypothesis and conclude that the independent variable produced an effect.

The results of the statistical test are indicated by a footnote in the summary table. In this case, the entry $p < .01$ notes that the F we have observed is larger than the value of F marking off the 1 percent level of significance; i.e., $F_{(.01)} = 5.95$. As explained earlier, an indication that the obtained F falls within the 1 percent rejection region does not necessarily mean that we set α at $p = .01$. This particular statement of the outcome of our analysis is more informative, allowing individual researchers to use their own significance levels in evaluating our finding. Since we adopted the 5 percent level of significance, we would have rejected the null hypothesis in any case.

chapter five

ASSUMPTIONS AND
ADDITIONAL CONSIDERATIONS

Certain assumptions concerning the distribution of scores within groups must be met if the analysis of variance is to "work" as described. The values listed in the F table are based on the theoretical F distribution. These values are appropriate for an analysis only when these distribution assumptions are satisfied. If they are not, then we have no simple way of determining whether or not $F_{observed}$ falls within the rejection region of the theoretical sampling distribution of this statistic—whatever it might be with a particular set of violations. The critical question for us, of course, is to see how our *conclusions* are affected by a failure of our experiment to meet these assumptions. Such a consideration is extremely important, since rarely will we find all of the assumptions met in the experiments we conduct. If even the slightest violation can result in a considerable change in the sampling distribution of the F statistic, then we are in trouble.

There has been an important development in the evaluation of the assumptions underlying the analysis of variance. It is a practical approach to the problem—in a sense, a "user's" approach. Monte Carlo experiments are performed, based on scores drawn at random from populations with characteristics *differing* from those assumed in the analysis. These populations are constructed to have the *same mean* but different shapes and different variances. The resultant sampling distribution of the *F* statistic, obtained from a large number of these random draws, is compared with the theoretical *F* distribution. Since the null hypothesis is true in these experiments (the population means are equal), the sampling distribution of the *F* statistic will equal the theoretical distribution of *F* only if the violations of the assumptions are *unimportant*. The degree to which the empirically derived sampling distribution deviates from the theoretical distribution provides an assessment of the practical consequences of these violations. As we will discover shortly, the sampling distribution of *F* is amazingly "robust"; that is, it is insensitive to even flagrant violations of the assumptions.

ASSUMPTIONS UNDERLYING THE SINGLE-FACTOR ANALYSIS OF VARIANCE

Normally Distributed Error Variance

The first assumption states that the individual treatment populations, from which the members of each treatment group are assumed to be randomly drawn, are normally distributed.[1] As a rough test of this assumption, we could look at the distribution of the *AS* scores within each group and estimate the general shape of the distribution. Or we could check for normality by means of a rather elaborate but objective test (see, for example, Hays, 1963, pp. 586–588). Suppose that the sample distributions are of approximately the same *non*normal shape—or, even worse, that the distributions for the different groups appear to have been drawn from populations with qualitatively different distributions. What does this do to the sampling distribution of *F*? Apparently, very little, especially if the groups contain equal numbers of subjects. This has been known by statisticians for some time (see Box, 1953). Monte Carlo experiments have also been performed. We will consider one of these studies in some detail.

In the Monte Carlo experiments, attention is focused upon the rejection region of the *F* distribution. When the sampling is from populations meeting all of the assumptions, the percentage of *F* ratios which actually fall in the rejection region matches very closely the percentage expected on the basis of the theoretical distribution. This point was demonstrated in Table 4-3, where the probabilities were obtained from a Monte Carlo study in which the scores for each "experiment" were drawn from the same normal distribution. An inspection of the table indicates a close correspondence between the obtained and expected probabilities for a number of possible rejection regions.

---

[1] This is equivalent to saying that the deviation of the members of the treatment populations from their respective population means (μ_i's) are normally distributed with a mean of zero.

An early Monte Carlo study performed by Norton (1952) is reported in detail by Lindquist (1953, pp. 78–90). Norton drew samples from distributions which were normal, leptokurtic (highly peaked), rectangular, moderately and markedly skewed, and J-shaped. He also conducted Monte Carlo tests where the scores were drawn from distributions having the same shape and from distributions having different shapes. He found that with homogeneous distributions, there was a close matching of empirical and theoretical percentages. The match was not quite as good when the populations were of markedly different form. In this latter case, the discrepancies were of the order of a 2–3 percent overestimation of the 5 percent significance level and of a 1–2 percent overestimation of the 1 percent significance level. This means, for example, that when an experimenter chooses an $\alpha = .05$, his *actual* α level may be as large as $p = .08$.

In short, Norton's study indicates that if we used the 5 percent rejection region, even for the most deviant comparisons, the empirically determined rejection region (the type I error) would be no larger than $\alpha = .08$. (This overestimation would probably have been less if Norton had used larger sample sizes. His sample sizes were 3 or 5.) Norton's and later studies tell us, then, that it is safe to conclude that violations of the normality assumption do not constitute a serious problem, except if the violations are especially severe. Under these circumstances, we need only worry about F's that fall close to the critical value of F defining the start of the rejection region.

Homogeneity of Error Variance

This assumption requires that the variances of the different treatment populations be equal. In terms of an experiment, the within-group mean squares for each group, which provide separate estimates of error variance, should be the same. Three methods are commonly used to test the homogeneity assumption. Two of these are computationally simple, but require equal sample sizes (the Cochran test and the Hartley test), while the other (the Bartlett test) is computationally complex, but accommodates unequal sample sizes.

Homogeneity of variance is tested in the Cochran test by dividing the largest within-group variance by the sum of the individual within-group variances. The Hartley test compares the largest within-group variance against the smallest within-group variance. The outcome of either test is evaluated by means of special tables. The Bartlett test is complicated and is no better than the Cochran and Hartley tests for testing the homogeneity assumption. [Winer (1962, pp. 92–96; 1971, pp. 205–210) discusses and provides examples of all three tests.]

There is a problem associated with these tests, however—a sensitivity to departures from *normality* as well as to the presence of heterogeneity. As a way to avoid this difficulty, Glass (1966) calls attention to a fourth test which is usually *not* sensitive to departures from normality. This test, proposed by Levene (1960), requires a recalculation of the basic sums of squares using transformed AS scores. (We will consider this test in the final section of this chapter.)

In assessing the significance of a set of differences among group means, we are interested in how seriously the theoretical sampling distribution of F is distorted by the presence of unequal variances, whether these differences are significant or not. As with deviations from normality, even sizable differences among the variances do not appear to distort the F distribution seriously. The work of Box (1954), for example, shows that with equal population means and with variances in the ratio of $1:2:3$, the proportion of F ratios falling within the 5 percent rejection region was .058. The results of a number of other studies [e.g., Norton (1952) for the F distribution; Boneau (1960) and Baker, Hardyck, and Petrinovich (1966) for a special two-group case of the F distribution (t)] suggest that the distortion is relatively slight when equal sample sizes are used. (Violations are more serious when unequal sizes are present.) Because of these findings, then, most researchers do not even bother to test the homogeneity assumption with their data.

Independence of Error Components

The deviation of each score from the grand mean of the population $(AS_{ij} - \mu)$ is thought to contain two components, a between-group treatment effect $(\mu_i - \mu)$ and a within-group deviation $(AS_{ij} - \mu_i)$, the latter forming the basis for our estimate of experimental error based on sample scores. A third assumption of the analysis of variance is that the error components are independent—independent within treatment groups as well as independent between treatment groups. Independence here means that each observation is in no way related to any other observation in the experiment. The random assignment of subjects to conditions is the procedure by which we obtain independence. Of course, this is just another way of saying that systematic biases must not be present in the assignment of subjects to conditions. This is not just a statistical assumption, but a basic requirement of experimental design as well. With nonindependence of error components between treatment groups, a confounding of variables is present, and we are unable to make unambiguous inferences concerning the independent influence of our independent variable on the behavior we are studying. This assumption, then, emphasizes the critical importance statistically, as well as experimentally, of ensuring the random assignment of subjects to the treatment groups.

Additivity of Components

The model underlying the analysis we have been discussing assumes that it is proper to view an AS score as the *sum* of effects. If we start with the familiar breakdown of the total deviation into between and within deviations,

$$AS_{ij} - \mu = (\mu_i - \mu) + (AS_{ij} - \mu_i),$$

and move μ from the left side of the equation to the right side, we have

$$AS_{ij} = \mu + (\mu_i - \mu) + (AS_{ij} - \mu_i).$$

That is, an AS_{ij} score is assumed to be made up of three parts: a part representing average performance in the overall population, a deviation reflecting the treatment effect, and a deviation reflecting experimental error.[2] Researchers do not appear to question this assumption of additivity, and little is said in psychological statistics texts about conditions in which the assumption is not tenable or in which a violation of the assumption can be recognized. Thus, it is mentioned here only for the sake of completeness.

UNEQUAL SAMPLE SIZES

As we have noted, most experiments contain an equal number of subjects in each of the treatment conditions. The most obvious reason for this is perhaps the tacit intention to estimate each of the population means with the same degree of precision. There is no compelling need for equal sample sizes in the single-factor analysis of variance, although the same cannot be said without qualification in analyses involving two or more independent variables. In fact, the argument could be made that the individual sample sizes should be chosen with the expectation of precision in mind. That is, if an experimenter had reason to believe that a particular group would be more or less variable than the others (as might be the case in comparing control and experimental groups, for example), he could run a larger number of subjects in the more variable group. [Winer (1962, p. 27; 1971, p. 29) states that the most sensitive design makes sample size proportional to respective population variances.] In this situation, the unequal sample sizes are *planned*.[3] What happens when the inequality is not planned, but occurs because of an inadvertent loss of subjects? We will consider the implications of this latter event in some detail.

Why should subjects fail to complete the experiment? In animal studies, subjects are frequently lost through death and sickness. In human studies, in which testing is to continue over several days, subjects are discarded when they fail to complete the experimental sequence. In a memory study, for instance, some of the subjects may fail to return for their terminal retention test a week later, perhaps because of illness or a conflicting appointment. Subjects also may

---

[2] An additional assumption that we are making is that $\sum (\mu_i - \mu) = 0$. This assumption is a specification of the *fixed-effects model*, which is appropriate for most of the research in the behavioral sciences. This and additional models are discussed in Chapter 16. For the single-factor experiment, however, there is no difference in the statistical analysis dictated by the different models. Thus, we can ignore the topic at this time.

[3] On the other hand, we noted in the preceding section that violations of the homogeneity assumption are more serious when sample sizes are unequal. Consequently, you should seek expert guidance if you find yourself planning to follow Winer's advice.

be lost when studies require them to reach a performance criterion, such as a certain level of mastery; those who fail to do so are eliminated from the experiment. A third class of situations occurs when some of the subjects fail to produce responses that meet the criteria established for the response measure. Suppose we are interested in the speed with which *correct responses* are made. If a subject fails to give a correct response, he cannot contribute to the analysis. Or suppose we want to analyze the percentage of times *errors* produced on some task are of a particular type. If a subject fails to make any errors, he cannot contribute to the analysis. In such situations, subjects are eliminated from the analysis because they fail to give scorable responses.

It is of *critical* importance to determine the *implication* of these losses. That is, we have assigned our subjects to the experimental conditions in such a way that any differences among the groups at the start of the experiment will be attributed to chance factors. It is this fundamental assumption which allows us to test the null hypothesis. We are not concerned with the loss of subjects per se, but with the question: Has the loss of subjects, for whatever reason, resulted in a loss of *randomness*? If it has, either we must find a way to restore it or simply junk the experiment. No form of statistical juggling will rectify this situation. If randomness may still be safely assumed or has been restored, we can proceed with the statistical analysis of the data.

In each situation, we have to determine whether or not the reason for the subject loss is in any way associated with particular experimental treatments. In animal research, for instance, certain experimental conditions (such as operations, drugs, high levels of food or water deprivation, exhausting training procedures) may actually be responsible for the loss of the subjects. If this were the case, only the strongest and healthiest animals would survive, and the result would be an obvious confounding of subject differences and treatment conditions: the difficult conditions would contain a larger proportion of healthy animals than the less trying conditions. Replacing the lost subjects with new animals drawn from the same population will not provide an adequate solution, since the replacement subjects will not "match" the ones who were lost. If it can be shown that the loss of subjects was approximately the same from all of the conditions or that the loss was not related to the experimental treatments, then we may be able to continue with the analysis.

The same considerations are relevant when human subjects fail to complete the experiment. In the memory study we mentioned, it is likely that more subjects will be lost with the longer retention intervals, where the subjects have a greater "opportunity" to get sick. It is not known whether or not the loss of these subjects affects randomness. A researcher could attempt to see if the subjects who were lost and the subjects who were retained were equivalent in learning, although equality at this point in the experiment does not necessarily mean that the two sets of subjects would have been equivalent at recall. In some experiments, an attempt is made to impose the same subject loss on *all* conditions.

For example, suppose we require all subjects to return for the later retention test, and we follow the rule of discarding any subject who fails to return. The subject who is tested at the long interval and does not return is dropped from the experiment by default. But so is the subject who is tested at a shorter interval and fails to return for the later appointment.

The loss of subjects through failure to reach a criterion of mastery poses similar problems. Clearly, subjects who fail to learn are by definition poorer learners. If one group suffers a greater loss, which may very well happen if the conditions differ in difficulty, the subjects "making" it in the difficult condition represent a greater proportion of fast learners than those completing the training in the easier conditions. The replacement of subjects lost in the difficult condition would not solve this problem, since the replacement subjects would not match in ability the subjects who were discarded. One possibility is to compare the different groups at a lower criterion—one that will allow *all* of the subjects to be included. In this way, *no* subjects will be lost. Such a solution will be adequate if the researcher feels he will obtain the information he needs from the smaller sample of behavior.

Some experimenters solve this problem by artificially imposing a subject selection upon the groups that suffer fewer or no losses. Thus, if it can be assumed that only the poorer subjects were dropped from the more difficult conditions for failure to reach the performance criterion, then it might be possible to drop an equal number of the *poorest* subjects from *all* of the treatment conditions. A similar procedure is sometimes followed when subjects fail to give scorable responses. Suppose, for example, that an investigator is studying the speed of correct response under a number of different treatment conditions. As we have pointed out, subjects may fail to give a correct response and thus not provide a speed score. Some researchers attempt to resolve this difficulty by excluding subjects with the poorest record from the other conditions in order to "restore" equivalence of the groups. In all of these situations, however, it is assumed that the subjects whose data are discarded in the manner described are subjects who would have failed to reach the criterion or to have given any correct responses *if they had been in the condition producing the failures*. This is often a questionable assumption, but it must be made before any meaningful inferences can be drawn from the data so adjusted.

Clearly, then, the loss of subjects is of paramount concern to the experimenter. We have seen that if the loss of subjects is related to the phenomenon under study, randomness is destroyed, and a systematic bias may be added to the differences among the means which cannot be disentangled from the influence of the treatment effects. This is a problem of experimental design which must be solved by the researcher. If he can convince himself (and others) that the subject loss could not have resulted in a bias, there are statistical procedures available which will allow him to analyze his results. We will discuss these methods in Chapter 17.

THE VARIANCE AS A DESCRIPTIVE STATISTIC

For most of us, our research hypotheses are couched in terms of differences that may be observed among the treatment means. Usually, we have little sustained interest in the within-group variances, except with regard to their role in the estimation of experimental error; we look at the variances only to test the homogeneity assumption of the statistical analysis. This does not always have to be the case. Important changes in behavior caused by the different treatments may not be revealed in average performance. Or, if we look for them, systematic differences among the treatment conditions might be reflected in average performance *and* in the variability of the subjects within these conditions.

Examples of the Variance Reflecting Treatment Effects

Suppose, for example, that subjects employ a number of different strategies in performing a particular task. If they are asked to study a prose passage for an eventual test of comprehension, some may try to extract basic idea units while others may attempt to commit the entire passage to memory. The variability of their performance will reflect any differential efficiency that may be associated with these strategies—extracting idea units may be more efficient in general than learning by rote—in addition to any difference in ability that may exist among subjects. Suppose that subjects in a standard, noninstructed condition are contrasted with subjects in a condition in which they are required to perform the task with a particular strategy. Conceivably, such a comparison would not show much of a difference between the means of the two treatment groups, and a statistical analysis might lead to the conclusion that no treatment effect was present. On the other hand, the subjects in the "restricted" or instructed condition might be *more variable* in performance than the subjects in the "free" or uninstructed condition. Subjects forced to abandon their usual strategy might experience great difficulty in switching to the new strategy, which, moreover, might even be incompatible with the old one. Any such negative transfer resulting from a forced switch in strategies would show up as an increase of within-group variability for the instructed condition.

Consider another experiment, focused on the effect of administering a mild electric shock to college students each time they make an error on a motor-tracking task. Suppose that the task consists of tracking a moving object with some sighting device. The score for each subject is the number of errors he makes during a 10-minute tracking period. There are two groups; one receives a shock each time a subject loses track of the object, and one does not. How might the experiment turn out? Subjects differ greatly in how they respond even to the threat of shock—some try harder while others "freeze" and perform poorly. If subjects reacted differentially in this experiment, there should be a marked increase in variance for the shock group, with some subjects reducing and others increasing their tracking errors. In fact, it is conceivable that the number of subjects responding "positively" to shock would be equal to the number of subjects responding "negatively," the result being no effect upon average tracking errors for the two conditions.

Thus, in some situations a comparison of variances may lead to some interesting speculations about individual differences and the way in which subjects within a group respond to the experimental treatments. These comparisons may reveal important clues as to the processes responsible for whatever effects are observed among the treatment means.

Statistical Analyses

If we are interested in determining whether or not the different treatments affected the variances of the conditions differentially, we are essentially considering the following null and alternative hypotheses:

$$H_0: \sigma_1^2 = \sigma_2^2 = \cdots = \sigma_a^2,$$

$$H_1: \text{all } \sigma_i^2\text{'s not equal.}$$

We could evaluate the null hypothesis by means of either the Cochran, the Hartley, or the Bartlett test, but, as we have noted, these tests are affected by departures from normality as well as by the presence of heterogeneity of variance. If we are interested only in a rough test of the homogeneity assumption of an analysis of variance, these tests are satisfactory. On the other hand, if we have a systematic interest in the differences among the variances, we want a test which is sensitive primarily to differences among the within-group variances. Such a test has been proposed by Levene (1960).

Briefly, the test consists of an ordinary analysis of variance performed on *transformed AS* scores, which we will refer to as Z scores. A Z score is defined as a within-group deviation score with the sign disregarded (an *absolute* deviation score). That is,

$$Z_{ij} = |AS_{ij} - \bar{A}_i|.$$

We will consider an example in a moment. Levene was able to show with Monte Carlo procedures that an analysis of variance of the Z scores was sensitive to differences in within-group *variances* and for all practical purposes unaffected by deviations from normality. It is interesting to note that this test was developed *empirically*—it evolved from a number of Monte Carlo experiments. Levene turned to the Monte Carlo procedure when the mathematical justification of the test proved to be unmanageable. The important point is that the test does what it was designed to do: it provides a simple test for heterogeneity of variance which is relatively insensitive to violations of the normality assumption. We will now work through an example of the analysis.

The numerical example is based on the data originally given in Table 3-3.

TABLE 5-1   *Numerical Example: The Levene Test for Homogeneity of Variance*

AS MATRIX: BASIC AS SCORES AND WITHIN-GROUP DEVIATIONS

a_1		a_2		a_3	
AS_{1j}	$(AS_{1j} - \bar{A}_1)$	AS_{2j}	$(AS_{2j} - \bar{A}_2)$	AS_{3j}	$(AS_{3j} - \bar{A}_3)$
16	16–15	4	4–6	2	2–9
18	18–15	6	6–6	10	10–9
10	10–15	8	8–6	9	9–9
12	12–15	10	10–6	13	13–9
19	19–15	2	2–6	11	11–9

AS MATRIX: TRANSFORMED SCORES, $Z_{ij} = |AS_{ij} - \bar{A}_i|$

	a_1	a_2	a_3
	1	2	7
	3	0	1
	5	2	0
	3	4	4
	4	4	2
$\sum\limits_{j}^{s} Z_{ij}$:	16	12	14
$\sum\limits_{j}^{s} (Z_{ij})^2$:	60	40	70

SUMMARY OF THE ANALYSIS

Source	Calculations	SS	df	MS	F
A	119.20 − 117.60 =	1.60	2	.80	< 1
S/A	170 − 119.20 =	50.80	12	4.23	
Total	170 − 117.60 =	52.40	14		

These scores are presented again in the upper portion of Table 5-1. To the right of each AS score is listed the deviation of that score from the relevant group mean. (The means for the three groups in order are 15, 6, and 9.) The transformed deviations (Z) are found in the middle portion of the table. For example, for the first subject in the second group:

$$Z_{21} = |AS_{21} - \bar{A}_2| = |4 - 6| = |-2| = 2.$$

The next step is to conduct a one-factor analysis of variance on the Z scores, treating them as we would any other set of scores. For this test, we will use the following definitions of different quantities:

$$A_i = \sum_j^s Z_{ij} \quad \text{and} \quad T = \sum Z.$$

From the data in Table 5-1,

$$SS_A = \frac{\sum (A)^2}{s} - \frac{(T)^2}{as}$$

$$= \frac{(16)^2 + (12)^2 + (14)^2}{5} - \frac{(16 + 12 + 14)^2}{3(5)},$$

$$SS_{S/A} = \sum (Z)^2 - \frac{\sum (A)^2}{s}$$

$$= [(1)^2 + (3)^2 + \cdots + (4)^2 + (2)^2] - \frac{(16)^2 + (12)^2 + (14)^2}{5},$$

and

$$SS_T = \sum (Z)^2 - \frac{(T)^2}{as}$$

$$= [(1)^2 + (3)^2 + \cdots + (4)^2 + (2)^2] - \frac{(16 + 12 + 14)^2}{3(5)}.$$

The results of these calculations are summarized in the bottom portion of Table 5-1.

The remainder of the analysis is completed in this section of the table. The F ratio is formed in the usual way:

$$F = \frac{MS_A}{MS_{S/A}},$$

and is evaluated in the F tables with the df associated with the numerator and denominator terms. This analysis indicates that the variances are homogeneous.

chapter six

COMPARISONS AMONG TREATMENT MEANS

We have discussed the logic behind the statistical analysis of the completely randomized single-factor experiment. For most researchers, however, the completion of the analysis as outlined in previous chapters is merely the *first step* in the analysis of their data. The next three chapters will consider additional analyses that the researcher may use in his comprehensive examination of the data he has collected.

INTRODUCTION

The Need for Analytical Comparisons

THE SS_A AS A COMPOSITE OF PAIRWISE COMPARISONS   The between-groups sum of squares, the SS_A, was defined in Chapter 3 in terms of the deviation of the group means from the grand mean:

$$SS_A = s \sum (\bar{A}_i - \bar{T})^2.$$

An alternative form of this equation shows that the SS_A reflects the degree to which the group means differ from one another:

$$SS_A = \frac{s \sum (\bar{A}_i - \bar{A}_{i'})^2}{a}, \tag{6-1}$$

where i and i' represent different levels of factor A and where $i < i'$. [This restriction is necessary to specify all *unique* pairs of means. Without this restriction, we would be told to form the difference between two means in *both* directions ($\bar{A}_1 - \bar{A}_2$ and $\bar{A}_2 - \bar{A}_1$, for example), specifying that $i < i'$ singles out one of these differences (namely, $\bar{A}_1 - \bar{A}_2$).]

As an example, consider the data presented in Table 3-3. There were three levels of factor A and $s = 5$ observations per group. The three means were as follows: $\bar{A}_1 = 15.00$, $\bar{A}_2 = 6.00$, and $\bar{A}_3 = 9.00$. Substituting in Eq. (6-1), we have

$$SS_A = \frac{5[(15.00 - 6.00)^2 + (15.00 - 9.00)^2 + (6.00 - 9.00)^2]}{3}$$

$$= \frac{5[(9.00)^2 + (6.00)^2 + (-3.00)^2]}{3}$$

$$= \frac{5(126.00)}{3} = 210.00.$$

This value is identical to the one obtained by the standard defining formula:

$$SS_A = s \sum (\bar{A}_i - \bar{T})^2$$

$$= 5[(15.00 - 10.00)^2 + (6.00 - 10.00)^2 + (9.00 - 10.00)^2]$$

$$= 5[(5.00)^2 + (-4.00)^2 + (-1.00)^2]$$

$$= 5(42.00) = 210.00.$$

THE OMNIBUS F TEST   The analysis outlined in the preceding chapters provides a procedure to guide us in drawing inferences about differences that we observe among the means of the treatment conditions. The alternative form of the defining formula for the SS_A [i.e., Eq. (6-1)] indicates that the resulting F ratio can be viewed as representing a simultaneous test of the hypothesis that all possible comparisons between pairs of treatment means are zero. (This property has led some authors to refer to an F ratio based on $a > 2$ treatment levels as the "omnibus" or overall F.)

We have decided that if the value of the F ratio is significant, we will conclude that treatment effects are present (i.e., the treatment means are not equal), and if the F is not significant, we will conclude just the opposite (the treatment means are equal). With a nonsignificant F, we are prepared to assert that there are no real differences among the treatment means and that the particular sample means we have observed show differences which are reasonably accounted for by experimental error. We will stop the analysis there. Why analyze any further when the differences can be presumed to be chance differences?

In contrast, a *significant* F allows, if not *demands*, a further analysis of the data. By accepting the alternative hypothesis, we are concluding that differences among the treatment means are present. But *which* differences are the real ones and which are not? As we have noted before, the alternative hypothesis is inexact and, consequently, so must be our conclusion. Suppose, for example, we are contrasting the following four means: 5.25, 4.90, 5.10, and 10.50, and that the F from the single-factor analysis is significant. What have we been told? Simply that the four population means are *not* equal to one another. Nothing is said about *particular* differences among the means. An inspection of the means in this example suggests that the treatment effects are not spread equally over the four means—one group deviates from the other three, while these latter three do not deviate greatly from one another. The single-factor analysis does not locate the *source* (or sources) of the treatment effects. All that the analysis does is to indicate that there are real differences among the treatment means, somewhere. It is our job in this and the next two chapters to see how we can identify the sources contributing to the significant omnibus F.

Problems in Conducting Additional Comparisons

INCREASE IN TYPE I ERRORS   In evaluating the outcome of any experiment, we control the probability of making a type I error—rejecting the null hypothesis when it is true—by choosing an α level. If α is set at $p = .05$, we know that 5 percent of the time we will reject the null hypothesis when in fact there are no differences among the population means. Suppose we conduct a large number of experiments and use this same α level for each experiment. In any one of these experiments, the chances are 1 in 20 that we will make a type I error when the null hypothesis is true. Another way of looking at the type I error is to consider the *number* of type I errors we may expect to make on the average when the null hypothesis is true. This number is found by multiplying α times the number of experiments; if we conduct 20 experiments, then we expect to make one type I error, .05(20), and if we conduct 100 experiments, we expect to make five type I errors, .05(100). It is obvious that by increasing the number of experiments we conduct and analyze, we are increasing the *number* of type I errors as well.

Now, suppose we shift our attention from a number of independent experiments to a single experiment in which $a > 2$ and in which independent comparisons between pairs of means are contemplated.[1] The same argument holds. The more comparisons we conduct, the more type I errors we will make, when H_0 is true for these comparisons. In talking about this relationship, the distinction is often made between the type I error rate *per comparison* and the error rate *experimentwise*. (We will refer to these two error rates as *PC* and *EW*, respectively.) The *PC* error rate, which we will continue to call α, uses the *comparison* as the conceptual unit for the error rate. If we evaluated several comparisons

---

[1] The distinction between independent and nonindependent comparisons will be made shortly.

in an experiment, each at $\alpha = .05$, we would be using a PC error rate; our probability of making a type I error would be .05 for each of the separate comparisons. In contrast, the type I EW error rate, α_{EW}, considers the probability of making *one or more* type I errors in the set of comparisons under scrutiny.

The relationship between the two error rates is expressed by

$$\alpha_{EW} = 1 - (1 - \alpha)^c, \tag{6-2}$$

where c represents the number of independent comparisons that are conducted. With the PC error rate set at $\alpha = .05$ and with $c = 3$ comparisons contemplated, the EW type I error rate is

$$\alpha_{EW} = 1 - (1 - .05)^3 = 1 - (.95)^3 = 1 - .857 = .143.$$

If we were working at the 1 percent significance level,

$$\alpha_{EW} = 1 - (1 - .01)^3 = 1 - (.99)^3 = 1 - .970 = .030.$$

The experimentwise error rate is approximated by

$$\alpha_{EW} \approx c(\alpha), \tag{6-2a}$$

but this approximation is accurate only for small values of α and for small numbers of comparisons. In the present example, with $\alpha = .05$, the

$$\alpha_{EW} \approx 3(.05) \approx .15,$$

as compared to the value of .143 obtained with Eq. (6-2). For the smaller α level ($p = .01$), the values of α_{EW} are identical to two decimal places.

When additional comparisons are involved in the analysis of an experiment, researchers have different attitudes about which conceptual unit for the error rate is most appropriate. The point to be emphasized now is that when we conduct additional comparisons on a set of means, there is an EW error rate with which we must contend and this error rate increases directly with the number of comparisons tested.

INDEPENDENCE OF COMPARISONS   The formula for the EW error rate, Eq. (6-2), holds only for independent comparisons. We will not always restrict ourselves to independent comparisons, however. Thus, it is important to have some "feeling" for the differences between comparisons which are independent and those which are not. See Chapter 7 for a definition of independence.

Suppose there are three conditions in our experiment and we want to make all possible comparisons between pairs of means. We can represent the results of the three comparisons as

$$\bar{A}_1 - \bar{A}_2 = X, \quad \bar{A}_1 - \bar{A}_3 = Y, \quad \text{and} \quad \bar{A}_2 - \bar{A}_3 = Z.$$

It can be shown that these comparisons do not contain independent pieces of information, since we can calculate the actual value of one of them by knowing the values of the other two. For instance, if we solve for $\bar{A}_1$ in the first equation, we have

$$\bar{A}_1 = \bar{A}_2 + X.$$

Substituting this value for $\bar{A}_1$ in the second equation, we obtain

$$\bar{A}_2 + X - \bar{A}_3 = Y.$$

By rearranging the terms, we can produce the algebraic equivalent to the third equation as

$$\bar{A}_2 - \bar{A}_3 = Y - X.$$

Thus, by merely knowing the results of the first two comparisons, we can calculate the third comparison.

The calculation of the EW error rate in this sort of situation is difficult, since the formula given by Eq. (6-2) holds only for a set of mutually independent comparisons (see Harter, 1957, for a discussion of the problem). Nevertheless, it is still accurate to say that the EW error rate increases as the number of independent and nonindependent comparisons that we conduct increases.

Summary

One purpose of this and the next two chapters is to consider ways by which we can learn to live with these difficulties. We should keep in mind, however, that an omnibus F, which is significant at, say, $\alpha = .05$, does give us the assurance that there is *at least one* comparison which will be significant at $p < .05$. It is our job as researchers to identify these comparisons—to extract from our data just as much useful information as possible. In a sense, then, the omnibus F test is a *signal* which indicates how reasonable it is to continue with a more analytical treatment of our data.

PLANNED VERSUS POST-HOC COMPARISONS

Most experiments are designed with specific hypotheses in mind. An experimenter hopes he has included the appropriate groups which will allow him to test these hypotheses. At this point, of course, the main consideration is *experimental* in nature. That is, statistical theory can indicate the correct procedures to follow in testing a particular hypothesis, but it has little to say about the relevance of the actual experiment—the logic, the specific groups chosen, the methods and procedures, and so on. A poorly conceived, designed, and executed study can be impeccably analyzed, so that there is not the slightest thing wrong with any part of the *statistical* analysis. But these statistical "virtues" will not in any way save an experimentally unsound experiment.

Assume that a researcher has designed an experimentally acceptable study. The point that interests us here is that he intends to make particular comparisons just as soon as the data have been collected. These *planned comparisons* can be made whether the omnibus F is significant or not. In fact, as we will see, planned comparisons are usually conducted *instead* of the omnibus F. With planned comparisons, the experimenter is interested not in the simultaneous test of all comparisons between pairs of means but in the ones which have *experimental relevance*—the ones which prompted the experiment in the first place. In contrast, *unplanned* or *post-hoc comparisons* are not decided on until after the experimenter has collected data and seen the results. These comparisons are performed only if the omnibus F is significant.

Let us consider in detail the special features of these two types of comparisons.

An Example of Planned Comparisons

Consider a concrete example of an experiment designed with some explicit comparisons in mind. Suppose that subjects are given a list of 40 common English words to learn and that the method used allows them to recall these words in any order they want. The list is presented for six trials, each trial consisting of a study portion, in which the words are presented to the subjects, and a test portion, in which the subjects attempt to recall the words. Thus, each subject sees the list six times and is tested six times. Subjects are randomly assigned to five different conditions of training, which are summarized in Table 6-1.

For the first two groups, the words are presented all at once on a piece of paper for 2 minutes; different orderings of the 40 words are used on the six trials. The groups differ with regard to the arrangement of the words on the sheet of paper—for one group the words appear in a column and for the other group they are scattered around on the paper. The remaining three groups also study the list for a total of 2 minutes, but the words are presented one at a time, at a constant rate, on a mechanical device called a memory drum. For groups 3 and 4, each word is presented once for 3 seconds; the total presentation time for the whole list of words is 120 seconds (3 seconds × 40 words). The two groups differ with regard to the presentation of the words on successive trials. Group 3 receives the *same* presentation order on all six trials, while group 4 receives *different* presentation orders. The final group also receives the materials on the memory drum, but at a faster rate of presentation (1 second per word). However, in order to equate total study time per word, the words are presented three times before the recall test is administered. As with group 4, the presentation order is changed at the start of each study trial. In summary, there are five different conditions of training. What they all have in common is that the list of words is presented for a total of 2 minutes before recall is taken.

The hypothesis under test is the *total-time hypothesis*. This hypothesis states that learning will be the *same* for these different groups just so long as the total time for study is held constant. It does not matter how the words are presented, all at once or one at a time, at a fast rate or at a slow rate, in the same order on successive study trials or in different orders, scrambled on a page or in a neat column array. The expectation, then, is that the groups will not differ in performance over the six training trials.

We could test this hypothesis by comparing the five groups simultaneously in an overall analysis of variance. If this omnibus F were significant, we would know that the total-time hypothesis did not hold in this experiment. We would *not* know, however, which of the groups were responsible for its failure. The way in which the experiment was designed suggests a number of *meaningful* comparisons which represent more *analytical* tests of the total-time hypothesis.

Four such comparisons are indicated in Table 6-1. The first comparison contrasts the two groups receiving the words on a sheet of paper (groups 1 and 2) with two of the groups receiving the words on the memory drum (groups 4 and 5). The question asked here is whether or not performance will be affected by forcing subjects to study the words in a rigid pattern. The total-time hypothesis would say no. On the other hand, it would seem reasonable to expect that subjects who are free to distribute their study time among the 40 words as they wish may be able to organize the material in such a way as to aid recall; subjects who are studying the words one at a time for a fixed 3-second period may not be able to organize the material as effectively. Thus, an organizational theory of learning and memory would predict better performance by groups 1 and 2, relative to groups 4 and 5. (Groups 1 and 2 and groups 4 and 5 have been combined to provide more stable estimates of the paper and drum methods of presentation, respectively. The plus and minus signs denote the groups to be contrasted.) Group 3 was *not* included in this comparison because the subjects in that group received the words in the same order on successive trials, while subjects in the other four groups received the words in different orders.

TABLE 6-1   *An Example of Planned Comparisons*

	Group 1: Paper, varied order, column array	Group 2: Paper, varied order, scattered array	Group 3: Drum, same order, 3-sec. rate	Group 4: Drum, varied order, 3-sec. rate	Group 5: Drum, varied order, 1-sec. rate
Comp. 1	+	+		−	−
Comp. 2	+	−			
Comp. 3				+	−
Comp. 4			+	−	

The second comparison focuses upon the two "paper" groups and asks whether or not the *type of array* will affect performance. The total-time hypothesis would again say no. There is some suggestion in the literature that subjects will form more organizational groupings of the words in the scattered condition than in the column condition. An organizational theory maintains that the formation of these organizational groupings will aid performance. Thus, this latter theory would predict higher recall by the group receiving the scattered array.

The next comparison involves groups 4 and 5, groups differing in the rates at which the words are presented. This comparison asks whether or not performance will be affected when the exposure time is varied. The total-time hypothesis would say no. On the other hand, it is conceivable that subjects given a more leisurely study of each word (group 4) may have time to create organizational groupings, while subjects given a fast exposure (group 5) may not be able to do so, even though they are given the same total time to study each word. If this speculation is correct, an organizational theory would predict a difference in favor of the longer presentation rate.

The final comparison contrasts groups 3 and 4. The only difference between these two conditions is the use of the same or different orderings of the words on successive study trials. While the total-time hypothesis again would predict no difference in performance, there are other hypotheses which do. For example, some investigators have speculated that a constant presentation order provides the subject with stable serial-position cues which are not possible when the order varies from trial to trial. It is thought that this additional set of cues will aid the subject in recall. Thus, these researchers would predict better performance for group 3.

The object of this example is to illustrate that experiments are designed with meaningful comparisons in mind. These comparisons are planned and statistical tests of them are conducted *instead* of the omnibus F. The planned comparisons enumerated in Table 6-1 provide detailed information concerning the success or failure of the total-time hypothesis. If we knew only that the omnibus F was significant, we would not know *where* the hypothesis was deficient. The use of planned comparisons allows us to pinpoint the specific conditions under which the hypothesis does and does not hold.

Independence of Planned Comparisons

It is clear, then, that tests of planned comparisons are a desirable alternative to the omnibus F test. What is not clear, however, is whether or not any restrictions are placed upon the nature and the number of these comparisons we may plan to test. Authors of statistical source books for psychologists are not in agreement on this issue. Some maintain that planned comparisons must be independent in the sense that they should provide nonredundant information. At one point in his discussion, Hays (1963), for example, refers to this property of independence as a *requirement* (p. 484). Similarly, Kirk (1968) suggests that we should distinguish between two classes of planned comparisons, redundant and nonredundant, and that we should place the former comparisons in the *same* category as *post-hoc* comparisons (p. 86). In contrast, Winer (1962) states that "in practice the comparisons that are constructed are those having some meaning in terms of the experimental variables; whether these comparisons are [redundant] or not makes little or no difference" (p. 69).

Winer's comments make good sense. The *critical* feature of planned comparisons is their *a priori* nature, not their independence. There are just so many meaningful comparisons that we can plan before the start of an experiment; most of these will provide independent information. Occasionally, we will think of comparisons which are *partially* redundant, but which may provide important information that is not completely obtainable from the other independent planned comparisons.

Consider the comparisons outlined in Table 6-1. Each represents a meaningful question. By using procedures which we will discuss in the next chapter, we could show that the first three comparisons provide nonredundant information, while the fourth comparison is not independent of comparisons 1 and 3. Each of the four comparisons asks important and interesting questions, however. In short, then, we will treat all planned comparisons the same way and evaluate each at the same *per comparison* error rate.[2]

Unplanned or Post-Hoc Comparisons

Unplanned or post-hoc comparisons may be described as data "sifting," where an experimenter is sorting through a large number of comparisons in the hope of finding something significant. In some cases, he may be assessing the significance of a difference between two means which *now* has relevance to him. That is, it may not have occurred to him before the start of the experiment that a comparison between two particular groups was of any interest. However, after he has examined the data and noticed a rather sizable difference between the two means and has thought about the theoretical meaning of this difference, he now wants to determine the significance of this comparison. If the comparison is significant, he may want to incorporate this new finding into his theoretical framework and use it to help generate further hypotheses. In other cases, the researcher may still have no specific interest in any particular differences. He might consider conducting an analysis which is designed to test a large number of comparisons and to indicate which means appear to cluster together and which do not. In either case, there is the very real problem that the experimenter may be capitalizing on chance fluctuations. In the first situation, he has selected groups which are widely separated but which make some sort of sense to him. He probably would not have looked at these same groups if they had not

---

[2] Occasionally, an experimenter may be worried about the *EW* error rate with planned comparisons. The Dunn test, which we will discuss in Chapter 8, provides a method for dealing with this problem.

differed. In the second situation, he is waiting to find out which differences are significant and *then* to search for a meaningful interpretation of the data.

However we look at these two situations, it is clear that the experimenter has selected a few comparisons—those comparisons with significant differences—from a pool containing a large number of possible comparisons. We must take this fact into consideration when calculating the experimentwise (EW) error rate. The post-hoc comparisons we choose to test are the ones which have passed through our rough screening of the potential comparisons. The ones which we do not test formally have been tested *implicitly*. Thus, post-hoc comparisons are usually treated differently from planned comparisons, to adjust for the increased EW rate resulting from the sizable number of comparisons involved. In Chapter 8 we will consider several procedures which have been devised to cope with this problem.

COMPARISONS BETWEEN TREATMENT MEANS

We have seen in Eq. (6-1) that a sum of squares, which is based on the deviation of three or more treatment means from the overall mean, is equivalent to an average of all possible comparisons between *pairs* of means. In this and in subsequent sections we will be considering procedures for making contrasts which essentially reduce to comparisons between pairs of means. In some cases these comparisons will involve simple contrasts between pairs of treatment means; in others they will involve more complex contrasts. The means in these latter comparisons are based on combinations of two or more treatment means. All of these comparisons share the common feature that ultimately they can be reduced to a contrast between two means and, therefore, are based on a *single df*. Comparisons of this sort are referred to variously as *comparisons*, *contrasts*, or *single-df comparisons*. We will refer to such comparisons as *comparisons* (or *contrasts*) *between means*.

Not all questions we will want to ask of our data reduce to comparisons between means, however. Occasionally, we will want to test the significance of subsets of two or more means, simply asking whether or not the means differ among themselves. For instance, suppose there are four treatment conditions, one a control condition and the others experimental treatments of some sort. It might make sense to ask two questions: (1) Do the *combined* experimental groups differ from the control condition—i.e., is there a general or an average experimental effect? (2) Do the experimental groups differ among themselves? In the first case we have a comparison between two means (the control mean versus an average of the three experimental means), while in the second case we have a comparison among the three experimental means.

A Comparison as a Sum of Weighted Means

Any comparison between pairs of means can be represented by two steps: (1) the multiplication (or weighting) of the means by a set of numbers called *coefficients*, and (2) an algebraic summation of these weighted means. A comparison between two means, for example, may be indicated as

$$(1)(\bar{A}_1) + (-1)(\bar{A}_2) = \bar{A}_1 - \bar{A}_2$$

or

$$(-1)(\bar{A}_1) + (1)(\bar{A}_2) = \bar{A}_2 - \bar{A}_1,$$

depending upon the particular direction of the difference that interests us. In either case, the sum of the treatment means, weighted by the coefficients $(1, -1)$ or $(-1, 1)$, results in the comparisons we want.

The system may be extended to experiments with more than two treatments. We will consider first the general formula for a comparison and then apply the formula to several examples. As we have indicated, a comparison (C) may be expressed as a sum of weighted means. Specifically,

$$C = (c_1)(\bar{A}_1) + (c_2)(\bar{A}_2) + \cdots + (c_a)(\bar{A}_a).$$

We obtain a comparison by weighting each mean by a specific coefficient (c_i) and then summing the set of weighted means. These calculations are summarized by the following formula:

$$C = \sum (c_i)(\bar{A}_i), \tag{6-3}$$

where the c_i's represent the set of coefficients. The pairing of a coefficient with a mean is dictated by the particular comparison desired. To qualify as a comparison, at least two of the coefficients must be numbers other than zero *and* the *sum* of the *coefficients* must equal zero.[3] That is,

$$\sum c_i = c_1 + c_2 + \cdots + c_a = 0. \tag{6-4}$$

The reason for the first restriction is obvious: if fewer than two coefficients were nonzero, there would be no comparison. The reason for the second restriction is to ensure that a comparison is independent of the overall mean of the experiment. Hays (1963, pp. 472–473) discusses this point and explains why this independence is desirable, saying that "in most instances, we want to ask questions about combinations of population means that will be unrelated to any consideration of what the over-all mean of the combined populations is estimated to be" (p. 473).

Suppose we have three treatment groups: group 1 is a control condition and groups 2 and 3 receive different experimental treatments. Two logical comparisons which we might consider making are (1) a contrast between the mean for the control group ($\bar{A}_1$) and the average of the means for the two experimental groups $[(\bar{A}_2 + \bar{A}_3)/2]$ and (2) a contrast between the mean of one experimental group ($\bar{A}_2$) and the mean of the other ($\bar{A}_3$). The first comparison would indicate whether or not there was a *general* experimental effect, while the second would show any difference between the two experimental treatments.

---

[3] Some authors also use the term *linear* when referring to this type of comparison or contrast. We have refrained from using this expression in order to avoid confusion with estimates of linear trend, a topic which we will consider later in the next chapter.

We may express these comparisons in terms of Eq. (6-3). Specifically, for the first comparison (C_1),

$$C_1 = (1)(\bar{A}_1) + (-\tfrac{1}{2})(\bar{A}_2) + (-\tfrac{1}{2})(\bar{A}_3).$$

If we perform some algebra,

$$C_1 = \bar{A}_1 - \frac{\bar{A}_2 + \bar{A}_3}{2},$$

which is exactly the contrast we wanted. For the second comparison (C_2),

$$C_2 = (0)(\bar{A}_1) + (1)(\bar{A}_2) + (-1)(\bar{A}_3)$$
$$= \bar{A}_2 - \bar{A}_3.$$

Both sets of coefficients, $(1, -\tfrac{1}{2}, -\tfrac{1}{2})$ and $(0, 1, -1)$, sum to zero, which satisfies the requirements of Eq. (6-4), and they "perform" the comparisons that we intended—that is, they result in the appropriate contrasts between means.

Consider an example with five means. If we wanted to compare $\bar{A}_1$ with $\bar{A}_4$, the coefficients would be $(1, 0, 0, -1, 0)$ and Eq. (6-3) would become

$$C = (1)(\bar{A}_1) + (0)(\bar{A}_2) + (0)(\bar{A}_3) + (-1)(\bar{A}_4) + (0)(\bar{A}_5)$$
$$= \bar{A}_1 - \bar{A}_4.$$

Take a more complicated comparison, a contrast between the combined means for groups 2 and 5 $[(\bar{A}_2 + \bar{A}_5)/2]$ and the combined means for groups 3 and 4 $[(\bar{A}_3 + \bar{A}_4)/2]$. In terms of coefficients, this comparison may be represented as $(0, \tfrac{1}{2}, -\tfrac{1}{2}, -\tfrac{1}{2}, \tfrac{1}{2})$; Eq. (6-3) now becomes

$$C = (0)(\bar{A}_1) + (\tfrac{1}{2})(\bar{A}_2) + (-\tfrac{1}{2})(\bar{A}_3) + (-\tfrac{1}{2})(\bar{A}_4) + (\tfrac{1}{2})(\bar{A}_5).$$

If we collect terms with the same coefficients and rewrite the equation, we can see that the desired comparison has been specified in this statement. That is,

$$C = [(\tfrac{1}{2})(\bar{A}_2) + (\tfrac{1}{2})(\bar{A}_5)] + [(-\tfrac{1}{2})(\bar{A}_3) + (-\tfrac{1}{2})(\bar{A}_4)]$$
$$= \frac{\bar{A}_2 + \bar{A}_5}{2} - \frac{\bar{A}_3 + \bar{A}_4}{2}.$$

Finally, suppose we want to compare the combined means for groups 2 and 4 with the combined means for groups 1, 3, and 5. Coefficients representing this comparison are $(-\tfrac{1}{3}, \tfrac{1}{2}, -\tfrac{1}{3}, \tfrac{1}{2}, -\tfrac{1}{3})$. From Eq. (6-3),

$$C = (-\tfrac{1}{3})(\bar{A}_1) + (\tfrac{1}{2})(\bar{A}_2) + (-\tfrac{1}{3})(\bar{A}_3) + (\tfrac{1}{2})(\bar{A}_4) + (-\tfrac{1}{3})(\bar{A}_5).$$

Again, algebraic simplification reveals the comparison we had in mind:

$$C = [(\tfrac{1}{2})(\bar{A}_2) + (\tfrac{1}{2})(\bar{A}_4)] + [(-\tfrac{1}{3})(\bar{A}_1) + (-\tfrac{1}{3})(\bar{A}_3) + (-\tfrac{1}{3})(\bar{A}_5)]$$
$$= \frac{\bar{A}_2 + \bar{A}_4}{2} - \frac{\bar{A}_1 + \bar{A}_3 + \bar{A}_5}{3}.$$

These last three comparisons are abstract examples. We would usually choose comparisons which ask *meaningful* questions of the data. What we have seen is that if we can frame these questions explicitly, indicating which mean or average of means will be compared with what, coefficients can be found which reflect these comparisons. We can then use Eq. (6-3) to calculate the actual result of the comparison.

Usefulness of the Coefficients and Eq. (6-3)

These examples illustrate the fact that comparisons involving a set of treatment means may be specified by different sets of coefficients. We also saw that by using these coefficients to weight the corresponding treatment means, we could produce the comparison represented by the coefficients. There are several reasons why it is useful to express comparisons in terms of a sum of weighted means—i.e., in terms of Eq. (6-3); these points will be illustrated later with actual examples. We will simply list them at this time in order to justify the amount of attention we will give to this particular procedure in the sections that follow.

First, the procedure is *general*; it may be used to compare the means of two groups as well as for complicated comparisons between combined means in experiments with any number of levels. Second, special sets of coefficients are available for the analytical analysis of experiments in which *quantitative* independent variables are present—i.e., where the levels of the independent variables differ in *amount*. Third, the statistical evaluation of these different comparisons is easily accomplished by using the coefficients to compute the sums of squares associated with the comparisons. Fourth, we will see that the independence of two or more comparisons is readily determined by comparing the sets of coefficients. Thus, it will be possible to ascertain whether or not several planned comparisons are mutually independent by comparing the coefficients associated with the comparisons we plan to make. Finally, sets of coefficients may be used to represent sources of variance in designs with two or more independent variables. Not only is this an interesting way of thinking about the analyses of multifactor experiments, but sets of coefficients may be used to illustrate the independence of sources of variance in these designs. (This point is explored in detail in Appendix A.)

Sums of Squares for Comparisons Between Treatment Means

COMPUTATIONAL FORMULA   The computational formula for the sum of squares for a comparison may be written in terms of the treatment means or in terms of the treatment sums. We will consider the formula expressed both ways, but in our actual analyses we will use treatment sums, as they are easier to work with. The computational formula with means is not too removed from Eq. (6-3), the formula for the sum of weighted means. Specifically,

$$SS_{A_{comp.}} = \frac{s[\sum (c_i)(\bar{A}_i)]^2}{\sum (c_i)^2},$$ (6-5)

where the quantity within the brackets is the sum of the weighted means, s is the sample size, and the denominator is the sum of the squared coefficients. It should be noted that Eq. (6-5) assumes an equal number of subjects in each treatment condition. The analysis of experiments with unequal sample sizes is discussed in Chapter 17.

A transformation of Eq. (6-5) to accommodate treatment *sums* rather than treatment means is given by

$$SS_{A_{comp.}} = \frac{[\sum (c_i)(A_i)]^2}{s[\sum (c_i)^2]}.$$ (6-6)

The correspondence between the two formulas is apparent—the only differences are in the use of sums and in the location of s in the denominator rather than in the numerator.

TABLE 6-2 *Numerical Example of Two Comparisons*

	Treatment Levels		
	a_1	a_2	a_3
A_i	75	30	45
Comparison 1	1	$-\frac{1}{2}$	$-\frac{1}{2}$
Comparison 2	0	1	-1

NUMERICAL EXAMPLE   For an example of these calculations, we will take the data originally listed in Table 3-3. In this example, $a = 3$ and $s = 5$. The totals for each group are presented again in Table 6-2, along with the coefficients representing the two comparisons we were discussing previously. That is, comparison 1 $(1, -\frac{1}{2}, -\frac{1}{2})$ consisted of a contrast of the group at a_1 (control group) with the average of the groups at a_2 and a_3 (experimental groups), while comparison 2 $(0, 1, -1)$ consisted of a comparison between the groups at a_2 and a_3. Applying the operations of Eq. (6-6) to the first comparison, we obtain

$$SS_{A_{comp. 1}} = \frac{[(1)(75) + (-\frac{1}{2})(30) + (-\frac{1}{2})(45)]^2}{5[(1)^2 + (-\frac{1}{2})^2 + (-\frac{1}{2})^2]}$$

$$= \frac{(75 - 15 - 22.50)^2}{5(1 + \frac{1}{4} + \frac{1}{4})}$$

$$= \frac{(37.50)^2}{5(1.50)} = \frac{1406.25}{7.50} = 187.50.$$

And for the second comparison,

$$SS_{A_{comp.\,2}} = \frac{[(0)(75) + (1)(30) + (-1)(45)]^2}{5[(0)^2 + (1)^2 + (-1)^2]}$$

$$= \frac{(0 + 30 - 45)^2}{5(0 + 1 + 1)}$$

$$= \frac{(-15)^2}{5(2)} = \frac{225}{10} = 22.50.$$

These two sums of squares have been entered in a new summary table, Table 6-3.

TABLE 6-3 *Analysis of Variance*

Source	SS	df	MS	F
Treatment (A)	(210.00)	(2)		
Comp. 1	187.50	1	187.50	13.23**
Comp. 2	22.50	1	22.50	1.59*
Within (S/A)	170.00	12	14.17	
Total	380.00	14		

* $p > .10$.
** $p < .01$.

EVALUATION OF COMPARISONS   If the comparisons listed in Table 6-2 were *planned* comparisons, we would probably not even bother to perform the omnibus F test. Table 6-3 does present the SS_A calculated in the last chapter (see Table 4-2). It should be noted that the two comparisons we have just computed completely account for or "use up" the total between-groups sum of squares. That is,

$$SS_{A_{comp.\,1}} + SS_{A_{comp.\,2}} = 187.50 + 22.50 = 210.00 = SS_A.$$

This will happen only when we have calculated a complete set of *orthogonal* (or independent) comparisons. (Just how we determine orthogonality will be discussed in Chapter 7.) The df for each of the comparisons is 1. The reason for the single df is that we are essentially comparing *two* means in each of the contrasts. In comparison 1, for example, we are comparing $\bar{A}_1$ against another mean, the average of $\bar{A}_2$ and $\bar{A}_3$; in comparison 2, we are clearly comparing two means, $\bar{A}_2$ and $\bar{A}_3$. In both cases we are comparing two means, and the df associated with the corresponding sums of squares is 1.

The mean square is calculated in the usual way (SS/df), and the F ratio is formed as follows:[4]

$$F = \frac{MS_{A_{comp.}}}{MS_{S/A}}, \tag{6-7}$$

[4] The use of the $MS_{S/A}$ as the error term assumes homogeneity of within-group variances. If this assumption is not met, the analysis becomes complicated (see Kirk, 1968, p. 74 and pp. 97–98). In this case, advice of a statistician should be sought.

and is evaluated in the F table under the appropriate entry for the df associated with the numerator ($df = 1$) and with the denominator [$df = a(s - 1)$]. If this is a planned comparison, the α level will be the per comparison rate.

The hypotheses being tested in our two comparisons are

COMPARISON 1 H_0: $\mu_1 = (\mu_2 + \mu_3)/2$,

H_1: $\mu_1 \neq (\mu_2 + \mu_3)/2$;

COMPARISON 2 H_0: $\mu_2 = \mu_3$,

H_1: $\mu_2 \neq \mu_3$.

While it can be shown that these two comparisons use independent information in their construction, it should be mentioned that the two F ratios are not, strictly speaking, independent. The reason for this state of affairs is that the $MS_{S/A}$ is used to test both of the comparisons. It appears, however, that this lack of *statistical* independence of the tests does not present a practical problem as long as the df for the denominator of the F ratio are reasonably large (cf. Hays, 1963, p. 467; Kirk, 1968, p. 74).

The within-groups mean square for these data, previously calculated in Chapter 4, is presented in Table 6-3. The results of the two F tests are indicated in the table. Specifically, they show that variability among the treatment means is produced primarily by the difference between the mean of group 1 (the control in our example) and the mean of groups 2 and 3 combined (the experimental groups in our example). The great advantage of this analysis is in the additional information that it provides. If we had looked at the overall F ratio, as we did in Chapter 4, we would have rejected the null hypothesis and concluded that the three treatment means do differ. With the present analysis, we are able to *pinpoint* the locus of these differences.

CONSTRUCTION OF COEFFICIENTS   When we initially looked at a set of coefficients and the sum of the resultant weighted means, the coefficients were direct translations of the desired comparisons. In our first comparison, for example, the coefficients $(1, -\frac{1}{2}, -\frac{1}{2})$ provided the appropriate weights to effect a comparison between the mean at a_1 and the average means at a_2 and a_3. In the *calculation of the sum of squares* for this comparison, actually *any* set will do, provided the *relative* weights of the groups remain the same. That is, we could use $(2, -1, -1)$ or $(4, -2, -2)$ or even $(250, -125, -125)$ for that matter; each of these sets of coefficients preserves the same $2:1:1$ weighting. The reason that the *absolute* values of the coefficients do not matter is that any difference produced in the numerator of Eq. (6-6) is exactly compensated for by a change in the denominator term. Suppose we were to use $(2, -1, -1)$ to calculate the sum of squares. We would have

$$SS_{A_{comp.}} = \frac{[\sum (c_i)(A_i)]^2}{s[\sum (c_i)^2]}$$

$$= \frac{[(2)(75) + (-1)(30) + (-1)(45)]^2}{5[(2)^2 + (-1)^2 + (-1)^2]}$$

$$= \frac{(150 - 30 - 45)^2}{5(4 + 1 + 1)}$$

$$= \frac{(75)^2}{5(6)} = \frac{5625}{30} = 187.50.$$

Or with $(250, -125, -125)$,

$$SS_{A_{comp.}} = \frac{[(250)(75) + (-125)(30) + (-125)(45)]^2}{5[(250)^2 + (-125)^2 + (-125)^2]}$$

$$= \frac{(18,750 - 3750 - 5625)^2}{5(62,500 + 15,625 + 15,625)}$$

$$= \frac{(9375)^2}{5(93,750)} = \frac{87,890,625}{468,750} = 187.50.$$

These two sets of calculations yielded the same value found with the set $(1, -\frac{1}{2}, -\frac{1}{2})$.

Because fractions are often involved when coefficients are written in the manner originally suggested, rounding-off errors and errors in placing decimal points may ensue. Thus, it is more reasonable to eliminate fractional coefficients altogether and to use the set of coefficients with the smallest absolute sum. (The use of the smallest absolute sum will reduce the size of the numbers entering into the calculations.) In the present example, the set with the smallest absolute sum is $(2, -1, -1)$.

A Comparison as a Correlation

We have indicated earlier the usefulness of the general formula for a comparison. For this reason, it is important to develop an understanding of how the formula "works." At one level of explanation, we have already seen that the sum of the weighted means actually represents the contrasts we have specified. In this sense, then, the formula has some face validity, some intuitive meaning. At another, more statistical level, it is possible to show that a comparison is related to a *correlation* between the coefficients defining the comparison and the corresponding treatment means. We will expand upon this point in the next several paragraphs.

Suppose we have two numbers, each reflecting different aspects of a set of things. If the "things" are people, the two numbers might be an IQ score and a grade-point average in college. We say that a correlation exists between the two sets of numbers when the values of one set (IQ) can be used to predict the individual values of the other set (grade-point average). We can carry this notion over to the quantities involved in a comparison. The "things" in an experiment are the treatment groups, and each has two numbers associated with it. One of these is the *coefficient*, which, in conjunction with the other coefficients in the set, reflects a particular comparison among the treatment groups. The other is the treatment mean itself, which reflects in part the effect of the differential treatments. In correlational terms, we can ask whether or not the *set of coefficients* can *predict* or account for the *differences* among the set of treatment means. If there is *no* predictability—i.e, the correlation is *zero*—then the sums of the weighted means will be zero also. On the other hand, if there is some predictability, the correlation *and* the sum of the weighted means will take on a nonzero value. Said another way, the coefficients specify a particular comparison involving the treatment groups, and the sum of the weighted means reflects the degree to which this comparison *describes* or *accounts for* the obtained data.

To be more specific, we can express the sum of squares associated with a particular comparison as follows:

$$SS_{A_{\text{comp.}}} = (r^2_{\text{comp.}})(SS_A), \tag{6-8}$$

where $r^2_{\text{comp.}}$ is the product-moment correlation of the coefficients and the treatment means (or sums). (While it is not critical for your understanding of this argument, the derivation is given in footnote 5.)

As an example, consider the two comparisons we have calculated already. The square of the product-moment correlation ($r^2_{\text{comp.}}$), relating the set of coefficients and the treatment means, is .893 for comparison 1 and .107 for comparison 2. Substituting in Eq. (6-8), we find

---

[5] The formula for $r^2_{\text{comp.}}$ is derived from the computational formula for the product-moment correlation (r). Specifically,

$$r^2 = \frac{[\sum(X_i)(Y_i) - (\sum X_i)(\sum Y_i)/s]^2}{[\sum(X_i)^2 - (\sum X_i)^2/s][\sum(Y_i)^2 - (\sum Y_i)^2/s]},$$

where X_i and Y_i are different sets of scores on the same individual. Substituting the *coefficients* (c_i) for the X_i scores, the *treatment means* ($\bar{A}_i$) for the Y_i scores, and the *number of means* (a) for the number of scores (s), we obtain $r^2_{\text{comp.}}$. That is,

$$r^2_{\text{comp.}} = \frac{[\sum(c_i)(\bar{A}_i) - (\sum c_i)(\sum \bar{A}_i)/a]^2}{[\sum(c_i)^2 - (\sum c_i)^2/a][\sum(\bar{A}_i)^2 - (\sum \bar{A}_i)^2/a]}.$$

If we remember that $\sum c_i = 0$, the equation simplifies to

$$r^2_{\text{comp.}} = \frac{[\sum(c_i)(\bar{A}_i)]^2}{[\sum(c_i)^2][\sum(\bar{A}_i)^2 - (\sum \bar{A}_i)^2/a]}.$$

Simple algebra transforms this equation to Eq. (6-10), given on the next page.

$$SS_{A_{comp.\,1}} = (.893)(210.00) = 187.53,$$

$$SS_{A_{comp.\,2}} = (.107)(210.00) = 22.47.$$

These two values agree quite closely with the sums of squares obtained with Eq. (6-6)—187.50 and 22.50, respectively.

As an interesting twist to this argument, we can ask a different question: how much of the SS_A is accounted for by a particular comparison? We can translate this reasonable question into a percentage by forming the ratio

$$\frac{SS_{A_{comp.}}}{SS_A} \qquad (6\text{-}9)$$

and multiplying by 100.[6] For our example, the percentage of variability associated with comparison 1 is

$$\frac{187.50}{210.00} \times 100 = 89.3 \text{ percent}$$

and with comparison 2 is

$$\frac{22.50}{210.00} \times 100 = 10.7 \text{ percent}.$$

The relationship between Eq. (6-8) and Eq. (6-9) is obvious; $r_{comp.}^2$ represents the proportion of between-groups variance associated with a particular comparison. That is,

$$r_{comp.}^2 = \frac{SS_{A_{comp.}}}{SS_A}. \qquad (6\text{-}10)$$

Thus, we can view a comparison as reflecting a correlation between the weighting coefficients, on the one hand, and the treatment means, on the other. The coefficients represent an *idealized outcome* of an experiment, and the sum of the weighted means $\left[\sum (c_i)(\bar{A}_i)\right]$ reflects in part the degree to which the actual treatment means match or correlate with the particular comparison. If the matching is close, the $SS_{A_{comp.}}$ will "contain" a large proportion of the units of variation due to the SS_A. If the matching is poor or nonexistent, the $SS_{A_{comp.}}$ will reflect only error variance. The coefficients are analytical detectors which "resonate" to the presence of a particular kind of relationship among the treatment means. We will find many uses for them in the analyses considered in this book.

---

[6] Vaughan and Corballis (1969, pp. 210–211) suggest the use of a different ratio, one based on estimates of treatment *effects* rather than on sums of squares.

chapter seven

ORTHOGONAL ANALYSES

In Chapter 6 we considered the use and construction of analytical comparisons involving the treatment means. In the present chapter we will focus upon comparisons that exhibit a particular property to one another: *orthogonality*. We will first discuss the general meaning of orthogonality and then consider a specialized and useful application of orthogonal comparisons—the assessment of trend.

INTRODUCTION TO ORTHOGONAL COMPARISONS

Comparisons which are orthogonal extract independent pieces of information from our data. A numerical test of the orthogonality of any two comparisons is provided by the following relationship between the two sets of coefficients:

$$\sum (c_i)(c_i') = 0, \tag{7-1}$$

where c_i and c_i' are the coefficients for a particular group in the two comparisons. As an illustration of Eq. (7-1), consider the two comparisons we have been discussing throughout the last chapter: $(1, -\frac{1}{2}, -\frac{1}{2})$ and $(0, 1, -1)$. In order to qualify as a comparison, each set of coefficients must satisfy Eq. (6-4): $\sum c_i = 0$. For these two comparisons,

$$(1) + (-\tfrac{1}{2}) + (-\tfrac{1}{2}) = 0 \quad \text{and} \quad (0) + (1) + (-1) = 0.$$

To test for orthogonality, we substitute corresponding coefficients into Eq. (7-1) and determine the sum of the products. In this example,

$$\sum (c_i)(c_i') = (1)(0) + (-\tfrac{1}{2})(1) + (-\tfrac{1}{2})(-1)$$
$$= 0 - \tfrac{1}{2} + \tfrac{1}{2} = 0.$$

In contrast, consider two comparisons that are not orthogonal, such as $(1, -1, 0)$ and $(1, 0, -1)$. Both sets of coefficients obviously satisfy Eq. (6-4) and so represent comparisons, but they fail the test of independence:

$$\sum (c_i)(c_i') = (1)(1) + (-1)(0) + (0)(-1)$$
$$= 1 + 0 + 0 = 1.$$

A more complicated example is found in the comparisons we outlined earlier for a study contrasting methods of presentation in a learning experiment. These comparisons, which were originally summarized in Table 6-1, are listed

TABLE 7-1 *Example of a Test for Mutual Orthogonality*

	Group 1: Paper, varied order, Column array	Group 2: Paper, varied order, Scattered array	Group 3: Drum, same order, 3-sec. rate	Group 4: Drum, varied order, 3-sec. rate	Group 5: Drum, varied order, 1-sec. rate		Sum
			COMPARISONS[a]				
Comp. 1:	1	1	0	-1	-1	$=$	0
Comp. 2:	1	-1	0	0	0	$=$	0
Comp. 3:	0	0	0	1	-1	$=$	0
Comp. 4:	0	0	1	-1	0	$=$	0
			TESTS FOR ORTHOGONALITY[b]				
Comp. × Comp.							
1 × 2:	1	-1	0	0	0	$=$	0
1 × 3:	0	0	0	-1	1	$=$	0
1 × 4:	0	0	0	1	0	$=$	1
2 × 3:	0	0	0	0	0	$=$	0
2 × 4:	0	0	0	0	0	$=$	0
3 × 4:	0	0	0	-1	0	$=$	-1

[a] Test for comparison: $\sum c_i = 0$.
[b] Test for orthogonality: $\sum (c_i)(c_i') = 0$.

again in the upper portion of Table 7-1. As we have noted previously, the absolute values of the coefficients are not critical. What has to be present is the desired relative weights. Comparison 1, for example, could be written as $(-1, -1, 0, 1, 1)$ or as $(\frac{1}{2}, \frac{1}{2}, 0, -\frac{1}{2}, -\frac{1}{2})$ and still produce the same sum of squares. Each of the four comparisons qualifies as a contrast—i.e., the co-efficients sum to zero, as shown in the last column on the right. The six different tests of independence are enumerated in the bottom half of the table. Each test contrasts a different pair of comparisons. As an example of the calculations, consider the test of comparisons 1 and 3:

$$\sum (c_i)(c'_i) = (1)(0) + (1)(0) + (0)(0) + (-1)(1) + (-1)(-1).$$

These products are listed in the row labeled "1 × 3," and the sum of these products, zero, is indicated in the last column of the table. An inspection of the sums for the different pairs of contrasts reveals that comparison 4 is not orthog-onal either to comparison 1 or to comparison 3. The remaining comparisons, however, are all orthogonal (1 × 2, 1 × 3, 2 × 3, and 2 × 4). If we just con-sider comparisons 1, 2, and 3, we can say that they are *mutually* orthogonal to one another, since each possible pair of comparisons is orthogonal.

A fourth comparison (4') which would be orthogonal to the first three is one that compares group 3 with the average of the remaining groups. In terms of coefficients, the set is $(-1, -1, 4, -1, -1)$ or, with fractions, $(-\frac{1}{4}, -\frac{1}{4}, 1, -\frac{1}{4}, -\frac{1}{4})$. To test for orthogonality,

$1 \times 4'$: $\sum (c_i)(c'_i) = (1)(-1) + (1)(-1) + (0)(4) + (-1)(-1) + (-1)(-1)$

$$= -1 - 1 + 0 + 1 + 1 = 0,$$

$2 \times 4'$: $\sum (c_i)(c'_i) = (1)(-1) + (-1)(-1) + (0)(4) + (0)(-1) + (0)(-1)$

$$= -1 + 1 + 0 + 0 + 0 = 0,$$

$3 \times 4'$: $\sum (c_i)(c'_i) = (0)(-1) + (0)(-1) + (0)(4) + (1)(-1) + (-1)(-1)$

$$= 0 + 0 + 0 - 1 + 1 = 0.$$

Thus, we have constructed a set of mutually orthogonal comparisons. But what usable information do we obtain from this new comparison? One difference between group 3 and the others is the order of the words on successive trials—the *same* order is used for group 3 and *different* orders are used for the other groups. There are other differences as well, however. Group 3 receives the words on a memory drum; two of the remaining groups receive the words on the drum and two on a piece of paper. Group 3 receives the material at a 3-second rate of exposure per word; the same rate is used for group 4, but group 5 receives the words at a 1-second rate and groups 1 and 2 receive the words all at once. Since more than one difference is reflected in this new contrast, any difference that is observed cannot be unequivocally attributed to *one* of the differences. The comparison is useless. This demonstration stresses the point we made earlier: we are interested only in *meaningful* comparisons. Whether or not these comparisons are mutually orthogonal is of little or no importance.

The Meaning of Orthogonality

What does it mean to say that two comparisons are orthogonal? We have been using the terms *independent* and *nonredundant* to refer to orthogonal comparisons. When two comparisons are orthogonal, they provide independent or nonoverlapping pieces of information about the results of an experiment. That is, the information derived from one comparison is *unrelated* to the information derived from another, orthogonal comparison.

The meaning of orthogonality becomes clearer if we consider the relationship between two sets of coefficients. For orthogonal comparisons, the numbers in one set of coefficients are *completely unrelated* to the numbers in the other set. To emphasize this point, we can express orthogonality in terms of a product-moment correlation between two sets of coefficients. Briefly, and not too technically, suppose we were to calculate the product-moment correlation for two sets of coefficients. If we were to consider the *numerator* of the computational formula for this correlation, written in terms of the two sets of coefficients (c_i and c_i'), we would have

$$\sum (c_i)(c_i') - \frac{(\sum c_i)(\sum c_i')}{a}.$$

Since the sum of a set of coefficients must equal zero [Eq. (7-1)], the righthand term drops out and the numerator of the product-moment correlation becomes

$$\sum (c_i)(c_i') - \frac{(0)(0)}{a}$$

$$= \sum (c_i)(c_i').$$

When comparisons are orthogonal, this sum is *zero*. If the numerator of the product-moment correlation is zero, then the *correlation* must be *zero*. On the other hand, if the numerator is not zero, then the correlation will be some negative or positive number.

We have added an important meaning to the concept of orthogonality: orthogonal comparisons represent *uncorrelated* pieces of information. Again, as we noted before, orthogonality or independence refers to the information afforded by the sets of comparisons and *not* to the statistical tests themselves. Comparisons evaluated by the same denominator term are not *statistically* independent. However, most experimental applications have a sufficient number of df associated with the denominator term to pose no practical problem.

Number of Orthogonal Comparisons

Just so many questions reflecting independent bits of information can be asked of any given set of data. The number of such comparisons is equal to the df for the SS_A—that is, $a - 1$. Formally, we can say that

with a treatment means, the total number of comparisons which are orthogonal to each other and to $\bar{T}$ is equal to $a - 1$.

If we have three means, for example, it is only possible to construct two orthogonal comparisons. Actually, the *total number* of possible comparisons involving three means is six, namely, $\bar{A}_1$ vs. $\bar{A}_2$, $\bar{A}_1$ vs. $\bar{A}_3$, $\bar{A}_2$ vs. $\bar{A}_3$, $\bar{A}_1$ vs. $(\bar{A}_2 + \bar{A}_3)/2$, $\bar{A}_2$ vs. $(\bar{A}_1 + \bar{A}_3)/2$, and $\bar{A}_3$ vs. $(\bar{A}_1 + \bar{A}_2)/2$. However, a set of orthogonal comparisons will contain no more than two of the six possible comparisons.

Orthogonal Comparisons and the SS_A

An important point which should be mentioned is that the sums of squares produced by a complete set of orthogonal comparisons account for the SS_A completely. That is, if we calculate the sums of squares associated with $a - 1$ mutually orthogonal comparisons, we exhaust all of the independent information in our data. In symbols,

$$SS_A = \sum SS_{A\text{comp.}}, \qquad (7\text{-}2)$$

where $\sum SS_{A\text{comp.}}$ represents a complete set of orthogonal comparisons.

We have already demonstrated that Eq. (7-2) holds for the analysis summarized in Table 6-3 by showing that

$$SS_{A\text{comp. 1}} + SS_{A\text{comp. 2}} = SS_A.$$

Suppose we apply two *non*orthogonal comparisons to the same set of data. Specifically,

	a_1	a_2	a_3
A_i:	75	30	45
s:	5	5	5
Comp. 1:	1	-1	0
Comp. 2:	1	0	-1

The two comparisons are not orthogonal; i.e.,

$$\sum (c_i)(c_i') = (1)(1) + (-1)(0) + (0)(-1) = 1 + 0 + 0 = 1$$

From the formula for a comparison, Eq. (6-6),

$$SS_{A\text{comp.}} = \frac{[\sum (c_i)(A_i)]^2}{s[\sum (c_i)^2]},$$

and

$$SS_{A_{\text{comp. 1}}} = \frac{[(1)(75) + (-1)(30) + (0)(45)]^2}{5[(1)^2 + (-1)^2 + (0)^2]}$$

$$= \frac{(75 - 30 + 0)^2}{5(1 + 1 + 0)} = \frac{(45)^2}{5(2)} = \frac{2025}{10} = 202.50,$$

and

$$SS_{A_{\text{comp. 2}}} = \frac{[(1)(75) + (0)(30) + (-1)(45)]^2}{5[(1)^2 + (0)^2 + (-1)^2]}$$

$$= \frac{(75 + 0 - 45)^2}{5(1 + 0 + 1)} = \frac{(30)^2}{5(2)} = \frac{900}{10} = 90.00.$$

The sum of these two comparisons, $202.50 + 90.00 = 292.50$, greatly exceeds the total for the SS_A given in Table 6-3 ($SS_A = 210.00$). Accumulating more units of variation than were actually obtained in an experiment is a vivid way to illustrate the redundancy of two nonorthogonal comparisons.

Finally, notice that we are not necessarily interested in the results of all of the $a - 1$ contrasts in a set of orthogonal comparisons. We are concerned only with comparisons that have a specific experimental meaning to us, and these may or may not constitute a complete orthogonal set. The main attractive feature, of course, is that a properly constructed set of comparisons represents an efficient breakdown of the results of an experiment. But efficiency is not everything, and we will form incomplete sets of orthogonal comparisons and sets of nonorthogonal comparisons when they are dictated by the nature of the questions we want to ask of our data.

AN ADDITIONAL ILLUSTRATION OF EQ. (7-2)   The equality stated in Eq. (7-2) is extremely important to understand. What is being said is that the sum of squares obtained from a set of a means is a *composite* of the sums of squares associated with a set of $a - 1$ orthogonal comparisons. As we saw in the preceding paragraph, not just any collection of comparisons will do the trick. There must be $a - 1$ of them, and they must be *mutually orthogonal*. Consider the numerical example in Table 7-2. There are four groups with $s = 5$ observations in each. The treatment sums are listed at the top of the table. If we calculate the SS_A in the usual way, we get

$$SS_A = \frac{\sum (A)^2}{s} - \frac{(T)^2}{as}$$

$$= \frac{(15)^2 + (10)^2 + (12)^2 + (18)^2}{5} - \frac{(15 + 10 + 12 + 18)^2}{4(5)}$$

$$= \frac{793}{5} - \frac{3025}{20} = 158.600 - 151.250 = 7.350.$$

We will now calculate this quantity by obtaining the sums of squares for three different sets of orthogonal comparisons. We know from the preceding section that a complete set of orthogonal comparisons contains $a - 1$ comparisons, each of which satisfies Eq. (6-4) by having the coefficients sum to zero, and each pair of which passes the test for orthogonality [Eq. (7-1)]. Each set of comparisons presented in Table 7-2 has these properties.

TABLE 7-2   *Three Sets of Orthogonal Comparisons*

	a_1	a_2	a_3	a_4
A_i:	15	10	12	18
SET I				
Comp. 1:	3	-1	-1	-1
Comp. 2:	0	2	-1	-1
Comp. 3:	0	0	1	-1
SET II				
Comp. 1:	1	1	-1	-1
Comp. 2:	1	-1	0	0
Comp. 3:	0	0	-1	1
SET III				
Comp. 1:	1	-1	-1	1
Comp. 2:	1	0	0	-1
Comp. 3:	0	1	-1	0

The sum of squares for each comparison is calculated by substituting values from Table 7-2 into Eq. (6-6):

$$SS_{A_{comp.}} = \frac{[\sum (c_i)(A_i)]^2}{s[\sum (c_i)^2]}.$$

The sums of squares for the three comparisons in set I are

$$SS_{A_{comp. 1}} = \frac{[(3)(15) + (-1)(10) + (-1)(12) + (-1)(18)]^2}{5[(3)^2 + (-1)^2 + (-1)^2 + (-1)^2]}$$

$$= \frac{(5)^2}{5(12)} = .417,$$

$$SS_{A_{comp. 2}} = \frac{[(0)(15) + (2)(10) + (-1)(12) + (-1)(18)]^2}{5[(0)^2 + (2)^2 + (-1)^2 + (-1)^2]}$$

$$= \frac{(-10)^2}{5(6)} = 3.333,$$

$$SS_{A_{comp.\,3}} = \frac{[(0)(15) + (0)(10) + (1)(12) + (-1)(18)]^2}{5[(0)^2 + (0)^2 + (1)^2 + (-1)^2]}$$

$$= \frac{(-6)^2}{5(2)} = 3.600.$$

The sum of these individual sums of squares, $.417 + 3.333 + 3.600$, equals the SS_A (7.350).

Following the same procedure for the comparisons in set II,

$$SS_{A_{comp.\,1}} = \frac{[(1)(15) + (1)(10) + (-1)(12) + (-1)(18)]^2}{5[(1)^2 + (1)^2 + (-1)^2 + (-1)^2]}$$

$$= \frac{(-5)^2}{5(4)} = 1.250,$$

$$SS_{A_{comp.\,2}} = \frac{[(1)(15) + (-1)(10) + (0)(12) + (0)(18)]^2}{5[(1)^2 + (-1)^2 + (0)^2 + (0)^2]}$$

$$= \frac{(5)^2}{5(2)} = 2.500,$$

$$SS_{A_{comp.\,3}} = \frac{[(0)(15) + (0)(10) + (-1)(12) + (1)(18)]^2}{5[(0)^2 + (0)^2 + (-1)^2 + (1)^2]}$$

$$= \frac{(6)^2}{5(2)} = 3.600.$$

Again, the sum of the three sums of squares, $1.250 + 2.500 + 3.600 = 7.350$, uses up all of the variability associated with the SS_A.

Finally, for the third set, we have

$$SS_{A_{comp.\,1}} = \frac{[(1)(15) + (-1)(10) + (-1)(12) + (1)(18)]^2}{5[(1)^2 + (-1)^2 + (-1)^2 + (1)^2]}$$

$$= \frac{(11)^2}{5(4)} = 6.050,$$

$$SS_{A_{comp.\,2}} = \frac{[(1)(15) + (0)(10) + (0)(12) + (-1)(18)]^2}{5[(1)^2 + (0)^2 + (0)^2 + (-1)^2]}$$

$$= \frac{(-3)^2}{5(2)} = .900,$$

$$SS_{A_{comp.\,3}} = \frac{[(0)(15) + (1)(10) + (-1)(12) + (0)(18)]^2}{5[(0)^2 + (1)^2 + (-1)^2 + (0)^2]}$$

$$= \frac{(-2)^2}{5(2)} = .400.$$

This set, too, adds up to the SS_A.

In this example, we used three completely different sets of orthogonal comparisons. That is, not only are the three comparisons within a set mutually orthogonal, but each of the comparisons is used only once in the entire example. For each of the sets, Eq. (7-2) holds, indicating that the SS_A can be represented as the sum of $a - 1 = 3$ orthogonal comparisons.

ORTHOGONAL COMPARISONS FOR TREND

Analytical Questions About Trend

The comparisons we have discussed so far in this and in the last chapter are appropriate for the analysis of *qualitative* independent variables. The experiment summarized in Table 7-1 is a good example, with a number of different methods of presentation being compared. The contrast between the two modes of presentation (drum and paper) or between orders of presentation (same or different), for example, reflects the manipulation of qualitative independent variables. With such manipulations, we find that we can and want to ask meaningful questions about the difference between two treatments or combinations of treatments. The comparisons flow directly from the questions being asked.

Analytical analyses of experiments with *quantitative* independent variables take a different form. With a quantitative variable, the treatment levels represent different *amounts* of a single common variable. The levels can be ordered or spaced along the stimulus dimension in terms of the amount of the variable. Examples of quantitative or scaled independent variables are the number of hours of food deprivation, different dosage levels of a particular drug, rates of stimulus presentation, and the intensity of the unconditioned stimulus in a conditioning experiment.

With a quantitative variable, we are often interested in the *shape* or the *form* of the function relating the independent and dependent variables. Moreover, we are generally *not* interested in making orthogonal comparisons of the sort we discussed in the preceding sections. That is, if we have selected for inclusion in our study more than two levels of a quantitative independent variable, we would probably not be concerned with differences between groups representing contiguous points on the independent variable. Whether or not such comparisons between contiguous means are significant depends upon the *shape* of the function between the two points in question. If we believe that there are no abrupt breaks in nature—i.e., that a function will be continuous over the extent of the independent variable studied—then it is unimportant to test the separation of contiguous means, because we are really interested in the overall relationship between the independent and dependent variables.

An analysis of the shape of a function, or *trend analysis* as it is called, is dictated when we find ourselves asking questions that focus on the "ups and downs" of a function. We might, for example, find ourselves asking whether it is accurate to describe the outcome of an experiment as representing a *linear* function (a steady rise or fall in the treatment means as the independent variable is increased) or a *nonlinear* function of some sort (involving, for example, one or more reversals of direction). If the actual trend reflected in the data is important for our understanding of the experiment, then a trend analysis is most appropriate.

Purposes of Trend Analyses

Tests for trend are motivated by two sorts of concern, one based on theoretical predictions and one which is purely empirical or descriptive in nature. In the first case, we may only want to know whether or not the function exhibits a particular shape that is critical for our theory. Theories of stimulus generalization, for example, sometimes make specific statements concerning the shape of the function relating performance to different points on a stimulus dimension. Under these circumstances we would probably focus our attention on comparisons that are sensitive to this question. In the second case, our interest in trend is *post hoc*—we are looking for the *simplest* function that will describe our results adequately.

Let's see how a trend analysis can help in the description of a set of data. Suppose that we have conducted a memory experiment in which retention tests were administered to different groups of subjects at seven different intervals following the termination of learning. The results of this hypothetical experiment are presented in Fig. 7-1. How might we describe these data? We would probably *not* be satisfied with a description that said the following: "The retention function first rises, dips, rises again, falls precipitously this time, rises slightly, and then dips once more." This statement quite accurately describes the picture we obtain when we connect successive points on the independent variable; however, our job is not just to report functional relationships, but to make speculations concerning the basic processes underlying these relationships. We will develop this point in some detail.

Suppose we felt that the function in Fig. 7-1 was the result of different memory processes interacting over these time intervals. It would be unreasonable to postulate a *single* process as being responsible for this function. What sort of hypothetical process would follow the ups and downs of the function depicted in Fig. 7-1? A more likely theoretical explanation would postulate *several* memory processes, each following a different course with time. One process could be thought to increase and decrease *early* during the retention interval, followed by a second process that reached a peak at the fourth retention interval. Then something has to be postulated to explain the rapid drop in the curve following this high point. And so on—an extremely complicated theory.

Most of us would hope that nature is not *that* complicated! Thus, we find ourselves looking for an *idealized* relationship—one which still reasonably describes the data, but requires the assumption of the *fewest* processes and

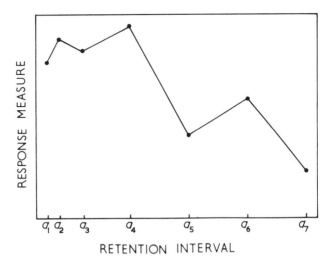

RESPONSE MEASURE

q_1 q_2 q_3 q_4 q_5 q_6 q_7

RETENTION INTERVAL

Fig. 7-1   Recall as a function of the retention interval.

interactions of processes. Therefore, we assume that experimental error is responsible, in part, for the jagged nature of the obtained function and that with increased precision, as would be afforded by an increased number of subjects and an increased number of retention intervals, the idealized curve would appear. Of course, we would like to be able to reach some sort of tentative conclusion now, before these more precise data are collected, if they ever are. What we need is a procedure which provides an assessment of the "strength" of the various fluctuations observed in the retention curve and which tells us the generalized form that the underlying function might take. Both of these goals— a test of theoretical predictions and data description—are achieved by means of an analysis of the trend into a set of orthogonal components, a procedure we will consider shortly.

Components of Trend

As mentioned previously, we are often searching for the simplest function to describe our data. A linear function is the least complex and would be the first one that normally we would consider. To say that a function is linear means that the curve either rises or drops at the same rate between any two points along the independent variable; a straight line may be used to describe the data. The data plotted in Fig. 7-1 can be described fairly adequately by a linear function. That is, a straight line with a downward slope reflects the variation among the data points fairly well. If the linear function actually represents the trend among the population means, we could devise a relatively simple explanation of the forgetting—a theory in which there is a *single* process changing at a constant rate with time would be sufficient.

Of course, the linear function does not fit the data of Fig. 7-1 all that well. A closer inspection of the curve seems to suggest that there is a consistent rise over the shorter retention intervals and *then* a linear drop over the longer intervals. A function that allows a single reversal of direction, e.g., a rise followed by a fall, is one containing a *quadratic* component. Assuming that the reversal of direction in Fig. 7-1 is a correct description of the real world, we would find it necessary to complicate our earlier one-process theory. One way to explain the quadratic component is to postulate an additional process with a different time course, whose influence is superimposed on the first. For instance, we could hypothesize a consolidation process, in which memory traces grow in strength for a short time following learning, as being responsible for the initial rise in the retention curve. We could then add another process, decay or interference with the memory trace, for example, as being fully responsible for forgetting after the consolidation process ceases to function. Presumably, both processes would be operating during the shorter retention intervals.

If we still felt that a function containing both a linear function (the constant downward trend) and a quadratic function (the early rise and fall) did not adequately fit the data, we might add higher-order components—components containing two or more reversals. A curve which has *two* reversals of slope contains a *cubic* component, *three* reversals a *quartic* component, and so on. As the number of slope reversals increases, the complexity of the theoretical interpretations increases considerably. Most existing theories in psychology make predictions about the linear and quadratic components only. Thus, our discussion of trend will concentrate primarily upon the analysis of these two components, although the method of analysis is easily extended to allow an assessment of the higher-order components.

CHOICE OF INTERVALS   Suppose we conduct an experiment in which we include five points on some stimulus dimension. We probably will include two groups at the extremes of the dimension to ensure that we "capture" the full range of effectiveness of the independent variable. How should we locate the other three groups?

One's first reaction might be to place them at equally spaced intervals. While many factors influence the choice of the specific intervals, the overriding consideration is the selection of levels that will "pick up" important changes in the response measure. Only if the function relating the independent and dependent variables is *linear* will equally spaced intervals be the best choice. This may be seen in Fig. 7-2. The function plotted in the two lefthand graphs is linear. Equally spaced intervals (upper graph) result in equal changes between successive intervals, while unequal intervals (lower graph) result in small changes where the intervals are closely spaced and large changes where they are spread out. In a sense, then, no interval is "wasted" in the first situation, while two of the intervals are wasted in the second. But what happens when the function is not linear? One possible outcome is depicted in the two graphs on the right.

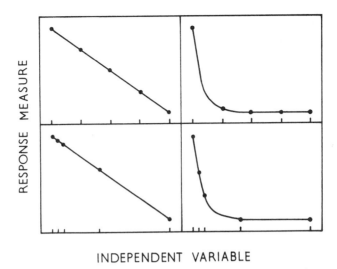

INDEPENDENT VARIABLE

Fig. 7-2   Spacing of points along a stimulus dimension.

Here, the situation is reversed. An equal spacing of intervals (upper graph) results in three intervals which show very little change and one interval which brackets around the point in the function where the maximum change is occurring. Unequal spacing (lower graph) does not waste any of the intervals, since the intervals are closely spaced where there is a precipitous change and widely spaced where only small changes occur.

The "trick" in designing an experiment, of course, is to know the shape of the function ahead of time so that we can make an efficient choice of our intervals. In most research applications, we usually do have enough information to provide a basis for a rational choice in the spacing. Often we will want to employ intervals that are not equal. This poses no insurmountable problem for a component analysis of trend—only some additional calculations.

Method of Orthogonal Polynomials

Many functional relationships in psychology may be adequately fitted by a *polynomial*, an algebraic expression having two or more terms. There are different orders of polynomials, depending upon the number of terms in the equation. The fewer and the lower the level of the terms, the simpler the function. For example, the linear or first-order equation is written

$$Y = b_0 + (b_1)(X),$$

where b_0 and b_1 are constants which must be estimated from the data, X represents points on the independent variable, and Y refers to values on the dependent variable. If we are dealing with treatment means, X is the numerical value taken by the different treatment levels and Y is the corresponding treatment mean predicted from the equation. The quadratic or second-order equation is given by

$$Y = b_0 + (b_1)(X) + (b_2)(X^2),$$

where the b's are constants estimated from the data, and X and Y refer to values on the independent and dependent variables, respectively. In general, the highest-degree polynomial that may be used to describe a set of a means is $a - 1$. The equation at the $a - 1$ order takes the following form:

$$Y = b_0 + (b_1)(X) + (b_2)(X^2) + \cdots + (b_{a-1})(X^{a-1}).$$

What we will be doing in these analyses is to see how well one of the *lower-degree* polynomials—linear or quadratic, for example—can describe the functional relationship. The procedure by which we accomplish this assessment is called the *method of orthogonal polynomials*. Briefly, a polynomial can be viewed as a sum of orthogonal polynomials. The general formula is given in Eq. (7-3):

$$Y = b_0' + (b_1')(c_{1i}) + (b_2')(c_{2i}) + \cdots + (b_{a-1}')(c_{(a-1)i}). \tag{7-3}$$

In this equation, the b' terms are constants, which are easily computed from the data, and the c_i terms are specialized *coefficients*, namely *orthogonal polynomial coefficients*. The c_{1i} coefficients represent the *linear* set of coefficients, the c_{2i} represent the *quadratic* set of coefficients, and so on.

The procedure we follow in the analysis is really quite simple—in spite of the formidable appearance of Eq. (7-3). Actually, we usually do not even bother with Eq. (7-3) but turn to the statistical analysis directly. The only time that Eq. (7-3) is useful is when we want to draw or to plot the idealized function. What we will accomplish in the analysis is to determine which of the b' terms are significantly different from zero. The b' terms are *slope* or *trend* constants. When one of the constants is zero, that particular component of trend is *absent* from the array of treatment means; when a constant takes on a nonzero value, that particular trend is present. In order to assess the significance of the different trend components, we use the polynomial coefficients to calculate the sums of squares associated with each trend component. The procedures are identical to the ones we use to calculate the sums of squares associated with *any* comparison. That is, we weight treatment sums with orthogonal polynomial coefficients and then substitute these values in Eq. (6-6).

In summary, then, whether we are interested in testing only the trend components specified by theory (planned comparisons) or are searching for a simplified polynomial to describe our data, the procedure is the same. Specifically, we determine the significance of a trend component by methods we have considered already. Depending upon which components are significant—i.e., have a significant nonzero value—Eq. (7-3) is then revised and simplified, with the nonsignificant components being dropped from the equation. We use the orthogonal polynomial coefficients, each of which is sensitive to a different trend component, to discover those trend components that may be important for an understanding of our data. The only new idea introduced by the method of orthogonal polynomials is that a functional relationship may be partitioned or decoded into orthogonal components of trend; otherwise, the method is like any other analysis involving orthogonal comparisons.

ILLUSTRATION OF THE COMPONENT ANALYSIS   We can see how the method of orthogonal polynomials works by watching what happens to the different trend components when the orthogonal polynomial coefficients are applied to sets of data reflecting different types of trend. Suppose we have five treatment groups that are equally spaced on some continuum. We can see from Eq. (7-3) that the highest-order polynomial possible in this experiment is $a - 1 = 4$. We will use the method of orthogonal polynomials to determine which terms can be dropped from the fourth-degree equation.

To do this, we need a different set of coefficients for each of the orthogonal trend components, namely, the linear, quadratic, cubic, and quartic components. As long as the levels of our independent variable are equally spaced, as they are in this example, we can look up the sets of coefficients in Table C-2 of Appendix C. (If the levels are not equally spaced, we will have to calculate the sets of coefficients by a method outlined in Appendix B.) The coefficients listed in Table C-2 are for all components up to the *quintic* (fifth-order polynomial) for experiments where a ranges from 3 to 10. More extensive tables are available in Fisher and Yates (e.g., 1953). For the present example, under the row entry of $k = 5$ groups, we have the following:

Coefficients	Levels of Factor A				
	a_1	a_2	a_3	a_4	a_5
Linear (c_{1i})	-2	-1	0	1	2
Quadratic (c_{2i})	2	-1	-2	-1	2
Cubic (c_{3i})	-1	2	0	-2	1
Quartic (c_{4i})	1	-4	6	-4	1

Let's look at the coefficients carefully. First, we observe that the five coefficients in each of the four sets sum to zero; hence, they satisfy the basic requirement for comparison: $\sum c_i = 0$. Second, the four sets are all mutually orthogonal, which we may verify by forming the cross products of corresponding coefficients and showing that they sum to zero: $\sum (c_i)(c_i') = 0$. All of the sets of coefficients, at any value of k in Table C-2, meet these two requirements. Third, each set of coefficients in this present example reflects a different trend component. Consider the plot of the linear coefficients which appear in the first panel of Fig. 7-3. All that is present is a linear trend, a straight line. In the second panel, the quadratic coefficients are plotted; here there is a symmetrical curve with a single reversal of trend—a quadratic function. There is no "tilt" to the curve, indicating the absence of any linear trend. The cubic and quartic coefficients are presented in the third and fourth panels, respectively. The cubic coefficients show two reversals of trend and the quartic coefficients show three reversals of trend. Each set of coefficients mirrors the trend that it will "search out" in the analysis of an actual set of data.

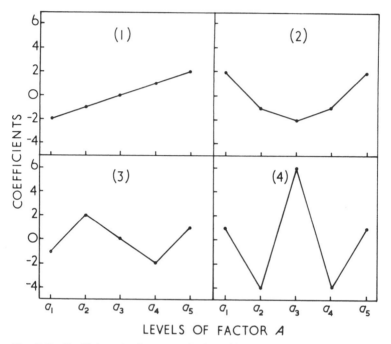

Fig. 7-3 Coefficients for linear, quadratic, cubic, and quartic trend components.

A comparison reflects the degree to which there is a *correlation* between the set of coefficients and the treatment means (pp. 101–103). In the present context, a *perfect correlation* between the linear coefficients, say, and the treatment means would indicate that the data were *perfectly fitted* by a first-degree polynomial—a linear equation. We will now turn to some hypothetical data, which have been constructed to show particular trends and to demonstrate the sensitivity of the different sets of coefficients in detecting the presence of these trends.

Consider the results for three different situations (Examples A, B, and C). The treatment means for each example are listed in Table 7-3 and are plotted in Fig. 7-4. The data for Example A reflect a perfect *linear* trend. The coefficients for the four orthogonal trend components are given in the first section of the table. In order to calculate the sum of squares for a comparison, we would substitute the coefficients for a particular component and the treatment means in Eq. (6-5):

$$SS_{A_{comp.}} = \frac{s[\sum (c_i)(\bar{A}_i)]^2}{\sum (c_i)^2}.$$

(We are working with treatment means, but the demonstration could be given using the treatment sums instead.) The important quantity in Eq. (6-5), of course, is the quantity within the brackets, $\sum (c_i)(\bar{A}_i)$; if this quantity is zero, the $SS_{A_{comp.}}$ will be zero, and if this quantity is either a positive or a negative number, the $SS_{A_{comp.}}$ will be some positive value. For this demonstration, then, we will look only at this quantity and see whether a particular trend is present or absent.

TABLE 7-3   *Illustration of Trend Components*

	Treatment Levels					
	a_1	a_2	a_3	a_4	a_5	Sum
COEFFICIENTS						
Linear (c_{1i})	-2	-1	0	1	2	$= 0$
Quadratic (c_{2i})	2	-1	-2	-1	2	$= 0$
Cubic (c_{3i})	-1	2	0	-2	1	$= 0$
Quartic (c_{4i})	1	-4	6	-4	1	$= 0$
EXAMPLE A						
$\bar{A}_i$:	8	9	10	11	12	
$(c_{1i})(\bar{A}_i)$:	-16	-9	0	11	24	$= 10$
$(c_{2i})(\bar{A}_i)$:	16	-9	-20	-11	24	$= 0$
$(c_{3i})(\bar{A}_i)$:	-8	18	0	-22	12	$= 0$
$(c_{4i})(\bar{A}_i)$:	8	-36	60	-44	12	$= 0$
EXAMPLE B						
$\bar{A}_i$:	8	11	12	11	8	
$(c_{1i})(\bar{A}_i)$:	-16	-11	0	11	16	$= 0$
$(c_{2i})(\bar{A}_i)$:	16	-11	-24	-11	16	$= -14$
$(c_{3i})(\bar{A}_i)$:	-8	22	0	-22	8	$= 0$
$(c_{4i})(\bar{A}_i)$:	8	-44	72	-44	8	$= 0$
EXAMPLE C						
$\bar{A}_i$:	6	10	12	12	10	
$(c_{1i})(\bar{A}_i)$:	-12	-10	0	12	20	$= 10$
$(c_{2i})(\bar{A}_i)$:	12	-10	-24	-12	20	$= -14$
$(c_{3i})(\bar{A}_i)$:	-6	20	0	-24	10	$= 0$
$(c_{4i})(\bar{A}_i)$:	6	-40	72	-48	10	$= 0$

For the linear component in Example A,

$$\sum (c_{1i})(\bar{A}_i) = (-2)(8) + (-1)(9) + (0)(10) + (1)(11) + (2)(12).$$

These calculations are completed in Table 7-3, showing a positive value of 10. The sums of the weighted means for the other three components are obtained in the same fashion, and the results are also presented in the table. The remaining three are all equal to zero, indicating the absence of any corresponding trend. (We would not expect to obtain sums of zero in an actual experiment, of course. When no particular trend is present in an array of means, we expect the sum of the weighted means still to take on some nonzero value, but a value that reflects the presence of experimental error.) Thus, the analysis indicates that only a linear trend is present in Example A.

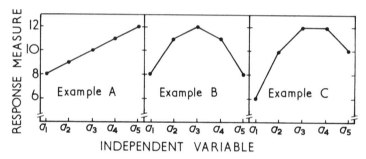

Fig. 7-4   Plot of artificial data presented in Table 7-3.

An inspection of the means for Example B reveals a perfect *curvilinear* trend. Consider the sum of the weighted means for the quadratic component:

$$\sum (c_{2i})(\bar{A}_i) = (2)(8) + (-1)(11) + (-2)(12) + (-1)(11) + (2)(8)$$
$$= 16 - 11 - 24 - 11 + 16 = -14.$$

Notice that the *coefficients* for the quadratic component describe a quadratic trend which is exactly the *reverse* of the one observed in the treatment *means*. This negative correlation between the coefficients and the means is reflected in the *negative* sum of the weighted means. What would happen if the signs of the coefficients were reversed? In this case,

$$\sum (c_{2i})(\bar{A}_i) = (-2)(8) + (1)(11) + (2)(12) + (1)(11) + (-2)(8)$$
$$= -16 + 11 + 24 + 11 - 16 = 14.$$

Since the coefficients and means vary in the *same* directions, the correlation is positive and so is the sum of the weighted means. Either set of coefficients will produce the same sum of squares for the quadratic component, however. The reason is that in Eq. (6-5),

$$SS_{A_{\text{quadratic}}} = \frac{s[\sum (c_{2i})(\bar{A}_i)]^2}{\sum (c_{2i})^2},$$

the sum is *squared* and all of the other terms remain the same. Returning to the other three orthogonal trend components in this example, we see that the sum of the weighted means is zero.

In the first two examples, we have seen that the sets of coefficients are able to pull out of the data *single trends* when they are the only trends present. Example C demonstrates that this analysis can isolate *two components* when they are acting together to determine performance. Look carefully at the plot of the means in Fig. 7-4. We can see that there is a general upward linear slope; we could fit a straight line through the data points and this line would have a positive slope. There is also a rise and then a fall to the curve, indicating the presence of a curvilinear trend as well. The results of applying the four sets of coefficients to these treatment means are recorded in the table. The sums of the weighted means are 10 and -14 for the linear and quadratic components, respectively, and zero for the other two. If we look back at Examples A and B, we see that the sums for the linear component in Example A and for the quadratic component in Example B are equal to the corresponding sums in Example C. This happened because of the way in which the three sets of data were constructed for this illustration. More specifically, the means for Example C were obtained by combining the two trend components in Examples A and B.

In summary, then, these examples demonstrate that the method of orthogonal polynomials applies a set of independent "decoders" to the treatment means and that these decoders "resonate" to the presence of a particular *form* of relationship between the independent and dependent variables and to no other.

Numerical Example

As an example of an analysis using the method of orthogonal polynomials, consider an experiment designed to test the proposition that subjects learn better when the training is distributed over a period of time than when the training is massed all at once. If we wanted to, we could investigate this question with just two groups, one group receiving massed training and another group receiving distributed training of some sort. But a more comprehensive investigation would include a number of different conditions of distributed training.

Consider the following experiment. Subjects are given some material to learn for 10 trials, with the independent variable, intertrial interval (the interval between successive trials), being manipulated at intervals of 0 seconds (the massed condition), 20, 40, and 60 seconds (the distributed conditions). This means that one group of subjects receives no spacing between successive trials, another group receives 20 seconds between trials, another group 40 seconds, and a final group 60 seconds. Suppose that $s = 20$ subjects are included in each of the four independent groups. The results of this hypothetical experiment, expressed in terms of the number of correct responses over the 10 learning trials, are given in the upper half of Table 7-4.

The sums of squares based on these data are as follows:

$$SS_A = \frac{\sum (A)^2}{s} - \frac{(T)^2}{as}$$

$$= \frac{(309)^2 + (429)^2 + (452)^2 + (401)^2}{20} - \frac{(1591)^2}{4(20)},$$

$$SS_{S/A} = \sum (AS)^2 - \frac{\sum (A)^2}{s}$$

$$= 33,715 - \frac{(309)^2 + (429)^2 + (452)^2 + (401)^2}{20},$$

$$SS_T = \sum (AS)^2 - \frac{(T)^2}{as}$$

$$= 33,715 - \frac{(1591)^2}{4(20)}.$$

These calculations are completed in the lower half of Table 7-4.

An evaluation of the F ratio indicates that we can reject the null hypothesis and conclude that intertrial interval is an effective variable in the learning of this material. As we have noted, however, this analysis does not tell us anything about the *form* of the relationship between learning and the length of the intertrial interval—only that it is unlikely that the population means are equal.

TABLE 7-4 *Numerical Example: Overall Analysis*

BASIC DATA

Intertrial Interval (A)

	0 sec., a_1	20 sec., a_2	40 sec., a_3	60 sec., a_4	Sum
A_i:	309	429	452	401	1591
s:	20	20	20	20	80
$\bar{A}_i$:	15.45	21.45	22.60	20.05	
$\sum_j^s (AS_{ij})^2$:	5175	9461	10,550	8529	33,715

SUMMARY OF THE ANALYSIS

Source	Calculations	SS	df	MS	F
A	32,231.35 − 31,641.01 =	590.34	3	196.78	10.08*
S/A	33,715 − 32,231.35 =	1483.65	76	19.52	
Total	33,715 − 31,641.01 =	2073.99	79		

* $p < .01$.

An inspection of the means in Table 7-4 suggests that a spacing interval between learning trials has an increasing beneficial effect up to a certain point (somewhere between 40 and 60 seconds), after which performance tends to decline. An assessment of this trend can be accomplished easily by the method of orthogonal polynomials. In this analysis, we will assume that we planned to conduct a component analysis of trend before the data were collected. In fact, there is even a theory that predicts exactly this finding (Underwood, 1961).

Whatever the case, it is of interest to find out more about the form of the relationship between the length of the intertrial interval and learning. Since the four levels are evenly spaced on the independent variable, we can use the orthogonal polynomial coefficients that are listed in Table C-2 of Appendix C. Also listed in the table are the sums of the squared coefficients $[\sum (c_i)^2]$, which are needed for the analysis. The coefficients and sums for the three possible components (linear, quadratic, and cubic) are presented in the upper half of Table 7-5. For convenience, the treatment sums (A_i) are also included in the table.

TABLE 7-5 *Numerical Example: Trend Analysis*

	Intertrial Interval (A)				
	0 Sec., a_1	20 Sec., a_2	40 Sec., a_3	60 Sec., a_4	
A_i:	309	429	452	401	
	COEFFICIENTS				$\Sigma (c_i)^2$
Linear (c_{1i}):	-3	-1	1	3	20
Quadratic (c_{2i}):	1	-1	-1	1	4
Cubic (c_{3i}):	-1	3	-3	1	20
	COMPUTATIONS				SUM
$(c_{1i})(A_i)$:	-927	-429	452	1203	299
$(c_{2i})(A_i)$:	309	-429	-452	401	-171
$(c_{3i})(A_i)$:	-309	1287	-1356	401	23

The formula for the $SS_{A\text{comp.}}$ is given by Eq. (6-6):

$$SS_{A\text{comp.}} = \frac{[\sum (c_i)(A_i)]^2}{s[\sum (c_i)^2]}.$$

For the quantity within the brackets, we have

$$\sum (c_{1i})(A_i) = (-3)(309) + (-1)(429) + (1)(452) + (3)(401),$$

$$\sum (c_{2i})(A_i) = (1)(309) + (-1)(429) + (-1)(452) + (1)(401),$$

$$\sum (c_{3i})(A_i) = (-1)(309) + (3)(429) + (-3)(452) + (1)(401).$$

These calculations are completed in the bottom half of Table 7-5. The next step is to substitute values from the tables into Eq. (6-6). We have, for the linear component,

$$SS_{A_{\text{linear}}} = \frac{(299)^2}{20(20)} = \frac{89,401}{400} = 223.50,$$

for the quadratic component,

$$SS_{A_{\text{quadratic}}} = \frac{(-171)^2}{20(4)} = \frac{29,241}{80} = 365.51,$$

and for the cubic component,

$$SS_{A_{\text{cubic}}} = \frac{(23)^2}{20(20)} = \frac{529}{400} = 1.32.$$

TABLE 7-6   *Summary of the Trend Analysis*

Source	SS	df	MS	F
Intertrial Interval (A)	(590.34)	(3)		
Linear	223.50	1	223.50	11.45*
Quadratic	365.51	1	365.51	18.72*
Cubic	1.32	1	1.32	<1
S/A	1483.65	76	19.52	
Total	2073.99	79		

* $p < .01$.

These three component sums of squares are presented together in an analysis-of-variance summary table in Table 7-6. Except for errors from rounding off, the three orthogonal components sum to the SS_A we obtained earlier:

$$\sum SS_{A_{\text{comp.}}} = 223.50 + 365.51 + 1.32 = 590.33 \approx SS_A.$$

The F ratios are formed by dividing the component mean squares by the overall error variance, the $MS_{S/A}$. As indicated in the table, the linear and quadratic components are significant.

Order of Testing Components

We have indicated already that it is possible to extract $a - 1$ orthogonal trend components from a set of a treatment means. Usually, we will not be directly interested in the presence or absence of trends beyond the linear and quadratic components. Of course, if a theory makes a specific prediction concerning a higher-order component, we would certainly test that prediction by isolating the variance due to that particular form of trend. We might only look at the variability associated with a single trend component, if, for theoretical reasons, this component was singled out. These comparisons are planned and are conducted as we have outlined. When there is no theory to guide the analysis or when we want to probe further into the higher-order components not specified by a theory—that is, when we are "hunting" for significant components—the comparisons are essentially post hoc. Under these circumstances, researchers often take a different sort of orientation. One change is the way in which an experimenter conducts the analysis, the other is the way he evaluates the significance of components he has isolated. We will consider the first change here and the second in Chapter 8.[1]

With a significant overall F, we are interested in discovering the trend components that jointly will describe the outcome of the experiment fairly accurately. The first step is to calculate the linear sum of squares and to test the significance of this component. In order to decide whether or not to continue searching for other significant components, we perform another "omnibus" F test based on the sums of squares remaining after the linear component has been removed. That is, we will test the significance of

$$SS_{A_{\text{residual}}} = SS_A - SS_{A_{\text{linear}}}.$$

The "residual" sum of squares has

$$df = df_A - df_{A_{\text{linear}}} = (a - 1) - 1,$$

and the corresponding mean square is evaluated against the $MS_{S/A}$. If this F is significant, then we can extract the next higher component, the quadratic in this case. If the F is not significant, we stop. (We subject the residual sum of squares to a test of significance for the same reason that we perform an omnibus F test—in the absence of any particular hypotheses, to see whether there is any variation among the means to worry about.)

If we continued with the analysis and extracted the quadratic component, we would test the significance of this component and then test the new residual sum of squares:

$$SS_{A_{\text{residual}}} = SS_A - SS_{A_{\text{linear}}} - SS_{A_{\text{quadratic}}},$$

which is associated with

$$df = df_A - df_{A_{\text{linear}}} - df_{A_{\text{quadratic}}}$$
$$= (a - 1) - 1 - 1.$$

If this F is not significant, we stop extracting components; if it is, we continue with the process.

It should be pointed out again, however, that little is gained by way of behavioral insight when we find significant higher-order components. The main purpose of this sort of analysis is to see just how well fairly simple

[1] To anticipate, we might consider using the Dunn method to evaluate the significance of the comparisons (see Chapter 8).

polynomials (linear and quadratic) fit the data as a first approximation. But even with this limitation, the orthogonal analysis of trend provides an extremely powerful analytical tool for the researcher.

Construction of the Polynomial Function

It is sometimes useful to be able to express the results of a trend analysis by means of a polynomial function containing only those components which are of interest or which have been shown to be significant. What we want is a formula that will allow us to draw a function containing the components suggested by the analysis of trend. We start with Eq. (7-3), the equation for a polynomial written in terms of orthogonal polynomial coefficients:

$$Y = b_0' + (b_1')(c_{1i}) + (b_2')(c_{2i}) + \cdots + (b_{a-1}')(c_{(a-1)i}),$$

where the b' terms are slope constants and the c_i terms are orthogonal polynomial coefficients. The results of the statistical analysis allow us to drop from Eq. (7-3) terms that are not significant. Finally, we have to calculate the b' terms and then solve for the predicted means with the resultant equation.

As an example, we will consider the experiment we have just analyzed. For $a = 4$, the highest-order polynomial possible would be $a - 1 = 3$. Thus, we might consider at first a third-order polynomial to describe the data:

$$Y = b_0' + (b_1')(c_{1i}) + (b_2')(c_{2i}) + (b_3')(c_{3i}).$$

Theory, as well as the statistical analysis, suggested that the function could be simplified to include only the linear and quadratic components. Consequently, we would drop the last term—i.e., set b_3' equal to zero—and work with the equation,

$$Y = b_0' + (b_1')(c_{1i}) + (b_2')(c_{2i}). \tag{7-4}$$

Our task now is to solve for the three different constants (the b' terms). This is simple: $b_0' = \overline{T}$ and

$$b' = \frac{\sum (c_i)(A_i)}{s\left[\sum (c_i)^2\right]},$$

for the remaining b' terms. From the data in Table 7-5,

$$b_0' = \overline{T} = \frac{1591}{80} = 19.888,$$

$$b_1' = \frac{\sum (c_{1i})(A_i)}{s\left[\sum (c_{1i})^2\right]} = \frac{299}{20(20)} = .748,$$

$$b_2' = \frac{\sum (c_{2i})(A_i)}{s\left[\sum (c_{2i})^2\right]} = \frac{-171}{20(4)} = -2.138.$$

Substituting in Eq. (7-4), we are now able to calculate the values of the predicted treatment means $(\bar{A}_i')$. Specifically,

$$\bar{A}_i' = 19.888 + (.748)(c_{1i}) - (2.138)(c_{2i}). \tag{7-5}$$

Substituting the coefficients for the different levels of factor A,

$$\bar{A}_1' = 19.888 + (.748)(-3) - (2.138)(1)$$

$$= 19.888 - 2.244 - 2.138 = 15.506,$$

$$\bar{A}_2' = 19.888 + (.748)(-1) - (2.138)(-1)$$

$$= 19.888 - .748 + 2.138 = 21.278,$$

$$\bar{A}_3' = 19.888 + (.748)(1) - (2.138)(-1)$$

$$= 19.888 + .748 + 2.138 = 22.774,$$

$$\bar{A}_4' = 19.888 + (.748)(3) - (2.138)(1)$$

$$= 19.888 + 2.244 - 2.138 = 19.994.$$

The final results of these calculations are entered in column 2 of Table 7-7. For comparison purposes, the actual means are presented in column 1 of the table. The predicted means closely approximate the obtained means.

TABLE 7-7   *Prediction of Treatment Means from Two Polynomials*

	(1) $\bar{A}_i$	(2) $\bar{A}_i'$ (Lin. + Quad.)	(3) $\bar{A}_i'$ (Lin. + Quad. + Cub.)
a_1:	15.45	15.51	15.448
a_2:	21.45	21.28	21.452
a_3:	22.60	22.77	22.600
a_4:	20.05	19.99	20.052

The extreme closeness of the prediction is the result of the fact that together the linear and quadratic components account for nearly all of the units of variation due to factor A (the SS_A). The only way we can obtain a *perfect* prediction is to include *all* the components that have any units of variation associated with them. There is only one component remaining in our example, $SS_{A_{\text{cubic}}} = 1.32$. If we include this component in our prediction, we simply add the term $(b_3')(c_{3i})$ to Eq. (7-5). For this example,

$$b_3' = \frac{\sum(c_{3i})(A_i)}{s[\sum(c_{3i})^2]} = \frac{23}{20(20)} = .058.$$

Thus, we would add the quantity $(.058)(c_{3i})$ to Eq. (7-5) to obtain the revised prediction. The amounts added or subtracted from the original prediction (column 2 of Table 7-7) are

$$(.058)(-1) = -.058, \qquad (.058)(3) = .174, \qquad (.058)(-3) = -.174,$$

and

$$(.058)(1) = .058,$$

for levels a_1 to a_4, respectively. The new predictions are presented in column 3 of Table 7-7. Except for rounding error, the predictions are *exact*.

The closeness of these last predictions is no point for celebration, however, since the predictions will *always* be exact when we write a polynomial that contains *all* of the orthogonal components. Said another way, we can always find a polynomial of the $a - 1$ order to fit a set of a means. But this is not why we turn to a trend analysis. We are *not* interested in the fitting of curves per se, but in the attempt to see how the *simple* functions—ones including linear and quadratic components—perform as predictors of the obtained values. The method of orthogonal polynomials provides a procedure by which we can isolate the different components and assess their significance. The success of this analysis is reflected in the size of the ratio relating the sums of squares for the significant components to the SS_A and in the closeness with which a polynomial using only these components (that is, setting all other components to zero) can predict the obtained means.

Limitations of the Analysis

We should mention several limitations of the analysis of trend. First, we must continually remind ourselves that our only knowledge about the underlying function for the population comes from the limited number of points we have selected for the experiment. We assess the importance of different orthogonal trend components on the basis of the means we *do* have. How do we know that the same underlying trend would be suggested if other points had been selected for the experiment? Is it accurate to draw a continuous function between the points that we do have—would values of the independent variable falling between the ones included in the experiment fall on the revised polynomial? In our example, we are asking whether we can predict from the curve specified by Eq. (7-5) such values on the independent variable as an intertrial interval of 10 seconds or of 50 seconds.

A related and more serious question concerns the shape of the function *outside* of the two extreme values on the independent variable included in the experiment. Translated to our experiment, we are asking about the shape of the function beyond the shortest and the longest intervals included in the study. Consider the function depicted in Fig. 7-5. We will assume that it represents the function in the population. Our experiment has focused on one portion of the continuum, the band between 0 and 60 seconds. On the basis of a trend analysis, we concluded that there is a linear and quadratic component. But the under-

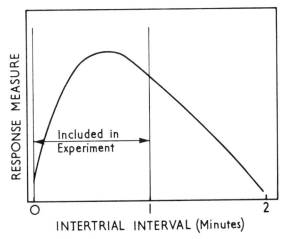

RESPONSE MEASURE

Included in
Experiment

O   I   2

INTERTRIAL INTERVAL (Minutes)

Fig. 7-5 Hypothetical function relating the length of the intertrial interval to some measure of learning.

lying function is *quadratic*. We would have seen this clearly had we included a 2-minute intertrial interval, for instance. All that we can say about this function is what we have found within the band we selected for the experiment. We did have a cue in this experiment that a quadratic trend was present from the reversal of trend between 40 and 60 seconds. On the other hand, the reversal of trend does not necessarily mean that performance will continue to drop as we increase the intertrial interval; perhaps it will level off. We cannot tell from this experiment. Still, we know that the function does reverse itself between 40 and 60 seconds. Imagine what would have happened if we had *not* included the 60-second condition. We would have concluded that only a *linear* trend was present and would not have suspected the reversal.

The point of this discussion is to stress a fundamental limitation of trend analysis: any inferences concerning the underlying trend in the population are really based upon a very limited number of data points. As Hays (1963) puts it, "Inferences are to be made about a hypothetical population in which [the] *only possible* values... [of the independent variable]... are those actually represented in the experiment" (p. 551).

Other limitations are not as serious as the one we have just considered. One is that the orthogonal polynomial coefficients in Table C-2 of Appendix C assume equal spacings on the independent variable. We are able to solve this difficulty by calculating sets of orthogonal polynomial coefficients that are appropriate to the actual spacings represented in an experiment (see Appendix B). A trend analysis also assumes an equal number of subjects in each of the treatment conditions. Trend analyses of experiments with unequal sample sizes are discussed in Chapter 17. Finally, the analysis is based upon the assumption that the polynomial is the appropriate mathematical function to describe a set of data. In some areas of psychology, certain phenomena are better described by an exponential function or by a logarithmic function. Nevertheless, the method of orthogonal polynomials still can approximate these alternative functions fairly well. If more precision is required, the advice of a statistician should be obtained.

In spite of these limitations, however, the analysis of trend by the method of orthogonal polynomials is a useful analytical tool for the researcher. In later chapters we will see that we can extend the method to more complicated experiments to ask even more detailed questions of a set of data.

chapter eight

MULTIPLE COMPARISONS

Planned comparisons are specified before the start of the experiment and are conducted in lieu of the overall F test. Unplanned or post-hoc comparisons take the form of data sifting—a search for interesting findings to evaluate, but a search with no particular hypotheses in mind. On occasion every researcher will find that comparisons prompted by a look at the data are the most revealing and provocative findings of the entire experiment.

Post-hoc comparisons often take the form of an intensive "milking" of a set of results—e.g., the comparison of all possible pairs of treatment means. The motivation, of course, is to extract the maximum amount of information from any given study. Another reason for conducting post-hoc comparisons is that the results of such tests often lead to future experiments. An interesting comparison, significant or not, may form the basis for a new experiment. In the next study, for example, we might choose to manipulate more extensively the different treatments contributing to the comparison we isolated.

As we discussed in Chapter 6, there is a serious problem with post-hoc comparisons. To repeat, the more comparisons we conduct, the more type I errors we will commit. The *experimentwise (EW) error rate*—the probability of making one or more type I errors in a set of comparisons—provides an index of this relationship. We saw that even with planned orthogonal comparisons the *EW* error rate increases with the number of comparisons. Equation (6-2) expresses the relationship formally as

$$\alpha_{EW} = 1 - (1 - \alpha)^c$$

or approximately as

$$\alpha_{EW} \approx c(\alpha),$$

where α is the per comparison error rate and c is the number of comparisons.

There are several different approaches to the solution of this difficulty. The solution common to all post-hoc techniques is to reduce the size of the critical rejection region. If we make it more difficult to reject the null hypothesis, fewer type I errors will be committed and the *EW* error rate will thus be reduced. Just how much of an "adjustment" is made depends upon a number of factors, such as the experimenter's willingness to make type I errors in general, the number of post-hoc comparisons he makes, and the pool of comparisons from which he chooses those he does test. As we will see, there is no general agreement among researchers concerning these points. [See Petrinovich and Hardyck (1969) for a useful analysis of this problem.]

We will now consider a number of procedures which have been developed to cope with the increased *EW* error rate with a particular form of post-hoc comparison, often called *multiple comparisons*.[1] The critical feature distinguishing planned and unplanned comparisons is the post-hoc nature of the latter. Multiple comparisons refer to post-hoc comparisons in which large numbers of contrasts are performed, with each mean entering into multiple numbers of comparisons. Multiple comparisons are easily recognized, since they generally involve the evaluation of all possible comparisons between means in a set of means. This set usually consists of the *a* treatment means in the experiment, but a smaller subset may be used when there is an a priori justification for the creation of the subset.

Our discussion of tests designed to control *EW* error rate of multiple comparisons will be divided into four parts. The first set of tests we will discuss is concerned with comparisons between all possible pairs of means, while the second set expands the pool of comparisons to include not only these simple contrasts but those involving differences between complex combinations of means. The third type of test restricts attention to a smaller set of comparisons than do the first two. Finally, we will discuss a test that accommodates all possible comparisons between a control group and a number of experimental groups.

[1] For a comprehensive summary and comparison of these techniques, see Kirk (1968, pp. 87–98) and Winer (1962, pp. 77–89; 1971, pp. 185–201).

THE LEAST SIGNIFICANT DIFFERENCE TEST (LSD)

The starting point for our discussion is a procedure in which *no correction* is made for comparisons conducted after the discovery of a significant overall F. This procedure, called the *least significant difference* (LSD), requires that the omnibus null hypothesis be rejected and consists of the unrestricted assessment of comparisons involving the treatment means. In general, the significance of any comparison is determined by forming the F ratio specified previously in Eq. (6-7):

$$F = \frac{MS_{A_{comp.}}}{MS_{S/A}},$$

which is evaluated against the tabled value of F at α and the df associated with the numerator and denominator terms. An alternative formula is useful when comparisons involve differences between pairs of means, where the least significant difference (LSD) is given by

$$LSD = \sqrt{F(1, df_{S/A})}\sqrt{\frac{2(MS_{S/A})}{s}}. \tag{8-1}$$

This value represents the critical difference that must exist between two means to be significant at the chosen value of α. If a number of such comparisons are to be conducted, it is more convenient to use Eq. (8-1) and simply compare the differences between pairs of means with the value obtained for LSD rather than to form the corresponding F ratios specified in Eq. (6-7).

The LSD test achieves no control over the EW error rate; i.e., no corrections are made for the *number* of post-hoc comparisons conducted with this test. It essentially treats planned and post-hoc comparisons on an equal basis with one exception: the LSD test requires a significant omnibus F test, while planned comparisons do not.

Not all researchers agree that the LSD test is the appropriate procedure for post-hoc comparisons, and so we will discuss in detail the various adjustment procedures made available to us by statisticians. In the final section of this chapter we will worry about the problem of choosing from among these approaches to the problem of multiple comparisons.

ALL POSSIBLE COMPARISONS BETWEEN PAIRS OF MEANS

If we can imagine designing an experiment in which we really have *no* a priori hypotheses to test, then we might consider a mechanical procedure for isolating the source(s) responsible for the significant treatment effect that we obtained with an omnibus F test. The procedure is simple enough. We arrange our means (or the treatment totals) in ascending order of magnitude on the dependent variable and commence to test the significance of the differences. This systematic "fishing" from the "pool" of all possible pairwise comparisons greatly increases the number of comparisons we are effectively considering and, therefore, the probability that we will make more type I errors.

We will discuss procedures which, in different ways, accomplish the adjustment in the size of the critical differences. There are three general approaches to this problem. At one extreme, we can use the LSD test and simply pay no attention to the *EW* error rate. At the other extreme, we can protect ourselves for all possible comparisons between means and combinations of means, whether we conduct all of the comparisons or not. The Tukey and Scheffé tests are of this nature. These tests effectively *reduce* the per comparison error rate (α) in order to control α_{EW}. Somewhere in the middle are tests for which the size of the adjustment depends upon the number of means encompassed between the means being compared. The Newman-Keuls and Duncan tests represent this approach. They occupy the middle ground, since the *effective EW* error rate lies somewhere between the uncorrected case and the Scheffé-Tukey case. In all of these discussions, we will assume that an equal number of subjects are placed in each treatment condition. (An adaptation of these procedures to the case with unequal sample sizes is presented in Chapter 17.) We will describe and compare the procedures and then work out a numerical example illustrating their use in an analysis.

Newman–Keuls Test

As indicated in the preceding paragraph, two procedures adjust the size of the critical region according to the means spanned in comparisons of the sort we are discussing here. Because of the separate adjustments, these are known as *layer* or *stairstep* methods. This differential adjustment is thought to be reasonable, since it is known that the relative frequency of extreme differences occurring by chance increases as the number of means contained between the smallest and largest means increases. In essence, what is being done is to reduce the α level systematically as the number of steps between means increases.

Suppose the groups were arranged in order according to the size of the means. In order to make all possible comparisons between pairs of means, we could compare first means that are adjacent, then means that are one step removed, then means that are two steps removed, until we reached the comparison of the smallest and largest means in the experiment. Each of these sets of comparisons will be evaluated at a different per comparison α level. In actually performing these comparisons, we will find it more efficient to deal directly with *differences* between group *totals*, rather than with separate F ratios for each comparison. The Newman-Keuls procedure sets the critical range (CR) between the sums of two groups as

$$CR_{\text{N-K}} = q(r, df_{S/A})\sqrt{s(MS_{S/A})},$$ (8-2)

where q represents an entry in the table of the Studentized Range Statistic (Table C-3 of Appendix C), r is the number of treatment groups considered together (see next paragraph), $df_{S/A}$ are the df associated with the error term in the overall analysis of variance (the $MS_{S/A}$) [that is, $df_{S/A} = a(s - 1)$], and s is the sample size.

If we look at Table C-3, we will see that for any particular value of $df_{S/A}$, called df_{error} in the table, the value of q increases with r. (Note that r refers to all of the groups encompassed within any given comparison, *including* the two groups being compared. Thus, if we are comparing adjacent groups, $r = 2$, groups that are one step removed, $r = 3$, groups that are two steps removed, $r = 4$, and so on.) The actual procedure is simple enough: we calculate $\sqrt{s(MS_{S/A})}$, a value that will be used for all of the comparisons, look up the appropriate values of q, and perform the multiplication indicated in Eq. (8-2). After this is accomplished, we are in a position to compare obtained differences with the appropriate critical ranges that we have calculated. Later in this section we will see an example of how this is accomplished.

The important characteristic of the Newman-Keuls technique is that the adjustment procedure sets the type I error at α for each comparison, no matter what the value of r may be. When $r = 2$, there is no correction and the difference is evaluated with an uncorrected critical range. When $r > 2$, a correction is applied; the correction is such that the per comparison rate, even for the most extreme groups which encompass the means for all the other groups, is α. There will still be a sizeable EW error rate, of course, but not as great as there would be if no correction were made at all.

Duncan Test

An alternative stairstep procedure has been proposed by Duncan (1955). There is the same individualized correction for comparisons representing different numbers of steps as we saw in the Newman-Keuls procedure, but the correction is not as severe. We should note that Scheffé (1957, p. 78) has questioned the mathematical justification of the Duncan method, although there has been no formal documentation of this objection. In any case, we will examine the method, since we often will encounter it in research reports.

The procedure for calculating the critical range with the Duncan method is the same as with the Newman-Keuls method, except that another specialized statistic (q') is needed for the calculations. The critical range is found by

$$CR_D = q'(r, df_{S/A})\sqrt{s(MS_{S/A})}. \tag{8-3}$$

[Tables of q' may be found in Edwards (1968, pp. 430–434) and Kirk (1968, p. 533). In Edwards, r and $df_{S/A}$ are listed as "k" and "df," respectively; in Kirk, they are listed as "r" and "$error\ df$."]

Tukey Test

The Newman-Keuls and Duncan tests result in critical ranges which change for different values of r. The next two tests we will discuss, the Tukey and the Scheffé tests, produce a *single* critical range for the evaluation of all differences between pairs of treatment groups. The purpose of these two tests is to control the EW error rate for *all* comparisons that can be made with a set of treatment groups. The tests treat all comparisons alike—i.e., they evaluate each comparison at the *same* adjusted α level. All multiple comparisons are viewed in the same light—they are comparisons made after the data have been inspected. The Tukey method is based on the Studentized Range Statistic (q), while the Scheffé procedure uses the F distribution. As we will see, the Tukey critical range is smaller than the one obtained with the Scheffé method for this type of comparison (between pairs of groups).

The systematic proposal of the Tukey test, often called the HSD (honestly significant difference) test, was made by Tukey (1953) in an unpublished manuscript. An excellent and detailed presentation of this test can be found in Guenther (1964, pp. 54–57). The formula for the CR is given by

$$CR_T = q(r_{max}, df_{S/A})\sqrt{s(MS_{S/A})}, \tag{8-4}$$

where $r_{max} = a$, the number of treatment groups. The Tukey test holds the EW error rate constant at the significance level chosen for the q statistic for all possible comparisons involving treatment means.

Scheffé Test

The Scheffé test (Scheffé, 1953) also sets the EW error rate for all possible comparisons that might be conducted between two or more groups. The critical range for the Scheffé test is specified in Eq. (8-5):

$$CR_S = \sqrt{(a-1)F(df_A, df_{S/A})}\sqrt{2s(MS_{S/A})}, \tag{8-5}$$

where a is the number of treatment groups, $F(df_A, df_{S/A})$ is the critical value from the F table (Table C-1), $df_A = a - 1$, $df_{S/A}$ is the number of df corresponding to the $MS_{S/A}$, and s is the sample size in each treatment group.

Comparison of the Different Methods

A vivid comparison of the various correction procedures can be obtained by rewriting the equations for the critical ranges so that they may be compared over various values of r. It is also useful for comparison purposes to include the value required for the LSD test (or planned comparisons) as a sort of reference point. The degree to which the multiple-comparison methods exceed this critical value provides an index of the severity of the corrections.

The four equations for the critical range, written in a form to facilitate comparison, are

LSD or planned comparisons: $CR_{LSD} = \sqrt{F(1, df_{S/A})}\sqrt{2s(MS_{S/A})}$,

Duncan:
$$CR_D = \frac{q'(r, df_{S/A})}{\sqrt{2}}\sqrt{2s(MS_{S/A})},$$

Newman-Keuls:
$$CR_{N-K} = \frac{q(r, df_{S/A})}{\sqrt{2}}\sqrt{2s(MS_{S/A})},$$

Tukey:
$$CR_T = \frac{q(r_{max}, df_{S/A})}{\sqrt{2}}\sqrt{2s(MS_{S/A})},$$

Scheffé:
$$CR_S = \sqrt{(a - 1)F(df_A, df_{S/A})}\sqrt{2s(MS_{S/A})}.$$

With these equations written this way, we can forget about the second factor, $\sqrt{2s(MS_{S/A})}$, and compare the first factors directly. This has been done in Table 8-1. For this comparison, we have set $\alpha = .05$, $a = 10$, and $s = 13$, and necessarily, $df_{S/A} = a(s - 1) = 10(13 - 1) = 120$. The appropriate values of F needed for this comparison of methods are $F(1, 120) = 3.92$ for the LSD test and $F(9, 120) = 1.96$ for the Scheffé test. The values for q are found in Table C-3 in the row at $df_{error} = df_{S/A} = 120$. The q' values are 2.80, 2.95, 3.04, 3.12, 3.17, 3.22, 3.25, 3.29, and 3.31 for increasing values of r. (We have used 1.414 as a solution to $\sqrt{2}$ in these calculations.)

The results of these substitutions are given in the body of Table 8-1. Several points should be noted from this display. First, the values for LSD, Tukey, and Scheffé comparisons are constant at all levels of r; the LSD and Scheffé comparisons form the smallest and largest critical ranges, respectively. Second, the critical ranges for the Duncan and Newman-Keuls procedures are equal to that required of an LSD comparison when adjacent groups are considered (i.e., at $r = 2$). Third, the critical ranges for the Newman-Keuls and Tukey procedures are equal at $r = r_{max} = a = 10$. Fourth, while the critical ranges for the Duncan and Newman-Keuls methods increase with r, the increase is considerably less for the Duncan test.

TABLE 8-1 *Comparison of Different Multiple-Comparison Techniques*

Comparison Techniques	Values of r								
	2	3	4	5	6	7	8	9	10
LSD or planned comparisons	1.98	1.98	1.98	1.98	1.98	1.98	1.98	1.98	1.98
Duncan test	1.98	2.09	2.15	2.21	2.24	2.28	2.30	2.33	2.34
Newman-Keuls test	1.98	2.38	2.60	2.77	2.90	3.00	3.08	3.16	3.22
Tukey test	3.22	3.22	3.22	3.22	3.22	3.22	3.22	3.22	3.22
Scheffé test	4.20	4.20	4.20	4.20	4.20	4.20	4.20	4.20	4.20

We can see in Table 8-1, then, just where and by how much the critical range is increased by the different tests. In terms of protection from making EW type I errors, it is clear that the Tukey and Scheffé methods afford the greatest protection, with the Duncan and Newman-Keuls methods providing an intermediate amount.[2]

TABLE 8-2 *Analysis of Variance*

Source	SS	df	MS	F
A	209.69	4	52.42	3.97*
S/A	528.80	40	13.22	
Total	738.49	44		

* $p < .01$.

Numerical Example

As an example, suppose we performed an experiment with $a = 5$ treatment groups and $s = 9$ subjects in each group. The results of the single-factor analysis of variance are presented in Table 8-2. The omnibus F test indicates that the null hypothesis is rejected at $p < .01$. The actual treatment sums (A_i) for the different groups are given in Table 8-3. Assuming that we have no a priori hypotheses about the outcome of this experiment, we are now interested in determining the locus of the significant omnibus F. (As noted previously, post-hoc tests in general are *not* conducted when the overall F is *not* significant.)

The particular arrangement of Table 8-3 was chosen to facilitate the systematic comparison of all pairs of groups and to allow a contrast of the different corrections for the multiple comparisons. The treatment *sums* are listed in ascending order along both dimensions of the table. Entries within the body of this portion of the table represent the differences between the two treatment sums at each intersection of a column and row. In the first row, for example, $A_2 - A_3 = 7$, $A_4 - A_3 = 15$, and so on. Numbers are not entered for comparisons below the last diagonal in the table, since the listing would be an exact mirror image of the numbers above the diagonal.

The three columns to the right of the treatment comparisons list the values necessary to evaluate the significance of the difference scores by the Newman-Keuls and the Duncan methods. The column labeled r refers to the number of groups bracketed in any given comparison. The comparisons appearing in the *diagonal* at $r = 2$ involve adjacent sums; thus, only two groups are bracketed. The differences given in the diagonal at $r = 3$ involve sums that are one step removed; hence, $r = 3$. The next two columns in the table give the critical

---

[2] This conclusion is born out in an empirical comparison of these techniques by Petrinovich and Hardyck (1969).

ranges ($\alpha = .05$) for each value of r as required by the Newman-Keuls test (CR_{N-K}) and the Duncan test (CR_D), respectively. The formula for CR_{N-K} is given by Eq. (8-2):

$$CR_{N-K} = q(r, df_{S/A})\sqrt{s(MS_{S/A})}.$$

The first step is to calculate the quantity under the radical:

$$\sqrt{s(MS_{S/A})} = \sqrt{9(13.22)} = \sqrt{118.98} = 10.91.$$

This quantity, 10.91, serves as a constant multiplier for all values of $q(r, df_{S/A})$, which are found in Table C-3. The q values for $df_{S/A} = 40$ are 2.86, 3.44, 3.79, and 4.04 for $r = 2$ to 5, respectively. The corresponding values of CR_{N-K} are obtained by multiplying these numbers by 10.91:

$$CR_{N-K} = (2.86)(10.91), \quad (3.44)(10.91), \quad (3.79)(10.91), \quad \text{and} \quad (4.04)(10.91).$$

The results of these multiplications are, respectively,

$$CR_{N-K} = 31.20, \quad 37.53, \quad 41.35, \quad \text{and} \quad 44.08.$$

These values are recorded in Table 8-3.

The calculations for the critical ranges for the Duncan test are the same, except that $q'(r, df_{S/A})$ are found in a table not included in Appendix C. For $df_{S/A} = 40$, q' values are 2.86, 3.01, 3.10, and 3.17 for increasing values of r. A multiplication of these values by the constant 10.91, calculated previously, gives

$$CR_D = (2.86)(10.91), \quad (3.01)(10.91), \quad (3.10)(10.91), \quad \text{and} \quad (3.17)(10.91).$$

A completion of the respective multiplications yields

$$CR_D = 31.20, \quad 32.84, \quad 33.82, \quad \text{and} \quad 34.58.$$

These critical ranges are entered in the last column of Table 8-3.

TABLE 8-3 *Numerical Example of Multiple Comparisons*

	Levels (Ordered by Size of Treatment Totals):							
	a_3	a_2	a_4	a_5	a_1			
A_i:	64	71	79	103	115	r	CR_{N-K}	CR_D
$A_3 = 64$	—	7	15	$39^{a,b}$	$51^{a,b,c,d,e}$	5	44.08	34.58
$A_2 = 71$		—	8	32^a	$44^{a,b,c}$	4	41.35	33.82
$A_4 = 79$			—	24	$36^{a,b}$	3	37.53	32.84
$A_5 = 103$				—	12	2	31.20	31.20
$A_1 = 115$					—	—	—	—

[a] $p < .05$, LSD test. [b] $p < .05$, Duncan test. [c] $p < .05$, Newman-Keuls test. [d] $p < .05$, Tukey test. [e] $p < .05$, Scheffé test.

We are now ready to perform the Newman-Keuls and Duncan tests. There is a systematic pattern to the evaluation procedure. We start first with the largest difference between two treatment sums, which appears in the upper right-hand corner of Table 8-3. If this difference is significant, we continue testing the differences to the left in the first row. In essence, then, we are considering all of the comparisons involving the *smallest* treatment sum. Significance is evaluated by comparing the obtained difference with the appropriate critical range—(i.e., the CR corresponding to the correct value of r.) The diagonal lines in Table 8-3 make this easy. As soon as a nonsignificant range is encountered, we shift down one row and continue our right-to-left evaluation. This procedure is reiterated until the *first* test of a new row is negative. At this point, the testing sequence is terminated.

We will follow this procedure with the Newman-Keuls test. The largest range (51) exceeds the critical range indicated for $r = 5$ in Table 8-3 (44.08). This fact can be recorded in the table by an asterisk placed next to the significant range. (We have a letter superscript, c, to indicate the outcome of this test.) Moving to the left, we find that the next difference (39) is compared with the critical range at $r = 4$ ($CR_{N-K} = 41.35$). Since the obtained difference is smaller than the relevant critical range, we drop to the next row and to the difference on the far right. This difference (44) exceeds the required critical value at $r = 4$ ($CR_{N-K} = 41.35$) and is labeled significant. The next difference in the second row does not reach significance; thus, we now evaluate the largest difference in the third row. Since this difference (36) is not significant and it is also the first comparison in this row, we discontinue the testing procedure.

The Duncan test is conducted in the same manner, but using, of course, the relevant set of critical ranges (CR_D) in Table 8-3. Significant differences by the Duncan test are indicated by the superscript b.

The Tukey and Scheffé tests require the calculation of a single critical range that will be used in the evaluation of all of the comparisons. For the Tukey test,

$$CR_T = q(r_{max}, df_{S/A})\sqrt{s(MS_{S/A})}$$
$$= q(5, 40)\sqrt{9(13.22)}$$
$$= (4.04)\sqrt{118.98} = (4.04)(10.91) = 44.08.$$

(This critical range equals the CR_{N-K} at $r = 5$.) For the Scheffé test,

$$CR_S = \sqrt{(a - 1)F(df_A, df_{S/A})}\sqrt{2s(MS_{S/A})}$$
$$= \sqrt{(5 - 1)F(4, 40)}\sqrt{2(9)(13.22)}$$
$$= \sqrt{4(2.61)}\sqrt{237.96}$$
$$= \sqrt{4(2.61)(237.96)} = \sqrt{2484.30} = 49.84.$$

The same sequence of testing is followed as before, except that all differences are evaluated in the Tukey test against the $CR_T = 44.08$ and in the Scheffé test against the $CR_S = 49.84$. With either test, only the largest difference (51) is significant. The superscripts d and e, respectively, register this fact in Table 8-3.

Finally, for comparison purposes, these pairwise contrasts are assessed by means of a critical range appropriate for the LSD test. The critical range for any two-group comparison in this example is

$$CR_{LSD} = \sqrt{F(1, 40)}\sqrt{2s(MS_{S/A})}.$$

Substituting the relevant values, we obtain

$$CR_{LSD} = \sqrt{4.08}\sqrt{2(9)(13.22)} = \sqrt{4.08}\sqrt{237.96}$$
$$= \sqrt{970.88} = 31.16.$$

The results of the testing procedure, using 31.16 as the critical range, are indicated by the superscript, a, in Table 8-3.

Usually we summarize the results of this type of multiple comparison by underscoring sets of treatment sums (or means) that do not differ significantly.

TABLE 8-4 *Summary of Multiple Comparisons*

Comparison Techniques	A_i:	a_3 64	a_2 71	a_4 79	a_5 103	a_1 115
		Levels				
LSD test						
Duncan test						
Newman-Keuls test						
Tukey test						
Scheffé test						

This has been done in Table 8-4 for the different tests we conducted. Take the Duncan test, for example. An inspection of the first row of Table 8-3 reveals that the comparison between A_3 and A_4, which includes A_2, is not significant. We can summarize this finding by underscoring these three treatment sums. The second row shows that A_2 and A_5 do not differ, and so we can connect these sums as well as A_4 by underscoring. The next row indicates that A_4 and A_5 do not differ, but this fact is already included in the previous statement. In the final row, we see that the difference between A_5 and A_1 is not significant; these two sums are joined by underscoring.

The underscoring provides an efficient way of communicating the results of the statistical analysis. The procedure also points up difficulties an experimenter will encounter when he tries to interpret his findings. For example, the patterning of the bands of statistical equivalence (conditions grouped by the same underscoring) usually can not be explained in any simple manner. That is, the different treatments represented by the conditions so grouped will rarely reflect sufficient commonality to allow a reasonable interpretation of the grouping or the pattern of the groupings. This difficulty may be accentuated whenever two or more bands have the same treatment conditions in common. In the Duncan test, for example, bands 1 and 2 both contain treatments a_2 and a_4 and bands 2 and 3 both contain a_5. The occurrence of this sort of overlap will blur any commonality discovered within any particular band. Still, if an experimenter is really at the point where he must resort to this sort of analysis, he may welcome any useful information that can be extracted from the outcome of the statistical test.

The other sets of tests that we conducted are also summarized in Table 8-4. The tests have been listed in order of increasing *conservatism* toward type I errors. An inspection of this table indicates that this difference in tests is reflected in the number of the bands of groups with nonsignificant sums as well as in the width of these bands. Of the multiple-comparison techniques, the Duncan test is clearly the least conservative and, in this example, the Tukey and Scheffé tests are the most conservative. If type I errors are to be avoided, the latter two tests are the ones to use. But this reduction of type I errors costs us something, something that we will want to worry about—a *decreased sensitivity* in detecting real differences when they are present. We are referring, of course, to the fact that we pay for the use of a smaller critical region for testing the null hypothesis by making an increased number of type II errors. We will come back to this really difficult problem at the end of this chapter.

ALL POSSIBLE COMPARISONS BETWEEN COMPLEX COMBINATIONS OF MEANS

The Tukey and Scheffé tests may be extended to multiple comparisons that represent contrasts involving more than two groups. A good example would be a post-hoc trend analysis. In this case, the way in which the treatment means are weighted is complicated, and each treatment group is essentially involved in the determination of each trend component. Other examples of these more complex multiple comparisons are contrasts between two means where one or both consist of an average of two or more different groups. We considered comparisons of this sort in Chapter 6. In the numerical example of the last section, where there were five treatment groups, three of the groups might have represented control treatments of some sort and the remaining two experimental treatments. It might be meaningful to compare the performance of the three combined control groups with the performance of the two combined experimental groups. Or, it might make more sense to compare each of the control groups separately with the combined experimental groups. Or, there may be some justification for making all four of these comparisons.

We rarely see these latter sorts of contrasts treated as post-hoc comparisons, however. The reason is that for a comparison to be experimentally *meaningful*, there must be some rationale for combining groups. Even though a particular comparison is *possible*, we are not going to form experimentally heterogeneous sets of groupings and contrast them. No meaningful inference can be drawn from such contrasts. The point is that if meaningful comparisons involving combined groups are possible, we would probably have thought of these comparisons at the outset and included the contrasts as *planned comparisons*. But, in any case, there may be times when multiple comparisons of this sort are relevant, and we should know how the Tukey and Scheffé methods accommodate them.

Both procedures already take into consideration these sorts of multiple comparisons. They differ, however, in the way we perform the evaluation of a comparison. We will take as an example the data we worked with in the last section. As an illustration of the calculations, we will compare two of the groups $[(\bar{A}_1 + \bar{A}_5)/2]$ with the remaining three groups $[(\bar{A}_2 + \bar{A}_3 + \bar{A}_4)/3]$. We have already discussed how to make these sorts of comparisons in Chapter 6.

Scheffé Test

The first step is to calculate the sum of squares associated with this comparison. As before, we will work with the treatment sums rather than the treatment means in the computations. For this example, we have the following arrangement:

	a_1	a_2	a_3	a_4	a_5
			Levels		
A_i:	115	71	64	79	103
c_i:	3	-2	-2	-2	3

Substituting these values in Eq. (6-6), we have

$$SS_{A_{comp.}} = \frac{[\sum (c_i)(A_i)]^2}{s[\sum (c_i)^2]}$$

$$= \frac{[(3)(115) + (-2)(71) + (-2)(64) + (-2)(79) + (3)(103)]^2}{9[(3)^2 + (-2)^2 + (-2)^2 + (-2)^2 + (3)^2]}$$

$$= \frac{(654 - 428)^2}{9(30)} = \frac{(226)^2}{270} = 189.17.$$

The next operation is to form an F ratio. Since we are still contrasting only two means in this comparison, the df for the $SS_{A_{comp.}}$ is $df = 1$ and the $MS_{A_{comp.}} = 189.17/1 = 189.17$. The appropriate F ratio is specified in Eq. (6-7) and consists simply of dividing the $MS_{A_{comp.}}$ by the $MS_{S/A}$. In this case,

$$F = \frac{189.17}{13.22} = 14.31.$$

It is at the point of evaluating the significance of the F ratio that the Scheffé correction is applied. Instead of evaluating the obtained F in the normal F table, we compare it with a special F value, F_S. This quantity is defined as

$$F_S = (a - 1)F(df_A, df_{S/A}), \tag{8-6}$$

where $F(df_A, df_{S/A})$ is found in Table C-1 at the desired α level. When translated into the present example (at $\alpha = .05$),

$$F_S = (5 - 1)F(4, 40)$$

$$= 4(2.61) = 10.44.$$

Since the obtained F of 14.31 exceeds this critical value demanded by the Scheffé test (10.44), we can reject the null hypothesis.

The main advantage of the Scheffé test is that the EW error rate ($\alpha_{EW} = .05$ in this example) remains at .05 or less, no matter how many multiple comparisons are conducted. Thus, after the establishment of a significant omnibus F test, we can consider *any* comparison, orthogonal or not, and still guarantee that our α_{EW} will be within a certain specified maximum.

Tukey Test

The Tukey method accomplishes the same sort of control of the EW error rate, but by a different route. In the Scheffé test, we obtained an F for the comparison in the usual fashion, but evaluated the significance of the F ratio with an adjusted F (F_S). In the Tukey test, we calculate the sum of the weighted treatment totals $[\sum (c_i)(A_i)]$ and compare the sum with the *critical* sum specified by

$$\text{Tukey critical sum} = q(r_{max}, df_{S/A})\sqrt{s(MS_{S/A})} \; [(\tfrac{1}{2})(\sum |c_i|)]. \tag{8-7}$$

We have already considered the first two terms of Eq. (8-7) in the section on pairwise comparisons. To refresh memories, $q(r_{max}, df_{S/A})$ refers to the Studentized Range Statistic (Table C-3), r_{max} to the maximum number of steps between means (a), and the other quantities are familiar. The third term of the equation specifies the *absolute sum* of the coefficients (that is, a sum of the coefficients, disregarding signs). This term provides an adjustment for different sorts of comparisons. When just two groups are involved,

$$(\tfrac{1}{2})(\sum |c_i|) = (\tfrac{1}{2})(1 + 1) = 1,$$

and the term drops out of the equation. Under these circumstances, Eq. (8-7) is identical to Eq. (8-4), p. 138. When more than two means are involved, adjustments for the different sets of coefficients are made.

We have already calculated the sum of the weighted treatment sums in the example of the Scheffé comparison: $\sum (c_i)(A_i) = 226$. All that is left is to determine the Tukey critical sum from Eq. (8-7):

$$\text{Tukey critical sum} = q(5, 40)\sqrt{9(13.22)}\ [(\tfrac{1}{2})(3 + 2 + 2 + 2 + 3)]$$
$$= (4.04)\sqrt{118.98}\ [(\tfrac{1}{2})(12)]$$
$$= (4.04)(10.91)(6) = 264.46.$$

The obtained sum (226) does *not* exceed the critical sum (264.46), and so the comparison is not significant.

It will be recalled that when we compared the Tukey and Scheffé tests for comparisons between pairs of means (Table 8-1), the Tukey test was more sensitive in detecting differences that were present. That is, a smaller critical range was required for significance under the Tukey test than under the Scheffé test. Exactly the opposite is true when multiple comparisons involve three or more means: the Scheffé test is more sensitive. In short, then, the two multiple-comparison techniques have differential sensitivity; the Tukey test is more sensitive when comparisons involve two groups and the Scheffé test is more sensitive when comparisons involve more than two groups.

RESTRICTED SET OF COMPARISONS BETWEEN MEANS (DUNN TEST)

The multiple-comparison tests we have been considering are designed to control the number of type I errors in an experiment where the set of comparisons is quite large, comprising all possible contrasts between pairs of means or between complex combinations of means. Often, however, we will not be interested in an enumeration of a complete set of comparisons. Instead, we will want to make a limited number of post-hoc comparisons. Under these circumstances, the Dunn test (Dunn, 1961) is appropriate.

Essentially what is done in this test is to start with an acceptable EW error rate (α_{EW}) and to apportion this probability among the comparisons contemplated. More specifically, we will use

$$\alpha_{\text{comp.}} = \frac{\alpha_{EW}}{c}$$

to evaluate the significance of each comparison. If there were five comparisons and $\alpha_{EW} = .01$, for example, then each comparison would be evaluated at $\alpha_{\text{comp.}} = (.01)/5 = .002$. The $\alpha_{\text{comp.}}$ need not be divided equally over the comparisons in the set, but according to an experimenter's concern for the balance between type I and type II errors. For example, if there were five tests to be conducted and we were working at $\alpha_{EW} = .05$, we could divide the α_{EW} equally among the comparisons: $\alpha_{comp.} = (.05)/5 = .01$. Or, we could divide the probabilities unequally—for example, .02, .01, .01, .005, and .005. Any division is acceptable as long as the sum of the individual probabilities equals $\alpha_{EW} = .05$.

The main problem with the Dunn test is in the selection of the comparisons to be tested. It may be that an investigator can specify a set of comparisons that he will make, given a particular outcome of an experiment. Or, once he has inspected the results of the experiment, a logical set of post-hoc comparisons may suggest itself. If it is not possible to restrict the number of comparisons in logical groups, however, the decision to use the Dunn test becomes questionable. For example, suppose the overall F test is significant and we decide to look at contrasts between pairs of means. We have no particular hypothesis in mind in conducting these contrasts—we just want to identify the locus of the significant overall effect. It would be inappropriate to pick out the five largest differences, say, and use the Dunn procedure to assess their significance. Under these circumstances, we would be selecting comparisons on the basis of the *size* of the differences and capitalizing on chance factors. The procedures discussed in an earlier section would be the correct ones to use, because the *total pool* of comparisons, from which these five were chosen, contains *all possible* contrasts between pairs of means. In short, the advantage of the Dunn procedure—of allowing flexibility in the assignment of the *EW* error rates in post-hoc comparisons—is also the biggest stumbling block in its use.

Numerical Example

As an example, suppose we single out three post-hoc comparisons which are of experimental interest to us from the data presented in Table 8-3. (In this experiment, $a = 5$, $s = 9$, and $MS_{S/A} = 13.22$.) We can apportion the per comparison error rates either equally or unequally among the different comparisons. We will consider these two situations in turn.

The critical range (CR) for the Dunn test in the first case is given by

$$CR_{Dunn} = d(c, df_{S/A})\sqrt{2s(MS_{S/A})}, \qquad (8\text{-}8)$$

where d is an entry in a special table prepared by Dunn (1961) and found in Table C-4; the other terms in Eq. (8-8) are familiar ones. To find the value of d, we enter the table under the number of comparisons (c), the number of df for the error term (in this case, $df_{error} = df_{S/A}$), and the desired probability level—.05 or .01. In the present example, at $p = .05$,

$$CR_{Dunn} = d(3, 40)\sqrt{2(9)(13.22)}$$

$$= (2.50)\sqrt{237.96} = (2.50)(15.43) = 38.58.$$

If any of the comparisons exceeds 38.58, it is considered significant. This critical range represents a per comparison rate of $\alpha_{comp.} = (.05)/3 = .017$.

In comparison with the multiple-comparison tests computed for this example, the CR_{Dunn} is larger than any of the CR's for the Duncan test and for the Newman-Keuls test at $r = 2$ and 3 (see Table 8-3, p. 141); it is smaller than the critical ranges for the Tukey test ($CR_T = 44.08$) and the Scheffé test ($CR_S = 49.84$).

When more complicated comparisons between means are contemplated, it is more convenient to calculate the F in the normal manner and to evaluate it against the following:

$$F_D = [d(c, df_{S/A})]^2. \tag{8-9}$$

For the present example,

$$F_D = [d(3, 40)]^2$$
$$= (2.50)^2 = 6.25.$$

The Dunn test is not as simple as we have just indicated when the error rate is not the same for each of the c comparisons. In this situation, we will have to find values of d at uncommon probability levels—i.e., values other than .05 and .01. When this happens, it is convenient to use the unit-normal distribution and approximate the value of d. (This approximation will work only for comparisons where $df = 1$.) The value of d at the α level of significance is found by

$$d(c, df_{S/A}) = z + \frac{z^3 + z}{4(df_{S/A} - 2)}, \tag{8-10}$$

where z represents the point on the unit-normal distribution, expressed as a deviation from the mean, above which $\frac{1}{2}(\alpha) \times 100$ percent of the curve falls.[3]

As an example, we will work out something we can verify in Table C-4—say, the value of $d(5, 40)$ at $\alpha_{EW} = .05$. What we need is the value of $d(5, 40)$ at a rate of $\alpha_{comp.} = (.05)/5 = .01$. From a table of the unit-normal curve, available in most introductory statistics texts, the value of z above which $(\frac{1}{2})(.01) \times 100 = .5$ percent of the area of the curve falls is 2.576. Substituting in Eq. (8-10), we have

$$d(5, 40) = 2.576 + \frac{(2.576)^3 + 2.576}{4(40 - 2)}$$

$$= 2.576 + \frac{17.094 + 2.576}{4(38)}$$

$$= 2.576 + \frac{19.670}{152}$$

$$= 2.576 + .129 = 2.705.$$

The value of $d(5, 40)$ from Table C-4 is 2.71.

---

[3] In more common terminology, we are referring to a *two-tailed* test, locating 1/2 of the α level for positive values of z and 1/2 for negative values of z.

COMPARISONS BETWEEN A CONTROL AND
SEVERAL EXPERIMENTAL GROUPS (DUNNETT TEST)

When we include a control condition in an experiment, we are often interested in a number of different comparisons. As a first step in the analysis, we might compare the control group with the average score for the experimental groups combined—a sort of overall control-experimental contrast. Additionally, we might evaluate the significance of any differences observed among the experimental groups alone—a sort of omnibus F for the experimental groups. Finally, we would probably consider multiple comparisons involving a contrast of each of the experimental groups with the single control group. Because of the necessary increase in the number of comparisons when a single control group is compared with several experimental groups, we might want to exercise some control over the EW error rate.

The Dunnett test is a specialized multiple-comparison test that compensates for the increased number of type I errors, but is not as 'corrective' as are the Scheffé or Tukey tests. This test holds constant the EW error rate so that even when all control-experimental group comparisons are conducted, the probability of making one or more type I errors is no larger than α_{EW}. The Dunnett test is chosen over the other multiple-comparison tests because it takes into consideration only a limited number of comparisons—the control-experimental contrasts. The Tukey and Scheffé tests consider all possible comparisons between two means.

The procedures followed in the Dunnett test can be expressed to parallel those elaborated for the more general multiple-comparison techniques. In brief, we calculate a critical control-experimental difference for a given α_{EW} level, analogous to the critical range of the tests previously discussed, and compare observed differences against this standard. Only if a difference exceeds this standard is it considered significant. The formula for calculating the critical control-experimental differences is given by

$$\text{critical C-E difference} = q_D(k, df_{S/A})\sqrt{2s(MS_{S/A})}, \qquad (8\text{-}11)$$

where q_D is obtained from Table C-5 at some α_{EW} level and k consists of the total number of groups (control and experimental groups). The other terms are familiar.

As an example, consider the data presented in Table 8-5. These data were drawn from an experiment comparing the amounts of memory loss for several different experimental conditions. There are three experimental groups, differing in the types of interfering activities they received between learning and recall. A control group received a neutral task during the period in which the experimental subjects were experiencing interference. There were $s = 16$ subjects in each group. The values necessary for the analysis of these data are given in the upper portion of the table. For the actual analysis, we find

TABLE 8-5 *Numerical Example: Dunnett Test*

BASIC DATA

	Control	E_1	E_2	E_3	Sum
A_i:	161	79	52	142	434
$\sum_{j}^{s}(AS_{ij})^2$:	1747	523	324	1421	4015

SUMMARY OF THE ANALYSIS

Source	Calculations	SS	df	MS	F
A	3439.38 − 2943.06 =	496.32	3	165.44	17.25*
S/A	4015 − 3439.38 =	575.62	60	9.59	
Total	4015 − 2943.06 =	1071.94	63		

* $p < .01$.

$$SS_A = \frac{\sum(A)^2}{s} - \frac{(T)^2}{as}$$

$$= \frac{(161)^2 + (79)^2 + (52)^2 + (142)^2}{16} - \frac{(434)^2}{4(16)},$$

$$SS_{S/A} = \sum(AS)^2 - \frac{\sum(A)^2}{s}$$

$$= 4015 - \frac{(161)^2 + (79)^2 + (52)^2 + (142)^2}{16},$$

$$SS_T = \sum(AS)^2 - \frac{(T)^2}{as}$$

$$= 4015 - \frac{(434)^2}{4(16)}.$$

The results of these calculations are entered in the bottom portion of the table. The single-factor analysis of variance, summarized in Table 8-5, reveals a significant overall treatment effect.

While other questions might be asked of the data (e.g., questions about meaningful comparisons among the *experimental* groups), it is of interest to determine whether or not each of the experimental groups showed a significant loss relative to the control group. In order to calculate the critical C-E difference, we need to obtain q_D. Although the argument could be made that only differences in favor of the control group make any sense, most researchers would prefer to choose what is termed a *nondirectional* alternative hypothesis. What this means is that we want to be alert to positive as well as negative differences in the experiment. If we set our significance level at $\alpha_{EW} = .05$, we will set aside half of the rejection region for positive deviations and the other half for negative deviations. Such a procedure is often called a *two-tailed test*. [Under certain circumstances, an experimenter may be willing to consider differences in either a positive or negative direction only. Such a prediction would be reflected by a *directional* alternative hypothesis and the statistical test would be called a *one-tailed test*. The use of a directional test is controversial, however, and rarely seen in the current research literature. See Hays (1963, pp. 282–286) for a discussion of directional and nondirectional tests.]

To find the value of q_D, we locate the part of Table C-5 labeled "two-tailed comparisons" and look for the entry at $k = 4$, $df_{error} = df_{S/A} = 60$, and $\alpha_{EW} = .05$. (A directional test would be conducted with the values given in the part of Table C-5 labeled "one-tailed comparisons".) For this combination, $q_D = 2.41$. Substituting into Eq. (8-11) gives as the critical control-experimental difference

$$q_D(4, 60)\sqrt{2s(MS_{S/A})} = (2.41)\sqrt{2(16)(9.59)} = (2.41)\sqrt{306.88}$$

$$= (2.41)(17.52) = 42.22.$$

This is the difference that must be exceeded in order to allow the rejection of the null hypothesis that the control group and a particular experimental group are equal. The observed differences are

C vs. E_1: $161 - 79 = 82$,

C vs. E_2: $161 - 52 = 109$,

C vs. E_3: $161 - 142 = 19$.

Since both E_1 and E_2 produce differences that are greater than the critical C-E difference (42.22), we can conclude that the specific interfering activities represented by these two groups produced a significant memory deficit. The third experimental treatment, E_3, did not result in a significant loss of memory.

PRACTICAL CONSIDERATIONS IN THE SELECTION OF A MULTIPLE-COMPARISON TEST

By now you are probably bewildered by the different techniques that have been devised to assess the significance of multiple comparisons. It is important not to lose sight of the main reason for analyzing these post-hoc comparisons differently from planned ones—namely, the increase in the number of type I errors when additional comparisons are conducted. As a reminder of some terminology, the probability that one or more type I errors will be made in a set of comparisons is called the *experimentwise* (*EW*) error rate (α_{EW}), while the probability of making a type I error in any given comparison is called the *per comparison (PC)* error rate (α). We saw in Eq. (6-2a) that

$$\alpha_{EW} \approx c(\alpha),$$

where c is the number of comparisons being conducted.

Let us consider what Eq. (6-2a) tells us. If we want to set α at some level, say .05, and we will not budge from that level, the only way we can reduce α_{EW} is to *decrease* the number of comparisons we make. If we feel that we must hold α_{EW} at some level, not necessarily the same as the α level, we can accomplish this goal either by reducing the number of comparisons or by decreasing the PC error rate (α) or by both. Since few investigators will tolerate a restriction on the number of comparisons they choose to make, the only possible way to reduce the EW error rate is to *lower* the PC rate (α). This is exactly what the various multiple-comparison techniques do. But an important consequence of lowering the α level is the necessary *increase* in another sort of error, the type II error. We saw in Chapter 4 that any change in the probability of making a type I error will result in the opposite change in the probability of making a type II error. Therefore, before we go any further in this discussion, we must consider again the meaning and the implication of reducing the α level in order to produce a reduction in the EW error rate.

Type I Versus Type II Errors

We have just argued that by demanding larger differences for post-hoc comparisons in general, we are of necessity decreasing our PC type I error rate. We have noted, also, that the price is a more frequent failure to recognize a real difference when it is present in our data—i.e., an increased number of type II errors. It is evident that we must strike a balance between these two types of errors—between a sort of scientific conservativism, on the one hand, where we resist changing the status quo by rejecting the null hypothesis, and a scientific liberalism, on the other hand, where we are receptive to the possibility of finding new facts. The real question is: which is worse—letting into a science an unknown, but relatively small number of bogus "facts," which committing a type I error implies, or overlooking a potentially important difference, either because it is small or it was attenuated by experimental error?

How serious is it to make a type I error? It can be argued that generally we are overly concerned about type I errors. In any active research area, we can be fairly confident of our decision to reject the null hypothesis when our results duplicate what others have found. Such independent demonstrations greatly reduce the chances that our particular result is a "fluke." Another advantage of working in an active area is that we can reasonably assume that our experiment will be repeated in some form or another. This replication will usually not represent an exact duplication of the experiment, but will focus upon critical features of the manipulations. The replication may be performed by others or by ourselves in an experiment that is based upon the implications of the earlier finding. With replications being conducted, we can be assured that an incorrect finding—a type I error—will be caught eventually. Of course, this "corrective" nature of science takes time, and an incorrect rejection of a null hypothesis has a way of persisting long after the conclusion should have been reversed by researchers in the field. Perhaps the most responsible approach is to hold back reporting an entirely new or startling finding until the *researcher* has repeated it once or twice. If he continues to obtain the same pattern of results, he can assume a high degree of confidence in the reliability of this phenomenon.

Not everyone views type I errors the same way. Bakan (1969), for example, suggests that "... when a type I error is committed, it has the effect of stopping investigation" (p. 427). He argues that a false rejection of a null hypothesis gains a certain degree of respectability and that "even the strict repetition of an experiment and not getting significance in the same way does not speak against the result already reported in the literature" (pp. 427–428). It is true that even bogus phenomena collect a certain amount of inertia which makes them difficult to erase from the records. [Gardner (1966) offers an interesting example of the chain of events in following up a provocative finding that may have been a type I error.] At worst, then, we might have a number of experiments being conducted which eventually result in the retroactive removal from the literature of the original type I error. We have lost some time and some energy, but we did give the new "fact" a fair chance of being verified. Thus, a type I error does not appear to retard greatly the development of a research area.

Then what about a type II error? Committing a type II error has a different effect upon an empirically based science. To be more specific, we might decide *not* to follow up a particular finding by virtue of the fact that a particular outcome is *not* significant. This possibility is serious enough with planned comparisons or with an omnibus F, but it is even more of a problem when we are dealing with multiple-comparison techniques—tests which, we have noted, are less sensitive in detecting differences (avoiding type II errors) than are planned tests. The situation is different, then, from that created by a type I error. If we increase our type I error, we also increase our chances of finding some small, but interesting *real* effects. If we increase our type II error, we may slow down progress in our field. Again, replication and new experiments which focus upon these originally "weak" findings are the answer. Just one replication, for example, can tell us whether or not the original observation represented a real difference. Placing too much emphasis upon minimizing type I errors might discourage these replications and extensions.

In short, we should be very worried about discarding interesting and provocative differences merely because they do not reach significance by a post-hoc procedure. The same point was made for general hypothesis testing in Chapter 4. If something makes sense, but is not statistically significant, then by all means we should pursue it. The results of statistical analyses should be seen as guides for the development of theories and the design of new experiments.

If we are persistent, we should discover our type I errors and the incorrectness of our original conclusions quickly enough.

Choice of Conceptual Unit for Error Rate

We have been through the arguments for the adoption of the *experiment*, rather than the individual *comparison*, as the conceptual unit upon which to base our error rate. Briefly, they amount to this: a particular comparison between two treatment conditions, say, should be evaluated under the same *EW* error rate, whether the experiment in which these conditions appear consists of two groups or of ten groups. As Myers (1966) puts it, "... we want a criterion for significance such that the [*EW* error rate] is constant regardless of the number of treatment groups. Only in this way can we adequately compare the results of the same comparison in different experiments" (p. 333). And Glass and Stanley (1970), "... a *contrast* between method *A* and method *B* always means the same thing whether it stands alone or is imbedded in a factor with a dozen levels" (p. 388). The equation of *EW* error rates in the two situations is essentially accomplished by lowering the *per comparison* error rate. This procedure reduces the type I error and increases the type II error for the particular *comparison* in the larger experiment relative to the same comparison in the smaller experiment.

Let us twist the argument around. Suppose we contrast two experiments, both of which include a comparison between treatment 1 and treatment 2. We will also assume that the obtained treatment effects for the two conditions are identical in the two experiments. Furthermore, the estimate of error variance, the $MS_{S/A}$, will be assumed to be equal. The only difference is that for one experiment treatments 1 and 2 and one additional treatment are included, while in the other experiment ten other treatments are also included. If the contrast between treatments 1 and 2 is considered to be a planned comparison, the conclusions will be the same. This is because the comparison in the two experiments is evaluated at the same *PC* α level. (The larger experiment is slightly more sensitive in detecting treatment effects, but we will not worry about that difference.)

What if these two comparisons are evaluated by means of a multiple-comparison test with α_{EW} *equal* in the two experiments? Clearly, the *PC* error rates will be quite different. Consider the Scheffé correction, against which the significance of any comparison will be evaluated:

$$F_S = (a - 1)F(df_A, df_{S/A}).$$

We will assume that there are $s = 6$ observations in each group in the two experiments and that the *EW* error rate is set at $\alpha_{EW} = .05$. For the experiment with $a = 3$ groups, where the $df_{S/A} = a(s - 1) = 3(6 - 1) = 15$,

$$F_S = (3 - 1)F(2, 15) = 2(3.68) = 7.36.$$

For the experiment with $a = 12$ groups, the $df_{S/A} = a(s - 1) = 12(6 - 1) = 60$, and

$$F_S = (12 - 1)F(11, 60) = 11(1.95) = 21.45.$$

The F associated with the comparison of interest must exceed these two values of F_S in order to be considered significant. If we translate these values of F_S into PC error rates, α in the small experiment is approximately .007 and α in the large experiment is approximately .00001—quite a difference in the type I error rate for this particular comparison when the contrast is evaluated by means of a post-hoc test!

This example illustrates clearly the dilemma we face when deciding what to do about post-hoc comparisons. If we are concerned about the number of type I errors that will be made over the course of the analysis, we will want to hold the EW error rate in check at some level. The sensitivity of the analysis in detecting differences between means, however, is sharply reduced. The unfortunate aspect of all this is that no approach to the problem is logically correct. Just as our selection of the α level in an experiment is arbitrary, so is the selection of the EW error rate. At least for the PC rate, researchers tend to agree upon .05 as an acceptable type I error—not so large as to allow a large number of false conclusions concerning the presence of differences between means, but not so small as to greatly reduce our chances of detecting real differences when they are present. But what about the α_{EW} level? What is an unacceptably large EW error rate—$\alpha_{EW} = .05, .10,$ or .20?

Some authors seem to suggest the use of an EW error rate that is equal to the PC error rate (e.g., Petrinovich and Hardyck, 1969). If $\alpha = .05$, then the α_{EW} is set at .05 also. There is no justification for this procedure, except an appeal to a principle of symmetry. What we really need is some perspective through which to view the *implications* of a low or a high EW error rate.

One way to look at the problem is to compare the EW error rate for an experiment in which five comparisons are *planned* with an experiment in which five post-hoc comparisons are conducted *after* the significance of the overall F has been established. The EW error rates in these two situations are approximately the *same*, namely, $\alpha_{EW} \approx 5(\alpha)$. Or, suppose we compare the analyses of five independent, two-group *experiments* with five planned *comparisons* within a single experiment. The *cumulative* type I error rate in the first case is again approximately equal to the EW error rate in the second case.

These last two examples—planned comparisons and independent experiments—illustrate exactly what is meant by a PC type I error rate. The probability is α that we will falsely reject the null hypothesis for each comparison we conduct. If we make more than one comparison, either in a single experiment or taken over a series of independent experiments, our cumulative type I error rates (EW error rate in the case of a single experiment) will be roughly equivalent. No serious researcher is worried about such a state of affairs. The increase in cumulative type I errors follows directly from the decision to make type I errors in the first place. Within an experiment or over our lifetimes, we expect to make a type I error 5 per cent of the time when the null hypothesis is true and our *PC* rate is set at $\alpha = .05$. Thus, when we talk about the probability of making one or more type I errors in a set of comparisons (within the same experiment or within a set of independent experiments), we are simply using an index that is sensitive to the *cumulative* probability. Our standard for any single comparison is not changed.

The decision concerning the *EW* error rate, then, reflects our attitudes towards type I errors in general. We have to weigh the seriousness of a type I error against the seriousness of a type II error. The result of such an assessment will dictate not only our choice of a *PC* error rate, but the *EW* error rate as well.

We will now consider the relative merits of the different multiple-comparison techniques. In so doing, we will have to keep in mind our attitude toward the two types of errors. Once this decision is made, the selection of an appropriate test is relatively simple.

A Summary of Multiple-Comparison Techniques

Hopkins and Chadbourn (1967) offer a useful summary of different multiple-comparison tests in terms of a series of separate decisions. A modified version of this summary appears in Table 8-6. The main function of this display of the tests is to indicate the relationship among the different methods and procedures; it is *not* meant to be a fixed and rigid plan for analysis. Let us examine the various courses of action outlined there.

INITIAL ANALYSES   We begin our analysis by deciding upon a per comparison α level. Our first decision is between an omnibus *F* test and a set of planned comparisons. If planned comparisons are decided upon, they will usually be few—there is a limited number of meaningful questions we can ask before the conduct of an experiment. The position taken in this book is that planned comparisons need not be orthogonal (see pp. 92–93). The *F* for the omnibus test is evaluated against $F(df_A, df_{S/A})$, while the *F*'s for the planned comparisons are evaluated against $F(df_{A_{\text{comp.}}}, df_{S/A})$.

DECISION TO CONTROL α_{EW} Assuming that the omnibus *F* test is significant, we now want to isolate the comparisons that are responsible for the differences among the means. At this point in the analysis we have to decide whether or not the control of the *EW* error rate is a critical feature of our evaluation procedure. As we have seen, some investigators do not feel so disposed and thus will choose to use the LSD test, where no correction is applied to the *PC* error rate for multiple comparisons. Others will be concerned with the problem of the increased *EW* error rate resulting from these tests and thus will have to choose from among the various correction procedures we have been discussing in this chapter.

BASE FOR CONTROL OF α_{EW} We have considered two basic ways of accomplishing these corrections: (1) the layer or stairstep approach, a graduated adjustment depending upon the number of steps between means being compared, and (2) the experimentwise approach, which holds the type I error rate at a fixed level for a set of comparisons. The decision to branch here is an important one. For a given *PC* error rate, the layer methods are more sensitive in detecting real differences when they are present, but they are also less conservative towards type I errors. Thus, when we select a layer approach to the problem, in essence we show less concern for type I errors over the experiment than when we choose an experimentwise approach. The logic behind the experimentwise methods is relatively simple to follow, but the layer methods are difficult to understand intuitively. Some authors of statistics texts [e.g., Guenther (1964), Hays (1963), and Myers (1966)] do not even mention layer methods in their discussion of multiple comparisons; others indicate that these methods are not well understood (cf. Glass and Stanley, 1970, p. 388).

In spite of this lack of enthusiasm by authors of statistics texts, layer methods remain quite popular with researchers. Perhaps the main reason for this popularity is their greater sensitivity in detecting real differences. But this is the *wrong reason* for selecting a layer method over an experimentwise method. If we are concerned about the *EW* error rate, it would make more sense to decide upon the error rate *first* and *then* choose the multiple-comparison that is most appropriate or most convenient, selecting the *PC* error rate accordingly. The reason for choosing a layer method is that an investigator wants a *graded adjustment*, not because the layer methods are more sensitive in detecting differences than are the experimentwise methods. Any differences in sensitivity between the two approaches are easily removed by operating at a *higher PC* error rate for the experimentwise tests than for the layer tests. If we had considered using a layer test at $\alpha = .05$, for example, we could obtain approximately the same *EW* error rate by selecting a higher probability for an experimentwise test, such as .10 or .20.

If we decide to use the layer method, we can choose between the Newman-Keuls and the Duncan procedures. If we decide to use the experimentwise procedures, a number of further decisions must be made.

CHOICES AMONG EXPERIMENTWISE METHODS   If we restrict our attention to a set of comparisons involving experimental groups and a control group, the choice is easy—we will select the Dunnett test. Its advantage is that attention is directed toward a smaller set of comparisons than with the other tests; hence, the adjustment for increased type I errors is less with the Dunnett test.

The next choice involves a decision between the Dunn test and either the Scheffé or the Tukey test. The Dunn test is useful when only a few multiple comparisons are to be tested. This extremely flexible procedure should receive more attention than it does in the analysis of our experiments. We have already mentioned one of the difficulties with the Dunn method, however: the problem

TABLE 8-6 *Summary of Multiple-Comparison Tests*[a]

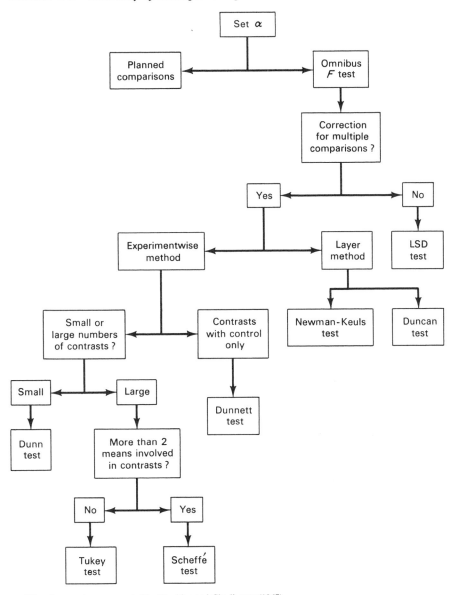

[a] Based on a schema presented by Hopkins and Chadbourn (1967).

of specifying the restricted pool of comparisons that will be selected for testing. Another point to keep in mind is that the test is more sensitive in detecting real differences when the number of comparisons is small and when the number of groups is large. Dunn (1961) has published convenient tables that tell us when her technique is more sensitive than the Scheffé test (Table 4, p. 57) and the Tukey test (Table 5, p. 61).

The final choice indicated in Table 8-6 is the decision between the Scheffé and Tukey procedures. Both hold the EW error rate at a given level (or lower) for all possible comparisons—comparisons between individual means or between combinations of means. The tests differ in a number of ways. (1) The Tukey test uses the q statistic, while the Scheffé test uses the F statistic. (2) Several authors have pointed out that the Scheffé test, since it is based on the F distribution, is relatively insensitive to violations of the assumptions of normality and homogeneity of variance, while little is known about effects of these violations on the q distribution. The results of Monte Carlo studies (Petrinovich and Hardyck, 1969) show that such violations "... seem to make little difference to the Tukey and Scheffé methods, except as these violations also affect the obtained value of F" (p. 53). (3) The Tukey test assumes equal sample sizes, while the Scheffé test does not. As we will see in Chapter 17, this difference does not pose a stumbling block for the Tukey procedure. (4) The Tukey test is more sensitive in detecting real differences between pairs of means, while the Scheffé test is more sensitive in detecting real differences between complex combinations of means. This last point is the critical one: we should choose Tukey when attention will be directed to comparisons between pairs of means and choose Scheffé for other comparisons.

Recommendations

Obviously, the first recommendation is to design an experiment so that the hypotheses of primary interest can be tested unambiguously by means of planned comparisons. The advantage of planned over post-hoc comparisons is so great that it is foolish not to decide upon some specific contrasts before the start of the experiment.

TWO EXTREME POSITIONS   What is our next step then? The procedures we adopt depend upon our attitude towards the EW type I error rate. We have already discussed this basic problem. Suppose we consider two extreme points of view. One represents the position that post-hoc corrections are potentially damaging to a developing, research-oriented science because they increase our type II errors (failures to recognize real differences when they are present). Associated with this point of view is the following argument: Implicit with the decision to operate at a PC error rate of $\alpha = .05$, say, is the expectation that a type I error will be committed on the average once in every twenty comparisons when the null hypothesis is true. The more comparisons we make, the greater is the probability that we will make at least one type I error. The concern for the EW error is based upon the conduct of large numbers of multiple comparisons within a single experiment. But there is an analogous problem when we consider the "between-experiment" EW error rate cumulating over a number of independent experiments. Since this latter type of error rate does not seem to bother active researchers, why should the usual EW rate be of such alarming concern?

An even stronger position can be taken—namely, that the *significance* of post-hoc comparisons should rarely be assessed. Our experiments are usually not designed to provide a sensitive test for many of these comparisons, and so a type II error will frequently be made. Testing a comparison and finding it *not* to be significant has a way of stopping an avenue of inquiry or an explanation that might have had rewarding consequences in future investigations. Related to this point is the fact that many experimenters often discount the significance of post-hoc comparisons anyway. Conclusions based on the outcome of post-hoc comparisons are typically not as strong as those based on planned comparisons. Additionally, we find that post-hoc comparisons are not considered all that critical to the theory leading to the experiment—they *are* suggestive of future research or of possible alternative interpretations of the data. For these various reasons, then, we can avoid making decisions between post-hoc comparisons simply by treating them as planned comparisons or by not evaluating them at all.

At the other extreme, of course, are the methods that control the EW error rate for each and every possible comparison that could be conducted with a set of data. The Tukey and Scheffé tests are of this sort. A user of these tests has made a decision to avoid type I errors at all costs. It is instructive to consider the number of comparisons included in this "protection." The number of these possible comparisons increases drastically as the number of independent groups increases. Edwards (1968, p. 151) enumerates all 25 comparisons that can be constructed with $a = 4$ treatment groups. For the experiment given in Table 8-3, where $a = 5$, there are **90** comparisons possible:

10 involving contrasts between single groups,
30 between a single group and a combination of 2 different groups,
20 between a single group and a combination of 3 different groups,
 5 between a single group and a combination of 4 different groups,
15 between 2-group versus 2-group combinations, and
10 between 2-group versus 3-group combinations.

The Scheffé and Tukey tests represent logical end points: protection for the *maximum number* of comparisons we can make with a treatment groups. But do these 105 comparisons constitute the pool from which we actually draw *our* comparisons? It is unlikely that they do. We may be searching for significant differences, but we are not that indiscriminate! Thus, we are "penalizing" ourselves unduly by using these two tests.

A COMPROMISE POSITION   If we are committed to doing something about the EW error rate, an alternative course of action offers a compromise solution. We could attempt to estimate our usable or *functional* pool of comparisons and then use the Dunn test. Probably the largest pool of comparisons we would ever consider is one containing all possible comparisons between pairs of means. There are $a(a-1)/2$ of these. For $a = 5$, for example, there are $5(5-1)/2 = 5(4)/2 = 20/2 = 10$ of these comparisons. Look at the other types of comparisons included in the pool of 105 comparisons we enumerated in the last paragraph. Rarely would we be interested in any of the other 95 comparisons that are formed by averaging two or more groups. That is, an averaging of groups cannot be done haphazardly—there must be some behavioral meaning in any combination we consider. If such meaningful comparisons are possible, they will probably have been specified ahead of time and included as planned comparisons in the first place!

In using the Dunn test, we face the problem we discussed earlier of being able to enumerate the functional pool of comparisons. Sometimes the logic of the experimental design will limit the number of comparisons considered. Other times it may be possible to divide the a groups into "natural" groupings and conduct a limited number of comparisons within these smaller sets. It would be inappropriate, however, to consider only those comparisons that, because of their size, are suggested after an inspection of the data. If we have been unable to define a pool of comparisons either experimentally or logically, we might consider including in the functional pool (represented by c in the Dunn test) all comparisons of the type or types selected for testing. If these are comparisons between pairs of single means, for example, then the functional pool consists of all such comparisons.

Summary

As we mentioned earlier, it is not possible to offer a plan of analysis that is based purely on logical grounds. Much is a matter of attitude toward the relative importance of type I and type II errors. The arguments in favor of different approaches have been given in detail in this and other sections of the chapter. The basic decision lies in the choice between uncorrected post-hoc comparisons and a correction of some sort. As we have seen, there is an even more fundamental choice, namely, to consider eliminating the *statistical evaluation* of post-hoc comparisons altogether. This does not mean that a researcher will close his eyes to comparisons other than those he planned. On the contrary, he, too, will sift through his data as carefully as any other investigator. What makes this approach refreshing is its emphasis on the fact that most researchers design experiments to answer specific questions. The experimental design and the comparisons planned are directed primarily at that target. Any other comparisons an experimenter decides to make after the data are examined need not be assessed statistically. Even if a comparison *is* significant, a researcher will usually reserve judgment until he has observed the finding again in another experiment.

The indiscriminate use of a statistical test as a means for sorting multiple comparisons into two piles—those that we must pay attention to (the significant comparisons) and those that we will ignore (the nonsignificant comparisons)—is a rigid and unimaginative procedure. A more reasonable approach is to sort on the basis of the *meaningfulness* of the comparisons. A particular outcome of a planned comparison may be bolstered by a number of relevant post-hoc comparisons. The significance or nonsignificance of these comparisons is less critical than the *pattern* of the outcomes. The adequacy of any interpretation of our data, which evolves from a consideration of planned and unplanned comparisons, will usually be brought to test in our next experiment. In short, then, we can view post-hoc statistical tests as less important than the extraction of meaningful comparisons which can shed some light on our current interpretation of a set of data.

This particular view of post-hoc comparisons is not a popular one in psychology, but it deserves serious attention. Most researchers elect to test the significance of post-hoc comparisons and to pay a penalty for it. If we decide that corrections for multiple comparisons should be applied to our experiment, then we can base our plan purely on considerations of sensitivity in detecting real differences between treatment groups. (1) Our first decision is to select an EW error rate. Unfortunately, there is no agreement among researchers as to an "acceptable" level; just how large a correction we select is basically up to us. As yet no psychological journal requires the use of a particular EW error rate—or, for that matter, the use of a particular multiple-comparison technique. We do have to convince others of the repeatability of our findings in order to get them published, and so we are not entirely free to select an especially lax criterion of rejection. Perhaps the proscriptions will appear in the future, but when they do they will be accompanied, it is hoped, by a clear statement and defense of the rationale behind this choice. (2) If the number of comparisons is less than $a(a - 1)/2$, the number of two-group comparisons possible with a means, we should use the Dunn test. This particular number is quite close to the critical values listed by Dunn (1961) in comparing her test with the Tukey and Scheffé tests. (3) Otherwise, we should use the Tukey test if our comparisons are between pairs of means and the Scheffé test if our comparisons involve more complex contrasts between means.

EXERCISES FOR PART II[1]

1. Find the critical values of F for the following situations:
   (a) $F(4, 30)$ at $\alpha = .05$.   (b) $F(1, 120)$ at $\alpha = .001$.
   (c) $a = 7, s = 5, \alpha = .10$.   (d) $a = 3, s = 9, \alpha = .25$.

2. Perform an analysis of variance on the following set of scores:

AS Matrix

a_1	a_2	a_3
8	9	2
0	4	0
9	8	5
4	1	7
2	8	7

3. In an experiment involving $a = 5$ treatments, the following measures were obtained:

AS Matrix

a_1	a_2	a_3	a_4	a_5
13	7	12	10	13
9	4	11	12	6
8	4	4	9	14
7	1	9	7	12
8	10	5	15	13
6	7	10	14	10
6	5	2	10	8
7	9	8	17	4
6	5	3	14	9
10	8	6	12	11

   (a) Determine whether or not there is homogeneity of variance. Use the Levene test
   (pp. 81–83).
   (b) Analyze the results using the analysis of variance.

4. An experiment is conducted with $s = 5$ subjects in each of the $a = 6$ treatment conditions; the sums are given below.
   (a) Perform an analysis of variance in the usual manner.
   (b) Calculate the $MS_{S/A}$ by the alternative method of obtaining the average of the variances for the six groups.

	a_1	a_2	a_3	a_4	a_5	a_6
A_i:	15	10	25	35	25	20
$\sum\limits_{j}^{s}(AS_{ij})^2$:	65	35	130	275	150	102

[1] The answers to these problems are found in Appendix D.

5. An experimenter is investigating the effects of two drugs on the activity of rats. Drug A is a depressant and drug B a stimulant. Half of the subjects receiving either drug are given a low dosage and half a high dosage. The experimenter also runs a control group that is given an injection of an inert substance, such as saline solution. Five different groups are represented in the experiment, each containing $s = 4$ rats assigned randomly from the stock of laboratory rats on hand. The animals are injected and then their activity is observed for a fixed period of time. The treatment sums for each group of four rats are given below:

	Drug A		Drug B	
Control a_1	Low a_2	High a_3	Low a_4	High a_5
60	55	32	66	92

The within-groups mean square, $MS_{S/A}$, is found to be 37.00.

(a) Perform a one-way analysis of variance on these data.

(b) Construct a set of coefficients that will provide the following comparisons:

    (1) Control versus combined experimental groups.

    (2) Drug A versus drug B.

    (3) Low versus high dosage for drug A.

    (4) Low versus high dosage for drug B.

(c) Show that these four comparisons are mutually orthogonal.

(d) Extract the sums of squares associated with these comparisons and test their significance.

6. For an experiment with $a = 6$ levels, find a set of $a - 1$ orthogonal comparisons and demonstrate that they are mutually orthogonal. Apply this set of comparisons to the data given below and show that the sum of squares associated with a set of orthogonal comparisons equals the SS_A.

	a_1	a_2	a_3	a_4	a_5	a_6
Treatment sums:	15	10	5	15	20	25

Assume that there are $s = 10$ subjects in each treatment condition.

7. Consider an experiment with $a = 5$ levels. This means, of course, that the SS_A is associated with $a - 1 = 4$ df and that this sum of squares may be divided into four independent comparisons. Listed below are four "starts" at constructing a set of orthogonal comparisons. Complete each of these sets, retaining the comparisons that have been specified already.

(a)	a_1	a_2	a_3	a_4	a_5
Comp. 1:	4	-1	-1	-1	-1
Comp. 2:	0	-1	-1	3	-1

(b)	a_1	a_2	a_3	a_4	a_5
Comp. 1:	3	0	-1	-1	-1
Comp. 2:	0	0	1	-1	0

(c)	a_1	a_2	a_3	a_4	a_5
Comp. 1:	1	0	0	0	-1
Comp. 2:	0	0	1	-1	0

(d)	a_1	a_2	a_3	a_4	a_5
Comp. 1:	3	3	-2	-2	-2
Comp. 2:	0	0	-1	2	-1

8. In this experiment $a = 5$ levels that are equally spaced on some stimulus dimension. We will assume $s = 8$ subjects in each treatment condition and that $\sum (AS)^2 = 1285$. Suppose we obtained the following sums:

a_1	a_2	a_3	a_4	a_5
34	60	47	20	48

(a) Perform a one-way analysis of variance with these data.
(b) Conduct a trend analysis using the coefficients of the orthogonal polynomial.

9. Suppose we have an experiment with independent groups of $s = 7$ subjects randomly assigned to each of 8 treatment conditions. The error term, $MS_{S/A} = 58.65$. The treatment sums are given below:

a_1	a_2	a_3	a_4	a_5	a_6	a_7	a_8
316	333	307	373	398	227	123	436

(a) Is the omnibus F significant?
(b) Conduct multiple comparisons on all comparisons between pairs of groups with the Newman-Keuls and Tukey tests, using $\alpha = .05$. Summarize these tests two ways: (1) by means of a table (see Table 8-3, p. 141) and (2) by means of a listing of overlapping conditions (see Table 8-4, p. 143).

10. Assume that we have a control group and seven experimental groups, with $s = 16$ subjects for each group. The $MS_{S/A} = 28.75$. The totals for each group are given below:

C	E_1	E_2	E_3	E_4	E_5	E_6	E_7
289	270	241	279	191	213	205	198

(a) Is the overall F significant?
(b) Use Dunnett's test to determine which of the treatment means is significantly different from the mean of the control group. Use a two-tailed test at $\alpha = .05$.
(c) Make the same set of comparisons with the Scheffé procedure, $\alpha = .05$. Do your conclusions change?

PART III

Factorial Experiments With Two Factors

In this part we will consider experiments where treatment conditions are classified with respect to the levels represented on *two* independent variables. In Part IV we will go on to discuss experiments involving the concomitant manipulation of three or more independent variables. In all of these discussions we will be assuming that subjects serve in only one of the treatment conditions, that they provide only a single score or observation, and that they are randomly assigned to one of the conditions. Formally, we refer to these sorts of experiments as *completely randomized designs.*[1]

Numerical examples illustrating arithmetic operations discussed in this section may be found at the end of Part III (pp. 247–250).

[1] We will be assuming the so-called *fixed-effects model*, which is appropriate for most of the research in the behavioral sciences. This and other models are discussed in Chapter 16.

chapter nine

THE ADVANTAGES OF FACTORIAL
DESIGN AND ITS UNIQUE
CONTRIBUTION: INTERACTION

The most common means by which two or more independent variables are manipulated in an experiment is a *factorial arrangement of the treatments* or, more simply, a *factorial experiment* or *design*. We will use these terms interchangeably. In a factorial design, the experiment includes every possible combination of the levels of the independent variables. Suppose, for example, that two variables are manipulated concurrently in a study—the magnitude of the food reward given to a hungry rat for completing a run through a maze and the difficulty of the maze he will be given to learn. We will assume there are three levels of food magnitude (small, medium, and large) and two levels of maze difficulty (easy and hard). The factorial arrangement of the treatment conditions is specified by the six cells in Table 9-1. We will often call such an arrangement a factorial *matrix* or simply a matrix. The cells in the matrix represent the following treatment combinations: small-easy, small-hard, medium-easy, medium-hard, large-easy, and large-hard. Each magnitude of reward (represented by the columns) is combined with each type of maze (represented by the rows). Factorial designs are sometimes referred to as experiments in which the independent variables are completely *crossed*. We can think of the crossing in terms of a *multiplication* of the levels of the different independent variables. In the present example, the treatment combinations may be enumerated by multiplying (small + medium + large) by (easy + hard) to produce the six treatment combinations of the design.

TABLE 9-1   *An Example of a Two-Variable Factorial Experiment*

Type of Maze	Reward Magnitude		
	Small	Medium	Large
Easy			
Hard			

ADVANTAGES OF THE FACTORIAL EXPERIMENT

A great deal of the research in the behavioral sciences consists of the identification of variables contributing to a given phenomenon. Quite typically, an experiment may be designed to focus attention upon a single factor. If the experimenter thinks a factor is important, he may attempt to establish the functional relationship between the independent and dependent variables by including a number of levels of the variable in a single-factor experiment. A main characteristic of this type of investigation is that it represents an assessment of how a variable operates under "ideal" conditions—with all other important variables held constant across the different conditions. An alternative approach is to study the influence of one independent variable in conjunction with variations in one or more additional independent variables. Here the primary question is whether or not a particular variable studied concurrently with other variables will show the same effect as it would when studied in isolation.

Both types of experiments certainly have their place in the behavioral sciences. The manipulation of a single variable in an experiment is most useful when its combination with other independent variables is relatively simple. When the combination is complex, the results of single-factor experiments will give an inaccurate picture of the effect of the variable under study.

The factorial experiment is probably most effective at the *reconstructive* stage of a science, where investigators begin to approximate the "real" world by manipulating a number of independent variables simultaneously. Of course, the type of experiment chosen by a researcher depends upon the complexity with which the phenomenon under study is determined. But it is clear that the factorial experiment has advantages of economy, control, and generality.

Economy

Suppose we are putting together a reading series for use in elementary schools and that we have reason to believe that the format of the books will influence reading speed. Two independent variables that might be of interest are the length of the printed lines and the contrast between the printed letters and the paper. Assume that we choose three line lengths (3, 5, and 7 inches) and three different levels of contrast (low, medium, and high). If we were to manipulate the variables in two separate single-factor experiments, the designs might look like those presented in the upper part of Table 9-2. In the experiment on the left, there is a total of 45 subjects (Ss), with $s = 15$ subjects assigned to each of the three length conditions. In the experiment on the right, the same number of subjects ($s = 15$) would be randomly assigned to each of the three levels of contrast. Other than differences in line length, on the one hand, and print-paper contrast, on the other, all of the subjects would be treated alike. At the completion of the two experiments, we would be able to analyze the data with the techniques discussed in Part II and make statements concerning the influence of line length and contrast on speed of reading.

TABLE 9-2 *Comparison of One- and Two-Factor Designs*

SEPARATE SINGLE-FACTOR EXPERIMENTS

Line Length (Inches)			Print-Paper Contrast		
3	5	7	Low	Medium	High
15 Ss[a]	15 Ss	15 Ss	15 Ss	15 Ss	15 Ss

FACTORIAL ARRANGEMENT

Print-Paper Contrast	Line Length (Inches)		
	3	5	7
Low	5 Ss	5 Ss	5 Ss
Medium	5 Ss	5 Ss	5 Ss
High	5 Ss	5 Ss	5 Ss

[a] S = subject.

Compare these two single-factor experiments with the factorial design presented in the bottom half of Table 9-2, in which the same two variables are manipulated simultaneously. In this experiment the two independent variables are completely crossed, meaning that all possible combinations of the three levels of the two variables are represented. Since each variable has three levels in this example, there is a total of $3 \times 3 = 9$ unique treatment groups. This design would be called a 3×3 factorial (read "three by three"). It should be noted that the sample size in each of the groups is $s = 5$. This number was chosen to provide a comparison with the two single-factor experiments. That is, we start this experiment by obtaining 45 school children; we then randomly assign 5 subjects to serve in each of the 9 treatment combinations.

After the experiment is completed, we will have 5 reading scores in each cell of the matrix. What if we want to obtain an estimate of the average effects of line length on reading speed? This information is obtained easily enough by collapsing across the levels of the other variable (contrast) and dividing by the number of scores ($s = 15$). That is, the mean for the 3-inch condition is found by summing the 15 reading scores in the first column of the matrix (5 scores each from the low-, medium-, and high-contrast conditions) and dividing by $s = 15$. The average performance of the subjects receiving 5- and 7-inch lines is obtained in a similar fashion. Turn now to a determination of the average effects of the other independent variable. The average effects of the low-, medium-, and high-contrast conditions are calculated by collapsing across the length classification—i.e., adding together the scores from the three levels of line length for each of the contrast conditions, and dividing by $s = 15$.

These average estimates of the influence of line length and of contrast are based upon the *same* number of subjects (15) as were the estimates provided by the two single-factor experiments. But note, the factorial experiment produces these estimates much more economically, with only half the number of subjects. The economy of the factorial design represents a distinct advantage over separate single-factor studies.

Experimental Control

In the preceding example, both of the independent variables were of scientific interest to us. That is, we were interested in the influence of each of the variables on reading speed. (This was implied when we considered conducting two single-factor experiments.) There will be times when we turn to a factorial experiment, not so much to obtain information on the two variables, but as a way of controlling important but unwanted sources of variability. (We will discuss this use of the factorial design more thoroughly in Chapter 15.)

The most common example of the use of a factorial experiment to control variability is with *subject variables*. Suppose we wanted to study the length variable in a single-factor experiment, but we knew that differences in the intelligence of the subjects would contribute to an especially large within-groups mean square. Under these circumstances, we would need a fairly strong between-groups effect to produce a significant F ratio. One way to solve this problem would be to select a group of subjects who are relatively homogeneous in intelligence (e.g., restrict IQ to the range 100–110) and to assign them at random to the three length conditions. The within-groups mean square will be smaller in this case, since the variability of subjects treated alike will be smaller with the restricted groups of subjects than with the unrestricted ones.

One drawback with this procedure is that the results of our experiment will be limited in generality; that is, we could only generalize our results to people in the 100–110 range. It is exactly in this situation that the factorial experiment is ideal. In this case the two factors would be line length and IQ. More specifically, if we form a number of levels of IQ and randomly assign the subjects within these levels to the three length conditions, we will receive the benefit of a reduced error term. We will not now consider in detail how this comes about, except to say that our estimate of error variance, the within-groups mean square, is still based upon the variability of subjects treated alike and that the variability within each length-IQ condition is less than would be the case if subjects were unselected. (We will discuss this type of design in Chapter 23.)

Generality of Results

In the single-factor experiment, all variables except the one being manipulated are maintained at the same level across the different treatment groups. Such a procedure is necessary, of course, to "guarantee" that the differences observed among the treatment conditions are due solely to the operation of the independent variable. One consequence of this control is a certain lack of generality of the results; that is, the particular pattern of results may be unique to the specific values of other relevant stimulus variables maintained at a constant level throughout the course of the experiment.

The factorial experiment provides one solution to this limitation by allowing the effect of an independent variable to be averaged over several different levels of another relevant variable. As we noted in discussing the factorial arrangement in Table 9-2, the importance of line length for reading speed is assessed by comparing the scores of all of the 3-, 5-, and 7-inch subjects, one third of whom were tested at each of the three contrast levels included in the experiment. Thus, in the factorial experiment, the effect of line length represents a more general effect, averaged over three levels of contrast, than in the case of the single-factor experiment where only *one* print-paper contrast would be used. We refer to the overall effect of one independent variable, obtained by combining the scores over the different levels of the second variable, as its *main effect*. Similarly, the main effect of contrast is found by collapsing across the groups of subjects differing in lengths of line. This second main effect also represents a more general effect than would be obtained in the corresponding single-factor experiment.

The comparison between a single-factor experiment and a factorial experiment is accurate, however, only up to a point. The factorial experiment will provide the same type of information as its single-factor counterpart only when there is no *interaction* between the two independent variables. What this means is that when the effects of one of the independent variables (line length, say) are the *same* at each of the levels of the other variable (contrast) —i.e., there is *no* interaction—the main effect of line length will be the *same* as the treatment effects of line length in the single-factor experiment. On the other hand, when the effects of line length are different at the different levels of contrast (i.e., there *is* an interaction), the information provided by the main effect will *not* be the same. This is not as bad as it may sound, since the researcher will have discovered something that is *not* obtainable from the single-factor experiment, namely, the unique manner in which the two independent variables combine jointly to influence behavior. When an interaction is present, an investigator will not be interested in the main effects anyway—anything that he might say about the effects of one independent variable must be qualified by a consideration of the levels of the other. We will consider the concept of interaction next.

INTERACTION

Interaction is the one new concept that is introduced by the factorial experiment. Main effects have essentially the same meaning as in the single-factor analysis of variance and they are calculated in exactly the same way. Moreover, as we will see in later chapters, factorials with three or more variables involve no additional principles. Thus, it is important to understand the single-factor analysis of variance, since many of the principles and procedures found in this simplest of experimental designs, such as partitioning of sums of squares, the logic of hypothesis testing, and planned and post-hoc comparisons, are also found in the more complicated designs. By the same token, the two-factor analysis of variance forms a building block for designs involving three or more variables, with the concept of interaction linking them all together.

TABLE 9-3   *Example of No Interaction*

| Contrast (Factor B) | Line Length (Factor A) | | | |
	3 inches (a_1)	5 inches (a_2)	7 inches (a_3)	Mean
Low (b_1)	.89	2.22	2.89	2.00
Medium (b_2)	3.89	5.22	5.89	5.00
High (b_3)	4.22	5.55	6.22	5.33
Mean	3.00	4.33	5.00	4.11

An Example of No Interaction

One way to understand what an interaction means is to take a concrete example in which an interaction is either present or absent. Table 9-3 presents some hypothetical results for the experiment on reading speed we have been discussing. Assume that an equal number of subjects are run in each of the nine conditions and that the values presented in the table represent the mean reading scores obtained in the experiment. The main effect of line length (factor A) is obtained by summing (or collapsing across) the three cell means for the different contrasts and then averaging these sums. The last row of the table gives these means for the three length conditions. These averages are called the column *marginal* means of the matrix. Thus, the average reading speed for subjects in the 3-inch condition is found by combining the means from the three contrast conditions and obtaining an average. In this case, we have

$$\bar{A}_1 = \frac{.89 + 3.89 + 4.22}{3} = \frac{9.00}{3} = 3.00.$$

This average reflects how fast the subjects read with 3-inch lines under three different conditions of print-paper contrast. We can obtain similar averages for the subjects reading the 5- and 7-inch materials. These are given in the other two columns.

In a like fashion, the *row* marginal averages give us information concerning the general effect of different print-paper contrasts. That is, the average reading speed for subjects in the low-contrast condition is given by an average of the means for the three length conditions. Thus,

$$\bar{B}_1 = \frac{.89 + 2.22 + 2.89}{3} = \frac{6.00}{3} = 2.00.$$

This averaging has been completed for the other contrast conditions and appears in the final column of the table.

Let's look at the two sets of marginal averages. They have been plotted in the upper two graphs of Fig. 9-1. (For the purposes of this example, we have assumed that the levels of the contrast variable are equally spaced.) In both cases we see that the independent variables influence reading scores positively, performance increasing with increases in either line length or print-paper contrast. These plots can be thought of as general descriptions of the overall effects of the two independent variables.

Now, would we say that these overall relationships are *representative* of the results obtained in the "single-factor" experiments found *within* the body of Table 9-3? There are two sets of these experiments—those reflected by the means in different rows and those reflected by the means in different columns. In the first case we are looking at the effect of varying line length (factor A) at the three different levels of contrast (factor B), while in the second case we are considering the effect of varying contrast (factor B) at the three different levels of line length (factor A). We will refer to the first set of "single-factor" experiments (the cells in the individual rows) as the *simple main effects of factor A* and to the second set (the cells in the individual columns) as the *simple main effects of factor B*. The question, then, is whether or not the simple main effects of either.factor are representative of the *main* effect of the corresponding factor.

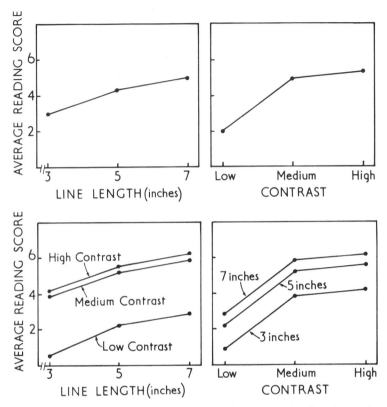

Fig. 9-1   Plot of data presented in Table 9-3; an example of no interaction.

Consider, then, the data within the body of the table. These means are presented in two double-classification plots in the lower portion of Fig. 9-1. The classification is accomplished by marking off one of the independent variables along the baseline—line length in the graph on the left—and connecting the means produced by groups receiving the same level of the other independent variable—contrast in this case. In either plotting of the results, it is clear that the *form* of the functional relationship obtained with one of the independent variables is *exactly the same* at each level of the second independent variable. The sets of functions are *parallel*, meaning that the simple main effects of either variable are the same and equal to the corresponding main effect.

An Example of Interaction

Table 9-4 presents a second set of hypothetical results using the same experimental design. Note that the same main effects are present; i.e., the means in the margins of Table 9-4 are identical to the corresponding means in Table 9-3.

There is a big difference, however, when we look at the simple main effects. To facilitate the comparisons of the simple main effects, the data within the body of the table have been plotted in Fig. 9-2. In either plot, we can see that the form of the relationship depicted by the simple main effects is *not* the same as that depicted by the row or column marginal means (the main effects). In short, then, an interaction is present.

TABLE 9-4   *Example of Interaction*

| Contrast (Factor B) | Line Length (Factor A) | | | |
	3 inches (a_1)	5 inches (a_2)	7 inches (a_3)	Mean
Low (b_1)	1.00	2.00	3.00	2.00
Medium (b_2)	3.00	5.00	7.00	5.00
High (b_3)	5.00	6.00	5.00	5.33
Mean	3.00	4.33	5.00	4.11

To be more specific, consider the simple main effects of line length at level b_1—the means in the first row of Table 9-4. This row is a "single-factor" experiment in which subjects from three levels of line length are tested, but *all* with a low print-paper contrast. These three means are presented in the left-hand graph of Fig. 9-2. An inspection of the figure indicates that the relationship is positive and even linear. The simple main effect at b_2 (the second row) also shows a positive linear trend for the subjects receiving the medium materials, but it is steeper than for the low-contrast case. But see what happens to the subjects tested with the high-contrast materials. In this third "single-factor" experiment the relationship is curvilinear: the reading scores first increase and then decrease with line length.

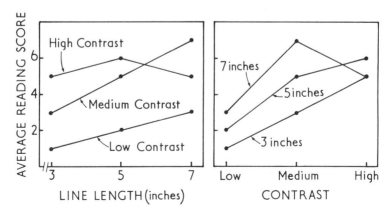

Fig. 9-2   Plot of data presented in Table 9-4; an example of interaction.

We can see the same sort of deviation of the simple main effects when we look at the means in each of the three *columns*. Here we are considering "single-factor" experiments in which contrast is varied but length is held constant. For the simple main effect of contrast for 3-inch lines (the first column) we can see that the relationship is linear. For the simple main effect for 5-inch lines (the second column) the relationship is not as sharply defined, with the function starting to "bend over" from the linear trend. In the final column (7-inch lines) we have an actual reversal of the trend—i.e., a curvilinear relationship, maximum performance being found with a medium contrast.

With either plot of the data, we can determine at a glance that the particular form of the relationship between the independent variable plotted on the baseline (line length or contrast)—i.e., the shape of the curve drawn between successive points on the baseline—is not the same at the three different levels of the other independent variable. A simple way to describe this situation is to say that the three curves are *not parallel*. When we find that an interaction is present, it is usually a good idea to plot the results of the experiment just as we have done in Fig. 9-2. The shape or form of the interaction will become readily apparent. We do not typically plot the data both ways, but choose for the baseline the independent variable that makes the most sense for the research hypotheses under consideration. Whichever way the data are plotted, an interaction will be revealed by nonparallel curves for the conditions plotted within the body of the figure.

Two Definitions of Interaction

VERBAL DEFINITION   Now that we have specific examples of interaction and of lack of interaction, it is a good time to give a relatively formal definition. We say that

two variables interact when the effect of one variable changes at different levels of the second variable.

An alternative way of defining interaction is to refer to the simple main effects, since a simple main effect *is* the effect of one variable at a specific level of the other variable. Thus,

an interaction is present when the simple main effects of one variable are not the same at different levels of the second variable.

In the first example, the simple main effects of either variable are identical and therefore equal to the corresponding main effects. This means that row and column marginal means are perfectly representative of the effects of the two independent variables and that any subsequent analyses will generally focus upon the marginal means rather than the individual treatment means. Stated another way, we can describe and analyze the effects of one of the independent variables without considering the specific levels of the other variable.

In the second example, the simple main effects of line length (the function relating line length and reading speed) are not the same at all levels of print-paper contrast. Stated in terms of the other variable, the simple main effects of print-paper contrast (the function relating contrast and reading speed) are not the same at all levels of line length. Either way, the data presented in Table 9-4 and plotted in Fig. 9-2 fit the definition of interaction. The presence of an interaction indicates that conclusions based on the two main effects will not fully describe the data. Each of the variables must be interpreted with the levels of the other variable in mind. To this end, any analyses conducted after the establishment of a significant interaction will tend to concentrate upon the individual treatment means rather than upon the overall marginal means.

Often the term *additive* is used to describe the joint effects of two non-interacting variables. What this means is that the effect of one variable simply adds to the effect of the second variable. When an interaction is present, the combination is *nonadditive*—i.e., an additional effect must be added to specify the joint effects of the two variables. This effect, of course, is the interaction.

ARITHMETIC DEFINITION OF INTERACTION   We can translate the definition of interaction into a simple arithmetic definition and test. From the verbal statement, an interaction is present when the effects of one variable (factor A, say) change at different levels of the other variable (factor B). We have seen in Chapter 6 that it is possible to view the sum of squares for factor A in terms of differences between *pairs* of A means (pp. 85–86). It is also possible to define an interaction in terms of two of the levels of factor A rather than all a of them. That is, an interaction exists when the difference between two means at *any two* levels of factor A (a_i and $a_{i'}$) changes at *any two* levels of factor B (b_j and $b_{j'}$). (We are again referring to simple main effects, but this time defining the manipulation in terms of two levels of factor A.)

To be more specific, consider the following 2×2 "factorial":

	a_i	$a_{i'}$
b_j	$\overline{AB}_{ij}$	$\overline{AB}_{i'j}$
$b_{j'}$	$\overline{AB}_{ij'}$	$\overline{AB}_{i'j'}$

where the $\overline{AB}$ terms represent means obtained under the four possible treatment combinations, ab_{ij}, $ab_{i'j}$, $ab_{ij'}$, and $ab_{i'j'}$. An interaction is present if the effect of the differential A treatment (a_i versus $a_{i'}$) at one level of factor B (i.e., b_j) is not equal to the corresponding effect at another level of factor B ($b_{j'}$). In terms of simple main effects, an interaction is present when

$$A \text{ at } b_j \neq A \text{ at } b_{j'},$$

where the expression "A at b_j" represents the simple main effect of A (a_i versus $a_{i'}$ in this case) at level b_j and the expression "A at $b_{j'}$" represents the same contrast at level $b_{j'}$. Stated more quantitatively, in terms of the sets of $\overline{AB}$ means in the two rows of the table, an interaction is present when

$$\overline{AB}_{ij} - \overline{AB}_{i'j} \neq \overline{AB}_{ij'} - \overline{AB}_{i'j'}$$

or

$$(\overline{AB}_{ij} - \overline{AB}_{i'j}) - (\overline{AB}_{ij'} - \overline{AB}_{i'j'}) \neq 0. \tag{9-1a}$$

Alternatively, we may state this definition in terms of simple main effects of factor B:

$$B \text{ at } a_i \neq B \text{ at } a_{i'},$$

and in terms of the sets of means in the two columns:

$$\overline{AB}_{ij} - \overline{AB}_{ij'} \neq \overline{AB}_{i'j} - \overline{AB}_{i'j'}$$

or

$$(\overline{AB}_{ij} - \overline{AB}_{ij'}) - (\overline{AB}_{i'j} - \overline{AB}_{i'j'}) \neq 0. \tag{9-1b}$$

A number of these 2×2 factorial arrangements may be formed from any two-way factorial with more than two levels of either or both independent variables by simply letting the pairs of subscripts (i and i'; and j and j') take on different values. In a 3×3 factorial, for example, where $a = 3$ and $b = 3$, we can form 2×2 factorials from the crossing of a_1 and a_2 with levels b_1 and b_2, or of a_1 and a_2 with b_1 and b_3, or of a_1 and a_2 with b_2 and b_3, or of a_1 and a_3 with b_1 and b_2, and so on. Finding a nonzero value for *any* one of the possible 2×2 arrangements is sufficient cause to conclude that an interaction effect is present. (We would still have to assess the significance of the interaction, but for the moment we will assume that the means are free of experimental error.)

Consider the example of an interaction presented in Table 9-4. Setting $i = 1, i' = 2, j = 1$, and $j' = 2$, and substituting in Eq. (9-1a),

$$\begin{aligned}(\overline{AB}_{11} - \overline{AB}_{21}) - (\overline{AB}_{12} - \overline{AB}_{22}) &= (1.00 - 2.00) - (3.00 - 5.00) \\ &= (-1.00) - (-2.00) = 1.00.\end{aligned}$$

The nonzero value indicates that an interaction effect is present. Setting $i = 2, i' = 3, j = 1$, and $j' = 3$,

$$\begin{aligned}(\overline{AB}_{21} - \overline{AB}_{31}) - (\overline{AB}_{23} - \overline{AB}_{33}) &= (2.00 - 3.00) - (6.00 - 5.00) \\ &= (-1.00) - (1.00) = -2.00,\end{aligned}$$

also indicating an interaction. For an example of no interaction, we can look at the data in Table 9-3. Setting $i = 2, i' = 3, j = 1$, and $j' = 2$,

$$\begin{aligned}(\overline{AB}_{21} - \overline{AB}_{31}) - (\overline{AB}_{22} - \overline{AB}_{32}) &= (2.22 - 2.89) - (5.22 - 5.89) \\ &= (-.67) - (-.67) = 0;\end{aligned}$$

setting $i = 1, i' = 3, j = 1, j' = 3$,

$$\begin{aligned}(\overline{AB}_{11} - \overline{AB}_{31}) - (\overline{AB}_{13} - \overline{AB}_{33}) &= (.89 - 2.89) - (4.22 - 6.22) \\ &= (-2.00) - (-2.00) = 0.\end{aligned}$$

With this particular set of data, all possible 2×2 arrangements will equal zero—a necessary outcome when an interaction is absent.

We will find little need for these arithmetic tests in detecting the presence or absence of interaction in a two-factor experiment, since obviously an inspection of a double-classification plot of the data is simpler. That is, if there is no interaction, the fact that Eq. (9-1a) and Eq. (9-1b) equal zero implies that the sets of curves in the figure are *parallel*; if there is an interaction, the equations will give nonzero values which implies that the curves are *not* parallel. We will find use for the arithmetic test when we consider more complicated factorials, where the visual test is often unrevealing of interactions.

Implications of Interaction for Theory

The presence of an interaction often requires more complexity in our theoretical explanations of the data than would be the case if no interaction were present. Consider the two different outcomes we have been discussing. Both examples indicate the importance of the two independent variables. In the first case, where there is no interaction, the effect of one of the independent variables adds to the effect of the other variable. The combination is simple. In the second case, on the other hand, the combination is complex—it will take a considerable amount of theoretical ingenuity to explain why the relationship between line length and average reading score is different with the three types of print-paper contrast or why the relationship between contrast and average reading score is different for the different line lengths.

The discussion above has focussed upon the complexity of post-hoc explanations of a set of data when an interaction is found. In an increasing number of experiments being reported in the literature, interactions not only are predicted but represent the major interest of the studies. Consider, for example, research in developmental psychology. Gollin (1965) indicates that it is not particularly revealing of developmental processes simply to compare a number of different age groups on a given task. Instead, he suggests that more interesting information is obtained from the discovery of *interactions* involving some manipulated independent variables and the age dimension. To show that two age groups differ on one task but not on another allows us to speculate about different developmental processes present in the two groups and required of the two tasks. To find a main effect of age or of task suggests very little about the processes involved in the phenomena under study. As Gollin puts it, "The uncovering of both the similarity *and* the difference in performance obviously gives us an order of information about the two groups which is quite different than if we had simply demonstrated that they did or did not differ on one or the other task" (p. 166).

The discovery or the prediction of interactions may lead to a greater understanding of the behavior under study. Lashley's classic study of the effect of the amount of brain damage on maze learning by rats is an excellent example.

Lashley varied the amount of cortical tissue destroyed from a small amount (1–10 percent) to a large amount (over 50 percent) and tested these animals on three mazes differing in difficulty. He found very slight differences among the operated groups on the easiest maze, but extremely dramatic differences on the most difficult maze. If Lashley had run his animals on only one of the mazes, he would have missed this important finding: that the destruction of cortical materials affects primarily the acquisition of complex learning tasks. That is, there is no uniform *overall* learning deficit. The effect of brain damage depends upon the complexity of the material being acquired.

In short, then, if behavior is complexly determined, we will need factorial experiments to isolate and to tease out these complexities. The factorial allows us to manipulate two or more independent variables concurrently and to obtain some idea as to how the variables combine to produce the behavior. An assessment of the interaction provides a hint as to the rules of combination.

Further Examples of Interaction and Lack of Interaction

In order to broaden (and to test) your understanding of the two-variable or $A \times B$ interaction and to get some practice in extracting information from double-classification tables and plots, consider the hypothetical outcomes of a 4×3 factorial experiment in which factor A is represented at four levels and factor B at three. The means for each set of 12 treatment combinations are presented in Table 9-5.

We have seen that the means (or sums) in the margins of a two-factor matrix reflect the main effects of the two independent variables and that the means within the body of the matrix reflect the presence or absence of an interaction. In this discussion we will assume that if any differences are present among the column marginal sums or among the row marginal sums, a corresponding main effect is present, and that if the effect of one independent variable changes at the different levels of the other independent variable, an interaction is present. (As we will see, the *significance* of main effects and of interaction effects is assessed by means of an F ratio.) We will look at eight examples, representing each of the possible combinations of the presence or absence of the two main effects and the interaction effect.

Consider the first example in Table 9-5. This example represents a completely negative study, none of the three effects being present. This state of affairs is illustrated by the identical 12 means in the body of the matrix. The column marginal sums are equal, indicating the absence of a main effect of factor A; similarly, the equal row marginal sums mean an absence of a main effect of factor B. A plot of the 12 means in panel 1 of Fig. 9-3 indicates that no $A \times B$ interaction is present in the data. The second example illustrates a case in which only factor A affects performance. We may see this by inspecting the column sums, which are not equal, and the row sums, which are equal. There is also no interaction, as may be seen in panel 2 of the figure—the three curves at b_1, b_2,

TABLE 9-5 *Eight Different Outcomes of the Same Two-Factor Experiment*

Levels of Factor B	Levels of Factor A a_1	a_2	a_3	a_4	Sum	Levels of Factor B	Levels of Factor A a_1	a_2	a_3	a_4	Sum
			(1)						(2)		
b_1:	4	4	4	4	16	b_1:	2	4	6	8	20
b_2:	4	4	4	4	16	b_2:	2	4	6	8	20
b_3:	4	4	4	4	16	b_3:	2	4	6	8	20
Sum	12	12	12	12	48	Sum:	6	12	18	24	60
			(3)						(4)		
b_1:	7	7	7	7	28	b_1:	5	6	7	8	26
b_2:	6	6	6	6	24	b_2:	4	5	6	7	22
b_3:	3	3	3	3	12	b_3:	2	3	4	5	14
Sum:	16	16	16	16	64	Sum:	11	14	17	20	62
			(5)						(6)		
b_1:	1	3	5	7	16	b_1:	1	3	5	7	16
b_2:	4	4	4	4	16	b_2:	2	3.3	4.7	6	16
b_3:	7	5	3	1	16	b_3:	4	4	4	4	16
Sum:	12	12	12	12	48	Sum:	7	10.3	13.7	17	48
			(7)						(8)		
b_1:	4	5	6	7	22	b_1:	1	3	5	7	16
b_2:	4	4	4	4	16	b_2:	1	2	3	4	10
b_3:	4	3	2	1	10	b_3:	1	1	1	1	4
Sum:	12	12	12	12	48	Sum:	3	6	9	12	30

and b_3 have the identical shape. In the next example, the marginal sums show that there is a main effect of factor *B* but no effect of factor *A*. Again, no interaction is present, since the three curves at the different levels of factor *B* are parallel. The outcome in example 4 indicates that a main effect of both independent variables is present. This may be seen in the two sets of marginal totals. The plot in Fig. 9-3 shows that the effect of factor *A* is the same at each of the levels of factor *B*—i.e., there is no interaction.

The last four examples contain $A \times B$ interactions. Look at the marginal sums for example 5. There are no differences among the column sums and no differences among the row sums; hence, there are no main effects of factors *A* and *B*, respectively. On the basis of the main effects, then, we might conclude that our manipulations were ineffective. But look at the cell means within the body of the matrix. The two independent variables produce quite striking effects. The simple main effect of factor *A* is positive at b_1, absent at b_2, and negative at b_3. The $A \times B$ interaction is so severe that the simple main effects

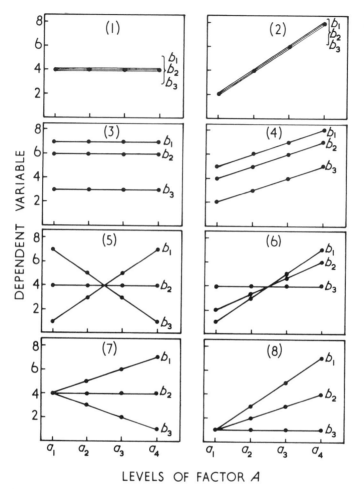

Fig. 9-3   Plot of data presented in Table 9-5.

of the two variables have been canceled. This example stresses the point that the main effects reflect treatment *averages* and as such do not necessarily reflect the constituent parts.

The next two examples show situations in which there is an interaction and one main effect. The main effect in example 6 is revealed in the column sums— i.e., a main effect of factor A—while the interaction is readily apparent in the plot of the cell means in panel 6 of Fig. 9-3. In this case, the effect of factor A is quite substantial at b_1 and nonexistent at b_3. In example 7 the situation is reversed; the row sums indicate a main effect of factor B and the nonparallel lines in panel 7 indicate an interaction of the two variables. The final experiment (example 8) provides an instance in which all three effects are present. Not only is there a main effect for each of the two variables (see the column and row totals), but the form of the function relating factor A to the dependent variable is different at each level of factor B, indicating the presence of an $A \times B$ interaction.

We have seen that it is possible to obtain eight different combinations of the presence or absence of the two main effects and of the interaction effects. Obviously, there is an infinite number of ways in which the actual means may turn out to reflect one of these combinations. The presence of main effects is revealed by the variation among the marginal sums of the two-way matrix, and the presence of an $A \times B$ interaction is revealed by the appearance of non-parallel lines in a double-classification plot of the means within the body of the data matrix. We are now ready to see how we can obtain variances which will reflect these three effects and how we can test their significance.

chapter ten

RATIONALE AND RULES FOR
CALCULATION OF THE
MAJOR EFFECTS

We saw in Chapter 3 how the total sum of squares could be partitioned into two parts: (1) a part reflecting the deviation of the treatment groups from the overall mean (the between-groups sum of squares—SS_{bg}) and (2) a part reflecting the variability of subjects treated alike (the within-groups sum of squares—SS_{wg}). We then discussed how we could test the null hypothesis. In subsequent chapters of Part II we saw that we could ask more refined questions of the data by dividing the SS_{bg} into component sums of squares. The analysis of the factorial experiment follows a similar pattern, except that the SS_{bg} is *not* of systematic interest. That is, we are primarily interested in the *further division* of the SS_{bg} into three orthogonal components: (1) a sum of squares reflecting the main effect of factor A (SS_A), (2) a sum of squares reflecting the main effect of factor B (SS_B), and (3) a sum of squares representing the $A \times B$ interaction ($SS_{A \times B}$). In this chapter we will consider only the most common case, having the same number of subjects in each of the treatment conditions. The analysis of experiments with unequal sample sizes is discussed in Chapter 17.

PARTITIONING THE TOTAL SUM OF SQUARES

Design and Notation

We will pause at this point to expand the notational system so that we can make explicit the operations needed for the analysis of the two-way factorial. The system we will use is summarized in Table 10-1. The factorial arrangement of the two independent variables, illustrated with $a = 2$ and $b = 3$, is enumerated in the upper portion of the table. We have indicated that there is a total of $ab = 2(3) = 6$ treatment conditions, each with a sample of s different subjects who have been randomly assigned to the different conditions.

A basic observation or score in this design is denoted ABS_{ijk} to indicate that it represents the score of a single subject in a particular combination of the levels

TABLE 10-1 *Design and Notation for the Two-Factor Design*

EXPERIMENTAL DESIGN

Factor A

Factor B	a_1	a_2
b_1	$s = 4$	$s = 4$
b_2	$s = 4$	$s = 4$
b_3	$s = 4$	$s = 4$

ABS MATRIX

Treatment Combinations

ab_{11}	ab_{12}	ab_{13}	ab_{21}	ab_{22}	ab_{23}
ABS_{111}	ABS_{121}	ABS_{131}	ABS_{211}	ABS_{221}	ABS_{231}
ABS_{112}	ABS_{122}	ABS_{132}	ABS_{212}	ABS_{222}	ABS_{232}
ABS_{113}	ABS_{123}	ABS_{133}	ABS_{213}	ABS_{223}	ABS_{233}
ABS_{114}	ABS_{124}	ABS_{134}	ABS_{214}	ABS_{224}	ABS_{234}

AB MATRIX[a]

Levels of Factor A

Levels of Factor B	a_1	a_2	Marginal Sum
		Sum	→
b_1	AB_{11}	AB_{21}	B_1
b_2	AB_{12}	AB_{22}	B_2 Sum
b_3	AB_{13}	AB_{23}	B_3
Marginal Sum	A_1	A_2	T
		Sum	→

[a] Note: $AB_{ij} = \sum\limits_{k}^{s} ABS_{ijk}$.

of factors A and B. These scores are arranged in the ABS matrix which appears in the middle portion of the table. If it is necessary to specify a particular score in one of the treatment conditions, we will use all three subscripts—one for the level of factor A (the i subscript), one for the level of factor B (the j subscript), and one for the score within the treatment cell (the k subscript).[1] As in the single-factor case, however, we will drop the subscripts whenever there is no ambiguity as to the arithmetic operations being specified.

An AB matrix, where the remainder of the notational system is explicated, is presented in the bottom portion of Table 10-1. The basic entry within the body of this matrix (often called the *cells* of the matrix) is the quantity AB_{ij}. This quantity represents the sum of the ABS scores at a particular combination of levels of the two factors. These are the totals that we would obtain if we summed the $s = 4$ ABS scores in any one column of the ABS matrix. For example,

$$\sum ABS_{21k} = ABS_{211} + ABS_{212} + ABS_{213} + ABS_{214} = AB_{21}.$$

More formally,

$$\sum_{k}^{s} ABS_{ijk} = AB_{ij}.$$

One way to see how the notation works is to think of the summation as canceling the relevant letter and subscript from the ABS_{ijk} designation. In this case, we are summing over the k subscript:

$$\sum_{k}^{s} ABS_{ijk} = AB\cancel{S}_{ij\cancel{k}} = AB_{ij}.$$

We will also refer to these sums as the *treatment sums* or *totals*. They form the basic ingredient in the determination of the sums of squares associated with different experimental treatments.

In order to calculate the two main effects, we will have to obtain the column and row totals shown in the margin of the matrix and hereafter referred to as the column and row marginal totals, respectively. These sums are found by collapsing across (i.e., summing over) the other subscript. More specifically, column marginal totals are formed by summing the cell totals in all of the rows for each of the a columns. These totals are denoted A_i in exactly the same manner as were the treatment sums in the single-factor case. More explicitly,

$$\sum_{j}^{b} AB_{ij} = A\cancel{B}_{i\cancel{j}} = A_{i}.$$

The row marginal totals are calculated in an analogous manner, summing the cell totals in all of the columns for each of the b rows. These are referred to as

---

[1] With these subscripts,

$$i = 1, 2, \ldots, a, \quad j = 1, 2, \ldots, b, \quad \text{and} \quad k = 1, 2, \ldots, s.$$

B_j. That is,

$$\sum_i^a AB_{ij} = AB_{\cdot j} = B_j.$$

Finally, the grand total is obtained by summing either set of marginal totals:

$$T = \sum A = \sum B.$$

Component Deviation Scores

Suppose factor A was manipulated at $a = 3$ levels and factor B at $b = 2$ levels, so that we had a total of $ab = 3(2) = 6$ different treatment groups, each containing s subjects. As a first step, it is useful to think of the six treatment means as coming from a single-factor experiment. According to the formulas given in Chapter 3, the variability of the abs subjects can then be broken down into

$$SS_T = SS_{bg} + SS_{wg}.$$

Up to this point, then, there is nothing new to the analysis. We will now refine the SS_{bg}.

The SS_{bg} is based upon the deviation of each individual treatment mean from the total mean—i.e., $\overline{AB}_{ij} - \overline{T}$. Consider the deviation score produced by a group of subjects receiving a particular treatment combination represented by the combination of level a_i and level b_j (ab_{ij}). This deviation score can be influenced by three sources of variability:

$$\overline{AB}_{ij} - \overline{T} = (A_i \text{ effect}) + (B_j \text{ effect}) + (A_i \times B_j \text{ interaction effect}).$$

Each of these effects can be expressed as a deviation score involving familiar quantities:

$$\overline{AB}_{ij} - \overline{T} = (\overline{A}_i - \overline{T}) + (\overline{B}_j - \overline{T}) + (\overline{AB}_{ij} - \overline{A}_i - \overline{B}_j + \overline{T}). \qquad (10\text{-}1)$$

Suppose we try to understand Eq. (10-1) a little better. First, we can verify that the equation is correct by performing the indicated additions and subtractions. To be more specific, there is only one $\overline{AB}_{ij}$ on the righthand side of Eq. (10-1) and so it will stay, but $\overline{A}_i$ and $\overline{B}_j$ will both drop out, since each appears once as a positive quantity and once as a negative quantity. The final term, $\overline{T}$, appears three times on the right—twice as a negative quantity and once as a positive quantity. Thus, we are left with the same expression, $\overline{AB}_{ij} - \overline{T}$, on both sides of the equation.

The second point concerns the specification of the interaction effect. To show that the third quantity on the right of Eq. (10-1) reflects an interaction, we can redefine an interaction as a *residual* deviation score. That is, the interaction effect represents whatever is left of the deviation of the individual treatment mean from $\overline{T}$ that cannot be accounted for by the two relevant main effects. In symbols,

$$\text{interaction effect} = (\text{deviation from } \overline{T}) - (A_i \text{ effect}) - (B_j \text{ effect})$$
$$= (\overline{AB}_{ij} - \overline{T}) - (\overline{A}_i - \overline{T}) - (\overline{B}_j - \overline{T}).$$

Performing some simple algebra, we obtain

$$\text{interaction effect} = \overline{AB}_{ij} - \overline{T} - \overline{A}_i + \overline{T} - \overline{B}_j + \overline{T}$$
$$= \overline{AB}_{ij} - \overline{A}_i - \overline{B}_j + \overline{T}.$$

We are now ready to consider the deviation scores for the individual subjects in the different treatment groups. We can easily expand Eq. (10-1) to accommodate the deviation of any given subject (ABS_{ijk}) from the mean of all of the subjects ($\overline{T}$). A complete subdivision of the total deviation ($ABS_{ijk} - \overline{T}$) is given by

$$ABS_{ijk} - \overline{T} = (\overline{A}_i - \overline{T}) + (\overline{B}_j - \overline{T}) + (\overline{AB}_{ij} - \overline{A}_i - \overline{B}_j + \overline{T})$$
$$+ (ABS_{ijk} - \overline{AB}_{ij}). \tag{10-2}$$

In words, the deviation of a subject from the grand mean can be broken down into four separate components: (1) the treatment effect at level a_i, (2) the treatment effect at level b_j, (3) the interaction effect at the combination of levels a_i and b_j, and (4) the deviation of the subject from his individual treatment mean.

Now that we have enumerated the component deviation scores for each subject, they can be squared and summed to produce the corresponding sums of squares for the analysis. However, rather than looking at the actual defining formulas, which preserve the "meaning" of Eq. (10-2), we will move directly to the computational formulas. These formulas are much easier to use than the defining formulas. Thus, except for the explication of the component deviation scores [i.e., Eq. (10-2)], no real purpose is served by looking at the defining formulas for the different sums of squares. We will now turn to a specification of these computational formulas.

RULES FOR GENERATING COMPUTATIONAL FORMULAS

In this section we will consider a set of rules which allow the generation of the computational formulas for the sums of squares obtained from *any* factorial experiment. The system will be introduced here in the context of the two-way factorial, but (as we will see in later chapters) it can be applied to a large variety of experimental designs. The method we will discuss, a modified version of the one presented by Myers (1966), is based on an isomorphic relationship between the *df* statement for a given source of variance and the corresponding formula for the sum of squares. The main purpose of this section is to introduce this useful scheme for constructing the computational formulas for the different component sums of squares. In the next section we will summarize the complete analysis and discuss in more detail the meaning behind some of the operations.

The system consists of three basic steps. First, we identify the sources of variance which are extracted in a standard analysis of variance. Second, we write the df statement for each of these sources. Finally, we construct the computational formulas from the different df statements.

Identification of Sources of Variance

There is a simple rule for specifying the sources of variance. We have already discussed what these sources would be in the present case, but it is useful to see how the rule applies in a situation with which we are familiar. This rule "works" with completely randomized designs of the sort we are discussing in the present major section and in Part IV.

(1) List all factors, including the within-groups factor, and (2) Form all possible interactions with these factors, omitting the within-groups factor.

For the two-factor design, step 1 results in a listing of

$$A, B, \text{ and } S/AB.$$

(The within-groups factor, S/AB, represents the variability due to subjects treated alike; that is, this source consists of the variability of subjects in each of the ab groups, pooled or summed over these different groups.) Step 2 results in the listing of a single interaction:

$$A \times B.$$

Degrees of Freedom

We will discuss the meaning of degrees of freedom in the next section. For the present we will just consider formulas that specify the df's for the different sources of variance we have identified. For the two main effects, the df's are simply the number of levels for each factor minus 1:

$$df_A = a - 1 \quad \text{and} \quad df_B = b - 1.$$

For the $A \times B$ interaction, the df are the product of the df's associated with factors A and B. More specifically,

$$df_{A \times B} = (df_A)(df_B) = (a - 1)(b - 1). \tag{10-3}$$

The calculation of the df for the within-groups source, S/AB, is more complicated. The variability for this source is due to a subject factor (factor S), and for this factor

$$df_S = s - 1.$$

However, since this factor is present in each of the ab treatment conditions, the df for S/AB is found by multiplying df_S times the total number of these groups, ab:

$$df_{S/AB} = (df_S)(ab) = (s - 1)(ab) = ab(s - 1).$$

The last expression on the right represents the df statement in the most common form. Finally, the df for the total sum of squares consist of the total number of observations (abs) minus 1:

$$df_T = abs - 1.$$

Construction of Computational Formulas

Table 10-2 summarizes the steps followed in the generation of the computational formulas for the different sums of squares in a two-way analysis of variance. The sources of variance are listed in the first column; the df's associated with these sources are listed in the second column. We will outline the construction procedure as a series of steps.

FIRST STEP   **Write the expanded df statement** for the source of variance. This first step represents the backbone of the computational scheme. It should present no difficulty, since it requires only the performance of the multiplications specified in the df statements in column 2 of Table 10-2. After completing any necessary multiplication, we arrange the sets of letters according to decreasing numbers of letters. When present, "1" is listed last. The expanded df statements are given in column 3 of the table.

Each term in these expanded df statements—single letters, combination of letters, or "1"—denotes a different term in the computational formulas, and the expanded df statements themselves indicate how these terms are to be combined to produce the different sums of squares. We will now construct the computational expressions for each of these quantities.

Look over the expanded df statements. Except for "1," each term appears once in the first position to the left. Thus, we will construct the computational expressions for these terms in the rows where they appear in the first position. (The last row of the table lists the term associated with "1" in the expanded df statements.)

SECOND STEP   For each letter in the first terms, **substitute capital letters; for "1" substitute "T."** This has been done in column 4 of the table. These letters and combinations of letters denote sums in particular matrices. (We have omitted subscripts, as they will not be necessary for the computational formulas.) That is, A refers to the overall total for any level of factor A, B to the overall total for any level of factor B, AB to the total for any cell in the AB matrix, ABS to the score for a single subject in the ABS matrix, and T to the sum of all of the scores in the experiment.

THIRD STEP   Next, we **square and sum all such totals or scores.** This step is enumerated in column 5 of the table. Consistent with the conventions adopted for this book, single summation signs without limits and quantities without subscripts are used, since the summation is taken over *all* such quantities. That is, the summation in the first row includes all a of the squared totals, in the second row all b of the squared totals, in the third row all ab of the squared totals, and in the fourth and fifth rows all abs of the squared scores.

FOURTH STEP   In this step we **select the appropriate divisor** for each term. We find these numbers easily by starting with the total number of observations in the experiment (*abs*) and *eliminating* those letters that appear in each numerator. This step is completed in column 6.

FIFTH STEP   The final operation on these first terms is to **represent each term by a code letter.** The principle behind the code is obvious, as a comparison of column 6 and column 7 will reveal. That is, the letter(s) within brackets correspond to the letter(s) used to represent the quantities which are squared in the numerator of the coded term.

SIXTH STEP   The **computational formulas are written in coded form** in the last column of the table. The particular combination of terms for each sum of squares is specified by the corresponding *df* statement in column 3. It is interesting to note the correspondence between these coded formulas and the respective deviation scores in Eq. (10-2).

Summary

This system is general and may be applied to all of the designs we will consider in this book. In addition, we will see in Chapter 15 that the formulas for other sorts of analyses can be generated by the same underlying system. The system elaborated here ensures that we will never "forget" the computational formulas, since we can very easily *reconstruct* them. Some of the steps will drop out with practice, and (as we will see in Chapter 15) shorthand forms can be used to simplify the formulas still further. You should not lose touch with the basic system, however, as it will prove extremely useful in generating formulas for the more complex designs considered in Parts IV and V.

In the next section we will consider the computational formulas again, but this time in conjunction with the remaining steps in the analysis of variance.

TABLE 10-2 *Construction of the Computational Formulas from the Expanded df Statements*

First Term

(1) Source	(2) df	(3) Expanded df	(4) Substitution	(5) Square and Sum	(6) Selection of Denominator	(7) Letter Code	(8) Computational Formula (Coded)[a]
A	$a-1$	$a-1$	A	$\sum(A)^2$	$\dfrac{\sum(A)^2}{abs} = \dfrac{\sum(A)^2}{bs}$	$[A]$	$[A] - [T]$
B	$b-1$	$b-1$	B	$\sum(B)^2$	$\dfrac{\sum(B)^2}{abs} = \dfrac{\sum(B)^2}{as}$	$[B]$	$[B] - [T]$
$A \times B$	$(a-1)(b-1)$	$ab-a-b+1$	AB	$\sum(AB)^2$	$\dfrac{\sum(AB)^2}{abs} = \dfrac{\sum(AB)^2}{s}$	$[AB]$	$[AB] - [A] - [B] + [T]$
S/AB	$ab(s-1)$	$abs-ab$	ABS	$\sum(ABS)^2$	$\dfrac{\sum(ABS)^2}{abs} = \sum(ABS)^2$	$[ABS]$	$[ABS] - [AB]$
Total	$abs-1$	$abs-1$	T	$(T)^2$	$\dfrac{(T)^2}{abs} = \dfrac{(T)^2}{abs}$	$[T]$	$[ABS] - [T]$

[a] Bracketed letters represent complete terms in the computational formulas; a particular term is identified by the letter(s) appearing in the numerator.

SUMMARY OF THE ANALYSIS OF VARIANCE

Sums of Squares

The computational formulas for the component sums of squares are presented in Table 10-3. Each term in the computational formulas is expressed in its complete form only once—when it first appears in the analysis. Thereafter, each term is designated by the letter code in which a particular term is identified by the letter or letters appearing in the numerator. The totals required for the SS_A are the column marginal totals in the AB matrix presented in Table 10-1 (p. 188). The totals required for the SS_B come from the row marginal totals in the AB matrix. The totals for the first term in the computational formula for the $SS_{A \times B}$ are the individual cell totals found within the body of the AB matrix. Finally, the scores for the first term in the formula for the $SS_{S/AB}$ appear in the ABS matrix.

The within-groups sum of squares ($SS_{S/AB}$) reflects the variability of subjects treated alike. That is, it consists of the variability of subjects receiving the same treatment combination, pooled over all of the ab treatment groups. While the correspondence between the computational formula and the deviation score ($ABS_{ijk} - \overline{AB}_{ij}$) is apparent, the fact that this sum of squares represents a pooling of the separate within-group sums of squares for the different ab groups is not.[2]

It is informative to see how computational rule number 1 (pp. 44–45) applies to the different formulas in Table 10-3. This rule states that we always divide a numerator term by the number of observations summed to calculate

TABLE 10-3 *Computational Formulas: Two-Factor Analysis of Variance*

Source	Computational Formula[a]	df	MS	F[b]
A	$\dfrac{\sum (A)^2}{bs} - \dfrac{(T)^2}{abs}$	$a - 1$	$\dfrac{SS_A}{df_A}$	$\dfrac{MS_A}{MS_{S/AB}}$
B	$\dfrac{\sum (B)^2}{as} - [T]$	$b - 1$	$\dfrac{SS_B}{df_B}$	$\dfrac{MS_B}{MS_{S/AB}}$
$A \times B$	$\dfrac{\sum (AB)^2}{s} - [A] - [B] + [T]$	$(a - 1)(b - 1)$	$\dfrac{SS_{A \times B}}{df_{A \times B}}$	$\dfrac{MS_{A \times B}}{MS_{S/AB}}$
Within (S/AB)	$\sum (ABS)^2 - [AB]$	$ab(s - 1)$	$\dfrac{SS_{S/AB}}{df_{S/AB}}$	
Total	$\sum (ABS)^2 - [T]$	$abs - 1$		

[a] Bracketed letters represent complete terms in the computational formulas; a particular term is identified by the letter(s) appearing in the numerator.
[b] The *fixed-effects model* is assumed (see footnote 3, p. 200).

[2] This fact is demonstrated in Exercise 2 for this part (p. 247).

one of the quantities that is squared. For the first term in the formula for the SS_A, we square sums that have been obtained by collapsing across the different levels of factor B. With s subjects and b groups, there are bs observations contributing to any one of the marginal sums (A_i). Thus, the rule applies, and we divide the numerator by the number of observations represented by each marginal sum (bs). The same is true for the second term of the computational formula, where the squared quantity (T) is the grand sum of all of the abs observations in the experiment. For the first term for the SS_B, the squared totals are the marginal sums B_j, which are obtained by summing across the different levels of factor A; there are as observations when this is done. The rule holds again. For the first term for the $SS_{A \times B}$ we are asked to square AB sums, each of which contains s observations, and this is the number by which we divide the numerator. For the $SS_{S/AB}$ and the SS_T the squared term (ABS) is based on a single observation, and so we can think of the quantity $\sum (ABS)^2$ as being divided by 1. In each case, then, computational rule number 1 continues to hold.

Degrees of Freedom

The df for any source of variance satisfy the statement given in Eq. (4-2): the df equal the number of independent observations upon which each sum of squares is based minus the number of restraints operating on these observations. For the two main effects, the observations involved are the marginal sums (or means) for the rows and columns. For the SS_A the number of observations is a; since the column marginal totals (A_i) must sum to the grand total (T), there is one restraint. Thus,

$$df_A = a - 1.$$

This restraint is symbolized in Table 10-4 by an **X** placed in the margin at a_4. (This level was arbitrarily picked; any of the a levels would do.) For the SS_B the number of observations is b; since the marginal row totals (B_j) must also sum to T, one restraint is placed on the independence of these observations. Thus,

$$df_B = b - 1.$$

This restraint is symbolized by an **X** placed in the margin at b_3.

The df for the $SS_{A \times B}$ are obtained from Eq. (10-3):

$$df_{A \times B} = (a - 1)(b - 1),$$

the product of the df associated with the two main effects. We may understand this formula by considering the cells within the AB matrix presented in Table 10-4. The question basically is how many of the AB totals are *free* to vary once certain restrictions of the matrix are met. We have already seen that the marginal sums for the columns and rows must satisfy the requirement that

$$\sum A = \sum B = T.$$

TABLE 10-4   *Representation of df Associated with the SS_A, SS_B, and $SS_{A \times B}$*

	Factor A				
Factor B	a_1	a_2	a_3	a_4	Sum
b_1				X	B_1
b_2				X	B_2
b_3	X	X	X	X	X
Sum	A_1	A_2	A_3	X	T

What about the AB_{ij} sums within the body of the matrix? For any one of the columns, the sum of the cell totals must equal the corresponding marginal total. This places one restriction on each of the columns; these restrictions are represented by **X**'s in the row at level b_3. (This row was again picked arbitrarily.) A similar restriction is placed on the rows: the sum of the cell totals in any one of the rows must equal the corresponding marginal totals. These restrictions are indicated by **X**'s in the column at level a_4. The unmarked cells, then, represent the *df* for the $A \times B$ interaction. This rectangle is bounded on one side by $a - 1$ columns and on the other side by $b - 1$ rows, and the total number of "free" cells without **X**'s is the quantity $(a - 1)(b - 1)$.

The *df* for the within-groups sum of squares ($SS_{S/AB}$) follow the same general rule for the determination of the number of *df.* Since this sum of squares consists of a within-group sum of squares that is pooled over the *ab* groups, we can start by finding the *df* for each individual cell in the matrix:

$$df_{S/AB_{ij}} = s - 1.$$

One *df* is lost because of the restriction that the *s* different *ABS* scores must sum to the cell total (AB_{ij}). Now, if we sum the *df*'s over the *ab* cells, we obtain

$$df_{S/AB} = \sum df_{S/AB_{ij}} = ab(s - 1).$$

Mean Squares and F Ratios

The mean squares are found by dividing each sum of squares by its corresponding *df*:

$$MS = \frac{SS}{df}.$$

These are enumerated in the fourth column of Table 10-3. The F ratios are formed in each case by dividing the mean squares by the $MS_{S/AB}$:

$$F_A = \frac{MS_A}{MS_{S/AB}}, \quad F_B = \frac{MS_B}{MS_{S/AB}}, \quad F_{A \times B} = \frac{MS_{A \times B}}{MS_{S/AB}}.$$

These F ratios are evaluated in the F table under the appropriate numerator and denominator df's.

The logic behind the construction of these ratios is the same as that offered in the single-factor case. Briefly, each mean square in the numerator of the F ratio is assumed to provide a population estimate of the particular effect plus error variance. The denominator in the F ratio ($MS_{S/AB}$) is assumed to provide an estimate of error variance alone. The null hypothesis in each case is that the population treatment effects (the effects due to factor A, to factor B, and to the interaction of the two factors) are zero. The within-groups mean square ($MS_{S/AB}$) is the appropriate error term for the three mean squares because the numerator mean squares (MS_A, MS_B, and $MS_{A \times B}$) and the denominator mean square ($MS_{S/AB}$) are independent estimates of error variance when the null hypothesis is true. Under these circumstances, the expected values of the three F ratios will be approximately 1.0. We follow the same decision rules as outlined for the single-factor case (pp. 63–65). A significant F indicates that the null hypothesis is untenable, and we then accept the alternative hypothesis that there are treatment effects present.

Orthogonality of the Two-Way Analysis

It is possible to show that the SS_A, SS_B, and $SS_{A \times B}$ are mutually orthogonal— i.e., that they provide independent information about the outcome of the experiment. (See Appendix A for a proof of this statement.) As we noted in Chapter 7, these tests are not *statistically* independent, since the same error term is used to form each F ratio. This, however, does not appear to present a problem for our interpretation of the results of an experiment. The three sources of variance extracted in the analysis we have been discussing represent an efficient way of dividing up the df associated with the total between-groups sum of squares. It would certainly be possible to divide this sum of squares into a *different* set of orthogonal comparisons. Nevertheless, investigators present most factorial experiments in a way that makes obvious their intention to extract and to evaluate the sources of variance listed in Table 10-3. In actuality, then, we can think of the analysis of a two-way factorial experiment as consisting of a set of *planned orthogonal comparisons*. But we are not restricted to these comparisons alone. Often we will want to isolate the locus of a significant main effect or of an interaction. Procedures for accomplishing these comparisons will be discussed in subsequent chapters of Part III.

ASSUMPTIONS UNDERLYING THE ANALYSIS

Except for the basic structural model, the assumptions for the two-factor experiment are the same as those we enumerated for the single-factor case. First, the model under which we have been operating merely specifies the components of variance with which we are already familiar.[3] Briefly,

$$ABS_{ijk} = \mu + (\mu_i - \mu) + (\mu_j - \mu) + (\mu_{ij} - \mu_i - \mu_j + \mu) + (ABS_{ijk} - \mu_{ij}).$$

That is, ABS_{ijk} can be represented by the sum of the following quantities: (1) the overall mean of the population (μ), (2) the treatment effect at level $a_i (\mu_i - \mu)$, (3) the treatment effect at level $b_j (\mu_j - \mu)$, (4) the interaction effect at cell $ab_{ij} (\mu_{ij} - \mu_i - \mu_j + \mu)$, and (5) experimental error $(ABS_{ijk} - \mu_{ij})$.

In order for the F ratios to be distributed as F, three additional assumptions must be met: (1) each of the ab treatment populations is normally distributed, (2) the variances of the treatment populations are equal, and (3) the error components $(ABS_{ijk} - \mu_{ij})$ are independent within groups and between treatment groups as well.

As we noted in the previous discussion of assumptions underlying the single-factor analysis of variance (see pp. 74–77), the assumptions that the within-group variances are normally distributed and homogeneous are not critical when the sample sizes are of a reasonable size (greater than 10, say) and are equal. The same conclusion holds for the two-factor experiment. In short, we can safely disregard all except major violations of these two assumptions. The assumption of independence of the individual error components, of course, continues to be important. As we saw in Chapter 5, independence is achieved by randomly assigning subjects to the different treatment conditions. If each subject is equally likely to be given any one of the ab treatments, then the ABS scores and hence, $ABS_{ijk} - \mu_{ij}$, will be independent.

NUMERICAL EXAMPLE

We are now ready for a numerical example showing all of the steps required for the analysis of a two-way factorial experiment. The example consists of a hypothetical investigation of the role of drive level and magnitude of reward on the learning of a discrimination problem by monkeys. The animals are given five trials a day for four days on a set of 20 "oddity" problems. In this task, three objects (two the same, one different) are presented to the monkeys, and the subject's task is to learn to select the nonduplicated (odd) object. A food reward is placed in a well underneath the correct object. A trial consists of the presentation of the three objects and the monkey's selection of one of them. The response measure is the number of correct selections in the 20 training trials. One of the independent variables (factor A) is the magnitude of the food reward, either 1, 3, or 5 grapes, while the other variable (factor B) is the drive level of the animals, either 1 hour of food deprivation or 24 hours of food deprivation. Four monkeys are randomly assigned to each treatment combination. Thus, the design is a 3×2 factorial with $s = 4$ subjects. The individual ABS scores appear in the upper portion of Table 10-5.

---

[3] For a more complete description of the statistical model, see Chapter 16.

The individual cell sums (AB_{ij}) are entered into an AB matrix in the middle portion of the table. Each cell total is obtained by summing the four observations in each cell. For cell ab_{11},

$$AB_{11} = \sum ABS_{11k} = 1 + 4 + 0 + 7 = 12.$$

After obtaining these cell sums, it is usually a good idea to plot the cell means so that we can see more readily whether or not we have obtained an interaction. This has been done in Fig. 10-1 (the means are presented in the bottom portion of the table). The figure shows a rather sizable interaction of the two variables. It appears that magnitude (factor A) has little differential effect upon correct responding by hungry monkeys and an increasing positive effect with less hungry monkeys. In other words, hungry animals are unaffected by the differences in the size of the food reward, while less hungry animals are. Now that we have a "feel" for the way the experiment came out (and what the analysis should reveal), we can proceed with the calculations.

TABLE 10-5   *Numerical Example: Two-Factor Analysis*

ABS MATRIX (INDIVIDUAL OBSERVATIONS)

Treatment Combinations

ab_{11}	ab_{12}	ab_{21}	ab_{22}	ab_{31}	ab_{32}
1	15	13	6	9	14
4	6	5	18	16	7
0	10	7	9	18	6
7	13	15	15	13	13

AB MATRIX (SUMS)

Amount of Food (Factor A)

Drive (Factor B)	1 Grape (a_1)	3 Grapes (a_2)	5 Grapes (a_3)	Sum
1 hour (b_1)	12	40	56	108
24 hours (b_2)	44	48	40	132
Sum	56	88	96	240

AB MATRIX (MEANS)

Factor A

Factor B	a_1	a_2	a_3
b_1	3.0	10.0	14.0
b_2	11.0	12.0	10.0

The first step is to substitute these data into the computational formulas for the sums of squares given in Table 10-3. We will perform these operations in two steps: (1) the calculation of the basic terms entering into the computational formulas and (2) the addition and subtraction of these terms in the actual determination of the various sums of squares. We will now solve for these basic quantities and identify each by means of the letter code. Working first with the AB matrix, we obtain

$$[T] = \frac{(T)^2}{abs} = \frac{(240)^2}{3(2)(4)} = \frac{57,600}{24} = 2400.00,$$

$$[A] = \frac{\sum (A)^2}{bs} = \frac{(56)^2 + (88)^2 + (96)^2}{2(4)} = \frac{20,096}{8} = 2512.00,$$

$$[B] = \frac{\sum (B)^2}{as} = \frac{(108)^2 + (132)^2}{3(4)} = \frac{29,088}{12} = 2424.00,$$

and

$$[AB] = \frac{\sum (AB)^2}{s} = \frac{(12)^2 + (44)^2 + \cdots + (56)^2 + (40)^2}{4}$$

$$= \frac{10,720}{4} = 2680.00.$$

The final calculation requires the scores presented in the ABS matrix:

$$[ABS] = \sum (ABS)^2 = (1)^2 + (4)^2 + \cdots + (6)^2 + (13)^2 = 3010.$$

We can now obtain the sums of squares by combining the quantities we have just calculated in the patterns specified in Tables 10-2 or 10-3. This has been done twice in Table 10-6. In the upper portion of the table we have indicated the actual numbers entering into the determination of each sum of squares,

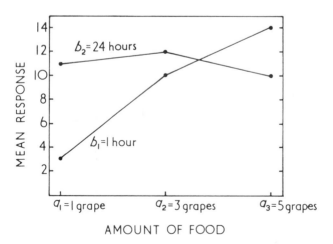

Fig. 10-1   Plot of data presented in Table 10-5.

TABLE 10-6 *Summary of the Analysis*

UNCODED

Source	Calculations	SS	df	MS	F
A	$2512.00 - 2400.00 =$	112.00	2	56.00	3.06
B	$2424.00 - 2400.00 =$	24.00	1	24.00	1.31
A × B	$2680.00 - 2512.00 - 2424.00 + 2400.00 =$	144.00	2	72.00	3.93*
S/AB	$3010 - 2680.00 =$	330.00	18	18.33	
Total	$3010 - 2400.00 =$	610.00	23		

* $p < .05$.

CALCULATIONS CODED BY LETTERS IN BRACKETS

Source	Calculations[a]	SS	df	MS	F
A	$2512.00 - 2400.00 =$	112.00	2	56.00	3.06
B	$2424.00 - [T] =$	24.00	1	24.00	1.31
A × B	$2680.00 - [A] - [B] + [T] =$	144.00	2	72.00	3.93*
S/AB	$3010 - [AB] =$	330.00	18	18.33	
Total	$[ABS] - [T] =$	610.00	23		

* $p < .05$.
[a] Bracketed letters represent complete terms in the computational formulas; a particular term is identified by the letter(s) appearing in the numerator.

while in the lower portion we have represented the same operations by replacing calculations that recur in subsequent rows of the table with the coded quantities. This latter representation is the form that the summary tables will usually take in the remainder of the book. The coding reduces the amount of writing needed to capture the critical steps in the analysis, and it emphasizes the pattern in which sums of squares are calculated.

The final steps of the analysis are recorded on the right sides of both tables in an analysis-of-variance summary table. We should check for computational errors in our calculations by summing the component sums of squares to verify that the total equals the SS_T. The df's are found by a simple substitution in the corresponding formulas:

$$df_A = a - 1 = 3 - 1 = 2,$$

$$df_B = b - 1 = 2 - 1 = 1,$$

$$df_{A \times B} = (a - 1)(b - 1) = (3 - 1)(2 - 1) = 2(1) = 2,$$

$$df_{S/AB} = ab(s - 1) = 3(2)(4 - 1) = 3(2)(3) = 18,$$

$$df_T = abs - 1 = 3(2)(4) - 1 = 24 - 1 = 23.$$

The mean squares are obtained by dividing each sum of squares by the appropriate df. Finally, each mean square reflecting the contribution of a different component of interest is tested against the mean square representing experimental error—i.e., the within-groups mean square ($MS_{S/AB}$). The observed F ratios are compared with the critical values of F listed in Table C-1. In this example, only the interaction source of variance reaches an acceptable level of significance.

Interpretation of Main Effects

In this example, clearly, we would be foolish to conclude that magnitude of reward and food deprivation were ineffective variables merely on the basis of the nonsignificant main effects. On the contrary, both independent variables influence learning, but their influence is masked by the presence of an $A \times B$ interaction. A significant interaction tells us that the variables do affect behavior, but only in combination with particular levels of another variable. In this experiment, the amount of reward does not produce differences in learning when the monkeys are hungry ($b_2 = 24$ hours), but it does produce an impressive effect when the animals are only slightly hungry ($b_1 = 1$ hour). We can restate this interaction in terms of the other independent variable. That is, drive is relatively ineffective when the animals are given 3 or 5 grapes (a_2 and a_3, respectively), but hungry animals show learning superior to that of less hungry animals when the reward is small ($a_1 = 1$ grape).

In general, the interpretation of any main effect depends upon the presence or absence of significant interaction effects. If there is no interaction, the outcome of the F tests involving the main effects can be interpreted without qualification. With an interaction, on the other hand, the meaning of these F tests must be interpreted with caution. We have already seen that the presence of an interaction and nonsignificant main effects does not mean that the independent variables are ineffective.

But what if the interaction is significant *and* we find one or even two significant main effects? The interpretation of these main effects will also be tempered by a consideration of the interaction; nevertheless, there might still be interest in the *main effects* as such. Consider the example presented in Fig. 10-2. On the left, the two curves do not cross within the limits of the factor A selected for the experiment. In spite of the interaction showing that the largest difference between b_1 and b_2 is found at a_2, it is also true that b_1 is *consistently* above b_2. This is an example of an *ordinal interaction*, where the relative ranking of the levels of factor B in this case does *not* change at the different levels of factor A. In this situation, it would be appropriate to conclude that in general the treatment represented by level b_1 results in performance that is higher than the treatment at level b_2. If we replot (on the right), with factor B on the baseline, we see what is called a *disordinal interaction*. In this view of the experiment, the rank order of the levels of factor A *changes* at the different levels of factor B. No general conclusion may be reached concerning the influence of factor A.

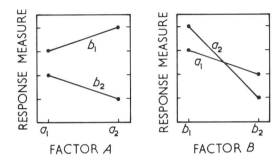

Fig. 10-2 Example of an ordinal interaction (left panel) and of a disordinal interaction (right panel).

The example shows that the ordinality of an interaction depends upon how the results are plotted. Thus, before significant main effects are interpreted and if there is an interaction present, it is wise to plot the data both ways (or to look at the values within the AB matrix both with regard to the rows and to the columns) to see whether or not ordinality exists. If it does, the main effect may be interpreted as a main effect. If it does not, the main effect cannot be interpreted independently of the interaction.

chapter eleven

COMPARISONS AMONG
THE MARGINAL MEANS
AND SIMPLE MAIN EFFECTS

In Part II we considered the varieties of analytical comparisons we might choose to make either in lieu of the omnibus F statistic (planned comparisons) or following a significant omnibus F (post-hoc comparisons). All of the procedures presented in the earlier chapters are applicable and easily adapted to factorial experiments. Since the basic ideas are the same, we need not pursue these procedures as deeply as we did in Chapters 6, 7, and 8.

One important difference between the single-factor experiment and factorial experiments is apparent, however. While an investigator may conduct a one-way analysis with no planned comparisons in mind, this seldom happens in a factorial experiment. That is, the design of a factorial experiment almost *implies* a set of planned orthogonal comparisons. We are referring, of course, to the extraction of sums of squares for the two main effects and the interaction. Relatively few factorial experiments are contemplated without these specific comparisons assumed. It is difficult to conceive of a situation in which a researcher would lump all of the *ab* treatment means in an omnibus F test when the experiment is a factorial. Moreover, we will generally not see researchers throwing the individual cell means into an undifferentiated pool and then forming all possible contrasts between pairs of means after the analysis of variance is completed. In a very real sense, a researcher who decides upon a factorial design to investigate a particular phenomenon knows a great deal about this phenomenon—at least enough to select the variables to include in the factorial design. He might still want to pursue additional analyses after the analysis of the factorial is completed, but these contrasts are more likely to be restricted to a small number of comparisons.

Previously, we drew a distinction between planned and post-hoc comparisons and discussed the construction and testing of different types of orthogonal comparisons. These comments are equally applicable to the analysis of factorial experiments. (You might find it useful to review relevant sections of Chapters 6 and 7 at various points in the present discussion.) Here, we will consider first comparisons involving the means representing the main effects of the two variables—i.e., the two sets of means in the margins of the AB matrix. For the remainder of the chapter and in Chapter 12 we will discuss analytical comparisons involving the means responsible for the interaction of the two variables—i.e., the individual cell means within the body of the matrix. As we have noted previously, a significant $A \times B$ interaction will influence our interpretation of main effects. By the same token, our additional comparisons will also be affected. That is, if the interaction is not significant, we will perform our post-hoc comparisons on the *marginal means* of the matrix. If the interaction *is* significant, we will dig within the body of the AB matrix and attempt to pinpoint the source (or sources) of the significant interaction.

COMPARISONS INVOLVING MARGINAL MEANS

The marginal means for any one variable are obtained by collapsing across, or in essence eliminating, the classification of the other variable. We have two sets of marginal means, one for each of the two independent variables. We can actually think of each set of means as coming from two single-factor experiments. Thus, we can conduct all of the planned and post-hoc comparisons on the row and column marginal means that we would have considered if the means did in fact come from single-factor studies. We have already noted that the reasoning behind the analytical comparisons performed on the marginal means and those conducted with a bona fide single-factor experiment is the same. We will look at these analyses and see how easily the formulas in Part II are modified to accommodate the marginal means from a factorial experiment. All that we have to do is to take account of the number of observations actually involved in the comparisons being made; this is the only change in the formulas.

The significance of comparisons is also evaluated by a within-groups mean square, which in the two-factor case is the $MS_{S/AB}$. At first glance, one might have thought that an estimate more analogous to the single-factor analysis would be one based upon subjects receiving the same level of factor A or factor B, forgetting about the B classification or the A classification, respectively. We can see that such a variance would not represent an estimate of "pure" experimental error, but the additional contribution of the other variable at each level of the variable of interest. Only the error term for the two-factor analysis provides the sort of estimate we need—one that assesses the *unsystematic* variability produced in our particular experiment.

Comparisons: General

In this section, we will be interested in comparisons between means that are based upon the row and column totals. As we have indicated, the only change in the formula for the sum of squares associated with a comparison is an adjustment for the number of observations represented in a given column mean or row mean. If we are interested in comparisons involving the $\bar{A}_i$ means, representing the main effect of factor A, we are combining the AB_{ij} cell sums in any given column of the matrix (see Table 10-1, p. 188). There are b sums (i.e., rows) in each column, and each cell sum is based on s observations. Hence, the number of observations is bs. The adaptation of Eq. (6-6) to the factorial case is given by

$$SS_{A_{comp.}} = \frac{[\sum (c_i)(A_i)]^2}{bs[\sum (c_i)^2]}, \tag{11-1a}$$

where the c_i terms are the coefficients representing the comparison being conducted, the A_i terms are the marginal sums, and bs is the number of observations. Look back at Eq. (6-6) on p. 98; the only change is the substitution of bs for s.

It is really not necessary to present the formula in terms of factor B also, since the identification of a particular as factor A or B in an actual experiment is purely arbitrary. We will consider corresponding formulas in these initial discussions, however, and omit them later on. If we are comparing $\bar{B}_j$ means, we will be summing the a cell sums in each row. In this case, there are a such sums (i.e., columns) in each row and s observations in each cell. Thus, the number of observations is as. The formula becomes

$$SS_{B_{comp.}} = \frac{[\sum (c_j)(B_j)]^2}{as[\sum (c_j)^2]}, \tag{11-1b}$$

where the c_j terms are the coefficients, the B_j terms are the marginal sums, and as is the number of observations.

After this point the procedure is identical to that outlined for the single-factor case. The F ratios for comparisons of either type are

$$F = \frac{MS_{A_{comp.}}}{MS_{S/AB}} \quad \text{and} \quad F = \frac{MS_{B_{comp.}}}{MS_{S/AB}}, \tag{11-2}$$

where the denominator is the estimate of error variance calculated for the two-factor analysis of variance—i.e., the pooled within-groups variance.[1] The df for the numerator and denominator for both F ratios are $df_{num.} = 1$ and $df_{denom.} = ab(s - 1)$.

NUMERICAL EXAMPLE   As an example, consider the data in Table 10-5 (p. 201) and suppose that we wanted to compare two means, $\bar{A}_1$ and $\bar{A}_3$ (1 grape versus 5 grapes). For this comparison, the coefficients would be $(1, 0, -1)$ for levels a_1, a_2, and a_3, respectively. For this comparison, then, we have the following:

	a_1	a_2	a_3
Coefficients (c_i):	1	0	-1
Marginal sums (A_i):	56	88	96

Substituting in Eq. (11-1a),

$$SS_{A_{comp.}} = \frac{[(1)(56) + (0)(88) + (-1)(96)]^2}{2(4)[(1)^2 + (0)^2 + (-1)^2]}$$

$$= \frac{(-40)^2}{8(2)} = \frac{1600}{16} = 100.00.$$

The mean square is

$$MS_{A_{comp.}} = \frac{100.00}{1} = 100.00.$$

The F ratio is found by using Eq. (11-2):

$$F = \frac{100.00}{18.33} = 5.46.$$

[The value for the $MS_{S/AB}$ (18.33) was taken from Table 10-6 (p. 203).] Since the critical value of $F(1, 18) = 4.41$ at $\alpha = .05$, the null hypothesis is rejected and we can conclude that the two means are different.

Orthogonal Comparisons

The construction of orthogonal comparisons follows the same rules as those discussed in Chapter 7 (see pp. 105–108). As was the case for the single-factor experiment, the number of orthogonal comparisons that can be constructed with the means for either factor A or factor B is dictated by the df for each

---

[1] The use of the $MS_{S/AB}$ as the error term assumes homogeneity of within-group variances. If this assumption is not met, the analysis becomes complicated (see Kirk, 1968, p. 74 and pp. 97–98). In this case, professional advice should be sought.

source of variance. In general,

$$SS_{\text{main effect}} = \sum SS_{\text{comp.}}, \tag{11-3}$$

where the summation includes a complete set of orthogonal comparisons.

Analysis of Trend

If either or both variables can be thought to represent points along a stimulus dimension, the respective main effects may be partitioned into orthogonal components of trend. The formulas and procedures discussed in Chapter 7 (pp. 113–132) are still appropriate. In general, we will be interested in this analysis only if the $A \times B$ interaction is *not* significant. If the interaction is significant, we might consider conducting a trend analysis on the individual *cell* means; we will consider such an analysis in the next chapter.

Multiple Comparisons

COMPARISONS BETWEEN PAIRS OF MEANS   The calculations necessary to assess comparisons between pairs of marginal means are identical to those enumerated in Chapter 8. The formulas for the critical ranges (CR), written in terms of factor A in a two-factor design, are simply

$$CR_{\text{N-K}} = q(r, df_{S/AB})\sqrt{bs(MS_{S/AB})}, \tag{11-4}$$

$$CR_{\text{D}} = q'(r, df_{S/AB})\sqrt{bs(MS_{S/AB})}, \tag{11-5}$$

$$CR_{\text{T}} = q(r_{\text{max}}, df_{S/AB})\sqrt{bs(MS_{S/AB})}, \tag{11-6}$$

and

$$CR_{\text{S}} = \sqrt{(a - 1)F(df_A, df_{S/AB})}\sqrt{2bs(MS_{S/AB})}. \tag{11-7}$$

If you refer back to Chapter 8, you can see that the only real change is in the use of bs instead of s. In all other respects, these post-hoc tests are conducted exactly as outlined in Chapter 8 (see pp. 140–144).

COMPLEX COMPARISONS BETWEEN MEANS   If we were interested in taking the most conservative point of view toward experimentwise error rate—i.e., protecting ourselves from making no more than $\alpha \times 100$ percent type I errors in any and all possible comparisons—then we would probably use the Scheffé test discussed in Chapter 8 (pp. 145–146). With this test, we calculate the mean squares for the comparisons of interest and form an F ratio as indicated in Eq. (11-2), evaluating the $MS_{A_{\text{comp.}}}$ against the $MS_{S/AB}$ from the factorial analysis. The final step is to evaluate the observed F against the value of F

corrected by Scheffé's method:

$$F_S = (a - 1)F(df_A, df_{S/AB}). \tag{11-8}$$

For the example in Table 10-6 (p. 203).

$$F_S = (3 - 1)F(2, 18) = 2(3.55) = 7.10, \text{ at } \alpha = .05.$$

SUMMARY   The selection of an appropriate multiple-comparison technique was discussed in detail in Chapter 8. Those comments are relevant to the present analyses. As indicated earlier in this section, individual comparisons between means are not found as frequently in factorial designs as they are in single-factor experiments. This statement applies even more strongly to post-hoc comparisons conducted on marginal means. The reason is that interpretation of differences in the marginal means must be cautious whenever a significant $A \times B$ interaction is present. Under these circumstances we are likely to be less interested in the main effects and to pay much more attention to subsequent analyses of the individual cell means in an attempt to isolate the particular treatment conditions that are responsible for the interaction.

COMPARISONS INVOLVING CELL MEANS

As with the omnibus F test in a single-factor design, a significant interaction in a two-factor design is not very informative by itself. The presence of an interaction merely indicates that the main effects of the two variables do not predict perfectly the individual cell means—that some variability among the cell means is not fully attributable to the two independent variables. While an interaction may take any number of forms, only a few of these will be "tolerable" to the researcher. Most investigators do not wish just for an interaction—any interaction—when they design a factorial experiment. They are expecting a *certain pattern* of results. In a real sense, many comparisons that they conduct involving the cell means represent an attempt to assess the veracity of their predictions. These analyses are actually planned comparisons and often are not orthogonal to other comparisons that have been made or will be made. Thus, it is difficult to draw a neat line between the planned-orthogonal comparisons and the often nonorthogonal, post-hoc comparisons. Each researcher has the responsibility to determine the specific sorts of comparisons he will conduct. If the pattern of the cell means comes out as he predicted, why should he be forced to treat any additional comparisons designed to point up these predictions as post-hoc and assess their significance with a less sensitive testing procedure? On the other hand, an indiscriminate search for tenable post-hoc comparisons should be held in check by a more stringent standard of rejection.

We next consider a useful analysis designed to isolate the sources of the interaction effect, a determination of the *simple main effects of the interaction*. Then, in Chapter 12, we will continue our discussion of analyses involving the cell means by considering the analysis of trend, interaction of comparisons, and multiple comparisons.

ANALYSIS OF SIMPLE MAIN EFFECTS

At times, our analysis of a significant interaction merely consists of an inspection of its pattern or form. If the expected outcome is obtained and the interaction is significant, our analysis may stop at this point. But at other times we will be interested in the significance of separate components of the interaction. Suppose we see that factor A has a particular effect at one level of factor B, say b_1, perhaps no effect at another level, b_2, and even a different outcome at a third level, b_3. It might be important to establish that certain differences would have been significant had a *single-factor* experiment been conducted at that level of factor B. That is, it may be critical theoretically to show that a *particular* outcome is significant, *in addition* to the question of whether or not the pattern is different for the variable at different levels of factor B.

	Learn B	
Test	Yes	No
Immediate	Group 1	Group 2
Delay	Group 3	Group 4

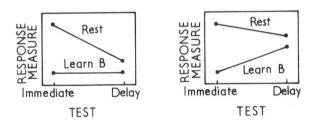

Fig. 11-1   Two possible outcomes (lower portion) of the same 2 × 2 factorial experiment (upper portion).

As an example, consider the following four groups:

Group 1: Learn A, Learn B,   Test A,
Group 2: Learn A, $-----$,   Test A,
Group 3: Learn A, Learn B, $-------------------$,   Test A,
Group 4: Learn A, $-------------------------$,   Test A.

All groups learn task A and are tested on task A subsequently. The difference between the first two groups is that group 1 learns task B before the test, while group 2 is given a rest activity instead (represented by the dashes). Groups 3 and 4 match groups 1 and 2, respectively, except for the delay of the final test.

This experiment, a 2 × 2 factorial, is diagramed in the upper half of Fig. 11-1. There are two independent variables: the presence or absence of a second task (task B) and the time of the test, after a short interval ("immediate") or delayed. There is reason to believe that group 1 will do more poorly on the test than will group 2; this outcome has been called *extinction*. Several theories postulate that extinguished material can "recover" with time. This would mean that groups 3 and 4 should show less of a difference on the test than groups 1 and 2—i.e., that extinction has dissipated. In terms of the 2 × 2, there should be an interaction of the two independent variables. However, certain theories also predict what is termed an *absolute* recovery, an actual *improvement* in performance by group 3 relative to group 1. To assess the significance of such a finding, we will need to analyze the simple main effects. Two possible outcomes of this experiment are presented in the bottom half of Fig. 11-1. Both graphs show an interaction, but only the one on the right shows absolute recovery.

In this example a test of the simple main effects is required by theory. Most of the time, however, we analyze simple main effects with the hope that additional information concerning the nature of the interaction may be revealed. We will consider a numerical example showing the usefulness of this analytical tool.

Numerical Example

The *AB* matrix of a 4 × 3 factorial experiment is presented in the upper portion of Table 11-1. In this example, factor *A* is manipulated at $a = 4$ levels, factor *B* at $b = 3$ levels, and there are $s = 3$ subjects in each treatment condition. The cell means have been plotted in Fig. 11-2. Inspection of the data indicates that factor *B* has produced a rather substantial effect, while the influence of factor *A* is masked in part by an $A \times B$ interaction. More specifically, it appears that factor *A* is relatively ineffective at levels b_1 and b_2 but shows a sizable effect at level b_3.

Substituting the data from Table 11-1 into the computational formulas for the basic quantities needed for the sums of squares, we obtain

$$[T] = \frac{(T)^2}{abs} = \frac{(276)^2}{4(3)(3)} = \frac{76{,}176}{36} = 2116.00,$$

$$[A] = \frac{\sum (A)^2}{bs} = \frac{(57)^2 + (71)^2 + (75)^2 + (73)^2}{3(3)} = \frac{19{,}244}{9} = 2138.22,$$

$$[B] = \frac{\sum (B)^2}{as} = \frac{(74)^2 + (88)^2 + (114)^2}{4(3)} = \frac{26{,}216}{12} = 2184.67,$$

TABLE 11-1   *Two-Factor Analysis of Variance*

AB MATRIX

Factor A

Factor B	a_1	a_2	a_3	a_4	Sum
b_1	18	20	17	19	74
b_2	21	21	24	22	88
b_3	18	30	34	32	114
Sum	57	71	75	73	276

$$\sum (ABS)^2 = 2291$$

SUMMARY OF THE ANALYSIS

Source	Calculations[a]	SS	df	MS	F
A	$2138.22 - 2116.00 =$	22.22	3	7.41	3.50*
B	$2184.67 - [T] =$	68.67	2	34.34	16.20**
$A \times B$	$2240.00 - [A] - [B] + [T] =$	33.11	6	5.52	2.60*
S/AB	$2291 - [AB] =$	51.00	24	2.12	
Total	$[ABS] - [T] =$	175.00	35		

* $p < .05$.
** $p < .01$.
[a] Bracketed letters represent complete terms in the computational formulas; a particular term is identified by the letter(s) appearing in the numerator.

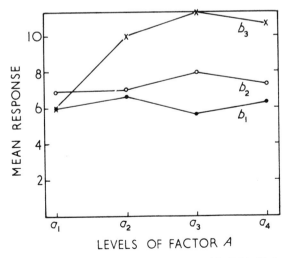

Fig. 11-2   Plot of data presented in Table 11-1.

$$[AB] = \frac{\sum (AB)^2}{s} = \frac{(18)^2 + (21)^2 + \cdots + (22)^2 + (32)^2}{3}$$

$$= \frac{6720}{3} = 2240.00,$$

$$[ABS] = \sum (ABS)^2 = 2291.$$

The completion of these calculations is given in the bottom half of Table 11-1. The F tests show that all three sources are significant. Of main concern, of course, is the interaction. We cannot interpret the results of the main effects without considering the contribution of the interaction. Would it be accurate to say that factor A, in general, exerts a significant effect on behavior? We would probably want to qualify this statement with the specification that this is true only at a particular level of factor B, namely, b_3. Similarly, but not as dramatically, factor B is apparently not effective at level a_1. An analysis of the simple main effects will allow a statistical assessment of these observations.

Simple Main Effects: Factor A

While we would usually calculate the simple main effects for only one of the independent variables, we will present an analysis of both sets for this example. Consider the simple main effects of factor A. A simple main effect of this factor at b_1, for example, represents the variability of the four cell means at levels a_1, a_2, a_3, and a_4 about the overall *marginal mean*, $\bar{B}_1$. Table 11-2 illustrates

TABLE 11-2 *Means Involved in the Simple Main Effects of Factor A*

Factor B	Factor A a_1	a_2	a_3	a_4	Marginal Mean	Effect
b_1	$\overline{AB}_{11}$	$\overline{AB}_{21}$	$\overline{AB}_{31}$	$\overline{AB}_{41}$	$\bar{B}_1$	$\longrightarrow A$ at b_1
b_2	$\overline{AB}_{12}$	$\overline{AB}_{22}$	$\overline{AB}_{32}$	$\overline{AB}_{42}$	$\bar{B}_2$	$\longrightarrow A$ at b_2
b_3	$\overline{AB}_{13}$	$\overline{AB}_{23}$	$\overline{AB}_{33}$	$\overline{AB}_{43}$	$\bar{B}_3$	$\longrightarrow A$ at b_3
Marginal Mean	$\bar{A}_1$	$\bar{A}_2$	$\bar{A}_3$	$\bar{A}_4$	T	$\longrightarrow A$ main effect

the nature of this source of variance. The sum of squares we are referring to involves the set of means at level b_1. Written in terms of deviation scores, the formula for this sum of squares is

$$SS_{A\,at\,b_1} = s(\overline{AB}_{11} - \bar{B}_1)^2 + s(\overline{AB}_{21} - \bar{B}_1)^2 + s(\overline{AB}_{31} - \bar{B}_1)^2 + s(\overline{AB}_{41} - \bar{B}_1)^2$$

$$= s \sum (\overline{AB}_{i1} - \bar{B}_1)^2.$$

If we write this formula in its computational form, we have

$$SS_{A \text{ at } b_1} = \left[\frac{(AB_{11})^2}{s} + \frac{(AB_{21})^2}{s} + \frac{(AB_{31})^2}{s} + \frac{(AB_{41})^2}{s} \right] - \frac{(B_1)^2}{as}$$

$$= \frac{\sum (AB_{i1})^2}{s} - \frac{(B_1)^2}{as}.$$

In a sense, then, we are conducting a single-factor analysis on the means within the box, obtaining the sum of squares due to factor A, with factor B fixed at level b_1.

In the last paragraph we were looking at level b_1. The means involved in the determination of the two remaining simple main effects are also indicated in Table 11-2. We will now write the general formula for the simple main effects of factor A. (General rules for the development of the formulas are presented in Chapter 15.) The computational formula for any level of factor B (level b_j) is given by[2]

$$SS_{A \text{ at } b_j} = \frac{\sum\limits_{i}^{a} (AB_{ij})^2}{s} - \frac{(B_j)^2}{as}. \tag{11-9}$$

The formulas are more easily understood when we see them "working" in an actual analysis. For the data in Table 11-1,

$$SS_{A \text{ at } b_1} = \frac{\sum (AB_{i1})^2}{s} - \frac{(B_1)^2}{as}$$

$$= \frac{(18)^2 + (20)^2 + (17)^2 + (19)^2}{3} - \frac{(74)^2}{4(3)},$$

$$SS_{A \text{ at } b_2} = \frac{\sum (AB_{i2})^2}{s} - \frac{(B_2)^2}{as}$$

$$= \frac{(21)^2 + (21)^2 + (24)^2 + (22)^2}{3} - \frac{(88)^2}{4(3)},$$

$$SS_{A \text{ at } b_3} = \frac{\sum (AB_{i3})^2}{s} - \frac{(B_3)^2}{as}$$

$$= \frac{(18)^2 + (30)^2 + (34)^2 + (32)^2}{3} - \frac{(114)^2}{4(3)}.$$

[2] Here the summation sign is adorned with notation, while in the last paragraph it was not; the reason is the need to specify that the summation is to be performed over the i subscript—i.e., over the levels of factor A. We are singling out only one set of AB_{ij} sums: those at level b_j. We did not have this problem in the last paragraph because the subset of quantities (the cell sums at level b_1, AB_{i1}) is unambiguously designated and the summation is taken over all of the cell totals in this subset.

(It should be noted that computational rule number 1 applies to these calculations; i.e., we use as a denominator the number of observations contained in any one of the numbers that we square.) The calculations are completed in Table 11-3.

It may not be evident, but each simple main effect contains *two* treatment effects: (1) a portion of the $A \times B$ interaction *and* (2) a portion of the *main effect* of factor A. That is, while the $SS_{A \times B}$ is independent of (i.e., orthogonal to) the SS_A, the simple main effects of factor A are not. What this means, then, is that a significant simple main effect does *not* represent significant interaction effects at that particular level of the other independent variable but, rather, the variability of the interaction and main effects combined. We may see this by summing the complete set of simple main effects and finding that

$$\sum SS_{A \text{ at } b_j} = SS_{A \times B} + SS_A. \tag{11-10}$$

In words, the sum of the simple main effects of factor A equals the total of the sums of squares associated with factor A and the $A \times B$ interaction. What Eq. (11-10) tells us is that an analysis of simple main effects is *not* a breakdown of the $SS_{A \times B}$ into a complete set of orthogonal comparisons.[3]

TABLE 11-3 *Analysis of the Simple Main Effects of Factor A (Data from Table 11-1)*

Source	Calculations	SS	df	MS	F
A at b_1	$458.00 - 456.33 =$	1.67	3	.56	<1
A at b_2	$647.33 - 645.33 =$	2.00	3	.67	<1
A at b_3	$1134.67 - 1083.00 =$	51.67	3	17.22	8.12*
S/AB			24	2.12	

*$p < .01$.

One useful application of Eq. (11-10) is to provide a check for our arithmetic. That is, if the sum of the simple main effects does not equal the sum of the $SS_{A \times B}$ and the SS_A, then we know that we have made an error in our calculations. Applying Eq. (11-10) to the present example,

$$1.67 + 2.00 + 51.67 \overset{?}{=} 33.11 + 22.22$$

$$55.34 \approx 55.33.$$

The remainder of the analysis is summarized in Table 11-3. The df for each simple main effect equals one less than the number of cell sums; i.e.,

$$df_{A \text{ at } b_j} = a - 1.$$

[3] Marascuilo and Levin (1970) make this point quite clearly and offer a procedure by which the significance of interaction effects alone may be evaluated.

The sum of these df's also equals the sum of the df associated with the $SS_{A \times B}$ and SS_A. Specifically,

$$\sum df_{A \text{ at } b_j} = b(a - 1) = ab - b$$

and

$$df_{A \times B} + df_A = (a - 1)(b - 1) + (a - 1)$$
$$= ab - a - b + 1 + a - 1$$
$$= ab - b.$$

The mean sums of squares are obtained by dividing each sum of squares by the appropriate df. The error term for each of these mean squares is the within-groups mean square from the original analysis, $MS_{S/AB}$. That is,

$$F = \frac{MS_{A \text{ at } b_j}}{MS_{S/AB}},$$

unless there is heterogeneity of within-group variances. If heterogeneity is present, one solution is to use an error term which is based on the within-group variability of only those observations involved in the calculation of that particular simple main effect, rather than one which pools all observations in the experiment. In this case, then,

$$F = \frac{MS_{A \text{ at } b_j}}{MS_{S/AB \text{ at } b_j}}.$$

[See Winer for a related procedure (1962, pp. 240–241; 1971, p. 444).]

We will assume homogeneity in our example. The resultant F's listed in Table 11-3 substantiate statistically what we observed in our earlier perusal of Fig. 11-2, namely, that factor A is effective only at level b_3 and that the significant main effect was entirely the result of the variation represented in this particular row of Table 11-1.

Simple Main Effects: Factor B

An analogous analysis can be conducted on the simple main effects of factor B—i.e., the effect of the B manipulations at the different levels of factor A. The means entering into the calculations of these effects are specified in Table 11-4. Consider the simple main effects of factor B at a_1. In this case, we are interested in the deviation of the cell means in the column at a_1 $(\overline{AB}_{1j})$ from the marginal mean $(\overline{A}_1)$. These deviations consist of

$$(\overline{AB}_{11} - \overline{A}_1), \quad (\overline{AB}_{12} - \overline{A}_1), \quad \text{and} \quad (\overline{AB}_{13} - \overline{A}_1).$$

The means contributing to the simple main effects at levels a_2, a_3, and a_4

TABLE 11-4   *Means Involved in the Simple Main Effects of Factor B*

Factor A

Factor B	a_1	a_2	a_3	a_4	Marginal Mean
b_1	$\overline{AB}_{11}$	$\overline{AB}_{21}$	$\overline{AB}_{31}$	$\overline{AB}_{41}$	$\overline{B}_1$
b_2	$\overline{AB}_{12}$	$\overline{AB}_{22}$	$\overline{AB}_{32}$	$\overline{AB}_{42}$	$\overline{B}_2$
b_3	$\overline{AB}_{13}$	$\overline{AB}_{23}$	$\overline{AB}_{33}$	$\overline{AB}_{43}$	$\overline{B}_3$
Sum	$\overline{A}_1$	$\overline{A}_2$	$\overline{A}_3$	$\overline{A}_4$	$\overline{T}$
Marginal Mean	B at a_1	B at a_2	B at a_3	B at a_4	B main effect

are also indicated in the table. The means in the final column are used to calculate the main effect of factor B. The deviation scores at level a_i are

$$(\overline{AB}_{i1} - \overline{A}_i), \quad (\overline{AB}_{i2} - \overline{A}_i), \quad \text{and} \quad (\overline{AB}_{i3} - \overline{A}_i).$$

The computational formula for the simple main effect of factor B at a_1 becomes

$$SS_{B\,at\,a_1} = \frac{\sum (AB_{1j})^2}{s} - \frac{(A_1)^2}{bs},$$

and the general formula at a_i is given by

$$SS_{B\,at\,a_i} = \frac{\sum_{j}^{b} (AB_{ij})^2}{s} - \frac{(A_i)^2}{bs}. \qquad (11\text{-}11)$$

The calculations are illustrated with the data from Table 11-1:

$$SS_{B\,at\,a_1} = \frac{\sum (AB_{1j})^2}{s} - \frac{(A_1)^2}{bs}$$

$$= \frac{(18)^2 + (21)^2 + (18)^2}{3} - \frac{(57)^2}{3(3)},$$

$$SS_{B\,at\,a_2} = \frac{\sum (AB_{2j})^2}{s} - \frac{(A_2)^2}{bs}$$

$$= \frac{(20)^2 + (21)^2 + (30)^2}{3} - \frac{(71)^2}{3(3)},$$

$$SS_{B \, at \, a_3} = \frac{\sum (AB_{3j})^2}{s} - \frac{(A_3)^2}{bs}$$

$$= \frac{(17)^2 + (24)^2 + (34)^2}{3} - \frac{(75)^2}{3(3)},$$

$$SS_{B \, at \, a_4} = \frac{\sum (AB_{4j})^2}{s} - \frac{(A_4)^2}{bs}$$

$$= \frac{(19)^2 + (22)^2 + (32)^2}{3} - \frac{(73)^2}{3(3)}.$$

The sums of squares for these simple main effects are presented in Table 11-5.

TABLE 11-5 *Analysis of the Simple Main Effects of Factor B*
(Data from Table 11-1)

Source	Calculations	SS	df	MS	F
B at a_1	363.00 − 361.00 =	2.00	2	1.00	<1
B at a_2	580.33 − 560.11 =	20.22	2	10.11	4.77*
B at a_3	673.67 − 625.00 =	48.67	2	24.34	11.48**
B at a_4	623.00 − 592.11 =	30.89	2	15.44	7.28**
S/AB			24	2.12	

* $p < .05$.
** $p < .01$.

As a computational check, we can adapt Eq. (11-10) for use with the simple main effects of factor B:

$$\sum SS_{B \, at \, a_i} = SS_{A \times B} + SS_B,$$

$$2.00 + 20.22 + 48.67 + 30.89 \overset{?}{=} 33.11 + 68.67$$

$$101.78 = 101.78.$$

The df for any one of these simple main effects is one less than the number of cell means:

$$df_{B \, at \, a_i} = b - 1.$$

The F ratios are formed by the same rules given in the previous discussion:

$$F = \frac{MS_{B \, at \, a_i}}{MS_{S/AB}},$$

unless there is heterogeneity of variance. The results of the F tests are presented in the last column of Table 11-5. They show that there is a significant effect of factor B at all levels of factor A except a_1.

Summary

These analyses are relatively simple to compute and provide a means by which we can identify the sources of a significant interaction. Experimenters are willing to accept the fact that the simple main effects are not orthogonal to the comparisons conducted in the standard analysis of variance. Moreover, it is common practice to evaluate the F's at a per comparison rate (α) rather than be concerned with the experimentwise error rate. It is true that there may be a greater frequency of type I errors by virtue of the increased number of comparisons being conducted, but this is a small price to pay for the possibility of isolating important sources of variance. At this point the researcher's concern for understanding the meaning of his data takes precedence over his concern for an increased frequency of type I errors. Moreover, we have already obtained evidence that there is *some* variability present among the different means that cannot reasonably be attributed to error variance. Under these circumstances, we would want to protect ourselves *more* against committing *type II* errors.

chapter twelve

ADDITIONAL COMPARISONS INVOLVING CELL MEANS: ANALYSIS OF TREND, INTERACTION OF COMPARISONS, AND MULTIPLE COMPARISONS

In the last chapter we discussed an analysis conducted on the cell means—the analysis of simple main effects. In this chapter we will consider additional comparisons conducted on the cell means: analysis of trend, interaction of comparisons, and multiple comparisons. All of these procedures share the same purpose of shedding light on the factor or factors responsible for a significant interaction.

ANALYSIS OF TREND

When the levels of one (or both) of the variables of the factorial represent points along a quantitative dimension or scale, it may be of interest to extract information concerning trend components contributing to the main effect of that variable. The analysis of orthogonal components of trend for a main effect is essentially the same as that presented for the single-factor design. The only difference is an adjustment for the number of observations. If the $A \times B$ interaction is significant, however, we will want to interpret any analysis of the main effect with caution and pay considerable attention to the specific form that the interaction takes. We saw in Chapter 11 that a useful method of analysis is to assess the simple main effects. In the case where one of the variables is amenable to a trend analysis, it may be more meaningful or revealing to partition the interaction into *independent trend components*. What we will obtain from such an analysis is an assessment of the degree to which the $A \times B$ interaction is localized in the linear component, the quadratic component, and so on.

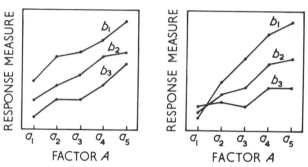

Fig. 12-1   Example of the presence (right panel) and the absence (left panel) of an $A_{\text{linear}} \times B$ interaction.

Suppose we performed a 5×3 factorial experiment where the $a = 5$ levels are equally spaced on some quantitative scale. Two possible outcomes of this experiment are presented in Fig. 12-1. If we consider the functions at each level of factor B, they are all primarily linear in shape; i.e., a straight line drawn through each set of five means would provide a relatively accurate description of the data. The graph on the left depicts a case where the slopes of the three curves at b_1, b_2, and b_3 are approximately equal; hence, a linear component of the interaction does *not* appear to be present. In contrast, the graph on the right represents an interaction which is almost entirely located in the linear component. That is, straight lines drawn through the means at b_1, b_2, and b_3, which accurately describe the three functions, have different slopes.

To say that the linear component of the interaction is significant, then, is to indicate that the particular linear function for factor A is not the same for the different levels of factor B. Said another way, it means that the overall linear component based on the *marginal means* $(\overline{A}_i)$ is not representative of the individual linear components based on the *cell means* $(\overline{AB}_{ij})$. In essence, we are comparing the slopes of idealized linear functions (represented by the linear coefficients) drawn through the cell means at different levels of factor B. If we find that the $SS_{A \times B}$ is due largely to the interaction of the linear functions—i.e., to the differences in slope—we will have pinpointed the source of the interaction to a particular mathematical component of the function relating variations in the independent variable (factor A in this case) to the behavior under study. A significant quadratic component of the interaction has a similar meaning: idealized quadratic functions drawn through the cell means at the different levels of factor B have different curvatures. Whether anything can be made out of these sorts of findings, of course, depends upon the particular area of research and the creativity of the investigator.

We will discuss a situation in which factor A is the one being subjected to a trend analysis, but you should find no difficulty in translating the manipulations to factor B, since the designation of variables is arbitrary. When both factors are quantitative, we can conduct an analysis of trend on both of them. This poses no problem if we are interested only in the analysis of the two main effects, as would be the case when the interaction is not significant. If it is, however, the breakdown of the *interaction* sum of squares can be quite complicated.[1]

Numerical Example

Suppose we are studying the effects of switching from a serial list of words that has just been learned to a second list made up of pairs of words taken from the serial list. One independent variable (factor A) consists of a variation in the number of training trials on the serial list (3, 6, 9, and 12 trials). The other independent variable (factor B) consists of two types of transfer lists—$b_1 = $ a list containing pairs of words which preserve the original serial order of consecutive words and $b_2 = $ a list containing pairs of words which do not preserve the serial order. [If we represent the serial list itself as A–B–C–D, pairs in the second list which preserve serial order (b_1) will look like A–B and C–D, for example, while pairs in the second list which do not preserve serial order (b_2), might look like B–D and C–A.]

There is a theory of serial learning which states that during the initial phases of learning, subjects will be forming associations between contiguous words in the serial list, such as A–B, B–C, C–D, and so on. Transfer to the list preserving these contiguous associations (b_1) should be positive, while transfer to the list scrambling these associations (b_2) should be negative. Increasing the amount

---

[1] It is possible to isolate variability due to the interaction of a trend component for one quantitative variable with the same or different trend component for another quantitative variable. The range of applications of such an analysis at present is quite limited in behavioral research. Not only is it difficult to visualize these interactions (such as an interaction of the linear component of factor A with the quadratic or cubic component of factor B), but few theories in psychology are sufficiently precise to *predict* these interactions or even to be able to *assimilate* them when they are unearthed. For these reasons, then, we will not discuss this particular analysis (although see footnote 2, p. 243). Numerical examples are found in a number of places, however: e.g., Kirk (1968, pp. 191–198), Myers (1966, pp. 357–369) and Winer (1962, pp. 273–278; 1971, pp. 478–484). If you are curious as to what these interactions look like, Kirk (p. 191) and Winer (1962, p. 278; 1971, p. 484) show them by means of a three-dimensional plot and Myers (p. 359) illustrates an interaction by plotting actual regression coefficients.

of training on the serial list (factor A) should increase both these positive and negative effects. The theory also maintains that at higher degrees of serial learning contiguous associations are discarded in favor of a serial organization or structure (Youssef, 1967). Thus, it is predicted that the positive and negative transfer will later decrease as the serial list becomes overlearned.

In short, the design is a 4×2 factorial experiment. Since we have equal steps on the stimulus scale for factor A (differences of 3 trials), we can use the table of coefficients for orthogonal polynomials, Table C-2 of Appendix C. We know, however, that equal spacing of the levels is not a requirement of the analysis, as we can construct our own coefficients. (See Appendix B for a specification of these procedures.)

The results of this experiment are summarized in the upper portion of Table 12-1. For this example, the number of subjects in each of the individual cells is $s = 5$. (The response measure is the number of correct responses on the first transfer trial.) In order to show the outcome of the experiment more clearly, the cell means have been plotted in Fig. 12-2. An inspection of this

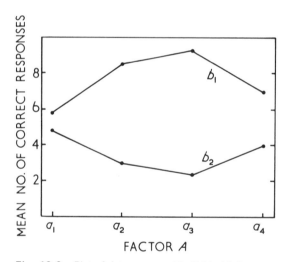

Fig. 12-2   Plot of data presented in Table 12-1.

figure reveals a relatively large effect due to factor B—there is a large difference between the two transfer lists—and there is an interaction of the two independent variables. The form of the interaction is such as to support the theory we mentioned: that the function relating factor A (the number of training trials) to transfer performance is curvilinear, but that the functions run in opposite directions at the two levels of factor B. More specifically, performance first increases and then decreases at b_1 (the list maintaining contiguous associations), while it initially decreases and then increases at b_2 (the list scrambling contiguous associations).

TABLE 12-1 *Two-Factor Analysis of Variance*

AB MATRIX

	a_1	a_2	a_3	a_4	Sum
b_1	29	42	46	35	152
b_2	24	15	12	20	71
Sum	53	57	58	55	223

$$\sum (ABS)^2 = 1613$$

SUMMARY OF THE ANALYSIS

Source	Calculations[a]	SS	df	MS	F
A	$1244.700 - 1243.225 =$	1.475	3	.492	<1
B	$1407.250 - [T] =$	164.025	1	164.025	33.90**
$A \times B$	$1458.200 - [A] - [B] + [T] =$	49.475	3	16.492	3.41*
S/AB	$1613 - [AB] =$	154.800	32	4.838	
Total	$[ABS] - [T] =$	369.775	39		

* $p < .05$.
** $p < .01$.
[a] Bracketed letters represent complete terms in the computational formulas; a particular term is identified by the letter(s) appearing in the numerator.

Analysis of the Factorial

Before assessing these trends, we will perform the usual analysis of variance. (Since we made specific predictions concerning the *form* of the interaction, we could have proceeded directly to the trend analysis.) From the formulas for the basic terms in Table 10-3, we find

$$[T] = \frac{(T)^2}{abs} = \frac{(223)^2}{4(2)(5)} = \frac{49,729}{40} = 1243.225,$$

$$[A] = \frac{\sum (A)^2}{bs} = \frac{(53)^2 + (57)^2 + (58)^2 + (55)^2}{2(5)} = \frac{12,447}{10} = 1244.700,$$

$$[B] = \frac{\sum (B)^2}{as} = \frac{(152)^2 + (71)^2}{4(5)} = \frac{28,145}{20} = 1407.250,$$

$$[AB] = \frac{\sum (AB)^2}{s} = \frac{(29)^2 + (24)^2 + \cdots + (35)^2 + (20)^2}{5} = \frac{7291}{5} = 1458.200,$$

and

$$[ABS] = \sum (ABS)^2 = 1613.$$

The analysis is completed in the bottom half of Table 12-1. Since the $A \times B$ interaction is significant, the significance or nonsignificance of the two main effects is not of cardinal importance, although it is true that the list with contiguous pairs is consistently better than the list with scrambled pairs. [This is an example of an *ordinal* interaction (see pp. 204–205).] We can see from Fig. 12-2 that the lack of a main effect of factor A is due to the compensating effects of the variable at the two levels of factor B. Similarly, we would not want to conclude that the effect of factor B is best indexed by the two marginal means. We see instead that the size of the difference between b_1 and b_2 varies depending upon the particular level of factor A we consider.

Trend Analysis

BASIC CALCULATIONS   We will depart from our usual procedure of presenting formulas before calculations. Instead, we will consider first the calculation of some basic ingredients needed for the analysis. These are most easily performed as a series of steps.

First, we arrange the AB matrix in a convenient form, as indicated in the upper portion of Table 12-2. Second, we list the sets of coefficients of the orthogonal polynomials, which have been obtained in Table C-2. The coefficients are presented in the middle portion of the table. (Since our interest is in the quadratic component of the interaction, we could have focused on this component alone. For the sake of completeness, however, we will extract all three of the trend components.) Finally, we multiply each coefficient times corresponding sums in the AB matrix and enter the product in a specialized AB *trend matrix*. Trend matrices for the linear, quadratic, and cubic components are presented separately in the bottom portion of the table.

Consider the AB matrix for the linear component. The entries in the first row are obtained by multiplying each AB sum at b_1 (AB_{i1}) by corresponding linear coefficients (c_{1i}). That is,

$$(c_{11})(AB_{11}) = (-3)(29) = -87,$$
$$(c_{12})(AB_{21}) = (-1)(42) = -42,$$
$$(c_{13})(AB_{31}) = (1)(46) = 46,$$
$$(c_{14})(AB_{41}) = (3)(35) = 105.$$

The entries in the second row are obtained by multiplying the linear coefficients times corresponding AB sums at b_2 (AB_{i2}). The final row in the specialized matrix contains column marginal totals—entries that may be obtained by summing the two products in each column. For example,

$$(c_{11})(A_1) = (c_{11})(AB_{11}) + (c_{11})(AB_{12}) = (-87) + (-72) = -159.$$

Alternatively, they may be calculated directly by substituting in $(c_{1i})(A_i)$; thus,

$$(c_{11})(A_1) = (-3)(53) = -159,$$
$$(c_{12})(A_2) = (-1)(57) = -57,$$
$$(c_{13})(A_3) = (1)(58) = 58,$$
$$(c_{14})(A_4) = (3)(55) = 165.$$

It is usually a good idea to calculate these products both by summing and by direct calculation, since computational errors are quite easy to commit in this analysis. The entries in the remaining two AB trend matrices are obtained in the same way, but using the appropriate sets of coefficients.

TABLE 12-2 *Trend Analysis: Basic Calculations*

AB MATRIX

Levels of	Levels of Factor A			
Factor B	a_1	a_2	a_3	a_4
b_1:	29	42	46	35
b_2:	24	15	12	20
Sum (A_i):	53	57	58	55

COEFFICIENTS

	a_1	a_2	a_3	a_4	$\sum (c_i)^2$
Linear (c_{1i}):	-3	-1	1	3	20
Quadratic (c_{2i}):	1	-1	-1	1	4
Cubic (c_{3i}):	-1	3	-3	1	20

AB TREND MATRICES

	a_1	a_2	a_3	a_4	Sum
	LINEAR TREND				
Level b_1—$(c_{1i})(AB_{i1})$:	-87	-42	46	105	22
Level b_2—$(c_{1i})(AB_{i2})$:	-72	-15	12	60	-15
$(c_{1i})(A_i)$:	-159	-57	58	165	7
	QUADRATIC TREND				
Level b_1—$(c_{2i})(AB_{i1})$:	29	-42	-46	35	-24
Level b_2—$(c_{2i})(AB_{i2})$:	24	-15	-12	20	17
$(c_{2i})(A_i)$:	53	-57	-58	55	-7
	CUBIC TREND				
Level b_1—$(c_{3i})(AB_{i1})$:	-29	126	-138	35	-6
Level b_2—$(c_{3i})(AB_{i2})$:	-24	45	-36	20	5
$(c_{3i})(A_i)$:	-53	171	-174	55	-1

MAIN EFFECT OF FACTOR A We can now proceed with the analysis. Even though our interest lies in the interaction trend components, we must still calculate the trend components for the main effect of factor A. To calculate the orthogonal trend components of the A main effect, we simply substitute values from the AB trend matrices (bottom portion of Table 12-2) in the general formula for a comparison, Eq. (11-1a):

$$SS_{A_{comp.}} = \frac{[\sum (c_i)(A_i)]^2}{bs[\sum (c_i)^2]}.$$

For the linear component,

$$SS_{A_{linear}} = \frac{[\sum (c_{1i})(A_i)]^2}{bs[\sum (c_{1i})^2]},$$

where the c_{1i} terms are the linear coefficients, the A_i terms are the marginal sums at each level of factor A, and bs is the number of observations contributing to each treatment sum. The formulas for the other components are identical, except for the substitution of corresponding sets of coefficients (c_{2i} for the quadratic component and c_{3i} for the cubic component).

We have already calculated these basic quantities and entered them in Table 12-2. The numerator terms are the grand sums for each AB trend matrix:

$$\sum (c_{1i})(A_i) = 7, \qquad \sum (c_{2i})(A_i) = -7, \qquad \sum (c_{3i})(A_i) = -1.$$

The quantity $\sum (c_i)^2$ is found in the middle portion of the table. Substituting in the formula, then,

$$SS_{A_{linear}} = \frac{[\sum (c_{1i})(A_i)]^2}{bs[\sum (c_{1i})^2]} = \frac{(7)^2}{2(5)(20)} = \frac{49}{200},$$

$$SS_{A_{quadratic}} = \frac{[\sum (c_{2i})(A_i)]^2}{bs[\sum (c_{2i})^2]} = \frac{(-7)^2}{2(5)(4)} = \frac{49}{40},$$

$$SS_{A_{cubic}} = \frac{[\sum (c_{3i})(A_i)]^2}{bs[\sum (c_{3i})^2]} = \frac{(-1)^2}{2(5)(20)} = \frac{1}{200}.$$

The results of these calculations are entered in Table 12-3. Note that the sum of these trend components equals the main effect of factor A:

$$\sum SS_{A_{comp.}} = .245 + 1.225 + .005 = 1.475 = SS_A.$$

As we saw in Chapter 6, each of these comparisons is associated with a single df. The F ratio for these comparisons is specified in Eq. (11-2):

$$F = \frac{MS_{A_{comp.}}}{MS_{S/AB}}.$$

These calculations are enumerated in the table. None of these sources of variance is significant.

$A \times B$ INTERACTION   The extraction of the orthogonal trend components of the $A \times B$ interaction follows directly from an intuitive description of their meaning. One definition of an interaction, we recall, is that it consists of the variation among cell means remaining after we have subtracted any variation due to the two main effects. The interaction trend component also represents residual variation. That is, a *trend component* of the interaction consists of the variability among the individual trend components at the different levels of factor B remaining *after* we have subtracted the variability due to the trend component of the main effect. In symbols,

$$SS_{A_{comp.} \times B} = \frac{\sum\limits_{j}^{b}\left[\sum\limits_{i}^{a}(c_i)(AB_{ij})\right]^2}{s\left[\sum(c_i)^2\right]} - SS_{A_{comp.}}. \qquad (12\text{-}1)$$

The first term on the right of the equation is the sum of the individual trend components at each level of factor B. This quantity contains trend components for the $A \times B$ interaction *and* the main effect of factor A as well. Thus, we obtain the trend component for the interaction by subtracting from this sum of squares the component main effect. (General rules for the development of the formulas are presented in Chapter 15.)

TABLE 12-3   *Summary of the Trend Analysis*

Source	Calculations	SS	df	MS	F
A:	=	(1.475)	(3)		
Linear	=	.245	1	.245	<1
Quadratic	=	1.225	1	1.225	<1
Cubic	=	.005	1	.005	<1
B:	=	164.025	1	164.025	33.90*
$A \times B$:	=	(49.475)	(3)		
Linear	7.090 − .245 =	6.845	1	6.845	1.41
Quadratic	43.250 − 1.225 =	42.025	1	42.025	8.69*
Cubic	.610 − .005 =	.605	1	.605	<1
S/AB	=	154.800	32	4.838	
Total	=	369.775	39		

* $p < .01$.

Let us see how these formulas work out in our example. Again, we have already performed the basic calculations specified in Eq. (12-1). That is, we can obtain the quantity

$$\sum_{i}^{a}(c_i)(AB_{ij})$$

from the marginal sums in Table 12-2, and the $SS_{A_{comp.}}$ has been computed and entered in Table 12-3. Substituting in Eq. (12-1),

$$SS_{A_{comp.} \times B} = \frac{\sum\limits_{j}^{b}\left[\sum\limits_{i}^{a}(c_i)(AB_{ij})\right]^2}{s\left[\sum(c_i)^2\right]} - SS_{A_{comp.}},$$

we have

$$SS_{A_{linear} \times B} = \frac{(22)^2 + (-15)^2}{5(20)} - .245 = \frac{709}{100} - .245,$$

$$SS_{A_{quadratic} \times B} = \frac{(-24)^2 + (17)^2}{5(4)} - 1.225 = \frac{865}{20} - 1.225,$$

$$SS_{A_{cubic} \times B} = \frac{(-6)^2 + (5)^2}{5(20)} - .005 = \frac{61}{100} - .005.$$

The results of these calculations are entered in Table 12-3. As a computational check, we should see whether the sum of these trend components equals the $SS_{A \times B}$. That is,

$$\sum SS_{A_{comp.} \times B} = 6.845 + 42.025 + .605 = 49.475 = SS_{A \times B}.$$

The df for each component source of variance is given by

$$df_{A_{comp.} \times B} = b - 1. \tag{12-2}$$

To understand how we arrived at Eq. (12-2), consider the formula giving the df for an interaction:

$$df_{A \times B} = (df_A)(df_B) = (a - 1)(b - 1).$$

This formula can be modified to show the df associated with a trend component of the interaction:

$$df_{A_{comp.} \times B} = (df_{A_{comp.}})(df_B) = 1(b - 1) = b - 1.$$

For the present example,

$$df_{A_{comp.} \times B} = 2 - 1 = 1.$$

The F tests are conducted by using Eq. (11-2):

$$F = \frac{MS_{A_{comp.} \times B}}{MS_{S/AB}}.$$

These tests are summarized in Table 12-3. The results of this analysis confirm our earlier observations that the $A \times B$ interaction is due largely to the divergent quadratic trends. We can quantify this conclusion by calculating the percentage of the $SS_{A \times B}$ "accounted for" by the quadratic component.

In this case, we can say that

$$\frac{42.025}{49.475} \times 100 = 84.9 \text{ percent}$$

of the interaction sum of squares is produced by the interaction of the two quadratic trends for levels b_1 and b_2.

Trend Analysis of Simple Main Effects

It is possible to partition simple main effects into orthogonal trend components. Consider the example we have just analyzed, where we discovered that there is a significant quadratic component of the $A \times B$ interaction. Perhaps we would like to determine whether the curvilinear trend at b_1 is significant by itself or whether the trend at b_2 is significant by itself. The analysis is essentially a combination of the trend analysis and an analysis of simple main effects.

Briefly, what we will be doing is to calculate the sum of squares for the quadratic component at b_1 and at b_2 and to evaluate them separately. As in the analysis of the simple main effects, we can act as if our calculations were being performed on two single-factor experiments, one at b_1 and one at b_2. That is, we will isolate a row of sums at b_1, for example, and compute the quadratic trend component for those sums. We have the following "single-factor" experiment at b_1:

	a_1	a_2	a_3	a_4
b_1:	AB_{11}	AB_{21}	AB_{31}	AB_{41}

and we simply calculate the sum of squares associated with the quadratic component on these sums. In symbols,

$$SS_{A_{\text{quadratic at } b_1}} = \frac{[(c_{21})(AB_{11}) + (c_{22})(AB_{21}) + (c_{23})(AB_{31}) + (c_{24})(AB_{41})]^2}{s[\sum (c_{2i})^2]}$$

$$= \frac{[\sum (c_{2i})(AB_{i1})]^2}{s[\sum (c_{2i})^2]}.$$

For the general case,

$$SS_{A_{\text{comp. at } b_j}} = \frac{\left[\sum_{i}^{a} (c_i)(AB_{ij})\right]^2}{s[\sum (c_i)^2]}. \tag{12-3}$$

We calculated all of the quantities we need in the previous analysis (Table 12-2). The main ingredient,

$$\sum_{i}^{a} (c_{2i})(AB_{ij}),$$

is found in the AB matrix for the quadratic trend. Substituting in Eq. (12-3), we have

$$SS_{A\text{quadratic at }b_1} = \frac{[\sum (c_{2i})(AB_{i1})]^2}{s[\sum (c_{2i})^2]} = \frac{(-24)^2}{5(4)} = \frac{576}{20}$$

$$= 28.800,$$

$$SS_{A\text{quadratic at }b_2} = \frac{[\sum (c_{2i})(AB_{i2})]^2}{s[\sum (c_{2i})^2]} = \frac{(17)^2}{5(4)} = \frac{289}{20}$$

$$= 14.450.$$

In the last chapter, we saw that for simple main effects

$$\sum SS_{A\text{ at }b_j} = SS_{A \times B} + SS_A.$$

This relationship can be extended to the present analysis:

$$\sum SS_{A\text{quadratic at }b_j} = SS_{A\text{quadratic} \times B} + SS_{A\text{quadratic}},$$

$$28.800 + 14.450 \stackrel{?}{=} 42.025 + 1.225,$$

$$43.250 = 43.250.$$

The df associated with each component simple main effect are given by

$$df_{A\text{comp. at }b_j} = df_{A\text{comp.}} = 1.$$

The two F ratios become

$$F = \frac{MS_{A\text{quadratic at }b_1}}{MS_{S/AB}} = \frac{28.800/1}{4.838} = \frac{28.800}{4.838} = 5.95$$

and

$$F = \frac{MS_{A\text{quadratic at }b_2}}{MS_{S/AB}} = \frac{14.450/1}{4.838} = \frac{14.450}{4.838} = 2.99.$$

These F's are evaluated at $df_{\text{num.}} = 1$ and $df_{\text{denom.}} = 32$; at $\alpha = .05$, $F(1, 32) \approx 4.17$. Thus, the curvilinear trend with the material retaining some semblance of the serial order is significant, while the reverse trend with the material consisting of scrambled pairs is not.

INTERACTION OF COMPARISONS BETWEEN MEANS

The $A_{comp.} \times B$ Interaction

The analysis of the trend components of the $A \times B$ interaction is actually a special case of the more general situation in which the $SS_{A \times B}$ is broken down into a set of comparisons. The analysis is important enough to warrant an additional example, this time with comparisons which involve a *qualitative* variable—unlike the comparisons of the last section, which involved a quantitative variable. In the most common analysis we will see of this type, comparisons involving one of the independent factors (factor A, say) are extended to the $A \times B$ interaction. More specifically, we will be asking whether or not a particular comparison involving the factor A treatments *changes* at the different levels of factor B.

We will return to the experiment we considered in Chapter 6, where five different methods of presenting a list of words were compared in a learning experiment. The words were presented either one at a time on a memory drum or all at once on a sheet of paper; under the former mode, the words might be presented at a 1-second or a 3-second rate; under the latter, they might be presented in a column or scrambled over the sheet of paper. For each of these four groups, the order of the words was varied on successive study trials. A final group received the words on a memory drum at a 3-second rate, but in the same order on each study trial. These five methods of presentation constitute factor A and are enumerated in the upper portion of Table 12-4. A second independent variable is introduced in this example (factor B): the frequency with which the words appear in the language (either infrequently or frequently). The design is a 5×2 factorial that is summarized in Table 12-4.

TABLE 12-4 *Factorial Experiment and Two Planned Comparisons*

EXPERIMENTAL DESIGN

Methods of Presentation (Factor A)

Word Frequency (Factor B)	Paper, Varied Order, Column (a_1)	Paper, Varied Order, Scattered (a_2)	Drum, Same Order, 3-Sec. Rate (a_3)	Drum, Varied Order, 3-Sec. Rate (a_4)	Drum, Varied Order, 1-Sec. Rate (a_5)
Infrequent (b_1)					
Frequent (b_2)					

COMPARISONS

	a_1	a_2	a_3	a_4	a_5
Comp. 1	1	1	0	-1	-1
Comp. 2	1	-1	0	0	0

We previously described four comparisons among the presentation conditions which might be of interest to us as planned comparisons (see pp. 90–92). For our purposes, however, we will consider only Comp. 1 and 2; these have been listed in the bottom portion of Table 12-4. Comparison 1 consists of a contrast between the presentation by the memory drum and the sheet of paper, while Comp. 2 contrasts the two methods of word ordering in the two "paper" conditions, the column array and the scrambled array. In Chapter 6 these manipulations were in the form of a single-factor experiment. We can ask the same questions in the present experiment, if we pay attention to the analysis of the A main effect—i.e., if we conduct Comp. 1 and 2 on the $\bar{A}_i$ treatment means. But what about a possible interaction of these two comparisons with the other independent variable, word frequency? Would we expect infrequent words to show the same advantage, say, for the "paper" presentation (Comp. 1) as do the frequent words? Would we expect the same sort of difference between the two methods of presenting the words on the sheet of paper (Comp. 2) with the two classes of words? These questions concern the interaction of the two *comparisons* with factor B, word frequency.

The method of analysis is identical to that outlined for a trend analysis, except that coefficients reflecting the comparisons mentioned are substituted for the coefficients of orthogonal polynomials. In fact, we can follow step by step the procedures outlined in the trend analysis of the last section. Nevertheless, in order to make these steps explicit, we will work an example with a qualitative independent variable.

NUMERICAL EXAMPLE   Assume that we performed the experiment summarized in Table 12-4 and obtained the set of treatment sums listed in the AB matrix of Table 12-5. (For this example, $s = 5$ subjects.) The coefficients for the two comparisons are presented again in the middle portion of the table. Consider the outcome of the experiment in terms of these comparisons. In Comp. 1, we are contrasting the two paper conditions (a_1 and a_2) with the two drum conditions in which word ordering varied on successive trials (a_4 and a_5). The means for this contrast at b_1 and b_2 (infrequent and frequent words, respectively) are:

	Paper	Drum	Average
Infrequent	2.40	5.20	3.80
Frequent	14.70	9.00	11.85
Average	8.55	7.10	7.82

An inspection of the marginal averages of this matrix shows, in general, that infrequent words are not as well learned as frequent ones and that there is a slight advantage to the paper condition. The means within the matrix indicate a striking interaction, with the drum method producing better performance than the paper method when infrequent words are learned, while just the reverse is true when frequent words are learned.

What about the other comparison? In this comparison, we are contrasting two ways of presenting the words in the paper condition, in a column (a_1) or scrambled (a_2). The outcome of the experiment for the two types of material is as follows:

	Column	Scrambled	Average
Infrequent	2.60	2.20	2.40
Frequent	12.60	16.80	14.70
Average	7.60	9.50	8.55

Looking at the means within the body of the matrix, we can see that the type of array makes little difference with infrequent words, but that the scrambled arrangement is superior with frequent words.

The basic calculation required to obtain sums of squares for these comparisons consists of the weighting of the totals by the relevant coefficients. In the formula for the $SS_{A_{comp.}}$, the weighting is conducted on the A_i treatment totals:

$$(c_i)(A_i),$$

while in the formula for the $SS_{A_{comp.} \times B}$ the weighting is conducted on the AB_{ij} totals:

$$(c_i)(AB_{ij}).$$

The results of these multiplications are presented in the bottom portion of Table 12-5. The entries in this section of the table are obtained by multiplying each set of coefficients and the corresponding AB_{ij} sums at b_1 and b_2 (these products are needed for the calculation of the interaction sums of squares) and the corresponding A_i column sums (these products are needed for the calculation of the main effects). For example, the entries in the second row for Comp. 1 are obtained by multiplying the coefficients for Comp. 1 times the AB_{ij} sums at b_2:

$$(c_{1i})(AB_{i2}): \quad (1)(63), \ (1)(84), \ (0)(47), \ (-1)(48), \ \text{and} \ (-1)(42).$$

The final column of this portion of the table presents the sum of these weighted totals. The sum of the weighted AB_{ij} totals is represented by

$$\sum_i^a (c_i)(AB_{ij}),$$

and the sum of the weighted A_i totals is represented by

$$\sum_i^a (c_i)(A_i).$$

These quantities, presented in the last column of the table, will be substituted directly into the computational formulas.

The formula for the main effect of a comparison ($SS_{A_{comp.}}$) is given by Eq. (11-1a). For the two comparisons of the present example,

TABLE 12-5 *Numerical Example: Analysis of the $A_{comp.} \times B$ Interaction*

AB MATRIX

Factor A

Factor B	a_1	a_2	a_3	a_4	a_5
b_1:	13	11	25	23	29
b_2:	63	84	47	48	42
Sum (A_i):	76	95	72	71	71

COEFFICIENTS

	a_1	a_2	a_3	a_4	a_5	$\sum(c_i)^2$
Comp. 1 (c_{1i}):	1	1	0	-1	-1	4
Comp. 2 (c_{2i}):	1	-1	0	0	0	2

COMPUTATIONS

	a_1	a_2	a_3	a_4	a_5	Sum
			COMP. 1			
Level b_1—$(c_{1i})(AB_{i1})$:	13	11	0	-23	-29	-28
Level b_2—$(c_{1i})(AB_{i2})$:	63	84	0	-48	-42	57
$(c_{1i})(A_i)$:	76	95	0	-71	-71	29
			COMP. 2			
Level b_1—$(c_{2i})(AB_{i1})$:	13	-11	0	0	0	2
Level b_2—$(c_{2i})(AB_{i2})$:	63	-84	0	0	0	-21
$(c_{2i})(A_i)$:	76	-95	0	0	0	-19

$$SS_{A_{comp. 1}} = \frac{[\sum(c_{1i})(A_i)]^2}{bs[\sum(c_{1i})^2]} = \frac{(29)^2}{2(5)(4)} = \frac{841}{40} = 21.02,$$

and

$$SS_{A_{comp. 2}} = \frac{[\sum(c_{2i})(A_i)]^2}{bs[\sum(c_{2i})^2]} = \frac{(-19)^2}{2(5)(2)} = \frac{361}{20} = 18.05.$$

The *df* associated with each comparison is 1. The error term for these comparisons would be the $MS_{S/AB}$.

The formula for the interaction of a comparison with factor B ($SS_{A_{comp.} \times B}$) is given by Eq. (12-1). Applied to the present set of data,

$$SS_{A_{comp.\,1} \times B} = \frac{\sum\limits_{j}^{b}\left[\sum\limits_{i}^{a}(c_{1i})(AB_{ij})\right]^2}{s\left[\sum(c_{1i})^2\right]} - SS_{A_{comp.\,1}}$$

$$= \frac{(-28)^2 + (57)^2}{5(4)} - 21.02$$

$$= \frac{4033}{20} - 21.02 = 201.65 - 21.02 = 180.63$$

and

$$SS_{A_{comp.\,2} \times B} = \frac{\sum\limits_{j}^{b}\left[\sum\limits_{i}^{a}(c_{2i})(AB_{ij})\right]^2}{s\left[\sum(c_{2i})^2\right]} - SS_{A_{comp.\,2}} \quad .$$

$$= \frac{(2)^2 + (-21)^2}{5(2)} - 18.05$$

$$= \frac{445}{10} - 18.05 = 44.50 - 18.05 = 26.45.$$

The df for these comparisons are given by Eq. (12-2):

$$df_{A_{comp.} \times B} = b - 1 = 2 - 1 = 1.$$

The error term for these comparisons would also be the $MS_{S/AB}$.

We have gone over these calculations quite rapidly. If you need more explanation, you should refer to the detailed example of the trend analysis in the last section. We will consider next the analysis of the overall $A \times B$ interaction into interactions between $A_{comp.}$ and $B_{comp.}$.

The $A_{comp.} \times B_{comp.}$ Interaction

A much less common situation is one in which meaningful comparisons are entertained for *both* independent variables and the possibility of *their interaction* is assessed. In the present example, we could add a third level to factor B, e.g., high-frequency words having high emotional content. These new words would be matched with the other high-frequency words on all characteristics except emotionality. Thus, the three levels of factor B now would be

b_1: low-frequency words with average emotional content,
b_2: high-frequency words with average emotional content, and
b_3: high-frequency words with high emotional content.

Two comparisons that might be of interest would be the contrast we considered in the last section (b_1 versus b_2) and a contrast between the sets of words varying in emotionality (b_2 versus b_3). In terms of coefficients, these comparisons are represented by

	b_1	b_2	b_3
Comp. 1 (c_{1j}):	1	-1	0
Comp. 2 (c_{2j}):	0	1	-1

It will be noted that these two comparisons are *not* independent, since the test for orthogonality,

$$\sum (c_{1j})(c_{2j}) = 0,$$

does not hold. Specifically,

$$\sum (c_{1j})(c_{2j}) = (1)(0) + (-1)(1) + (0)(-1)$$
$$= 0 - 1 + 0 = -1.$$

On the other hand, the two comparisons do ask meaningful experimental questions; i.e., does the frequency of these words affect performance (Comp. 1) and does the emotionality of high-frequency words affect performance (Comp. 2)? It is perfectly sensible, therefore, to perform the analysis with both of them.

NATURE OF THE ANALYSIS   We will now extend the comparisons involving the A treatments and those involving the B treatments to the analysis of the $A \times B$ interaction. Suppose we consider the questions that could be asked:

	Comparisons Involving Factor A	
Comparisons Involving Factor B	Comp. 1: Paper vs. Drum	Comp. 2: Column vs. Scrambled
Comp. 1: Low vs. high frequency	$A_{comp. 1} \times B_{comp. 1}$	$A_{comp. 2} \times B_{comp. 1}$
Comp. 2: Ave. vs. high emotionality	$A_{comp. 1} \times B_{comp. 2}$	$A_{comp. 2} \times B_{comp. 2}$

Each of the two comparisons for the two factors may be crossed to form a different interaction. The questions being asked in each of these "cells" are as follows:

$A_{comp. 1} \times B_{comp. 1}$: Is the difference between the two modes of presentation the same with low- and high-frequency words?

$A_{comp. 1} \times B_{comp. 2}$: Is the difference between the two modes of presentation the same with av.- and high-emotionality words?

$A_{comp. 2} \times B_{comp. 1}$: Is the difference between the two types of array the same with low- and high-frequency words?

$A_{comp. 2} \times B_{comp. 2}$: Is the difference between the two types of array the same with av.- and high-emotionality words?

In the complete analysis, we would extract the main effects of the two sets of comparisons as well as their interactions. The steps in the calculation of the $SS_{A_{comp.1}}$ and the $SS_{A_{comp.2}}$ were outlined in the last section. That is, we obtain the sums of the weighted A_i totals and substitute in Eq. (11-1a). Exactly the same steps are followed in the calculation of the $SS_{B_{comp.1}}$ and the $SS_{B_{comp.2}}$, except that we obtain the sums of the weighted B_j totals and substitute in Eq. (11-1b):

$$SS_{B_{comp.}} = \frac{[\sum (c_j)(B_j)]^2}{as[\sum (c_j)^2]}.$$

Since our interest is in the interaction of the A and B comparisons, we can proceed directly to a consideration of their calculation.

The actual calculations are quite simple. The main change is in the construction of the coefficients for weighting the AB_{ij} sums. These coefficients (d_{ij}) are simply the *products* of the two coefficients for A and B for each of the combinations of i and j. Formally, they are defined as

$$d_{ij} = (c_i)(c_j),$$

for any pairs of comparisons. In the present example, there are $ab = 5(3) = 15$ different treatment conditions and a uniquely specified coefficient for each one of the resulting AB_{ij} totals. The 15 coefficients are enumerated in the upper portion of Table 12-6. Here the coefficients for a comparison among the a treatments are represented along the columns, the coefficients for a comparison among the b treatments are represented along the rows, and the corresponding products (d_{ij}) by the cell entries within the body of the matrix.

The remainder of the table specifies the actual interaction coefficients for two of the four interactions involving A and B comparisons we have discussed. The d_{ij} coefficients for the $A_{comp.1} \times B_{comp.1}$ interaction, for instance, are presented in the middle section of Table 12-6. The coefficients for the two comparisons involved are listed along the columns $(A_{comp.1})$ and the rows $(B_{comp.1})$. The entries within the body of the matrix are obtained by multiplying corresponding column and row coefficients. For the first row $(j = 1)$,

$$d_{i1}: \quad (1)(1), \ (1)(1), \ (0)(1), \ (-1)(1), \ \text{and} \ (-1)(1);$$

for the second row $(j = 2)$,

$$d_{i2}: \quad (1)(-1), \ (1)(-1), \ (0)(-1), \ (-1)(-1), \ \text{and} \ (-1)(-1);$$

and for the third row $(j = 3)$,

$$d_{i3}: \quad (1)(0), \ (1)(0), \ (0)(0), \ (-1)(0), \ \text{and} \ (-1)(0).$$

The results of these multiplications are presented in the body of the table. The d_{ij} coefficients for another interaction, $A_{comp.1} \times B_{comp.2}$, is given in the bottom portion of the table. (The other two interactions form the basis of Problem 9 in the exercises to Part III.)

TABLE 12-6 *Numerical Example: Analysis of the $A_{comp.} \times B_{comp.}$ Interaction*

INTERACTION COEFFICIENTS (d_{ij})

Levels of Factor A

Levels of Factor B	(a_1) c_1	(a_2) c_2	(a_3) c_3	(a_4) c_4	(a_5) c_5
$(b_1)\, c_1$	d_{11}	d_{21}	d_{31}	d_{41}	d_{51}
$(b_2)\, c_2$	d_{12}	d_{22}	d_{32}	d_{42}	d_{52}
$(b_3)\, c_3$	d_{13}	d_{23}	d_{33}	d_{43}	d_{53}

$A_{comp.\,1} \times B_{comp.\,1}$

Coefficients ($A_{comp.\,1}$)

Coefficients ($B_{comp.\,1}$)	1	1	0	-1	-1	Sum
1	1	1	0	-1	-1	0
-1	-1	-1	0	1	1	0
0	0	0	0	0	0	0
Sum	0	0	0	0	0	0

$A_{comp.\,1} \times B_{comp.\,2}$

Coefficients ($A_{comp.\,1}$)

Coefficients ($B_{comp.\,2}$)	1	1	0	-1	-1	Sum
0	0	0	0	0	0	0
1	1	1	0	-1	-1	0
-1	-1	-1	0	1	1	0
Sum	0	0	0	0	0	0

The sums of squares for these component interactions are given by

$$SS_{A_{comp.} \times B_{comp.}} = \frac{[\sum (d_{ij})(AB_{ij})]^2}{s[\sum (d_{ij})^2]}. \tag{12-4}$$

In words, we simply calculate a sum of *all* of the weighted AB_{ij} totals, square this quantity, and divide by the product formed by multiplying the number of observations (s) and the sum of the squared coefficients. This sum of squares has

$$df_{A_{comp.} \times B_{comp.}} = (df_{A_{comp.}})(df_{B_{comp.}})$$
$$= 1(1) = 1.$$

The denominator for the F ratio is the overall error term, the $MS_{S/AB}$.

TABLE 12-7 *AB Matrix for the Numerical Example*

Levels of Factor B	Levels of Factor A				
	a_1	a_2	a_3	a_4	a_5
b_1	21	13	22	29	18
b_2	75	85	63	50	69
b_3	92	58	51	44	46

NUMERICAL EXAMPLE   As an example of the calculations involved in Eq. (12-4), we will use the AB_{ij} sums presented in Table 12-7. For these data we will again assume $s = 5$ subjects in each treatment condition. Substituting the coefficients from Table 12-6 and the data from Table 12-7 in Eq. (12-4), we have

$$SS_{A_{\text{comp. 1}} \times B_{\text{comp. 1}}} = \frac{[(1)(21) + (-1)(75) + \cdots + (1)(69) + (0)(46)]^2}{5[(1)^2 + (-1)^2 + \cdots + (1)^2 + (0)^2]}$$

$$= \frac{(-54)^2}{5(8)} = \frac{2916}{40} = 72.90$$

and

$$SS_{A_{\text{comp. 1}} \times B_{\text{comp. 2}}} = \frac{[(0)(21) + (1)(75) + \cdots + (-1)(69) + (1)(46)]^2}{5[(0)^2 + (1)^2 + \cdots + (-1)^2 + (1)^2]}$$

$$= \frac{(-19)^2}{5(8)} = \frac{361}{40} = 9.02.$$

Summary

Both analyses considered so far in the chapter represent methods for asking extremely precise questions about the nature of a two-way interaction. As we have pointed out, the methods discussed here may be used with quantitative as well as with qualitative independent variables. We have seen that the same computational formulas are employed to analyze a qualitative variable in this section and a quantitative variable in the preceding section. Moreover, we have just looked at an even more specialized analysis: that of the $A_{\text{comp.}} \times B_{\text{comp.}}$ interaction.[2]

The construction of comparisons, a useful tool in the analysis of the single-factor experiment, is equally useful in the analysis of the factorial experiment. If we can formulate interesting questions about a main effect (or the independent

[2] This analysis may also be used if both independent variables are quantitative. Under these circumstances, we would construct sets of d_{ij} coefficients for the $A_{\text{linear}} \times B_{\text{linear}}$, $A_{\text{linear}} \times B_{\text{quadratic}}$, $A_{\text{quadratic}} \times B_{\text{linear}}, \ldots,$ interactions. We indicated in footnote 1 (p. 225) that such analyses are rare in psychological research and will probably wait upon the emergence of precise quantitative theories of behavior that can assimilate the outcome of such an analysis.

variable in a single-factor experiment) and express these questions in terms of a set of coefficients, then we can extend the same questions to the $A \times B$ interaction. In Chapter 6 we asked a number of analytical questions about the outcome of the experiment we have been discussing in this present section, indicating that different theories predicted different outcomes for these comparisons (see pp. 90–92). In the context of the two factorial experiments considered in this section, the interaction of these comparisons with the other independent variable may provide important information about the correctness of one or the other of the theories. Perhaps a given prediction is critical only under certain conditions of testing, or with certain types of material. The analyses we have outlined in this section will allow us to investigate these possibilities.

MULTIPLE COMPARISONS

It was argued in the last chapter that although multiple comparisons involving individual cell means are not frequently encountered in the literature, they can and certainly should be conducted if there are interesting questions that may be asked of the data. It is highly unlikely that we would ever want to compare a mean found in one row-cell combination with the mean found in another row-cell combination, *unless* either the rows or the columns were the *same*. That is, we might want to compare cell means within a particular level of factor A or within a particular level of factor B, but rarely would we want to compare a mean from cell ab_{11} with the mean from cell ab_{23} or ab_{22}, for example. In order to obtain unambiguous information from a comparison, we have to let only one factor vary between two means. In the comparisons where we hold either the level of factor A or the level of factor B constant, this is the case. In the other comparisons, where the levels of both factors vary, any difference observed between these means will be difficult to interpret. In short, we will generally restrict our post-hoc comparisons to analyses of the *simple main effects*—i.e., to differences between the means at a particular level of factor A or of factor B.

Since we will usually restrict the number of multiple comparisons we conduct on the cell means, we should seriously consider turning to the Dunn test if we want to exert some control over the experimentwise (EW) error rate. (The Dunn test is discussed in detail in Chapter 8, pp. 147–149.) Briefly, this test simply apportions the EW error rate among the comparisons that will be made. The Newman-Keuls and Duncan tests provide protection for all possible comparisons between pairs of means, while the Tukey and Scheffé tests protect us for these and complex comparisons as well.

In general, the procedures discussed in Chapter 8 are applicable to the case where we want to make multiple comparisons between cell means in *one* particular row or column. The only real change in the formulas is the use of the $MS_{S/AB}$ instead of the $MS_{S/A}$. In terms of differences between treatment sums, the critical range (CR) for the Tukey test, for example, becomes

$$CR_T = q(r_{max}, df_{S/AB})\sqrt{s(MS_{S/AB})}, \qquad (12\text{-}5)$$

where values of the q statistic are found in Table C-3 of Appendix C and r_{max} equals the total number of cells in a particular row or column. For the Scheffé test,

$$CR_S = \sqrt{(a - 1)F(df_A, df_{S/AB})} \sqrt{2s(MS_{S/AB})}, \qquad (12\text{-}6a)$$

if we are comparing cell means within a particular row, and

$$CR_S = \sqrt{(b - 1)F(df_B, df_{S/AB})} \sqrt{2s(MS_{S/AB})}, \qquad (12\text{-}6b)$$

if we are comparing cell means within a particular column. The other tests are modified similarly.

We have just considered the case where comparisons will be restricted to the means of one column or of one row. What about the other extreme, where an experimenter decides to lump all of the ab cell means together for his multiple comparisons? We have argued that it is unlikely that we would ever be interested in making such "heterogeneous" comparisons, but there may be situations in which such a procedure is justified. If an experimenter is really intent upon comparing any and all means in the AB matrix, then he should use either the Tukey or Scheffé methods and take ab as the number of means in his pool. If only comparisons between *pairs* of means will be conducted, then the Tukey method is used; the critical range (CR) for differences between cell sums is given by

$$CR_T = q(ab, df_{S/AB})\sqrt{s(MS_{S/AB})}, \qquad (12\text{-}7)$$

where ab, the total number of cell means, replaces the r_{max} in Eq. (12-5). If complex comparisons are also contemplated, then the Scheffé test is better; under these circumstances, the F ratios for these comparisons are obtained in the usual way and evaluated against

$$F_S = (ab - 1)F(ab - 1, df_{S/AB}). \qquad (12\text{-}8)$$

Of course, when most experimenters resort to multiple comparisons, they are more likely to operate between these two extremes. That is, they will make comparisons within a column or row, but will probably conduct these same comparisons within *all* of the columns or rows. It is not appropriate to use the first set of corrections [e.g., Eq. (12-5), Eq. (12-6a), or Eq. (12-6b)], as these fix the EW error rate at α_{EW} for the comparisons in only *one* of the columns or rows. To elaborate on this point, suppose an experimenter uses the Scheffé test and sets the EW error rate for comparisons involving means in one row at $\alpha_{EW} = .10$. If he makes the same correction for comparisons in the other rows, his *actual EW* error rate for the total number of multiple comparisons is *not* .10, but a value equal to .10 *times* the number of rows. It is also not appropriate to use the second set of corrections [e.g., Eq. (12-7) and Eq. (12-8)], as these take into consideration far more comparisons than are contemplated in this analysis.

The most reasonable solution to this problem, assuming that an experimenter is making all of these comparisons and is concerned about controlling the EW error rate, is to use a modification of the Dunn procedure. He would proceed as follows: (1) Decide upon an acceptable EW error rate (α_{EW}). (2) Divide the α_{EW} by the number of columns or rows. (3) Use this *divided EW* error rate (either α_{EW}/a or α_{EW}/b) as the α level for *each* column or row, respectively. (4) Choose between the Tukey and Scheffé tests. If the Tukey test is chosen, substitute the number of means in a column or row for r_{max} in Eq. (12-5).[3] If the Scheffé test is chosen, use the correction

$$F_S = (a - 1)F(df_A, df_{S/AB}),\qquad (12\text{-}9a)$$

if the comparisons involve variations in factor A, and

$$F_S = (b - 1)F(df_B, df_{S/AB}),\qquad (12\text{-}9b)$$

if the comparisons involve variations in factor B. This procedure will guarantee that the EW error rate is α_{EW} or less for these particular comparisons.

A fairly frequent comparison among cell means is between experimental treatments and a control treatment. If a single control group is appropriate to all of the experimental groups, then the analysis follows procedures different from those considered in this chapter. [See Winer (1962, pp. 263–267; 1971, pp. 468–473).] More commonly, we will see the case in which one of the levels of factor A, say, is a control and the others are experimental treatments, and there is a different control at each level of factor B. Under these circumstances, we may want to compare each individual experimental group with its relevant control, and Dunnett's test is appropriate. Briefly, we obtain differences between cell sums for each control-experimental contrast and evaluate these differences against a critical difference given by

$$\text{critical C-E difference} = q_D(k, df_{S/AB})\sqrt{2s(MS_{S/AB})},\qquad (12\text{-}10)$$

where the value of q_D is found in Table C-5 and k represents the total number of groups (control and experimental).

---

[3] In practice, it may be difficult to use the Tukey procedure since the "divided" EW error rate can result in a value for which tabled values of the q statistic are not available.

EXERCISES FOR PART III[1]

1. The individual AB cell means for a 4×2 factorial experiment are given below in a set of six examples. Indicate for each example whether or not an interaction is present. Illustrate your decision by using the arithmetic test for interaction (cf. pp. 179–181).

(a)

	a_1	a_2	a_3	a_4
b_1	10	12	14	16
b_2	8	10	12	14

(b)

	a_1	a_2	a_3	a_4
b_1	10	14	12	16
b_2	7	11	9	13

(c)

	a_1	a_2	a_3	a_4
b_1	10	14	12	16
b_2	12	10	8	14

(d)

	a_1	a_2	a_3	a_4
b_1	10	12	14	16
b_2	14	12	10	8

(e)

	a_1	a_2	a_3	a_4
b_1	10	12	14	16
b_2	8	9	10	11

(f)

	a_1	a_2	a_3	a_4
b_1	12	12	8	12
b_2	8	8	12	8

2. The purpose of this problem is to show that the within-groups mean square ($MS_{S/AB}$) is an average of the individual mean squares obtained from the ab different treatment combinations. With the data provided in Table 10-5 (p. 201), calculate the separate within-group mean squares ($MS_{S/AB_{ij}}$). The average of these mean squares will equal the $MS_{S/AB}$ listed in Table 10-6 (p. 203). For your information,

$$SS_{S/AB_{ij}} = \sum_{k}^{s} (ABS_{ijk})^2 - \frac{(AB_{ij})^2}{s}$$

and

$$MS_{S/AB_{ij}} = \frac{SS_{S/AB_{ij}}}{s - 1}.$$

3. A two-variable factorial experiment is designed in which factor A consists of $a = 5$ equally spaced levels of shock intensity and factor B consists of $b = 3$ discrimination tasks of different difficulty (b_1 = easy, b_2 = medium, and b_3 = hard). There are $s = 5$ rats assigned to each of the $ab = 5(3) = 15$ treatment conditions. The task for the animals is to learn to avoid the shock by solving the discrimination task within a 10-second period. The response measure consists of the number of learning trials needed to reach the criterion of an avoidance of the shock on three consecutive trials. The data are given in the accompanying ABS matrix.

[1] The answers to these problems are found in Appendix D.

ABS Matrix

Treatment Conditions

a_1 b_1	a_1 b_2	a_1 b_3	a_2 b_1	a_2 b_2	a_2 b_3	a_3 b_1	a_3 b_2	a_3 b_3	a_4 b_1	a_4 b_2	a_4 b_3	a_5 b_1	a_5 b_2	a_5 b_3
6	14	15	5	12	14	8	11	16	13	14	16	15	15	17
7	18	18	11	10	17	11	10	20	12	19	18	19	12	15
3	12	14	6	15	15	13	15	17	10	17	19	13	16	19
4	13	13	5	14	11	9	17	13	14	12	11	17	18	14
9	11	15	7	11	14	7	12	16	9	13	14	12	13	16

(a) Conduct the usual factorial analysis.

(b) In (a) you will find the $A \times B$ interaction to be significant. Since factor A represents a quantitative variable, we can attempt to refine our description of the interaction by partitioning the trend components. Conduct a trend analysis of the $A \times B$ interaction, assuming that we have no a priori notion of which trends will be significant.

(c) You will discover in (b) that the interaction is concentrated in the *linear component*. It is now of interest to refine this finding even more carefully. One way to accomplish this is to obtain the *simple linear* effects of the $A \times B$ interaction. That is, test the significance of the linear component at each of the levels of factor B.

4. Consider the factorial design displayed in the accompanying *ABS* matrix and the scores produced by the $s = 3$ subjects in each of the treatment conditions.

ABS Matrix

Treatment Conditions

a_1 b_1	a_1 b_2	a_1 b_3	a_1 b_4	a_1 b_5	a_2 b_1	a_2 b_2	a_2 b_3	a_2 b_4	a_2 b_5	a_3 b_1	a_3 b_2	a_3 b_3	a_3 b_4	a_3 b_5
10	11	9	12	9	11	15	19	8	11	8	12	11	10	11
9	8	7	7	9	8	12	16	9	12	11	9	7	9	9
7	8	9	6	11	6	16	20	7	8	10	8	7	7	8

(a) Conduct an analysis of variance on these data.

(b) Since the $A \times B$ interaction is significant, it is of some interest to examine the simple main effects of the interaction. For this example, test the significance of the simple main effects of factor B.

(c) From the analysis in (b), you will see that the locus of the interaction is found among the cell means at a_2 (the $\overline{AB}_{2j}$ means). Use the Scheffé procedure to isolate the significant clusters of cell means at this level of factor A. (Set $\alpha_{EW} = .05$.)

(d) Suppose we were interested in conducting comparisons between pairs of means. What are the critical ranges (CR's) with the Tukey test ($\alpha_{EW} = .05$) for the following sets of comparisons?

(1) Comparisons between the $\bar{A}_i$ means.
(2) Comparisons between the $\bar{B}_j$ means.
(3) Comparisons between the $\overline{AB}_{ij}$ means in *one row* of the AB matrix—i.e., at one level of b_j.
(4) Comparisons between *all* the $\overline{AB}_{ij}$ means in the AB matrix.
(5) Comparisons between the $\overline{AB}_{ij}$ means within *each* of the rows—i.e., at each of the levels of factor B. (Set α_{EW} at .05 for the *total set* of comparisons.)

5. The AB matrix from a 4×2 factorial experiment with $s = 10$ subjects is given below:

	a_1	a_2	a_3	a_4
b_1	44	31	60	72
b_2	22	14	31	61

For these data, $\sum (ABS)^2 = 3361$.
(a) Perform an analysis of variance.
(b) Suppose we are interested in several comparisons between the different levels of factor A. Since the $A \times B$ interaction is *not* significant, it makes sense to conduct meaningful comparisons involving the $\bar{A}_i$ means—i.e., collapsing across factor B. Assess the significance of the following set of orthogonal comparisons: (1) a_1 versus a_3, (2) a_2 versus the combination of a_1, a_3, and a_4, and (3) a_4 versus the combination of a_1 and a_3. Show that these comparisons are mutually orthogonal and that the sum of the sums of squares associated with these comparisons equals the SS_A.

6. In order to conserve space, most psychology journals do not publish analysis-of-variance summary tables, except where the analysis is complicated and where there are many significant sources of variance. Thus, the most that we can expect to find is a table of means and a report of the obtained values of F. At times, however, we will wish that the researcher had extracted a certain comparison which is of particular interest to us or had conducted a multiple comparison between pairs of means. We can perform these analyses *ourselves* even though the researcher has not provided us with a detailed summary of the analysis—i.e., sums of squares. Suppose we have been given the following table of means:

	a_1	a_2	a_3
b_1	11	12	10
b_2	3	10	14

and we have been told that only the $A \times B$ interaction is significant, $F = 3.93, p < .05$. Assuming that there are $s = 4$ subjects in each treatment condition, reconstruct the entire summary table, the SS's, the df's, and the F's.

7. Suppose we have a 2×2 factorial design with $s = 10$ subjects in each treatment condition and that we obtain the following cell sums:

	a_1	a_2
b_1	30	80
b_2	40	20

(a) Calculate the SS_A, SS_B, and $SS_{A \times B}$.

(b) See if you can work out a way of calculating these same quantities by constructing a set of three *orthogonal comparisons*.

8. Subjects are asked to perform a tracking task under different incentive conditions (factor A). In one condition, subjects are given no specific inducement for good performance on the task. In the remaining three conditions, subjects are provided three types of incentive for good performance: verbal praise, monetary reward, and credit toward a course grade. One half of the subjects in each group are tested on a relatively simple tracking task, the other half on a complex tracking task. There are $s = 5$ subjects randomly assigned to each of the $ab = 4(2) = 8$ treatment conditions. The experimenter is interested in the effectiveness of incentives with simple and complex tasks. The response measure is the number of minutes out of 15 minutes that a subject can maintain a 90 percent accuracy on the tracking task. The sums for each treatment group are given below:

	Incentive Conditions (A)			
Tasks (B)	None	Verbal	Monetary	Course Credit
Simple	70	72	65	69
Complex	32	48	53	47

For this example, $\sum (ABS)^2 = 5582$.

(a) Conduct an analysis of variance on these data.

(b) One obvious comparison we might consider making among the incentive conditions is a contrast between the condition with no explicit incentive provided the subjects (None) and the combined incentive conditions (Verbal + Monetary + Course Credit). We will refer to this contrast as Comp. 1. Another obvious comparison is among the three incentive conditions (Comp. 2). The first comparison indicates whether or not incentive made a difference, while the second determines whether or not the three types of incentives were equally effective. It will be noted, however, that the $A \times B$ interaction is significant. This means, of course, that we will have to worry about the influence of the different incentives on the two tracking tasks. It is meaningful, then, to look separately at the interactions of these two comparisons with factor B. Thus, partition the $SS_{A \times B}$ into these two components:
(1) the sum of squares associated with the interaction of Comp. 1 and factor B and
(2) the sum of squares associated with the interaction of Comp. 2 and factor B.

9. In discussing comparisons involving one variable interacting with comparisons involving the other variable (see pp. 240–243), we considered four subcomponents of an $A \times B$ interaction. At that time we calculated the sums of squares for only two of the four subcomponents. Your task is to complete the analysis by obtaining the sums of squares for the other two components: $A_{comp.\,2} \times B_{comp.\,1}$ and $A_{comp.\,2} \times B_{comp.\,2}$.

PART IV

Higher-order Factorial Experiments

The analysis of experiments involving three or more independent variables introduces no new concepts or procedures. Our task in the first three chapters of this part is to see how the basic analyses of one- and two-factor experiments are extended to these multifactor experiments. (As in the preceding discussions, we will assume a completely randomized design; i.e., subjects are randomly assigned to a single treatment condition.)

In Chapters 13 and 14 we will consider in detail the relatively common three-factor design, again with an equal number of subjects in each basic treatment cell. Then (Chapter 15) we will consider the general case—the analysis of experiments with any number of independent variables—including rules that allow the construction of computational formulas for two types of analytical comparisons often conducted after the main analysis: comparisons involving pairs of means and analyses of simple effects. In Chapter 16 we will

Numerical examples illustrating arithmetic operations discussed in this section may be found at the end of Part IV (pp. 387–392).

consider a number of theoretical models and the effects they have on the analysis of variance. Part IV concludes by dealing with two special cases: the analysis of experiments with unequal numbers of subjects in the different treatment conditions (Chapter 17) and the analysis of experiments with "nested" independent variables (Chapter 18).

chapter thirteen

THE THREE-FACTOR CASE: INTERACTION AND THE BASIC ANALYSIS

Let us begin with a typical experiment in which three variables are arranged in a completely crossed fashion. As before, this means that each possible combination of the levels associated with each variable is represented in the design. The two-way factorial was represented by a rectangle, the levels of factor A defining the columns and the levels of factor B defining the rows. Continuing with this geometrical display, we can represent the three-way factorial as a rectangular solid in which the levels of factors A and B mark off the "width" and "height," respectively, and the levels of the third factor, C, mark off the "depth." This may be seen in Fig. 13-1.

It is instructive to think about the ingredients that go into a three-factor design. Consider the display presented in Table 13-1. In the top section of the table, each of the independent variables is represented in a different single-factor experiment. We have seen in Chapter 9 that the two-way factorial is in essence constructed from two single-factor experiments. Three such two-way factorial experiments are possible with three independent variables: a crossing

253

of factors A and B, a crossing of factors A and C, and a crossing of factors B and C. These experiments are enumerated in the middle section of the table. Finally, a three-way factorial can be viewed as a two-way factorial crossed with a third factor. Three of these crossings are possible and they are listed in the bottom section of the table. Each one of these instances of a three-way factorial specifies the same set of treatment combinations.

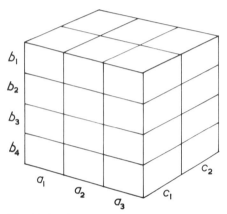

Fig. 13-1   Geometric display of a 3 × 4 × 2 factorial design.

We will usually display a three-way factorial in the first arrangement on the left. For consistency with the earlier chapters, we will continue to identify factor A with the columns and factor B with the rows; factor C, then, will be represented as individual AB matrices as in Table 13-1. We will refer to this display as an ABC matrix. Whether we look at the geometrical display of the three-way factorial or the ABC matrix, we can see that all possible $abc = 3(4)(2) = 24$ combinations of the three independent variables are enumerated, either as individual cubes of the rectangular solid (Fig. 13-1) or as individual cells in the ABC matrix (Table 13-1). This particular design would be referred to as a 3 × 4 × 2 factorial.

Suppose we consider Table 13-1 in reverse. We start with the three-way factorials at the bottom. By collapsing across any one of the three independent variables and combining the scores contained therein, we will obtain a two-dimensional data matrix: an AB matrix when we collapse across the levels of factor C, an AC matrix when we collapse across the levels of factor B, and a BC matrix when we collapse across the levels of factor A. From these three matrices we can obtain information concerning the respective two-way interactions, which represent interactions averaged over the levels of the remaining

TABLE 13-1   *Relationship Between the Three-Way Factorial and Lower-Order Designs*

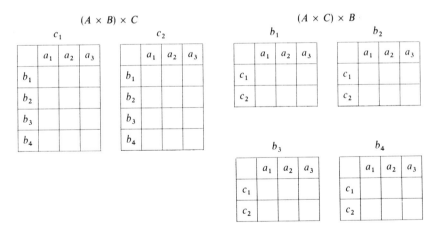

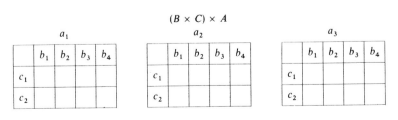

independent variable. Because of the collapsing, these interactions will not necessarily be the same as those obtained from a standard two-way factorial.[1]

From the two-way matrices we can obtain information concerning respective main effects for each of the three independent variables. These main effects are estimates of the effects of one of the independent variables averaged over the levels of the other two independent variables. In addition to the main effects and two-way interactions, which may be investigated with appropriate two-way factorial experiments, we obtain from the ABC matrix information about the manner in which the three variables combine to affect the behavior we are studying. That is, we are able to determine the presence or absence of a *three-way interaction*.

THREE-WAY INTERACTION

An Example of a Three-Way Interaction

The three-way interaction is called by a number of names, such as the *three-way*, the *second-order*, the *triple*, or the $A \times B \times C$ interaction. We will use these labels interchangeably. One way to understand the meaning of this higher-order interaction is to look at a concrete example. This illustration comes from an experiment reported by Wallace and Underwood (1964), in which the main purpose was an assessment of the triple interaction. To understand why this was the case, we must consider some of the reasoning behind this experiment.

Briefly, Wallace and Underwood began with the assumption that the presentation of a common word will elicit from the subject an implicit associative response; e.g., a subject may think of the word *table* upon the presentation of the word *chair*, or of *apple* upon the presentation of the word *orange*. These associations are thought to be the result of experience with a language. Linguistic associations are assumed to facilitate learning when they correspond to the requirements of the learning task and to interfere with learning when they do not. One implication of this theory was tested in the experiment by including, as two of the independent variables, the *strength* of the linguistic associations and the *type* of learning task.

The degree of strength (factor A) was varied by constructing learning materials from two pools of words. One pool contained groups of words from the same conceptual class, such as FRUITS: *apple, peach, pear*; or COLORS: *green, blue, red*; or PARTS OF THE BODY: *leg, head, arm*. The other pool contained no words from the same conceptual class—e.g., *fly, saw, snow, car, sun*, and so on. It was assumed that words from the same category are highly associated, while words

---

[1] These interactions will be identical only when there is no three-way interaction, a concept we will discuss in the next section. An analogous statement was made in Chapter 9 when we considered the main effects in a two-way factorial, where we estimated the effects of one of the independent variables averaged over the levels of the other independent variable.

from different categories are not. Two types of learning tasks (factor *B*) were compared: a free-recall task in which subjects may recall a series of words in any order they wish and a paired-associate task in which they are required to learn specific word pairs. A crossing of these two factors results in two free-recall lists and two paired-associate lists. In each case, one of the lists contained words of a low degree of association and another contained words of a high degree of association. The free-recall lists were constructed by randomly ordering the words from a given pool, while the paired-associate lists were constructed by randomly forming *pairs* of words from the pool.

It was predicted that there would be an interaction between these two independent variables. More specifically, it was anticipated that the presence of strong interword associations would *facilitate* free-recall learning in that the high interconnections among the words within a group would facilitate the recall of the separate words. Thus, the high list would be learned more quickly than the low list. In direct contrast, it was predicted that strong interword associations would *retard* paired-associate learning, since the interconnections among the words would be in conflict with the arbitrary pairs that the subjects were required to learn. Thus, the high list would be learned more slowly than the low list. In short, then, they predicted an interaction between factors *A* and *B*—namely, that associative strength (factor *A*) would have opposite effects on the two learning tasks (factor *B*).

For the third independent variable, Wallace and Underwood compared the learning of these tasks and materials by college students and by mental retardates. This final variable was introduced with the thought that the degree of linguistic development was being "manipulated." It was assumed that college students have stronger and more extensive linguistic habits than do mental retardates. Therefore, it was predicted that associative strength would have *less* effect upon the performance of retarded subjects than it would on the performance of college students. That is, the negative and positive effects of associative strength (the *A* × *B* interaction), which we described in the last paragraph, should be found with college students, but greatly diminished or even absent with retardates.

TABLE 13-2 *Experimental Design of Wallace and Underwood* (1964)

| | COLLEGE STUDENTS | | | MENTAL RETARDATES | |
| | Degree of Association | | | Degree of Association | |
Task	Low	High	Task	Low	High
Free recall			Free recall		
Paired associate			Paired associate		

The complete design is specified in Table 13-2. Each of the three independent variables (strength, task, and type of subject) is represented by two levels.

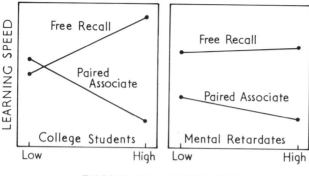

Fig. 13-2   Speed of learning as a function of learning task, degree of association, and type of subject. (From Wallace and Underwood, 1964, by permission of the authors and the American Psychological Association.)

Thus, there are $abc = 2(2)(2) = 8$ treatment combinations in the experiment. The results of the experiment are reproduced in Fig. 13-2. It will be noted that the expected Strength × Task $(A \times B)$ interaction was obtained with the college students but was virtually nonexistent with the mental retardates. This pattern of results represents an interaction of *three* independent variables. For Wallace and Underwood, the outcome provided strong support for their theoretical speculations. That is, they found that assumed linguistic associations could facilitate as well as interfere with learning and that the magnitude of these opposed effects seemed to depend upon the degree of linguistic development of the subjects.

Definitions of the Three-Way Interaction

VERBAL DEFINITION   The interaction of *two* variables, as defined in Chapter 9, is a situation in which the effect of one variable changes at different levels of the second variable. The definition of the three-way interaction is a direct translation. That is, we say that

> **three variables interact when the *interaction* of two of the variables changes at different levels of the *third* variable.**

We can see that this definition is satisfied by the data summarized in Fig. 13-2. More specifically, the two-way interaction of strength and task is *different* for college students (one level of the third variable) than it is for mental retardates (the other level of the third variable).

When considering interactions, many students have difficulty making the transition from two to three independent variables. Suppose we go back to an interaction of two variables. Recall from our discussion in Chapter 9 that a two-way interaction is present when the *simple main effects* of one of the variables are not the same at the different levels of the other variable. By analogy,

a three-way interaction is present when the *simple interaction* effects of two variables are not the same at different levels of the third variable.

Three simple interactions are possible in the three-factor experiment: the $A \times B$ interaction effects at the different levels of factor C ($A \times B$ at c_k), the $A \times C$ interaction effects at the different levels of factor B ($A \times C$ at b_j), and the $B \times C$ interaction effects at the different levels of factor A ($B \times C$ at a_i). When there is a three-way interaction, the simple interaction effects for any one of the sets will not be the same at the different levels of the corresponding third variable.

It is important to note that the simple interaction effects merely need to be different—they do not need to represent significant two-way interactions themselves. This is why Fig. 13-2 is such a good example. If we had conducted the experiment only with retardates as subjects, we would *not* have observed the two-way interaction; under these circumstances we would have concluded that associative strength produces no effect with either type of learning task. However, if we had conducted this experiment only with college students, we would have concluded that there is a severe interaction of the two variables. In short, when we consider the results of these separate "two-factor" experiments together in a three-factor design, we can see that no one summary statement is possible—we *must* indicate that the two independent variables, associative strength and learning task, produce a different pattern of results with the two types of subjects. Said another way, the presence of an $A \times B \times C$ interaction signals the fact that the interpretation of the two-way interactions, which we obtain by collapsing across the levels of one of the variables, must be made with caution, just as an $A \times B$ interaction in the two-factor case means that the interpretation of the main effects must be made with caution. Translated to our example, we can see that a general statement describing the interaction of associative strength and learning task cannot be made without a specification of the type of subject being tested.

ARITHMETIC DEFINITION   Interactions of any degree or order are most easily communicated to others by a plot of the results of the experiment. Unfortunately, however, visual inspection of a three-way plot does not always offer a simple test of the presence or absence of a triple interaction.[2] There is an arithmetic test which will tell us whether or not a triple interaction is reflected in a set of means. The test is an extension of the one presented in Chapter 9

[2] An exception is a three-dimensional display of the results of the experiment. Winer (1962, pp. 178–184; 1971, pp. 351–359) presents a useful discussion of this method of representation.

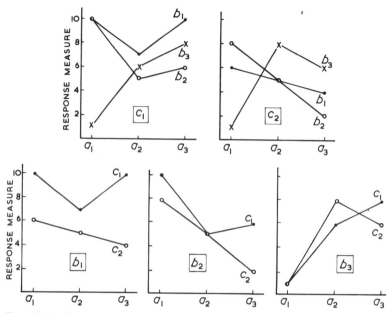

Fig. 13-3 Two plots of the data presented in Table 13-3. (The representation of factors B and C is reversed in the two plots.)

and follows directly from the verbal definition of the three-way interaction. First, however, we will consider a numerical example.

The data from a $3 \times 3 \times 2$ factorial experiment are presented in Table 13-3. The entries in the ABC matrix are means and we will assume that they are not subject to experimental error. (It is obvious that this is never the case in an actual experiment, but as an illustration of possible outcomes of experiments, it is convenient to make this assumption.) For ease of detecting the presence or absence of interactions, the means have been plotted two ways in Fig. 13-3. In the upper panel, the levels of factor A are marked off on the baseline, the levels of factor B are indicated by connected points within the body of each graph, and the levels of factor C are represented by separate double-classification plots. Is an $A \times B \times C$ interaction present in these data? Consider the simple $A \times B$ interactions. At both c_1 and at c_2 there is clearly an $A \times B$

TABLE 13-3   *Treatment Means for a $3 \times 3 \times 2$ Factorial*

	c_1				c_2		
	a_1	a_2	a_3		a_1	a_2	a_3
b_1	10	7	10	b_1	6	5	4
b_2	10	5	6	b_2	8	5	2
b_3	1	6	8	b_3	1	8	6

interaction. The critical question, however, is whether the two interactions are the same or different. It is certainly difficult to tell, but most readers would probably say that they are different. The truth of the matter is that the two simple interactions are *identical*, meaning that no triple interaction is present.

The same data have been replotted in the lower panel with the representation of factors B and C reversed. An inspection of the three simple interaction effects indicates an $A \times C$ interaction at each level of factor B. Are these interactions the same or are they different? Again, you will probably want to say that they are different, but since you have been told that there is no three-way interaction, then a rational answer (and the correct one) would be that they are the same! The reason it is difficult to "see" the absence of the triple interaction in this example is that all three of the *two-way interactions* ($A \times B$, $A \times C$, and $B \times C$) *are* represented in the data.

Consider two more examples. The data plotted in Fig. 13-4 are based on the same experiment presented in Table 13-3, except that this time one or two of the two-way interactions have been systematically "removed." In the upper panel, the only interaction present is the one involving factors A and B. We can see that the $A \times B$ interaction is identical in form at the two levels of factor C; hence, there is no triple interaction. In the lower panel we have "restored" the $B \times C$ interaction. Look again at the simple $A \times B$ interactions

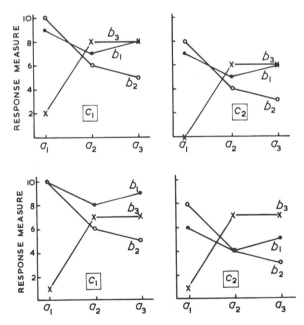

Fig. 13-4 The upper example contains an $A \times B$ interaction, while the lower example contains the same $A \times B$ interaction in addition to a $B \times C$ interaction.

at c_1 and at c_2. Can you still tell that they are of the same form? They are, but it is more difficult to see than in the first case.

The point of all this is to illustrate the difficulty of visually detecting a three-way interaction when two-way interactions are present. In Chapter 9 we considered a simple arithmetic test for a two-way interaction, one which involves the construction of basic 2×2 arrangements from any two levels of factor A (a_i and $a_{i'}$) and any two levels of factor B (b_j and $b_{j'}$). We will do the same thing with the triple interaction, except that we will add two levels of factor C (c_k and $c_{k'}$).

Consider the basic matrix given below:

	c_k			$c_{k'}$	
	a_i	$a_{i'}$		a_i	$a_{i'}$
b_j	$\overline{ABC}_{ijk}$	$\overline{ABC}_{i'jk}$	b_j	$\overline{ABC}_{ijk'}$	$\overline{ABC}_{i'jk'}$
$b_{j'}$	$\overline{ABC}_{ij'k}$	$\overline{ABC}_{i'j'k}$	$b_{j'}$	$\overline{ABC}_{ij'k'}$	$\overline{ABC}_{i'j'k'}$

The $\overline{ABC}$ means entered in the matrix are the means obtained under the eight possible treatment combinations, considering any pair of levels for the three factors. We have defined the three-way interaction in terms of simple interaction effects. Using the matrix above, a three-way interaction is present if

$$(A \times B \text{ at } c_k) \neq (A \times B \text{ at } c_{k'})$$

or

$$(A \times B \text{ at } c_k) - (A \times B \text{ at } c_{k'}) \neq 0.$$

Similar statements can be made for the other two sets of simple interaction effects. In essence, what we are contrasting is the $A \times B$ interaction on the left with the $A \times B$ interaction on the right.

We have seen that a two-way interaction is defined in terms of the effect of one variable at the levels of the other variable. If we apply this definition to the means in the portion of the ABC matrix at c_k, we have

$$(A \times B \text{ at } c_k) = (\overline{ABC}_{ijk} - \overline{ABC}_{i'jk}) - (\overline{ABC}_{ij'k} - \overline{ABC}_{i'j'k}).$$

We are comparing the difference between the two means at the treatment combination of bc_{jk}, which reflects a treatment effect of factor A, with the corresponding difference at $bc_{j'k}$. We can apply the same definition to the means in the ABC matrix at $c_{k'}$:

$$(A \times B \text{ at } c_{k'}) = (\overline{ABC}_{ijk'} - \overline{ABC}_{i'jk'}) - (\overline{ABC}_{ij'k'} - \overline{ABC}_{i'j'k'}).$$

Putting this all together, we have an arithmetic test of a three-way interaction. More specifically, a triple interaction is present if

$$(A \times B \text{ at } c_k) - (A \times B \text{ at } c_{k'}) \neq 0,$$

$$\begin{aligned}
&[(\overline{ABC}_{ijk} - \overline{ABC}_{i'jk}) - (\overline{ABC}_{ij'k} - \overline{ABC}_{i'j'k})] \\
&\quad - [(\overline{ABC}_{ijk'} - \overline{ABC}_{i'jk'}) - (\overline{ABC}_{ij'k'} - \overline{ABC}_{i'j'k'})] \neq 0.
\end{aligned} \tag{13-1}$$

If Eq. (13-1) does not equal zero, for any one of the possible $2 \times 2 \times 2$ factorials formed by taking any two levels of each variable, then a three-way interaction is present.

TABLE 13-4 *Arithmetic Test for a Three-Way Interaction*

	$c_1\ (k = 1)$				$c_2\ (k' = 2)$		
	a_1	a_2 $(i = 2)$	a_3 $(i' = 3)$		a_1	a_2 $(i = 2)$	a_3 $(i' = 3)$
$b_1\ (j = 1)$	$-$	7	10	$b_1\ (j = 1)$	$-$	5	4
b_2	$-$	$-$	$-$	b_2	$-$	$-$	$-$
$b_3\ (j' = 3)$	$-$	6	8	$b_3\ (j' = 3)$	$-$	8	6

	$c_1\ (k = 1)$				$c_2\ (k' = 2)$		
	a_1 $(i = 1)$	a_2	a_3 $(i' = 3)$		a_1 $(i = 1)$	a_2	a_3 $(i' = 3)$
b_1	$-$	$-$	$-$	b_1	$-$	$-$	$-$
$b_2\ (j = 2)$	10	$-$	6	$b_2\ (j = 2)$	8	$-$	2
$b_3\ (j' = 3)$	1	$-$	8	$b_3\ (j' = 3)$	1	$-$	6

We have maintained that there is no triple interaction in the data presented in Table 13-3. To test this assertion, suppose we apply Eq. (13-1) to the means in the matrix defined by $i = 2$, $i' = 3$, $j = 1$, $j' = 3$, $k = 1$, and $k' = 2$. For this combination, the lefthand side of Eq. (13-1) becomes

$$[(\overline{ABC}_{211} - \overline{ABC}_{311}) - (\overline{ABC}_{231} - \overline{ABC}_{331})]$$
$$- [(\overline{ABC}_{212} - \overline{ABC}_{312}) - (\overline{ABC}_{232} - \overline{ABC}_{332})].$$

The specific eight means involved in this $2 \times 2 \times 2$ factorial are indicated in the upper portion of Table 13-4. Substituting the means into the equation, we have

$$[(7 - 10) - (6 - 8)] - [(5 - 4) - (8 - 6)] = [(-3) - (-2)] - [(1) - (2)]$$
$$= (-3 + 2) - (1 - 2)$$
$$= (-1) - (-1)$$
$$= -1 + 1$$
$$= 0.$$

Setting $i = 1$, $i' = 3$, $j = 2$, $j' = 3$, $k = 1$, and $k' = 2$, we have

$$[(\overline{ABC}_{121} - \overline{ABC}_{321}) - (\overline{ABC}_{131} - \overline{ABC}_{331})]$$
$$- [(\overline{ABC}_{122} - \overline{ABC}_{322}) - (\overline{ABC}_{132} - \overline{ABC}_{332})].$$

These means are specified in the lower portion of Table 13-4. Carrying on with the substitution,

$$[(10 - 6) - (1 - 8)] - [(8 - 2) - (1 - 6)] = [(4) - (-7)] - [(6) - (-5)]$$
$$= (4 + 7) - (6 + 5)$$
$$= 11 - 11$$
$$= 0.$$

COMMENT   The arithmetic test specified by Eq. (13-1) is useful primarily as a way of increasing our understanding of interaction. It is not a practical method for detecting three-way interactions—for several reasons. First, although only *one* nonzero value is needed to demonstrate the *presence* of interaction, essentially all of the possible combinations must be evaluated to establish the *absence* of interaction. Second, with actual data, even a *nonzero* value for Eq. (13-1) is not sufficient cause to conclude that an interaction is present—the statistical significance of the interaction must be assessed before this conclusion is made. Finally, the interaction sum of squares can be viewed as a composite or average of the interactions found in all of the arrangements possible by forming pairs of levels for the three independent variables. Since we must calculate this quantity anyway, there is no need to turn to Eq. (13-1). The arithmetic test is useful as a probe, however, to show that a three-way interaction *is* present numerically in a set of data, even if we cannot see it in the plot of the means.

The important lesson to be drawn from this discussion is our reliance upon the results of the statistical analysis. If we find out that the three-way interaction is *not* significant, we will immediately focus our attention on the two-way interactions—even though the data display may *still* seem to reflect the higher-order interaction! If it *is* significant, we can *then* worry about "seeing" it in the data plot. Even more critical, however, we will have to worry about finding an *interpretation* of its meaning.

Additional Illustrations of Interaction and Noninteraction

Additional examples of interaction and noninteraction are found in Exercises 1 and 2 at the end of Part IV. These problems are designed to test your understanding of the definition of the triple interaction, as well as of two-way interactions and of main effects. Another example is provided by the numerical example used to illustrate the analyses discussed in this chapter. This example contains a three-way interaction (see Fig. 13-5). Exercises 3 and 4 provide additional numerical examples, one with a significant higher-order interaction and one without.

It is much easier to grasp the meaning of a second-order interaction when the experiment is your own and you have gone through the agonizing steps in planning the experiment than when it is an example in a statistics text, where the independent variables are represented by theoretically neutral letters. A researcher does not turn to a three-way factorial unless he has thought about the real possibilities of the higher-order interaction—of what it will mean if it does materialize as predicted and what it will mean if it does not. Wallace and Underwood, for example, already knew that associative strength would show opposite results with the free-recall and paired-associate tasks. Their intent was to test their theoretical interpretation of this interaction by manipulating a *third* independent variable that would reduce or eliminate this interaction. This variable, represented by a contrast of college students and mental retardates, was assumed to be a way of reducing the strength of linguistic associations without changing the nature of the materials. Their prediction of a three-way interaction followed directly from their original theoretical explanation and their assumption of the effects of comparing college students and mental retardates.

The point is that we usually build up to a three-way interaction by the logic of our own research. You should understand precisely what is meant by a higher-order interaction, so that you will know when you are predicting its occurrence or nonoccurrence in a three-way factorial. To this end, the "neutral" examples in the exercises to this part will prove useful.

COMPUTATIONAL FORMULAS AND ANALYSIS SUMMARY

Design and Notation

Before turning to the actual analysis, we will discuss the notation needed to specify the various calculations. The notational system is illustrated in Tables 13-5(a) and 13-5(b). The basic design is summarized in the upper portion of Table 13-5(a). Inspection indicates that the design is a $3 \times 2 \times 2$ factorial, factor A being represented with $a = 3$ levels, factor B with $b = 2$ levels, and factor C with $c = 2$ levels. We have also indicated that there are $s = 3$ subjects randomly assigned to each of the $abc = 3(2)(2) = 12$ treatment conditions.

A basic score or individual observation becomes $ABCS_{ijkl}$ in the notational system for the three-factor design. The four capital letters are needed to designate the score of a single subject in a particular combination of the levels of the factors A, B, and C. These $ABCS$ scores are enumerated in the $ABCS$ matrix in the lower half of Table 13-5(a). When it is necessary to specify a particular observation in one of the abc treatment conditions, we will do so by using four subscripts, namely, an i to refer to the level of factor A, a j to refer to the level of factor B, a k to refer to the level of factor C, and an l to refer to

TABLE 13-5(a) *Design and Notation for the Three-Factor Design*

EXPERIMENTAL DESIGN

Factor C

	c_1			c_2		
	Factor A			Factor A		
Factor B	a_1	a_2	a_3	a_1	a_2	a_3
b_1	$s = 3$	$s = 3$	$s = 3$	$s = 3$	$s = 3$	$s = 3$
b_2	$s = 3$	$s = 3$	$s = 3$	$s = 3$	$s = 3$	$s = 3$

$ABCS$ MATRIX

Treatment Combinations

abc_{111}	abc_{121}	$\cdots$	abc_{312}	abc_{322}
$ABCS_{1111}$	$ABCS_{1211}$	$\cdots$	$ABCS_{3121}$	$ABCS_{3221}$
$ABCS_{1112}$	$ABCS_{1212}$	$\cdots$	$ABCS_{3122}$	$ABCS_{3222}$
$ABCS_{1113}$	$ABCS_{1213}$	$\cdots$	$ABCS_{3123}$	$ABCS_{3223}$

the specific subject in the ijkth cell.[3] We will use notational subscripts only when we must in order to avoid ambiguity in the calculations.

Table 13-5(b) presents the four matrices from which we will calculate the different treatment effects. The first is the ABC matrix. This matrix contains the totals for each of the abc treatment conditions; they are denoted as ABC_{ijk}. The ABC_{ijk} sums are obtained by adding up the individual $ABCS_{ijkl}$ scores in each of the abc cells or groups. We have seen that there are s of these scores in each group. More formally, then, a cell sum is defined as

$$ABC_{ijk} = \sum_{l}^{s} ABCS_{ijkl}.$$

The notation may be better understood if we cancel the letter and the subscript involved in this summation. That is,

$$\sum_{l}^{s} ABCS_{ijkl} = ABC\cancel{S}_{ijk\cancel{l}} = ABC_{ijk}.$$

For an example of the summation,

$$ABC_{312} = ABCS_{3121} + ABCS_{3122} + ABCS_{3123}.$$

The other three matrices presented in Table 13-5(b) are two-factor matrices formed when the levels of a third factor are disregarded—i.e., summed across

---

[3] With these subscripts,

$$i = 1, 2, \ldots, a, \quad j = 1, 2, \ldots, b, \quad k = 1, 2, \ldots, c, \quad \text{and} \quad l = 1, 2, \ldots, s.$$

or collapsed over. Thus, the AB matrix superimposes the lefthand and right-hand portions of the ABC matrix, eliminating the C classification. Any sum listed within the body of the AB matrix is obtained by combining corresponding treatment sums from the different levels of factor C. That is,

$$\sum_{k}^{c} ABC_{ijk} = AB\mathcal{C}_{ijk} = AB_{ij}.$$

For example,

$$AB_{11} = ABC_{111} + ABC_{112} \quad \text{and} \quad AB_{32} = ABC_{321} + ABC_{322}.$$

The marginal totals in the AB matrix represent familiar ground, the column marginal totals are the A_i sums, the row marginal totals are the B_j sums, and the sum of either the row marginal totals or the column marginal totals is the grand sum (T).

The AC and BC matrices are formed in a similar way. The totals within the body of the AC matrix are obtained by summing corresponding totals from the different levels of factor B. That is,

$$\sum_{j}^{b} ABC_{ijk} = A\mathcal{B}C_{ijk} = AC_{ik},$$

TABLE 13-5(b)   *Summary Matrices for the Three-Factor Design*

ABC MATRIX

	c_1			c_2		
	a_1	a_2	a_3	a_1	a_2	a_3
b_1	ABC_{111}	ABC_{211}	ABC_{311}	ABC_{112}	ABC_{212}	ABC_{312}
b_2	ABC_{121}	ABC_{221}	ABC_{321}	ABC_{122}	ABC_{222}	ABC_{322}

AB MATRIX

	a_1	a_2	a_3	Sum
b_1	AB_{11}	AB_{21}	AB_{31}	B_1
b_2	AB_{12}	AB_{22}	AB_{32}	B_2
Sum	A_1	A_2	A_3	T

AC MATRIX

	a_1	a_2	a_3	Sum
c_1	AC_{11}	AC_{21}	AC_{31}	C_1
c_2	AC_{12}	AC_{22}	AC_{32}	C_2
Sum	A_1	A_2	A_3	T

BC MATRIX

	c_1	c_2	Sum
b_1	BC_{11}	BC_{12}	B_1
b_2	BC_{21}	BC_{22}	B_2
Sum	C_1	C_2	T

and, as an example,

$$AC_{22} = ABC_{212} + ABC_{222} \quad \text{and} \quad AC_{31} = ABC_{311} + ABC_{321}.$$

The marginal totals of the AC matrix provide the A_i sums (column marginal totals), the C_k sums (row marginal totals), and T (the sum of either the row or column marginal totals).

Turning finally to the BC matrix, we see that the totals within the body of this matrix are found by collapsing across the levels of factor A. Specifically,

$$\sum_i^a ABC_{ijk} = ABC_{.jk} = BC_{jk}.$$

For the sum at bc_{12},

$$BC_{12} = ABC_{112} + ABC_{212} + ABC_{312},$$

and at bc_{21},

$$BC_{21} = ABC_{121} + ABC_{221} + ABC_{321}.$$

The marginal totals of the BC matrix duplicate totals obtainable from the AB and AC matrices—namely, the C_k sums (column marginal totals), the B_j sums (row marginal totals), and T.

Partitioning the Total Sum of Squares

In the three-way factorial presented in Table 13-5(a), there are s subjects in each cell of the ABC matrix and, thus, $abcs = 12s$ subjects in the entire experiment. As with any completely randomized experiment, the variability of the individual scores from the overall mean (the SS_T) can be partitioned into a between-groups sum of squares (SS_{bg}—the variability of the $\overline{ABC}$ treatment means from $\overline{T}$) and a within-groups sum of squares (SS_{wg}—the variability of subjects treated alike, pooled over the specific treatment conditions). As with the two-factor analysis described in Chapter 10, we can subdivide the SS_{bg} into a set of useful components.

We have already hinted at the nature of these sources of variance. That is, the SS_{bg} can be partitioned into a set of three main effects (one for each independent variable), a set of three two-way interactions ($A \times B$, $A \times C$, and $B \times C$), and the three-way interaction. In symbols,

$$SS_{bg} = SS_A + SS_B + SS_C + SS_{A \times B} + SS_{A \times C} + SS_{B \times C} + SS_{A \times B \times C}. \quad (13\text{-}2)$$

It is a simple step to include in Eq. (13-2) the variability of the individual subjects:

$$
\begin{aligned}
SS_T &= SS_{bg} + SS_{wg} \\
&= SS_A + SS_B + SS_C + SS_{A \times B} + SS_{A \times C} + SS_{B \times C} \\
&\quad + SS_{A \times B \times C} + SS_{S/ABC}.
\end{aligned}
\quad (13\text{-}3)
$$

The last source of variance, the $SS_{S/ABC}$, is the within-groups sum of squares and refers to the pooled sums of squares of subjects within each abc treatment condition. We will now construct the computational formulas for these component sums of squares.

Generation of Formulas from *df* Statements

In Chapter 10 we considered a procedure by which the computational formulas for the sums of squares are constructed from the corresponding *df* statements. We will apply the same set of rules to the present analysis. The development of the formulas takes place in three basic steps, through which we will work quickly. If further guidance is required, refer back to the earlier discussion (pp. 191–195).

IDENTIFICATION OF SOURCES OF VARIANCE   This step has been completed by Eq. (13-3), but we will still follow the rules given in Chapter 10. Specifically,

1. **List factors:** A, B, C, and S/ABC, and
2. **Form interactions:** $A \times B$, $A \times C$, $B \times C$, and $A \times B \times C$.

These sources of variance are presented in column 1 of Table 13-6.

DEGREES OF FREEDOM   The *df* associated with each source of variance are listed in column 2. The *df* for the main effects equal the number of treatment levels minus 1. The *df* for the interaction sums of squares are found by multiplying the *df*'s associated with the factors specified by the interaction:

$$df_{A \times B} = (df_A)(df_B) = (a - 1)(b - 1),$$

$$df_{A \times C} = (df_A)(df_C) = (a - 1)(c - 1),$$

$$df_{B \times C} = (df_B)(df_C) = (b - 1)(c - 1),$$

$$df_{A \times B \times C} = (df_A)(df_B)(df_C) = (a - 1)(b - 1)(c - 1).$$

In each case, the *df* reflect the number of cells in the corresponding data matrices that are free to vary (see pp. 197–198).

The *df* for the $SS_{S/ABC}$ are calculated by pooling the *df* associated with factor S, i.e., $s - 1$, over the abc treatment groups:

$$df_{S/ABC} = abc(df_S) = abc(s - 1).$$

The *df* for the SS_T are one less than the total number of observations in the experiment; i.e.,

$$df_T = abcs - 1.$$

CONSTRUCTION OF THE COMPUTATIONAL FORMULAS   The remaining steps in the generation of the computational formulas for the sums of squares are specified in columns 3 through 7 of Table 13-6. We start in column 3 with the

TABLE 13-6 Construction of the Computational Formulas from the Expanded df Statements

(1) Source	(2) df	(3) df Expanded	First Term			
			(4) Square and Sum	(5) Selection of Denominator	(6) Letter Code	(7) Computational Formula (Coded)
A	$a-1$	$a-1$	$\sum (A)^2$	$\dfrac{\sum (A)^2}{abcs} = \dfrac{\sum (A)^2}{bcs}$	$[A]$	$[A]-[T]$
B	$b-1$	$b-1$	$\sum (B)^2$	$\dfrac{\sum (B)^2}{abcs} = \dfrac{\sum (B)^2}{acs}$	$[B]$	$[B]-[T]$
C	$c-1$	$c-1$	$\sum (C)^2$	$\dfrac{\sum (C)^2}{abcs} = \dfrac{\sum (C)^2}{abs}$	$[C]$	$[C]-[T]$
$A \times B$	$(a-1)(b-1)$	$ab-a-b+1$	$\sum (AB)^2$	$\dfrac{\sum (AB)^2}{abcs} = \dfrac{\sum (AB)^2}{cs}$	$[AB]$	$[AB]-[A]-[B]+[T]$
$A \times C$	$(a-1)(c-1)$	$ac-a-c+1$	$\sum (AC)^2$	$\dfrac{\sum (AC)^2}{abcs} = \dfrac{\sum (AC)^2}{bs}$	$[AC]$	$[AC]-[A]-[C]+[T]$
$B \times C$	$(b-1)(c-1)$	$bc-b-c+1$	$\sum (BC)^2$	$\dfrac{\sum (BC)^2}{abcs} = \dfrac{\sum (BC)^2}{as}$	$[BC]$	$[BC]-[B]-[C]+[T]$
$A \times B \times C$	$(a-1)(b-1)(c-1)$	$abc-ab-ac-bc$ $+a+b+c-1$	$\sum (ABC)^2$	$\dfrac{\sum (ABC)^2}{abcs} = \dfrac{\sum (ABC)^2}{s}$	$[ABC]$	$[ABC]-[AB]-[AC]-[BC]$ $+[A]+[B]+[C]-[T]$
S/ABC	$abc(s-1)$	$abcs-abc$	$\sum (ABCS)^2$	$\dfrac{\sum (ABCS)^2}{abcs} = \sum (ABCS)^2$	$[ABCS]$	$[ABCS]-[ABC]$
Total	$abcs-1$	$abcs-1$	$\sum (ABCS)^2$	$\dfrac{\sum (ABCS)^2}{abcs} = \sum (ABCS)^2$	$[ABCS]$	$[ABCS]-[T]$
	1	1	$(T)^2$	$\dfrac{(T)^2}{abcs} = \dfrac{(T)^2}{abcs}$	$[T]$	

expanded *df* statements, which as we have seen, provide all the information we need to evolve the computational formulas. The next three columns represent the construction of basic terms which appear in the computational formulas for the component sums of squares. These are the first terms in each formula. (The last row lists the term associated with "1" in the expanded *df* statements.) By working with the first terms, we can minimize our writing chores. In column 4, we have combined steps 2 and 3 from Chapter 10; that is, we have written the first terms for column 3 as totals—or, in the case of S/ABC and "Total" as individual observations, squared and then summed all of these quantities that are possible.

In column 5 we complete the construction of the terms by dividing each numerator by the total number of observations (*abcs* in this design), deleting letters in the denominator which appear in the numerator, and rewriting the term. The final operation on the first terms is to represent each one by the letter code we have been using in the preceding chapters. The computational formulas for the sums of squares, written in coded form, are given in column 7 of the table. The particular combination of terms for each sum of squares is specified by the corresponding *df* statement in column 3.

Summary of the Analysis of Variance

SUMS OF SQUARES AND *df*'s   The formulas for the sums of squares and the respective *df*'s are presented again in Table 13-7.

MEAN SQUARES AND F RATIOS   The mean squares are obtained by dividing each component sum of squares by its corresponding *df* as indicated in Table 13-7. Each of these mean squares, except the $MS_{S/ABC}$, provides an estimate of the population treatment effects (main effects or interaction) plus error variance.[4] The $MS_{S/ABC}$ provides an independent estimate of error variance. The null hypothesis in each case specifies the absence of population treatment effects, while the alternative hypothesis specifies their presence. When the null hypothesis is true, ratios formed by dividing these mean squares by the $MS_{S/ABC}$ are distributed as F (with appropriate numerator and denominator *df*'s). Obtained F ratios which exceed theoretical values at some significance level (α) lead to the rejection of the null hypothesis and the acceptance of the alternative hypothesis.

ASSUMPTIONS   The assumptions underlying the analysis just outlined are the same as those we have listed for the one-way and the two-way analyses of variance (see pp. 74–77 and pp. 199–200, respectively).

---

[4] This statement is correct only for the *fixed-effects model*, which is appropriate for most research applications. See Chapter 16 (pp. 333–343) for a discussion of the different models and how the analysis is changed under the alternative ones (in particular, see Table 16-4, p. 342).

TABLE 13-7 *Computational Formulas for the Three-Way Factorial*

Source	Sum of Squares[a]	df	MS	F[b]
A	$\dfrac{\sum (A)^2}{bcs} - \dfrac{(T)^2}{abcs}$	$a - 1$	$\dfrac{SS_A}{df_A}$	$\dfrac{MS_A}{MS_{S/ABC}}$
B	$\dfrac{\sum (B)^2}{acs} - [T]$	$b - 1$	$\dfrac{SS_B}{df_B}$	$\dfrac{MS_B}{MS_{S/ABC}}$
C	$\dfrac{\sum (C)^2}{abs} - [T]$	$c - 1$	$\dfrac{SS_C}{df_C}$	$\dfrac{MS_C}{MS_{S/ABC}}$
$A \times B$	$\dfrac{\sum (AB)^2}{cs} - [A] - [B] + [T]$	$(a-1)(b-1)$	$\dfrac{SS_{A \times B}}{df_{A \times B}}$	$\dfrac{MS_{A \times B}}{MS_{S/ABC}}$
$A \times C$	$\dfrac{\sum (AC)^2}{bs} - [A] - [C] + [T]$	$(a-1)(c-1)$	$\dfrac{SS_{A \times C}}{df_{A \times C}}$	$\dfrac{MS_{A \times C}}{MS_{S/ABC}}$
$B \times C$	$\dfrac{\sum (BC)^2}{as} - [B] - [C] + [T]$	$(b-1)(c-1)$	$\dfrac{SS_{B \times C}}{df_{B \times C}}$	$\dfrac{MS_{B \times C}}{MS_{S/ABC}}$
$A \times B \times C$	$\dfrac{\sum (ABC)^2}{s} - [AB] - [AC] - [BC]$ $+ [A] + [B] + [C] - [T]$	$(a-1)(b-1)(c-1)$	$\dfrac{SS_{A \times B \times C}}{df_{A \times B \times C}}$	$\dfrac{MS_{A \times B \times C}}{MS_{S/ABC}}$
S/ABC	$\sum (ABCS)^2 - [ABC]$	$abc(s-1)$	$\dfrac{SS_{S/ABC}}{df_{S/ABC}}$	
Total	$[ABCS] - [T]$	$abcs - 1$		

[a] Bracketed letters represent complete terms in the computational formulas; a particular term is identified by the letter(s) appearing in the numerator.
[b] The *fixed-effects model* is assumed.

NUMERICAL EXAMPLE

Background

A numerical example of the basic analyses is drawn from a reasonable, but hypothetical, study in human memory. In a typical study of memory, different groups of subjects are given a test on a list of verbal materials at different periods of time following the learning of the list. These intervals between training and testing are called *retention intervals*. Any decrement in performance observed over the retention intervals is called forgetting. A common explanation of forgetting is that interference from linguistic sources is responsible for any losses detected in the experiment. It has been assumed that this interference comes from linguistic habits which conflict with the material being learned. We will focus on one source of this interference, namely, conflicting linguistic habits that the subject encounters during the retention interval—after the learning is completed but before the memory test is administered.

Suppose we manipulate the *amount* of linguistic activity that a subject experiences during the interval by confining subjects to the laboratory and exposing them to an activity that *minimizes* linguistic experience or to one that *maximizes* it. What we are proposing, then, is a factorial design with two independent variables, length of the retention interval and type of interval activity, and we are predicting an interaction, namely, greater forgetting for the "maximum" condition than for the "minimum" condition. In order to establish the critical nature of the linguistic activity, we will also compare the effect of these different activities upon the forgetting of different kinds of verbal materials— materials that have a low, medium, or high correspondence to the language. The expectation is that linguistic experience will interfere greatly with the materials of low correspondence and only slightly with the materials of high correspondence.

If we piece together all these speculations, we see that we are predicting an interaction of the three independent variables. Specifically, we are predicting (1) that with increased linguistic activity, we will observe small amounts of forgetting with the high material and large amounts of forgetting with the low material over the different retention intervals and (2) that with reduced activity, we will observe approximately the same small amounts of forgetting with the different types of material. The first expectation specifies a two-way interaction of type of material and the length of the retention interval at one level of the third variable, increased linguistic activity, and the second expectation specifies the *absence* of an interaction of these two variables at the other level of the third variable, reduced linguistic activity. In short, a triple interaction is predicted because the interaction of two variables is expected to be different at the two levels of the third variable.

The Design

The factorial design is summarized by the ABC matrix presented in the upper portion of Table 13-8. There are three retention intervals (1, 4, and 7 hours), three types of materials that will be learned (low, medium, and high), and two types of linguistic activity (minimum and maximum)—a $3 \times 3 \times 2$ factorial. These independent variables have been arbitrarily designated factors A, B, and C, respectively. Each treatment cell in the ABC matrix contains $s = 15$ subjects. Although the individual $ABCS$ scores are not given, a sufficient amount of information is provided to allow the completion of the analysis—i.e., the values of the cell sums (ABC_{ijk}) and the quantity, $\sum (ABCS)^2$. The cell totals are entered in the ABC matrix, and the sum of the squared $ABCS$ scores is given in the bottom righthand corner of the table.

A reasonable first step is to plot the means calculated from the sums in the ABC matrix to give us some indication as to how the experiment came out. This has been done in Fig. 13-5. It will be noted that the retention functions for the condition in which subjects are given minimum linguistic activity show a small amount of forgetting and roughly parallel curves; i.e., the forgetting is the same for all three types of material. The display on the right, where the interval activity maximizes linguistic involvement, shows an increase in forgetting as the material deviates more and more from that found in the language; in short, there appears to be a higher-order interaction. We now have to assess the significance of this effect.

TABLE 13-8 *Design and Results of a Three-Way Factorial*

ABC MATRIX

Interval Activity (Factor C)

Material	Minimum (c_1)			Maximum (c_2)		
	Retention Interval (Factor A)			Retention Interval (Factor A)		
(Factor B)	1 Hour (a_1)	4 Hours (a_2)	7 Hours (a_3)	1 Hour (a_1)	4 Hours (a_2)	7 Hours (a_3)
Low (b_1)	205	198	182	209	178	146
Medium (b_2)	210	193	177	203	182	169
High (b_3)	208	197	179	211	197	182

AB MATRIX

	a_1	a_2	a_3	Sum
b_1	414	376	328	1118
b_2	413	375	346	1134
b_3	419	394	361	1174
Sum	1246	1145	1035	3426

AC MATRIX

	a_1	a_2	a_3	Sum
c_1	623	588	538	1749
c_2	623	557	497	1677
Sum	1246	1145	1035	3426

BC MATRIX

	c_1	c_2	Sum
b_1	585	533	1118
b_2	580	554	1134
b_3	584	590	1174
Sum	1749	1677	3426

$\sum (ABCS)^2 = 44,187$

The Analysis

We begin by preparing the necessary two-way matrices; these are presented in the bottom portion of Table 13-8. The marginal totals of the two-way matrices provide the sums needed to calculate the three main effects. The totals within the body of the matrices provide the additional sums needed to calculate the three two-way interactions. The cell totals in the ABC matrix are used in the calculation of the three-way interaction and the within-groups sum of squares. In order to guard against computational errors in the formation of

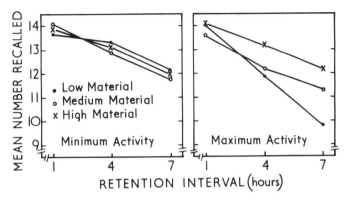

Fig. 13-5   Mean recall as a function of retention interval (factor *A*), type of material (factor *B*), and interval activity (factor *C*).

these matrices, it is a good idea to verify for each two-way matrix that the sum of the row and column marginal totals equals the grand sum, *T*.

We are now ready to calculate the basic terms entering into the computational formulas for the sums of squares. From any of the two-way matrices,

$$[T] = \frac{(T)^2}{abcs} = \frac{(3426)^2}{3(3)(2)(15)} = \frac{11,737,476}{270} = 43,472.13.$$

From the margins of either the *AB* or *AC* matrix, we have

$$[A] = \frac{\sum (A)^2}{bcs} = \frac{(1246)^2 + (1145)^2 + (1035)^2}{3(2)(15)} = \frac{3,934,766}{90} = 43,719.62.$$

From either the *AB* or *BC* matrix,

$$[B] = \frac{\sum (B)^2}{acs} = \frac{(1118)^2 + (1134)^2 + (1174)^2}{3(2)(15)} = \frac{3,914,156}{90} = 43,490.62,$$

and from either the *AC* or *BC* matrix,

$$[C] = \frac{\sum (C)^2}{abs} = \frac{(1749)^2 + (1677)^2}{3(3)(15)} = \frac{5,871,330}{135} = 43,491.33.$$

Our next task is the computation of the first terms entering into the determination of the *SS*'s for the two-way interactions. From the *AB* matrix,

$$[AB] = \frac{\sum (AB)^2}{cs} = \frac{(414)^2 + (413)^2 + \cdots + (346)^2 + (361)^2}{2(15)}$$

$$= \frac{1,312,384}{30} = 43,746.13,$$

from the AC matrix,

$$[AC] = \frac{\sum (AC)^2}{bs} = \frac{(623)^2 + (623)^2 + \cdots + (538)^2 + (497)^2}{3(15)}$$

$$= \frac{1,968,704}{45} = 43,748.98,$$

and from the BC matrix,

$$[BC] = \frac{\sum (BC)^2}{as} = \frac{(585)^2 + (580)^2 + \cdots + (554)^2 + (590)^2}{3(15)}$$

$$= \frac{1,958,786}{45} = 43,528.58.$$

We next obtain the first term of the $SS_{A \times B \times C}$. The totals needed for this sum of squares are found in the ABC matrix:

$$[ABC] = \frac{\sum (ABC)^2}{s} = \frac{(205)^2 + (210)^2 + \cdots + (169)^2 + (182)^2}{15}$$

$$= \frac{657,174}{15} = 43,811.60.$$

The final quantity needed for the $SS_{S/ABC}$ and the SS_T has been provided in Table 13-8:

$$[ABCS] = \sum (ABCS)^2 = 44,187.$$

TABLE 13-9 *Summary of the Analysis of Variance*

Source	Calculations[a]	SS	df	MS	F
Retention Interval (A)	$43,719.62 - 43,472.13 =$	247.49	2	123.74	83.05***
Material (B)	$43,490.62 - [T] =$	18.49	2	9.24	6.20***
Interval Activity (C)	$43,491.33 - [T] =$	19.20	1	19.20	12.89***
$A \times B$	$43,746.13 - [A] - [B] + [T] =$	8.02	4	2.00	1.34
$A \times C$	$43,748.98 - [A] - [C] + [T] =$	10.16	2	5.08	3.41*
$B \times C$	$43,528.58 - [B] - [C] + [T] =$	18.76	2	9.38	6.30***
$A \times B \times C$	$43,811.60 - [AB] - [AC] - [BC]$ $+ [A] + [B] + [C] - [T] =$	17.35	4	4.34	2.91**
S/ABC	$44,187 - [ABC] =$	375.40	252	1.49	
Total	$[ABCS] - [T] =$	714.87	269		

* $p < .05$.   ** $p < .025$.   *** $p < .01$.

[a] Bracketed letters represent complete terms in the computational formulas; a particular term is identified by the letter(s) appearing in the numerator.

These basic quantities and the patterns in which we combine them to calculate the sums of squares are entered in the second column of Table 13-9. The final steps in the analysis are summarized in the remaining columns of the table. The sum of the component sums of squares is compared with the SS_T to provide a partial computational check on the operations. The results of the F tests are given in the final column of the table. All factors are significant, except the $A \times B$ interaction. The important challenge now is to be able to assess the "meaning" of these various statistical comparisons.

Additional Analyses

We started this example with a discussion of what we were hoping to find with the experiment and why. More specifically, we predicted that the type of material learned would be an important determiner of forgetting, but only when the retention interval was filled with a large amount of linguistic activity. An inspection of Fig. 13-5 indicates that such an outcome was obtained. Moreover, we can see that the corresponding three-way interaction is significant. There are several factors that should be considered at this point.

SIMPLE INTERACTION EFFECTS   One obvious analysis would be to attempt to identify the source or locus of the significant triple interaction. To conclude that a three-way interaction is present simply means that the variation among the treatment means cannot be entirely accounted for by the main effects and the two-way interactions; the test for interaction is an omnibus F test. We are familiar with this problem, of course, as the same thing was true when we found a significant main effect or interaction in the one-way and two-way cases.

We have spent a good deal of time considering analyses that are intended to isolate the components or factors contributing to a significant main effect or interaction. We discussed in Chapter 11 an analysis specifically designed to analyze a significant $A \times B$ interaction: an analysis of the *simple main effects.* We saw that this analysis was a direct and useful way of extracting information from a significant two-way interaction. The same sort of analysis may be adapted for use with the higher-order interactions. For the triple interaction, the analysis becomes an isolation of the *simple interaction effects.*

In the present example, this analysis is obvious. That is, we predicted that there would be no interaction between the type of learning material and the length of the retention interval for the subjects given minimal linguistic activity, while we specified a particular type of interaction between the two variables for the subjects given the maximal linguistic activity. In this case, then, an analysis of the simple interaction effects of the three-way interaction would consist of separate analyses of the Interval × Material interaction at the two levels of the activity variable. We will discuss how this is accomplished in the next chapter.

INTERPRETATION OF LOWER-ORDER EFFECTS   A second point we should consider also stems from the fact that the three-way interaction is significant.

Specifically, there is little reason for us to be greatly interested in the outcomes of the other F tests. The reason is that in every one of these comparisons we must remind ourselves of the fact that the higher-order interaction is significant. Consider the two-way interactions, for example. We found in our analysis a significant interaction of retention interval and activity (see Table 13-9). To see what this interaction looks like, we can inspect the relevant sums in Table 13-8 or, better, we can plot the data. This has been done in the lefthand panel of Fig. 13-6. The nature of this interaction is clear from the plot: the forgetting curve is steeper for the maximum condition than for the minimum condition. Knowing what we now know, however, we would say that this summary of the results, which disregards the type of learning material, is too crude for our purposes, since it "hides" the important three-way interaction. Look back at Fig. 13-5. The retention functions are essentially identical for the high material under the two activity conditions. With this information known to us, we certainly would *not* want to offer a general conclusion that greater forgetting is always associated with greater linguistic activity; we would want to qualify this statement with a specification of the nature of the material being learned.

We see a similar difficulty in the plot of the Material × Activity interaction in the right panel of Fig. 13-6. (The three levels of the learning material have been arbitrarily spaced equally on the baseline of the figure.) We can see here that the type of material produces no effect under the minimum condition and a large effect under the maximum condition. Again, inspection of Fig. 13-5 indicates that this is *not true* at the shortest retention interval, where all of the scores are approximately the same; it is only at the longer intervals that this interaction shows itself strongly. Thus, with either of the significant two-way interactions, we find it necessary to recognize the presence of the significant three-way interaction. We are not satisfied with these simplified statements

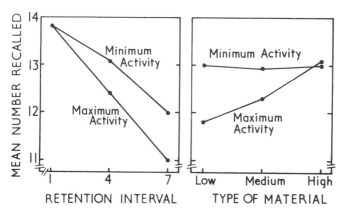

Fig. 13-6   Plot of the A × C (or Interval × Activity) interaction (left panel) and the B × C (or Material × Activity) interaction (right panel).

because they do not accurately reflect the characteristics of the phenomenon as we know it now.

What conclusions can we draw from the three significant *main effects*? Clearly, we have found a sizable amount of forgetting, but we must qualify this statement, since the exact amount depends upon the type of activity filling the retention interval and the type of material that was learned. Consider the main effect of Material. In general, the material corresponding to linguistic habits is recalled better than material that does not. But again we must qualify this conclusion, because we also know that this effect is most pronounced at the longer intervals and under the condition of maximal linguistic activity. Looking at the final main effect, we see that less is recalled by subjects in the maximum condition than in the minimum condition. However, it is also clear that the effect of the two types of activity does not show itself until four hours have passed, and that this is true primarily for the material of low correspondence to language.

In summary, then, any statements concerning the main effects and two-way interactions in our example are *not accurate descriptions* of how the three independent variables affected behavior. It is convenient to remember that the order in which we *interpret* the outcomes of an analysis of variance is exactly the *reverse* of the order in which we extract the component sums of squares. In the present example, we have seen that the significant triple interaction reduces our interest in any of the lower-order effects. If the higher-order interaction had *not* been significant, then we would have immediately shifted our attention to the next level of effects—the two-way interactions. The reason for looking at these interactions before considering the main effects is the same: a significant two-way interaction limits our interest in the main effects of the two variables entering into the interaction. (We discussed this point previously in the context of the two-way factorial.) If an independent variable does *not* interact with a second independent variable, then its main effect may be interpreted unambiguously. Otherwise, we will give most of our attention to an interpretation of any significant interactions that might appear in our analysis.

It is possible, in the higher-order designs, to have one or more variables which do not interact with the other variables. Under these circumstances, the main effects of any *noninteracting* variables may be interpreted without qualification. For example, suppose the following sources of variance are significant: A, C, and $A \times B$. The main effect of factor C may be interpreted without qualification, while any interpretation of the main effect of factor A must be tempered by a consideration of the $A \times B$ interaction. (Exercise 3 for Part IV illustrates such a situation.)

Of course, we should not be dismayed by the reduced interest in the lower-level sources of variance when the higher-level sources are significant. It was exactly for the possibility of an interaction that we included the different variables in a factorial experiment. We suspected that the influence of any one of the variables would depend upon the levels of the other critical variables, and this is what we discovered from this analysis. If the interactions had not been significant, we could have developed a relatively simple explanation of the behavior we have been studying. Since they are significant, we must attempt to construct an explanation that will account for the complicated way in which the different variables combined to influence behavior.

SUPPLEMENTARY ANALYSES   So far in our discussion, we have mentioned analyses that we might consider conducting on a single set of data, such as the set presented in Table 13-8. These data represent one measure of memory: the number of words correctly recalled. Other sorts of data from the same experiment may provide additional information concerning the most reasonable interpretation of the basic results. The main interest here was in memory for correct words. Perhaps the errors that the subject made during learning and during the retention test may provide useful supplementary information. For instance, the errors that subjects made with the low material might reflect the intrusion of relatively strong linguistic habits. Such a finding would lend support to the assumption that linguistic habits are an important source of interference in learning and forgetting. Similarly, an analysis of the actual verbal activity undertaken by each subject in the maximum condition may prove to be revealing. It might be shown, for example, that the subjects who are the most active linguistically during the retention interval will show a greater interaction of material and retention interval than those who are less active.

The statistical analysis of the results obtained from supplementary measures may be patterned after the main analysis, or it may focus upon a particular interaction or a comparison between selected groups. Often these supplementary analyses occur to an investigator *after* he has conducted the main analysis and is trying to interpret the meaning of the different outcomes. Given that he has found a significant three-way interaction, for example, what kinds of differences might he expect to find with the supplementary response measures? Considering the post-hoc nature of these questions, we might consider a post-hoc correction of some sort. On the other hand, we might avoid this problem by omitting a formal statistical analysis. That is, we might simply indicate that certain comparisons are *suggestive* of a particular interpretation and forego the formal analysis. Too often researchers use statistical analyses at this point as a sort of stamp of approval or disapproval. The blind use of a statistical test on measures or comparisons which were not originally incorporated into the design of the experiment will tend to suppress potentially interesting findings. We usually expect an experiment not only to answer the questions that we put to it but also to suggest new avenues of approach to a problem. We must be careful not to stifle these unexpected findings by the use of the same relatively stringent statistical standards we reserve for the main analysis.

We cannot cover the subject of supplementary analyses in any systematic fashion, because they will usually be unique to a particular research problem or even to a particular experiment. We simply wish to point out that very few researchers stop with a single analysis. Instead, they comb their data and press their ingenuity to extract additional information concerning the nature of the phenomenon being studied. If one of the supplementary measures presents a different picture, this finding may become the basis for a new explanation of the outcome of the experiment or the jumping-off point for a new experiment. We must pay as much attention to supplementary analyses as to the analysis of the main response measure. We need to be aware, however, that any increase in the number of comparisons we conduct, whether with the main response measure or with supplementary measures, will increase our *experimentwise* error rate. Just what you do about this problem is fundamentally your own decision.

chapter fourteen

THE THREE-FACTOR CASE: SIMPLE EFFECTS AND COMPARISONS

In Chapter 12 we argued that an investigator would probably not be interested in making a large number of multiple comparisons with a two-way factorial. The reason is that the researcher, who knows enough about the phenomenon under study to manipulate two variables that he feels are relevant and may interact, does not intend to sift through his data in an indiscriminate fashion, searching for significant differences. Such a procedure is *unanalytical*, since comparisons between cells which do not occupy the same row or column in the *AB* matrix will be difficult, if not impossible, to interpret. The same argument holds for the higher-order factorials. Our main interest, therefore, will be in analyses that can ask *analytical* questions of our data.

We will consider two such analyses in this chapter. The first approach, the analysis of simple effects, attempts to isolate the source or sources of a higher-order interaction in terms of simple effects. The second approach, the analysis of comparisons, accomplishes the same goal by assessing the contribution of specific comparisons to the interaction. To conclude the chapter we shall discuss multiple comparisons.

ANALYSIS OF SIMPLE EFFECTS

In the analysis of a two-way factorial, simple effects took only one form—namely, simple main effects of the interaction. In the analysis of higher-order factorials, various types of simple effects are possible. In the three-factor design, for example, the simple effects of two-way interactions as well as of the three-way interaction can be examined. We will discuss first the evaluation of significant two-way interactions.

Simple Main Effects of a Two-Way Interaction

As we argued in the last chapter, we will probably undertake a detailed analysis of a significant two-way interaction only when the three-way interaction is *not* significant. With a significant triple interaction, anything that we may say about two-way interactions and main effects will be colored by the presence of the higher-order interaction. But if the $A \times B \times C$ interaction is not significant, then we can consider the two-way interactions directly, without ambiguity. One useful analysis of a significant two-way interaction is a determination of the simple main effects of the interaction.

We saw in Chapter 11 that simple main effects consist of a separate determination of the effect of one of the independent variables at the different levels of the other variable. If we were looking at the variation due to factor A, we would calculate separate estimates of this variation at each of the b levels of factor B. We can translate this analysis to the three-way factorial directly. With a significant $B \times C$ interaction, say, we could consider the simple main effects of factor B at the different levels of factor C or the reverse: the simple main effects of factor C at the levels of factor B. Similar analyses may, of course, be conducted with significant $A \times B$ and $A \times C$ interactions. As before, our goal in these analyses is to pinpoint the source of a particular interaction effect.

COMPUTATIONAL FORMULAS   The meaning of this analysis and the procedures to be followed are exactly those outlined in Chapter 11 (see pp. 213–222). Briefly, we locate the particular two-way matrix that contains the cell sums in which we are interested: the AB matrix for the $A \times B$ interaction, the AC matrix for the $A \times C$ interaction, or the BC matrix for the $B \times C$ interaction. Then we calculate a set of sums of squares representing the variability of one of the variables at the different levels of the other variable. For any one of these interactions, the two variables can serve either function. That is, we could look at the $B \times C$ interaction in terms of the variability due to factor B at the different levels of factor C or the variability due to factor C at the different levels of factor B. The particular way that we choose to perform the analysis depends upon the most meaningful way to look at the data.

Suppose we were looking at the interaction of retention interval and material from the numerical example in the last chapter. It makes more sense to determine the magnitude of the effect attributable to the increasing retention interval (i.e., forgetting) for the different types of learning materials than to consider the variation due to material at each retention interval. We are interested in the course of forgetting and not in the recall of different lists at 1 hour or at 4 hours or at 7 hours.

The computational formulas presented in Chapter 11 for the analysis of simple main effects need only an adjustment for the number of observations. To be more specific, suppose we wanted to determine the simple main effects of factor A at the levels of factor B. The computational formula for Chapter 11 took the form:

$$SS_{A \text{ at } b_j} = \frac{\sum_{i}^{a} (AB_{ij})^2}{s} - \frac{(B_j)^2}{as}.$$

The only change needed for the three-way factorial is in the denominators, to accommodate the fact that each AB_{ij} sum contains cs observations and each B_j sum contains acs observations. Specifically,

$$SS_{A \text{ at } b_j} = \frac{\sum_{i}^{a} (AB_{ij})^2}{cs} - \frac{(B_j)^2}{acs}. \tag{14-1}$$

The new denominators, of course, reflect the operation of computational rule number 1: we divide by the number of observations contributing to the basic totals. An easy way to determine the modification is to note that each term in the computational formula contains the letters representing the total number of observations in the three-way factorial, namely, $abcs$. Two of the letters, ab, appear in the numerator of the first term in Eq. (14-1) and the remaining two, cs, appear in the denominator; the letter b appears in the numerator of the second term and the letters acs appear in the denominator. (This property is true for all computational formulas and will be discussed in Chapter 15.)

Computational formulas for other simple main effects follow this pattern. Consider, for example, the simple main effects of factor C at the levels of factor B. For this analysis, we would be concentrating on the BC matrix and the deviation of the means in the body of the matrix from corresponding $\bar{B}_j$ means in the row margins [see Table 13-5(b), p. 267]. The sum of squares at the b_j level is given by

$$SS_{C \text{ at } b_j} = \frac{\sum_{k}^{c} (BC_{jk})^2}{as} - \frac{(B_j)^2}{acs}. \tag{14-2}$$

The numerators reflect the attention being paid to variability due to factor C at the levels of factor B and the denominators reflect the application of computational rule number 1. (Again, note that the letters $abcs$ are represented in each term.)

The df for simple main effects are simply the df's associated with the corresponding main effects: $a - 1$ for simple main effects of factor A, $b - 1$ for simple main effects of factor B, and $c - 1$ for simple main effects of factor C. Each mean square is tested against the overall within-groups error term, $MS_{S/ABC}$, and the resulting F is evaluated at the appropriate numerator and denominator df's.

NUMERICAL EXAMPLE   We will not formally work out a numerical example here. Except for the change in the denominators, the calculations are identical to those followed in the two-factor case. (A worked example of this analysis is found in Chapter 11, pp. 216–221.) You can also find an example of this sort of analysis applied to the three-factor case in Exercise 3 for Part IV (pp. 388–389).

Simple Interaction Effects of the Three-Way Interaction

Assuming that the triple interaction is significant, we will undoubtedly want to probe into the ABC matrix to locate the critical combinations of variables responsible for the interaction. Two such analyses are possible. One of these, the analysis of the *simple interaction effects*, will be considered in this section. The alternative way in which we can analyze the variability associated with a significant three-way interaction is to assess the effect of *one* variable, factor A say, at all possible combinations of levels of the other *two* variables, factors B and C. This analysis will be presented in the section that follows.

Although the analysis of the simple interaction effects is more complicated than the one we have just considered, it does follow the same general procedure. For the simple main effects, we determined the variation due to one of the variables at the different levels of the other. For the simple interaction effects, on the other hand, we determine the variation due to the *interaction* of two of the variables at each of the levels of the third. This breakdown may be made three different ways: We can look at the $A \times B$ interactions at the c levels of factor C, or at the $A \times C$ interactions at the b levels of factor B, or at the $B \times C$ interactions at the a levels of factor A. The particular breakdown chosen for the analysis again depends upon the most meaningful way for the researcher to think about the three-way interaction.

COMPUTATIONAL FORMULAS   The analysis is conducted as it has been described—we actually obtain a set of two-way interactions, using the general formulas we have been employing all along. For instance, if we choose to calculate the $A \times B$ interaction at the different levels of factor C, we would focus our attention on the ABC matrix, where we will find a separate AB matrix for each level of factor C. We would then calculate the $A \times B$ interaction based on the data of a given matrix just as if the matrix were in fact a two-way interaction in a *two-factor* experiment.

To understand the computational formulas, it is perhaps best to work through a numerical example. We will do that in a moment. But first, refer to the ABC matrix in Table 13-5(b) (p. 267). Suppose we wanted to calculate the simple $A \times B$ interaction at c_2. For the $A \times B$ interaction in the *two-factor case*, we would obtain a quantity involving the AB sums, subtract quantities based on the column and row marginal sums (A_i and B_j), and then add a quantity using the grand total of the matrix (T). We will go through exactly the same calculations for the simple $A \times B$ interaction at c_2 except that we will be using sums and marginal totals from a portion of the ABC matrix. Thus, the designation of the totals involved and, of course, the denominator terms, must reflect this difference. Specifically,

$$SS_{A \times B \text{ at } c_2} = \frac{\sum (ABC_{ij2})^2}{s} - \frac{\sum (AC_{i2})^2}{bs} - \frac{\sum (BC_{j2})^2}{as} + \frac{(C_2)^2}{abs}.$$

Note that the C classification is present in each of the four terms and that it is *not* acted upon, i.e., summed across. This indicates that the C subscript (k) remains *constant* throughout the arithmetic operations: all that will vary will be the levels of factors A and B. The computational formula for the $A \times B$ interaction at *any* level of factor C appears more formidable because of the multiple summation signs and additional notation:

$$SS_{A \times B \text{ at } c_k} = \frac{\sum_{i}^{a} \sum_{j}^{b} (ABC_{ijk})^2}{s} - \frac{\sum_{i}^{a} (AC_{ik})^2}{bs} - \frac{\sum_{j}^{b} (BC_{jk})^2}{as} + \frac{(C_k)^2}{abs}. \quad (14\text{-}3)$$

We will introduce in Chapter 15 a set of computational rules which will allow you to write the computational formulas for any one of the three possible simple interaction effects. For the time being, it is sufficient to point out that the four letters *abcs*, representing the total number of observations, are again present in each of the terms in Eq. (14-3), either in the designation of a sum or as the denominator of the term.

NUMERICAL EXAMPLE   It will be recalled that the triple interaction was significant in the example used to illustrate the three-factor analysis of variance in the last chapter. We saw in Fig. 13-5 that the interaction appeared to result from the fact that the forgetting curves for subjects recalling the different types of materials were the same when the retention interval was filled with a minimum amount of linguistic activity, and they were different when the interval was filled with a large amount of linguistic activity. An analysis of the simple interaction effects might provide statistical support for these observations.

For convenience, the ABC matrix is reported in the upper half of Table 14-1. To facilitate the calculations, marginal sums have been obtained for the AB matrix at c_1 and the one at c_2. Applying Eq. (14-3) to the data appearing in the

AB matrix at c_1 (minimum activity), we find

$$SS_{A \times B \, at \, c_1} = \frac{\sum (ABC_{ij1})^2}{s} - \frac{\sum (AC_{i1})^2}{bs} - \frac{\sum (BC_{j1})^2}{as} + \frac{(C_1)^2}{abs}$$

$$= \frac{(205)^2 + (210)^2 + \cdots + (177)^2 + (179)^2}{15}$$

$$- \frac{(623)^2 + (588)^2 + (538)^2}{3(15)} - \frac{(585)^2 + (580)^2 + (584)^2}{3(15)}$$

$$+ \frac{(1749)^2}{3(3)(15)},$$

and applying it to the data appearing in the AB matrix at c_2 (maximum activity), we have

$$SS_{A \times B \, at \, c_2} = \frac{\sum (ABC_{ij2})^2}{s} - \frac{\sum (AC_{i2})^2}{bs} - \frac{\sum (BC_{j2})^2}{as} + \frac{(C_2)^2}{abs}$$

$$= \frac{(209)^2 + (203)^2 + \cdots + (169)^2 + (182)^2}{15}$$

$$- \frac{(623)^2 + (557)^2 + (497)^2}{3(15)} - \frac{(533)^2 + (554)^2 + (590)^2}{3(15)}$$

$$+ \frac{(1677)^2}{3(3)(15)}.$$

These calculations are completed in the lower half of Table 14-1.

Like the simple main effects of the two-way interaction, the sum of the simple interaction effects of the three-way interaction contains two sources of variance, the three-way interaction and the *two-way interaction* we have been considering. In symbols,

$$\sum SS_{A \times B \, at \, c_k} = SS_{A \times B \times C} + SS_{A \times B}. \qquad (14\text{-}4)$$

In our example, the values for the lefthand sums of squares come from Table 14-1 and those for the righthand sums of squares from Table 13-9 (p. 276). Substituting in Eq. (14-4),

$$2.31 + 23.07 \overset{?}{=} 17.35 + 8.02$$

$$25.38 \approx 25.37.$$

The df are calculated in the usual way by applying the formula for interaction df, Eq. (10-3). Here,

$$df_{A \times B} = (a - 1)(b - 1) = (3 - 1)(3 - 1) = 2(2) = 4$$

for both of the simple interaction effects. Note that these df also satisfy Eq. (14-4).

TABLE 14-1 *Numerical Example: Simple Interaction Effects*

ABC MATRIX

Interval Activity (C)

Materials (B)	Minimum (c_1)				Maximum (c_2)			
	Retention Interval (A)				Retention Interval (A)			
	1 Hour (a_1)	4 Hours (a_2)	7 Hours (a_3)	Sum	1 Hour (a_1)	4 Hours (a_2)	7 Hours (a_3)	Sum
Low (b_1)	205	198	182	585	209	178	146	533
Medium (b_2)	210	193	177	580	203	182	169	554
High (b_3)	208	197	179	584	211	197	182	590
Sum	623	588	538	1749	623	557	497	1677

SUMMARY OF THE ANALYSIS

Source	Calculations	SS	df	MS	F
$A \times B$ at c_1	22,743.00 − 22,740.38 −22,659.58 + 22,659.27 =	2.31	4	.58	<1
$A \times B$ at c_2	21,068.60 − 21,008.60 − 20,869.00 + 20,832.07 =	23.07	4	5.77	3.87*
S/ABC			252	1.49	

* $p < .01$.

That is, the sum of the df associated with the simple interaction effects equals the df for the $SS_{A \times B \times C}$ plus $SS_{A \times B}$. For this example,

$$\sum df_{A \times B \text{ at } c_k} = df_{A \times B \times C} + df_{A \times B}$$
$$= (a - 1)(b - 1)(c - 1) + (a - 1)(b - 1)$$
$$= (3 - 1)(3 - 1)(2 - 1) + (3 - 1)(3 - 1)$$
$$= 2(2)(1) + 2(2)$$
$$= 4 + 4 = 8.$$

The F ratios are formed in the usual way by

$$F = \frac{MS_{A \times B \text{ at } c_k}}{MS_{S/ABC}}, \qquad (14\text{-}5)$$

unless there is heterogeneity of within-group variance.[1] The results of the F tests, summarized in Table 14-1, indicate that the interaction of retention

---

[1] Under these circumstances, separate error terms based on the pooled within-group mean squares should be calculated for each of the AB matrices at the different levels of factor C.

interval and materials is not significant when the interval is filled with minimum linguistic activity and is significant when it contains maximum linguistic activity.

Simple Main Effects of the Three-Way Interaction

We have indicated that there is an alternative way of attempting to isolate the comparisons responsible for a significant three-way interaction. This analysis concentrates on a type of simple main effect for one independent variable at all combinations of the other *two* variables. Suppose the variable of interest is factor A. What this analysis amounts to is a determination of the variability due to factor A alone for each of the different *bc rows* in the ABC matrix [see Table 13-5(b), p. 267]. This set of comparisons is sometimes referred to as an analysis of the *simple, simple main effects* of factor A. We can understand this awkward terminology when we realize that in this analysis we are *two steps* removed from an *actual* main effect. That is, the main effect of factor A is based upon sums that collapse across two variables, factors B and C. The simple main effects of factor A at the levels of factor B (or factor C), which we discussed in an earlier section, are based upon sums that collapse across one variable, factor C (or factor B). The simple, simple main effects of factor A are based upon individual ABC cell sums—all classifications are retained. Simple main effects and simple, simple main effects are still *main* effects, however, since only the sums at the different levels of *one* variable, factor A, are considered.

COMPUTATIONAL FORMULAS   All that we will be doing in an analysis of the simple main effects of the triple interaction is to calculate a set of sums of squares reflecting what in essence is a one-way analysis of variance. Again, the computational formulas tend to hide this relationship because of the need to specify particular subsets of ABC_{ijk} sums. The formulas for these simple main effects are given by

$$SS_{A \text{ at } bc_{jk}} = \frac{\sum\limits_{i}^{a}(ABC_{ijk})^2}{s} - \frac{(BC_{jk})^2}{as}, \tag{14-6a}$$

$$SS_{B \text{ at } ac_{ik}} = \frac{\sum\limits_{j}^{b}(ABC_{ijk})^2}{s} - \frac{(AC_{ik})^2}{bs}, \tag{14-6b}$$

and

$$SS_{C \text{ at } ab_{ij}} = \frac{\sum\limits_{k}^{c}(ABC_{ijk})^2}{s} - \frac{(AB_{ij})^2}{cs}. \tag{14-6c}$$

Each simple main effect can be thought of as a main effect in a single-factor experiment, where the levels of two other factors are held constant.

The df for these simple main effects are those associated with the corresponding main effects: $a - 1, b - 1$, and $c - 1$ for Eqs. (14-6a), (14-6b), and (14-6c), respectively. The mean squares and F ratios are obtained in the usual fashion.

NUMERICAL EXAMPLE   As an example, we will compute the simple main effect of factor A at a particular combination of factors B and C, namely, bc_{11}. Again we will refer to the ABC matrix of Table 14-1, but this time we will concentrate on the rows of the matrix. Applying Eq. (14-6a) to the first row of the lefthand matrix (bc_{11}), we have

$$SS_{A \text{ at } bc_{11}} = \frac{\sum (ABC_{i11})^2}{s} - \frac{(BC_{11})^2}{as}$$

$$= \frac{(205)^2 + (198)^2 + (182)^2}{15} - \frac{(585)^2}{3(15)}$$

$$= 7623.53 - 7605.00 = 18.53.$$

COMMENT   Just how we decide to analyze a three-way interaction depends upon the experimental questions we want to ask. In some cases, our hypothesis implies an interest in the simple interaction effects. That is, we are interested in how the interaction of two independent variables will change when a third variable is introduced. Wallace and Underwood (see Fig. 13-2, p. 258), for example, were looking at the form of the *interaction* of tasks and degree of association for college students and mental retardates. They were not interested in the simple main effects, such as the effect of associative strength for college students learning paired associates or the effect of associative strength for college students learning by free recall. On the other hand, there may be situations in which such a breakdown of the three-way interaction provides useful information. This will happen when we are really interested in the presence or absence of an effect of one of the independent variables in the "separate experiments" formed at the combination of levels of the other two variables.

Another way to evaluate the usefulness of an analysis of simple main effects is to consider the different sources of variance contributing to the sum of the simple main effects of the triple interaction. That is,

$$\sum SS_{A \text{ at } bc_{jk}} = SS_{A \times B \times C} + SS_{A \times B} + SS_{A \times C} + SS_A. \tag{14-7}$$

Consider what Eq. (14-7) implies: an analysis of simple main effects is relatively useless when sources other than the triple interaction contribute greatly to the variability of the means involved. In the present example, the *main* effect of factor A is an important source of variability. If we had completed the analysis of the simple main effects we began in the numerical example, we would have found them *all* to be significant. What would we have learned from this analysis? Very little, except that significant forgetting was obtained for all combinations of materials and activity. In short, then, the analysis of the simple main effects of the triple interaction does not serve a useful *analytical* function in this example because of the presence of the other sources of variance in addition to that associated with the interaction itself. The most appropriate analysis of this experiment is the analysis of the simple *interaction* effects, since the comparisons reflect a direct test of the hypothesis being considered.

Relationship Between Simple Effects and the Standard Analysis

A useful way of summarizing the analysis of simple effects is to consider how the different analyses are related to the standard analysis of variance. We have already indicated that the *interpretation* of the standard analysis begins with the three-way interaction, moves on to the two-way interactions, if the higher-order interaction is not significant, and ends up with the main effects, if a particular factor does not enter into an interaction with another variable. The analyses of simple effects of two-way and three-way interactions are undertaken when an interaction is significant and the researcher wants to determine the locus of the effect. (He will also turn to these analyses when they represent meaningful or analytical questions of the data.)

Table 14-2 summarizes the relationship between the analyses we have been discussing in this section and the standard analysis. At the top of the table is listed the statistical evaluation of the $A \times B \times C$ interaction. If the interaction is significant, we will probably branch to the right and pay little attention to analyses involving two-way matrices (i.e., two-way interactions) and main effects. On the other hand, if the interaction is not significant, we will immediately be interested in the significance of the three two-way interactions, branching to the left. We will consider these two main branches separately.

With a significant triple interaction, the most likely subsequent analysis would be an assessment of simple two-way interactions. As we have seen, there are three directions such an analysis may take—one for each possible two-way interaction. We have indicated one of these in the table. The particular interaction selected will be dictated by the logic of the experimental hypotheses tested by such an analysis. The statistical tests of the simple interaction effects should reveal one or more significant sources, and an experimenter may elect to probe further into these significant interactions. Such a determination represents an analysis of the simple main effects (or simple, simple main effects) and in our example may involve either of the two factors contributing to the simple interaction: the simple main effects of factor A at combinations of factors B and C or the simple main effects of factor B at combinations of factors A and C.

The lefthand branch is followed when the three-way interaction is not significant. The reason for considering the two-way interactions at this point are (1) they are now interpretable because the triple interaction is not significant, and (2) if present, they will reduce our interest in the main effects involved in the interaction or interactions. A significant two-way interaction may be subjected

TABLE 14-2 *Relationship Between Simple Effects and the Standard Analysis of Variance*

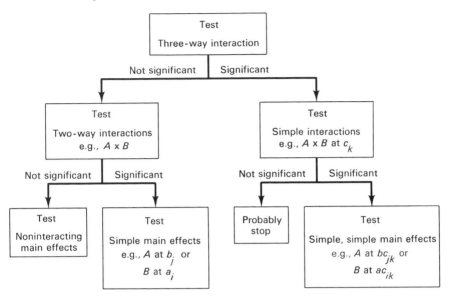

to further analysis in the form of simple main effects. If the $A \times B$ interaction is involved, the simple main effects tested would be those due to either factor A or factor B, the choice being based upon the logic of the research hypotheses. Main effects will be of systematic interest only when they do *not* enter into interactions with other independent variables. In our example, suppose that the only significant interaction was the $A \times B$ interaction. In this case we would be able to consider the main effect of the noninteracting variable, factor C, without ambiguity.

A NOTE OF CAUTION   The summary of the analyses outlined in Table 14-2 is not intended to represent a general blueprint or obligatory plan for the analysis of three-factor experiments. On the contrary, statistical analyses are the servants of the *researcher* and should be chosen to focus upon the comparisons that are of interest to him. Table 14-2 does provide a useful summary of a variety of statistical tests, showing how analyses of simple effects are related to the standard three-way analysis of variance.

COMPARISONS BETWEEN MEANS

We have seen in previous chapters how sets of coefficients may be used to assess the variability associated with comparisons between means. In the single-factor experiment, these comparisons obviously involved contrasts among the different treatment means. In the two-factor experiment, the comparisons were of two sorts: those involving row or column marginal means and those involving the individual cell means in the AB matrix. We were interested in the former comparisons when the $A \times B$ interaction was not significant and in the latter comparisons when it was. Of course, if we had theoretical reasons for looking at certain comparisons involving cell means, we would do so regardless of the significance of the interaction. Similar analyses may be conducted with the data obtained from a three-way factorial.

In the case of the experiment with three independent variables combined factorially, the number and the complexity of the possible comparisons are much greater than in the case with two variables. We will consider the formulas for these comparisons in general and illustrate their use with a specialized set of comparisons, i.e., orthogonal trend components. The analysis is the same for any type of comparison. The critical feature is the set of weighting factors specified by the coefficients. We discussed in Chapter 6 how.these sets may be constructed (see pp. 100–101).

We have argued that there is no necessary restriction on the nature or the number of these comparisons. For instance, they do not have to be mutually orthogonal, nor must their number be less than or equal to the number of df associated with the sum of squares being analyzed. The only restriction is that comparisons should reflect contrasts that have some theoretical meaning. It makes no difference whether comparisons are orthogonal or not, just so long as they are interesting contrasts. Of course, we realize that relative to the standard analysis we are increasing our experimentwise error rate by making these analytical comparisons. The question of orthogonality does not change this fact. On the other hand, the number of comparisons we actually conduct in an analysis is restricted, not for statistical reasons, but because of our inability to come up with many interesting comparisons.

Suppose we have selected a comparison involving the different A treatments. If this were a single-factor experiment, we would calculate the variability due to this comparison by working directly with the treatment sums. If this were a two-factor experiment, our comparison could be conducted on the A_i sums and on the AB_{ij} sums as well. In the first case, we would be analyzing components of variation making up the main effect of factor A, while in the second case, we would be analyzing the components making up the $A \times B$ interaction. An example of this analysis was presented in Chapter 12.

In the three-factor experiment, the situation becomes more complicated. Again continuing with a comparison involving the A treatments, we can look at this comparison wherever factor A enters into a source of variance, namely, the A main effect (SS_A), two of the two-way interactions ($SS_{A \times B}$ and $SS_{A \times C}$), and the three-way interaction ($SS_{A \times B \times C}$). Assume that the basic comparison involves a contrast between the treatment at level a_1 and the treatment at level a_2. As a main effect, we are asking about the extent to which the overall mean at a_1 differs from the overall mean at a_2. As a component of the $A \times B$

interaction, we are asking whether or not the difference between a_1 and a_2 is the same at the different levels of factor B; i.e., is there an interaction of the comparison with factor B? Similarly, as a component of the $A \times C$ interaction, the contrast becomes the question of an interaction of the comparison with factor C. Finally, in terms of the three-way interaction, we are determining whether or not the *interaction* of the comparison with factor B is the same at the different levels of factor C (or whether or not the interaction of the comparison with factor C is the same at the different levels of factor B). We will now consider the computational formulas with which these analyses are accomplished.

Computational Formulas[2]

We have already indicated that analyses we have encountered in the one-way and two-way factorials can be extended to the three-way factorial. Again, if the $A \times B \times C$ interaction is significant, we will probably not consider an evaluation of comparisons at the lower levels, unless, of course, we have an explicit reason for testing hypotheses concerning comparisons exhibited in the main effects and two-way interactions. On the other hand, if the higher-order interaction is not significant, we might want to turn to an evaluation of these other comparisons, i.e., the interactions of the comparison with one or both of the independent factors when the interactions are significant and the main effect when they are not.

MAIN EFFECT   We will begin with the formula used to assess the presence of a particular comparison in the *main effect* of factor A. In this case the formula is identical to the one presented in Chapter 11, Eq. (11-1a), except for an adjustment for the number of observations. Specifically,

$$SS_{A_{comp.}} = \frac{[\sum (c_i)(A_i)]^2}{bcs[\sum (c_i)^2]}, \tag{14-8}$$

where the c_i terms represent the coefficients reflecting the comparison and the number bcs represents the number of observations upon which each A_i sum is based. (A convenient way to find this latter quantity is to delete from the total number of observations, $abcs$ in the three-factor experiment, the letter or letters used to represent the sum in the denominator.) This sum of squares has $df = 1$ and is tested against the $MS_{S/ABC}$.

TWO-WAY INTERACTIONS   The analysis of the interaction of a comparison and a second factor was discussed in Chapter 12 (pp. 235–239). We have noted that in the three-factor case two such interactions may be analyzed: the $A \times B$ and the $A \times C$ interactions. Starting with the first interaction, since it represents

---

[2] Rules for constructing the computational formulas for these types of comparisons are presented in Chapter 15 (pp. 321–325).

familiar ground, we have

$$SS_{A_{comp.} \times B} = \frac{\sum\limits_{j}^{b}\left[\sum\limits_{i}^{a}(c_i)(AB_{ij})\right]^2}{cs\left[\sum (c_i)^2\right]} - SS_{A_{comp.}}. \tag{14-9a}$$

The formula is identical to Eq. (12-1) except for the division by cs, the number of observations contributing to each AB_{ij} sum, instead of s in the two-way case. The first part of Eq. (14-9a) is a composite, consisting of the combination of the sums of squares associated with this comparison at each level of factor B. Since this term contains two sources of variance, the $SS_{A_{comp.} \times B}$ and the $SS_{A_{comp.}}$, the subtraction of the second quantity results in the desired sum of squares.

The computational formula for the corresponding analysis of the $A \times C$ interaction is analogous to Eq. (14-9a):

$$SS_{A_{comp.} \times C} = \frac{\sum\limits_{k}^{c}\left[\sum\limits_{i}^{a}(c_i)(AC_{ik})\right]^2}{bs\left[\sum (c_i)^2\right]} - SS_{A_{comp.}}. \tag{14-9b}$$

The similarity of this equation to Eq. (14-9a) is apparent. Again, bs, a component of the divisor in the first term, equals the number of observations upon which the AC_{ik} sums are based.

The df for the two sets of comparisons are given by

$$df_{A_{comp.} \times B} = (df_{A_{comp.}})(df_B) = 1(b-1) = b-1 \tag{14-10a}$$

and

$$df_{A_{comp.} \times C} = (df_{A_{comp.}})(df_C) = 1(c-1) = c-1. \tag{14-10b}$$

These comparisons are tested by the within-groups mean square, $MS_{S/ABC}$.

THE THREE-WAY INTERACTION   Now we can consider the extraction of the comparison from the three-way interaction. We have indicated already the nature of this quantity. That is, it reflects the extent to which the interaction of the comparison with one of the two independent variables changes at the different levels of the other independent variable. We will refer to this source of variance as $A_{comp.} \times B \times C$. The formula specifying the calculations necessary to compute such a comparison is given by

$$SS_{A_{comp.} \times B \times C} = \frac{\sum\limits_{j}^{b}\sum\limits_{k}^{c}\left[\sum\limits_{i}^{a}(c_i)(ABC_{ijk})\right]^2}{s\left[\sum (c_i)^2\right]} - SS_{A_{comp.} \times B}$$
$$- SS_{A_{comp.} \times C} - SS_{A_{comp.}}. \tag{14-11}$$

Consider the first term on the right of Eq. (14-11). Looking inside the brackets in the numerator of this term, we can see that we are dealing with the cell sums from the ABC matrix. We are asked to multiply these sums by coefficients corresponding to the levels of factor A and to sum these products over the levels of factor A. This is done for each unique combination of the levels of factors B and C. Finally, these sums are squared and collected over the levels of factors B and C. In essence, then, we have combined a set of numbers that reflects the degree to which each bc combination shows the comparison under scrutiny. This sum is then divided by the product formed by multiplying the number of observations in each cell of the matrix (s) by the sum of the squared coefficients.

Let us consider the rest of Eq. (14-11). We have already seen that the first term combines the comparisons for each combination of the other two variables (factors B and C). Thus, this sum of squares contains *three* other sources of variability in addition to the three-way interaction—the $SS_{A_{comp.} \times B}$, the $SS_{A_{comp.} \times C}$, and the $SS_{A_{comp.}}$. We find the component of the three-way interaction, then, by subtracting these three quantities from the first term of Eq. (14-11).

The df for a component of the three-way interaction is given by

$$df_{A_{comp.} \times B \times C} = (df_{A_{comp.}})(df_B)(df_C) = 1(b - 1)(c - 1)$$
$$= (b - 1)(c - 1). \qquad (14\text{-}12)$$

The F ratio is obtained by the use of

$$F = \frac{MS_{A_{comp.} \times B \times C}}{MS_{S/ABC}}.$$

We are now ready for a numerical example.

Numerical Example

We will illustrate the general analysis by working through the calculations necessary to extract the trend components of the three-way interaction using the data from Table 13-8. If we refer back to the plot of these data in Fig. 13-5 (p. 275), we can see that the different forgetting curves all appear to be linear. Thus, we would expect to find most of the interaction being associated with the linear rather than the quadratic trend component. Stated again, it appears that the retention curves are best described by a linear function; thus the higher-order interaction is largely the result of the presence of one sort of patterning of the *linear* component for the three types of material under the condition of minimum linguistic activity (i.e., parallel, downward slope) and of a different patterning under the conditions of maximum linguistic activity (i.e., diverging, downward slope).

The sums we will need for this analysis are taken from Table 13-8 and are presented again in Table 14-3. We will need three matrices, ABC, AB, and AC; the BC matrix is not involved in this particular analysis. Note that the row marginal totals have been replaced with entries called "linear sum" and "quadratic sum." We will explain this arrangement in a moment.

The partitioning is accomplished by means of the coefficients of the orthogonal polynomial. (As we have indicated, however, the analysis is appropriate to any comparison that may be expressed in terms of coefficients.) Since the levels of the retention interval are equally spaced, we can use the coefficients that are listed in Table C-2 of Appendix C. If they were not equally spaced, we would have to construct our own set. (See Appendix B for a discussion of how this is accomplished.) With three points along the dimension and $df = 2$ for the quantitative variable, we will be able to extract two orthogonal trend components, the linear and the quadratic. From Table C-2 we obtain the following:

Coefficients	a_1	a_2	a_3	$\sum (c_i)^2$
Linear (c_{1i}):	-1	0	1	2
Quadratic (c_{2i}):	1	-2	1	6

Although we are interested only in the analysis of the three-way interaction, a consideration of Eq. (14-11) indicates that we must also obtain a breakdown of the main effect of A and the $A \times B$ and the $A \times C$ interactions.

CALCULATION OF WEIGHTED SUMS   It is convenient to perform the calculations in two steps, first forming all necessary weighted sums and then actually determining the sums of squares. An inspection of the computational formulas we will be using indicates that we will need the following sums of weighted totals:

$$\sum_i^a (c_i)(A_i) \qquad \text{for the } SS_{A_{\text{comp.}}} \qquad \text{[see Eq. (14-8)]},$$

$$\sum_i^a (c_i)(AB_{ij}) \qquad \text{for the } SS_{A_{\text{comp.}} \times B} \qquad \text{[see Eq. (14-9a)]},$$

$$\sum_i^a (c_i)(AC_{ik}) \qquad \text{for the } SS_{A_{\text{comp.}} \times C} \qquad \text{[see Eq. (14-9b)]},$$

and

$$\sum_i^a (c_i)(ABC_{ijk}) \qquad \text{for the } SS_{A_{\text{comp.}} \times B \times C} \qquad \text{[see Eq. (14-11)]}.$$

Each treatment total specified by these equations is found in the different data matrices presented in Table 14-3. The A_i totals are found in the last row of the AB and AC matrices, the AB_{ij} totals are the entries within the body of the AB matrix, the AC_{ik} totals are the entries in the AC matrix, and the ABC_{ijk} totals are the entries in the ABC matrix. In short, we will need the sums of the weighted totals for *each row* in the three matrices presented in Table 14-3. The results of these operations using the linear and quadratic coefficients are entered in the last two columns of each matrix.

As an example of the calculations, we will indicate one set of weighted totals for each matrix. Starting with the ABC matrix and the sums in the first row of the c_2 half of the matrix:

$$\sum_i^a (c_{1i})(ABC_{i12}) = (-1)(209) + (0)(178) + (1)(146)$$

for the linear component and

$$\sum_i^a (c_{2i})(ABC_{i12}) = (1)(209) + (-2)(178) + (1)(146)$$

for the quadratic component. The weighted sums for this and the other five rows of the ABC matrix are presented in the linear and quadratic columns of Table 14-3. From the body of the AB matrix and the totals at level b_2,

$$\sum_i^a (c_{1i})(AB_{i2}) = (-1)(413) + (0)(375) + (1)(346)$$

for the linear component and

$$\sum_i^a (c_{2i})(AB_{i2}) = (1)(413) + (-2)(375) + (1)(346)$$

for the quadratic component. The sums of the weighted totals for this and the other levels of B are found in the table. The column marginal totals for this matrix provide the A_i totals. Applying the weights to these totals,

$$\sum_i^a (c_{1i})(A_i) = (-1)(1246) + (0)(1145) + (1)(1035)$$

for the linear component and

$$\sum_i^a (c_{2i})(A_i) = (1)(1246) + (-2)(1145) + (1)(1035)$$

for the quadratic component. (These sums can also be obtained from the column marginal totals of the AC matrix.) Finally, from the body of the AC matrix and the totals at level c_1,

$$\sum_i^a (c_{1i})(AC_{i1}) = (-1)(623) + (0)(588) + (1)(538)$$

for the linear component and

$$\sum_i^a (c_{2i})(AC_{i1}) = (1)(623) + (-2)(588) + (1)(538)$$

for the quadratic component.

TABLE 14-3   *Numerical Example: Trend Analysis*

ABC MATRIX

Minimum Activity (c_1)

Materials (B)	1 Hour (a_1)	4 Hours (a_2)	7 Hours (a_3)	Linear Sum	Quadratic Sum
Low (b_1)	205	198	182	-23	-9
Medium (b_2)	210	193	177	-33	1
High (b_3)	208	197	179	-29	-7

Maximum Activity (c_2)

Materials (B)	1 Hour (a_1)	4 Hours (a_2)	7 Hours (a_3)	Linear Sum	Quadratic Sum
Low (b_1)	209	178	146	-63	-1
Medium (b_2)	203	182	169	-34	8
High (b_3)	211	197	182	-29	-1

AB MATRIX

	a_1	a_2	a_3	Linear Sum	Quadratic Sum
b_1	414	376	328	-86	-10
b_2	413	375	346	-67	9
b_3	419	394	361	-58	-8
Sum	1246	1145	1035	-211	-9

AC MATRIX

	a_1	a_2	a_3	Linear Sum	Quadratic Sum
c_1	623	588	538	-85	-15
c_2	623	557	497	-126	6
Sum	1246	1145	1035	-211	-9

As a convenient computational check, we should verify that the sums of the entries in the linear and quadratic columns of each matrix equal the corresponding sum of the weighted A_i totals. For the *ABC* matrix,

$$(-23) + (-33) + \cdots + (-34) + (-29) = -211$$

and

$$(-9) + (1) + \cdots + (8) + (-1) = -9;$$

for the *AB* matrix,

$$(-86) + (-67) + (-58) = -211$$

and

$$(-10) + (9) + (-8) = -9;$$

and for the AC matrix,

$$(-85) + (-126) = -211$$

and

$$(-15) + (6) = -9.$$

We are now ready to calculate the sums of squares.

CALCULATION OF THE SUMS OF SQUARES   For the $SS_{A_{comp.}}$, we substitute the values we have just obtained in Eq. (14-8):

$$SS_{A_{linear}} = \frac{\left[\sum (c_{1i})(A_i)\right]^2}{bcs\left[\sum (c_{1i})^2\right]} = \frac{(-211)^2}{3(2)(15)(2)} = \frac{44,521}{180},$$

$$SS_{A_{quadratic}} = \frac{\left[\sum (c_{2i})(A_i)\right]^2}{bcs\left[\sum (c_{2i})^2\right]} = \frac{(-9)^2}{3(2)(15)(6)} = \frac{81}{540}.$$

The respective sums of squares are entered into the summary of the analysis presented in Table 14-4. (Note that the two component sums of squares add to the SS_A. That is,

$$SS_A = SS_{A_{linear}} + SS_{A_{quadratic}} = 247.34 + .15 = 247.49.)$$

These two component sums of squares are each associated with $df = 1$, and the mean squares are tested against the $MS_{S/ABC}$.

For the $A \times B$ interaction, we substitute in Eq. (14-9a):

$$SS_{A_{linear} \times B} = \frac{\sum\limits_{j}^{b}\left[\sum\limits_{i}^{a}(c_{1i})(AB_{ij})\right]^2}{cs\left[\sum (c_{1i})^2\right]} - SS_{A_{linear}}$$

$$= \frac{(-86)^2 + (-67)^2 + (-58)^2}{2(15)(2)} - 247.34,$$

$$SS_{A_{quadratic} \times B} = \frac{\sum\limits_{j}^{b}\left[\sum\limits_{i}^{a}(c_{2i})(AB_{ij})\right]^2}{cs\left[\sum (c_{2i})^2\right]} - SS_{A_{quadratic}}$$

$$= \frac{(-10)^2 + (9)^2 + (-8)^2}{2(15)(6)} - .15.$$

These calculations are completed in Table 14-4. The two resulting sums of squares, 6.81 and 1.21, sum to the $SS_{A \times B}$. The df for these components are

TABLE 14-4 *Summary of the Trend Analysis*

Source	Calculations	SS	df	MS	F
Retention Interval (A)		(247.49)	(2)		
Linear		247.34	1	247.34	166.00**
Quadratic		.15	1	.15	<1
Material (B)		18.49	2	9.24	6.20**
Interval Activity (C)		19.20	1	19.20	12.89**
A × B		(8.02)	(4)		
Linear	254.15 − 247.34 =	6.81	2	3.40	2.28
Quadratic	1.36 − .15 =	1.21	2	.60	<1
A × C		(10.16)	(2)		
Linear	256.68 − 247.34 =	9.34	1	9.34	6.27*
Quadratic	.97 − .15 =	.82	1	.82	<1
B × C		18.76	2	9.38	6.30**
A × B × C		(17.35)	(4)		
Linear	280.83 − 6.81 − 9.34 − 247.34 =	17.34	2	8.67	5.82*
Quadratic	2.19 − 1.21 − .82 − .15 =	.01	2	.00	<1
S/ABC		375.40	252	1.49	
Total		714.87	269		

* $p < .025$.   ** $p < .01$.

calculated from Eq. (14-10a):

$$df_{A_{\text{linear}} \times B} = df_{A_{\text{quadratic}} \times B} = b - 1 = 3 - 1 = 2.$$

Again, the F ratio is formed by dividing the mean squares of these components by the $MS_{S/ABC}$.

For the $A \times C$ interaction, we use Eq. (14-9b). Substituting in this equation,

$$SS_{A_{\text{linear}} \times C} = \frac{\sum\limits_{k}^{c} \left[\sum\limits_{i}^{a} (c_{1i})(AC_{ik}) \right]^2}{bs\left[\sum (c_{1i})^2 \right]} - SS_{A_{\text{linear}}}$$

$$= \frac{(-85)^2 + (-126)^2}{3(15)(2)} - 247.34,$$

$$SS_{A_{\text{quadratic}} \times C} = \frac{\sum\limits_{k}^{c} \left[\sum\limits_{i}^{a} (c_{2i})(AC_{ik}) \right]^2}{bs\left[\sum (c_{2i})^2 \right]} - SS_{A_{\text{quadratic}}}$$

$$= \frac{(-15)^2 + (6)^2}{3(15)(6)} - .15.$$

The results of these calculations are given in Table 14-4. As a check, we can see that the two component sums of squares, 9.34 and .82, sum to the $SS_{A \times C}$. The df for the two components are equal and are obtained from Eq. (14-10b):

$$df_{A_{\text{linear}} \times C} = df_{A_{\text{quadratic}} \times C} = c - 1 = 2 - 1 = 1.$$

The variation due to these components is assessed by means of the $MS_{S/ABC}$.

The final step in this long process is the extraction of the information we wanted originally, the trend components of the three-way interaction. Substituting in Eq. (14-11) gives

$$SS_{A_{\text{linear}} \times B \times C} = \frac{\sum\limits_{j}^{b} \sum\limits_{k}^{c} \left[\sum\limits_{i}^{a} (c_{1i})(ABC_{ijk}) \right]^2}{s\left[\sum (c_{1i})^2 \right]} - SS_{A_{\text{linear}} \times B}$$

$$- SS_{A_{\text{linear}} \times C} - SS_{A_{\text{linear}}}$$

$$= \frac{(-23)^2 + (-33)^2 + \cdots + (-34)^2 + (-29)^2}{15(2)}$$

$$- 6.81 - 9.34 - 247.34,$$

$$SS_{A_{\text{quadratic}} \times B \times C} = \frac{\sum\limits_{j}^{b} \sum\limits_{k}^{c} \left[\sum\limits_{i}^{a} (c_{2i})(ABC_{ijk}) \right]^2}{s\left[\sum (c_{2i})^2 \right]} - SS_{A_{\text{quadratic}} \times B}$$

$$- SS_{A_{\text{quadratic}} \times C} - SS_{A_{\text{quadratic}}}$$

$$= \frac{(-9)^2 + (1)^2 + \cdots + (8)^2 + (-1)^2}{15(6)}$$

$$- 1.21 - .82 - .15.$$

These calculations are completed in Table 14-4. As a check, we can see that the two components sum to the $SS_{A \times B \times C}$:

$$SS_{A \times B \times C} = 17.34 + .01 = 17.35.$$

We find the df associated with these comparisons from Eq. (14-12):

$$df_{A_{\text{linear}} \times B \times C} = df_{A_{\text{quadratic}} \times B \times C} = (b - 1)(c - 1)$$

$$= (3 - 1)(2 - 1) = 2(1) = 2.$$

These variances are evaluated against the $MS_{S/ABC}$. The analysis reveals that the linear component accounts for nearly all of the variance due to the three-way interaction. In terms of a percentage, the linear component represents

$$\frac{17.34}{17.35} \times 100 = 99.9 \text{ percent}$$

of the $SS_{A \times B \times C}$.

Practical Considerations

The analysis substantiates statistically what was apparent from a visual inspection of the data presented in Fig. 13-5. As we have noted in presenting trend analyses in previous chapters, these statistical refinements of our data can be extremely useful in pinpointing the *form* of a given relationship between independent and dependent variables. On the other hand, we should realize that for this sort of analysis to have any importance it should have implications for theory. In the present example, what difference does it make if the higher-order interaction is located primarily in the interaction of the linear component of the retention functions? The theory, as it was presented in these pages, merely predicted an interaction of a particular type—it did not specify the orthogonal trend component(s) that would be involved. (If it did, of course, the theory would be very precise indeed.) In some research areas there is speculation concerning the shapes of the functions relating the independent and dependent variables. In discrimination learning, for example, there have been different theoretical statements concerning the shape of the gradient of stimulus generalization; in the area of motivation, there have been theories that predict an inverted-U shaped function (a quadratic component) relating performance and drive level. Under these circumstances the analysis of the trend components of the interactions may carry with it comparisons of important theoretical interest.

MULTIPLE COMPARISONS

As we have indicated a number of times, multiple comparisons are rarely conducted on individual means in a factorial experiment. If such comparisons are considered useful and informative, then certainly we should make them. The strongest argument against multiple comparisons is that they might not be interpretable when they cut across two classifications. If a difference is found between $\overline{ABC}_{111}$ and $\overline{ABC}_{122}$, say, can we attribute this difference to the change in the level of factor B or to the change in the level of factor C or to both changes? If the second group in the comparison were at level abc_{121} or abc_{112}, we could pinpoint the source of the difference as specifically factor B or factor C, respectively. With two changes, it will be difficult. In many cases the researcher's interest lies in the entire pattern of changes in behavior associated with the different levels of a particular variable—not in the specific differences between two of the levels of the variable. In our long-enduring example, we would have little reason to compare one group tested after 1 hour with a group tested after 4 hours. When manipulating a quantitative variable, for example, we usually assume a continuous dimension and that performance will be continuous function of the independent variable. Hence, our interest is in the *trend* described by the means obtained at *all* of the points selected from a particular dimension.

The different adjustments for multiple comparisons are easily adapted for use in the three-way factorial. All of these procedures employ the $MS_{S/ABC}$ and the df associated with it.[3] The only modification in the formulas is the substitution of the appropriate number of observations. Take, for example, the determination of the critical range between treatment sums for the Tukey test. (In all of these formulas, r_{max} will be replaced with a direct designation of the number of means being compared.) If we are making comparisons between the $\bar{A}_i$ means,

$$CR_T = q(a, df_{S/ABC})\sqrt{bcs(MS_{S/ABC})}, \qquad (14\text{-}13\text{a})$$

where q is a statistic found in Table C-3 of Appendix C, a is the total number of means, and bcs is the number of observations upon which each mean is based.

We saw in Chapter 12 that when comparisons are made between means in the AB matrix, the magnitude of the correction depends upon the pool of means from which the comparisons are drawn. If we are comparing the $\overline{AB}_{ij}$ means at a *particular level* of factor B,

$$CR_T = q(a, df_{S/ABC})\sqrt{cs(MS_{S/ABC})}. \qquad (14\text{-}13\text{b})$$

On the other hand, if we can justify drawing our comparisons from the total pool of ab means, then

$$CR_T = q(ab, df_{S/ABC})\sqrt{cs(MS_{S/ABC})}. \qquad (14\text{-}13\text{c})$$

If the comparisons involve the means in the body of the AC matrix or the BC matrix, similar corrections are applied.

Finally, if we are comparing the $\overline{ABC}_{ijk}$ means at *one* particular combination of factors B and C,

$$CR_T = q(a, df_{S/ABC})\sqrt{s(MS_{S/ABC})}, \qquad (14\text{-}13\text{d})$$

while if we are selecting contrasts from the *total pool* of abc means,

$$CR_T = q(abc, df_{S/ABC})\sqrt{s(MS_{S/ABC})}. \qquad (14\text{-}13\text{e})$$

The principle for adapting the formula is simple. There are two points of variation in these formulas—the size of the pool from which the comparisons will be drawn and the number of observations upon which each mean is based. The formulas for the other comparison techniques are adapted in a similar fashion. Care must be taken in selecting the appropriate correction, as the

---

[3] Separate error terms may be necessary if the within-group variances are heterogeneous.

adjustment is considerably greater when the pool is taken to be $r_{max} = a$, as in Eq. (14-13d), than when $r_{max} = abc$, as in Eq. (14-13e).[4]

If we wish to take the most conservative approach and to control the experimentwise error rate for any possible comparison between two means, then we will select the Scheffé test. With this test, we calculate the mean squares for the comparisons we want to make and test them against the $MS_{S/ABC}$. We then compare the obtained F's against Scheffé's corrected F, i.e., F_S. To indicate the form of the correction, consider the values of F_S for the following comparisons:

(1) between the $\bar{A}_i$ means:

$$F_S = (a - 1)F(a - 1, df_{S/ABC});$$ (14-14a)

(2) between the $\overline{AB}_{ij}$ means at one level of factor B:

$$F_S = (a - 1)F(a - 1, df_{S/ABC});$$ (14-14b)

(3) between all of the $\overline{AB}_{ij}$ means:

$$F_S = (ab - 1)F(ab - 1, df_{S/ABC});$$ (14-14c)

(4) between the $\overline{ABC}_{ijk}$ means at one combination of factors B and C:

$$F_S = (a - 1)F(a - 1, df_{S/ABC});$$ (14-14d)

(5) between all of the $\overline{ABC}_{ijk}$ means:

$$F_S = (abc - 1)F(abc - 1, df_{S/ABC}).$$ (14-14e)

Again, the pattern of the different corrections is obvious. As with the Tukey procedure, the critical factor is the size of the basic pool from which the comparisons are drawn.

To repeat earlier comments, these procedures for controlling the experimentwise error rate with multiple comparisons often protect the researcher against a very large set of comparisons that he will never make. This is especially true in factorial experiments, where a meaningful pool of means from which comparisons will be constructed is generally *not* the total set of *ab* means in the two-way factorial or the set of *abc* means in the three-way factorial. Instead, most of the time we will want to restrict our comparisons to sets of *logical*, i.e., interpretable, groupings. Thus, we will usually make comparisons that involve the variation of only one independent variable at a time. Not to be aware of this fact in the statistical adjustments will result in an overly conservative and unrealistic correction for a large number of multiple comparisons that

---

[4] The correction applied by Eq. (14-13d) guarantees that the experimentwise error rate is no larger than the selected probability for all possible comparisons between pairs of $\overline{ABC}_{ijk}$ means in *one* particular bc_{jk} combination. If similar comparisons will be conducted at other combinations, the experimentwise error rate will be greater than in the first case unless an additional correction is made. This point is discussed in Chapter 12 (pp. 244–246).

will never be conducted. If a restricted set can be justified, then any of the comparison techniques can be adapted for use with this set. Assuming that the comparisons involve the ABC_{ijk} means,

$$CR_T = q(r_{set}, df_{S/ABC})\sqrt{s(MS_{S/ABC})},\qquad(14\text{-}15)$$

where r_{set} equals the number of means in the comparison pool. For the Scheffé correction,

$$F_S = (r_{set} - 1)F(r_{set} - 1, df_{S/ABC}),\qquad(14\text{-}16)$$

where r_{set} has the same meaning as in Eq. (14-15).

An alternative procedure was proposed in Chapter 12, namely, to divide the experimentwise error rate (α_{EW}) by the number of post-hoc comparisons (c) that will be considered and to use this resultant probability, α_{EW}/c, as the per comparison error rate (α). This individualized approach for multiple comparisons, patterned after the Dunn procedure, may prove extremely useful in the analysis of factorial experiments. (For a general description of this method, see pp. 147–149, and for a discussion of its application to the analysis of a factorial, see p. 246.)

chapter fifteen

ANALYSIS OF THE
GENERAL CASE

We have discussed in detail the analysis of completely randomized experiments—from experiments in which a single independent variable is manipulated to factorial experiments in which two or three independent variables are manipulated concurrently. These designs represent a large majority of the experiments conducted in the behavioral sciences. Occasionally, we will encounter experiments in which more than three independent variables are included in the design. As we will see, it is relatively easy to extend the analyses we have considered so far to these higher-order factorial experiments. Before we discuss the analysis of the general case, however, we will consider again and in more detail the uses of multifactor experiments in the behavioral sciences.

USE OF MULTIFACTOR EXPERIMENTS IN THE BEHAVIORAL SCIENCES

Advantages and Disadvantages

ADVANTAGES   The advantages listed in Chapter 9 for the two-way factorial are even more compelling for the higher-order factorials. Of these, perhaps the most important is the closer approximation to the "real" world—the greater *external validity* that is afforded by the controlled multifactor experiment. With the inclusion of additional relevant independent variables, we begin to reach the point where in effect we "understand" the behavior under study. Presumably our theoretical explanations will keep abreast of the elaboration of our designs and they will begin to take on the flavor of a comprehensive, general theory of behavior. At the present time, factorials with more than three independent variables of experimental interest are still rare in the literature, a fact that probably reflects the level of development in the behavioral sciences. However, we can say that when a theoretical explanation is "ready" for predictions involving a number of independent variables, the factorial experiment provides an analytical and useful tool for the testing of these predictions.

Other advantages of the higher-order factorials should also be mentioned. They are efficient, providing information about the influence of an increased number of independent variables at very little increase in cost (i.e., subjects, time, and energy). Further, the multifactor experiment allows the determination of the way in which the different variables *combine* to influence behavior jointly. We are referring, of course, to the assessment of interactions. The three-way factorial, for example, produces 4 interactions, the four-way factorial contains 11 interactions, and the five-way factorial contains 26. The point is that higher-order factorials are satisfyingly analytical and rich with factual information.

DISADVANTAGES   We pay a price for this "luxury," however, and this is the possibility of *too much* complexity. This may sound like a direct contradiction of the preceding paragraphs, and in a sense it is. The inclusion of a large number of independent variables in an experiment carries with it the *potential* of a significant higher-order interaction involving *all* of the manipulated variables. Such an interaction would require an extremely complicated statement just to describe the outcome. With the two-way factorial, an interaction indicates that any description of the influence of one of the factors demands a consideration of the specific levels represented by the other factor. With a three-way factorial, a significant higher-order interaction implies that any description of one of the two-way *interactions* must be made with reference to the specific levels selected for a third factor. Interactions involving four or more variables require even more complicated descriptions. Now, if it is difficult merely to *summarize* the pattern of a particular interaction, imagine the problem we will have in *explaining* these results. Obviously, if a significant higher-order interaction exerts an important influence on the phenomenon we are studying, we cannot ignore its presence. On the other hand, we might make faster progress by attempting to understand the results of the simpler designs before attempting to tackle the more complex. We will return to this issue presently.

Another point concerns economy. As we add variables to a factorial, the number of different treatment groups expands greatly. A 3×3 design requires a total of 9 treatment combinations, while a $3 \times 3 \times 3$ needs 27 and a $3 \times 3 \times$

3×3 needs 81. If we hold constant the total number of subjects we will use in the experiment, the number of subjects in each specific treatment group (s) must get smaller and smaller as we increase the number of treatment groups. Suppose (picking a large round number) we had available a pool of 200 subjects. With this pool of subjects, we could include as the maximum number of subjects in each treatment condition, and still maintain equal sample size, $s = 22$ subjects in the 3×3 design, $s = 7$ subjects in the $3 \times 3 \times 3$ design, and $s = 2$ in the $3 \times 3 \times 3 \times 3$ design. The gain in economy breaks down at some point, since we are also concerned about the *reliability* associated with each of the basic treatment means. In human learning, for example, the minimum sample size acceptable to researchers ranges from 8 to 12 subjects.[1] If we set this minimum at $s = 10$, say, we will need only 90 subjects in the two-factor experiment, 270 subjects in the three-factor experiment, and 810 subjects in the four-factor experiment.

This important concern for the reliability or stability of the *individual* treatment means clearly reduces some of the apparent efficiency of the factorial experiment. Additionally, an ambitious factorial experiment, when adjusted to a reasonable sample size, may require many more subjects than are available. In the present example, for instance, the demand for subjects in the three-factor and four-factor experiments far exceeds the 200 subjects that are available for testing.

There are several solutions to this problem. One that we often see is the selection of a "minimal" factorial design, each variable being represented by only two levels—a 2^v design, where v equals the number of independent variables. The drawback to this procedure is that we may lose important information by failing to provide for a more comprehensive sampling of the different variables. The selection of the levels for each variable is arbitrary but, if it is done in some realistic fashion, the chance of missing some important behavioral change associated with any variable is reduced as the number of levels is increased. A second solution is the use of a *confounded factorial*, a design that we will not be able to consider in this book.[2] Third, we could use a *repeated-measures design*, in which each subject serves in more than one experimental condition. If each subject served in two conditions, for example, the total number of subjects would be half those required if independent groups were used. We will consider this type of design in Part V. Of course, some phenomena are best studied with

---

[1] This number depends upon the size of the within-groups variance. The larger the variability of subjects treated alike, the more subjects that will be required to reach a given criterion of stability. [Stability generally refers to the size of the *confidence interval* drawn around the sample means. The size of this interval depends upon the α level acceptable to an experimenter, the sample size (s), and the size of the within-groups mean square. For any given α level, a constant interval may be achieved by applying the following formula: $(MS_{wg})/\sqrt{s}$. Any increase in the MS_{wg} requires a corresponding increase in the sample size in order to ensure the maintenance of a constant confidence interval.]

[2] For a discussion of this type of factorial design, see Kirk (1968, pp. 319–454) and Winer (1962, pp. 379–513; 1971, pp. 604–684).

independent groups, so that the repeated-measures design does not provide a general solution to this problem. Finally, if we are able to obtain additional information about the subjects before the start of the experiment, it may be possible to use specialized designs and analyses that require fewer subjects to achieve a given degree of precision. These are discussed in Part VI.

PREDICTION OF HIGHER-ORDER INTERACTIONS   Complex designs allow the analytical study of behavior under conditions approximating the functional stimulating environment. A question often asked, however, concerns the *interpretation* of significant higher-order interactions when and if they appear. Can anyone conceive of a four-way factorial in which a significant four-way interaction is predicted? Not too long ago, the same question was asked about three-way designs—and probably before that about two-way designs; yet these latter types of designs are now relatively commonplace in certain areas of the behavioral sciences (e.g., experimental psychology).

The answer to this very reasonable question is that complex factorial experiments seem to *evolve* from less complex ones. That is, if a particular two-way interaction has cropped up in a number of different experiments, the effect will be "accepted" by the scientific community as a "fact." Eventually, theories will be developed to attempt to explain this fact. At this point, it is usually not too difficult to think of a *third* independent variable that will interact with the other two. By the same token, as we begin to assimilate the meaning of a particular three-way interaction, we will be able to think of a *fourth* independent variable whose interaction with the other three variables provides an interesting test of the current theoretical interpretations of the earlier finding. Suppose we consider an example based on a three-factor experiment with which we are already familiar.

In the Wallace and Underwood study (see pp. 256–258), three independent variables were manipulated in a factorial arrangement: associative strength, type of learning task, and presumed linguistic development (college students versus retardates). A significant triple interaction was found, with associative strength having a positive effect in free-recall learning and a negative effect in paired-associate learning, but *only* with college students. The investigators assumed that the critical mechanism involved was the *implicit associative response*, the strength of which may be governed in a number of ways. In their experiment, strength was varied two ways, specifically, the nature of the materials and the degree of linguistic development. Suppose we add another independent factor along these lines—one that involves what we may call associative pretraining. What if we added a factor (factor D) consisting of two levels: pretra ning with the clusters of words that will subsequently be used in the main phase of the experiment (level d_1) and no pretraining (level d_2)?[3] The experi-

---

[3] We might consider substituting pretraining with *irrelevant* material for the condition with no pretraining (level d_2) so that all groups would be equated on the degree of laboratory experience before the critical learning tasks are introduced.

ment now could be described as the crossing of strength, task, linguistic development, and pretraining. Further, suppose we assume this pretraining to be such that it will strengthen the weak linguistic habits of the retardates and leave the habits of the college students, which are probably near some maximum strength already, unchanged. If this assumption is correct, we should again find the three-way interaction of Wallace and Underwood (strength × task × normality) with the subjects at d_2 (no pretraining) and the elimination or the reduction of the same interaction with the subjects at d_1 (pretraining). Note that this latter expectation can be made even more explicit—the positive and negative effects of associative strength observed with the two learning tasks should be present now with *both types* of subjects, college students and retardates.

Whether this four-way factorial is feasible to run or even of theoretical interest is not the point here. What we have seen is that a higher-order factorial can *evolve* from a significant three-way interaction. If we can explain an interaction at one level of complexity, as Wallace and Underwood did in their interpretation of the interaction of strength, task, and type of subject, we will probably be able to conjure up an interesting test of this explanation by predicting an interaction of an even higher order. It may be for this reason that we see so few higher-order designs in the behavioral sciences—the theoretical development in many research areas has not yet reached a point where higher-order designs are useful (i.e., would be interpretable if higher-order interactions were significant). The factorial experiment is not adapted to the "shotgun" approach that is simply looking for relevant variables. The results of such an attempt are likely to be wholly uninterpretable. It is, rather, a device for advancing a field which has reached an appropriate stage of theoretical development.

We have been arguing for an analytical evolution of factorial experiments. We should know how a variable "reacts" in relative isolation, and often this requires an extensive analysis of the function relating variations in the independent variable to behavior. Armed with this knowledge and perhaps an idea concerning the processes that may be responsible for this functional relationship, we can then increase the complexity of our design.

Internal Validity and Experimental Control

In the design of any experiment, we attempt to hold constant as many factors as we can that may influence the behavior we are studying. We test all animals in the same apparatus, perhaps with the same experimenter, and often under a high degree of control of the experimental environment (temperature, illumination, background noise, and so on). Ideally, we would like to be able to hold physically constant all important variables except the ones under systematic study. Factors which we are unable to control in this fashion, or which are not sufficiently important to control, we allow to vary randomly across the treatment conditions. Thus, randomization of these so-called "nuisance" factors is the major way in which we obtain *internal validity*—i.e., the elimination of biases which, if present, might invalidate any conclusions drawn concerning the manipulations in the experiment.

Another way of achieving internal validity is through the *counterbalancing* of materials across conditions. A simple experiment on transfer of training provides a good example. In a transfer study, an experimenter is interested in a comparison of a subject's performance on two tasks (A and B) that are learned in succession. To be able to compare the two tasks and to attribute any differences to transfer, we must guarantee that they are equal in difficulty. We could determine this through a preliminary comparison of the two tasks, but a far easier method is simply to balance the order in which the tasks are presented. For half of the subjects the tasks are learned in the order, A-B; for the other half, the tasks are learned in the reverse order, B-A. The order in which the tasks are presented thus becomes a control factor. While this balancing of material achieves internal validity, it also is an experimental necessity—the problem of differential difficulty of the two tasks must be solved before any meaning can be attached to differences observed in the experiment.

There is an important difference between these two methods of achieving internal validity. The first method (randomization) spreads the influence of uncontrolled variables over the treatment groups equally. These variables do not systematically affect the treatment means, and so any bias is removed. They do, however, influence the *sensitivity* of the experiment, because any variability due to nuisance variables becomes "deposited" in the error term— i.e., results in an increase in the variability of subjects treated alike. With a larger error term, our ability to detect the presence of real treatment effects is reduced. In contrast, the second method achieves control without affecting the size of the within-groups mean square;[4] instead, lists or stimulus orders or balancing procedures are introduced into the design as *independent variables*, and any variance due to control factors may be isolated and kept distinctly apart from the within-groups variance.

External Validity and the Multifactor Design

We have seen that in order to achieve an acceptable degree of internal validity, we must greatly restrict the conditions under which we study a given phenomenon. This implies, then, that most of our research is of limited generality. The degree to which we *can* generalize our findings beyond the present conditions of testing has been called the *external validity* of an experiment. Frequently, a researcher will introduce a factor into his experiment solely in the hope of increasing the external validity of the experiment. Where one set of stimulus materials is sufficient, two or three will be used; where one experimenter could

---

[4] An exception to this statement is when some characteristic of subjects, e.g., intelligence, becomes a control factor. Such a situation is considered in Chapter 23.

conduct the experiment, several are employed; where one arrangement of a list of words will suffice, a number of orderings are constructed. In most cases these factors can be thought of as independent variables added to the main experimental design; thus, they effectively transform a two-factor or a three-factor experiment into an experiment of greater complexity.

These factors are certainly not introduced into an experiment because of their inherent interest. Moreover, it is clear that the resultant increase in external validity is really not very great in any far-reaching sense. In spite of these qualifications, control factors still serve an important function in establishing the generalizability of a phenomenon. To be more specific, suppose we are interested in the effect of different stimulants on reading comprehension. Since different groups of subjects receive different stimulants, we could test all of the subjects on the *same* passage of prose material. There is no compelling reason to include two or more passages, as there can be no confounding of the passage with the stimulants. Most experimenters, however, would feel more comfortable with the experiment if additional passages *were* introduced. The reason is the possibility that the outcome of the experiment may be due to some unknown peculiarity of the single passage used in the experiment. For one reason or another drug A produces better performance than drug B, but only with a particular passage. This may sound far-fetched to the beginning student, but it is observed all too frequently in actual research situations.

If an independent variable by definition requires different sets of materials, one also feels a little uneasy with only one set per condition. Consider an experiment concerned with the perception of words varying in three degrees of pleasantness. Obviously, we would need three different lists of words, one containing pleasant words, one containing neutral words, and one containing unpleasant words. Suppose we constructed these three lists and conducted the experiment—one list per condition. How could we be sure that these lists were *representative* of the pools of words from which they were drawn? Certainly, we would feel "safer" if more than one list per condition were prepared.

To illustrate the importance of control factors such as lists or stimulus orderings, we will consider an experiment by Underwood and Richardson (1956). These investigators were studying the effect of two independent variables —meaningfulness and within-task similarity—on the speed of serial learning. The basic design was a 2 × 2 factorial, two levels of each factor being represented. They constructed four lists of materials, one for each treatment combination. For reasons we will not go into, they found it desirable to construct 10 different random orderings of the materials within each of the four basic lists; thus, there were four basic sets of materials and 10 different orderings of each basic list. A total of 10 subjects was assigned randomly to each of the 4(10) = 40 serial lists. The average numbers of trials to learn the lists in the four treatment conditions are presented in Table 15-1.

Consider the *range* of the means for the 10 different lists within each treatment combination, which is also given in the table. Each set of lists differs only with

TABLE 15-1   *Trials to Learn Serial Lists*[a]

Similarity		Meaningfulness	
		Low	High
Low	Grand mean	29.2	19.3
	Range	20.5–38.3	16.7–22.2
High	Grand mean	42.6	25.9
	Range	33.0–52.0	19.5–33.0

[a] From Underwood and Richardson (1956).

respect to the specific *serial ordering* of the materials, and still the differences among these lists are substantial. What if only *one* serial ordering had been used for each level of the independent variable? It is entirely possible that by chance an easy order might be constructed for a difficult condition and just the reverse for an easier condition. If this were the case, the basic trend observed in Table 15-1 could be changed.

The point is that with only one serial ordering, just as with only one basic list, the results we obtain may be due in large measure to the unique characteristics of the materials used for the experiment. Thus, we will be more confident of our results when we include more than one list or more than one stimulus ordering.

TEST FOR GENERALITY   Now that we have seen why we introduce control factors into an experiment, either for the sake of internal validity or for an increase in external validity, the question is: what do we do about it? There are two approaches to this problem, and they depend upon the nature of the control factor. We have discussed two situations—one in which the control factor crosses with the experimental factors (e.g., the same three sets of materials being used in all of the experimental conditions) and one in which the control factor is *nested* within specific conditions (e.g., lists within levels of pleasantness or of meaningfulness or of similarity). We will consider the crossed case in this section, since the analysis of so-called nested factors has not yet been introduced (see Chapter 18 for a discussion of this particular situation).

The generality of results in which a control factor is completely crossed (i.e., represented at each treatment level or combination of treatment levels) is tested by the *interactions* between control factors and the experimental factors. A significant interaction essentially means that the results are associated with a particular combination of experimental and control factors, an outcome that severely limits the generality of the findings. That is, the presence of an interaction between stimulus sets or presentation orders indicates that conclusions drawn from the experiment must be more circumscribed than they are already: a given effect appears and disappears with different sets of materials, or the size of an effect varies with the different presentation orders.

PRACTICAL CONSIDERATIONS   We have indicated why control factors are introduced and how their isolation in the analysis of variance can provide a test for the generality of the findings. Moreover, there would seem to be no question concerning the form of the analysis; i.e., we would subdivide the total sum of squares into subcomponents reflecting both experimental and control factors. Thus, an experiment with two experimental factors and three control factors would be classified as a five-way factorial, with the SS_T being partitioned into 32 component sources of variance. It is perhaps safe to say that if this experiment were reported in one of our scientific journals, we would find it treated as a *two*-way factorial, the control factors being mentioned only in the method section of the research report. There is an obvious discrepancy, then, between the analysis that is reported and the one that is *implied* in the experimental design.

What has happened to the control factors in these cases? There are two explanations. First, the experimenter introduces a control factor only as an experimental necessity to guarantee *internal* validity. He is not concerned about the degree of external validity afforded by the control procedure; thus, he does nothing about it. Alternatively, the experimenter performs an analysis of the complete design and, finding no significant sources of variance involving the control factors, drops the control classifications from his analysis. That is, the five-factor experiment with two experimental factors and three control factors would revert back to a two-way factorial, just as if the control classifications had never been present. The issue we want to consider now is whether or not either of these alternative approaches is justified.

In the first case, the experimenter is operating in ignorance of the true state of affairs; in the second case, he is changing his underlying statistical model depending upon the outcome of his statistical tests. The first attitude is defensible in that the researcher does not express an overriding concern for external validity. The second smacks of statistical "opportunism," with the researcher retaining a control classification only when it is of benefit to him. That is, if he collapses across a control factor only when it *fails* to capture a significant amount of variance, he is creating a *bias* in the direction of an increased probability that null hypotheses are rejected. To be more specific, the fact that a control factor is significant, either as a main effect or as an interaction, implies that a sizable amount of variability is "removed" from the within-groups sum of squares. This means that there will be a smaller error term than would be the case if the control classification had been disregarded. On the other hand, the *absence* of significant effects involving the control factor may mean a smaller error term if the control factor is disregarded.

What we really need is a rational way of proceeding in our statistical analysis. Suppose we consider the *consequences* of maintaining the statistical model that includes the control classifications, no matter what the statistical outcome might be. If the variability associated with control factors proves to be significant, then we benefit from a reduction in the size of the within-groups mean square. On the other hand, if these sources are not significant, we have lost very little. That is, if control factors exert no influence whatsoever, corresponding F ratios will equal approximately 1.0; consequently, the within-groups mean square will be unchanged in the long run by the removal of sources of variance where the null hypothesis component is zero. The only "loss" is a reduction in power due to the fact that the control factors remove degrees of freedom from the within-groups error term which would have been present if the sources involving control factors had not been removed. In most cases, however, this loss of power is negligible.[5]

Note that this procedure does in fact collapse across control classifications, but only when it is appropriate to do so. That is, if interactions involving control factors are not significant, attention will be drawn to data matrices in which only experimental factors appear. Analytical comparisons will be conducted on the data contained within *these* matrices. Again, the only loss as compared to a total disregard of the control classifications is a small amount of power. If there are interactions involving control factors that prove to be significant, data matrices including the control classifications must now be inspected and differences evaluated.

In sum, then, the most consistent and rational approach would be the maintenance of control classifications in our statistical analyses. The only real complication is the necessity to calculate a large number of interaction sums of squares associated with the control factors. These, however, would have to be calculated anyway in order to test for the generality of the treatment effects.

Summary

Because of the fundamental importance of this type of design in the behavioral sciences, this discussion has stressed the disadvantages and problems associated with multifactor experiments. This emphasis should not be taken to mean a questioning of the usefulness of the factorial in the design of our experiments. On the contrary, the factorial experiment allows us to increase in a systematic way the complexity of our experimental manipulations. With the factorial, we can determine how two or more independent variables combine to influence behavior. In addition, the factorial experiment is easily adapted to include any number of control factors that will provide for an increase in internal and external validity. We will now see how simply the analyses we have considered in preceding chapters can be extended to factorial experiments with any number of independent variables.

[5] At sufficiently high degrees of freedom for the error term, i.e., $df_{error} > 20$, any reduction in power resulting from the extraction of sources of variability involving control factors is quite small.

GENERAL ANALYSIS OF FACTORIAL EXPERIMENTS

Granting that higher-order designs have an important role to play in the developing behavioral sciences, we must ask if there are general ways of treating such designs, no matter what their particular form. We have seen how a simple set of rules can be used to generate the computational formulas for two- and three-factor experiments. Fortunately, this system can be easily extended to factorial experiments with more than three independent variables.

Simplified Rules for Generating Computational Formulas

You would probably find little difficulty in applying the rules from Chapter 10 to generate the computational formulas for, say, a four-way design. As you become experienced with the pattern underlying the analysis of variance, you will be able to delete a number of the steps needed to construct the computational formulas. The shorthand formulas we will consider in this section do not specify in detail the operations required to calculate a given sum of squares, but they do provide sufficient information to complete the analysis once one is experienced with them.

BASIC FORMULA   The sources of variance are specified by the rule stated in Chapter 10 (p. 192). Once the sources have been identified, the next question concerns the computational formulas for the corresponding sums of squares. The basic formula for any term in the computational formulas is given by

$$\frac{\sum (\text{relevant sum})^2}{(\text{appropriate divisor})}. \tag{15-1}$$

That is, we identify the relevant sum, square it, combine all of the quantities in this particular set of squares, and divide this total by the number of observations summed prior to the squaring operation—i.e., computational rule number 1. (This latter number may be obtained by deleting from the expression denoting the total number of observations those letters that appear in the numerator term.)

COMPUTATIONAL RULE NUMBER 2   The next step in the construction of the formulas for the sums of squares consists of a systematic reiterative process in which we add and subtract other basic terms in accord with a second computational rule. This rule applies to sums of squares for main effects and for interactions. Each basic term is represented by the letter code we have been using. We start by writing down the first term for a sum of squares; this term is indicated by the combination of letters used to designate the source of variance. Next, we *subtract* coded quantities obtained by deleting *one* letter from the first term. Then we *add* coded quantities obtained by deleting *two* letters from the first term. Next, we *subtract* coded quantities obtained by removing *three* letters from the first term. This alternating procedure of adding-subtracting-adding is continued until all of the letters have been deleted, at which time we complete the operation by adding or subtracting $[T]$, depending upon which arithmetical operation was next in line.

In general, computational rule number 2 may be stated as follows:

$$SS_k = [\text{term with } k \text{ letters}] - [\text{terms with } k - 1 \text{ letters}]$$

$$+ [\text{terms with } k - 2 \text{ letters}] - [\text{terms with } k - 3 \text{ letters}]$$

$$+ \cdots \pm [\text{term with } k - k \text{ letters} = T], \tag{15-2}$$

where k denotes the letters (i.e., independent variables) representing the first term of the desired sum of squares.

For example, consider the computational formula for the $A \times B \times C$ interaction. Substituting in Eq. (15-2),

$$SS_{A \times B \times C} = [ABC]$$

$$- [AB] - [AC] - [BC]$$

$$+ [A] + [B] + [C]$$

$$- [T].$$

As another example, we will write the formula for the $A \times B \times C \times D$ interaction. From Eq. (15-2), we have

$$SS_{A \times B \times C \times D} = [ABCD]$$

$$- [ABC] - [ABD] - [ACD] - [BCD]$$

$$+ [AB] + [AC] + [AD] + [BC] + [BD] + [CD]$$

$$- [A] - [B] - [C] - [D]$$

$$+ [T].$$

COMMENT   The shorthand formulas are useful only when one has become completely familiar with the various computational operations.[6] The recurrent pattern is surprisingly simple and will be easy to identify and to apply in complex analyses. You should not lose touch with the basic system, however, as it will prove extremely helpful in generating the computational formulas for different analytical comparisons, for experiments with nested factors, and for designs with repeated measures, all of which we will consider shortly.

---

[6] A rule for calculating within-groups sums of squares goes as follows: From the first term, which consists of all of the letters in the design, subtract the coded quantity represented by the letter(s) appearing to the right of the diagonal in the designation of the within-group source of variance. For example, $SS_{S/ABC} = [ABCS] - [ABC]$ and $SS_{S/ABCD} = [ABCDS] - [ABCD]$.

GENERATION OF FORMULAS FOR COMPARISONS BETWEEN MEANS

Two of the most useful tools for extracting information from a factorial experiment are comparisons between pairs of means and analyses of simple effects of interactions. In this section and the next, we will consider rules for the construction of the computational formulas necessary for carrying out these statistical analyses. Both sets of rules are derived from the basic system we described earlier.

We have seen in earlier chapters how we may ask questions of a set of data by using comparisons that are defined in terms of coefficients (weights) and sums of weighted means. Coefficients may be constructed to reflect contrasts between pairs of means or between pairs of complex combinations of means. They may also be used to detect the presence of trend components when the levels of the independent variable represent points on a quantitative scale.

We will be concerned with a statement of rules which will apply to these sorts of comparisons in designs of any degree of complexity. For convenience, these rules are written in terms of factor A, although they are easily adapted to comparisons between means associated with levels of other factors in an experiment. The first point to note is that the computational formulas vary in two ways: (1) with regard to the basic *means* involved in the comparison and (2) with regard to the number of *observations*. The first variation changes the *nature* of the computational formulas, while the second changes them only slightly. We will devote separate sections to the first variation (the basic means involved) and discuss the second variation (number of observations) within these sections.

Comparisons Involving the $\overline{A}_i$ Means

The basic quantity entering into all computational formulas may be represented by the following ratio:

$$\frac{(\text{sum of weighted totals})^2}{(\text{number of observations})(\text{sum of squared coefficients})}. \tag{15-3}$$

The term inside the parenthesis in the numerator has the form

$$\sum_i^a (c_i)(Total_i). \tag{15-3a}$$

That is, the totals will always vary with regard to the A classification (the i subscript), the weights will always reflect contrasts involving this classification, and the summation will always result in a combination of weighted totals across the A classification. For comparisons involving the $\overline{A}_i$ means in any design, the numerator for Eq. (15-3) becomes

$$\left[\sum_{i}^{a} (c_i)(A_i) \right]^2 .$$

The denominator of Eq. (15-3) does require a slight change in the different designs. This poses no problem, however, because the only modification involved is a simple adjustment for the number of observations. This number can be obtained quite easily by deleting from the total number of observations in the experiment the letters appearing in the numerator. The remaining quantity in Eq. (15-3), the sum of the squared coefficients, requires no comment.

As an example, consider the following adaptations of Eq. (15-3) to two-, three-, and four-factor experiments, respectively:

$$SS_{A_{comp.}} = \frac{\left[\sum_{i}^{a} (c_i)(A_i) \right]^2}{bs\left[\sum (c_i)^2 \right]}, \quad \frac{\left[\sum_{i}^{a} (c_i)(A_i) \right]^2}{bcs\left[\sum (c_i)^2 \right]}, \quad \frac{\left[\sum_{i}^{a} (c_i)(A_i) \right]^2}{bcds\left[\sum (c_i)^2 \right]}.$$

The numerator is identical in all of these formulas; the only change is a reflection of the number of observations. More specifically, in the $A \times B$ design, where the total number of observations is abs, the number of observations contributing to each $\bar{A}_i$ is $abs = bs$; in the $A \times B \times C$, where the total number of observations is $abcs$, the number of observations contributing to each mean is $abcs = bcs$; and in the $A \times B \times C \times D$ design, where the total number of observations is $abcds$, the number of observations contributing to each mean is $abcds = bcds$.

Comparisons Involving Means in Higher-Order Matrices

At times we may want to compare means at different levels of factor A, where we hold the levels of the other variables in a matrix constant. For instance, we might compare two $\overline{AB}$ means at a particular level of factor B or two $\overline{ABC}$ means at a particular combination of factors B and C. (This sort of comparison is essentially a simple main effect of factor A at a specific level or combination of levels. The "main effect" in this case reflects a comparison between means varying with respect to factor A.)

These comparisons can be extracted relatively easily. We start with Eq. (15-3a) and substitute the appropriate cell totals for "$Total_i$." We can then substitute Eq. (15-3a) in the numerator of Eq. (15-3). The denominator is obtained exactly as we outlined in the last section. Thus, for a comparison among the $\overline{AB}$ means at level b_j, Eq. (15-3) becomes

$$SS_{A_{comp. \, at \, b_j}} = \frac{\left[\sum_{i}^{a} (c_i)(AB_{ij}) \right]^2}{s\left[\sum (c_i)^2 \right]}$$

in a two factor experiment. The formula is exactly the same in a three-factor experiment except for an adjustment for the number of observations; i.e., we will substitute $abcs = cs$ for the s in the equation given above.

For a comparison among the $\overline{ABC}$ means at a particular combination of levels b_j and c_k, we substitute the quantity ABC_{ijk} for "$Total_i$" in Eq. (15-3a) and then complete the substitution in Eq. (15-3). In a three-factor experiment, where the number of observations upon which the ABC_{ijk} totals are based is $abcs = s$, then Eq. (15-3) becomes

$$SS_{A_{\text{comp. at } bc_{jk}}} = \frac{\left[\sum\limits_{i}^{a} (c_i)(ABC_{ijk})\right]^2}{s\left[\sum (c_i)^2\right]}.$$

In a four-factor experiment, all that would change would be the number of observations. In this case, we would substitute $abcds = ds$ for the s in the equation.

Interaction with Comparisons

A common analysis in factorial experiments is the assessment of interactions of comparisons involving the A treatments with other independent variables. We covered this sort of analysis in Chapter 12 (see pp. 235–239) and in Chapter 14 (see pp. 295–304). Briefly, the question we asked in the first case is whether or not a particular comparison involving differences in A treatments is the same at different levels of factor B (the $A_{\text{comp.}} \times B$ interaction), and in the second case, whether or not an *interaction* of $A_{\text{comp.}}$ and factor B is the same at different levels of factor C (the $A_{\text{comp.}} \times B \times C$ interaction). The computational formulas for these sorts of analyses can be generated from the df statement in a manner analogous to that outlined for the standard analysis of variance.

We will illustrate the steps by constructing the computational formula for the $SS_{A_{\text{comp.}} \times B \times C}$ in a three-factor design (total number of observations $= abcs$). The computational formula will consist of a number of quantities, each of which stems from Eq. (15-3). We start with the expanded df statement, which will indicate the treatment totals to be included in Eq. (15-3) and the pattern of combination. For example,

$$df_{A_{\text{comp.}} \times B \times C} = (df_{A_{\text{comp.}}})(df_B)(df_C)$$
$$= a'(b - 1)(c - 1)$$
$$= a'bc - a'b - a'c + a',$$

where a' stands for the 1 df associated with the $A_{\text{comp.}}$. From the expanded df statement, we can write the treatment totals involved in each term of the formula:

$$SS_{A_{\text{comp.}} \times B \times C} = ABC - AB - AC + A.$$

The next step is to begin forming the numerator of Eq. (15-3) for each of these terms. Because the summation is over the i subscript only, notational subscripts and summation limits must be added:

$$SS_{A_{comp.} \times B \times C} = \left[\sum_i^a (c_i)(ABC_{ijk}) \right]^2 - \left[\sum_i^a (c_i)(AB_{ij}) \right]^2$$
$$- \left[\sum_i^a (c_i)(AC_{ik}) \right]^2 + \left[\sum_i^a (c_i)(A_i) \right]^2.$$

Since we are also obtaining these quantities over the levels of factors B and C, we have to perform summations over subscripts other than i. We make the summations explicit by adding a summation sign for each subscript excluding i:

$$SS_{A_{comp.} \times B \times C} = \sum_j^b \sum_k^c \left[\sum_i^a (c_i)(ABC_{ijk}) \right]^2 - \sum_j^b \left[\sum_i^a (c_i)(AB_{ij}) \right]^2$$
$$- \sum_k^c \left[\sum_i^a (c_i)(AC_{ik}) \right]^2 + \left[\sum_i^a (c_i)(A_i) \right]^2.$$

The final steps represent familiar ground. The number of observations upon which the weighted totals are based is obtained by deleting letters from the total number of observations ($abcs$ in this example) that appear in the numerator. For ABC_{ijk}, the number is $abcs = s$; for AB_{ij}, the number is $abcs = cs$; for AC_{ik}, the number is $abcs = bs$; and for A_i, the number is $abcs = bcs$. The final computational formula becomes

$$SS_{A_{comp.} \times B \times C} = \frac{\sum_j^b \sum_k^c \left[\sum_i^a (c_i)(ABC_{ijk}) \right]^2}{s[\sum (c_i)^2]} - \frac{\sum_j^b \left[\sum_i^a (c_i)(AB_{ij}) \right]^2}{cs[\sum (c_i)^2]}$$
$$- \frac{\sum_k^c \left[\sum_i^a (c_i)(AC_{ik}) \right]^2}{bs[\sum (c_i)^2]} + \frac{\left[\sum_i^a (c_i)(A_i) \right]^2}{bcs[\sum (c_i)^2]}. \tag{15-4}$$

If we refer back to Chapter 14, it will be noted that the computational formula given in Eq. (15-4) is different from that enumerated in Eq. (14-11). Specifically, Eq. (14-11) stated that the

$$SS_{A_{comp.} \times B \times C} = \frac{\sum_j^b \sum_k^c \left[\sum_i^a (c_i)(ABC_{ijk}) \right]^2}{s[\sum (c_i)^2]} - SS_{A_{comp.} \times B}$$
$$- SS_{A_{comp.} \times C} - SS_{A_{comp.}}.$$

The two equations can be shown to be algebraically equivalent. Equation (14-11) may appear to be simpler than Eq. (15-4), but remember, each of the sums of squares included in the equation involves computational formulas of its own. Equation (14-11) is more appropriate when we actually want to extract the lower-level sums of squares (the three sums of squares listed on the right of the equation), while Eq. (15-4) is more convenient when we want to calculate the sum of squares for the comparison directly, as might be the case if the three-way interaction proved to be significant.

GENERATION OF FORMULAS FOR SIMPLE EFFECTS OF INTERACTIONS

Following the discovery of a significant interaction, we will often want to conduct additional analyses in order to discover the locus of the interaction effects. Usually we will analyze the simple effects of interactions. With a significant two-way interaction, we might look at the variation of *one* of the variables at the different levels of the other variable; this is called an analysis of the simple main effects of the two-way interaction—"main effects" because we are assessing the effect of variations in *one* independent variable. We discussed this sort of analysis in Chapter 11 (see pp. 213–222).

With a significant three-way interaction we have two choices: (1) an analysis of the *interaction* of *two* of the independent variables at the different levels of the third variable and (2) an analysis of the effects of *one* independent variable at the different combinations of the other two variables. The first analysis is called an analysis of the simple interaction effects of the three-way interaction and the second analysis is called an analysis of the simple, simple main effects of the three-way interaction. We discussed these two analyses in Chapter 14 (see pp. 286–293).

In general, the higher the interaction, the more types of simple effects that may be inspected. For the four-way interaction, for example, there are three levels of analyses: (1) an analysis of the interaction of three variables at the different levels of the fourth variable, (2) an analysis of the interaction of two variables at the different combinations of the other two variables, and (3) an analysis of the effects of one variable at the different combinations of the other three variables.

The computational formulas for these types of analyses may be constructed by using the basic system we introduced earlier. We will illustrate the procedure by generating the formulas for analyses we have discussed already: the simple interaction effects and the simple, simple main effects of the three-way interaction.

Simple Interaction Effects

Taking the simple interaction effects first, we begin with a determination of the df statement for this sum of squares. We will consider the $A \times B$ interaction at the levels of factor C, although we could have considered the simple $A \times C$ or the simple $B \times C$ interactions just as well. The sum of squares for this quantity at level c_k is denoted at $SS_{A \times B \text{ at } c_k}$. The df are found by multiplying the *df* for the two variables:

$$df_{A \times B \text{ at } c_k} = (df_A)(df_B) = (a - 1)(b - 1).$$

If we expand this *df* statement, however, we will obtain an arrangement that is appropriate for the $SS_{A \times B}$ and *not* for the simple interaction effects. We have to modify the *df* statement in order to reflect the fact that we are dealing with one of the $A \times B$ interactions at level c_k. This may be accomplished by the simple expedient of adding the fixed factor (c_k) to the *df* statement. More specifically,

$$
\begin{aligned}
df_{A \times B \text{ at } c_k} &= (df_A)(df_B)(c_k) \\
&= (a - 1)(b - 1)(c_k) \\
&= ab(c_k) - a(c_k) - b(c_k) + c_k.
\end{aligned}
$$

We can now proceed with the construction of the computational formula. The only changes in the operations are (1) we introduce notational subscripts and summation limits because a restricted set of sums is being specified in the calculations and (2) we do not act upon the subscript for factor C, since it is fixed at level c_k for this analysis.

Continuing with the construction, then, we substitute capital letters and subscripts for corresponding terms in the *df* statement:

$$SS_{A \times B \text{ at } c_k} = ABC_{ijk} - AC_{ik} - BC_{jk} + C_k.$$

In the next step, we square each total and sum over the subscripts that are free to vary, namely, i and j (k is fixed):

$$SS_{A \times B \text{ at } c_k} = \sum_i^a \sum_j^b (ABC_{ijk})^2 - \sum_i^a (AC_{ik})^2 - \sum_j^b (BC_{jk})^2 + (C_k)^2.$$

We now select the appropriate divisors, dividing each term by the total number of observations (*abcs* in this case) and deleting letters also appearing in the numerator:

$$SS_{A \times B \text{ at } c_k} = \frac{\sum_i^a \sum_j^b (ABC_{ijk})^2}{ab\cancel{c}s} - \frac{\sum_i^a (AC_{ik})^2}{a\cancel{b}\cancel{c}s} - \frac{\sum_j^b (BC_{jk})^2}{\cancel{a}b\cancel{c}s} + \frac{(C_k)^2}{\cancel{a}\cancel{b}\cancel{c}s}.$$

Rewriting the equation gives us

$$SS_{A \times B \text{ at } c_k} = \frac{\sum_i^a \sum_j^b (ABC_{ijk})^2}{s} - \frac{\sum_i^a (AC_{ik})^2}{bs} - \frac{\sum_j^b (BC_{jk})^2}{as} + \frac{(C_k)^2}{abs},$$

which is identical to the one presented in Chapter 14 (see p. 287).

Simple, Simple Main Effects

The computational formulas for any simple effect may be obtained in the same manner. The main "trick" in adapting the basic system to the present analyses is to include the combination of levels of the constant factors in the *df* statement. For the simple, simple main effects of factor *A* at the combination of levels bc_{jk}, the *df* statement would be

$$df_{A\,at\,bc_{jk}} = (df_A)(bc_{jk})$$
$$= (a - 1)(bc_{jk}) = a(bc_{jk}) - bc_{jk}.$$

This statement leads directly to the critical sums involved, ABC_{ijk} and BC_{jk}, respectively, and indicates that the *jk* subscripts are fixed and will not be summed over. Starting the construction:

$$SS_{A\,at\,bc_{jk}} = ABC_{ijk} - BC_{jk}.$$

Squaring and summing over the *i* subscript, we have

$$SS_{A\,at\,bc_{jk}} = \sum_i^a (ABC_{ijk})^2 - (BC_{jk})^2.$$

Dividing each numerator by the total number of observations (*abcs*) and deleting letters also appearing in the numerator,

$$SS_{A\,at\,bc_{jk}} = \frac{\sum_i^a (ABC_{ijk})^2}{ab\cancel{c}s} - \frac{(BC_{jk})^2}{ab\cancel{c}s}.$$

Rewriting the equation,

$$SS_{A\,at\,bc_{jk}} = \frac{\sum_i^a (ABC_{ijk})^2}{s} - \frac{(BC_{jk})^2}{as},$$

which is identical to Eq. (14-6a) presented in Chapter 14 (p. 290).

Further Examples

In order to test your understanding of the procedure and to provide an additional example, turn to Exercise 7 for Part IV (p. 390). This exercise asks you to construct the formulas for the simple effects of the four-way interaction.

COMMENTS ABOUT ADDITIONAL COMPARISONS

Other methods of making additional comparisons, such as multiple-comparison techniques, are easily adapted for use with higher-order factorial experiments. The ease with which these computational formulas are modified has already been demonstrated in Chapter 12 (pp. 244–246) and in Chapter 14 (pp. 305–307). The formulas for even more complex experiments can be modified in an analogous manner. Because of the limited usefulness of these procedures in the factorial experiment, we will not discuss them in this chapter. As we have argued before, the number of comparisons between pairs of means that we will want to make is generally small. This is because it usually makes little sense allowing more than one factor to vary in any given comparison.

In contrast to the multiple-comparison techniques, the procedures we discussed in the preceding sections are considerably more *analytical*: with these methods variations in two or more factors may be assessed in a meaningful fashion. These take the form of interactions of comparisons with other independent variables and the systematic search for the contributing sources of a significant interaction. For any of these analyses to prove fruitful, however, they must reflect meaningful research questions. Knowing *how* to calculate the sum of squares for a particular comparison or simple effect ensures that these important statistical analyses will be at our disposal, but being able to generate the *questions* from which the analyses flow is of far more critical importance. On the other hand, a knowledge of what analytical tools are available and how to use them will help us to frame our questions in such a way that they can be answered by means of a straightforward analysis.

As a final point, we must continue to recognize the problem that exists whenever we undertake additional comparisons—namely, the increase in the experimentwise (EW) error rate. It is this increase, of course, which the multiple-comparison techniques are designed to control; but we have seen that these corrections are much too severe for the comparisons we will actually undertake. As we noted in Chapter 12 (pp. 244–246) and Chapter 14 (pp. 305–307), these techniques may be adapted to provide a correction for a more realistic pool of potential comparisons. Nevertheless, it is common practice for researchers to disregard the increase in the EW error rate with the sorts of analyses we have considered previously and to operate with uncorrected significance levels— i.e., the usual per comparison rate (α). We have also mentioned a compromise position between these two extremes: the Dunn procedure. With the Dunn technique an EW error rate is chosen, with the significance level used to evaluate the comparisons being divided among the comparisons actually being made (see pp. 147–149 and 158–160). Whatever course of action is taken depends ultimately upon our attitudes towards type I and type II errors. This point has been discussed in detail in the previous chapters.

chapter sixteen

STRUCTURAL MODELS OF
THE ANALYSIS OF VARIANCE

In the preceding chapters we have purposely minimized formal discussions of statistical theory. Considering the goals of this book, this is exactly what was promised—a discussion of the design and analysis of experiments from the point of view of the researcher. There is some utility, however, in examining briefly the statistical structure that underlies and justifies the analyses we have learned to conduct. This chapter, therefore, will dig more deeply into these statistical underpinnings. We will carry out this discussion within the context of the two-way factorial design. During the course of this examination, you will also be introduced to the distinction between *fixed* and *random* independent variables and will see how the presence of the latter type affects our evaluation of the significance of main effects and interactions.

A REVIEW OF THE LOGIC OF THE *F* TEST

Each analysis of variance we consider in this book is based upon a structural model of some sort. These models are written in terms of population parameters and specify the sources contributing to a single observation in the experiment. We saw in Chapter 10, for example, that the structural model could be expressed as

$$ABS_{ijk} = \mu + (\mu_i - \mu) + (\mu_j - \mu) + (\mu_{ij} - \mu_i - \mu_j + \mu) + (ABS_{ijk} - \mu_{ij}).$$

(16-1)

That is, an individual ABS_{ijk} score reflects the overall mean of the treatment populations (μ), the population treatment effect at level a_i ($\mu_i - \mu$), the population treatment effect at level b_j ($\mu_j - \mu$), the population interaction effect at the combination of level a_i and level b_j ($\mu_{ij} - \mu_i - \mu_j + \mu$), and experimental error ($ABS_{ijk} - \mu_{ij}$). The first three quantities on the right within parentheses are called factorial effects and the last is called experimental error.

In the analysis of variance, we make inferences concerning the presence or absence of these factorial effects by expressing them in terms of population variance components. These components are based on the deviations specified on the righthand side of Eq. (16-1). In general, a variance component for factorial effects has the following form:

$$\frac{\sum (\text{deviation})^2}{df_{\text{component}}}.$$

More specifically, we would have

$$\frac{\sum (\mu_i - \mu)^2}{a - 1}$$

as the variance component for factor A,

$$\frac{\sum (\mu_j - \mu)^2}{b - 1}$$

as the variance component for factor B, and

$$\frac{\sum (\mu_{ij} - \mu_i - \mu_j + \mu)^2}{(a - 1)(b - 1)}$$

as the variance component for the $A \times B$ interaction.

We will often see these components with Greek letters substituted for the deviations. For instance, if we set

$$\alpha_i = \mu_i - \mu,$$

$$\beta_j = \mu_j - \mu,$$

and

$$(\alpha\beta)_{ij} = \mu_{ij} - \mu_i - \mu_j + \mu,$$

then the corresponding components become

$$\frac{\sum (\alpha_i)^2}{a - 1}, \quad \frac{\sum (\beta_j)^2}{b - 1}, \quad \text{and} \quad \frac{\sum (\alpha\beta_{ij})^2}{(a - 1)(b - 1)}.$$

We will refer to these components as

$$\theta_\alpha^2, \quad \theta_\beta^2, \quad \text{and} \quad \theta_{(\alpha\beta)}^2,$$

respectively.[1] We will refer to the variance component associated with experimental error as

$$\sigma_\varepsilon^2.$$

We do not observe these components in an actual experiment, although we can use the mean squares calculated from the basic observations to provide *estimates* of these quantities. Unfortunately, however, the mean squares we obtain from the analysis of variance do not provide *direct* estimates of the variance components for the factorial effects. Instead, each mean square provides an estimate which represents a combination of two or more components, the number of which depends upon the structural model involved. For the two-way design we considered in Chapter 10, which as we will see represents the *fixed-effects model*, each mean square contains two components: the factorial component and the error component. We can see this point quite vividly by considering the *expected values* of the mean squares [$E(MS)$] for the two main effects and interaction. (The expected value in this situation is simply the mean of the sampling distribution of the statistic obtained with repeated random samplings from a given population.) In the present example,

$$E(MS_A) = \sigma_\varepsilon^2 + bs\theta_\alpha^2,$$

$$E(MS_B) = \sigma_\varepsilon^2 + as\theta_\beta^2,$$

and

$$E(MS_{A \times B}) = \sigma_\varepsilon^2 + s\theta_{(\alpha\beta)}^2.$$

(Note that each component is weighted by the number of observations contributing to the estimate of the corresponding population mean—i.e., bs for μ_i, as for μ_j, and s for μ_{ij}.) To round out the picture,

$$E(MS_{S/AB}) = \sigma_\varepsilon^2.$$

The essential logic behind the analysis of variance lies in the construction of ratios having the form

$$\frac{MS_{\text{effect}}}{MS_{\text{error}}}$$

---

[1] We have used the Greek letter theta (θ) to indicate that these variance components are *not* variance *estimates*. The estimation of variance components is discussed in Chapter 25.

where the expected value of the MS_{error} matches the expected value of the MS_{effect} in all respects except for the variance component reflecting the effect. Symbolically,

$$E(MS_{effect}) = \text{error} + \text{effect}$$

and

$$E(MS_{error}) = \text{error}.$$

Under the null hypothesis, the variance component reflecting the effect will be zero, the "effect" component (or *null hypothesis* component as it is often called) drops out, and

$$E(MS_{effect}) = E(MS_{error}).$$

Under these circumstances, then, the ratio

$$\frac{MS_{effect}}{MS_{error}}$$

will be distributed as $F(df_{effect}, df_{error})$, provided the usual assumptions of normality, homogeneity, and independence are satisfied. We can then relate the observed ratio to the tabled values of F and assess its significance through the application of the decision rules.

For the example we have been considering, we have already noted that

$$E(MS_{S/AB}) = \sigma_\varepsilon^2.$$

Consequently, this mean square is the appropriate error term for all three of the mean squares reflecting factorial effects—because in each case, when the null hypothesis is true, the null hypothesis component drops out and we are dividing one estimate of error variance by another independent estimate of error variance.

Summary

The F ratios for the analyses we have described in this and the preceding chapters—the completely randomized designs—are typically formed by using the within-groups mean square as the only error term. The use of this mean square as the error term in all of our analyses is based on a particular structural model, the *fixed-effects* model. We will consider this model in a moment and describe the other models that are sometimes found in the behavioral sciences—the *random* and *mixed* models. As we will see, however, no new calculations are involved. The only change in the analysis is in the selection of the appropriate error term. Moreover, the selection will be made from mean squares we will have calculated anyway. Thus, what must be discussed are the defining characteristics of the different models and rules for the selection of appropriate error terms under them.

DISTINCTION BETWEEN FIXED
AND RANDOM FACTORS

The whole distinction among the three models is the manner in which the levels of the independent variables are selected. To qualify as a *fixed factor*, the levels of an independent variable are selected arbitrarily and systematically. In contrast, to qualify as a *random factor*, the levels of an independent variable are selected *randomly* or unsystematically from a pool of possible levels. In the *fixed-effects model* all of the independent variables are fixed, while in the *random model* all of the independent variables are random. The *mixed model* represents an inclusion of both fixed and random factors in the same experiment.

From a statistical point of view, the main advantage of an experiment with random independent variables is the increased generality accorded the results. That is, the outcome of the experiment provides an undistorted picture of the influence of this variable on behavior—"undistorted" in that we can generalize our results to levels of the variable that we have not included in the experiment. On the other hand, the results obtained with fixed independent variables, where the selection is not random, are presumed to be limited to the particular levels chosen and not necessarily representative of the levels not selected for inclusion in the experiment.

In spite of this apparently important difference in the generalizability of results, most independent variables manipulated in the behavioral sciences are *fixed*. There are two major reasons for this. First, for many independent variables, the levels included in an experiment effectively exhaust the pool of possible levels. There may be only two or three drugs that produce a particular effect or only a handful of teaching methods that can be considered realistic alternatives to be used in a classroom. Under these circumstances there is no need to generalize, since as far as the researcher is concerned, he has included *all* of the levels of the factor in his experiment. The same thing is true when a quantitative variable is represented at a number of "representative" intervals (see Winer, 1962, pp. 142–143; 1971, pp. 312–313). We are referring here to the fact that a continuous dimension (such as age, intelligence, meaningfulness, stimulus intensity) may be divided coarsely into two, three, or more categories. When included in an experiment, these categories effectively constitute a complete enumeration of all possible categories (i.e., levels). Under these circumstances a researcher is justified in concluding that a particular independent variable produces such and such effect, without worrying about qualifying his statement with the clause, "under the specific levels chosen for this experiment."

A second and related point is that a researcher usually chooses his levels to be *representative* of the independent variable. Suppose we are varying the intensity of background noise in a psychophysical investigation and that we decide to include four levels of this variable in our experiment. If we consider the potential levels of the variable that we could use in our experiment, the number is exceedingly large. Even so, most researchers would not select the four levels randomly from this pool of potential levels. Instead they would be influenced by some or all of the following considerations: (1) to represent the full extent of the effective stimulus dimension in the experiment; (2) to choose levels that are expected to produce a reasonably large difference between adjacent levels; and (3) to attempt to "hit" points of inflection—points where there might be a change in the direction of the functional relation. *These* are the overriding considerations in the selection of the four levels, and they certainly are *not* met by a random-selection procedure which gives equal weight to all possible levels of the variable. With random selection there is no "guarantee" that the important points along the dimensions will be represented in the experiment.

In most of the examples of random factors found in statistics books it is clear that the variable is not to be *manipulated*, but to be *sampled*. For instance, an educator who wants to try out a number of methods of teaching reading in the second grade (a fixed factor) may choose as a second independent variable *schools* within a particular city or state. He cannot include all of the second graders in his experiment, but he clearly wants to extend his conclusions to the population of students *not* participating in the experiment. Thus, schools becomes a random factor. Other examples include (1) a sampling of the personalities of different experimenters, (2) order of presenting a large set of material, (3) hospitals in a particular locality, and (4) raters and ratees from different political parties. (*Subjects*, our familiar *s* in the designs we have considered so far, is usually assumed to be a random variable. This view is justified because the particular subjects in any given treatment condition are assigned *randomly* to that condition.)

In any case, it is easy to identify random independent variables. In order to sample from a population (such as hospitals, classes, stimulus orders), a researcher will have to specify the members of the population and the procedures designed to guarantee the random selection of members from this population. In applied areas of research (e.g., educational applications) random independent variables generally consist of samples of subject grouping (e.g., schools, classes, cities). In other areas (e.g., experimental psychology) perhaps the most frequent use of random factors is as control procedures (e.g., the random selection of presentation orders or of lists of stimulus materials). But even these applications are rare. The main reason is that in many situations, randomization is not an adequate control procedure.

Suppose, for example, that we were interested in determining whether or not unpleasant words are more difficult to perceive under minimal perceptual conditions (e.g., reduced illumination, blur, brief exposure) than neutral words or pleasant words. In the basic experiment, one group of subjects might be given 20 unpleasant words to recognize, another group 20 neutral words, and a third group 20 pleasant words. From the arguments given above, *pleasantness* is a fixed factor. Where does the experimenter obtain the samples of words? First, it will be necessary to rate a large number of words on "pleasantness" and on the basis of these ratings divide these words into the three categories. At this point, the researcher might decide to have several sets of words in each category. One way to obtain these sets is to select several random samples of 20 words each from a given category of word. *Sets* would then become a random independent variable that is included in the experiment. The design now would be a mixed model, pleasantness representing the fixed factor and sets representing the random factor.

Such an experiment would *not* be acceptable in this research area, however, for the important reason that *other* characteristics of words must be held *constant* across levels of pleasantness, and random sampling will not accomplish this requirement. Characteristics of words, such as frequency of occurrence in the language, word length, the initial letter of the word, the predictability of letter pairs within a word, and the number of similar words with which a target word may be confused, all have been shown to affect the probability of a correct perception.[2] If any of these characteristics varies along with pleasantness, the results of the experiment will be contaminated by their presence.

Thus, instead of selecting his stimulus sets by random sampling, a researcher may take great pains to *equate* unpleasant, neutral, and pleasant words on each of these characteristics. With the first approach, an experimenter will be able to generalize back to the original pools of words from which the stimulus sets were drawn; with the second, he will not be able to do so. From a scientific point of view, however, the first approach is virtually useless, since any differences obtained in the experiment may be attributed to any of the other characteristics that varied between the three types of words. In contrast, the second approach sacrifices generalizability for *analyzability*, since it permits any differences that may be observed to be attributed to the independent variable under study.

In short, then, an experimenter must know his research area very well before he introduces random independent variables of this sort. If a random factor is introduced, certain changes occur in the statistical evaluation of some of the factorial effects. We will now consider why designs with random factors complicate the analysis procedure.

THE EFFECT OF RANDOM FACTORS
UPON THE ANALYSIS

A critical requirement of a fixed factor is that the sum of the separate treatment effects (deviations) equals zero. For example, factor A is a fixed factor if

$$\sum (\mu_i - \mu) = 0.$$

Since μ is the mean of all of the μ_i's and since all of the levels of factor A are included in the experiment (and thus all of the μ_i's are included also), the sum

---

[2] This example was suggested by Dr. D. E. Broadbent in his Kenneth Craik Memorial Lecture, October 1970, Cambridge.

of the deviations of the μ_i's from the overall mean (μ) must equal zero. In an $A \times B$ experiment with both factors fixed,

$$\sum (\mu_i - \mu) = \sum \alpha_i = 0,$$
$$\sum (\mu_j - \mu) = \sum \beta_j = 0,$$

and

$$\sum (\mu_{ij} - \mu_i - \mu_j + \mu) = \sum (\alpha\beta)_{ij} = 0.$$

Additionally, and not so obviously, the interaction effects sum to zero for any row and for any column [see Winer (1962, p. 149; 1971, pp. 318–319)]. That is,

$$\sum_i^a (\alpha\beta)_{ij} = 0 \quad \text{and} \quad \sum_j^b (\alpha\beta)_{ij} = 0. \tag{16-2}$$

Under these assumptions, then, the $MS_{S/AB}$ becomes the appropriate error term for evaluating the significance of the two main effects and the $A \times B$ interaction.

A different situation exists for an experiment with a random factor present. Staying within the context of a two-way factorial, we can think of an AB matrix in which all possible levels of factor A are listed in one direction and all possible levels of factor B are listed in the other direction. Included in the cells of this matrix are the population interaction effects [the $(\alpha\beta)_{ij}$ terms]. For this *potential* AB matrix, Eq. (16-2) holds both for rows and for columns. If both independent variables are fixed factors, the potential AB matrix and the AB matrix actually represented in the experiment are the same. This is not true, however, if one or both of the factors are random.

Let us assume that factor A is random and factor B is fixed. This means that we would select at random a levels of factor A from the total population of levels present in the potential AB matrix, while we would include all of the levels of factor B. We will use a capital letter to refer to the number of *potential* levels of a factor and a lower-case letter to refer to the number of levels actually included in the experiment. In the present example we have an $a \times B$ factorial, with factor A random (since $a < A$) and factor B fixed (since $b = B$). To complete the other possibilities,

$A \times B$ designates an experiment with both factors fixed,

$A \times b$ designates an experiment in which factor A is fixed and factor B is random, and

$a \times b$ designates an experiment in which both factors are random.

Suppose we examine the consequences of crossing a random factor (factor A) with a fixed factor (factor B). A potential AB matrix is presented in the upper portion of Table 16-1. (For convenience the potential number of levels of factor A has been made small.) Entered in the body of the matrix are numbers representing the $(\alpha\beta)_{ij}$ interaction effects. Notice that for each row and column of this matrix, the sum of the effects equals zero. For purposes of this discussion, we will assume that there are no main effects in the population; thus, interaction

TABLE 16-1   *A Potential AB Matrix Contrasted with an Actual AB Matrix*

POTENTIAL AB MATRIX: $(\alpha\beta)_{ij}$ INTERACTION EFFECTS

Potential Levels of Factor B	Potential Levels of Factor A					Sum
	a_1	a_2	a_3	a_4	a_5	
b_1	3	2	-1	-2	-2	0
b_2	3	-1	1	-5	2	0
b_3	1	-2	3	-1	-1	0
b_4	-7	1	-3	8	1	0
Sum	0	0	0	0	0	

POTENTIAL AB MATRIX: POPULATION MEANS (μ_{ij})

Potential Levels of Factor B	Potential Levels of Factor A					Mean
	a_1	a_2	a_3	a_4	a_5	
b_1	13	12	9	8	8	10
b_2	13	9	11	5	12	10
b_3	11	8	13	9	9	10
b_4	3	11	7	18	11	10
Mean	10	10	10	10	10	

THE aB MATRIX: POPULATION MEANS (μ_{ij})

Levels of Factor B	Levels of Factor A^a			Mean
	$a_1 (a_2)$	$a_2 (a_3)$	$a_3 (a_5)$	
b_1	12	9	8	9.7
b_2	9	11	12	10.7
b_3	8	13	9	10.0
b_4	11	7	11	9.7
Mean	10.0	10.0	10.0	

[a] Corresponding levels in the AB matrix are indicated in parentheses.

effects are all that should be present. What this means is that we can specify the population cell means (the μ_{ij}'s) by simply knowing the appropriate $(\alpha\beta)_{ij}$ interaction effect and the overall mean (μ). That is,

$$\mu_{ij} = (\alpha\beta)_{ij} + \alpha_i + \beta_j + \mu$$
$$= (\alpha\beta)_{ij} + 0 + 0 + \mu$$
$$= (\alpha\beta)_{ij} + \mu.$$

If we set $\mu = 10$ and then add this quantity to all of the $(\alpha\beta)_{ij}$'s, we obtain an AB

matrix of population means (the μ_{ij}'s). This matrix appears in the middle portion of Table 16-1. If we include *all levels* of the two factors in our experiment, both main effects will be zero; this is because all of the column means are equal (the μ_i's) and all of the row means are equal (the μ_j's). On the other hand, there will be an interaction present. (We knew this from the upper matrix.)

In our example, however, we are going to sample randomly from the potential levels of factor A, but include *all* levels of factor B. One of the possible aB matrices is presented in the lower portion of Table 16-1. In this matrix we have simply taken three entire columns from the AB matrix of μ_{ij}'s given in the middle portion of the table. Consider what will happen to the main effects in this new matrix. For the random independent variable (factor A) the column marginal means are still equal and, therefore, the main effect will be zero. For the fixed independent variable (factor B), on the other hand, the row marginal means are *not* equal; consequently, a main effect will be observed.

This demonstration shows us that with a random independent variable present in a two-factor design, the $(\alpha\beta)_{ij}$ interaction effects will *intrude* upon the main effect of the *fixed* independent variable. If the situation had been reversed, with factor A fixed and factor B random, the main effect of factor A would have been affected by any interaction effects present. If both factors had been random, both main effects would have been affected by the interaction effects. The practical conclusion from this demonstration is that with random factors present, the expected values of main effects will contain the interaction component in addition to the components for the main effect and experimental error. This means that we will have to search for new error terms, since the expected value of the within-groups mean square ($MS_{S/AB}$ in this example) will continue to be σ_ε^2.

We will now consider a set of rules that will allow us to determine the appropriate error term for any combination of fixed or random factors with the designs we have been considering so far in this book. We will continue to extract exactly the same sums of squares from our experiments and to calculate the same mean squares. The only change will be in the specification of the appropriate error term.

SELECTION OF ERROR TERMS

Alternative Systems

The basic rule followed in the selection of an error term has been stated earlier. To repeat, a mean square qualifies as an error term if its expected value matches the expected value of the MS_{effect} in all respects except the null hypothesis component. To aid in this selection, authors usually present tables showing the expected values for the different sources. Sometimes they actually list the variance components for the different arrangements of fixed and random independent variables. A more efficient display consists of a listing of the variance components that remain or drop out depending upon the nature of the different independent variables [see Winer (1962, p. 172; 1971, p. 346) for a comprehensive example with a three-factor design.] In whatever way the expected values are listed, the selection procedure is the same: the variance components of the different sources are compared with the variance components of the effect, and an error term is discovered when a source matches the expectation of the effect except for the component reflecting the effect.

Since it is not practical to present such tables for higher-order factorials, most authors offer some sort of mechanical scheme for actually writing the expected values for each term listed in the analysis of variance summary table. [See, for example, Glass and Stanley (1970, pp. 479–481), Kirk (1968, pp. 208–212), Myers (1966, pp. 184–185), and Winer (1962, pp. 195–199; 1971, pp. 371–375).] Basically, these systems start with a statement of the components contributing to an individual observation, such as the one given in Eq. (16-1), and then require the listing of all of the variance components that would be present for a given mean square under the most complicated model—the random model. Rules are given for the deletion of different components as random factors are changed to fixed factors. On the basis of the variance components remaining after the deletion is accomplished, the researcher can now start the selection process described in the last paragraph.

The Present System

We will consider an equally mechanical procedure, but one which skips the rather tedious chore of determining the exact form of the different expected values.[3] Instead, the present system accomplishes the selection of an error term by focusing upon the *letters* used to designate each source of variance and asking a series of yes-no questions about the letters designating the effect to be tested and the letters designating the potential error terms. The answers will identify the correct error term. The advantage of this system is simplicity, its disadvantage the fact that it is a step removed from the logic of the F test—i.e., the actual matching of specific variance components. We can "restore" the essence of the basic logic, of course, by reminding ourselves that the error term produced by the simplified system contains exactly the same variance components as the mean square for the effect except for the null hypothesis component.

The first step in the discovery of the appropriate error term is to list the letters and the combinations of letters designating the different sources of variance normally extracted in the standard analysis. We will use capital letters to represent fixed factors and lower-case letters to represent random factors. We

[3] The author wishes to thank Dr. Albert Erlebacher for suggesting the rules for error-term selection that will be given here and in subsequent chapters.

TABLE 16-2   *Steps in the Selection of Appropriate Error Terms in the Completely Randomized Factorial Experiment[a] (All Factors Crossed)*

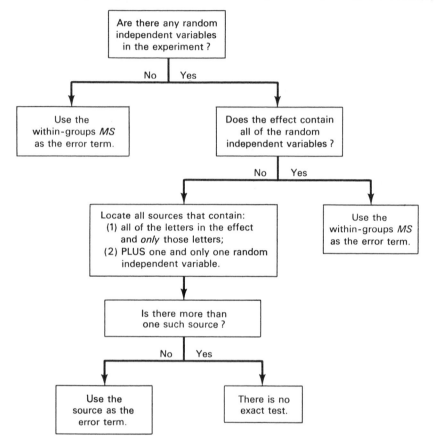

[a] *Source* refers to any subcomponent isolated in the standard analysis of variance; *effect* refers to the source containing only those letters denoting the treatment effect in question.

then go through an elimination procedure in which each source in the analysis of variance table is subjected to a test to see whether or not it qualifies as an error term for a given factorial effect. The test is presented in Table 16-2. We will illustrate the use of this test by working through two examples.

Examples

TWO-FACTOR EXPERIMENT   As our first illustration, consider the possible arrangements of fixed and random independent variables in a two-factor experiment. The four possibilities are enumerated in Table 16-3. For each case,

TABLE 16-3   *Error Terms for Different Structural Models: The Completely Randomized A × B Factorial*[a]

Both Factors Fixed		Factor A Random; Factor B Fixed		Factor A Fixed; Factor B Random		Both Factors Random	
Source	Error Term	Source	Error Term	Source	Error Term	Source	Error Term
A	Wg	a	Wg	A	$A \times b$	a	$a \times b$
B	Wg	B	$a \times B$	b	Wg	b	$a \times b$
$A \times B$	Wg	$a \times B$	Wg	$A \times b$	Wg	$a \times b$	Wg
Wg	—	Wg	—	Wg	—	Wg	—

[a] $Wg = MS_{S/AB}$.

the letters designating the sources of variance are listed in the first column and the error terms in the second. In the first case, both factors are fixed and the fixed-effects model is appropriate. Table 16-2 asks first whether there are any random independent variables in the experiment. Since the answer is "no," we follow the appropriate branch at this point and find that we use the within-groups mean square ($MS_{S/AB}$) as the error term for all sources.

The next case is an example of a mixed model; i.e., factor A is random and factor B is fixed. Considering the main effect of factor A, we move to the "yes" branch in response to the first question, since a random independent variable is present in the experiment. In response to the next question, whether the letter designation of the effect contains the random variable, factor A, we answer "yes" and find that the $MS_{S/AB}$ is the appropriate error term. For the main effect of factor B, we answer "no" to the second question, since the random variable, a, is *not* part of the letter designation of the effect. At this point we are asked to subject the sources of variance to a two-part criterion, selecting only those sources that match exactly the letters in the effect *plus one* random independent variable. For the final question, we simply check to see that there is only one source meeting these requirements; otherwise, there is no appropriate error term. Since the only other source that has the letter B in it is $a \times B$ and since it also contains the only random independent variable, the $MS_{A \times B}$ becomes the error term. The interaction effect itself, which contains the random independent variable, has the $MS_{S/AB}$ as the error term. The next case is also a mixed model and is worked out in a similar manner.

The final situation is a random model. The $MS_{A \times B}$ is used to evaluate both main effects because for each effect, the other letter (b for the A main effect and a for the B main effect) represents the additional random independent variable. The $MS_{S/AB}$ is the error term for the interaction, since both random variables are present in the designation of the effect.

THREE-FACTOR EXPERIMENT   The second illustration considers several arrangements of fixed and random factors in the three-factor design. Four

TABLE 16-4   *Error Terms for Different Structural Models: The Completely Randomized $A \times B \times C$ Factorial*[a]

All Factors Fixed		Factors A and B Fixed; Factor C Random		Factor A Fixed; Factors B and C Random		All Factors Random	
Source	Error Term	Source	Error Term	Source	Error Term	Source	Error Term
A	Wg	A	$A \times c$	A	none	a	none
B	Wg	B	$B \times c$	b	$b \times c$	b	none
C	Wg	c	Wg	c	$b \times c$	c	none
$A \times B$	Wg	$A \times B$	$A \times B \times c$	$A \times b$	$A \times b \times c$	$a \times b$	$a \times b \times c$
$A \times C$	Wg	$A \times c$	Wg	$A \times c$	$A \times b \times c$	$a \times c$	$a \times b \times c$
$B \times C$	Wg	$B \times c$	Wg	$b \times c$	Wg	$b \times c$	$a \times b \times c$
$A \times B \times C$	Wg	$A \times B \times c$	Wg	$A \times b \times c$	Wg	$a \times b \times c$	Wg
Wg	—	Wg	—	Wg	—	Wg	—

[a] $Wg = MS_{S/ABC}$.

different possibilities are presented in Table 16-4. In discussing the determination of the correct error terms, we will only summarize the reason for a given selection. If in doubt, you can verify the statement by working through the questions in Table 16-2. In the first case, where there are no random independent variables, the within-groups mean square ($MS_{S/ABC}$) is the error term for each of the sources of variance. In the second case, the only random independent variable is factor C. Thus, any effects involving factors A and B alone or together (i.e., A, B, and $A \times B$) are tested against appropriate interactions containing factor C (i.e., $A \times c$, $B \times c$, and $A \times B \times c$, respectively); since the remaining sources in the table "use up" the single random factor (i.e., c, $A \times c$, $B \times c$, and $A \times B \times c$), they are all tested against the $MS_{S/ABC}$.

Consider next the complication introduced in the next two cases. In the first of these, a search for an error term for the main effect of factor A, which is the single fixed factor in the experiment, indicates that *two* sources meet the selection criteria—$A \times b$ and $A \times c$—since both contain the letter A and one and only one random independent variable as well. Because more than one source survived this test, the final branch in Table 16-2 indicates that no exact error term is available.[4] (The same fate befalls all of the main effects in the final example, where all three factors are random.) It is possible to obtain tests of these factorial effects, but it involves the construction of what are called "quasi F ratios" [see Winer (1962, pp. 199–202; 1971, pp. 375–378)]. The selection of the remaining error terms in this example should be obvious.

---

[4] This does not mean that *both* mean squares are perfectly good error terms and that there is no adequate way to choose between them. On the contrary, finding that more than one source survives the selection criteria means that *no* single source matches the variance components of the $E(MS_{\text{effect}})$ except for the null hypothesis component. We would have to look at an actual enumeration of the different expected values to understand this point completely. For our purposes, however, the conclusion that no exact test exists is sufficient.

SUMMARY

We have seen that the introduction of random independent variables into a completely randomized experiment produces a serious complication in the formation of correct F ratios. The examples given in Table 16-4 indicate that some sources of variance, such as the MS_A, are evaluated against the within-groups mean square in one model, against an interaction mean square in another model, and only by approximate methods in other models. The series of questions enumerated in Table 16-2 directs us to the correct choice of error term in any possible design.

One drawback associated with the random and mixed models is the reduction in *power* when an interaction mean square replaces the within-groups mean square as the error term. This occurs because the *df* associated with an interaction mean square are considerably fewer in number than those associated with the within-groups mean square. (The relationship between denominator *df* and power is discussed in Chapter 24.) This problem and the fact that exact F tests may not be available, lead to the practical recommendation that the *consequences* of a mixed or random model be considered in detail *before* the start of any experiment.

chapter seventeen

ANALYSIS OF EXPERIMENTS
WITH UNEQUAL SAMPLE SIZES

So far, we have considered only cases in which equal numbers of subjects (s) are placed in each basic treatment condition. This approach was justified, since most experiments are conducted with equal sample sizes. Also, the specialized formulas needed for the analysis of experiments with unequal sample sizes might have diminished your comprehension of the computational simplicities of the formulas required for the case with equal sample sizes. We have already discussed some of the reasons we encounter experiments with unequal sample sizes. (It may be beneficial to review the discussion at this time—see pp. 77–79.)

There are really two problems associated with the analysis of the data from experiments with unequal numbers of subjects in the different treatment conditions. The first is of utmost importance: the unequal sample sizes must *not* have resulted from the systematic operation of psychological sources. In other words, the reason for the differential numbers of subjects must be *unrelated* to the experimental treatments. Otherwise, the benefit derived from a random assignment of subjects to conditions—a "guarantee" of equivalent groups of subjects in each treatment condition—is lost. If this in fact happens, the scientific value of the experimental results is greatly reduced unless some procedure is found that will restore the equivalency.

In the discussion that follows, we will assume that unequal sample sizes have occurred for reasons independent of the experimental conditions. A common reason for unequal sizes is the use of different intact groups of subjects, such as students in different classrooms, for the different treatment conditions. Since classes will rarely have the same numbers of students in attendance, unequal sample sizes will result. (With this sort of experiment, it is absolutely necessary to convince ourselves and others that the groups of subjects in these intact groups —e.g., classes—are equivalent with regard to abilities that are important for the task being studied. Subjects are not assigned to classes randomly and hence are not assigned to the treatments randomly even if the *classes* are.) Some common reasons for the loss of subjects are sickness or death or the failure to complete the experiment for reasons unrelated to the task itself.

The second problem is practical: How do we analyze the data? One method for dealing with unequal sample sizes is the random discarding of data so that the same number of subjects is represented in each of the treatment conditions. As we noted in Chapter 5, however, this solution has its difficulties. We will consider two statistical methods in general use which are designed to accommodate unequal sample sizes *without* discarding subjects' data. A third statistical procedure, the method of least squares, is much less frequently used and will not be discussed. A comprehensive elaboration of this method can be found in Kirk (1968, pp. 204–208) and Winer (1962, pp. 224–227 and pp. 291–297; 1971, pp. 404–416 and pp. 498–505). We will consider the analysis of one- and two-factor designs. Methods of analysis described in these two sections can be generalized to higher-order designs.

ONE-FACTOR DESIGN

Two Methods of Analysis

The two procedures commonly used to analyze experiments with unequal sample sizes differ only with regard to the calculation of the SS_A. Basically, the difference between the two methods lies in the way sample sizes are allowed to influence the size of the SS_A. In the case of the analysis of *unweighted* means, each treatment mean is allowed to contribute *equally* to the determination of the SS_A. In direct contrast, the analysis of *weighted* means allows each treatment mean to influence the SS_A by an amount which is proportional to the number of subjects in that condition. Thus, in the analysis of weighted means, groups with large numbers of subjects will "count" more in the analysis than will groups with small numbers of subjects; in the analysis of unweighted means, all groups will contribute equally.

The formulas given in Table 3-2 (p. 42) for the calculation of the sums of squares with equal sample size (s) are actually a special case of the formulas we will consider in this section. Let's compare the defining formula from Table 3-2 with the formula for weighted means:

$$\text{equal sample sizes:} \quad SS_A = s\left[\sum_{i}^{a} (\bar{A}_i - \bar{T})^2\right], \quad (17\text{-}1a)$$

$$\text{weighted means:} \quad SS_A = \sum_{i}^{a} s_i(\bar{A}_i - \bar{T})^2. \quad (17\text{-}1b)$$

A comparison of Eqs. (17-1a) and (17-1b) indicates that the *only* change is a differential weighting of the deviations of treatment means from $\bar{T}$ for the unequal sample sizes (s_i). With equal sizes, we can place s on either side of the summation sign, since it is a constant, while with unequal sizes, s_i must appear to the right of the summation sign. In either case, all that the weighting factor does is to ensure that each deviation of a group mean from the overall mean is multiplied by the number of subjects actually contributing to the individual mean. (Note that with equal numbers of subjects, the two formulas are equivalent.)

Consider next the defining formula for unweighted means:

$$SS_A = \tilde{s}\left[\sum_{i}^{a} (\bar{A}_i - \bar{T}')^2\right]. \quad (17\text{-}1c)$$

Looking first at the quantity within the brackets, we are squaring and then summing the deviation of the *group means* from the *average mean*, $\bar{T}'$. This latter quantity represents an *unweighted average* of the a treatment means. That is,

$$\bar{T}' = \frac{\sum \bar{A}}{a}.$$

(The prime is used to distinguish this unweighted average from the mean we use in the analysis of weighted means. This latter mean, $\bar{T}$, takes into consideration the numbers of subjects in each of the groups. With equal sample sizes, $\bar{T}' = \bar{T}$.) The final step in the calculations is the multiplication of the quantity within the brackets by an *average* sample size. The appropriate average, $\tilde{s}$, is called the *harmonic mean*. In the context of the present analysis,

$$\tilde{s} = \frac{a}{\dfrac{1}{s_1} + \dfrac{1}{s_2} + \cdots + \dfrac{1}{s_a}} = \frac{a}{\sum\left(\dfrac{1}{s_i}\right)}. \quad (17\text{-}2)$$

In words, we divide the total number of treatment means, a, by the sum of the reciprocals of the various sample sizes, s_i.

NUMERICAL EXAMPLE   Consider Example 1 presented in Table 17-1 and the data for a single-factor experiment with unequal sample sizes. We will determine the SS_A for the weighted-means analysis first. For these data,

$$\bar{T} = \frac{5 + 20 + 105}{5 + 10 + 35} = \frac{130}{50} = 2.60.$$

Substituting in Eq. (17-1b), we have

$$SS_A = \sum_i^a s_i(\bar{A}_i - \bar{T})^2$$

$$= 5(1.00 - 2.60)^2 + 10(2.00 - 2.60)^2 + 35(3.00 - 2.60)^2$$

$$= 5(-1.60)^2 + 10(-.60)^2 + 35(.40)^2$$

$$= 12.80 + 3.60 + 5.60 = 22.00.$$

TABLE 17-1   *The Results of Two Experiments with Unequal Sample Sizes*

	Example 1			Example 2		
	a_1	a_2	a_3	a_1	a_2	a_3
A_i:	5	20	105	A_i: 10	70	15
s_i:	5	10	35	s_i: 10	35	5
$\bar{A}_i$:	1.00	2.00	3.00	$\bar{A}_i$: 1.00	2.00	3.00

For the unweighted-means analysis, we will need to calculate the harmonic mean ($\tilde{s}$) and the unweighted average of the a treatment means ($\bar{T}'$) before we can substitute in Eq. (17-1c). For the harmonic mean of the sample sizes, we follow the operations specified in Eq. (17-2):

$$\tilde{s} = \frac{3}{\frac{1}{5} + \frac{1}{10} + \frac{1}{35}} = \frac{3}{.20 + .10 + .03} = \frac{3}{.33} = 9.09.$$

For the unweighted overall mean,

$$\bar{T}' = \frac{\sum \bar{A}}{a} = \frac{1.00 + 2.00 + 3.00}{3} = \frac{6.00}{3} = 2.00.$$

Substituting in Eq. (17-1c),

$$SS_A = \tilde{s}\left[\sum_i^a (\bar{A}_i - \bar{T}')^2\right]$$

$$= (9.09)[(1.00 - 2.00)^2 + (2.00 - 2.00)^2 + (3.00 - 2.00)^2]$$

$$= (9.09)[(-1.00)^2 + (0.00)^2 + (1.00)^2]$$

$$= (9.09)(2.00) = 18.18.$$

COMPARISON OF THE TWO METHODS   It is clear that the two methods produce different values for the treatment sum of squares. Which one is correct? Both values are correct in the sense that they were produced by legitimate formulas. A more relevant question, however, is: "Which one is *appropriate*?"

We will begin our answer by considering the second numerical example presented in Table 17-1. For the weighted-means analysis,

$$\bar{T} = \frac{10 + 70 + 15}{10 + 35 + 5} = \frac{95}{50} = 1.90.$$

Using Eq. (17-1b),

$$SS_A = 10(1.00 - 1.90)^2 + 35(2.00 - 1.90)^2 + 5(3.00 - 1.90)^2$$

$$= 10(-.90)^2 + 35(.10)^2 + 5(1.10)^2$$

$$= 8.10 + .35 + 6.05 = 14.50.$$

For the unweighted-means analysis, we need

$$\tilde{s} = \frac{3}{\frac{1}{10} + \frac{1}{35} + \frac{1}{5}} = \frac{3}{.10 + .03 + .20} = \frac{3}{.33} = 9.09$$

and

$$\bar{T}' = \frac{1.00 + 2.00 + 3.00}{3} = \frac{6.00}{3} = 2.00.$$

Completing the substitution in Eq. (17-1c),

$$SS_A = (9.09)[(1.00 - 2.00)^2 + (2.00 - 2.00)^2 + (3.00 - 2.00)^2]$$

$$= (9.09)[(-1.00)^2 + (0.00)^2 + (1.00)^2]$$

$$= (9.09)(2.00) = 18.18.$$

This second example clearly illustrates the basic difference between the two analyses. You will note that the *same* treatment means are present in the two examples and that the *same* sample sizes are also present. All that has been changed is the allocation of the three sample sizes to the treatment conditions. This change in the distribution of the numbers of subjects left unchanged the analysis performed on the unweighted means ($SS_A = 18.18$) but resulted in two different values when the analysis was performed on the weighted means ($SS_A = 22.00$ and 14.50). In brief, the unweighted-means analysis is unaffected by the differences in sample sizes, while the weighted-means analysis is.

It is difficult to conceive of practical situations in which researchers would want to use the analysis based on weighted means.[1] Given that we are able to

---

[1] As an example of a possible experiment, suppose we wanted to see whether or not subjects differing in IQ would have different sensory thresholds. Suppose that we use three IQ levels, low (81–100), medium (101–120), and high (121–140). Since we would not expect equal proportions of subjects to fall into these three categories in the population, we might want to maintain this proportionality in the experiment by using unequal sample sizes and an analysis based on weighted means.

accept a set of data as being free of bias in spite of unequal numbers of subjects in the different treatment conditions, we are implying that the *means* reflect the potential outcome had equal numbers of subjects been present. Therefore, our conclusions must be influenced by the differences among the *unadjusted* (i.e., unweighted) treatment means and not influenced in addition by the unequal sample sizes. Consequently, we will consider in further detail only the analysis of unweighted means. (If you ever can justify the use of the weighted means in an analysis, you can find the procedure explicated in most standard statistics texts.)

Analysis of Unweighted Means

DEFINING AND COMPUTATIONAL FORMULAS   The defining and computational formulas for the entire analysis are presented in Table 17-2. We have already discussed the defining formula for the SS_A. The computational formula for the SS_A is easily understood if we view the quantity within the brackets as representing a sum of squares based on A means that are treated as *single observations*. That is, for the first term within the brackets, each mean is squared, implicitly divided by 1, and the results are summed. In the second term, the means are summed to produce a total, T', which is squared and divided by the number of "observations" contributing to T'—i.e., a. As with the defining formula, the quantity within the brackets is multiplied by the harmonic mean of the sample sizes ($\tilde{s}$).

TABLE 17-2   *Defining and Computational Formulas: Analysis of Unweighted Means*

Source	Defining Formula[a]	Computational Formula[b]
A	$\tilde{s}[\sum(\bar{A} - \bar{T}')^2]$	$\tilde{s}\left[\sum(\bar{A})^2 - \dfrac{(T')^2}{a}\right]$
S/A	$\sum(AS - \bar{A})^2$	$\sum(AS)^2 - \sum\left[\dfrac{(A_i)^2}{s_i}\right]$

[a] $\bar{T}' = \dfrac{\sum \bar{A}}{a}$.   [b] $T' = \sum \bar{A}$.

The defining formula for the $SS_{S/A}$ is identical to the one presented for equal sample size in Table 3-2. The only change in the computational formula is in the second term—this small modification reflects the operation of computational rule number 1. That is, we are asked to sum the scores within each group, square and divide by the appropriate number of observations (s_i), and then sum the results of these divisions. (Subscripts have been included in these formulas so that the respective sample sizes, treatment sums and means may be specified.)

NUMERICAL EXAMPLE   The AS matrix from a fictitious experiment with unequal sample sizes is presented in Table 17-3. To illustrate the use of the

TABLE 17-3 *Numerical Example: AS Matrix*

Treatment Groups

	a_1	a_2	a_3	a_4
	3	16	5	19
	16	11	7	17
	12	14	14	12
	16	20	17	7
	18		18	17
			16	
A_i:	65	61	77	72
s_i:	5	4	6	5
$\bar{A}_i$:	13.00	15.25	12.83	14.40

computational formula for the SS_A, we will obtain first the quantity within the brackets:

$$\sum(\bar{A})^2 - \frac{(T')^2}{a} = [(13.00)^2 + (15.25)^2 + (12.83)^2 + (14.40)^2]$$

$$- \frac{(13.00 + 15.25 + 12.83 + 14.40)^2}{4}$$

$$= 773.53 - \frac{(55.48)^2}{4}$$

$$= 773.53 - 769.51 = 4.02.$$

We need next the harmonic mean of the sample sizes:

$$\tilde{s} = \frac{4}{\frac{1}{5} + \frac{1}{4} + \frac{1}{6} + \frac{1}{5}} = \frac{4}{.20 + .25 + .17 + .20} = \frac{4}{.82} = 4.88.$$

Finally, we have

$$SS_A = \tilde{s}\left[\sum(\bar{A})^2 - \frac{(T')^2}{a}\right]$$

$$= (4.88)(4.02) = 19.62.$$

For the within-groups sum of squares,

$$SS_{S/A} = \sum(AS)^2 - \sum\left[\frac{(A_i)^2}{s_i}\right]$$

$$= [(3)^2 + (16)^2 + \cdots + (7)^2 + (17)^2] - \left[\frac{(65)^2}{5} + \frac{(61)^2}{4} + \frac{(77)^2}{6} + \frac{(72)^2}{5}\right]$$

$$= 4233 - (845.00 + 930.25 + 988.17 + 1036.80)$$

$$= 4233 - 3800.22 = 432.78.$$

These two sums of squares are entered into a summary table (Table 17-4). (Note that with unweighted means, the component sums of squares typically do not add up to the SS_T. In this example, $SS_A + SS_{S/A} = 19.62 + 432.78 = 452.40$, while the SS_T, which we have not calculated here, is 451.75.)

TABLE 17-4 *Analysis of Unweighted Means*

Source	SS	df	MS	F
A	19.62	3	6.54	< 1
S/A	432.78	16	27.05	

The only change in the analysis at this point is in the calculation of the *df* for the $SS_{S/A}$, which in this case may be obtained by either of the following formulas:

$$df_{S/A} = \sum (s_i - 1)$$

or

$$= \sum s_i - a. \tag{17-3}$$

An application of the first expression requires the addition of the *df* for each group separately, i.e., $4 + 3 + 5 + 4 = 16$, which is algebraically equivalent to the second, i.e., $(5 + 4 + 6 + 5) - 4 = 20 - 4 = 16$.

The final calculations follow the formulas for the *MS* and *F* given in Table 4-1 (p. 53). The *F* in this particular example is less than 1.0 and hence need not even be referred to the *F* table. It should be obvious that we will not reject the null hypothesis with this set of data.

Comment   This analysis should entail an increased concern for violations of the assumptions underlying the analysis of variance. As we have seen, the *F* test is relatively insensitive to violations of these assumptions, but only when the sample sizes are equal. Serious distortions may appear when these violations occur in experiments with unequal sample sizes.

Analytical Comparisons

All the techniques and procedures discussed in Part II for conducting analytical comparisons among the different treatment means may be adapted for the analysis of an experiment with unequal sample sizes. With an equal number of subjects in each group, it is convenient to perform these analyses with the treatment *sums*, and this is how the formulas were presented earlier. With unequal sample sizes, we will use the treatment *means*. Just as we could analyze these latter data with either the weighted or the unweighted means, we can generally use either procedure in isolating interesting sources of variance with our analytical techniques. The choice between the two procedures involves the same issue that we discussed in connection with the overall analysis. That is, if the unequal sample sizes have nothing to do with the hypothesis under test, we will probably want to give equal weight to each treatment mean. On the other hand, if the unequal sizes reflect an underlying stratification in the population from which we are sampling, we will want to weight the means in direct proportion to the respective sample sizes. We will only consider formulas for comparisons conducted on the unweighted means.

COMPARISONS BETWEEN MEANS   The formula for equal sample sizes, written in terms of treatment *means*, is given by Eq. (6-5):

$$SS_{A_{comp.}} = \frac{s[\sum (c_i)(\bar{A}_i)]^2}{\sum (c_i)^2}.$$

The corresponding formula for *unweighted* means is

$$SS_{A_{comp.}} = \frac{\tilde{s}[\sum (c_i)(\bar{A}_i)]^2}{\sum (c_i)^2}. \tag{17-4}$$

Orthogonality of two comparisons may be established by means of the formula given for equal sample sizes, Eq. (7-1):

$$\sum (c_i)(c_i') = 0.$$

As an example of the calculations, we will conduct a comparison using the data presented in Table 17-3. Suppose we wanted to compare $\bar{A}_2$ against the mean of the other three groups combined. Coefficients corresponding to this comparison are $-1, +3, -1,$ and -1, respectively. We have already computed the harmonic mean for this example: $\tilde{s} = 4.88$. Substituting in Eq. (17-4),

$$SS_{A_{comp.}} = \frac{(4.88)[(-1)(13.00) + (3)(15.25) + (-1)(12.83) + (-1)(14.40)]^2}{(-1)^2 + (3)^2 + (-1)^2 + (-1)^2}$$

$$= \frac{(4.88)(5.52)^2}{12} = \frac{148.69}{12} = 12.39.$$

The remainder of the analysis is accomplished in the usual manner. There is 1 *df* associated with the sum of squares. Thus,

$$F = \frac{MS_{A_{comp.}}}{MS_{S/A}} = \frac{12.39/1}{27.05} = .46.$$

ANALYSIS OF TREND   Coefficients of orthogonal polynomials may be used to extract components of trend (linear, quadratic, and so on) from a set of data obtained from an experiment in which the treatment levels represent points on a quantitative dimension and unequal numbers of subjects are present at the different levels. For an analysis based on *unweighted* means, the sums of squares are calculated by means of Eq. (17-4). If the spacing of the levels along the stimulus dimension is equal, the coefficients are obtained from Table C-2 of Appendix C. If the spacing is unequal, the coefficients may be constructed by the method presented in Appendix B.

It would make little sense to conduct the analysis with *weighted means*, however, since our interest is in detecting the presence of trend components, and each point sampled on the simulus dimension—i.e., the levels of the independent variable—should contribute *equally* to the determination of this functional relationship. If we do justify the use of weighted means, which would happen rarely, we will find it necessary to construct our own set of orthogonal polynomials, one that is based on the particular sample sizes present at the different levels of factor *A*. Gaito (1965) discusses a method for accomplishing this task.

MULTIPLE COMPARISONS   The procedures described in Chapter 8 for making all possible comparisons between pairs of means may be conducted with experiments in which different numbers of subjects are present in the treatment conditions. Except for the Scheffé test, the various procedures assume equal sample sizes. To overcome this difficulty, Winer (1962, p. 101; 1971, p. 216) suggests the use of the harmonic mean ($\tilde{s}$) for *s* as long as the sample sizes do not differ "markedly." If we follow his suggestion, we will be constructing comparisons on *unweighted means*, since the differences in sample sizes will not contribute differentially to the corresponding means.

The formulas in Chapter 8 are written for use with treatment sums; the formulas for unequal sample sizes are written more conveniently for use with treatment means. Consider, for example, the formula for a critical range (*CR*) with the Tukey test;

$$CR_T = q(r_{max}, df_{S/A})\sqrt{s(MS_{S/A})},$$

where *q* represents an entry in Table C-3 for $r_{max} = a$ steps between ordered groups and for the *df* associated with the error term. To modify this formula for use with means, we simply divide both sides of the equation by *s* and then rearrange the expression:

$$\overline{CR}_T = \frac{CR_T}{s} = \frac{q(r_{max}, df_{S/A})\sqrt{s(MS_{S/A})}}{s}$$

$$= q(r_{max}, df_{S/A})\sqrt{\frac{MS_{S/A}}{s}}.$$

Instead of comparing the difference between two treatment *sums* against the critical range, CR_T, as we do with the original formula, we now compare the difference between two treatment *means* against the *average* critical range, $\overline{CR}_T$. The formulas for the other techniques are adapted for the use with means in a similar fashion.

To accommodate unequal sample sizes, the formulas are changed by substituting $\tilde{s}$ for *s*. Thus,

$$\overline{CR}_{N\text{-}K} = q(r, df_{S/A})\sqrt{\frac{MS_{S/A}}{\tilde{s}}}, \tag{17-6}$$

$$\bar{C} \tag{17-7}$$

$$\tag{17-8}$$

The Scheffé test may be

$$\overline{CR}_S \tag{17-9}$$

The steps followed in performing the set of multiple comparisons are the same as those outlined in Chapter 8 (see pp. 140–144). Winer (1962, pp. 101–103; 1971, pp. 216–218) provides a numerical example with the Newman-Keuls test.

The Scheffé correction for making complex comparisons between means is applied after the F ratio for the comparison is calculated from Eq. (17-4) by evaluating the significance against F_S:

$$F_S = (a - 1)F(df_A, df_{S/A}).$$

Dunnett's test for comparisons between a control and several experimental groups may also be adapted for unequal sample sizes and unweighted means. In this case we will be comparing differences between the mean for a control group and means for the experimental groups against an *average* critical difference, a value that is given by

$$\text{average critical C-E difference} = q_D(k, df_{S/A})\sqrt{\frac{2(MS_{S/A})}{\tilde{s}}}. \tag{17-10}$$

Otherwise, the procedure is unchanged from that given in Chapter 8 (see pp. 150–152).

TWO-WAY FACTORIAL

When unequal sample sizes appear in factorial designs, we must again decide whether to base our analyses on unweighted means or on weighted means. Again the critical question is: Do we want the main effects and interactions to be influenced by the differential sample sizes or do we want each cell mean to contribute equally to these effects? The position taken here is that only rarely will we consider the weighted-means analysis appropriate. That is, we will encounter few experiments in which unequal sample sizes form an integral part of the hypotheses being tested. For this reason, then, we will again confine our discussion to the unweighted-means analysis.

Before we turn to this analysis, we should say a few words about a further limitation placed on the weighted-means analysis when and if it is performed. More specifically, the sample sizes within any particular row (or column) of the

AB matrix must be in the same proportion as the sample sizes in all other rows (or columns).[2] If this proportionality is not present, it is possible for the analysis to produce marked distortions and the analysis may be invalid. Such a distortion does not occur with the unweighted-means analysis.[3]

Analysis of Unweighted Means

In Chapter 5, we considered a variety of reasons why unequal sample sizes might be found in an experiment where equal numbers of subjects had been planned. These were the result of some sort of subject loss—subjects failing to achieve a performance criterion or failing to return for a second testing session, equipment breakdown, experimenter error, and so on. In any given case, we must determine whether the loss is unrelated to the treatment conditions. If it is, the analysis may proceed; if it is not, other action is called for, such as artificially dropping subjects from particular conditions or even scrapping the experiment.

We should add to our worries another problem that might occur when subject losses are incurred. In most experiments, several control factors are present in the design in addition to the independent variables. These factors are usually equally represented in the different treatment conditions in the complete design. A loss of subjects may upset this balancing, and a possible confounding of the control factors and the experimental treatments may occur. In short, then, unequal sample sizes produced by subject loss represent an extremely serious experimental problem.[4]

If, in spite of all these considerations, we are still convinced that a meaningful analysis of the data is possible, we will find it necessary to use a new set of formulas. The analysis may be used in situations where the differences among the sample sizes are not great. In this analysis, the means for each treatment combination are taken to represent the means that would have been observed if equal sample sizes had been present. In essence, the analysis is conducted on the *individual means*, treating each cell mean as a *single observation*.

COMPUTATIONAL FORMULAS   The first step is to form an AB data matrix, with the individual treatment means entered in the body of the matrix as in the upper portion of Table 17-5. The sums in the two margins of this matrix are the sums of the set of means in a particular column or row. That is,

$$A_i' = \sum_j^b \overline{AB}_{ij}, \qquad B_j' = \sum_i^a \overline{AB}_{ij}, \quad \text{and} \quad T' = \sum \overline{AB}_{ij}.$$

---

[2] Myers (1966, pp. 102–104) provides a useful discussion of this type of proportionality.

[3] The weighted-means analysis, with proportional sample sizes, is discussed briefly by a number of authors, e.g., Kirk (1968, pp. 200–201) and Myers (1966, pp. 102–104). A numerical example is provided by Glass and Stanley (1970, pp. 432–439).

[4] When imbalances are produced as the result of subject loss, it is usually not possible to perform an analysis including the control factors. The reason is that the different combinations of treatments and control factors are not completely crossed because of the loss of subjects.

(To indicate that these marginal sums are different from the usual sums, primes have been introduced in their designation.)

The computational formulas are presented in the lower half of the table. The only differences between these formulas and those given in Table 10-3 (p. 196) are (1) the use of cell means as single scores, (2) the division of squared quantities by the *number of cell means* contributing to the quantity that is squared (computational rule number 1), and (3) the multiplication of a "sum of squares" by $\tilde{s}$, the harmonic mean of the sample sizes. For the two-factor design, the harmonic mean is defined as

$$\tilde{s} = \frac{ab}{\dfrac{1}{s_{11}} + \dfrac{1}{s_{12}} + \cdots + \dfrac{1}{s_{ab}}} = \frac{ab}{\sum \left(\dfrac{1}{s_{ij}}\right)}. \qquad (17\text{-}11)$$

That is, we divide the total number of cell means, ab, by the sum of the reciprocals of each sample size, s_{ij}. Returning to the computational formulas, if we look carefully at the quantities in brackets, we can see that they are exactly what we would use if we had only one observation per cell. It is important to note,

TABLE 17-5 *Computational Formulas: Two-Factor Analysis of Unweighted Means*

AB Matrix of Means

	a_1	a_2	$\cdots$	a_a	Sum
b_1	$\overline{AB}_{11}$	$\overline{AB}_{21}$	$\cdots$	$\overline{AB}_{a1}$	B_1'
b_2	$\overline{AB}_{12}$	$\overline{AB}_{22}$	$\cdots$	$\overline{AB}_{a2}$	B_2'
$\vdots$	$\vdots$				$\vdots$
b_b	$\overline{AB}_{1b}$	$\overline{AB}_{2b}$	$\cdots$	$\overline{AB}_{ab}$	B_b'
Sum	A_1'	A_2'	$\cdots$	A_a'	T'

Computational Formulas

Source	Computational Formula	df
A	$\tilde{s}\left[\dfrac{\sum (A')^2}{b} - \dfrac{(T')^2}{ab}\right]$	$a - 1$
B	$\tilde{s}\left[\dfrac{\sum (B')^2}{a} - \dfrac{(T')^2}{ab}\right]$	$b - 1$
$A \times B$	$\tilde{s}\left[\sum (\overline{AB})^2 - \dfrac{\sum (A')^2}{b} - \dfrac{\sum (B')^2}{a} + \dfrac{(T')^2}{ab}\right]$	$(a-1)(b-1)$
S/AB	$\sum (ABS)^2 - \sum \left[\dfrac{(AB_{ij})^2}{s_{ij}}\right]$	$\sum s_{ij} - ab$

however, that the $SS_{S/AB}$ is *not* adjusted by $\tilde{s}$. Essentially, this sum of squares represents a pooling of the sums of squares of subjects who have been treated alike.

The *df* are computed as in Table 10-3 except for $df_{S/AB}$. In this case,

$$df_{S/AB} = \sum (s_{ij} - 1),$$

a pooling of the *df* associated with each treatment cell. This formula may be rewritten as

$$df_{S/AB} = \sum s_{ij} - ab.$$

The calculation of the mean squares and the *F* ratios follows the formulas for equal sample size (see Table 10-3).

In summary, then, we use the cell means as unbiased estimates of the outcome of the experiment had equal sample sizes been present. We calculate the sums of squares on these means, using formulas that treat the means as if they were single observations, and multiply these "sums of squares" by the average (harmonic) number of subjects per treatment group. The analysis may seem laborious, but perhaps one should "suffer" a little for allowing unequal sample sizes to occur! We are now ready for a numerical example.

NUMERICAL EXAMPLE   We will consider an experiment in which unequal cell frequencies occur as the result of subdividing subjects within the different treatment conditions *after* the conduct of the experiment. This frequently happens when so-called subject variables are investigated and it is difficult to ensure an equal number of males and females, or of low- and high-anxiety subjects, for example, in each condition. The subjects are assigned randomly to all of the treatment conditions, and the assumption is that on the average the subjects of a particular type will be represented without bias in each of the conditions. The numbers of subjects in each subgroup would obviously not be equal.

As a hypothetical example, suppose an experimenter wanted to compare male and female subjects on a number of different problem-solving tasks, but that he decides it would be easier to separate the subjects *after* the experiment rather than before. He plans to compare three types of tasks (factor *A*), with $s = 20$ subjects solving each type. The dependent variable is the number of problems solved in five minutes. After the experiment, the subjects in each group are divided into males and females and scored separately (factor *B*). These scores and the sample sizes are presented in the upper half of Table 17-6. We will assume that $\sum (ABS)^2 = 2970$. The corresponding cell means are listed in the *AB* data matrix in the lower half of the table. Inspection of this latter matrix reveals that the problems differ in difficulty and that sex differences are not consistent across the tasks; i.e., there is a Task × Sex interaction. Since the subjects were assigned to the three types of tasks at random, there is no reason to believe that the assignment of males and females to the tasks was biased. Thus, an analysis of the unweighted means is appropriate.

TABLE 17-6 *Numerical Example: Unweighted-Means Analysis*

AB Matrix (Sums)

		Tasks (A)		
Sex (B)		a_1	a_2	a_3
Male (b_1)	Sum:	96	57	54
	s_{i1}:	13	11	8
Female (b_2)	Sum:	72	44	49
	s_{i2}:	7	9	12

AB Matrix (Means)

	a_1	a_2	a_3	Sum
b_1	7.38	5.18	6.75	19.31
b_2	10.29	4.89	4.08	19.26
Sum	17.67	10.07	10.83	38.57

The first step in the analysis is to obtain the six individual cell means ($\overline{AB}_{ij}$), which has been done in the lower half of Table 17-6. The cell means form the basis for the analysis, and we will treat them as if they were single observations. The values in the margins of the matrix are the sums of the cell means. The harmonic mean of the sample sizes is given by Eq. (17-11) and in this example equals

$$\tilde{s} = \frac{3(2)}{\frac{1}{13} + \frac{1}{11} + \frac{1}{8} + \frac{1}{7} + \frac{1}{9} + \frac{1}{12}}$$

$$= \frac{6}{.08 + .09 + .12 + .14 + .11 + .08}$$

$$= \frac{6}{.62} = 9.68.$$

The various sums of squares are computed on the cell means, using the computational formulas listed in Table 17-5. Substituting in these formulas, we have

$$SS_A = (9.68)\left[\frac{(17.67)^2 + (10.07)^2 + (10.83)^2}{2} - \frac{(38.57)^2}{2(3)}\right],$$

$$SS_B = (9.68)\left[\frac{(19.31)^2 + (19.26)^2}{3} - \frac{(38.57)^2}{2(3)}\right],$$

and

$$SS_{A \times B} = (9.68)\Bigg[(7.38)^2 + (10.29)^2 + \cdots + (6.75)^2 + (4.08)^2$$

$$-\frac{(17.67)^2 + (10.07)^2 + (10.83)^2}{2}$$

$$-\frac{(19.31)^2 + (19.26)^2}{3} + \frac{(38.57)^2}{2(3)}\Bigg].$$

These arithmetical operations are completed in Table 17-7. The calculation of the $SS_{S/AB}$ requires the use of the treatment *sums*, which we can find in the upper portion of Table 17-6. Specifically,

TABLE 17-7   *Summary of the Analysis*

Source	Calculations[a]		SS	df	MS	F
A	$(9.68)(265.46 - 247.94)$					
	$= (9.68)(17.52)$	$=$	169.59	2	84.80	10.28**
B	$(9.68)(247.94 - T')$					
	$= (9.68)(0.00)$	$=$	0.00	1	0.00	<1
$A \times B$	$(9.68)(273.30 - A' - B' + T')$					
	$= (9.68)(7.84)$		75.89	2	37.94	4.60*
S/AB	$2970 - 2524.54$	$=$	445.46	54	8.25	

[a] Letters represent complete terms in the computational formulas; a particular term is identified by the letter(s) appearing in the numerator.

* $p < .05$.
** $p < .01$.

$$SS_{S/AB} = 2970 - \left[\frac{(96)^2}{13} + \frac{(72)^2}{7} + \cdots + \frac{(54)^2}{8} + \frac{(49)^2}{12}\right].$$

The remaining steps in the analysis are enumerated in the table. We can see that the problem-solving tasks differed in difficulty and that there is a Task × Sex interaction.[5]

Analytical Comparisons

Any of the analyses discussed for use with unequal sample sizes in the one-factor design may be conducted with unequal sample sizes in the two-factor design. We will not go through these procedures nor their modified formulas here; the approach should be clear from the previous exposition. The one analysis which is new and will be discussed is the calculation of the simple main

[5] The interpretation of data obtained from an experiment in which characteristics of subjects are "manipulated" (sex, in this example) poses special problems for the researcher. Underwood (1957, pp. 112–125) provides a detailed discussion of these problems of inference.

effects of the interaction. The usefulness of this analysis was described earlier. Briefly, the analysis is undertaken in an attempt to pinpoint the locus of a significant $A \times B$ interaction. A simple main effect of factor A, say, consists of the variability due to factor A at a particular level of factor B. Or, viewed the other way, a simple main effect of factor B consists of the variability due to factor B at a particular level of factor A.

For the unweighted-means analysis, we will return to the data in Table 17-6. With a significant $A \times B$ interaction as we have in this example, it is reasonable to conduct an analysis of the simple main effects. One way to look at the interaction is to compare the scores for males and females on each of the problem-solving tasks. That is, we will determine the simple main effects of factor B at three levels of factor A. In this analysis, we will again work with the $\overline{AB}$ means, treating them as if they were single observations. Whatever value we find will then be multiplied by the harmonic mean of the sample sizes. The formula for the simple main effect of factor B at level a_i is given by

$$SS_{B \, at \, a_i} = \tilde{s} \left[\sum_{j}^{b} (\overline{AB}_{ij})^2 - \frac{(A'_i)^2}{b} \right].$$

Substituting in this general formula, we have

$$SS_{B \, at \, a_1} = \tilde{s} \left[\sum (\overline{AB}_{1j})^2 - \frac{(A'_1)^2}{b} \right]$$

$$= (9.68) \left[(7.38)^2 + (10.29)^2 - \frac{(17.67)^2}{2} \right],$$

$$SS_{B \, at \, a_2} = \tilde{s} \left[\sum (\overline{AB}_{2j})^2 - \frac{(A'_2)^2}{b} \right]$$

$$= (9.68) \left[(5.18)^2 + (4.89)^2 - \frac{(10.07)^2}{2} \right],$$

and

$$SS_{B \, at \, a_3} = \tilde{s} \left[\sum (\overline{AB}_{3j})^2 - \frac{(A'_3)^2}{b} \right]$$

$$= (9.68) \left[(6.75)^2 + (4.08)^2 - \frac{(10.83)^2}{2} \right].$$

These calculations are completed in Table 17-8. The sum of these three sums of squares should equal the sum of the $SS_{A \times B}$ and the SS_B, except for rounding error. For this example, the sum of the sums of squares for the simple main effects is $41.04 + .39 + 34.46 = 75.89$, which is identical to $SS_{A \times B} + SS_B = 75.89 + 0.00 = 75.89$. The analysis is completed and summarized in the table. Females seem to do better with the task represented at a_1, and males seem to do better with the task represented at a_3.

TABLE 17-8 *Analysis of Simple Main Effects*

Source	Calculations		SS	df	MS	F
B at a_1	$(9.68)(160.35 - 156.11)$					
	$= (9.68)(4.24)$	$=$	41.04	1	41.04	4.97*
B at a_2	$(9.68)(50.74 - 50.70)$					
	$= (9.68)(.04)$	$=$	.39	1	.39	<1
B at a_3	$(9.68)(62.21 - 58.64)$					
	$= (9.68)(3.57)$	$=$	34.56	1	34.56	4.19*
S/AB			445.46	54	8.25	

* $p < .05.$

SUMMARY

The analyses of data based on unequal sample sizes may be extended to the higher-order designs. The necessary formulas are adapted in a manner analogous to those we examined for the single-factor and two-way factorial experiments. As we have noted before, the analysis of unweighted means is the appropriate analysis for the sorts of cases we usually encounter in the behavioral sciences. As an alternative, equal sample size can always be obtained through the dropping of subjects' data from the cells with the greater numbers of subjects. Data can be eliminated randomly if the reason for the inequality of sample sizes is independent of the experimental treatments.

This method of solving the problems of unequal sample sizes results, of course, in an unnecessary loss of data—unnecessary because an analysis of unweighted means is applicable and this analysis uses the data from all of the subjects remaining after the loss. If subjects are dropped in an attempt to compensate for a serious subject selection (see Chapter 5, p. 79), equal sample sizes will result and the standard formulas may be used. The use of this compensatory dropping of subjects must be fully justified by the researcher. That is, he must be able to show that any destruction of the equivalence of groups, which is afforded by the random assignment of subjects to conditions, has been eliminated by the subsequent dropping of subjects from the unaffected or partially affected groups; otherwise, the analysis may be meaningless.

It should be clear, then, that the appearance of unequal sample sizes signals a careful scrutiny of the reason or reasons for the inequality. Unless it can be guaranteed that the groups are equivalent insofar as random assignment allows, the results of the experiment may not be interpretable. If inequalities are *planned*, the investigator must decide between the analysis based on weighted means and that based on unweighted means. Only if the differences in sample sizes represent a defining characteristic of an independent variable—as might be the case if a subject variable, such as IQ or socioeconomic status, were included in the experiment—can the analysis of weighted means be justified. Under these circumstances, the researcher may want to preserve in his experiment the relative proportions of subjects in the different classifications existing in the population. In most other cases the analysis of unweighted means is still appropriate. It is not wise to view these statements as unvarying principles, however. The logic of the experimental situation must dictate the most reasonable approach to the problem.

chapter eighteen

ANALYSIS OF EXPERIMENTS WITH NESTED FACTORS

The designs we have considered so far in this book are ones in which the factors in the experiment have been completely crossed: all possible combinations of the levels of the different independent variables are present in the experiment. An alternative to the complete crossing of factors is an arrangement in which one (or more) factors is *uniquely defined* at the different levels of another factor or combination of factors. That is, it is possible to have independent variables included in an experiment which do *not* cross with all of the other independent variables manipulated in the experiment. Such an arrangement is called *nesting*.

DISTINCTION BETWEEN CROSSING AND NESTING

A simple example should make clear the distinction between crossing and nesting of independent variables. Suppose we are interested in comparing

TABLE 18-1 *Comparison of Nested and Crossed Designs*

FACTOR B NESTED WITHIN FACTOR A

Languages (Factor A)

Passages (Factor B)	a_1	Passages (Factor B)	a_2	Passages (Factor B)	a_3
b_1		b_5		b_9	
b_2		b_6		b_{10}	
b_3		b_7		b_{11}	
b_4		b_8		b_{12}	

BOTH FACTORS CROSSED

Languages (Factor A)

Setting (Factor B)	a_1	a_2	a_3
b_1			
b_2			
b_3			
b_4			

the readability of three different artificial languages. In order to increase the generality of the results, we might consider introducing into the experiment several examples of these languages rather than just one example of each. The design is presented in the upper portion of Table 18-1. Factor A (types of languages) is represented by the three columns and factor B (passages) by the four rows. Note, however, that the geometrical display is *not* a rectangle, as would be the sorts of two-factor designs we considered in Part III, but rather, three separate columns. The reason for this change in the representation is that factor B does *not cross* with factor A—the four passages constructed from one artificial language are *unrelated* to the four passages constructed from the other languages. The first passage listed at a_1 bears no relationship to the first passage (or any other passage) at a_2 and a_3. It is not possible to produce a crossing of factor A and factor B that makes any sense. For this reason, then, we have labeled the levels of factor B uniquely at each level of factor A: levels b_1 to b_4 for the language represented at a_1, levels b_5 to b_8 for the language represented at a_2, and levels b_9 to b_{12} for the language represented at a_3.

We will use letters in conjunction with a diagonal to designate a nested factor. The letter to the *left* of the diagonal will designate the *nested* factor, while any letters to the *right* of the diagonal will designate the factor (or factors) within which the nesting occurs. In the present example, the nested factor would be represented by B/A, indicating that factor B is nested within factor A.[1]

Contrast this experiment with the one presented in the lower portion of the table. Here, the same three languages are compared (factor A), but this time the control factor is the type of setting in which the experiment is performed—classroom, laboratory, student commons, or whatever. Since the readability of each language is tested in each of the different settings, the two independent variables are crossed. It will be noted that the geometrical display of this experiment is accommodated by a rectangle, rather than by separate columns as in the case of an experiment with a nested factor.

It may have occurred to you that we have already seen an example of a nested factor—namely, the within-groups factor. In a single-factor design, for example, we can isolate variability due to factor A and to the pooled variability of subjects treated alike. While this latter source does not represent an independent variable of the sort we have considered, "subjects" can be thought of as a factor consisting of s different levels (i.e., s different subjects). "Subjects" does *not* cross with the levels of factor A—there is a different collection of s subjects in each of the a levels of the independent variable. Since the definition or meaning of "subjects" as a factor is different at each level of factor A, it qualifies as a nested factor. (This is why we referred to this source of variance as S/A, the variability of subjects nested within factor A.) One way that subjects could be made to cross with factor A is to have each of s subjects serve in *all* of the a treatment conditions. With this sort of arrangement, we would have an $A \times S$ (S for subjects) factorial, with each subject represented at all levels of factor A. We will discuss this type of design in Chapter 19.

In the discussion that follows, it will be assumed that you are familiar with the rules for generating the computational formulas for completely crossed factorial designs that we originally presented in Chapter 10 (see pp. 191–195). We will consider the general case first, seeing how the sources of variance can be identified and how the corresponding computational formulas can be constructed. We will illustrate the use of the computational rules with numerical examples of the types of nested designs typically found in the behavioral sciences. These appear to be of two general types—those for which the nested factor consists of intact subject groupings of some sort and those for which the nested factors consist of control or of experimental factors. Following these examples, we will see the complications that arise when random independent variables are introduced into an experiment with nested factors. Finally, we will discuss the possibility of viewing an experiment which is completely crossed in terms of nesting, when this alternative view provides a more direct test of the experimental hypotheses under consideration.

---

[1] Sources of variance containing nested factors usually represent a composite—a pooling of the individual components. Occasionally, it may make sense to evaluate these components separately. (For example, see the answer to Exercise 12 for Part IV.)

ANALYSIS OF EXPERIMENTS WITH NESTED
FACTORS: GENERAL

A computational scheme is presented in this section that will allow us to generate the computational formulas for the analysis of experiments with nested independent variables. The discussion consists of two parts—the identification of the sources of variance and the actual construction of the computational formulas for the corresponding sums of squares. As we will see, the first step is the most difficult, since we have to be able to specify the component sums of squares that result from the presence of the nested factor. The second step simply uses the df statement for the different sources as the key to the construction of the computational formulas.

Identification of Sources of Variance

In Chapter 10, we considered a rule that allowed the specification of the component sources of variance in the completely crossed design. We will have to expand this rule now, to handle the case in which nested factors occur.[2] The rule is stated in terms of the following three steps:

1. **List all factors including the within-groups factor;**
2. **Form all potential interactions, omitting the within-groups factor:**
   (a) **letters designating crossed factors and letters to the left of the diagonal for nested factors stay on the left of the diagonal, and**
   (b) **letters to the right of the diagonal for nested factors stay on the right of the diagonal (do not duplicate repeated letters);**
3. **Delete any interaction in which the same letter appears on both sides of the diagonal.**

The sources listed in the first step, together with any interactions surviving the third step, constitute a complete enumeration of the sources of variance that would be extracted in the standard analysis.

As an example, suppose we combined the two experiments presented in Table 18-1 into a single, three-factor experiment varying languages (factor A), passages (factor B), and setting (factor C); again, passages are nested within the three languages.[3] The design of this experiment is summarized in Table 18-2 as an ABC matrix. To find out the sources of variance that are isolated in the analysis, we will follow the rule step by step. First, we list the independent variables and the within-groups factor. This latter factor consists of the

---

[2] The rule is adapted from Glass and Stanley (1970, pp. 474–475). It also assumes that the same number of levels in the nested factor is present at each level of the factor in which it is nested. In Table 18-1, for example, factor B (passages) is nested in factor A (languages) and there are $b = 4$ passages for each of the $a = 3$ languages.

[3] Factor C has two levels in this example, while in Table 18-1 the independent variable was represented by four levels. The reason for the change was to avoid the impression that any of the independent variables had to have the same number of levels.

TABLE 18-2 *An Example of Nesting: Languages (Factor A), Passages Nested within Languages (Factor B), and Settings (Factor C)*

THE ABC MATRIX

	a_1		a_2		a_3	
	c_1	c_2	c_1	c_2	c_1	c_2
b_1			b_5		b_9	
b_2			b_6		b_{10}	
b_3			b_7		b_{11}	
b_4			b_8		b_{12}	

IDENTIFICATION OF THE SOURCES OF VARIANCE

1. **List factors:** A, B/A, C, and S/ABC.
2. **Find interactions:** $A \times B/A$, $A \times C$, $C \times B/A$, and $A \times C \times B/A$.
3. **Delete:** $A \times B/A$ and $A \times C \times B/A$.

variability of subjects treated alike pooled over the *abc* treatment combinations. These four factors are listed below the *ABC* matrix in Table 18-2. Next, we form all potential interactions with the independent variables—all possible two-way interactions and a three-way interaction. These are also listed in the table. Finally, we delete those interactions in which the same letters appear on both sides of the diagonal. The two terms lost in this step are indicated in the table.

It will be noted that there is no three-way interaction—this interaction obviously is not possible since the three factors do not cross. The two crossed factors do produce an interaction, since each level of factor C is represented at each level of factor A (see Table 18-2). The only other two-way interaction is the $C \times B/A$ interaction. To understand the meaning of this interaction, look separately at each of the three displays in Table 18-2. In the first, we see a crossing of factor C with the nested factor at level a_1; in the second we see a similar crossing with the nested factor at level a_2; and in the third, a crossing with the nested factor at level a_3. The $C \times B/A$ interaction, then, is a *pooling* of the $B \times C$ interactions at each level of factor A.

Suppose we attempt to make sense out of these sources of variance. Remember that factors B and C have been introduced to extend the generality of any differences in the readability of the three artificial languages. Our primary interest, then, is in the *main effect* of factor A. The main effect of factor C is presumably of little interest, since it will merely reflect the overall influence of different experimental settings. The remaining sources of variance *are* important for increasing the external validity (or generality) of the experiment. That is, the generality of any conclusion we may draw concerning factor A will be limited if these sources of variance are significant. The main effect of the nested factor (B/A) indicates whether the different passages which are drawn from the three languages are equally readable; if they are not, the generality of any overall effect of the languages may be restricted. The $A \times C$ interaction indicates whether the readability of the three languages changes in the different experimental settings; if it does, we will again question the generality of any overall differences in readability. Finally, the $C \times B/A$ interaction would reflect changes in the relative difficulty of a set of passages in the different settings at the various levels of factor A; if this occurred, we might find ourselves restricted in the conclusions that we would draw concerning the main effect of factor A.

Construction of the Computational Formulas

Now that we have listed the sources of variance, we can consider next the construction of the computational formulas for the analysis of variance. The sources of variance we obtained by applying the identification rule to the design and enumerated in Table 18-2 have been listed in the first column of Table 18-3. The next column gives the information that is critical for the construction of the computational formulas—namely, the df associated with the different sources of variance. The df for any source of variance may be obtained by means of the following rule:

Multiply (1) the product of the df's of factors to the *left* of the diagonal by (2) the product of the *levels* of factors to the *right* of the diagonal.

For sources involving only crossed factors, all of the factors are assumed to be on the *left* of the diagonal; the corresponding df's, therefore, are found by multiplying the df's of the factors so specified. We will consider only the df's for the sources containing nested factors:

$$df_{B/A} = (df_B)(a) = (b - 1)(a),$$

$$df_{C \times B/A} = [(df_C)(df_B)](a) = (c - 1)(b - 1)(a),$$

and

$$df_{S/ABC} = (df_S)[(a)(b)(c)] = (s - 1)(abc).$$

(The df for the within-groups factor have been included to show that their determination is consistent with the rule.) These df, with the letters rearranged in alphabetical order, are presented in the second column of Table 18-3.

The remaining steps represent a straightforward application of the system presented in Chapter 10. Briefly, the df statements are expanded in the third column. Next, the first term in each df statement is translated into a sum, which is squared and then summed. The results of these operations are found in the fourth column. In the next column, the denominator for each term is found by

TABLE 18-3 *Construction of the Computational Formulas for the Experiment Presented in Table 18-2*

(1) Source	(2) df	(3) df Expanded	(4) Square and Sum	(5) Selection of Denominator — First Term	(6) Letter Code	(7) Computational Formula (Coded)[a]
A	$a-1$	$a-1$	$\sum(A)^2$	$\dfrac{\sum(A)^2}{abcs} = \dfrac{\sum(A)^2}{bcs}$	$[A]$	$[A]-[T]$
B/A	$a(b-1)$	$ab-a$	$\sum(AB)^2$	$\dfrac{\sum(AB)^2}{abcs} = \dfrac{\sum(AB)^2}{cs}$	$[AB]$	$[AB]-[A]$
C	$c-1$	$c-1$	$\sum(C)^2$	$\dfrac{\sum(C)^2}{abcs} = \dfrac{\sum(C)^2}{abs}$	$[C]$	$[C]-[T]$
$A \times C$	$(a-1)(c-1)$	$ac-a-c+1$	$\sum(AC)^2$	$\dfrac{\sum(AC)^2}{abcs} = \dfrac{\sum(AC)^2}{bs}$	$[AC]$	$[AC]-[A]-[C]+[T]$
$C \times B/A$	$a(b-1)(c-1)$	$abc-ab-ac+a$	$\sum(ABC)^2$	$\dfrac{\sum(ABC)^2}{abcs} = \dfrac{\sum(ABC)^2}{s}$	$[ABC]$	$[ABC]-[AB]-[AC]+[A]$
S/ABC	$abc(s-1)$	$abcs-abc$	$\sum(ABCS)^2$	$\dfrac{\sum(ABCS)^2}{abcs} = \sum(ABCS)^2$	$[ABCS]$	$[ABCS]-[ABC]$
Total	$abcs-1$	$abcs-1$	$\sum(ABCS)^2$	$\dfrac{\sum(ABCS)^2}{abcs} = \sum(ABCS)^2$	$[ABCS]$	$[ABCS]-[T]$
	1	1	$(T)^2$	$\dfrac{(T)^2}{abcs} = \dfrac{(T)^2}{abcs}$	$[T]$	

[a] Bracketed letters represent complete terms in the computational formulas; a particular term is identified by the letter(s) appearing in the numerator.

dividing by the total number of observations, *abcs*, and deleting letters that occur in the numerator. These terms in the computational formulas are now coded by the letters appearing in the numerator (sixth column). Finally, in the last column, the computational formulas are written in coded form by substituting into the expanded *df* statements listed in column 3.

The remainder of the analysis requires little comment. The mean squares are found by dividing sums of squares by corresponding *df*'s. If all of the independent variables are fixed-effects factors, the appropriate error term is the $MS_{S/ABC}$. If random independent factors are present, a different mean square may be the appropriate error term. Rules for the selection of error terms are discussed subsequently (see pp. 383–385).

As promised, the only complication in the analysis of an experiment with nested independent variables is in the determination of the sources of variance that may be extracted in the analysis. After these sources have been identified, the *df* are obtained easily and the computational formulas are generated in a purely mechanical fashion. We will now work through two numerical examples to illustrate different applications of designs with nested factors in the behavioral sciences and to demonstrate the application of the rules to experimental data.

NESTING OF SUBJECT GROUPINGS WITHIN TREATMENTS

In some experiments, it is convenient and even desirable to include independent subgroupings of subjects within the different treatment conditions. There are situations, for example, in which it is much easier to administer the experiment to subgroups of subjects rather than to individual subjects. Perhaps the experiment can be conducted with a group procedure, but only one condition can be presented at a given time. The group procedure provides efficiency over the running of the subjects individually. If two or more such groups are assigned to each experimental condition, we have an example of the nesting of groups within treatments. Each of the groups is represented only once in one of the conditions of the experiment—they are *unique* to a single treatment condition.

We often see this sort of design employed when there is some attempt to sample groups from a much larger population, such as classes from a large school system or patients from different hospitals in a large city or in a state. It is not necessary that the subjects be tested in a group with group procedures, however. In the case of medical research, for instance, individual patients from several hospitals may be administered a particular treatment, while patients from other hospitals are given different treatments. The fact that patients from any given hospital receive only one of the treatments, rather than being represented in all of the treatment combinations, signifies a nested design. In this case, hospitals are nested within treatment conditions.

Nesting Versus Crossing

We will now look more carefully at this type of nested design. Suppose that an educator decides to compare a number of methods of teaching arithmetic (factor A) to children at a particular grade level. We will assume it is more convenient to administer one of the methods to the students in an entire classroom than to administer the different methods to an equal number of students in any given classroom. Presumably the researcher does not want the results of a given method to be tied to a particular class. Thus, he will include a number of different classes under each of the methods (factor B), and so this latter factor, classes, is nested within factor A (i.e., B/A).[4] That is, the particular classes associated with one method have nothing to do with the classes associated with the other methods.

It may be profitable to contrast this nested design with a factorial arrangement. Look at Table 18-4. In the case on the left, we have the nested design. Six classrooms are represented, two with each of three teaching methods. We will assume that there are $s = 21$ students in each of these classes. In the factorial design, which is presented on the right, the same six classrooms are represented, but each class contributes one-third of its members ($s = 7$) to each of the three methods. Notice the obvious differences between the two designs. For the factorial, each level of one variable (methods) is combined

TABLE 18-4 *A Comparison of Nested and Crossed Designs*

THE EXPERIMENTAL DESIGNS

Nested Design

Method 1	Method 2	Method 3
Class 1	Class 3	Class 5
Class 2	Class 4	Class 6

Crossed Design

Classes	Method 1	Method 2	Method 3
1			
2			
3			
4			
5			
6			

SOURCES OF VARIANCE AND df's

Source	df
Method (A):	2
Classes/Method (B/A):	3
S/AB	120
Total	125

Source	df
Method (A)	2
Class (B)	5
$A \times B$	10
S/AB	108
Total	125

[4] If he selects classes randomly, this variable becomes a random factor. On the other hand, if the classes used constitute the population of classes, the variable is a fixed-effects factor.

with each level of the other variable (classes). For the nested design this is not the case—the classroom representation is unique for each of the methods.

IDENTIFICATION OF SOURCES   As you may have inferred from the last section, the sources of variance identified and extracted in these two designs are different. To make this point explicit, we have partitioned the SS_T for the two designs in the bottom of Table 18-4. In both cases we obtain information concerning the three methods, and this comparison is associated with $df_A = a - 1 = 3 - 1 = 2$. In both cases, too, the df for the SS_T are identical. In the nested design,

$$df_T = abs - 1 = 3(2)(21) - 1 = 126 - 1 = 125,$$

and in the factorial design,

$$df_T = abs - 1 = 3(6)(7) - 1 = 126 - 1 = 125.$$

Let us now see how the two analyses differ.

The analysis of the factorial design requires little comment. The $SS_{S/AB}$ represents the variability of subjects treated alike, pooled over treatment combinations. In this example, there are $s = 7$ subjects in each method-class combination, giving

$$df_{S/AB} = ab(s - 1) = 3(6)(7 - 1) = 108.$$

For the nested design, we follow the rules from the last section:

1. **List factors:** A, B/A, and S/AB.
2. **Find interactions:** $A \times B/A$.
3. **Delete:** $A \times B/A$.

(The quantity $A \times B/A$ originally listed in step 2 is deleted in step 3 because the letter A appears on both sides of the diagonal.) The df for the nested factor are found by applying the df rule (p. 370):

$$df_{B/A} = (df_B)(a) = (b - 1)(a) = (2 - 1)(3) = 3.$$

The within-groups source of variance is based upon subjects treated alike. In this case, we are referring to the $s = 21$ subjects within each of the six different classes. The df for this source are

$$df_{S/AB} = ab(s - 1) = 3(2)(21 - 1) = 6(20) = 120.$$

COMMENT   What can we say about the relative merits of the two designs? The nested design is certainly simpler to conduct. On the other hand, the factorial provides more information; that is, we can find out whether or not the same differences among the methods are found with each of the different classes—a form of independent replication. Also, we know that any differences among classes (the teachers, the students, the class environment, or whatever) are spread equally across the three methods. The nested design, in contrast, has to depend upon the random assignment of the classes to the teaching methods to accomplish this. We will worry about this problem in the numerical example which follows.

Numerical Example

As an example of the nesting of groups within treatments, we will consider the results of an actual experiment.[5] In this study, subjects were given training on a list of unrelated words, followed by either 0, 2, 4, or 6 trials on a different set of words; then they were asked to recall all of the words they had learned

TABLE 18-5 *AB Matrix for an Experiment with Nesting of Subject Groupings (Entries Based on $s = 5$ Subjects)*

Trials (Factor A)

	0 Trials (a_1)		2 Trials (a_2)		4 Trials (a_3)		6 Trials (a_4)
b_1	85	b_7	57	b_{13}	45	b_{19}	28
b_2	66	b_8	56	b_{14}	41	b_{20}	49
b_3	58	b_9	58	b_{15}	45	b_{21}	40
b_4	80	b_{10}	48	b_{16}	32	b_{22}	30
b_5	74	b_{11}	48	b_{17}	49	b_{23}	42
b_6	77	b_{12}	54	b_{18}	33	b_{24}	53
Sum	440	Sum	321	Sum	245	Sum	242

in the experiment. The response measure of interest was the number of first-list words recalled. The independent variable, trials, will be called factor A. Subjects were run in groups of $s = 5$ subjects each. These groups consisted of volunteers who had agreed "independently" to serve in the experiment at the same time and date. The subjects within any group were treated identically. Six groups so formed were assigned to each of the four experimental conditions in a random fashion. Since the different groups were independent of one another, "groups" is a factor (factor B) which is nested within each treatment condition, i.e., B/A.

The results of this experiment are presented within the body of the AB matrix of Table 18-5. The entries in the matrix are the total numbers of words recalled by the 5 subjects within each subgroup. For these data, $\sum (ABS)^2 = 15,292$. An inspection of the totals for the four treatment conditions indicates

[5] Postman and Keppel (1967).

that there was a progressive decline in first-list recall as the number of trials on the second list increased. That is, learning a second list has an increasingly deleterious effect on the memory for the first list.

CALCULATION OF SUMS OF SQUARES   The sources of variance obtained from this analysis have been specified already in Table 18-4. There are three sources: A, B/A, and S/AB. We will construct the computational formulas from the corresponding df statements and then calculate the sums of squares with the data presented in Table 18-5. For the SS_A,

$$df_A = a - 1,$$

$$SS_A = \frac{\sum (A)^2}{abs} - \frac{(T)^2}{abs}$$

$$= \frac{(440)^2 + (321)^2 + (245)^2 + (242)^2}{6(5)} - \frac{(85 + 66 + \cdots + 42 + 53)^2}{4(6)(5)}.$$

For the $SS_{B/A}$,

$$df_{B/A} = a(b - 1) = ab - a,$$

$$SS_{B/A} = \frac{\sum (AB)^2}{abs} - \frac{\sum (A)^2}{abs}$$

$$= \frac{(85)^2 + (66)^2 + \cdots + (42)^2 + (53)^2}{5} - \frac{(440)^2 + (321)^2 + (245)^2 + (242)^2}{6(5)}.$$

For the $SS_{S/AB}$,

$$df_{S/AB} = ab(s - 1) = abs - ab,$$

$$SS_{S/AB} = \frac{\sum (ABS)^2}{abs} - \frac{\sum (AB)^2}{abs}$$

$$= 15{,}292 - \frac{(85)^2 + (66)^2 + \cdots + (42)^2 + (53)^2}{5}.$$

Finally, for the SS_T,

$$df_T = abs - 1,$$

$$SS_T = \frac{\sum (ABS)^2}{abs} - \frac{(T)^2}{abs}$$

$$= 15{,}292 - \frac{(85 + 66 + \cdots + 42 + 53)^2}{4(6)(5)}.$$

These calculations are summarized in Table 18-6.

TESTS OF SIGNIFICANCE   We are now ready to determine the significance of the main effect of factor A. At this point, however, the analysis introduces a complication in the selection of the appropriate error term against which to evaluate the MS_A. We saw with the one-way analysis of variance that the variability observed among the treatment conditions was potentially due to two components—the treatment effects and error variance. With this nested design, however, there is the possibility of a *third* component, the presence of an effect of the *nested* factor. In this experiment the groups were not matched on any relevant factors; rather, groups were constituted by whatever factors are responsible for volunteers' signing up at the same time and date for a

TABLE 18-6   *Summary of the Analysis*

Source	Calculations[a]	SS	df	MS	F
A	$13{,}841.00 - 12{,}979.20 =$	861.80	3	287.27	21.75*
B/A	$14{,}105.20 - [A] =$	264.20	20	13.21	1.07
S/AB	$15{,}292 - [AB] =$	1186.80	96	12.36	
Total	$[ABS] - [T] =$	2312.80	119		

[a] Bracketed letters represent complete terms in the computational formulas; a particular term is identified by the letter(s) appearing in the numerator.

* $p < .01$.

psychology experiment. There is every reason to believe, therefore, that real differences did exist among the $ab = 4(6) = 24$ groups before the start of the experiment. We rely upon the random assignment of the groups to conditions to spread these differences "evenly" (i.e., without bias) across the four treatment conditions. However, just as we do not expect the assignment of *subjects* to conditions in a completely randomized single-factor experiment to result in perfectly equivalent groups, we must not expect the assignment of *groups* to conditions to accomplish this either. Thus, the MS_A may reflect in part group differences, in addition to any systematic treatment effects and error variance.

Given this argument, then, if we use the $MS_{S/AB}$ as the error term with which to evaluate the MS_A, there may be a *bias* in favor of rejecting the null hypothesis. That is, the MS_A can be thought to contain three components (treatment effects, group effects, and error variance) and the $MS_{S/AB}$ to contain one (error variance). When the null hypothesis is true, the treatment component drops out and we have a quantity in the numerator of the F ratio which is *not* an unbiased, independent estimate of error variance—it includes variance due to differences among the different groups as well. This bias, since it will result in the false rejection of the null hypothesis at a rate greater than that specified by α, is called a *positive* bias.

We can avoid this bias by finding an error term which contains *all* of the components present in the MS_A *except* the treatment component. Such a source is the $MS_{B/A}$, which reflects the group component *and* error variance.

Thus, when the null hypothesis is *true*, the ratio

$$\frac{MS_A}{MS_{B/A}}$$

is distributed as F, with $df_{\text{num.}} = df_A$ and $df_{\text{denom.}} = df_{B/A}$. In the present example,

$$F = \frac{287.27}{13.21} = 21.75.$$

An inspection of the critical value of $F(3, 20)$ indicates that the null hypothesis is rejected handily.

The error term for the other mean square, the nested main effect, is the within-groups mean square ($MS_{S/AB}$). The formation of this ratio tests the hypothesis that there are no systematic group differences. That is, when the null hypothesis is *true*, we have one estimate of error variance divided by another independent estimate of error variance, the result of which is distributed as $F(df_{B/A}, df_{S/AB})$. As indicated in Table 18-6, the hypothesis is not rejected.

COMMENTS   The formation of the F ratios in this example was complicated by the fact that the nested factor is considered *random*, rather than fixed. That is, groups within treatment conditions (B/A) is just as much a random variable as is subjects within treatment conditions (S/AB) in the fixed-effects model. (We will consider subsequently a mechanical scheme for selecting the appropriate error term for experiments with nested factors.)

It has been mentioned already that we frequently see subject groupings incorporated into experiments in the behavioral sciences. Researchers often fail to appreciate what it means to have the *subgroups* assigned randomly to the experimental treatments and *not* the individual subjects. That is, random assignment of subjects (or subgroups) is used to ensure the *independence* of one statistical unit from another, either within a given treatment or between two treatments. Especially if *intact* groups are used (such as classes or wards or sections), there is every reason to believe that the subjects *within* any given group are not mutually independent of each other. The groups are usually not constituted randomly, and the subjects within these groups have usually shared a large number of common experiences. In addition, if the group is also tested in the experiment as a group, the subjects will have shared any unique features of the treatment that may have occurred by chance, such as an extraneous noise, a mistake by the experimenter, the administration of the conditions with faulty equipment. Under these circumstances, then, we cannot think of the s subjects in each subgroup as representing *independent* replications of the experiment. For this reason the analysis of such designs must be given close and expert attention. This general problem receives an excellent treatment by Glass and Stanley (1970, pp. 501–508).

NESTING OF CONTROL AND EXPERIMENTAL FACTORS

In this section we will consider the nesting of control and experimental factors. Actually, we see more of this general type of nesting reported in the literature than we do the nesting of groups within treatments. We will examine in this section an example in which a control factor is nested within the experimental conditions of a factorial. Briefly, such situations consist of the introduction of a control factor which is uniquely defined at the levels of the experimental factor. You have already been introduced to an example of this type of nesting in Table 18-1 and Table 18-2.

Nesting of experimental factors represents a nonfactorial elaboration or expansion of the levels of an independent variable in the experiment. The most common instances of this sort of nesting are found in experiments containing experimental-control comparisons. For example, an experiment relating drug dosage to the learning rate of rats might consist of a control treatment (no drug) which is contrasted with the experimental treatment (drug), the experimental treatment being represented by a number of different dosage levels. In this case, dosage level is a manipulation which cannot occur in the control condition; thus, dosage level is nested within the experimental condition.

Illustrative Example

DESIGN   The example we will work through uses the data from an experiment reported by Underwood and Richardson (1956), which we described briefly in an earlier chapter. The part of the experiment we will examine involves the determination of the relative learning difficulty of serial lists of nonsense syllables. The two independent variables of experimental interest were the similarity (factor A) and the meaningfulness (factor B) of the nonsense syllables within a given list. With two levels of each factor, the design is a 2×2 factorial. For reasons connected with other purposes of the experiment, Underwood and Richardson included a control factor in the experiment: the serial order (factor C) of the nonsense syllables within the different lists. Ten orders of each basic list were prepared. Since the syllables in one list were unrelated to the syllables in the other lists, the serial orders of the syllables are nested within each of the four lists. Thus, there were three independent variables in the experiment—the two crossed factors of experimental interest (factors A and B) and the nested control factor (factor C). Since this latter factor is nested within each of the ab treatment combinations, we will represent the source as C/AB.

COMPUTATIONS   The results of the experiment are summarized in the ABC matrix presented in Table 18-7.[6] The response measure consists of the number

---

[6] The data were kindly furnished by Dr. Benton J. Underwood.

of trials needed to attain one perfect recitation of the serial list. Each entry in this matrix represents a *sum* of the learning scores of $s = 10$ subjects receiving that particular list and list order; for the grand total of $abcs = 2(2)(10)(10) = 400$ subjects, $\sum (ABCS)^2 = 445,317$.

The first step in the analysis consists of the determination of the component sources of variance. Following the rule for the identification of the sources (p. 368), we have

1. **List factors:** A, B, C/AB, and S/ABC.
2. **Form interactions:** $A \times B$, $A \times C/AB$, $B \times C/AB$, and $A \times B \times C/AB$.
3. **Delete:** $A \times C/AB$, $B \times C/AB$, and $A \times B \times C/AB$.

The next two steps—the construction of the computational formulas and the calculation of the sums of squares—will be accomplished at the same time. We start by determining the *df* for each source (see p. 370). From the expanded

TABLE 18-7   *Numerical Example: Nesting of a Control Factor*

ABC Matrix

Similarity (A)

	Low (a_1)				High (a_2)		
	Meaningfulness (B)				Meaningfulness (B)		
Lists (C)	Low (b_1)	Lists (C)	High (b_2)	Lists (C)	Low (b_1)	Lists (C)	High (b_2)
c_1	277	c_{11}	207	c_{21}	520	c_{31}	277
c_2	270	c_{12}	187	c_{22}	413	c_{32}	295
c_3	269	c_{13}	206	c_{23}	503	c_{33}	197
c_4	331	c_{14}	178	c_{24}	461	c_{34}	223
c_5	305	c_{15}	172	c_{25}	385	c_{35}	232
c_6	273	c_{16}	204	c_{26}	361	c_{36}	195
c_7	383	c_{17}	222	c_{27}	330	c_{37}	280
c_8	372	c_{18}	167	c_{28}	446	c_{38}	260
c_9	233	c_{19}	167	c_{29}	419	c_{39}	297
c_{10}	205	c_{20}	217	c_{30}	419	c_{40}	330

AB Matrix

	a_1	a_2	Sum
b_1	2918	4257	7175
b_2	1927	2586	4513
Sum	4845	6843	11,688

df statements, and following the rules given in Chapter 10 (see pp. 193–195), we can write the computational formulas. Finally, we find the sums of squares by substituting the data provided in Table 18-7 into the computational formulas. The totals for the first three sums of squares come from the AB matrix in the lower half of Table 18-7. For the SS_A,

$$df_A = a - 1,$$

$$SS_A = \frac{\sum (A)^2}{abcs} - \frac{(T)^2}{abcs}$$

$$= \frac{(4845)^2 + (6843)^2}{2(10)(10)} - \frac{(11,688)^2}{2(2)(10)(10)}.$$

For the SS_B,

$$df_B = b - 1,$$

$$SS_B = \frac{\sum (B)^2}{abcs} - \frac{(T)^2}{abcs}$$

$$= \frac{(7175)^2 + (4513)^2}{2(10)(10)} - \frac{(11,688)^2}{2(2)(10)(10)}.$$

For the $SS_{A \times B}$,

$$df_{A \times B} = (a - 1)(b - 1) = ab - a - b + 1,$$

$$SS_{A \times B} = \frac{\sum (AB)^2}{abcs} - \frac{\sum (A)^2}{abcs} - \frac{\sum (B)^2}{abcs} + \frac{(T)^2}{abcs}$$

$$= \frac{(2918)^2 + (4257)^2 + (1927)^2 + (2586)^2}{10(10)} - \frac{(4845)^2 + (6843)^2}{2(10)(10)}$$

$$- \frac{(7175)^2 + (4513)^2}{2(10)(10)} + \frac{(11,688)^2}{2(2)(10)(10)}.$$

We will now turn to the two nested factors. For the main effect of C/AB,

$$df_{C/AB} = (df_C)[(a)(b)] = (c - 1)(ab) = abc - ab,$$

$$SS_{C/AB} = \frac{\sum (ABC)^2}{abcs} - \frac{\sum (AB)^2}{abcs}$$

$$= \frac{(277)^2 + (270)^2 + \cdots + (297)^2 + (330)^2}{10}$$

$$- \frac{(2918)^2 + (4257)^2 + (1927)^2 + (2586)^2}{10(10)}.$$

For the within-groups sum of squares,

$$df_{S/ABC} = (df_S)[(a)(b)(c)] = (s - 1)(abc) = abcs - abc,$$

$$SS_{S/ABC} = \frac{\sum (ABCS)^2}{abcs} - \frac{\sum (ABC)^2}{abcs}$$

$$= 445{,}317 - \frac{(277)^2 + (270)^2 + \cdots + (297)^2 + (330)^2}{10}.$$

For the final sum of squares,

$$df_T = abcs - 1,$$

$$SS_T = \frac{\sum (ABCS)^2}{abcs} - \frac{(T)^2}{abcs}$$

$$= 445{,}317 - \frac{(11{,}688)^2}{2(2)(10)(10)}.$$

The calculations for these sums of squares are completed in Table 18-8. Since the three independent variables were considered fixed-effects factors, the significance of all of the mean squares is evaluated with the $MS_{S/ABC}$. The results of these F tests are indicated in the last column of the summary table. The effects of experimental interest are all significant. The main effects indicate that a high-similarity list is more difficult to learn than a low-similarity list and that a list of high meaningfulness is easier to learn than a list of low meaningfulness. The $A \times B$ interaction indicates that similarity (factor A) has a greater effect at low meaningfulness (level b_1) than at high meaningfulness (level b_2). The main effect of the nested factor (C/AB) is not significant,

TABLE 18-8 *Summary of the Analysis*

Source	Calculations[a]		SS	df	MS	F
Similarity (A):	351,503.37					
	$-341{,}523.36 =$		9,980.01	1	9,980.01	53.93**
Meaningfulness (B):	$359{,}238.97 - [T] =$		17,715.61	1	17,715.61	95.74**
$A \times B$:	370,374.98					
	$-[A] - [B] + [T] =$		1,156.00	1	1,156.00	6.25*
Order/Treatments (C/AB):	$378{,}701.40 - [AB] =$		8,326.42	36	231.29	1.25
S/ABC:	$445{,}317 - [ABC] =$		66,615.60	360	185.04	
Total:	$[ABCS] - [T] =$		103,793.64	399		

[a] Bracketed letters represent complete terms in the computational formulas; a particular term is identified by the letter(s) appearing in the numerator.

* $p < .05$.
** $p < .01$.

indicating that the results are not due to a particular ordering of the stimulus materials.

SELECTION OF ERROR TERMS WHEN RANDOM FACTORS ARE PRESENT

Earlier, we considered the complications occurring when random independent variables are introduced into a completely randomized factorial experiment (see pp. 335–338). In this section we will simply acknowledge that error terms change in experiments with nested factors as well and turn immediately to a mechanical scheme for identifying the correct error term.

The system is an elaboration of the one presented in Table 16-2 (p. 340)—an elaboration necessitated by the presence of nested factors. The general principle of the system is to find the error term for a particular treatment effect by matching the letters used to designate the effect and the other sources of variance in the summary table. Following the convention established earlier, we will use lower-case letters to represent random independent variables and capital letters to represent fixed independent variables.

The scheme, presented in Table 18-9, consists of a series of tests designed to select out the exact error term, if one exists. The first question asks whether or not random independent variables are present in the experiment. If there are none—i.e., all of the factors are fixed—then the within-groups mean square is the correct error term. This was the case in the example we considered in the nesting of control factors. The example of the nesting of subject groupings was an exception, since the nested factor (groups within treatment conditions) can quite reasonably be thought of as a random independent variable. The summary table (Table 18-6) lists the following sources of variance:

A (the number of second-list learning trials),
b/A (groups within treatment conditions), and
S/Ab (the within-groups mean square).

Since the nested factor is considered to be random, we will follow the "yes" branch in Table 18-9 to the next question for each of the sources considered. For the MS_A, we ask whether the letter designating the effect contains all of the random independent variables. It does not (b is a random independent variable). Thus, we follow the "no" branch and consider a set of selection criteria: we are to examine all of the sources and select those that contain the letters in the effect and, in addition, one more random variable.[7] For the present example, only one source satisfies the different tests: b/A. More specifically, only b/A contains the letter in the effect (A) and a random

[7] Since no *extra* capital letters are present to the right of the diagonal, the qualification listed in the table is not relevant. For an example of the application of this aspect of the selection criteria, see Exercise 11 for Part IV (p. 391).

TABLE 18-9   *Steps in the Selection of Appropriate Error Terms in the Completely Randomized Factorial Experiment*[a] *(Nested Factors Present)*

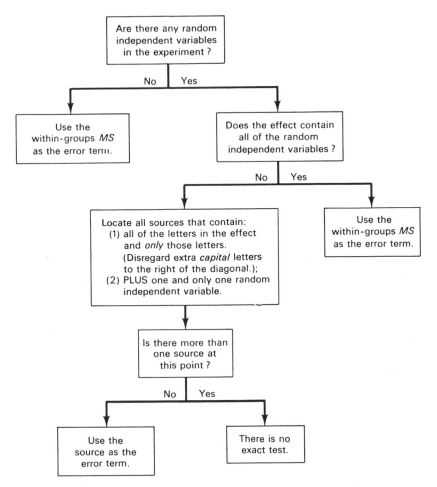

[a] *Source* refers to any subcomponent isolated in the standard analysis of variance; *effect* refers to the source containing only those letters denoting the treatment effect in question.

independent variable (b). Thus, we use the $MS_{b/A}$ as the error term for evaluating the significance of the MS_A.

The error term for the *nested factor* is found easily by using the selection scheme. Since the answer to the first question continues to be "yes" for this design, we ask whether or not the effect (b/A) contains all of the random independent variables. The answer is "yes," and we are told that the within-groups mean square $(MS_{S/Ab})$ is the correct error term.

We will not work out any further examples of the selection procedure. Additional illustrations are found in Exercise 11 for Part IV. A word of caution, however: careful consideration should be given to the nature of the independent variables before the start of the experiment. With random variables present in any type of experiment, the error terms will often have many fewer degrees of freedom than does the within-groups mean square. With a reduction in denominator df, there is a corresponding reduction in the power of the F test.[8] Professional advice should be sought if there is any doubt as to the feasibility or correctness of the analysis of any experiment with random independent factors.

INTERACTION AND NESTED MODELS
IN FACTORIAL DESIGNS

When considering a completely crossed two-factor experiment, we usually assume the structural model to be one which includes two main effects and interaction effects. On the basis of this model, then, we proceed to construct F ratios that provide tests of null hypotheses concerning the presence of these different effects. This is what we do in the standard analysis of variance. If the interaction is significant, we will generally want to attempt to identify the factors contributing to its significance. Two useful post-hoc analyses are available: an analysis of simple main effects and an analysis of interactions involving comparisons (e.g., $A_{comp.} \times B$ or $A \times B_{comp.}$ or $A_{comp.} \times B_{comp.}$). We may even resort to multiple comparisons of some sort, but we would probably restrict these to cell means within a particular column or row.

There may be times when an alternative structural model makes more experimental sense, even though the experiment is nominally a completely crossed factorial. If we wish to think of the manipulations of factor B as nested in factor A, for example, the sources of variance normally extracted in the standard analysis (A, B, $A \times B$, and S/AB) shift to the following:

A,

a set of B/A_i sources (one for each level of factor A), and

S/AB.

This means that any variability due to B and the $A \times B$ interaction in the standard analysis is combined and reapportioned to the nested sources. The practical implication of adopting this nested model is that tests of simple main effects (the effect of factor B at the different levels of factor A) are substituted for tests of the main effect of factor B and the $A \times B$ interaction.

---

[8] It is possible to overcome this difficulty by pooling sums of squares, but the implications of these procedures are not fully understood by statisticians and cannot be counted on until *after* the data are collected (see Myers, 1966, pp. 283–288). We will discuss pooling of sums of squares in Chapter 25.

The consequence is that it is possible for one or more simple main effects to be significant under the nested model, where they are evaluated directly, and remain undetected under the interaction model owing to a nonsignificant $A \times B$ interaction.[9]

It is not possible to say when the model with the interaction component is appropriate and the model with the nested component is not or the reverse. If an experimenter is asking research questions that imply the presence of different treatment effects of one independent variable at the different levels of another, then the model with the interaction component is correct—his main concern is in *differential effects* and not necessarily the significance of these effects in isolation (i.e., the significance of the simple main effects). On the other hand, if a researcher is thinking of the manipulations of one independent variable at the levels of another as if they were *separate experiments*, he *is* concerned about the significance of the simple main effects. As soon as he finds himself wanting to contrast a simple effect at one level against a simple effect at another level, however, he is asking a question that implies the interaction model.

The point is that there are alternative ways of looking at an experiment —e.g., with interaction effects or with nested effects—and these should at least be considered in the initial stages of the planning. If we are sufficiently wise, we can propose the structural model that is appropriate for a given phenomenon. This model will make clear the specific analysis that should be conducted. Any statistical model we adopt, however, must depend upon the nature of the questions we want to ask about the data. [Marascuilo and Levin (1970) offer a detailed discussion of these two models and of post-hoc comparisons that stem from them.]

---

[9] You may recall from Chapter 16 that an interaction mean square represents an *averaging* of the interaction effects for each cell of the particular matrix involved; consequently, in some circumstances significant effects will be obscured by a large number of nonsignificant ones.

EXERCISES FOR PART IV [1]

1. Table 1 presents the outcomes of 10 three-way factorial experiments. The design in each example is the same—a $2 \times 2 \times 2$ factorial. The main intent of this exercise is to test your ability to identify three-way interactions when they are present in a set of data. Indicate the presence or absence of a triple interaction for each example. (We will assume for this problem that these means are "error free.") When the three-way interaction is *not* present, indicate which, if any, of the two-way interactions are present. Finally, are there any main effects that may be interpreted unambiguously in any of these examples?

TABLE 1   *Hypothetical Outcomes for a $2 \times 2 \times 2$ Factorial Experiment*

	Treatment Conditions							
Examples	a_1 b_1 c_1	a_1 b_1 c_2	a_1 b_2 c_1	a_1 b_2 c_2	a_2 b_1 c_1	a_2 b_1 c_2	a_2 b_2 c_1	a_2 b_2 c_2
1	1	1	1	1	3	3	3	3
2	2	2	1	1	3	3	2	2
3	3	2	2	1	4	3	3	2
4	1	1	3	3	3	3	1	1
5	1	2	2	3	2	3	1	2
6	2	0	1	1	4	2	3	3
7	2	4	1	3	0	3	1	4
8	2	3	1	4	0	4	1	3
9	2	2	1	1	4	4	3	4
10	1	0	2	3	2	3	1	0

2. In each part of this exercise you will be given an ABC matrix for a $2 \times 2 \times 2$ factorial design. Some of the cell sums are filled in and some are left blank. Your task is to fill in the blank cells with numbers that will result in the presence of the sources of variance that are specified and no others. This means that the specified sources are to produce sums of squares that are *greater* than zero and the nonspecified sources are to produce sums of squares that are *equal* to zero. Be sure to convince yourself that you have accomplished this. One tedious, but infallible, way is to assume some cell frequency, such as $s = 10$, and solve for the different sums of squares.
   (a) Source present: SS_A.

	c_1			c_2	
	a_1	a_2		a_1	a_2
b_1	30	20	b_1		
b_2			b_2		

[1] The answers to these problems are found in Appendix D.

(b) Sources present: SS_A, SS_B, and SS_C.

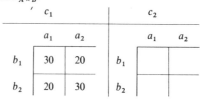

	c_1			c_2	
	a_1	a_2		a_1	a_2
b_1	30	20	b_1		15
b_2		30	b_2		

(c) Source present: $SS_{A \times B}$.

	c_1			c_2	
	a_1	a_2		a_1	a_2
b_1	30	20	b_1		
b_2	20	30	b_2		

(d) Sources present: SS_C and $SS_{A \times B}$.

	c_1			c_2	
	a_1	a_2		a_1	a_2
b_1	30	20	b_1		
b_2	20	30	b_2	30	

(e) Source present: $SS_{A \times B \times C}$.

	c_1			c_2	
	a_1	a_2		a_1	a_2
b_1	30	20	b_1		
b_2	20	30	b_2	30	

(f) Sources present: SS_C and $SS_{A \times B \times C}$.

	c_1			c_2	
	a_1	a_2		a_1	a_2
b_1	30	20	b_1		20
b_2	20	30	b_2		

3. Consider the results of a $3 \times 3 \times 2$ factorial experiment, presented below in an $ABCS$ matrix, in which there are $s = 4$ subjects in each treatment condition.

ABCS Matrix

Treatment Conditions

a_1 b_1 c_1	a_1 b_1 c_2	a_1 b_2 c_1	a_1 b_2 c_2	a_1 b_3 c_1	a_1 b_3 c_2	a_2 b_1 c_1	a_2 b_1 c_2	a_2 b_2 c_1	a_2 b_2 c_2	a_2 b_3 c_1	a_2 b_3 c_2	a_3 b_1 c_1	a_3 b_1 c_2	a_3 b_2 c_1	a_3 b_2 c_2	a_3 b_3 c_1	a_3 b_3 c_2
7	7	2	2	4	1	10	6	4	1	7	1	13	12	9	7	8	7
4	5	4	3	3	3	7	5	6	3	4	3	10	13	8	6	5	7
5	5	3	4	0	2	6	5	3	4	5	3	13	11	9	7	6	4
6	6	3	1	3	2	8	6	5	5	5	0	8	12	10	6	6	6

(a) Conduct an analysis of variance on these data.

(b) You will find that the $A \times B \times C$ interaction is not significant. This means, of course, that we can look at the two-way interactions and certain main effects for an adequate description of these results. Just as our interpretation of two-way interactions and main effects depends upon the significance or nonsignificance of the three-way interaction, our interpretation of *main* effects depends upon the significance or nonsignificance of the relevant two-way interactions. In the present example, the $A \times C$ interaction alone is significant. Thus, we might be interested in further analyses of this interaction. The two main effects (A and C), although significant in their own right, are not of much interest because any interpretation will have to be tempered with a consideration of the interaction of these two independent variables. In order to identify the locus of the interaction, test the significance of the simple main effects of factor C at the different levels of factor A.

(c) The one main effect that we might consider giving further attention is the main effect of factor B. This independent variable does not enter in any interactions with either or both factors A and C. We will assume that we are interested in making the following orthogonal comparisons involving the $\bar{B}_j$ means: (1) condition b_2 versus the combined effects of conditions b_1 and b_3, and (2) condition b_1 versus condition b_3. Test the significance of these comparisons.

4. Suppose a $4 \times 3 \times 2$ factorial design is conducted and the following results are obtained:

	c_1					c_2			
	a_1	a_2	a_3	a_4		a_1	a_2	a_3	a_4
b_1	35	46	49	55	b_1	37	49	56	65
b_2	42	51	55	62	b_2	40	38	44	42
b_3	29	40	45	49	b_3	27	23	19	14

For this problem, $s = 5$ and $\sum (ABCS)^2 = 9490$.

(a) Perform an analysis of variance with these data.

(b) From the analysis in (a), you will find that *all* sources of variance are significant. The critical source, however, is the three-way interaction. As mentioned in Exercise 3, any interpretation of two-way interactions as well as of main effects must be made in light of the way in which the three independent variables interact to produce the significant triple interaction. An inspection of the treatment sums suggests that one way of describing the interaction is to focus upon the simple $A \times B$ interaction effects at the two levels of factor C. (We could have just as well looked at the other two sets of simple interaction effects—the simple $A \times C$ interactions at the different levels of factor B and the simple $B \times C$ interactions at the different levels of factor A. Which set we consider in an actual experiment depends upon the independent variables we have manipulated and any hypotheses we may have about the outcome.) For this problem, then, test the significance of the simple $A \times B$ interaction effects.

(c) Suppose that factor A represents a quantitative variable and that the levels of this independent variable are equally spaced on this stimulus dimension. In terms of orthogonal trend components, how might the $A \times B \times C$ interaction be best described? That is, is the interaction reflected in a particular component of the orthogonal polynomial?

5. Although we will rarely choose to manipulate more than three independent variables for which we have experimental interest in a factorial arrangement, we will quite frequently form a four- or five-factor experiment when control factors are added to the design. Suppose that we do conduct a five-way factorial with factors A, B, and C reflecting manipulations for which we have a systematic interest and factors D and E representing control factors. We will randomly assign s subjects to each of the treatment combinations represented in the $ABCDE$ matrix.

(a) List all of the sources of variance associated with this design. Which of these will provide tests of the generality of the results?

(b) Write out the computational formulas for the following sums of squares: (1) $SS_{A \times B}$, (2) $SS_{B \times D}$, (3) $SS_{B \times C \times E}$, and (4) the within-groups sum of squares.

6. Continuing with the design described in Exercise 5, construct the computational formulas for the following comparisons: (a) $SS_{B_{comp.}}$, (b) $SS_{A \times B_{comp.}}$, and (c) $SS_{B_{comp. \, at \, ac_{ik}}}$.

7. Suppose you have conducted a four-way factorial experiment and have found the $A \times B \times C \times D$ interaction to be significant. In the hope of finding a way to interpret this interaction, you might turn to an analysis of the simple effects. There are three levels at which such an analysis may be conducted: an analysis of the simple three-way interactions at different levels of the fourth variable, an analysis of the simple two-way interactions at the different combinations of the two other variables, and an analysis of the simple main effects at the different combinations of the three other variables. Write the computational formulas for the first two levels of analysis. (Assume a completely randomized design with s subjects in each treatment condition.) In order to be able to check your answers with the ones provided, write the formulas for (a) the simple $A \times C \times D$ interactions at b_j, and (b) the simple $A \times D$ interactions at bc_{jk}.

8. What are the sources of variance normally extracted in an analysis of variance of a four-way factorial? Indicate the appropriate error term for each of these sources under the following conditions: (a) factors A, C, and D are fixed and factor B is random, and (b) factors B and D are fixed and factors A and C are random.

9. Consider the following scores in a completely randomized, single-factor experiment:

AS Matrix

a_1				a_2			a_3		a_4	
7	8	7	16	6	2	3	5	6	9	9
3	3	6	11	2	3	3	6	5	4	6
2	11	6	5	3	5	6	2	9	5	11
8	9	9	3	4	4	2	8	3	8	5
14	8	8	6	5	2	2	5	10	8	2
				0			7	14		

Analyze the results using unweighted means.

10. The following experiment, a 3×3 factorial, is conducted with unequal sample sizes:

ABS Matrix

	a_1	a_2	a_3
b_1	8, 10, 9, 12, 14, 7, 9, 13, 12, 12.	18, 12, 14, 12, 16, 17, 13, 16, 13, 15, 16, 14.	12, 12, 10, 14, 13, 10, 9, 10.
b_2	10, 6, 10, 11, 9, 6, 9, 6, 7, 7, 6, 12, 7, 8, 8.	16, 13, 14, 14, 15, 12, 18, 12, 15, 17, 20, 13, 13, 16, 15, 12, 14, 14.	22, 19, 20, 21, 18, 16, 18, 17, 19, 20, 19, 18.
b_3	10, 12, 8, 9, 12.	13, 8, 12, 13, 9, 9.	10, 9, 12, 12.

(a) Perform an analysis of the unweighted means.
(b) Suppose you wanted to obtain the simple main effects of factor B. How would you do it; i.e., what formula would you use? Assuming that you have an answer, extract these sums of squares and test their significance.

11. Imagine that a team of educators in California is planning to evaluate the relative effectiveness of three science books for sixth-grade children developed by competing publishers. Because they want to generalize their findings to all school systems in California, but cannot include them all in the study, they decide to sample randomly from the systems in the state. Furthermore, in order to reduce again the number of students tested, they plan to sample randomly sixth-grade classes from each of the systems selected. We will refer to the books as factor A, to school systems as factor B, and to the classes themselves as factor C. (We will assume that each class contains s students.)

(a) Suppose that the team plans to assign the three books to an equal number of classes from *each* of the systems selected for the study. (1) Which factors are nested? (2) Indicate the sources that may be obtained from this design and the appropriate error term for each source.
(b) Assume that the team plans to assign the three books to an equal number of school systems, but to have *all* of the classes randomly chosen within any particular system receive *only* that book. (1) Which factors are nested? (2) Indicate the sources of variance that may be obtained from this design and the appropriate error term for each source.

(c) Suppose that the evaluation is being conducted in a much smaller state than California and that it is possible to include *all* of the school systems in the experiment. (Continue to assume that classes within systems are selected randomly.) For the two designs described in (a) and (b) above, indicate the sources of variance that may now be obtained and the appropriate error term for each source.

12. A researcher is interested in comparing two different concept-formation tasks, one involving a disjunctive concept and the other involving a conjunctive concept, under three conditions of informative feedback—immediate knowledge of results, knowledge that is delayed by 10 seconds, and knowledge that is delayed by 30 seconds. The design, so far, is a 2×3 factorial. In order to increase the external validity of the experiment, the researcher includes *problems* as a third factor. The design is made explicit in the accompanying table. There are three feedback conditions (factor B)

ABC Matrix

Disjunctive Concept (a_1)				Conjunctive Concept (a_2)			
	Feedback Intervals (B)				Feedback Intervals (B)		
Problems (C)	0 Sec. (b_1)	10 Sec. (b_2)	30 Sec. (b_3)	Problems (C)	0 Sec. (b_1)	10 Sec. (b_2)	30 Sec. (b_3)
c_1	2	6	14	c_6	2	4	4
c_2	5	7	9	c_7	14	17	18
c_3	2	6	12	c_8	3	4	6
c_4	8	12	24	c_9	2	4	5
c_5	14	20	30	c_{10}	16	19	17

under the two types of conceptual tasks (factor A). In addition, there are five different examples of each of the two types of tasks (factor C). This is another way of saying that factor C is nested within factor A. The sums presented in the ABC matrix represent the numbers of trials required to reach a criterion of performance and are based on the scores of $s = 2$ subjects in each individual abc cell. For this example, $\sum (ABCS)^2 = 2509$. Perform an analysis of variance on these data. (Assume that factor C is fixed.)

PART V

Designs with Repeated Measures

In the preceding chapters we have considered the analysis of a large number of experimental designs, all of which have assumed the placement of independent groups of subjects in each treatment condition. Every design can be duplicated in a second type of arrangement with the *same* subjects receiving some or even all of the different treatment combinations. Such designs are said to contain *repeated measures*, and they represent a reasonable proportion of the experiments conducted in the behavioral sciences.

In Part V we will examine in detail the most common examples of designs with repeated measures, and in Chapter 21 consider computational rules and procedures for the general case. We will find that the computational formulas for the sources of variance due to the experimental factors—i.e., the main effects and interactions—remain unchanged. The only new procedures introduced by repeated measures involve the selection and calculation of the

Numerical examples illustrating arithmetic operations discussed in this section may be found at the end of Part V (pp. 470–474).

appropriate error term for a particular source of variance or comparison. For ease of development, single-factor experiments are considered first, then the multifactor designs, and then the general computational rules. Initially we will assume that the experimental factors are *fixed*; and later we will introduce random independent factors into the discussion.

ADVANTAGES AND DISADVANTAGES OF REPEATED-MEASURES DESIGNS

Advantages

The main advantage of this type of design is the control of subject heterogeneity—i.e., individual differences. Take as an example a single-factor experiment. When independent groups of subjects are present in the different conditions, it is likely that the groups will differ somewhat on any single attribute we wish to measure. These between-group differences, which are the natural outcome of the random assignment of subjects to conditions, will be superimposed over whatever treatment effects we may have been fortunate enough to produce by our experimental manipulations. But suppose we select only *one group* of subjects as opposed to the *a* different groups and have the subjects in this single group serve in all of the treatment conditions. On the face of it, such a procedure seems to guarantee treatment conditions with subjects of identical ability and implies that any differences observed among the treatment conditions reflect the effects of the treatment alone.

A moment's reflection, however, will indicate that this is an oversimplification. For this ideal outcome to result, a subject would have to perform *identically*, when serving in different conditions for which treatment effects were in fact *zero*. Such an expectation is unrealistic, since we do not expect identical scores even when a subject is repeatedly tested in the *same* condition of the experiment. Individuals will respond differently on each test for a whole host of reasons: changes in attention and motivation, learning about the task, and so on. Not only is a subject not the "same" individual on successive tests, but we also expect other uncontrolled sources of variability, such as variations in the physical environment or in the testing apparatus, to show themselves by producing differences between the treatment means. In short, then, the variance attributed to factor *A* will still contain an error component even when the same subjects are tested in all of the treatments.

On the other hand, changes in performance on successive applications of the different experimental treatments will probably *not* be as great as those produced through the random assignment of subjects to the different experimental conditions. The error component associated with factor *A*, therefore, should be *smaller* in the case of repeated measures than that expected in an experiment with independent groups of subjects. This reduction in error variance represents a direct increase in economy. There are also other ways in which the repeated-measures design is economical. The running time per observation, for example, may be cut drastically by the omission of detailed instructions that overlap the different treatment conditions. With animals as subjects, a great deal of time can be saved in the pretraining needed to "prepare" the animals for the experimental treatments.

In addition to an increase in efficiency, the repeated-measures design has become the modal experimental design with which to study such phenomena as learning, transfer, and practice effects of all sorts. In these research areas, the interest is in the changes in performance that result from successive experience with a task. In a learning experiment, for example, the experience consists of repeated exposures of the same learning task—number of trials becomes the independent variable. In a transfer experiment, the interest may be in the development of learning skills through experience with other tasks and materials. In these studies each subject receives each level of the independent variable, which in this case consists of the number of previous trials or tasks. It is not necessary to study learning or transfer with a repeated-measures design; it is possible, for instance, to study the effect of trials or of tasks with independent groups. But to do this, we need a group that is tested after one presentation or on one task, another that is tested after two presentations or on the second task alone, and so on. In the majority of cases such an alternative would be unnecessary and wasteful.[1] It is safe to say, therefore, that the repeated-measures design represents the most economical way of studying the positive and negative effects of practice.

Disadvantages

The main difficulty with the repeated-measures design is the very real possibility of *carry-over effects* from one treatment to another. We do not mean here the consistency in the behavior of a subject from condition to condition stemming from stable factors such as intelligence and past experience outside of the laboratory; instead, we are referring to the possibility that treatments already given to a subject may influence his performance under the treatment which is currently being administered. In the learning and transfer experiments, of course, carry-over effects are the *explicit* object of study. In other experiments, where repeated measures are chosen as an economical alternative to independent groups, carry-over effects present a serious problem, both statistically and behaviorally.

Subjects in our experiments are rarely passive organisms. Instead, they retain from previous experience in the laboratory some "residue," which may be positive or negative. A subject may show a general improvement

---

[1] There are times when the use of independent groups of subjects would serve an important analytical function. We will consider such a situation in the illustration of the computational chores in the single-factor design.

during the course of testing; in this case the carry-over effect is positive. Alternatively, fatigue may build up on the successive tests to produce a negative carry-over effect. In some research areas, we can effectively disregard these major sources of carry-over effects when we have reason to believe that performance has effectively reached an asymptote so that additional practice on the task does not produce any further improvement.[2] For instance, if we are studying sensory functioning or performance on motor tasks which are highly learned, we ordinarily assume that a general practice effect is not present. On the other hand, if fatigue is a major source of carry-over effects, it may be possible to eliminate its influence by introducing a rest of sufficient length between successive tasks.

If we have reason to believe that a carry-over effect is possible, then it is clear that the *current performance* of a subject will reflect in part the effect of the particular treatment being administered as well as any carry-over effect that may be present. If the effect is positive, then the first condition presented to a subject obviously will not benefit from practice, while the last condition will benefit maximally. If we use the same order in administering the treatments to all subjects, we will be unable to disentangle the contribution of the treatment effect from the contribution of the practice effect. In this case, the order of testing and the treatment conditions are confounded.

A common solution to this problem is to employ enough testing orders to ensure the equal occurrence of each experimental treatment at each stage of practice in the experiment. One such procedure is *counterbalancing*, illustrated in the upper portion of Table V-1.[3] In this example, four treatments are represented by the four columns. The different sequences in which the treatments are presented are indicated in the four rows. In the first sequence, for example, the subject receives the treatments in the order 1-2-3-4, while in the other three sequences, subjects receive the orders specified in the table. Each level of factor A is presented *once* as the first, as the second, as the third, and as the fourth task that different subjects receive. The purpose of this arrangement is to balance any effect of prior testing over the four treatment conditions equally. In order to maintain this balancing of treatments and stages of practice, additional subjects must be added in similar blocks of four. An alternative method is to choose testing orders randomly for each subject, relying on chance probabilities to produce a homogeneous representation of treatments and stages of testing.

Let us see how this might work out in practice. Consider the possible outcome of an experiment in the lefthand matrix in the bottom portion of the table. These data reflect scores of four subjects obtained by following the

[2] In order to ensure that all subjects have reached asymptotic performance, researchers frequently administer preliminary training designed to produce a desired stability in performance before the start of the actual experiment.

[3] A type of counterbalancing, in which each condition proceeds and follows all other conditions once, is described by Wagenaar (1969). Such "digram balanced" arrangements are desirable for most research applications. The sequences in Table V-1 exhibit this property.

TABLE V-1   *An Example of Counterbalancing*

A COUNTERBALANCING ARRANGEMENT

Treatments

Sequences	a_1	a_2	a_3	a_4
1	1	2	3	4
2	2	4	1	3
3	3	1	4	2
4	4	3	2	1

TWO HYPOTHETICAL OUTCOMES

Sequences	a_1	a_2	a_3	a_4	Sequences	a_1	a_2	a_3	a_4
1	1	8	13	15	1	2	8	12	12
2	5	12	6	14	2	5	12	8	12
3	8	4	14	11	3	6	4	12	12
4	9	11	10	7	4	10	11	11	11
Sum	23	35	43	47	Sum	23	35	43	47

counterbalancing scheme listed above in the table. The column marginal sums indicate the treatment effects found by collapsing over the four sequences. Suppose we had presented the conditions in only one of these orders, say the fourth sequence. If the scores in this row are any indication, a different outcome of the results would be observed—because the differences between treatments reflect the effects themselves *and* the effects of practice. This is true for the differences observed in any of these sequences. The counterbalancing scheme, however, where all four sequences are included, allows us to spread the practice effect equally over the four conditions.

To see how this occurs, it is convenient to plot the scores as a function of condition and of testing order. This has been done in the upper half of Fig. V-1. (The plotting was accomplished by noting from the upper portion of Table V-1 the order in which a given treatment condition was presented in the different sequences. For example, the treatment at a_2 was presented first in sequence 3, second in sequence 1, third in sequence 4, and fourth in sequence 2.) An inspection of the figure reveals a marked practice effect, but one that is the same for each treatment condition. That is, there is *no interaction* between testing order and treatments. Numerically, the same treatment effects are found at each of the orders of testing.

A very serious problem with counterbalancing may be present whether the balancing is achieved through the use of a systematic arrangement or through randomization. As an illustration, consider the outcome of a second example. These data are presented in the righthand matrix of the table and are plotted in the bottom half of the figure. While the data were arranged to show the

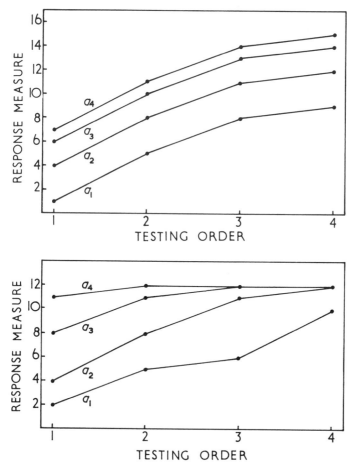

Fig. V-1   Plot of data presented in Table V-1.

same average treatment effects (i.e., the same column marginal sums), it is clear that they are not representative of the effects at the different stages of practice. When the four tasks are given first, the differences among the treatments are at a maximum. In contrast, when the tasks are given last in the sequences, the differences have very nearly disappeared. For whatever the cause, then, there is an *interaction* between testing order and treatments.

Counterbalancing and the random ordering of treatments, when used as methods of neutralizing the effects of practice, assume that the carry-over effect is the *same* for each ordering of the treatments. If there is an interaction, the treatment conditions are subjected to different practice effects. In the second example, the condition at a_1 gains markedly by being administered later in the testing, while the condition at a_4 gains essentially nothing. Just as the interaction of two independent variables complicated our interpretation of the main effects in a factorial experiment, the presence of differential practice effects distorts the picture of the influence of the independent variable in a repeated-measures design.

If the conditions are subject to differential carry-over effects, we are left with the original difficulty inherent with repeated-measures designs: a confounding of practice and treatment effects. We can always check on the possibility of an interaction—*after* the experiment is conducted—by plotting the data as we have in Fig. V-1 and determining whether or not there is an interaction of testing order and treatments. If an interaction is indicated, the only way of extracting unambiguous information concerning the influence of the independent variable is to restrict our attention to the *initial task* given to each subject. Performance at this point is uncontaminated by practice effects. Of course, such an analysis involves a retreat to the comparison of independent groups of subjects, and the researcher loses the advantages of the repeated-measures design. He may also be left with a relatively impoverished experiment —i.e., small numbers of subjects in each experimental condition.

It would be a mistake to conclude that all carry-over effects reflect rather general changes in the condition of the subject. In most situations there will be some amount of improvement (or a loss in performance) that is *nonspecific*, unrelated to the specific conditions represented by the earlier treatments and tasks. All too frequently, however, there will be *specific* carry-over effects. When this is a possibility, a repeated-measures design should not be used. For example, there may be specific positive or negative transfer from one condition to the next owing to an overlap of elements of the two tasks. Specific transfer of a different sort may be found with instructional variables which attempt to effect changes in a subject's perception of a task through the use of different instructions. If a subject is told that performance on a given task is a measure of intelligence, how will he view any future tasks that are presented to him? If a subject is told to learn a set of material by the use of one sort of strategy, will he be able to drop that method and adopt a new one when the conditions are switched? Typically, these sorts of manipulations cannot be counterbalanced. So-called "deception" experiments, in which subjects are led to believe that one thing will happen but are given another set of treatments, work only once. After the first deception, subjects will be suspicious of anything the experimenter tells them (or at least much more suspicious than they were already!). Or, if some of the experimental conditions are frightening or distasteful, how will a subject react when he is told that he will not be given that treatment in a subsequent condition? If he was given an electric shock for making incorrect responses in a task, will he be unaffected by this experience when he is now told that he will *not* be shocked in another condition? If a subject is given an "eventful" or interesting experimental treatment first, how will he perform on less eventful or even boring tasks that are given later in the testing sequence?

The point is that in all of these cases important carry-over effects exist and they are often *asymmetrical*. This means that there will be interactions between conditions and testing orders which call into question the appropriateness of a repeated-measures design in investigating these problems. Unless the carry-over or sequence effects represent the *primary* interest of the investigator, as in learning and transfer studies, the repeated-measures design should be given careful scrutiny before it is chosen for use in the investigation of a given problem.

A final disadvantage of the repeated-measures design is statistical. The statistical model justifying the analyses is highly restrictive in the sense that the basic observations are supposed to exhibit certain mathematical properties. We will consider these assumptions subsequently. For the moment, however, it is sufficient to observe that even when carry-over effects can be shown to be symmetrical and to have caused no distortion of the effects of the independent variable, the data may not fit the assumptions of the model, producing complications in the statistical analyses.

With these cautions in mind, let us consider the single-factor experiment in which subjects serve in each of the experimental conditions.

chapter nineteen

SINGLE-FACTOR DESIGNS

The simplest design in which repeated measures may be used is the single-factor experiment. In this repeated-measures design, *subjects* is treated as a second factor in the experiment. In the case of the one-factor design, both the independent factor (factor A) and subjects (factor S) are completely crossed; that is, each subject receives each of the a treatments. (In the higher-order designs, where two or more experimental factors are manipulated, such an arrangement is not necessary. We will discuss such situations in the next two chapters.)

DESIGN AND NOTATION

The single-factor design and the scores and totals that we will find necessary for the analysis are presented in Table 19-1. It is convenient and accurate to refer to this as an $(A \times S)$ design. The AS matrix has the levels of factor A

TABLE 19-1   *Notational System:* $(A \times S)$ *Design*

Levels of Factor A

Subjects	a_1	a_2	a_3	a_4	Sum
s_1	AS_{11}	AS_{21}	AS_{31}	AS_{41}	S_1
s_2	AS_{12}	AS_{22}	AS_{32}	AS_{42}	S_2
s_3	AS_{13}	AS_{23}	AS_{33}	AS_{43}	S_3
s_4	AS_{14}	AS_{24}	AS_{34}	AS_{44}	S_4
s_5	AS_{15}	AS_{25}	AS_{35}	AS_{45}	S_5
Sum	A_1	A_2	A_3	A_4	T

listed along the columns and the levels of factor S listed along the rows. Within any given row of the AS matrix appear the scores attained by a single subject (s_j) at the different levels of factor A, while in any given column are entered the scores produced by all s subjects at that particular level of factor A (a_i). Thus, each subject provides a different scores or observations in the experiment.

The notational system is identical to the one used for the single-factor experiment with independent groups of subjects. That is, the scores in the AS matrix are symbolized as AS_{ij}, where the subscript i denotes the particular level of factor A and runs from 1 to a, and the subscript j denotes one of the s different subjects (factor S) and runs from 1 to s. The marginal totals needed for the analysis are also presented in the table. It is here that the notation for the $(A \times S)$ design differs from the case with independent groups. Specifically, in addition to the usual column marginal totals, A_i, row marginal totals, S_j, are also calculated. The S_j terms consist of totals for each subject of his scores produced at each of the levels of factor A. Consistent with the previous notational system,

$$S_j = \sum_i^a AS_{ij}.$$

(Such a quantity was not possible in the completely randomized design, because different subjects were represented in each cell of the AS matrix.) The symbol T continues to signify the grand total of all individual AS_{ij} scores.

COMPUTATIONAL FORMULAS

We have already indicated that the $(A \times S)$ design represents a complete crossing of factors A and S. Because of this, the calculations required of this type of design follow those enumerated for the two-way design considered in Chapter 10. The only exception is that there is no within-groups factor in the $(A \times S)$ design. (Since there is only *one* score in each cell of the AS matrix, there can be no within-cell variability.) We will now consider the construction of the computational formulas. Following the procedures described in Chapter 10, we start with a listing of the sources of variance, namely, A, S, and $A \times S$. From these, we can write the df associated with each source and then the computational formulas, remembering that the total number of observations in the experiment is as:

$$df_A = a - 1,$$

$$SS_A = \frac{\sum (A)^2}{\cancel{a}s} - \frac{(T)^2}{as};$$

$$df_S = s - 1,$$

$$SS_S = \frac{\sum (S)^2}{a\cancel{s}} - \frac{(T)^2}{as};$$

$$df_{A \times S} = (a - 1)(s - 1) = as - a - s + 1,$$

$$SS_{A \times S} = \frac{\sum (AS)^2}{\cancel{a}\cancel{s}} - \frac{\sum (A)^2}{\cancel{a}s} - \frac{\sum (S)^2}{a\cancel{s}} + \frac{(T)^2}{as};$$

$$df_T = as - 1,$$

$$SS_T = \frac{\sum (AS)^2}{\cancel{a}\cancel{s}} - \frac{(T)^2}{as}.$$

The computational formulas are rewritten with the canceled letters removed in the second column of Table 19-2. The df associated with each source of variance were used to construct the computational formulas for the sums of squares and are obtained by following the usual rules. The mean squares are constructed by dividing sums of squares by the corresponding df's. The only new operations specified in Table 19-2 is the selection of the error term for the

TABLE 19-2 *Computational Formulas for the $(A \times S)$ Design*

Source	Sum of Squares[a]	df	MS	F[b]
A	$\dfrac{\sum (A)^2}{s} - \dfrac{(T)^2}{as}$	$a - 1$	$\dfrac{SS_A}{df_A}$	$\dfrac{MS_A}{MS_{A \times S}}$
S	$\dfrac{\sum (S)^2}{a} - [T]$	$s - 1$	$\dfrac{SS_S}{df_S}$	
$A \times S$	$\sum (AS)^2 - [A] - [S] + [T]$	$(a - 1)(s - 1)$	$\dfrac{SS_{A \times S}}{df_{A \times S}}$	
Total	$[AS] - [T]$	$as - 1$		

[a] Bracketed letters represent complete terms in the computational formulas; a particular term is identified by the letter(s) appearing in the numerator.
[b] Factor A is fixed.

MS_A. In the table, we have indicated that the interaction mean square $(MS_{A \times S})$ serves this function, but the justification of this choice will require some discussion. First, however, we will work through a numerical example.

NUMERICAL EXAMPLE

The data for this example are drawn from an actual experiment.[1] In this study, subjects learned a list of ten pairs of words on one day and recalled the pairs two days later. Following recall, the subjects learned a second list of pairs, and these were also recalled after a delay of two days. This cycle of learning-recall-learning-recall was continued for a number of lists, but we will consider only the data for the first six. The independent variable was the *ordinal position* of a particular list, i.e., whether the list was first, second, . . . , or sixth in the sequence. The main interest in the experiment was in the recall scores obtained two days following the learning of each of the different lists. It was hypothesized that recall would be best on the very first list and would worsen progressively as laboratory experience increased (i.e., with the other five lists). Such a research problem seems ideally suited for investigation with a repeated-measures design, because in order to produce a score on the sixth list a subject must receive the five other lists first. Why not use this necessity to advantage and have the same subject provide recall scores for all six of the lists learned and recalled successively every other day? A comparable design with independent groups would use six samples of subjects, one providing recall scores on the first list, another providing recall scores on the second list, and so on. This is a wasteful procedure unless there is an analytical reason for resorting to such an arrangement.[2]

There were $s = 8$ subjects in the experiment. Their recall data for the six lists are presented in the upper portion of Table 19-3. We can consider the particular lists that are learned and recalled by different subjects as having been assigned randomly to each subject from a larger pool of lists. Thus, there is no reason to believe that specific lists are confounded with the ordinal position of the lists. An inspection of the recall sums for each of the six lists reveals a dramatic deterioration in performance (from a mean recall of 6.12 correct responses on the first list to a mean recall of 1.62 correct responses on the

---

[1] Keppel, Postman, and Zavortink (1968).

[2] If a researcher were concerned about violations of the statistical assumptions of the repeated-measures design, he might resort to the completely randomized design. As we will see, however, this does not seem necessary. On the other hand, if a researcher wanted to separate learning and recall processes, he might consider a design in which different groups of subjects learned one, two, three, . . . , or six lists every other day, say, but then recalled *only* the *last* list in their particular series. This design, which attacks a slightly different problem, would allow some comment to be made about the effect of prior laboratory *learning* experience on the recall of a particular list that was uncontaminated by prior laboratory experience in *recalling* the previous lists as well. The possibility of investigation of this research question does not preclude the study presented in this example, which *is* most readily investigated with repeated measures.

TABLE 19-3 *Numerical Example: $(A \times S)$ Design*

AS MATRIX

Ordinal Position of the Lists (A)

Subjects (S)	a_1	a_2	a_3	a_4	a_5	a_6	Sum
s_1	7	3	2	2	1	1	16
s_2	4	8	3	8	1	2	26
s_3	7	6	3	1	5	4	26
s_4	8	6	1	0	2	0	17
s_5	7	2	3	0	1	3	16
s_6	6	3	3	1	1	1	15
s_7	4	2	0	0	0	0	6
s_8	6	7	5	1	3	2	24
Sum	49	37	20	13	14	13	146

SUMMARY OF THE ANALYSIS

Source	Calculations[a]	SS	df	MS	F
A	$588.00 - 444.08 =$	143.92	5	28.78	10.32*
S	$498.33 - [T] =$	54.25	7	7.75	
$A \times S$	$740 - [A] - [S] + [T] =$	97.75	35	2.79	
Total	$[AS] - [T] =$	295.92	47		

* $p < .01$.

[a] Bracketed letters represent complete terms in the computational formulas; a particular term is identified by the letter(s) appearing in the numerator.

last list) that tends to level off with the last three lists. The significance of this observation will now be assessed.

The first step in the analysis consists of the calculation of the basic quantities appearing in the computational formulas for the sums of squares. Using the formulas specified in Table 19-2 and the data of Table 19-3, we find

$$[T] = \frac{(T)^2}{as} = \frac{(146)^2}{6(8)} = \frac{21{,}316}{48} = 444.08,$$

$$[A] = \frac{\sum (A)^2}{s} = \frac{(49)^2 + (37)^2 + \cdots + (14)^2 + (13)^2}{8} = \frac{4704}{8} = 588.00,$$

$$[S] = \frac{\sum (S)^2}{a} = \frac{(16)^2 + (26)^2 + \cdots + (6)^2 + (24)^2}{6} = \frac{2990}{6} = 498.33,$$

and

$$[AS] = \sum (AS)^2 = (7)^2 + (4)^2 + \cdots + (0)^2 + (2)^2 = 740.$$

These numbers are entered in the lower portion of Table 19-3, where they are combined in the patterns indicated to produce the appropriate sums of squares. The remainder of the analysis follows directly from the formulas given in Table 19-2 and thus requires no comment. The main effect of factor A is clearly significant.

In the introduction to Part V, we indicated that the repeated-measures design is more sensitive in detecting differences among means than is a companion design with independent groups. We can see how this works out in the context of the present design. We will assume for this illustration that instead of eight different subjects being tested on each of the six lists, we have a sample of 48 subjects, 8 of whom were tested on list 1, 8 on list 2, and so on. With this change of design, the $SS_{S/A}$ will be formed by the usual formula:

$$df_{S/A} = a(s - 1) = as - a,$$

$$SS_{S/A} = \frac{\sum (AS)^2}{as} - \frac{\sum (A)^2}{as}$$

$$= [(7)^2 + (4)^2 + \cdots + (0)^2 + (2)^2] - \frac{(49)^2 + (37)^2 + \cdots + (14)^2 + (13)^2}{8}$$

$$= 740 - 588.00 = 152.00.$$

The df associated with the $SS_{S/A}$ may be obtained by means of the usual formula:

$$df_{S/A} = a(s - 1) = 6(8 - 1) = 42.$$

The $MS_{S/A}$ is obtained by dividing the $SS_{S/A}$ by the relevant df:

$$MS_{S/A} = \frac{152.00}{42} = 3.62,$$

and the resulting F ratio for the main effect of factor A now becomes

$$F = \frac{MS_A}{MS_{S/A}} = \frac{28.78}{3.62} = 7.95.$$

This F is smaller than the one obtained with the repeated-measures analysis, but it is still significant, $p < .01$.

The "sensitivity" that we have been talking about refers to the amount by which this "composite" mean square, $MS_{S/A}$, is reduced by extracting the main effect of *subjects* (factor S) from the sum of squares. A rough index of the relative efficiency of the two designs is given by

$$\text{relative efficiency} = \frac{MS_{S/A}}{MS_{A \times S}} \times 100.$$

In this example,

$$\text{relative efficiency} = \frac{3.62}{2.79} \times 100 = 130 \text{ percent.}$$

A value greater than 100 percent indicates that the repeated-measures design is more efficient than a corresponding design with independent groups. If the value is less than 100 percent, we should question the usefulness and even the *appropriateness* of the repeated-measures design in this situation. Any gain in relative efficiency must also be evaluated against the loss of *df* for the error term, since a larger value of F will be required for the rejection of the null hypothesis.[3]

ASSUMPTIONS

The statistical model underlying the analysis of variance is usually specified by expressing the basic AS_{ij} score as a sum of a number of quantities. (Such statements of the structural model for this and for other designs are found in most advanced statistics texts.) From this basic statement, the expected values of the mean squares normally extracted in the analysis are written in terms of population variance components. The error term for evaluating the main effect of factor A is found by locating a mean square, the expectation of which matches the expected value of the main effect (except for the population treatment component, of course). (This chain of events was described in more detail in Chapter 16.) The critical features of the statistical theory which will be discussed in this section are concerned with the justification of the $MS_{A \times S}$ as the error term for the MS_A and with certain conditions of homogeneity that are assumed for the treatment populations.

Justification of the Error Term

We will begin by noting that it is convenient to think of factor S as a *random factor* in repeated-measures designs.[4] That is, we generally assume that the subjects in the experiment represent a random sample from some population

---

[3] Kirk (1968) offers a general discussion of efficiency (pp. 8–9). He also presents a formula for relative efficiency which corrects for the differences in *df*'s (p. 148). An application of this correction to the numerical example reduces the index from 130 percent to 129 percent.

[4] It is also a random factor in the completely randomized design, but we have not yet had to think of the within-groups factor in these terms. This point will be clarified when we discuss repeated-measures designs where some factors are repeated and others are not.

even though we are unable to specify the population itself with any degree of precision. The importance of this assumption for the analysis involves a consideration of any Treatment × Subject interaction that may be present in the experiment. To be more specific, it will be recalled from the discussion of random factors in Chapter 16 that an interaction of a fixed factor with a random factor will intrude upon the main effect of the *fixed factor* (see pp. 335–338). In the present context, this means that in addition to a variance component reflecting population treatment effects and one reflecting experimental error, the expectation of the MS_A will also include a component reflecting the $A \times S$ interaction effects. However, since the expectation of the $MS_{A \times S}$ includes the interaction and error components, the appropriateness of the F ratio specified in Table 19-2 remains unchanged. That is,

$$E(MS_A) = \text{(treatment effects)} + \text{(interaction effects)} + \text{(error)}$$

and

$$E(MS_{A \times S}) = \text{(interaction effects)} + \text{(error)}.$$

The F ratio formed by dividing the MS_A by the $MS_{A \times S}$ is distributed as $F(df_A, df_{A \times S})$ when the null hypothesis is true and other conditions, which we will consider in a moment, are met.[5]

Homogeneity Assumptions

In our discussion of the analyses with independent groups, we essentially dismissed as unimportant violations of the distribution assumptions of normality and homogeneity of within-group variances. Statisticians agree that the F test is robust and insensitive to such violations with these sorts of designs. The same *cannot* be said, however, for the repeated-measures design. Of critical concern are the assumptions of *homogeneity of within-treatment variances* and *homogeneity of the covariance between pairs of treatment levels*. It is convenient to consider these assumptions and the consequences of failing to meet them in the context of repeated-measures designs in general. This discussion can be found in Chapter 21. For the present, then, we will simply acknowledge that a problem exists and suggest that you refer ahead to this presentation (pp. 462–467).

COMPARISONS INVOLVING THE TREATMENT MEANS

Error Terms for Comparisons

All of the types of comparisons discussed in Part II are available for the repeated-measures design. Moreover, the sums of squares for these comparisons

---

[5] The structural model underlying this analysis is sometimes called the *nonadditive* model, which emphasizes the fact that an $A \times S$ interaction is included. The *additive* model (see Myers, 1966, pp. 153–156), in which the interaction is absent, is not a reasonable model for repeated-measures designs in the behavioral sciences.

are calculated by means of the same computational formulas. There is one important difference, and this again lies in the selection of the error term. We have seen that the mean square used to test the main effect of factor A, $MS_{A \times S}$, is influenced by two components: experimental error and the Treatment × Subject interaction. In our evaluation of the treatment main effect, in which all a treatment means are compared, it makes intuitive sense to use a denominator based on all of the scores in the experiment. But when we consider *individual comparisons*, which do *not* include all of the treatment conditions, this overall interaction mean square may no longer be appropriate. That is, it is likely that the Treatment × Subject interaction is not the same for each comparison conducted and, thus, is not accurately estimated by the overall $MS_{A \times S}$. For this reason, then, it may be desirable to employ as an error term one that specifically includes this *Comparison* × Subject interaction. After all, it is *this* interaction that is presumably reflecting itself in the particular set of treatment means we are considering.

Note that the construction of different error terms for each comparison among treatment means was *not* mentioned in our discussion of designs involving independent groups. There is a good reason for this. In contrast to the case of repeated measures, the error term for a single-factor experiment with independent groups, $MS_{S/A}$, is in reality an average of a independent estimates of population error variance. Thus, any and all comparisons are best evaluated by the most stable estimate of error variance, the $MS_{S/A}$. Interestingly, when the assumption of homogeneous within-treatment variances is *not* upheld, separate error terms are calculated for any analytical comparisons that are conducted. That is, we obtain error terms that are based only on those scores involved in a particular comparison.

We have a problem, however, of finding a way to decide upon the correct course of action. Authors of psychological statistics books are not in agreement on this matter. Both Kirk (1968, pp. 144–145) and Winer (1962, pp. 112–115; 1971, pp. 269–271), for example, recommend the use of the "composite" error term, the $MS_{A \times S}$, in all analytical comparisons except in the analysis of trend components. Myers (1966) is silent on the topic as far as the $(A \times S)$ design is concerned, but recommends the extraction of error terms based upon the specific comparisons of interest for designs with two independent variables (see pp. 340–343 and pp. 365–368).

It is difficult to specify when the $MS_{A \times S}$ is the appropriate error term for analytical comparisons and when it is not. Suppose we consider the implications of choosing as a practical solution separate error terms for *all* cases. If we have a case where the overall error term is in fact appropriate (but we do not know this) and separate error terms are used, there will be no bias, since the overall error term and the separate error terms provide estimates of the same thing: error variance plus interaction effects.[6] On the other hand, if we have

---

[6] There is a loss of power due to the reduction in df for the denominator term of the F ratio.

a situation where the overall error term is *inappropriate*, the need for separate error terms is obvious. On the basis of these arguments, then, the analyses presented in this section will evaluate comparisons with error terms that are calculated from the actual scores responsible for the effects.

Comparisons Between Pairs of Means

A common comparison is one in which pairs of means are contrasted. Either mean may represent one treatment condition or an average of two or more treatments. We will consider two ways by which these comparisons can be conducted. The first, which essentially treats these comparisons as separate "Treatment" × Subject analyses, has the virtue of making explicit the numbers that are producing the sums of squares for the comparison and the error term. The second method, which uses specialized formulas, is general and can be applied to any type of comparison.

"DIRECT" METHOD   As an example of the two methods, we will work with the data presented in Table 19-3. Suppose we are interested in comparing the average recall of the first two lists. For the first method, we construct what amounts to a new AS matrix, but one that captures the comparison of interest. This has been done in the upper portion of Table 19-4: the two levels of factor A (a_1 and a_2) are represented by the columns and the subjects by the rows. The AS_{ij} scores within the body of the matrix come from the appropriate columns of Table 19-3. This new arrangement can be thought of as an ($A_{comp.} \times S$) design, and we will analyze the data with the same formulas as we used in the original analysis.

As in the main analysis, the total sum of squares for this particular AS matrix may be partitioned into three independent components: the $SS_{A_{comp.}}$, the SS_S, and the $SS_{A_{comp.} \times S}$. Applying the formulas of Table 19-2, we have

$$SS_{A_{comp.}} = \frac{(49)^2 + (37)^2}{8} - \frac{(86)^2}{2(8)},$$

$$SS_S = \frac{(10)^2 + (12)^2 + \cdots + (6)^2 + (13)^2}{2} - \frac{(86)^2}{2(8)},$$

$$SS_{A_{comp.} \times S} = [(7)^2 + (4)^2 + \cdots + (2)^2 + (7)^2] - \frac{(49)^2 + (37)^2}{8}$$
$$- \frac{(10)^2 + (12)^2 + \cdots + (6)^2 + (13)^2}{2} + \frac{(86)^2}{2(8)},$$

and

$$SS_T = [(7)^2 + (4)^2 + \cdots + (2)^2 + (7)^2] - \frac{(86)^2}{2(8)}.$$

The calculations are completed in the lower portion of Table 19-4.

TABLE 19-4 *Numerical Example: Comparison Between Two Means, Standard Formulas*

AS MATRIX

Subjects	a_1	a_2	Sum
s_1	7	3	10
s_2	4	8	12
s_3	7	6	13
s_4	8	6	14
s_5	7	2	9
s_6	6	3	9
s_7	4	2	6
s_8	6	7	13
Sum	49	37	86

SUMMARY OF THE ANALYSIS

Source	Calculations[a]	SS	df	MS	F
A[b]	$471.25 - 462.25 =$	9.00	1	9.00	2.17*
S	$488.00 - [T] =$	25.75	7	3.68	
$A \times S$	$526 - [A] - [S] + [T] =$	29.00	7	4.14	
Total	$[AS] - [T] =$	63.75	15		

[a] Bracketed letters represent complete terms in the computational formulas; a particular term is identified by the letter(s) appearing in the numerator.
[b] A refers to $A_{\text{comp.}}$ in this example.
* $p > .10$.

The remainder of the analysis is straightforward. The "main effect," the $MS_{A_{\text{comp.}}}$, is tested against the interaction mean square. The resulting F is not significant.[7] If we felt that it was appropriate to use the error term from the overall analysis, the $MS_{A \times S}$, we would form the ratio

$$F = \frac{MS_{A_{\text{comp.}}}}{MS_{A \times S}} = \frac{9.00}{2.79} = 3.23.$$

Even with the smaller denominator ($MS_{A \times S} = 2.79$ and $MS_{A_{\text{comp.}} \times S} = 4.14$) and the increased df in the denominator ($df_{A \times S} = 35$ and $df_{A_{\text{comp.}} \times S} = 7$), the conclusion remains unchanged—i.e., the null hypothesis is not rejected.

[7] A simplified computational formula is available for comparisons involving the difference between two means. We start with the same modified AS matrix, but obtain *difference scores* produced by subtracting a subject's score at one of the levels from his score at the other level. If we let D_j represent these difference scores (i.e., $D_j = AS_{ij} - AS_{i'j}$), then the F may be calculated directly from the following formula:

$$F = \frac{(s - 1)(\sum D)^2}{s(\sum D^2) - (\sum D)^2}.$$

A numerical illustration of the use of this formula is offered in Exercise 3 for Part V (p. 471).

METHOD OF WEIGHTED SUMS   The alternative analysis uses sums, weighted by coefficients, to extract the relevant sums of squares. The $SS_{A_{comp.}}$ is obtained directly by applying the basic formula for comparisons between pairs of means with which we have been operating since Chapter 6. Specifically,

$$SS_{A_{comp.}} = \frac{(\text{sum of weighted totals})^2}{(\text{no. of observations})(\text{sum of squared coefficients})} \quad (19\text{-}1)$$

$$= \frac{[\sum (c_i)(A_i)]^2}{s[\sum (c_i)^2]}, \quad (19\text{-}2)$$

where the c_i terms are the coefficients required of the comparisons. In the present example, the contrast between list 1 and list 2 may be represented as:

Lists:	1	2	3	4	5	6
c_i:	1	-1	0	0	0	0

If we were dealing with independent groups of subjects, all we would have to do would be to substitute these coefficients and the respective sums in Eq. (19-2), complete the indicated operations, compute the $MS_{A_{comp.}}$, and divide by the $MS_{S/A}$. Any and all comparisons would be evaluated against this single error term. As we indicated earlier, specialized error terms are computed for each comparison made between means obtained from the same set of subjects. We will use the rules outlined in Chapter 15 (pp. 321–325) to construct the computational formula for the $SS_{A_{comp.} \times S}$. Starting with the df statement,

$$df_{A_{comp.} \times S} = a'(s - 1) = a's - a',$$

where a' stands for the 1 df associated with the $A_{comp.}$. From the expanded df statement, we can construct the computational formula:

$$SS_{A_{comp.} \times S} = AS - A$$

$$= \left[\sum_i^a (c_i)(AS_{ij}) \right]^2 - \left[\sum_i^a (c_i)(A_i) \right]^2$$

$$= \frac{\sum_j^s \left[\sum_i^a (c_i)(AS_{ij}) \right]^2}{as[\sum (c_i)^2]} - \frac{\left[\sum_i^a (c_i)(A_i) \right]^2}{as[\sum (c_i)^2]}.$$

Finally, rewriting this last expression,

$$SS_{A_{comp.} \times S} = \frac{\sum_j^s \left[\sum_i^a (c_i)(AS_{ij}) \right]^2}{\sum (c_i)^2} - \frac{\left[\sum_i^a (c_i)(A_i) \right]^2}{s[\sum (c_i)^2]}. \quad (19\text{-}3)$$

The quantity represented by the first term on the right of Eq. (19-3) represents the results of applying the same set of coefficients to the scores for *each individual subject*, squaring these weighted sums, and dividing by the sum of the squared coefficients. The other summation sign, $\sum_j^s$, indicates that we combine these scores across the s subjects. The variation represented by this term consists of (1) the "main effect" of the comparison and (2) unique differences that are not accounted for by the main effect. Since it is the second component of variance that we want for our error term, we must subtract the first component, the $SS_{A_{comp.}}$. This is what we do in carrying out the operations specified in Eq. (19-3).

The data from Table 19-3 have been reproduced in Table 19-5 for this analysis. The coefficients defining the comparison are listed at the top of the table, with the recall scores for individual subjects given below the coefficients. Also included are the sums for each list. As our first step, we will calculate the sum of squares for the comparison itself. Substituting in Eq. (19-2), we have

$$SS_{A_{comp.}} = \frac{[(1)(49) + (-1)(37) + (0)(20) + (0)(13) + (0)(14) + (0)(13)]^2}{8[(1)^2 + (-1)^2 + (0)^2 + (0)^2 + (0)^2]}$$

$$= \frac{(12)^2}{8(2)} = \frac{144}{16} = 9.00.$$

TABLE 19-5 *Numerical Example: Comparison Between Two Means: Specialized Formulas*

AS MATRIX AND COEFFICIENTS

	a_1	a_2	a_3	a_4	a_5	a_6	
c_i:	1	−1	0	0	0	0	
Subjects							$\sum_i^a (c_i)(AS_{ij})$
s_1	7	3	2	2	1	1	4
s_2	4	8	3	8	1	2	−4
s_3	7	6	3	1	5	4	1
s_4	8	6	1	0	2	0	2
s_5	7	2	3	0	1	3	5
s_6	6	3	3	1	1	1	3
s_7	4	2	0	0	0	0	2
s_8	6	7	5	1	3	2	−1
Sum	49	37	20	13	14	13	12

SUMMARY OF THE ANALYSIS

Source	SS	df	MS	F
$A_{comp.}$	9.00	1	9.00	2.17*
$A_{comp.} \times S$	29.00	7	4.14	

* $p > .10$.

The result of these arithmetical operations is entered in the lower half of Table 19-5. The next step is to obtain the sum of squares for the error term. The quantities that we need are specified in Eq. (19-3). First, we must obtain the sum of the weighted recall scores for each of the subjects. For the second subject (s_2), for example,

$$\sum (c_i)(AS_{i2}) = (1)(4) + (-1)(8) + (0)(3) + (0)(8) + (0)(1) + (0)(2).$$

The result of this operation (-4) is given in the final column of the table. Sums for the remaining subjects are also listed in this column. A useful computational check is available at this point: the sum of these eight weighted totals must equal the sum of the cross-products obtained with the column (i.e., list) sums. Specifically,

$$\sum_{j}^{s} \left[\sum_{i}^{a} (c_i)(AS_{ij}) \right] = (4) + (-4) + \cdots + (2) + (-1) = 12$$

and

$$\sum_{i}^{a} (c_i)(A_i) = (1)(49) + (-1)(37) + \cdots + (0)(14) + (0)(13) = 12.$$

While it may not be apparent in this relatively simple example, it is quite easy to make computational errors in these calculations. This check will catch nearly all of them.

Now that we have the weighted sums for each of the eight subjects, we can complete Eq. (19-3).

$$SS_{A_{comp.} \times S} = \frac{(4)^2 + (-4)^2 + \cdots + (2)^2 + (-1)^2}{2} - \frac{(12)^2}{8(2)}$$

$$= \frac{76}{2} - \frac{144}{16} = 38.00 - 9.00 = 29.00.$$

This sum of squares is also listed in the summary table. If we compare the two sums of squares we have just calculated with those given in Table 19-4, we can see that the results are identical. The remainder of the analysis is obvious.

All other comparisons involving pairs of means are computed in the same fashion. Orthogonal comparisons are verified in the usual way (see pp. 105–106). We will now consider the application of a specialized set of coefficients to these data—namely, the extraction of orthogonal trend components.

Analysis of Trend

Most learning experiments are conducted with repeated-measures designs, and an analysis of trend is quite a common undertaking by researchers in this area. As discussed originally (Chapter 7, pp. 113–132), the method of orthogonal polynomials is a useful procedure by which independent components of trend may be isolated and tested for significance. A trend analysis may be conducted on any set of means; the only requirement is that the levels of the independent variable are drawn from a measured dimension. The analysis allows us to partition the sum of squares for the main effect, factor A, into $a - 1$ orthogonal components, each representing a different component of trend.

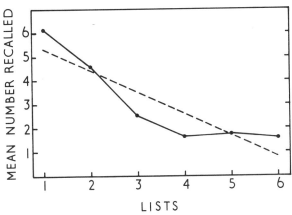

Fig. 19-1   Plot of data presented in Table 19-3 (solid line) and the best-fitting linear function describing these data points (dashed line).

The means for the numerical example we have been considering are plotted in Fig. 19-1. If we were to attempt to fit these data with a simple mathematical function, we would probably choose a straight line—i.e., the linear component of the orthogonal polynomial. This idealized function is superimposed upon the actual recall data in the figure. It is obvious, however, that the linear function does not fully describe the functional relationship reflected in the means. Recall drops on successive lists, but the magnitude of the drop decreases with the later lists. This observation suggests the presence of a *quadratic* component. It is clear that a "pure" quadratic function would not fit the data very well at all. On the other hand, a function combining the linear and the quadratic components would fare better than either one singly. We could continue adding higher-order components, and the composite "fit" would improve. It was argued in Chapter 7 that we are generally not interested in the actual fitting of a function to the data, however, but rather in the "capture" of basic, lower-level trends. Except in rare cases, higher-order trends are too complicated to interpret meaningfully. Thus, researchers usually extract only the lower-level components in the analyses they report. In our example, we will compute all five components in order to illustrate the calculations and to demonstrate the additive property of a complete set of orthogonal comparisons.

TABLE 19-6 *Numerical Example: Analysis of Trend*

ORTHOGONAL POLYNOMIAL COEFFICIENTS

Component	a_1	a_2	a_3	a_4	a_5	a_6	$\sum (c_i)^2$
Linear	−5	−3	−1	1	3	5	70
Quadratic	5	−1	−4	−4	−1	5	84
Cubic	−5	7	4	−4	−7	5	180
Quartic	1	−3	2	2	−3	1	28
Quintic	−1	5	−10	10	−5	1	252

AS MATRIX AND SUMS OF WEIGHTED RECALL SCORES

Subjects	a_1	a_2	a_3	a_4	a_5	a_6	Linear	Quadratic	Cubic	Quartic	Quintic
s_1	7	3	2	2	1	1	−36	20	−16	4	4
s_2	4	8	3	8	1	2	−26	−23	19	1	83
s_3	7	6	3	1	5	4	−20	28	0	−14	−18
s_4	8	6	1	0	2	0	−53	28	−8	−14	2
s_5	7	2	3	0	1	3	−26	35	−1	7	−29
s_6	6	3	3	1	1	1	−33	15	−3	3	−15
s_7	4	2	0	0	0	0	−26	18	−6	−2	6
s_8	6	7	5	1	3	2	−36	6	24	−10	−24
Sum	49	37	20	13	14	13	−256	127	9	−25	9

The values necessary to conduct a trend analysis of the recall data in our continuing example are presented in Table 19-6. Listed at the top of the table are the five sets of coefficients obtained from Table C-2 of Appendix C. Below the coefficients and on the left, the AS matrix containing the recall scores for the eight subjects on the six successive lists is presented again. The basic formulas for the analysis are specified by Eqs. (19-2) and (19-3). We need sums of the recall scores for individual subjects, weighted by the corresponding coefficients, and the sum of corresponding weighted list totals. The table is arranged to facilitate the calculation of these quantities.

As an example of the calculations for individual subjects, consider the third subject. For the numerator of the first term in Eq. (19-3), we need the quantity $\sum (c_i)(AS_{i3})$. Thus, the sum of the recall scores weighted by the linear coefficients is

$$(-5)(7) + (-3)(6) + (-1)(3) + (1)(1) + (3)(5) + (5)(4),$$

and by the quintic coefficients is

$$(-1)(7) + (5)(6) + (-10)(3) + (10)(1) + (-5)(5) + (1)(4).$$

The results of these calculations, −20 and −18, respectively, are recorded in the appropriate columns to the right of the AS matrix. The weighted sums for all components and subjects are obtained in the same manner. (Ordinarily, it is preferable to calculate the sums for a single *component* at a time, since it helps to avoid errors of computation.)

For the numerator in the second term of Eq. (19-3) and for Eq. (19-2), we need sums involving the list totals, i.e., $\sum (c_i)(A_i)$. To illustrate, the weighted sums found by applying the quadratic and cubic coefficients to the list totals are

$$(5)(49) + (-1)(37) + (-4)(20) + (-4)(13) + (-1)(14) + (5)(13)$$

and

$$(-5)(49) + (7)(37) + (4)(20) + (-4)(13) + (-7)(14) + (5)(13),$$

respectively. These weighted sums are listed in the corresponding columns of Table 19-6.

A useful computational check at this point is to verify for each component that the values calculated for the individual subjects sum to the value calculated on the list totals. That is,

linear: $(-36) + (-26) + \cdots + (-26) + (-36) = -256,$

quadratic: $(20) + (-23) + \cdots + (18) + (6) = 127,$

cubic: $(-16) + (19) + \cdots + (-6) + (24) = 9,$

quartic: $(4) + (1) + \cdots + (-2) + (-10) = -25,$

quintic: $(4) + (83) + \cdots + (6) + (-24) = 9.$

With a large number of identical numbers and changing signs, it is not rare to make an error of multiplication or of algebraic summation. Thus, the check is important.

The next step is to calculate the actual sums of squares associated with each orthogonal component. We will work on the partitioning of the SS_A first. Substituting in Eq. (19-2),

$$SS_{A_{comp.}} = \frac{[\sum (c_i)(A_i)]^2}{s[\sum (c_i)^2]},$$

we have

$$SS_{A_{linear}} = \frac{(-256)^2}{8(70)}, \quad SS_{A_{quadratic}} = \frac{(127)^2}{8(84)}, \quad SS_{A_{cubic}} = \frac{(9)^2}{8(180)},$$

$$SS_{A_{quartic}} = \frac{(-25)^2}{8(28)}, \quad \text{and} \quad SS_{A_{quintic}} = \frac{(9)^2}{8(252)}.$$

The results of these calculations are entered in an analysis summary table (Table 19-7). Note that the component sums of squares sum to the SS_A;

that is,

$$SS_{A_{\text{linear}}} + SS_{A_{\text{quadratic}}} + SS_{A_{\text{cubic}}} + SS_{A_{\text{quartic}}} + SS_{A_{\text{quintic}}}$$
$$= 117.03 + 24.00 + .06 + 2.79 + .04 = 143.92.$$

Our next task is to obtain the error terms $(MS_{A_{\text{comp.}} \times S})$ for each of the trend components.[8] We find the sums of squares by using Eq. (19-3), which asks us to sum the individual squared deviation scores of trend for each subject and to subtract the overall trend effect. More specifically,

$$SS_{A_{\text{comp.}} \times S} = \frac{\sum\limits_{j}^{s}\left[\sum\limits_{i}^{a}(c_i)(AS_{ij})\right]^2}{\sum(c_i)^2} - \frac{\left[\sum\limits_{i}^{a}(c_i)(A_i)\right]^2}{s\left[\sum(c_i)^2\right]}$$

and

$$SS_{A_{\text{linear}} \times S} = \frac{(-36)^2 + (-26)^2 + \cdots + (-26)^2 + (-36)^2}{70} - \frac{(-256)^2}{8(70)},$$

$$SS_{A_{\text{quadratic}} \times S} = \frac{(20)^2 + (-23)^2 + \cdots + (18)^2 + (6)^2}{84} - \frac{(127)^2}{8(84)},$$

$$SS_{A_{\text{cubic}} \times S} = \frac{(-16)^2 + (19)^2 + \cdots + (-6)^2 + (24)^2}{180} - \frac{(9)^2}{8(180)},$$

$$SS_{A_{\text{quartic}} \times S} = \frac{(4)^2 + (1)^2 + \cdots + (-2)^2 + (-10)^2}{28} - \frac{(-25)^2}{8(28)},$$

and

$$SS_{A_{\text{quintic}} \times S} = \frac{(4)^2 + (83)^2 + \cdots + (6)^2 + (-24)^2}{252} - \frac{(9)^2}{8(252)}.$$

The results of the arithmetical operations are summarized in Table 19-7. Except for rounding error, the sum of the orthogonal trend components equals the $SS_{A \times S}$. That is,

$$\sum SS_{A_{\text{comp.}} \times S} = 10.37 + 27.27 + 7.18 + 17.60 + 35.32 = 97.74,$$

and, from Table 19-3,

$$SS_{A \times S} = 97.75.$$

[8] The analysis illustrated here follows the recommendation of Grant (1956, p. 153) and is consistent with the analysis used to extract orthogonal trend components in more complicated designs. Winer (1962, pp. 132–135; 1971, pp. 296–300) and Kirk (1968, p. 145) suggest an alternative method for computing separate error terms, but they also indicate that there is a negative bias in the F test when this procedure is used. They give no explanation of the inconsistency between this method and the one they offer for the analysis of trend when additional independent variables are represented by independent groups of subjects.

TABLE 19-7 *Summary of the Analysis of Trend*

Source	SS	df	MS	F
Lists (A)	(143.92)	(5)		
Linear	117.03	1	117.03	79.07**
Quadratic	24.00	1	24.00	6.15*
Cubic	.06	1	.06	<1
Quartic	2.79	1	2.79	1.11
Quintic	.04	1	.04	<1
Subjects (S)	54.25	7	7.75	
A × S	(97.75)	(35)		
Linear	10.37	7	1.48	
Quadratic	27.27	7	3.90	
Cubic	7.18	7	1.03	
Quartic	17.60	7	2.51	
Quintic	35.32	7	5.05	
Total	295.92	47		

* $p < .05$.
** $p < .01$.

For each trend component, $df = 1$, while for the interaction component,

$$df_{A_{\text{comp.}} \times S} = (df_{A_{\text{comp.}}})(df_S) = 1(s - 1) = 7.$$

The F ratios are formed by dividing the component mean square for Lists by the corresponding interaction of Component and Subjects. For the linear and quadratic comparisons, for example,

$$F = \frac{MS_{A_{\text{linear}}}}{MS_{A_{\text{linear}} \times S}} = \frac{117.03}{1.48} = 79.07$$

and

$$F = \frac{MS_{A_{\text{quadratic}}}}{MS_{A_{\text{quadratic}} \times S}} = \frac{24.00}{3.90} = 6.15.$$

These two are the only components that reach an acceptable level of significance.[9] These two components result in the following ratio:

$$\frac{SS_{A_{\text{linear}}} + SS_{A_{\text{quadratic}}}}{SS_A} = \frac{117.03 + 24.00}{143.92} = \frac{141.03}{143.92}$$

$$= .98$$

and account for $.98 \times 100 = 98$ percent of the main effect of factor A (lists).

---

[9] These conclusions remain unchanged if the overall error term from the original analysis, $MS_{A \times S} = 2.79$, is used to evaluate the significance of the component sources of variance.

A final comment concerns the relative magnitudes of the five different error terms. We have argued that separate error terms are justified because of the possibility of different interactions between the comparison involved and subjects. This point is emphasized in the present example, where the ratio of the largest to the smallest mean square is nearly 5.

Multiple Comparisons

It is highly unlikely, in this example, that we would consider making all possible comparisons between pairs of lists, since the independent factor (ordinal position of the lists) represents a manipulation along a continuum of sorts. But at times, certainly, we will want to "protect" ourselves in making the multiple comparisons usually found when a qualitative independent variable has been manipulated. The formulas for the critical ranges are easily adapted to the case of repeated measures. From the logic of the earlier discussions in this chapter, we should expect to calculate a separate error term for each comparison we undertake.

In our previous discussions of multiple comparisons, we presented formulas that were written in terms of critical ranges. For the Newman-Keuls test, the critical range $(CR_{\text{N-K}})$ was given by

$$CR_{\text{N-K}} = q(r, df_{S/A})\sqrt{s(MS_{S/A})},$$

where q represents an entry in Table C-3 of Appendix C, r is the number of steps between ordered groups, and $MS_{S/A}$ is the within-groups error term. In Chapter 8 we conducted the Newman-Keuls test by calculating a critical range for each possible value of r and then comparing in a systematic fashion the obtained differences between groups with the appropriate critical ranges. This was an efficient procedure, since the $MS_{S/A}$ appeared in all of the calculations. In the $(A \times S)$ design, however, there will be a different error term for each of these comparisons. More specifically,

$$CR_{\text{N-K}} = q(r, df_{A' \times S})\sqrt{s(MS_{A' \times S})},$$

where $MS_{A' \times S}$ signifies the error term corresponding to the particular pair of groups being contrasted.[10] Instead of using this type of formula, it is actually easier to calculate the F for the comparison and to compare this value with an

---

[10] We have considered the arguments for the use of individualized error terms when evaluating comparisons with repeated measures (pp. 408–410). When we follow this strategy with *planned comparisons*, we use the $MS_{A_{\text{comp.}} \times S}$ as the error term and evaluate the resultant F with $df_{\text{denom.}} = df_{A_{\text{comp.}} \times S}$. A problem arises, however, when we attempt to apply the various corrections designed to control the experimentwise error rate. Specifically, there is the additional question as to the appropriate denominator df for the specialized statistics used with these techniques, e.g., the Studentized Range Statistic (q) and the Scheffé correction for the F test (F_S). Should we use the df associated with the individualized error term or with the overall error term? I have not been able to find a treatment of this subject in the psychological literature. The most conservative approach is to use the smaller number of df, which is, of course, the number of df associated with the separate

F that has been adjusted by the amount specified by the Newman-Keuls test. This critical value of F is given by

$$F_{\text{N-K}} = \frac{[q(r, df_{A' \times S})]^2}{2}.$$
(19-4)

That is, we square the appropriate value of q found in Table C-3 and divide by 2. The formulas for the other tests have a similar form:

$$F_{\text{D}} = \frac{[q'(r, df_{A' \times S})]^2}{2}$$
(19-5)

and

$$F_{\text{T}} = \frac{[q(r_{\max}, df_{A' \times S})]^2}{2}.$$
(19-6)

The formula for the Scheffé test is applicable for *any* comparison between two means, two-group comparisons as well as contrasts between combinations of groups. The critical value of F for the Scheffé test is found by

$$F_{\text{S}} = (a - 1)F(a - 1, df_{A' \times S}).$$
(19-7)

The detailed procedures involved in conducting these various multiple comparisons are outlined in Chapter 8 (pp. 140–147).

error term. Assuming that once a researcher has decided to control the experimentwise error rate, he will probably elect to take the conservative approach, I have written the formulas reflecting this decision. If the use of the overall error term is justified, the overall error term ($MS_{A \times S}$) and the appropriate df are substituted in the relevant formulas. In any case, you should seek the help of a professional statistician if you require a more definitive recommendation.

chapter twenty

TWO-FACTOR DESIGNS

When two independent variables are combined factorially, two types of repeated-measures designs are possible. Either the design may be *completely repeated*, with all subjects serving in all *ab* treatment combinations, or it may involve repeated measures for one factor and independent measures (i.e., groups) for the other. This latter design is frequently referred to as *mixed*.[1] That is, there are sources of variance that are produced by between-subject differences (independent groups) and by within-subject differences (repeated measures). We will distinguish between the two designs by placing the *repeated factor* (or factors) within a parenthesis. Thus, the completely repeated case will be designated as the $(A \times B \times S)$ design and the mixed case as the $A \times (B \times S)$ design. The factor within the parenthesis, B, involves the repeated measures. To round out the picture, the completely randomized two-factor design is

---

[1] Statisticians also use the term "split plot" which is descriptive of the early agricultural experiments using this sort of design.

TABLE 20-1   *Comparison of Two-Factor Designs*

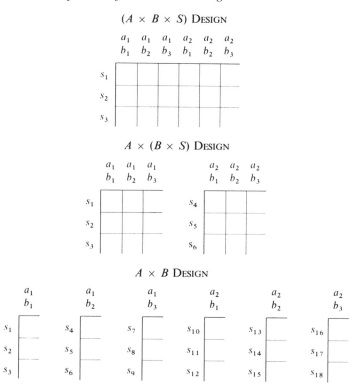

designated as usual without the parenthesis and without the specification of factor S, i.e., $A \times B$.

The distinction between the three types of designs may be readily seen in Table 20-1. For this display, the same 2×3 factorial, each containing a total of $abs = 18$ observations, is represented in the table. The upper display indicates that each of $s = 3$ subjects serves in all six of the treatment combinations. The middle display depicts the $A \times (B \times S)$ design. Here the same six treatment combinations are present, but any given subject serves in only three of them. Moreover, the particular set of three is explicitly specified, namely, that the same set of subjects (s_1, s_2, and s_3) serves in all three levels of factor B, but only in combination with the a_1 level of factor A, while a different set of subjects (s_4, s_5, and s_6) receives the three levels of factor B in combination with the a_2 level of factor A. It should be evident that factor S is a *nested factor* in the mixed design; i.e., factor S is nested within the different levels of factor A. In contrast, factor S is a *crossed factor* in the $(A \times B \times S)$ design, with the same set of subjects being represented at all levels of factors A and B. In the bottom panel of Table 20-1, the $A \times B$ design is depicted. In this case there are $s = 3$ *different* subjects in each of the six treatment combinations; no subject serves in more than one condition of the experiment. With this design, factor S is nested within the conditions produced by crossing factors A and B.

We will now consider the analysis of the two repeated-measures designs. The $(A \times B \times S)$ design will be presented first, since it introduces no new concepts. The $A \times (B \times S)$ design forces us to deal with nested factors and so it needs considerable exposition. It is important to understand the logic of the $A \times (B \times S)$ design, because it is a common design in the behavioral sciences and because the more complicated designs we will encounter in Chapter 21 are based upon this simplest representative of designs in which repeated and nonrepeated factors are mixed.

THE $(A \times B \times S)$ DESIGN

Notation

We saw that the $(A \times S)$ design was analyzed as a two-way factorial; similarly, the $(A \times B \times S)$ design will be treated as a three-way factorial. Thus, from our knowledge of the three-way design, we would expect to be able to extract sources of variance for three main effects (A, B, and S), three

TABLE 20-2   *Notational System:* $(A \times B \times S)$ *Design*

ABS MATRIX

Subject	a_1			a_2		
	b_1	b_2	b_3	b_1	b_2	b_3
s_1	ABS_{111}	ABS_{121}	ABS_{131}	ABS_{211}	ABS_{221}	ABS_{231}
s_2	ABS_{112}	ABS_{122}	ABS_{132}	ABS_{212}	ABS_{222}	ABS_{232}
s_3	ABS_{113}	ABS_{123}	ABS_{133}	ABS_{213}	ABS_{223}	ABS_{233}

AS MATRIX

	a_1	a_2	Sum
s_1	AS_{11}	AS_{21}	S_1
s_2	AS_{12}	AS_{22}	S_2
s_3	AS_{13}	AS_{23}	S_3
Sum	A_1	A_2	T

BS MATRIX

	b_1	b_2	b_3	Sum
s_1	BS_{11}	BS_{21}	BS_{31}	S_1
s_2	BS_{12}	BS_{22}	BS_{32}	S_2
s_3	BS_{13}	BS_{23}	BS_{33}	S_3
Sum	B_1	B_2	B_3	T

AB MATRIX

	b_1	b_2	b_3	Sum
a_1	AB_{11}	AB_{12}	AB_{13}	A_1
a_2	AB_{21}	AB_{22}	AB_{23}	A_2
Sum	B_1	B_2	B_3	T

two-way interactions ($A \times B$, $A \times S$, and $B \times S$), and the $A \times B \times S$ inter-action. The design and notational system are indicated in Table 20-2. The ABS matrix enumerates the basic scores obtained in the experiment. The two-way matrices provide a convenient way of obtaining all of the sums needed for the analysis. Consistent with the notation we have been using, a letter dropped from a designation signifies that a summation has occurred across that particular classification. That is, an AB_{ij} sum collapses across the scores for the s subjects, an AS_{ik} sum collapses across the b scores for each subject, and a BS_{jk} sum collapses across the a scores for each subject. For sums denoted by a single letter, we collapse across two levels of classification. An A_i sum, for example, collapses across both the j and k classifications.

Computational Formulas

SUMS OF SQUARES   The computational formulas needed for the analysis of this design are presented in Table 20-3. As we have noted already, the formulas for the sums of squares follow exactly those specified for the $A \times B \times C$ design if we substitute factor S for factor C and thus require no comment. (The only exception is the obvious absence of the within-groups factor, $SS_{S/ABC}$.) It will be noted that the sums of squares have *not* been arranged in a simple

TABLE 20-3   *Computational Formulas:* $(A \times B \times S)$ *Design*

Source	Computational Formula[a]	df	MS	F[b]
A	$\dfrac{\sum (A)^2}{bs} - \dfrac{(T)^2}{abs}$	$a - 1$	$\dfrac{SS_A}{df_A}$	$\dfrac{MS_A}{MS_{A \times S}}$
S	$\dfrac{\sum (S)^2}{ab} - [T]$	$s - 1$	$\dfrac{SS_S}{df_S}$	
$A \times S$	$\dfrac{\sum (AS)^2}{b} - [A] - [S] + [T]$	$(a - 1)(s - 1)$	$\dfrac{SS_{A \times S}}{df_{A \times S}}$	
B	$\dfrac{\sum (B)^2}{as} - [T]$	$b - 1$	$\dfrac{SS_B}{df_B}$	$\dfrac{MS_B}{MS_{B \times S}}$
$B \times S$	$\dfrac{\sum (BS)^2}{a} - [B] - [S] + [T]$	$(b - 1)(s - 1)$	$\dfrac{SS_{B \times S}}{df_{B \times S}}$	
$A \times B$	$\dfrac{\sum (AB)^2}{s} - [A] - [B] + [T]$	$(a - 1)(b - 1)$	$\dfrac{SS_{A \times B}}{df_{A \times B}}$	$\dfrac{MS_{A \times B}}{MS_{A \times B \times S}}$
$A \times B \times S$	$\sum (ABS)^2 - [AB] - [AS] - [BS]$ $+ [A] + [B] + [S] - [T]$	$(a - 1)(b - 1)$ $(s - 1)$	$\dfrac{SS_{A \times B \times S}}{df_{A \times B \times S}}$	
Total	$[ABS] - [T]$	$abs - 1$		

[a] Bracketed letters represent complete terms in the computational formulas; a particular term is identified by the letter(s) appearing in the numerator.
[b] Factors A and B are fixed.

ascending order from main effects to the higher-order interactions as we have done in the past. This deviation from the previous listings is to emphasize the error terms for the evaluation of the critical mean squares. It is intended that the analysis will be accomplished in the ordinal arrangement specified in the table.

ERROR TERMS[2]   In addition to the correspondence of the formulas for the sums of squares in the $(A \times B \times S)$ design to those in the $A \times B \times C$ design, the df and the mean squares are obtained in the usual manner. The main difference in the analysis is the selection of the appropriate error terms for the assessment of the main effects of factors A and B and their interaction. In the discussion of the $(A \times S)$ design, it was argued that we usually suspect the presence of a Treatment $\times$ Subject interaction in most behavioral studies. Since factor S is a random factor, this meant that the MS_A contained the interaction and error variance, in addition to any treatment effects. This posed no problem for the evaluation of the significance of factor A, since the interaction mean square $(MS_{A \times S})$ contained the interaction and error variance.

The same argument applies to the present situation. Consider the AS matrix in Table 20-2. This matrix displays the results of what may be viewed as an $(A \times S)$ experiment. The main effect of factor A contains a Treatment $\times$ Subject interaction, error variance, and a treatment effect. In this case, the error term is the $MS_{A \times S}$, because it reflects the interaction and error variance. Similarly, the BS matrix enumerates a $(B \times S)$ experiment. By the same argument offered for SS_A in the $(A \times S)$ design, the main effect of factor B contains a Treatment $\times$ Subject interaction, error variance, and treatment effects. The interaction in this case, however, is one involving the BS matrix. Thus, the appropriate error term for the MS_B is the $MS_{B \times S}$, which is assumed to reflect the relevant interaction and error variance. Finally, we have the $MS_{A \times B}$, which can also be thought to contain three components, a possible $A \times B$ interaction, an $A \times B \times$ Subjects interaction, and error variance. The mean square for the $A \times B \times S$ interaction contains the last two components $(A \times B \times$ Subjects interaction and error variance) and, thus, is an appropriate error term with which to test the significance of the $A \times B$ interaction.

In short, *we test the significance of any effect with a mean square that involves the interaction of that effect with factor S.* In the $(A \times B \times S)$ design, we test the MS_A with the $MS_{A \times S}$, the MS_B with the $MS_{B \times S}$, and the $MS_{A \times B}$ with the $MS_{A \times B \times S}$.

Suppose we consider the selection of the appropriate error terms in another way. In Chapter 16 we worked through a procedure by which we could select the correct error term when random independent variables were present in a completely randomized design. In the next chapter we will consider a similar procedure that is adapted for repeated-measures designs. For the time being,

---

[2] This analysis assumes homogeneity of variance and of covariance. See Chapter 21 (pp. 462–467) for a discussion of these assumptions.

however, it may help to relate these different notions if we return to Table 16-2 (p. 340) at this point in the discussion. In order to modify Table 16-2 for use with the $(A \times B \times S)$ design, we will treat factor S as a *random independent factor* and delete any reference to the within-groups mean square—which, of course, does not exist in this particular design. This means, then, that we can omit the first question at the top of the table and turn immediately to the question asked on the "yes" branch of the selection tree. Starting with the main effect of factor A, we can see that the effect (A) does not contain the random factor (S), and so we will follow the "no" branch in response to the second question. We are asked at this juncture to find a source that contains only the letter A plus a random variable. The obvious answer is the $A \times S$ interaction. Since there is only one such term, the $MS_{A \times S}$ is the correct error term. The same path is taken in our search for the error terms for the MS_B and the $MS_{A \times B}$. Neither contains the random factor, and the only sources satisfying the selection criteria are the $MS_{B \times S}$ and the $MS_{A \times B \times S}$, respectively.

TABLE 20-4   *Numerical Example: $(A \times B \times S)$ Design*

ABS MATRIX

	a_1				a_2			
---	b_1	b_2	b_3	b_4	b_1	b_2	b_3	b_4
s_1	3	5	9	6	5	6	11	7
s_2	7	11	12	11	10	12	18	15
s_3	9	13	14	12	10	15	15	14
s_4	4	8	11	7	6	9	13	9
s_5	1	3	5	4	3	5	9	7

AS MATRIX

	a_1	a_2	Sum
s_1	23	29	52
s_2	41	55	96
s_3	48	54	102
s_4	30	37	67
s_5	13	24	37
Sum	155	199	354

BS MATRIX

	b_1	b_2	b_3	b_4	Sum
s_1	8	11	20	13	52
s_2	17	23	30	26	96
s_3	19	28	29	26	102
s_4	10	17	24	16	67
s_5	4	8	14	11	37
Sum	58	87	117	92	354

AB MATRIX

	b_1	b_2	b_3	b_4	Sum
a_1	24	40	51	40	155
a_2	34	47	66	52	199
Sum	58	87	117	92	354

Numerical Example

The data for a hypothetical experiment are presented in Table 20-4. For the experimental factors, the design is a 2×4 factorial with repeated measures on both factors. There are $s = 5$ subjects, each of whom serves in each of the $ab = 2(4) = 8$ treatment combinations. The marginal totals specified in Table 20-2 have been computed in the different data matrices of Table 20-4. The calculation of the different sums of squares is familiar: Working with the AS matrix first, we have

$$[T] = \frac{(T)^2}{abs} = \frac{(354)^2}{2(4)(5)} = \frac{125,316}{40} = 3132.90,$$

$$[A] = \frac{\sum (A)^2}{bs} = \frac{(155)^2 + (199)^2}{4(5)} = \frac{63,626}{20} = 3181.30,$$

$$[S] = \frac{\sum (S)^2}{ab} = \frac{(52)^2 + (96)^2 + \cdots + (67)^2 + (37)^2}{2(4)} = \frac{28,182}{8} = 3522.75,$$

$$[AS] = \frac{\sum (AS)^2}{b} = \frac{(23)^2 + (41)^2 + \cdots + (37)^2 + (24)^2}{4} = \frac{14,310}{4} = 3577.50.$$

Turning next to the BS matrix,

$$[B] = \frac{\sum (B)^2}{as} = \frac{(58)^2 + (87)^2 + (117)^2 + (92)^2}{2(5)} = \frac{33,086}{10} = 3308.60,$$

$$[BS] = \frac{\sum (BS)^2}{a} = \frac{(8)^2 + (17)^2 + \cdots + (16)^2 + (11)^2}{2} = \frac{7428}{2} = 3714.00.$$

The AB matrix provides the sums for the first term of the $SS_{A \times B}$. Specifically,

$$[AB] = \frac{\sum (AB)^2}{s} = \frac{(24)^2 + (34)^2 + \cdots + (40)^2 + (52)^2}{5} = \frac{16,802}{5} = 3360.40.$$

We have to use the ABS matrix for the calculation of the first term of the $SS_{A \times B \times S}$:

$$[ABS] = \sum (ABS)^2 = (3)^2 + (7)^2 + \cdots + (9)^2 + (7)^2 = 3778.$$

These computations are recorded in Table 20-5 together with the additions and subtractions needed for the calculation of the different SS's. The F ratios for the three critical mean squares are formed by dividing the mean squares by the appropriate error terms. The analysis indicates significant differences between the two A conditions and among the four B conditions. The $A \times B$ interaction is not significant.

TABLE 20-5   *Summary of the Analysis*

Source	Calculations[a]	SS	df	MS	F
A	$3181.30 - 3132.90 =$	48.40	1	48.40	30.44*
S	$3522.75 - [T] =$	389.85	4	97.46	
$A \times S$	$3577.50 - [A] - [S] + [T] =$	6.35	4	1.59	
B	$3308.60 - [T] =$	175.70	3	58.57	45.05*
$B \times S$	$3714.00 - [B] - [S] + [T] =$	15.55	12	1.30	
$A \times B$	$3360.40 - [A] - [B] + [T] =$	3.40	3	1.13	2.31
$A \times B \times S$	$3778 - [AB] - [AS] - [BS]$ $+ [A] + [B] + [S] - [T] =$	5.85	12	.49	
Total	$[ABS] - [T] =$	645.10	39		

[a] Bracketed letters represent complete terms in the computational formulas; a particular term is identified by the letter(s) appearing in the numerator.

* $p < .01$.

Analytical Analyses

The different comparisons discussed and illustrated for the one-factor case may all be conducted with the data of the present experiment. The formulas for the application of these comparisons are available in Chapters 11 and 12, and you should refer to the discussion there. The main difficulty in the analyses, as applied to the two-factor repeated-measures design, is in the selection of the correct error terms. The considerations for the error terms in the $(A \times B \times S)$ design are the same as those outlined for the $(A \times S)$ design. To repeat, it is necessary to obtain error terms that will contain the *Comparison* × Subject interaction that is relevant to the comparison being tested. If we want to compare two levels of factor B, the error term is based upon only the scores entering into the means of interest. In symbols,

$$F = \frac{MS_{B_{comp.}}}{MS_{B_{comp.} \times S}}.$$

This ratio is evaluated in the F table against the df associated with the numerator and denominator terms constructed for the comparison. A similar procedure is followed for all other comparisons.

SIMPLE MAIN EFFECTS OF THE INTERACTION   If the $A \times B$ interaction is not significant, we will probably concentrate our efforts on an analysis of the main effects. On the other hand, if the interaction is significant, a common analysis is a test of the simple main effects of the interaction. Such an analysis is under-taken to attempt to identify the locus of the significant interaction. In this case, too, there will be separate error terms for each of the simple main effects. More specifically, suppose we wanted to study the simple main effects of factor B at the two levels of factor A. We can construct the computational formula for these sums of squares by the procedures outlined in Chapter 15 (see pp. 325–327).

That is,

$$df_{B \text{ at } a_i} = (df_B)(a_i) = (b - 1)(a_i)$$
$$= (a_i)b - a_i,$$

$$SS_{B \text{ at } a_i} = \frac{\sum\limits_{j}^{b} (AB_{ij})^2}{abs} - \frac{(A_i)^2}{abs}. \tag{20-1}$$

From the AB matrix in Table 20-4 we have for the simple main effects of factor B at a_1:

$$SS_{B \text{ at } a_1} = \frac{\sum (AB_{1j})^2}{s} - \frac{(A_1)^2}{bs}$$

$$= \frac{(24)^2 + (40)^2 + (51)^2 + (40)^2}{5} - \frac{(155)^2}{4(5)}$$

$$= 1275.40 - 1201.25 = 74.15.$$

The error term for the simple main effect is the *interaction* of this simple effect with factor S—i.e., the $B \times S$ interaction at a_i. Starting with the df statement,

$$df_{B \times S \text{ at } a_i} = (df_B)(df_S)(a_i) = (b - 1)(s - 1)(a_i)$$
$$= (a_i)bs - (a_i)b - (a_i)s + a_i,$$

TABLE 20-6   *Specialized ABS Matrix for the Analysis of a Simple Main Effect*

ABS MATRIX AT LEVEL a_1: NOTATION

	b_1	b_2	b_3	b_4	Sum
s_1	ABS_{111}	ABS_{121}	ABS_{131}	ABS_{141}	AS_{11}
s_2	ABS_{112}	ABS_{122}	ABS_{132}	ABS_{142}	AS_{12}
s_3	ABS_{113}	ABS_{123}	ABS_{133}	ABS_{143}	AS_{13}
s_4	ABS_{114}	ABS_{124}	ABS_{134}	ABS_{144}	AS_{14}
s_5	ABS_{115}	ABS_{125}	ABS_{135}	ABS_{145}	AS_{15}
Sum	AB_{11}	AB_{12}	AB_{13}	AB_{14}	A_1

ABS MATRIX AT LEVEL a_1: DATA

	b_1	b_2	b_3	b_4	Sum
s_1	3	5	9	6	23
s_2	7	11	12	11	41
s_3	9	13	14	12	48
s_4	4	8	11	7	30
s_5	1	3	5	4	13
Sum	24	40	51	40	155

we have

$$SS_{B \times S \text{ at } a_i} = \frac{\sum\limits_{j}^{b} \sum\limits_{k}^{s} (ABS_{ijk})^2}{abs} - \frac{\sum\limits_{j}^{b} (AB_{ij})^2}{abs} - \frac{\sum\limits_{k}^{s} (AS_{ik})^2}{abs} + \frac{(A_i)^2}{abs}. \quad (20\text{-}2)$$

At this point, the calculations are clearer if we work directly with the part of the ABS matrix that is specifically involved in the computations—i.e., the ABS matrix at level a_1. This partial matrix is presented in Table 20-6: the upper half of the table specifies the quantities involved, while the lower half provides the actual data needed to calculate the $MS_{B \times S \text{ at } a_1}$. More specifically,

$$SS_{B \times S \text{ at } a_1} = \sum (ABS_{1jk})^2 - \frac{\sum (AB_{1j})^2}{s} - \frac{\sum (AS_{1k})^2}{b} + \frac{(A_1)^2}{bs}$$

$$= [(3)^2 + (7)^2 + \cdots + (7)^2 + (4)^2]$$

$$\quad - \frac{(24)^2 + (40)^2 + (51)^2 + (140)^2}{5}$$

$$\quad - \frac{(23)^2 + (41)^2 + \cdots + (30)^2 + (13)^2}{4} + \frac{(155)^2}{4(5)}$$

$$= 1477 - 1275.40 - 1395.75 + 1201.25$$

$$= 7.10.$$

We are now ready to calculate the F ratio. First, the mean squares:

$$MS_{B \text{ at } a_1} = \frac{SS_{B \text{ at } a_1}}{b - 1} = \frac{74.15}{4 - 1} = \frac{74.15}{3} = 24.72,$$

$$MS_{B \times S \text{ at } a_1} = \frac{SS_{B \times S \text{ at } a_1}}{(b - 1)(s - 1)} = \frac{7.10}{(4 - 1)(5 - 1)} = \frac{7.10}{3(4)} = .59.$$

Finally,

$$F = \frac{MS_{B \text{ at } a_1}}{MS_{B \times S \text{ at } a_1}} = \frac{24.72}{.59} = 41.90,$$

which is significant at $p < .01$.

If we were interested in the simple main effects of the other factor, we would follow the same general procedure outlined in developing Eqs. (20-1) and (20-2). For example,

$$df_{A \text{ at } b_j} = (df_A)(b_j) = (a - 1)(b_j)$$

$$= a(b_j) - b_j,$$

$$SS_{A \text{ at } b_j} = \frac{\sum\limits_{i}^{a} (AB_{ij})^2}{abs} - \frac{(B_j)^2}{abs}.$$

For the corresponding error term,

$$df_{A \times S \text{ at } b_j} = (df_A)(df_S)(b_j) = (a - 1)(s - 1)(b_j)$$
$$= a(b_j)s - a(b_j) - (b_j)s + b_j,$$

$$SS_{A \times S \text{ at } b_j} = \frac{\sum\limits_{i}^{a} \sum\limits_{k}^{s} (ABS_{ijk})^2}{abs} - \frac{\sum\limits_{i}^{a} (AB_{ij})^2}{abs}$$
$$- \frac{\sum\limits_{k}^{s} (BS_{jk})^2}{abs} + \frac{(B_j)^2}{abs}.$$

COMPARISONS INVOLVING SPECIFIC MEANS   Any comparison, for which $df = 1$, may be expressed in terms of coefficients and a sum of treatment totals weighted by these coefficients. These include comparisons between pairs of single means and between pairs of complex means as well as analyses of trend. The computational formulas in all of the applications are the same. These procedures will be illustrated for the $A \times (B \times S)$ design (pp. 442–454), however, since the calculations are quite similar to those required for the $(A \times B \times S)$ design.

MULTIPLE COMPARISONS   If the $A \times B$ interaction is not significant, we may want to make multiple comparisons between the means contributing to the *main effects* of factors A and B. As with other comparisons, we would first arrange the data into a Comparison × Subject matrix. That is, we would have two scores for each subject, one for level a_i and the other for level $a_{i'}$, say. Next, we would calculate the sum of squares for the comparison and a sum of squares for the error term—i.e., the Comparison × Subject interaction. Finally, the F that we find is compared with an F that has been adjusted to correspond to the corrections demanded by the different procedures. These corrections are given in Eqs. (19-4), (19-5), (19-6), and (19-7). If the $A \times B$ interaction is significant, a procedure identical to the one just outlined is followed for comparisons involving pairs of means within the AB matrix. As noted in Chapter 12 (pp. 244–246), however, it is unlikely that we would consider making all possible comparisons between pairs of means. Instead, we would probably restrict our attention to comparisons within each level of factor A or of factor B.

THE $A \times (B \times S)$ DESIGN

Uses of the Design

This design represents a mixture of the two generic types of designs we have considered previously: independent groups, constituting the levels of one factor

(factor A), and repeated measures, constituting the levels of the other factor (factor B). The contrast between the "pure" repeated-measures design and the "mixed" design was given in Table 20-1 (p. 424). As we will see, the analysis of the mixed design combines features of the one-factor design with independent groups and the one-factor design with repeated measures. Consequently, the analysis will *not* be simple and will require a more complicated treatment of the data. The mixed design is "worth" it, however, since it is employed much more frequently than the $(A \times B \times S)$ design. Moreover, the partitioning of the component sums of squares and the identification of appropriate error terms that we will see in the $A \times (B \times S)$ design will serve as a model for the more complicated higher-order designs with which we frequently deal.

The most common example of this type of design is one in which the repeated factor represents *trials* or *successive tasks* in a learning experiment. Rarely will we be interested in an $(A \times S)$ experiment in which "trials" is the independent variable. The reason for this is, of course, that all we can hope to show with this type of experiment is that learning does or does not occur and if so, what the shape of the function is over trials (i.e., the levels of the independent variable). More typically, we will want to compare the learning curves for *different treatment groups*. Under these circumstances, the various "treatments" (factor A) will be administered to independent groups of subjects and all subjects will receive a certain number of learning trials (factor B). Thus, the experiment becomes an $A \times (B \times S)$ design. With this particular design, it is still possible to compare the different treatment groups on performance averaged over all of the learning trials. In addition to this information, however, it is also possible to compare the *shapes* of the learning curves for the different treatment groups. To be more specific, we can ask whether or not the effects of practice (trials) are the same for the different levels of factor A—i.e., whether or not there is an $A \times B$ interaction (in this case, a Treatment $\times$ Trials interaction).

Notation

The notational system for the $A \times (B \times S)$ design is presented in Table 20-7. We have indicated that factor S is a *nested* factor; i.e., there is a different set of subjects appearing in each level of factor A. This fact is made explicit in Table 20-7 by denoting the subjects at each level of factor A with different sets of numbers. An individual score, ABS_{ijk}, is specified by the three subscripts, with i indicating the level of factor A, j indicating the level of factor B, and k specifying a subject appearing in a particular level of factor A.

It is instructive to compare the sums necessary for the $A \times (B \times S)$ design with those needed for the $(A \times B \times S)$ design (Table 20-2). Missing from the present layout is the BS matrix. Instead, there are two "BS" matrices contained in the ABS matrix, one at a_1 and the other at a_2. As one might suspect, a difference in the summary matrices must imply a difference in the formulas used to calculate the sums of squares.

TABLE 20-7 *Notational System: $A \times (B \times S)$ Design*

ABS MATRIX

	a_1				a_2		
Subject	b_1	b_2	b_3	Subject	b_1	b_2	b_3
s_1	ABS_{111}	ABS_{121}	ABS_{131}	s_4	ABS_{214}	ABS_{224}	ABS_{234}
s_2	ABS_{112}	ABS_{122}	ABS_{132}	s_5	ABS_{215}	ABS_{225}	ABS_{235}
s_3	ABS_{113}	ABS_{123}	ABS_{133}	s_6	ABS_{216}	ABS_{226}	ABS_{236}

AB MATRIX

	a_1	a_2	Sum
b_1	AB_{11}	AB_{21}	B_1
b_2	AB_{12}	AB_{22}	B_2
b_3	AB_{13}	AB_{23}	B_3
Sum	A_1	A_2	T

AS MATRIX

	a_1		a_2
s_1	AS_{11}	s_4	AS_{24}
s_2	AS_{12}	s_5	AS_{25}
s_3	AS_{13}	s_6	AS_{26}
Sum	A_1	Sum	A_2

Computational Formulas

We will now develop the computational formulas for this design by using the procedures introduced in Chapter 10. This will be done in three steps: (1) the identification of the sources of variance, (2) the generation of the formulas for the corresponding sums of squares, and (3) the selection of the correct error terms.

IDENTIFICATION OF THE SOURCES OF VARIANCE   We can specify the sources of variance, which are extracted in the standard analysis of any design, by adapting the rules given in Chapter 18 for nested designs (p. 368). This modification simply includes the within-groups factor in the formation of all potential interactions (see step 2). In the case of the $A \times (B \times S)$ design, then, we have

1. **List factors:** A, B, and S/A;
2. **Form all potential interactions:** $A \times B$, $A \times S/A$, $B \times S/A$, and $A \times B \times S/A$; and
3. **Delete:** $A \times S/A$ and $A \times B \times S/A$.

The sources in the first step, plus those interactions remaining after impossible interactions are deleted in step 3 (those in which the same letter appears on both sides of the diagonal), constitute the components into which the total sum of squares is partitioned. These sources are presented in the first column of Table 20-8. We will not discuss the details of the identification rule here, except to refer you to the original representation in Chapter 18 (pp. 368–370) and to note that factor S is written in its appropriate form as a *nested* factor (S/A) in the first step.

Sums of squares   We will now construct the computational formulas for the corresponding sums of squares. The first step, which forms the backbone of the construction scheme, consists of writing the df statement. To aid in this process, a simple rule given in Chapter 18 (see p. 370) is repeated here. To find the df for any source,

Multiply (1) the product of the df's of factors to the *left* of the diagonal by (2) the product of the *levels* of factors to the *right* of the diagonal.

We will now construct the computational formulas in the order listed in Table 20-8 from the expanded df statements, using the steps outlined in Chapter 10 (see pp. 193–195). For the SS_A,

$$df_A = a - 1,$$

$$SS_A = \frac{\sum (A)^2}{abs} - \frac{(T)^2}{abs}.$$

For the $SS_{S/A}$,

$$df_{S/A} = (df_S)(a) = (s - 1)(a) = as - a,$$

$$SS_{S/A} = \frac{\sum (AS)^2}{abs} - \frac{\sum (A)^2}{abs}.$$

For the SS_B,

$$df_B = b - 1,$$

$$SS_B = \frac{\sum (B)^2}{abs} - \frac{(T)^2}{abs}.$$

For the $SS_{A \times B}$,

$$df_{A \times B} = (df_A)(df_B) = (a - 1)(b - 1) = ab - a - b + 1,$$

$$SS_{A \times B} = \frac{\sum (AB)^2}{abs} - \frac{\sum (A)^2}{abs} - \frac{\sum (B)^2}{abs} + \frac{(T)^2}{abs}.$$

For the $SS_{B \times S/A}$,

$$df_{B \times S/A} = [(df_B)(df_S)](a) = (b - 1)(s - 1)(a)$$

$$= abs - ab - as + a,$$

$$SS_{B \times S/A} = \frac{\sum (ABS)^2}{abs} - \frac{\sum (AB)^2}{abs} - \frac{\sum (AS)^2}{abs} + \frac{\sum (A)^2}{abs}.$$

Finally, for the SS_T,

$$df_T = abs - 1,$$

$$SS_T = \frac{\sum (ABS)^2}{abs} - \frac{(T)^2}{abs}.$$

TABLE 20-8 *Computational Formulas:* $A \times (B \times S)$ *Design*

Source	Sum of Squares[a]	df	MS	F[b]
A	$\dfrac{\sum (A)^2}{bs} - \dfrac{(T)^2}{abs}$	$a - 1$	$\dfrac{SS_A}{df_A}$	$\dfrac{MS_A}{MS_{S/A}}$
S/A	$\dfrac{\sum (AS)^2}{b} - [A]$	$a(s - 1)$	$\dfrac{SS_{S/A}}{df_{S/A}}$	
B	$\dfrac{\sum (B)^2}{as} - [T]$	$b - 1$	$\dfrac{SS_B}{df_B}$	$\dfrac{MS_B}{MS_{B \times S/A}}$
$A \times B$	$\dfrac{\sum (AB)^2}{s} - [A] - [B] + [T]$	$(a - 1)(b - 1)$	$\dfrac{SS_{A \times B}}{df_{A \times B}}$	$\dfrac{MS_{A \times B}}{MS_{B \times S/A}}$
$B \times S/A$	$\sum (ABS)^2 - [AB] - [AS] + [A]$	$a(b - 1)(s - 1)$	$\dfrac{SS_{B \times S/A}}{df_{B \times S/A}}$	
Total	$[ABS] - [T]$	$abs - 1$		

[a] Bracketed letters represent complete terms in the computational formulas; a particular term in identified by the letter(s) appearing in the numerator.
[b] Factors A and B are fixed.

These formulas, with the canceled letters in the denominators removed, are presented in the second column of Table 20-8.

SELECTION OF ERROR TERMS[3]   If we eliminate from the component sources of variance listed in Table 20-8 those sources reflecting treatment effects, we have two sources remaining to serve as potential error terms, namely, the S/A and the $B \times S/A$. In the next chapter we will discuss a rule which will identify the appropriate error term for sources of variance in any repeated-measures design. For the time being, however, we will simply acknowledge that the treatment mean square which is *not* based on repeated measures (the MS_A) is evaluated by the within-groups mean square (the $MS_{S/A}$), while the two treatment mean squares which *are* based on repeated measures (the MS_B and the $MS_{A \times B}$) are evaluated by a mean square reflecting an interaction of the repeated factor (B) with factor S, namely, the $MS_{B \times S/A}$.

Numerical Example

For comparison purposes, the numerical example uses the same set of data presented originally in Table 20-4 as an illustration of the calculations in the $(A \times B \times S)$ design. The data, recast to fit the $A \times (B \times S)$ design, are presented in Table 20-9. We will begin the analysis by calculating the basic quantities needed for the analysis from the computational formulas of Table 20-8. From

[3] This analysis assumes homogeneity of variance and of covariance. See Chapter 21 (pp. 462–467) for a discussion of these assumptions.

TABLE 20-9   *Numerical Example: $A \times (B \times S)$ Design*

ABS MATRIX

	a_1						a_2			
	b_1	b_2	b_3	b_4			b_1	b_2	b_3	b_4
s_1	3	5	9	6	27	s_6	5	6	11	7
s_2	7	11	12	11		s_7	10	12	18	15
s_3	9	13	14	12		s_8	10	15	15	14
s_4	4	8	11	7		s_9	6	9	13	9
s_5	1	3	5	4		s_{10}	3	5	9	7
	24									

AB MATRIX

	a_1	a_2	Sum
b_1	24	34	58
b_2	40	47	87
b_3	51	66	117
b_4	40	52	92
Sum	155	199	354

AS MATRIX

	a_1		a_2
s_1	23	s_6	29
s_2	41	s_7	55
s_3	48	s_8	54
s_4	30	s_9	37
s_5	13	s_{10}	24
Sum	155	Sum	199

the AB matrix,

$$[T] = \frac{(T)^2}{abs} = \frac{(354)^2}{2(4)(5)} = \frac{125{,}316}{40} = 3132.90.$$

From the AS matrix,

$$[A] = \frac{\sum (A)^2}{bs} = \frac{(155)^2 + (199)^2}{4(5)} = \frac{63{,}626}{20} = 3181.30,$$

$$[AS] = \frac{\sum (AS)^2}{b} = \frac{(23)^2 + (41)^2 + \cdots + (37)^2 + (24)^2}{4}$$

$$= \frac{14{,}310}{4} = 3577.50.$$

From the AB matrix,

$$[B] = \frac{\sum (B)^2}{as} = \frac{(58)^2 + (87)^2 + (117)^2 + (92)^2}{2(5)} = \frac{33{,}086}{10} = 3308.60,$$

$$[AB] = \frac{\sum (AB)^2}{s} = \frac{(24)^2 + (40)^2 + \cdots + (66)^2 + (52)^2}{5}$$

$$= \frac{16{,}802}{5} = 3360.40.$$

Finally, from the ABS matrix,

$$[ABS] = \sum (ABS)^2 = (3)^2 + (7)^2 + \cdots + (9)^2 + (7)^2 = 3778.$$

The results of these basic calculations are entered in the second column of Table 20-10. The coded representations of these numbers also in this column indicate how these terms are manipulated to produce the different sums of squares. The remaining steps in the analysis are summarized in the table.

TABLE 20-10 *Summary of the Analysis*

Source	Calculations[a]	SS	df	MS	F
A	$3181.30 - 3132.90 =$	48.40	1	48.40	<1
S/A	$3577.50 - [A] =$	396.20	8	49.52	
B	$3308.60 - [T] =$	175.70	3	58.57	65.81*
$A \times B$	$3360.40 - [A] - [B] + [T] =$	3.40	3	1.13	1.27
$B \times S/A$	$3778 - [AB] - [AS] + [A] =$	21.40	24	.89	
Total	$[ABS] - [T] =$	645.10	39		

[a] Bracketed letters represent complete terms in the computational formulas; a particular term is identified by the letter(s) appearing in the numerator.
* $p < .01$.

In comparing the results of the analysis of the two designs, we can see that the major change in the outcome of the three statistical tests is the shift from significance to nonsignificance of the main effect of factor A. To be more specific, the F ratio is less than 1 in the present analysis, while $F(1, 4) = 30.44$, $p < .01$ in the previous analysis (see Table 20-5, p. 430). It is important to see how this happened. A comparison of the two summary tables indicates that the size of the main effect of factor A remained unchanged in this new analysis; that is, the $MS_A = 48.40$ in both analyses. The dramatic decrease in the size of the F ratio must be due, then, to an *increase* in the size of the error term. Compare the error terms in the two designs: The $MS_{A \times S} = 1.59$ in the $(A \times B \times S)$ design and the $MS_{S/A} = 49.52$ in the $A \times (B \times S)$ design. It is also instructive to compare the sizes of the two error terms in the mixed design itself. This difference is considerable: 49.52 versus .89. Although these data are artificial, tenfold differences are not uncommon in the literature. The difference in the sizes of the error terms reflects the increased sensitivity of the repeated-measures portion of the $A \times (B \times S)$ design in detecting the influence of independent variables.

Further Discussion of the Mixed Design

The $A \times (B \times S)$ design has been called a "mixed" design which reflects in part that it represents a combination of two single-factor experiments, one with independent groups (factor A) and the other with repeated measures (factor B). This description is not completely accurate, however, since the two-factor design contains an $A \times B$ interaction which obviously cannot be present in either of the single-factor experiments. Nevertheless, the analogy is sufficiently close to give us a "feel" for the composite nature of the mixed design. Table 20-11 makes this point explicit. The component sources of variance for a completely randomized, single-factor experiment are listed in the first column. The component sources for a single-factor experiment with repeated measures are listed in the third column. [We will refer to this independent variable as factor B and to the experiment as a $(B \times S)$ design to facilitate the comparison of the designs.] The component sources of variance for the $A \times (B \times S)$ design are listed in the middle column of the table.

TABLE 20-11   *A Comparison of the Sources of Variance in Two Single-Factor Experiments with Those in the $A \times (B \times S)$ Design*

Completely Randomized Design	$A \times (B \times S)$ Design	$(B \times S)$ Design
A	A	
S/A	S/A	S
	B	B
	$B \times S/A$	$B \times S$
	$A \times B$	

An inspection of the table reveals that the completely randomized design is perfectly duplicated in the mixed design. The same could be said of the $(B \times S)$ design except that the designation of "subjects" is different. This comes about because factor S is a *crossed factor* in the $(B \times S)$ design, while it is actually *nested* within factor A in the mixed design.[4]

BETWEEN-SUBJECTS AND WITHIN-SUBJECT SOURCES   Another way of describing the combination of the two single-factor experiments in the mixed design is to note that some of the sources of variance extracted in the analysis are based upon *between-subject* differences, while others are based upon *within-subject* differences. A glance at Table 20-7 (p. 435) indicates that the scores in the AS matrix provide the ingredients necessary for the SS_A and the $SS_{S/A}$. The only difference between the scores in this AS matrix and those in the AS matrix of a single-factor experiment with independent groups is that these are a composite; i.e., tl :y are produced by summing the ABS scores over the B classification. In a single-factor experiment, the sum of these two sums of squares, $SS_A + SS_{S/A}$,

---

[4] Kirk (1968, pp. 252–255) presents an interesting demonstration that the $SS_{S/A}$ and the $SS_{B \times S/A}$ in the mixed design are in essence a within-groups sum of squares and a $B \times S$ sum of squares, respectively.

would equal the total sum of squares. Since this label might be confused in the mixed design with the "real" total sum of squares, SS_T, we often see the sum referred to as the *between-subjects* sum of squares ($SS_{bet.\,S}$). Sources of variance drawn from the repeated-measures portion of the experiment are said to constitute the *within-subject* sum of squares ($SS_{w.\,S}$). In fact, we often see the mixed design described in terms of the separation of the total variability of the individual *ABS* scores about the grand mean—i.e., the SS_T—into the $SS_{bet.\,S}$, which is based upon independent groups of subjects, and the $SS_{w.\,S}$, which is based upon repeated measures. In symbols,

$$SS_T = SS_{bet.\,S} + SS_{w.\,S}. \tag{20-3}$$

Authors of statistics books quite typically present the partitioning of the component sums of squares in the mixed design in two steps: (1) a coarse division of the SS_T into the $SS_{bet.\,S}$ and the $SS_{w.\,S}$, followed by (2) a more analytical division of these two sums of squares into sources of variance that reflect components having systematic interest. To be more specific,

$$SS_T = SS_{bet.\,S} + SS_{w.\,S}$$
$$= (SS_A + SS_{S/A}) + (SS_B + SS_{A \times B} + SS_{B \times S/A}).$$

The $SS_{bet.\,S}$ reflects the deviation of all *as* subjects from the overall mean; thus, $df_{bet.\,S} = as - 1$. The $SS_{w.\,S}$, on the other hand, reflects the deviation of each subject from his *own* mean, which is then pooled over the *as* subjects; thus, $df_{w.\,S} = as(b - 1)$.

The computational formulas for these two sums of squares can be constructed from the respective *df* statements. Since both sums of squares contain quantities we have calculated already, we can quickly compute them. Representing the quantities in coded form and substituting from Table 20-10, we have

$$df_{bet.\,S} = as - 1,$$

$$SS_{bet.\,S} = [AS] - [T] = 3577.50 - 3132.90 = 444.60;$$

$$df_{w.\,S} = as(b - 1) = abs - as,$$

$$SS_{w.\,S} = [ABS] - [AS] = 3778 - 3577.50 = 200.50.$$

Just to convince ourselves that these sums of squares contain the component sums of squares we have specified,

$$SS_A + SS_{S/A} = 48.40 + 396.20 = 444.60 = SS_{bet.S},$$

$$SS_B + SS_{A \times B} + SS_{B \times S/A} = 175.70 + 3.40 + 21.40$$
$$= 200.50 = SS_{w.\,S}.$$

SUMMARY   We have considered the analysis of the $A \times (B \times S)$ design in two ways. The earlier approach showed that the analysis evolves from an application of the rules for constructing the formulas for the analysis of variance.

The present approach followed a different line of argument, stressing the fact that the mixed design can be thought of as the conjunction of a completely randomized, single-factor experiment and a single-factor experiment with repeated measures.

ANALYTICAL ANALYSES

We considered the topic of analytical comparisons when we discussed the analysis of the $(A \times B \times S)$ design, and all of these procedures are available for the analysis of the $A \times (B \times S)$ design. Because of the mixed nature of the design, the selection of error terms is more complicated, however. In the $(A \times B \times S)$ design, where *all* treatment combinations involve repeated measures, we followed a simple rule, namely, to construct an error term that represents a Comparison $\times$ Subject interaction. The mixed design has no such consistent rule. We will now discuss a number of the more common analyses we might consider with this type of design.

Simple Main Effects

Following the discovery of a significant $A \times B$ interaction, we would undoubtedly begin a search for the locus of this effect. As we have seen in previous discussions, an analysis of the simple main effects is just such an analytical tool. Depending upon the experimental questions being asked, the simple main effects of one of the factors may be more revealing than one conducted on the other. If we are interested in the simple main effects of the *repeated factor* (factor B in the mixed design), we follow the same procedures outlined in the discussion of the $(A \times B \times S)$ design. Rather than duplicate the previous discussion, you are referred to pp. 430–433 for a presentation of the computational formulas and an illustration of the analysis. If, on the other hand, we are interested in the simple main effects of the *nonrepeated factor* (factor A in this design), the analysis is different. It is with these changes that we will concern ourselves in this section.

SIMPLE MAIN EFFECTS OF THE NONREPEATED FACTOR   We will use the procedures presented in Chapter 15 (see pp. 325–327) to construct the computational formula for the $SS_{A \text{ at } b_j}$. Specifically,

$$df_{A \text{ at } b_j} = (df_A)(b_j) = (a - 1)(b_j)$$

$$= a(b_j) - b_j,$$

$$SS_{A \text{ at } b_j} = \frac{\sum_{i}^{a} (AB_{ij})^2}{abs} - \frac{(B_j)^2}{abs}. \tag{20-4}$$

For these simple main effects, we are asked to calculate the variability due to factor A at the different levels of factor B. Reference to Table 20-7 (p. 435) indicates that we are considering the AB sums in successive rows of the AB matrix. As an example, we will use the data from Table 20-9 (p. 438) to calculate the simple main effect of A at b_3. From Eq. (20-4),

$$SS_{A\,\text{at}\,b_3} = \frac{\sum (AB_{i3})^2}{s} - \frac{(B_3)^2}{as}$$

$$= \frac{(51)^2 + (66)^2}{5} - \frac{(117)^2}{2(5)}$$

$$= 1391.40 - 1368.90 = 22.50.$$

Since only two means are being contrasted, the $df = 2 - 1 = 1$, but we could have computed this quantity from the df statement, remembering the convention we adopted in Chapter 15 that $b_j = 1$; i.e.,

$$df_{A\,\text{at}\,b_j} = (a - 1)(b_j) = (2 - 1)(1) = 1.$$

INDIVIDUAL ERROR TERMS   What is a reasonable error term with which to evaluate the significance of this source of variance? One possibility is a mean square that is based on the scores entering into this comparison. If we consider the means actually involved in this comparison, $\overline{AB}_{13}$ and $\overline{AB}_{23}$, we can see that they are based on the ABS scores obtained from two *independent groups* of subjects—one at each of the two levels of factor A. Thus, the appropriate error term would seem to be a sort of within-groups mean square based upon the scores of the independent groups of subjects at *this particular level* of factor B—i.e., the $MS_{S/A\,\text{at}\,b_3}$.

To construct the computational formula for the corresponding sum of squares, we start with the df statement:

$$df_{S/A\,\text{at}\,b_j} = (df_S)(a)(b_j),$$

where the first two quantities on the right represent the df associated with any within-groups sum of squares obtained in a single-factor experiment and the third quantity provides a means for designating a particular level of factor B (see pp. 326–327 for an explanation of this procedure). We can now obtain the computational formula from the expanded df statement using the procedures described in Chapter 15:

$$df_{S/A\,\text{at}\,b_j} = (s - 1)(a)(b_j) = a(b_j)s - a(b_j),$$

$$SS_{S/A\,\text{at}\,b_j} = \frac{\sum_{i}^{a} \sum_{k}^{s} (ABS_{ijk})^2}{abs} - \frac{\sum_{i}^{a} (AB_{ij})^2}{abs}. \tag{20-5}$$

The quantity specified in Eq. (20-5) is the same sum of squares that would be obtained if we were to consider the set of ABS scores at level b_j to have come from a single-factor design with independent groups of subjects.

The completion of the numerical example will help to clarify the nature of the calculations specified in Eq. (20-5). We have been looking at the simple main effect of factor A at b_3. The relevant portions of the ABS matrix have been duplicated in Table 20-12. The upper portion of the table enumerates the

TABLE 20-12 *ABS Matrix at Level b_3*

NOTATION

	ab_{13}			ab_{23}
s_1	ABS_{131}		s_6	ABS_{236}
s_2	ABS_{132}		s_7	ABS_{237}
s_3	ABS_{133}		s_8	ABS_{238}
s_4	ABS_{134}		s_9	ABS_{239}
s_5	ABS_{135}		s_{10}	ABS_{2310}
Sum	AB_{13}		Sum	AB_{23}

DATA

	ab_{13}			ab_{23}
s_1	9		s_6	11
s_2	12		s_7	18
s_3	14		s_8	15
s_4	11		s_9	13
s_5	5		s_{10}	9
Sum	51		Sum	66

notational representation of the scores, and the lower portion presents the corresponding scores from the ABS matrix. Substituting in Eq. (20-5),

$$SS_{S/A \text{ at } b_3} = \sum (ABS_{i3k})^2 - \frac{\sum (AB_{i3})^2}{s}$$

$$= [(9)^2 + (12)^2 + \cdots + (13)^2 + (9)^2] - \frac{(51)^2 + (66)^2}{5}$$

$$= 1487 - 1391.40 = 95.60.$$

Using the *df* statement from which we evolved Eq. (20-5), we find

$$df_{S/A \text{ at } b_3} = (5 - 1)(2)(1) = 8.$$

And so,

$$MS_{S/A \text{ at } b_3} = \frac{SS_{S/A \text{ at } b_3}}{df_{S/A \text{ at } b_3}} = \frac{95.60}{8} = 11.95.$$

Making use of our earlier calculations, the F ratio becomes

$$F = \frac{MS_{A \text{ at } b_3}}{MS_{S/A \text{ at } b_3}} = \frac{22.50}{11.95} = 1.88,$$

which, with 1 and 8 df's, is not significant, $p > .10$.

"HETEROGENEOUS" ERROR TERM   Winer (1962, pp. 310–312; 1971, pp. 529–532) and Kirk (1968, pp. 264–266) have proposed a qualitatively different sort of error term with which to evaluate simple main effects involving the nonrepeated factor. More specifically, they describe an error term that pools the two error terms in the overall analysis, the $MS_{S/A}$ and the $MS_{B \times S/A}$. This pooled error term, or *within-cell* mean square as they call it, is defined as follows:

$$MS_{\text{w. cell}} = \frac{SS_{S/A} + SS_{B \times S/A}}{df_{S/A} + df_{B \times S/A}}.$$

Using the results of the analysis presented in Table 20-10, we have

$$MS_{\text{w. cell}} = \frac{396.20 + 21.40}{8 + 24} = \frac{417.60}{32} = 13.05.$$

The F now becomes

$$F = \frac{MS_{A \text{ at } b_3}}{MS_{\text{w. cell}}} = \frac{22.50}{13.05} = 1.72,$$

which, with 1 and 32 df's, does not change the conclusion drawn from the analysis. The justification for the use of this pooled error term involves a consideration of the sources of variance included in simple main effects and the error terms used to test these sources (see Kirk, 1968, pp. 264–265).

DISCUSSION   Use of the heterogeneous error term seems dubious in most applications. In many cases it does not seem reasonable to allow the mean square intended to evaluate the variability observed at one level of factor B to be influenced by the variability at levels of factor B not entering into the analysis. Consider, for example, an independent variable commonly represented as a repeated factor, "trials" in a learning experiment. If we are evaluating the simple main effect of factor A at one level of factor B, trial 1 say, why should the error term be based in large part upon the variability of scores obtained under levels of factor B that have *not yet been administered*? But an even more compelling reason stems from the fact that in many cases there will be heterogeneity of variance and covariance (discussed in the next chapter) and, under these circumstances, separate error terms seem most appropriate. It does not seem possible to resolve this issue in the abstract. Any question one may have concerning the error term that is appropriate for a particular application should be resolved by the statistician and researcher on joint considerations.

Trend Analysis and Other Single *df* Comparisons

In this section we will discuss the analysis of comparisons which can be expressed in terms of coefficients. These analyses are conducted on the means contributing to the main effects of factors A and B, if the interaction is not significant, and upon the means in the AB matrix, if the interaction is significant. In this latter case, the comparisons generally take the form of interactions between the comparisons of one factor and the other factor itself—i.e., $A_{comp.} \times B$ or $A \times B_{comp.}$. Although the trend analysis represents a special case of single *df* comparisons, the only difference is in the nature of the coefficients. Thus, an analysis of trend can serve as a model for the analysis of comparisons of this sort.

This section will be divided into two parts. The first will consider the development of the computational formulas, drawing upon the rules presented in Chapter 15. The steps involved in the construction can serve as a model for similar analysis in more complicated designs with repeated measures. The second part consists of a numerical example of a trend analysis, which will illustrate the nature of these types of analyses.

COMPUTATIONAL FORMULAS   In this discussion we will assume that the comparisons are being conducted on the repeated factor (factor B), since it is on this factor that most of the comparisons are conducted in the mixed design.[5] The first thing we must do is to identify the sources of variance in which we will be interested. This is easy: we simply apply the comparison to all of the sources in the main analysis that contain factor B. That is,

SS_B will be divided into one or more $SS_{B_{comp.}}$;
$SS_{A \times B}$ will be divided into one or more $SS_{A \times B_{comp.}}$; and
$SS_{B \times S/A}$ will be divided into one or more $SS_{B_{comp.} \times S/A}$.

These three sources are listed as column entries in Table 20-13. The steps in the construction of the computational formulas are enumerated in the rows of the table; these steps are based on the procedures described in Chapter 15 (pp. 321–325). The three sets of *df* are written in the first row and expanded in the second. The symbol b' refers to the *df* associated with the $B_{comp.}$; thus, $b' = 1$. Steps 3–7 work with the *first term* of each computational formula.

---

[5] The analysis is different when the comparisons involve the nonrepeated factor. In brief, the error term for the $MS_{A_{comp.}}$ is the $MS_{S/A}$ and the error term for the $MS_{A_{comp.} \times B}$ is the $MS_{B \times S/A}$. See Myers (1966, pp. 368–396 and Table 14-2) for a more detailed discussion of this analysis.

Each of these terms has the general form,

$$\frac{(\text{sum of weighted totals})^2}{(\text{no. of observations})(\text{sum of squared coefficients})}, \qquad (20\text{-}6)$$

where the term inside the parenthesis in the numerator is defined as

$$\sum_{j}^{b} (c_j)(Total_j)^2. \qquad (20\text{-}6a)$$

The "total" in Eq. (20-6a) refers to the B_j terms for the $B_{\text{comp.}}$, to the AB_{ij} terms for the $A \times B_{\text{comp.}}$, and to the ABS_{ijk} terms for the $B_{\text{comp.}} \times S/A$. The numerator terms are constructed in steps 3 and 4, the weighted totals being summed in step 3 and these resultant sums being squared and summed over the remaining subscripts in step 4. (The final summation is needed to "collect" all of the squared sums of weighted totals of a given type that are present in the experiment.) At this point, the numerators are complete.

The next two steps develop the denominator terms. In step 5, the number of observations upon which each "total" is based is found by deleting from the total number of observations in the experiment (*abs*) the letter or letters appearing in the numerator (e.g., in step 4). The first terms are completed in step 6 by dividing the numerator portion by the denominator specified in Eq. (20-6). Each of these basic terms is given a letter code in step 7.

TABLE 20-13 *Construction of the Computational Formulas for df = 1 Comparisons in the $A \times (B \times S)$ Design*

Source

Steps	$B_{\text{comp.}}$	$A \times B_{\text{comp.}}$	$B_{\text{comp.}} \times S/A$
(1) *df*	b'	$(a-1)(b')$	$(b')(s-1)(a)$
(2) *df* expanded	b'	$ab' - b'$	$ab's - ab'$
		FIRST TERM OF THE FORMULA	
(3) Weight and sum over *j*	$\displaystyle\sum_{j}^{b}(c_j)(B_j)$	$\displaystyle\sum_{j}^{b}(c_j)(AB_{ij})$	$\displaystyle\sum_{j}^{b}(c_j)(ABS_{ijk})$
(4) Square and then sum over remaining subscripts	$\left[\displaystyle\sum_{j}^{b}(c_j)(B_j)\right]^2$	$\displaystyle\sum_{i}^{a}\left[\sum_{j}^{b}(c_j)(AB_{ij})\right]^2$	$\displaystyle\sum_{i}^{a}\sum_{k}^{s}\left[\sum_{j}^{b}(c_j)(ABS_{ijk})\right]^2$
(5) No. of observations	*abs*	*abs*	*abs*
(6) Divide by: (no. of observations)$\left[\sum(c_j)^2\right]$	$\dfrac{\left[\displaystyle\sum_{j}^{b}(c_j)(B_j)\right]^2}{as\left[\sum(c_j)^2\right]}$	$\dfrac{\displaystyle\sum_{i}^{a}\left[\sum_{j}^{b}(c_j)(AB_{ij})\right]^2}{s\left[\sum(c_j)^2\right]}$	$\dfrac{\displaystyle\sum_{i}^{a}\sum_{k}^{s}\left[\sum_{j}^{b}(c_j)(ABS_{ijk})\right]^2}{\sum(c_j)^2}$
(7) Letter code	$[B_c]$	$[AB_c]$	$[AB_cS]$
		COMPUTATIONAL FORMULA	
(8) Coded formula	$[B_c]$	$[AB_c] - [B_c]$	$[AB_cS] - [AB_c]$

The final step presents, in coded form, the computational formulas for the three sources. The patterns of combination indicated in this step are specified by the expanded df statement (step 2). We are now ready to use these formulas in a numerical example. This example consists of a specialized application of this sort of analysis: an analysis of trend.

TREND ANALYSIS   We have already indicated that a common use of the $A \times (B \times S)$ design is in the comparison of independent groups (factor A) over a number of trials (factor B). Since trial numbers (the levels of factor B) conveniently represent points which are equally spaced, we can ask questions concerning the nature of the functional relationship between trial number and performance. Such questions often take the form of an analytical assessment of the different components of trend present in the learning curves.

Before we begin the actual analysis, it must be stressed that the interpretation of any interaction of treatments and trials, as well as the interpretation of the meaning of the trend analysis itself, is often clouded by the fact that a performance ceiling is usually reached over the course of the training trials. That is, subjects either begin to attain the maximum performance or reach a physiological limit of some sort. Either way, the consequence of such a possibility is a *necessary* interaction with trials, if groups are separated on early trials and converge upon the performance ceiling on later trials. Under these circumstances, comparisons of different learning trends are generally meaningless. It might be possible to restrict attention entirely to the initial learning trials, where the ceiling is much less likely to have an influence upon the trends. Of course, there are many instances in which the mixed design does not involve trials, but other factors that reflect points on an ordered dimension. Trends based upon these conditions usually will not suffer from this problem.

The data presented in Table 20-9 will be used for the example of the analysis of trend. We will assume that the repeated factor consists of points taken from some ordered dimension (e.g., successive trials) and that we are interested in isolating the orthogonal trend components of the main effect of factor B and of the $A \times B$ interaction. The relevant portions of Table 20-9 are presented again in Table 20-14. In the upper section of the table, the coefficients for the linear, quadratic, and cubic components of the orthogonal polynomials are presented. (These were obtained from Table C-2 of Appendix C.) An inspection of row 3 of Table 20-13 reveals that we will need three basic quantities: the B_j sums, the AB_{ij} sums, and the ABS_{ijk} scores. These can be found in the AB and ABS matrices, and it is this portion of the original data that is duplicated on the left in the two remaining sections of Table 20-14.

It is convenient to conduct the analysis in a series of steps. The first step simply consists of the calculation of all of the sums of weighted totals specified in row 3 of Table 20-13. We will be obtaining, then, a sum for each of the rows in the ABS and AB matrices. Starting with the B_j totals at the bottom of the table,

$$\sum_j^b (c_{1j})(B_j) = (-3)(58) + (-1)(87) + (1)(117) + (3)(92),$$

$$\sum_j^b (c_{2j})(B_j) = (1)(58) + (-1)(87) + (-1)(117) + (1)(92),$$

$$\sum_j^b (c_{3j})(B_j) = (-1)(58) + (3)(87) + (-3)(117) + (1)(92).$$

The results of these operations are entered in the appropriate columns to the right of the actual totals.

Working with the AB_{ij} totals and in particular the totals at level a_2 (the AB_{2j} totals), we have

$$\sum_j^b (c_{1j})(AB_{2j}) = (-3)(34) + (-1)(47) + (1)(66) + (3)(52),$$

$$\sum_j^b (c_{2j})(AB_{2j}) = (1)(34) + (-1)(47) + (-1)(66) + (1)(52),$$

$$\sum_j^b (c_{3j})(AB_{2j}) = (-1)(34) + (3)(47) + (-3)(66) + (1)(52).$$

These sums appear on the right side of the table. The same sort of operation is performed to produce the sums for the AB_{ij} totals at level a_1; these appear in the table.

Finally, we will calculate the same sums on the individual ABS_{ijk} scores found in the different rows of the ABS matrix. For example, the second subject at level a_2 (s_7) provides the following sums:

$$\sum_j^b (c_{1j})(ABS_{2j7}) = (-3)(10) + (-1)(12) + (1)(18) + (3)(15),$$

$$\sum_j^b (c_{2j})(ABS_{2j7}) = (1)(10) + (-1)(12) + (-1)(18) + (1)(15),$$

$$\sum_j^b (c_{3j})(ABS_{2j7}) = (-1)(10) + (3)(12) + (-3)(18) + (1)(15).$$

The results of the calculations for this subject and for the remaining subjects are given in the three columns on the right of Table 20-14.

After calculating all of these weighted sums, it is a good idea to perform simple computational checks on the entries in the table. There are two sets of these. The first deals with the ABS matrix and verifies that the column totals for each

TABLE 20-14 *Numerical Example: Analysis of Trend*

ORTHOGONAL POLYNOMIAL COEFFICIENTS

Component	b_1	b_2	b_3	b_4	$\sum (c_j)^2$
Linear (c_{1j})	-3	-1	1	3	20
Quadratic (c_{2j})	1	-1	-1	1	4
Cubic (c_{3j})	-1	3	-3	1	20

ABS MATRIX AND SUMS OF WEIGHTED SCORES

	b_1	b_2	b_3	b_4	Linear	Quadratic	Cubic
					a_1		
s_1	3	5	9	6	13	-5	-9
s_2	7	11	12	11	13	-5	1
s_3	9	13	14	12	10	-6	0
s_4	4	8	11	7	12	-8	-6
s_5	1	3	5	4	11	-3	-3
					a_2		
s_6	5	6	11	7	11	-5	-13
s_7	10	12	18	15	21	-5	-13
s_8	10	15	15	14	12	-6	4
s_9	6	9	13	9	13	-7	-9
s_{10}	3	5	9	7	16	-4	-8

AB MATRIX AND SUMS OF WEIGHTED TOTALS

	b_1	b_2	b_3	b_4	Linear	Quadratic	Cubic
AB_{1j}	24	40	51	40	59	-27	-17
AB_{2j}	34	47	66	52	73	-27	-39
Sum (B_j)	58	87	117	92	132	-54	-56

level of factor A equal the corresponding entries in the AB matrix. For example, at level a_2 and for the cubic component,

$$(-13) + (-13) + (4) + (-9) + (-8) = -39.$$

The second computational check deals with the AB matrix and verifies that the column totals equal the corresponding column marginal entries. For the cubic component, for example,

$$(-17) + (-39) = -56.$$

We can now calculate the sums of squares for the trend analysis. We will begin by computing the *first terms* for each set of comparisons and then combine these quantities to produce the corresponding sums of squares. For the

$SS_{B_{comp.}}$, the first term (and in this case, the only term) is given by

$$[B_c] = \frac{\left[\sum\limits_{j}^{b} (c_j)(B_j)\right]^2}{as\left[\sum (c_j)^2\right]}.$$

Substituting the relevant data from Table 20-14, we have

$$[B_1] = \frac{(132)^2}{2(5)(20)} = \frac{17{,}424}{200} = 87.12,$$

$$[B_2] = \frac{(-54)^2}{2(5)(4)} = \frac{2916}{40} = 72.90,$$

$$[B_3] = \frac{(-56)^2}{2(5)(20)} = \frac{3136}{200} = 15.68.$$

For the $SS_{A \times B_{comp.}}$, the first term is given by

$$[AB_c] = \frac{\sum\limits_{i}^{a}\left[\sum\limits_{j}^{b} (c_j)(AB_{ij})\right]^2}{s\left[\sum (c_j)^2\right]}.$$

From the AB matrix of Table 20-14,

$$[AB_1] = \frac{(59)^2 + (73)^2}{5(20)} = \frac{8810}{100} = 88.10,$$

$$[AB_2] = \frac{(-27)^2 + (-27)^2}{5(4)} = \frac{1458}{20} = 72.90,$$

$$[AB_3] = \frac{(-17)^2 + (-39)^2}{5(20)} = \frac{1810}{100} = 18.10.$$

Finally, the first term for the $SS_{B_{comp.} \times S/A}$ is given by

$$[AB_cS] = \frac{\sum\limits_{i}^{a}\sum\limits_{k}^{s}\left[\sum\limits_{j}^{b} (c_j)(ABS_{ijk})\right]^2}{\sum (c_j)^2}.$$

Substituting the data from the ABS matrix of Table 20-14, we have

$$[AB_1S] = \frac{(13)^2 + (13)^2 + \cdots + (13)^2 + (16)^2}{20} = \frac{1834}{20} = 91.70,$$

$$[AB_2S] = \frac{(-5)^2 + (-5)^2 + \cdots + (-7)^2 + (-4)^2}{4} = \frac{310}{4} = 77.50,$$

$$[AB_3S] = \frac{(-9)^2 + (1)^2 + \cdots + (-9)^2 + (-8)^2}{20} = \frac{626}{20} = 31.30.$$

We are now in a position to calculate the sums of squares. For the comparisons involving the main effect of factor B.

$$SS_{B_{comp.}} = [B_c],$$

and so we can enter these quantities directly in the analysis summary (Table 20-15). For the $A \times B$ interaction,

$$SS_{A \times B_{comp.}} = [AB_c] - [B_c],$$

$$SS_{A \times B_{linear}} = 88.10 - 87.12 = .98,$$

$$SS_{A \times B_{quadratic}} = 72.90 - 72.90 = .00,$$

$$SS_{A \times B_{cubic}} = 18.10 - 15.68 = 2.42.$$

These quantities are also entered in Table 20-15. Finally, for the $B \times S/A$ interaction,

$$SS_{B_{comp.} \times S/A} = [AB_cS] - [AB_c],$$

$$SS_{B_{linear} \times S/A} = 91.70 - 88.10 = 3.60,$$

$$SS_{B_{quadratic} \times S/A} = 77.50 - 72.90 = 4.60,$$

$$SS_{B_{cubic} \times S/A} = 31.30 - 18.10 = 13.20.$$

These sums of squares are listed in the table.

There is a useful computational check that can be used at this point. It consists of the verification that the sum of each set of orthogonal components equals the corresponding sums of squares from the original analysis. For the three sets,

$$\sum SS_{B_{comp.}} = 87.12 + 72.90 + 15.68 = 175.70 = SS_B,$$

$$\sum SS_{A \times B_{comp.}} = .98 + .00 + 2.42 = 3.40 = SS_{A \times B},$$

$$\sum SS_{B_{comp.} \times S/A} = 3.60 + 4.60 + 13.20 = 21.40 = SS_{B \times S/A}.$$

Continuing with the analysis, the df are calculated for the component sums of squares. Using the df statements presented in Table 20-13,

$$df_{B_{comp.}} = 1,$$

$$df_{A \times B_{comp.}} = (df_A)(df_{B_{comp.}}) = (a - 1)(1)$$

$$= (2 - 1)(1) = 1,$$

$$df_{B_{comp.} \times S/A} = (df_{B_{comp.}})(df_S)(a) = (1)(s - 1)(2)$$

$$= (1)(5 - 1)(2) = 8.$$

It will be noted that the same computational checks are available with the

TABLE 20-15   *Summary of the Analysis of Trend*

Source	SS	df	MS	F
A	48.40	1	48.40	< 1
S/A	396.20	8	49.52	
B	(175.70)	(3)		
Linear	87.12	1	87.12	193.60*
Quadratic	72.90	1	72.90	125.69*
Cubic	15.68	1	15.68	9.50*
A × B	(3.40)	(3)		
Linear	.98	1	.98	2.18
Quadratic	.00	1	.00	< 1
Cubic	2.42	1	2.42	1.47
B × S/A	(21.40)	(24)		
Linear	3.60	8	.45	
Quadratic	4.60	8	.58	
Cubic	13.20	8	1.65	
Total	645.10	39		

* $p < .01$.

component df's as were available for the SS's. That is,

$$\sum df_{B_{comp.}} = 1 + 1 + 1 = 3 = df_B,$$

$$\sum df_{A \times B_{comp.}} = 1 + 1 + 1 = 3 = df_{A \times B},$$

$$\sum df_{B_{comp.} \times S/A} = 8 + 8 + 8 = 24 = df_{B \times S/A}.$$

The mean squares are calculated in the usual way.

The final step in the analysis is to calculate the different F ratios. Consistent with the analysis of trend in the $(A \times S)$ design, we will use different error terms to evaluate each of the trend components. To be more specific, the denominator terms for the F ratios involving the main effect and the interaction are the corresponding $MS_{B_{comp.} \times S/A}$. That is, for the trend components of the main effect,

$$F = \frac{MS_{B_{comp.}}}{MS_{B_{comp.} \times S/A}},$$

and for the components of the $A \times B$ interaction,

$$F = \frac{MS_{A \times B_{comp.}}}{MS_{B_{comp.} \times S/A}}.$$

For example, the F ratios for the two sets of linear components, the $MS_{B_{\text{linear}}}$ and the $MS_{A \times B_{\text{linear}}}$, are

$$F = \frac{87.12}{.45} = 193.60 \quad \text{and} \quad F = \frac{.98}{.45} = 2.18,$$

respectively. The results of these and the remaining statistical tests are presented in the table.[6]

SUMMARY   Since the $A \times B$ interaction was not significant in the original analysis (see Table 20-10), we would usually not be interested in isolating trend components of the interaction but would, instead, concern ourselves with the analysis of the main effect. This latter analysis indicates that each trend component is significant, although most of the variation among the means is accounted for by the linear and quadratic components. In terms of percentages, the linear component represents $87.12/175.70 \times 100 = 49.6$ percent of the main effect of factor B and the quadratic represents $72.90/175.70 \times 100 = 41.5$ percent of the main effect; the cubic component accounts for the remainder, $15.68/175.70 \times 100 = 8.9$ percent. If we look at the four $\bar{B}$ means, $\bar{B}_1 = 5.8$, $\bar{B}_2 = 8.7, \bar{B}_3 = 11.7$, and $\bar{B}_4 = 9.2$, we can "see" the first two components quite clearly: The means tend to increase with trial number (linear trend) but show a slight reversal at b_4 (quadratic trend). The slight cubic trend comes from the fact that the reversal in trend is not symmetrical, as if the curve would change its direction again.

Multiple Comparisons

Multiple comparisons are also complicated by the fact that some contrasts are based upon independent groups while others are based upon repeated measures. If we are concerned with the latter, the procedures discussed for the analysis of the main effect of factor B in the $(A \times B \times S)$ design are appropriate (see p. 433). For comparisons involving means contributing to the main effect of factor A, we should be able to use the procedures outlined for two-factor designs with independent groups (see Chapter 11, pp. 208–212). This involves the use of critical ranges and an error term based upon a pooled within-groups variance—in this case, the $MS_{S/A}$. The argument justifying this error term is the same given in the earlier chapters: that we assume homogeneity of population treatment variances for the different conditions of factor A.

Multiple comparisons between means contributing to the $A \times B$ interaction will undoubtedly be conducted within a particular level of either factor A or factor B, depending upon the experimental question of interest. If the

---

[6] The analysis is different in the $(A \times B \times S)$ design. Two sets of error terms are needed, one for the main effect (i.e., the $MS_{B_{\text{comp}} \times S}$) and one for the interaction (i.e., the $MS_{A \times B_{\text{comp}} \times S}$). The formulas for the comparisons themselves are unchanged. [See Myers (1966, Table 14-2, pp. 365–366) for more detail.]

comparisons involve the means appearing at one level of the repeated factor (B), separate error terms should be constructed for each contrast. [This is essentially the procedure outlined for the ($A \times B \times S$) design, p. 433.] If they involve the nonrepeated factor (A), we can use the within-groups variance pooled over the a groups at that particular level of factor B, exactly as we did in testing the significance of the simple main effect of factor A. Or, if the within-group variances appear to be heterogeneous, we should use a within-groups variance that pools only the two groups entering in a specific comparison. [See the discussion of the complications arising when separate error terms are used in conducting multiple comparisons in Chapter 19 (pp. 420–421).]

chapter twenty-one

HIGHER-ORDER FACTORIALS, HOMOGENEITY ASSUMPTIONS, AND STRUCTURAL MODELS

In this chapter we will consider the analysis of the general case in which repeated measures appear. First, we will examine the nature of the statistical analysis and see how simply the necessary computational formulas can be constructed through an application of procedures we have discussed in earlier chapters. Next, we will consider the homogeneity assumptions underlying the analysis of repeated-measures designs. Finally, we will worry about the implications for the evaluation of factorial effects when random independent variables are introduced into an experiment with repeated measures.

HIGHER-ORDER FACTORIALS

The statistical analysis of one- and two-factor experiments containing repeated measures was outlined in the last two chapters. The set of rules to be presented in this section can be applied to these designs as well as to factorial designs with three or more factors. It is obvious that with an increase in the number of factors, there is a corresponding increase in types of designs that are possible. With one factor, there was only the $(A \times S)$ design. With two factors, where one or both factors may be repeated, two basic designs were produced: the $A \times (B \times S)$ and the $(A \times B \times S)$ designs, respectively. The addition of a *third* factor makes possible designs in which one, two, or three factors are repeated: the $A \times B \times (C \times S)$, the $A \times (B \times C \times S)$, and the $(A \times B \times C \times S)$ designs, respectively. We find detailed discussions of the first two designs in a number of sources, e.g., Winer (1962, pp. 319–349; 1971, pp. 539–571) and Myers (1966, pp. 189–209). Four-factor designs appear often enough in the literature that we should know how to analyze designs of this complexity.

In this section we assume that the independent variables are *fixed*. In all of the analyses, the sums of squares associated with the independent variable (the main effects and the interaction) are obtained with exactly the same formulas required of completely randomized designs. The point at which completely randomized designs and designs with repeated measures diverge is, as you now know, in the choice of the appropriate error terms. We will discuss the analysis of repeated-measures designs in four steps: (1) the identification of the sources of variance, (2) the calculation of the corresponding degrees of freedom, (3) the construction of the computational formulas for the sums of squares, and (4) the selection of the error terms.

Identification of Sources of Variance

We have already considered schemes for specifying the sources of variance in completely randomized designs. As long as there is no nesting of the *independent* variables, a simplified rule is available to specify the sources of variance for designs with repeated measures:[1]

1. List the *independent* factors and all possible interactions of these factors; and
2. add factor *S* plus all interactions with factor *S* except those in which letters are duplicated.

In order to illustrate this new rule, we will apply it to three-factor designs with repeated measures. This has been done in Table 21-1. The first column of the table gives the results of the first part of the rule, listing all possible sources of variance involving the independent variables alone. This listing is appropriate for all three designs. The next three columns show the results of applying the second part of the rule to the different designs. In column 2, for example, we have the design in which all factors are repeated. Factor S becomes "S" in this case and crosses with each of the sources listed in column 1. For the next design, factors B and C involve repeated measures and factor S is nested within factor A. Under these circumstances, factor S becomes "S/A" and crosses

---

[1] With nesting present, we use the rule presented in Chapter 18 (p. 368), deleting from the second part of the rule the phrase "omitting the within-groups factor".

with all of the sources listed in column 1 except those containing the letter A. For the final design, only factor C involves repeated measures. This means that factor S is nested within factors A and B. In this case, factor S becomes "S/AB" and crosses only with C, since in all other cases letters are duplicated.

TABLE 21-1 *Sources of Variance in Three-Factor Designs with Repeated Measures*

(1) Basic Sources of Variance	(2) $(A \times B \times C \times S)$ Design	(3) $A \times (B \times C \times S)$ Design	(4) $A \times B \times (C \times S)$ Design
	Factor S: S	Factor S: S/A	Factor S: S/AB
A	$A \times S$	—	—
B	$B \times S$	$B \times S/A$	—
C	$C \times S$	$C \times S/A$	$C \times S/AB$
$A \times B$	$A \times B \times S$	—	—
$A \times C$	$A \times C \times S$	—	—
$B \times C$	$B \times C \times S$	$B \times C \times S/A$	—
$A \times B \times C$	$A \times B \times C \times S$	—	—

Calculation of Degrees of Freedom

The df statements for any source of variance are obtained by means of a rule presented in Chapter 18. To repeat, the df are found by

multiplying (1) the product of the df's of factors to the *left* of the diagonal by (2) the product of the *levels* of factors to the *right* of the diagonal.

For sources involving only crossed factors, the diagonal is assumed to be on the right. Thus, the df statements for all of the sources listed in columns 1 and 2 of Table 21-1 are found by multiplying the df's of the factors contained in any given source. For the sources listed in column 3,

$$df_{S/A} = (df_S)(a) = (s - 1)(a),$$

$$df_{B \times S/A} = [(df_B)(df_S)](a) = (b - 1)(s - 1)(a),$$

$$df_{C \times S/A} = [(df_C)(df_S)](a) = (c - 1)(s - 1)(a),$$

$$df_{B \times C \times S/A} = [(df_B)(df_C)(df_S)](a) = (b - 1)(c - 1)(s - 1)(a).$$

Finally, for the two sources listed in column 4,

$$df_{S/AB} = (df_S)[(a)(b)] = (s - 1)(ab),$$

$$df_{C \times S/AB} = [(df_C)(df_S)][(a)(b)] = (c - 1)(s - 1)(ab).$$

Construction of Computational Formulas

By now, the construction of the formulas for the sums of squares should be a familiar operation. We are given sufficient information from the expanded *df* statements to construct the basic terms entering into the different formulas and to specify the patterns in which these terms are combined to produce the complete computational formulas. These steps are explained in detail in Chapter 10 (pp. 191–195). Another piece of information provided by the expanded *df* statements is the different summary matrices into which the data of the experiment must be arranged. The term *abcs*, for example, indicates scores contained within the four-way classification of factors A, B, C, and S— i.e., the $ABCS$ matrix. Similarly, the term *bcs* indicates the totals contained within the three-way classification of factors B, C, and S—the BCS matrix.

Selection of Error Terms

The error terms for the different sources of variance can be found by means of the following principle:

If a source contains a repeated factor or factors, the error term is an *interaction* of factor S with the repeated factor(s); and
If a source contains no repeated factors, the error term is the within-groups factor, factor S.

Suppose we consider the second part of this rule first. We have seen in the $A \times (B \times S)$ design that the error term for the MS_A, which contains no repeated factors, is a within-groups mean square, the $MS_{S/A}$ in this case. This will be true in any design where repeated and nonrepeated factors are mixed—sources coming from that part of the experiment represented by independent groups are evaluated by a within-groups mean square. The first part of the rule, on the other hand, pertains to sources of variance based on repeated factors. In the examples we have considered earlier, the error term has always been an interaction of factor S and the repeated factor(s) involved. The same principle holds for all designs in which repeated measures appear.

EXAMPLES   We will use the three-factor designs we have been considering in this section as illustrations of this rule. Each of these designs appears in Table 21-2, with the sources reflecting treatment effects listed on the left and the appropriate error terms on the right. For convenience, we have segregated the sources according to the number of repeated factors contained in the source and, where applicable, grouped sources containing the same repeated factors. Consider first the $(A \times B \times C \times S)$ design. Since all sources in this design contain one or more repeated factors, only the first clause of the rule applies, and all of the error terms take the form of an interaction between the experimental factor(s) and factor S. Moreover, since each source contains a different

TABLE 21-2 *Identification of Error Terms in Three-Factor Designs with Repeated Measures*

($A \times B \times C \times S$) Design		$A \times (B \times C \times S)$ Design		$A \times B \times (C \times S)$ Design	
Source	Error Term	Source	Error Term	Source	Error Term
NO REPEATED FACTORS		NO REPEATED FACTORS		NO REPEATED FACTORS	
none	—	A	S/A	A	
ONE REPEATED FACTOR		ONE REPEATED FACTOR		B	S/AB
A	$A \times S$	B	$B \times S/A$	$A \times B$	
B	$B \times S$	$A \times B$		ONE REPEATED FACTOR	
C	$C \times S$			C	
TWO REPEATED FACTORS		C	$C \times S/A$	$A \times C$	$C \times S/AB$
$A \times B$	$A \times B \times S$	$A \times C$		$B \times C$	
$A \times C$	$A \times C \times S$	TWO REPEATED FACTORS		$A \times B \times C$	
$B \times C$	$B \times C \times S$	$B \times C$	$B \times C \times S/A$		
THREE REPEATED FACTORS		$A \times B \times C$			
$A \times B \times C$	$A \times B \times C \times S$				

combination of repeated factors, there is a unique error term for each one of them. These error terms are specified in Table 21-2.

In the $A \times (B \times C \times S)$ design, where factor A represents the single non-repeated factor, there are three classifications of sources: 0, 1, and 2 repeated factors. The MS_A contains no repeated factors. Thus, the second clause applies and the error term is the within-groups factor, the $MS_{S/A}$. Two sources contain the repeated factor "B" (B and $A \times B$) and two sources contain the repeated factor "C" (C and $A \times C$). The error term for each set of scores is an interaction of factor S (S/A) with the corresponding repeated factor—$B \times S/A$ and $C \times S/A$, respectively. Finally, two sources contain both of the repeated factors (the $B \times C$ and the $A \times B \times C$ interactions) and these are both evaluated by the interaction of the repeated factors (B and C) with factor S—the $B \times C \times S/A$ interaction.

The third example is the $A \times B \times (C \times S)$ design, in which only factor C is repeated. There are three sources of variance containing no repeated factors—A, B, and $A \times B$—and these are evaluated by the within-groups factor for this design, the $MS_{S/AB}$. The four remaining sources contain the single repeated factor—C, $A \times C$, $B \times C$, and $A \times B \times C$—and these are evaluated by the interaction of the repeated factor and the within-groups factor, $C \times S/AB$.

Summary   The application of the rule for selecting error terms in designs with more than three factors should be obvious. After segregating sources of variance according to the repeated factor (or factors) in common, we find the different error terms. As indicated in the rule, the error term for sources based on independent groups of subjects is the within-groups source. The error term(s) for the sources of variance obtained from repeated measures are interactions of the repeated factor(s) involved with factor S.

Concluding Comments

We have been able to specify the statistical analysis of three-factor designs by using a number of simple rules. From the information provided in the expanded *df* statements and from Table 21-2, it is possible to conduct the analysis of variance without any further specification of the calculations needed. In order to make this point explicitly, and to illustrate the analysis of relatively common three-factor designs, two of the exercises for Part V provide sets of data to be analyzed. Exercise 9 contains one repeated factor, the $A \times B \times (C \times S)$ design, and Exercise 10 contains two repeated factors, the $A \times (B \times C \times S)$ design.

The procedures outlined in this section place a minimal demand on our memory systems and still make possible the generation of the computational formulas for any type of factorial design incorporating repeated measures on one or more factors. These, together with the general procedures presented in the earlier chapters for completely randomized experiments, give you sufficient background to analyze the data from most of the experiments you will encounter in your professional life. We have not discussed the conduct of additional comparisons for these higher-order designs. The procedures for adapting these analyses to higher-order factorials have been illustrated in Chapters 16 and 20, and so they need not be repeated here. Finally, as a reminder, we have assumed in the selection of error terms that the factors of experimental interest are *fixed*. The complications arising from the introduction of random independent variables into a repeated-measures design will be discussed subsequently (pp. 467–470).

HOMOGENEITY ASSUMPTIONS IN THE ANALYSIS OF REPEATED-MEASURES DESIGNS

Homogeneity of Variance and of Covariance

In Chapters 19 and 20 we indicated that certain assumptions of the statistical model must be met before the analyses can be justified. The first is the assumption of *homogeneity of within-treatment variances*, which is analogous to the homogeneity assumption in the case of independent groups. That is, it specifies equal variability of the scores in each treatment population. The second assumption concerns the degree to which subjects maintain their relative standing in the various conditions defined by the repeated factor (or factors). To be more specific, the assumption states that the consistency observed for any pair of treatment conditions is the *same* for *all possible pairs* of treatment conditions. Said more formally, the second assumption specifies the *homogeneity of the covariance between pairs of treatment conditions*. This is a new assumption for us and requires some discussion.

Suppose we consider the simplest design with repeated measures, the $(A \times S)$ design. Since the same subjects appear in each of the treatment conditions in this design, we can obtain an index of the degree to which subjects maintain their relative standing to one another in the different treatment conditions. A familiar index of this consistency is the product-moment correlation. In the analysis of variance, however, it is convenient to employ an algebraically related measure of correlation: *covariance*. In the context of the $(A \times S)$ design, the sample covariance of any two levels of factor A, a_i and $a_{i'}$, is given by

$$\text{covariance} = \frac{\sum_{j}^{s}(AS_{ij} - \bar{A}_i)(AS_{i'j} - \bar{A}_{i'})}{s - 1}. \tag{21-1}$$

What we are asked to do in Eq. (21-1) is (1) to obtain two deviation scores for each of the s subjects, one representing his deviation from the mean at level a_i $(AS_{ij} - \bar{A}_i)$ and the other his deviation from the mean at level $a_{i'}$ $(AS_{i'j} - \bar{A}_{i'})$, (2) to multiply the two deviations, (3) to sum these products over the s subjects, and (4) to divide the sum by the quantity, $s - 1$. Note the similarity between Eq. (21-1) and the general equation for a sample *variance*. That is, the variance of the s scores at level a_i is given by

$$\text{variance} = \frac{\sum_{j}^{s}(AS_{ij} - \bar{A}_i)^2}{s - 1} = \frac{\sum_{j}^{s}(AS_{ij} - \bar{A}_i)(AS_{ij} - \bar{A}_i)}{s - 1}.$$

The last expression is identical to Eq. (21-1) except for the second deviation score.

We can now return to our discussion. The homogeneity assumption specifies the same consistency—equal covariances—for all pairs of treatment populations. Suppose there were $a = 3$ treatment levels, for example. With this design three pairs of treatment conditions are possible: levels a_1 and a_2, levels a_1 and a_3, and levels a_2 and a_3. Therefore, we must assume that the population covariances for these pairs of conditions are equal, i.e., homogeneous.

We would expect to find homogeneity of the covariances in the population were it not for the possibility of a Treatment × Subject interaction. Consider the implication of such an interaction: subjects react differently to the specific treatment conditions, either because of differential susceptibility to the treatments or to the presence of differential carry-over effects. Consequently, the relative standing of subjects will change from treatment to treatment, thus lowering the correlation between sets of scores *and* lowering it *differentially* for pairs of conditions. In short, then, the presence of a Treatment × Subject interaction may very well result in marked heterogeneity of covariance.

It has been asserted that Treatment × Subject interactions are to be expected in much of our research. In some areas, such as physiological psychology or research on sensory processes, the interaction may be relatively small. In some cases it may even be possible to minimize magnitude of these interactions by attempting to reduce or to eliminate carry-over effects from one treatment to another. This could be accomplished, for instance, by introducing time intervals between successive treatments. In contrast, one of the most typical applications of the repeated-measures design is the learning experiment in which "trials" is the independent variable. Under these circumstances it is quite likely to be the case that the assumptions of homogeneity of variance and of covariance are *not* met. That is, it is a common observation that within-trial variability decreases over trials (heterogeneity of variance) and that intertrial correlations (covariance) decrease as increasing numbers of trials intervene; i.e., the correlation between trials 1 and 2 will be higher than between trials 1 and 10, say. In one of the few tests of this assumption that has been reported, Cotton, Jensen, and Lewis (1962) examined the running times over 30 acquisition trials of 100 identically treated rats and showed dramatically that the assumption of homogeneous covariances did not hold.[2] The point of all of this is to stress the fact that a great many experiments with repeated measures will lead to a questioning of the assumptions of homogeneous variances and covariances.

Implications of Violations of the Homogeneity Assumptions

If the variance-covariance assumption is not met, then the F test of the treatment effect is known to be biased *positively*.[3] That is, the tabled value of F at $\alpha = .05$, say, actually represents a significance level that is *greater* than .05—e.g., $\alpha = .10$. What this means is that if we do not make an adjustment in our rejection procedure, we will be operating at a more "lenient" significance level than we had set originally. As a consequence, we will reject the null hypothesis falsely a greater percentage of the time than our statements of significance would imply.

As an illustration, consider the demonstration reported by Collier, Baker, Mandeville, and Hayes (1967) in which the computer and Monte Carlo procedures were used to provide an estimate of the magnitude of the bias in the standard analysis. Briefly, these investigators built different degrees of heterogeneity into different populations of scores, then sampled randomly from these populations and performed statistical analyses on the sets of sampled scores. All of the populations had the same mean. Thus, if a large number of such "experiments" were conducted, the resulting sampling distribution of F should approximate the theoretical distribution when the homogeneity assumptions are fully met. That is, 5 percent of the empirical F ratios should exceed the critical value of F at $\alpha = .05$. When violations of these assumptions are introduced, the extent to which empirical F ratios exceed the 5 percent value would provide an indication of the extent of the positive bias.

---

[2] The author is indebted to Dr. Norman E. Spear for suggesting this reference.

[3] The statistical evaluation of the homogeneity assumptions is complicated and involves matrix algebra. An example of the test is found in Kirk (1968, pp. 139–142) and in Winer (1962, p. 124, pp. 369–374; 1971, p. 282, pp. 594–599).

Collier et al. varied a number of characteristics of the distributions of scores to determine the effect on the empirical α level for the main effects and for the $A \times B$ interaction in the $A \times (B \times S)$ design. They obtained this information for 15 different conditions of heterogeneity, some clearly more deviant than would ever be expected in actual experimentation. The results of these determinations on the *nonrepeated factor*, A, indicated that approximately 5 percent of the F ratios exceeded the critical value of F. Thus, conclusions concerning the significance of the main effect of A are essentially uninfluenced by these severe violations of the homogeneity assumptions. As expected by theory, positive biases *did* appear for the comparisons involving *repeated measures*. If we take an average over the 15 different conditions of their study, we find for the main effect of factor B that 6.8 percent of the obtained F ratios exceeded the α level when $s = 5$ and 7.5 percent when $s = 15$. The corresponding values for the $A \times B$ interaction were slightly higher, 8.0 percent and 8.2 percent, respectively.

USE OF A "CORRECTED" F A solution to this problem is to evaluate an F ratio based on repeated measures against a critical value that assumes the presence of *maximal heterogeneity*. In practice, all that we do is to decrease the numerator and the denominator df's associated with the original F ratios by a factor equal to the df associated with the repeated factor (or factors) involved in any particular treatment effect. That is,

$$df_{num.} = \frac{df_{effect}}{df_{repeated\,factors}}$$

$$df_{denom.} = \frac{df_{error\,term}}{df_{repeated\,factors}}.$$

(21-2)

As an example, consider the correction for the $A \times (B \times S)$ design, which is discussed by Greenhouse and Geisser (1959). There is no adjustment required for the evaluation of the main effect of factor A because no repeated factors are involved. Thus,

$$F = \frac{MS_A}{MS_{S/A}}$$

continues to be evaluated with

$$df_{num.} = a - 1 \quad \text{and} \quad df_{denom.} = a(s - 1).$$

The df's are changed for the other two F ratios because of the presence of repeated factors. More specifically,

$$F = \frac{MS_B}{MS_{B \times S/A}}$$

is evaluated with

$$df_{num.} = \frac{b - 1}{b - 1} = 1$$

and

$$df_{\text{denom.}} = \frac{a(b-1)(s-1)}{b-1} = a(s-1);$$

and

$$F = \frac{MS_{A \times B}}{MS_{B \times S/A}}$$

is evaluated with

$$df_{\text{num.}} = \frac{(a-1)(b-1)}{b-1} = a-1$$

and

$$df_{\text{denom.}} = \frac{a(b-1)(s-1)}{b-1} = a(s-1).$$

The main difficulty with this type of correction is that it tends to *overcorrect*, leading to a reduction in the number of null hypotheses falsely rejected as expected by theory. In other words, the adjusted F ratios are now biased in a *negative* direction. (This negative bias was confirmed in the Monte Carlo study of Collier et al. They found that only about 2 percent of the F ratios exceeded the corrected critical values at $\alpha = .05$.) In short, then, if we proceed in the normal fashion and use an uncorrected value of F when there is heterogeneity, the test is positively biased; if we use the correction, the test is negatively biased.

HOTELLING'S T^2 It is obvious that the actual theoretical distributions of most cases will fall somewhere between homogeneity and maximum heterogeneity. Under these circumstances, there is available an *exact test* of the null hypothesis that allows us to calculate the critical values of F given the particular severity of the homogeneity violations in our experiment. This is Hotelling's T^2 statistic. The calculations are quite complicated, however, and you are referred to Kirk (1968, pp. 143–144) and to Winer (1962, pp. 632–635; 1971, pp. 305–308) for descriptions and examples of Hotelling's test.

Practical Considerations

We have seen that violations of the homogeneity assumptions can produce a positive bias in our decision process. Several courses of action are open to us. We can use the Greenhouse-Geisser correction, but this adjustment tends to produce a negatively biased F test. On the other hand, we could use Hotelling's procedure or a general multivariate approach, but these calculations are difficult, even with a desk calculator, and the analyses are beyond the scope of this book.

A practical, but less precise, approach is to make no formal correction. The study by Collier et al. suggests that we may actually be operating at $\alpha = .08$

when we base our decision rule on an uncorrected F nominally set at $\alpha = .05$. Most experimenters will still pay close attention to an F that is significant at $\alpha = .06–.08$, which is probably the range of α levels that result from the usual violations of the homogeneity assumptions that we encounter in our research. We have argued in previous chapters that an increased type I error can be tolerated in many cases, since we are also concerned about failing to recognize "real" differences when they are present—i.e., type II errors. The statistical procedures are guides to aid us in guessing at which facts are "real" and which are not. In the absence of any other information, rigid decision rules, where we maintain α at an arbitrary level, make some sense. But if a finding is interesting theoretically, we should not ignore its presence merely because it fails to exceed the critical F value or its corrected value. Agreement with previous experiments and internal consistency with other response measures in the current experiment are important factors that we should take into consideration when we are drawing inferences from our data. The pure statistical arguments represent one input contributing to our final decision. But they are not the only inputs, as we have argued here and elsewhere in the book.

STRUCTURAL MODELS AND ERROR-TERM SELECTION

In Chapter 16 we considered several statistical (or structural) models, which were distinguished by the nature of the independent variables present in the design. Two types of independent variables were described, those that are *fixed* and those that are *random*. Briefly, a random independent variable is one for which the levels of the factors included in the experiment are assumed to represent a random sample from a population of treatment levels. Schools are chosen randomly from a large metropolitan school system, for example, or sets of stimulus materials are chosen randomly from a large pool of materials. The intention of the researcher in these cases is to generalize from the sample of treatment levels included in the experiment to the population of treatment levels. A fixed independent variable, on the other hand, is one for which the levels included in the experiment are assumed to constitute the population of interest. That is, inferences are limited to the treatment levels actually present in an experiment. (See pp. 333–335 for an elaboration of the distinction between fixed and random independent variables.)

We have noted that most independent variables in the behavioral sciences are fixed. We must be prepared, however, for the possibility that we will encounter in our work or in the work of others cases in which random factors are present in repeated-measures designs. Just as was true for completely randomized designs, the introduction of random independent variables into repeated-measures designs changes the nature of the statistical analysis. These changes take the form of new error terms with which to evaluate the significance of the different treatment effects.

Selection Procedure

In Chapter 16 we discussed a scheme for discovering the error term in completely randomized designs when random independent variables are present. We can modify this scheme to accommodate repeated-measures designs. The selection procedure is outlined in Table 21-3 and consists of a series of questions directed towards the different sources of variance in the analysis of variance summary table. These questions concern a matching of the letters used to designate treatment effects and the letters of potential error terms. For convenience, fixed factors are represented by capital letters and random factors by small letters. Contrary to the earlier systems, which were intended for use with completely randomized designs, the system in Table 21-3 specifically includes factor S (nested or crossed) as a random factor. (In Chapter 16 factor S was called the "within-groups mean square," and the questions focused only on the independent variables.)

We should perhaps review the logic of error-term selection. For a source to qualify as an error term, it must "contain" the same theoretical components (i.e., have the same expected value) as the treatment mean square *except* for the so-called null hypothesis component. This latter component is the one that

TABLE 21-3   *Steps in the Selection of Appropriate Error Terms in Experiments (Crossed and Nested) with Repeated Measures*[a]

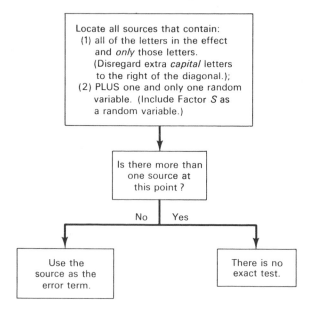

[a] *Source* refers to any subcomponent isolated in the standard analysis of variance; *effect* refers to the source containing only those letters denoting the treatment effect in question.

reflects the treatment effects and is assumed to be zero when the null hypothesis is true. If we say that there is no exact test for a particular treatment mean square, we mean that an exact matching of theoretical components is not possible.

Examples

We will illustrate the use of Table 21-3 by determining the error terms for four different $A \times (B \times S)$ designs. If you care to check the system against the actual expected values, you can do so by consulting Kirk (1968, pp. 275–276). The four designs represent all possible combinations of fixed and random factors and are enumerated in Table 21-4. The design on the left represents a situation in which *both* factors are fixed; it represents the model we have assumed in the earlier discussions of this design. The design on the right specifies two random independent variables. The two designs in the middle contain both types of factors.

We will begin with the model on the left. Starting with the main effect of factor A (A), we are asked at the top of Table 21-3 to locate all sources containing only A plus one random variable. This would be s/A. Since only one source qualifies, s/A is the error term. Considering next the main effect of factor B (B), we find only $B \times s/A$ satisfying the two criteria in the first test. [The source contains B and the random variable s and we can disregard the additional *capital* letter (A) to the *right* of the diagonal.] Finally, the error term for the $A \times B$ interaction must also be $B \times s/A$, since it is the only source that contains the letters in the effect (A and B) and one additional random variable, namely, s. [It will be noted, of course, that the selection scheme produces the same error terms as does the general method presented earlier (pp. 460–462).]

In the second example, factor A is random and factor B is fixed. For the main effect of factor A, only s/a satisfies the two selection criteria; it contains a and an additional random variable (s). For the main effect of factor B, only the $a \times B$ interaction satisfies the selection criteria and thus is the appropriate error term. For the interaction itself, the only term containing the two letters also contains an additional random variable and no extra letters (i.e., $B \times s/a$). This source is the correct error term.

TABLE 21-4   *Error Terms for Different Structural Models: The $A \times (B \times S)$ Design*

Both Factors Fixed		Factor A Random; Factor B Fixed		Factor A Fixed; Factor B Random		Both Factors Random	
Source	Error Term	Source	Error Term	Source	Error Term	Source	Error Term
A	s/A	a	s/a	A	none	a	none
s/A	—	s/a	—	s/A	—	s/a	—
B	$B \times s/A$	B	$a \times B$	b	$b \times s/A$	b	$a \times b$
$A \times B$	$B \times s/A$	$a \times B$	$B \times s/a$	$A \times b$	$b \times s/A$	$a \times b$	$b \times s/a$
$B \times s/A$	—	$B \times s/a$	—	$b \times s/A$	—	$b \times s/a$	—

In the third example, factor A is fixed and factor B is random. For the main effect of factor A, there are two sources containing A and one random variable, namely, s/A and $A \times b$. Since *both* sources also contain no additional letters other than the additional random variable, we conclude that there is no exact test.[4] The error term for the two remaining sources is the quantity $b \times s/A$; the reasons for this selection are the same as those given for these two sources in the first example and we need not go through the discussion again.

Similarly, the error terms for the final situation are selected for the same reasons terms were selected in other designs. That is, there is no exact error term for the main effect of factor A, since two sources of variance satisfy the selection criteria (see the third example). The error terms for the main effect of factor B and for the interaction are the same as those chosen for the second example and for the same reasons.

Summary

We have indicated already that random independent variables are an esoteric topic, since most researchers will rarely encounter an experiment in which it is profitable to view an independent variable as random. On the other hand, such situations do exist, and we should at least know how to change the evaluation procedures when they occur. The fact that an exact test is not available when a single independent variable is random in the $A \times (B \times S)$ design (third example in Table 21-4) indicates that we must be especially careful of random independent variables with repeated measures. The situation is not as critical in the completely randomized design, however, as an inspection of Table 16-3 (p. 341) and 16-4 (p. 342) will reveal. Only when three independent variables are present, two of which are random, does a similar problem exist in the completely randomized design.

EXERCISES FOR PART V[5]

1. An experiment is conducted in which 5 different dosage levels of a particular drug are administered to each of 8 different animals. The order in which the dosages are given is randomized for each animal. The response measure consists of the number of discrimination problems solved within a given time limit. The data in the accompanying AS matrix are obtained. Analyze the results of the experiment.

---

[4] Although a "quasi" F test is available (see, for example, Kirk, 1968, p. 276), a statistician should be consulted.

[5] The answers to the exercises are found in Appendix D.

AS MATRIX

Dosage Levels

	a_1	a_2	a_3	a_4	a_5
s_1	3	7	8	5	7
s_2	2	7	7	6	2
s_3	2	6	7	4	2
s_4	3	3	8	7	5
s_5	4	7	7	6	7
s_6	2	6	7	7	1
s_7	3	7	8	8	6
s_8	1	5	8	4	4

2. We will assume that the experimenter is interested in finding out more about the trend represented in his data listed in Exercise 1. An inspection of the means suggests a strong *curvilinear* trend; i.e., the best scores are obtained with intermediate levels of the drug. Test for the presence of a curvilinear trend by using coefficients of the orthogonal polynomials. (Assume that the drug levels are equally spaced.) Can you think of an alternative way of asking this same question?

3. In Chapter 19 (footnote 7, p. 411) we presented a simplified computational formula for conducting comparisons between two means when the same subjects produced scores under the two treatments. Use this alternative formula to calculate the F for the data presented in Table 19-4 (p. 411). Verify that the F obtained with this formula is identical to the one reported in the text, which was obtained with the standard formulas.

4. The 3×2 factorial in the ABS matrix shown here was conducted with $s = 5$ subjects serving in each of the $ab = 3(2) = 6$ treatment combinations. The order of the combinations was randomized for each subject. Analyze the data obtained from this experiment.

ABS MATRIX

	b_1			b_2		
	a_1	a_2	a_3	a_1	a_2	a_3
s_1	16	19	16	17	7	15
s_2	18	9	9	22	16	23
s_3	10	7	9	14	7	16
s_4	9	7	22	10	16	11
s_5	12	13	17	12	9	13

5. Subjects are given a digit-canceling task under three different conditions of monetary incentive. One group, a_1, are told that they will receive \$1 if they perform at some predetermined level; another group, a_2, are offered \$5 for the same performance; and a third group, a_3, are offered \$10 for this performance. Each subject (4 subjects per incentive group) is given four 30-second trials (factor B). The response measure consists of the number of digits canceled from a long series of digits within the time period.

The data from this experiment are given in the accompanying ABS matrix. Analyze these results.

ABS Matrix

	a_1					a_2					a_3			
	b_1	b_2	b_3	b_4		b_1	b_2	b_3	b_4		b_1	b_2	b_3	b_4
s_1	23	24	27	30	s_5	15	20	27	31	s_9	23	34	38	40
s_2	20	21	25	24	s_6	18	25	32	34	s_{10}	19	32	32	34
s_3	23	29	28	31	s_7	24	26	33	33	s_{11}	24	32	38	38
s_4	14	22	24	25	s_8	22	31	36	36	s_{12}	18	28	37	38

6. Perform the following comparisons on the data presented in Exercise 5:
   (a) A trend analysis over trials using the method of orthogonal polynomials.
   (b) A comparison of the three incentive conditions on each of the four training trials—i.e., an analysis of the simple main effects of factor A.

7. In discussing the appropriate error terms with which to evaluate the $MS_{B_{comp.}}$ and the $MS_{A \times B_{comp.}}$, we focused our attention on the $A \times (B \times S)$ design. We did indicate, however, what the error terms would have been if we had been dealing with the $(A \times B \times S)$ design (footnote 6, p. 454). As practice at constructing computational formulas for single-df comparisons, write the formulas for the $B_{comp.} \times S$ interaction, used in the $(A \times B \times S)$ design to evaluate the $MS_{B_{comp.}}$, and the $A \times B_{comp.} \times S$ interaction, used in this design to evaluate the $MS_{A \times B_{comp.}}$.

8. Consider the following experiment reported by Slobin (1966). Subjects were presented pictures depicting some sort of activity together with a sentence describing the objects in the pictures. The subjects' task was to indicate whether or not the sentence accurately described the picture. There were four independent variables in the experiment, three of which involved repeated measures and one of which involved independent groups. Thus, the design may be represented as an $A \times (B \times C \times D \times S)$ factorial.

   The three independent variables based on repeated measures were (1) 4 types of sentences (factor B), (2) the truth or falsity of the descriptive sentences (factor C), and (3) the reversibility or nonreversibility of the subject and object depicted in the picture (factor D). For this latter independent variable, reversibility refers to situations in which the "...object of action could also serve as the subject..." and nonreversibility refers to situations in which "...the object could not normally serve as the subject" (p. 219). Factor A consisted of groups of subjects drawn from five different age groups —i.e., groups of subjects whose average ages were 6, 8, 10, 12, and 20 years.

   In short, then, the experiment is a "mixed" design, with four independent variables, three of which involve repeated measures, and it contains a total of $abcd = 5(4)(2)(2) = 80$ treatment combinations. There were $s = 16$ subjects in each of the age groupings. Your task is to identify the treatment sources of variance and the appropriate error terms with which to evaluate their significance.

9. The influence of two variables, meaningfulness and intertrial spacing, is studied in a learning experiment. The design is a $2 \times 4 \times 5$ factorial, with the first variable consisting of two levels of meaningfulness (factor A), the second variable consisting of four levels of intertrial spacing (factor B), and the third variable consisting of five learning

trials (factor C). Each of the $ab = 2(4) = 8$ meaningfulness-spacing conditions contains $s = 3$ subjects and each subject receives all five of the learning trials. Thus, the design represents a so-called "mixed" design—i.e., an $A \times B \times (C \times S)$ design. The scores for each of the subjects on each of the learning trials are given in the accompanying $ABCS$ matrix. Analyze the results of the experiment.

$ABCS$ MATRIX

	a_1						a_2				
	c_1	c_2	c_3	c_4	c_5		c_1	c_2	c_3	c_4	c_5
					b_1						
s_1	3	1	4	6	7	s_4	3	3	5	7	7
s_2	1	2	5	5	5	s_5	0	1	3	2	4
s_3	4	6	7	7	8	s_6	2	5	6	6	7
					b_2						
s_7	0	4	4	7	8	s_{10}	1	3	6	5	6
s_8	2	3	5	7	8	s_{11}	0	4	6	7	6
s_9	0	4	4	4	8	s_{12}	2	2	3	5	7
					b_3						
s_{13}	1	3	3	4	4	s_{16}	2	3	5	7	8
s_{14}	1	3	3	5	6	s_{17}	0	4	5	8	8
s_{15}	1	4	7	7	8	s_{18}	1	4	5	7	7
					b_4						
s_{19}	3	5	8	7	6	s_{22}	1	4	4	5	8
s_{20}	0	2	3	6	4	s_{23}	1	2	4	6	8
s_{21}	2	1	2	5	5	s_{24}	2	5	6	7	7

10. The data for this problem were selected from an experiment reported by Postman (1964).[6] The main purpose of the experiment was to study the transfer of verbal habits as a function of a number of different independent variables. Each subject received three transfer "cycles," each containing two learning tasks; of primary interest was the performance on the second task. There were two types of second tasks (factor A), one in which there was no possibility of the transfer of specific habits from task 1 to task 2 (level a_1) and the other in which a subject could use the habits learned on the first task to help with the learning of the second task (level a_2). We have mentioned already that each subject received three transfer cycles (factor B). Within each of these cycles a subject received the same sort of transfer task (a_1 or a_2) that he had been receiving previously; the actual learning tasks themselves were different from cycle to cycle. The final independent variable was trials on task 2 (factor C). Specifically, all subjects were given $c = 4$ trials on each of the transfer tasks in the three cycles.

---

[6] The data were generously made available by Dr. Leo J. Postman. The data presented in the problem are a random sample of the subjects actually serving in the experiment; this was done to reduce the labor of calculation.

One group of subjects received the a_1 transfer task and a different group of subjects received the a_2 transfer task. All subjects received the four trials on task 2 in all three transfer cycles. Thus, the design was an $A \times (B \times C \times S)$ factorial. The dependent variable was the number of correct responses given on each trial of task 2. The questions being asked were: Would subjects differ on the two transfer tasks? Would they differ by the same amount on each of the transfer trials? Would these differences change as subjects gained experience over the three transfer cycles? For the data given in the accompanying $ABCS$ matrix there are $s = 6$ subjects in each of the two transfer tasks.

$ABCS$ MATRIX

	Cycle 1 (b_1)				Cycle 2 (b_2)				Cycle 3 (b_3)			
	c_1	c_2	c_3	c_4	c_1	c_2	c_3	c_4	c_1	c_2	c_3	c_4
						Task a_1						
s_1	1	3	6	6	3	5	6	6	2	4	6	7
s_2	2	4	4	5	2	4	6	7	2	4	6	6
s_3	3	3	4	6	1	2	5	7	3	4	5	7
s_4	2	4	5	7	2	5	6	7	3	4	5	6
s_5	3	4	6	7	4	6	6	7	2	5	5	6
s_6	2	4	4	6	2	4	5	6	1	4	5	6
						Task a_2						
s_7	4	5	6	6	4	4	7	6	5	6	7	8
s_8	1	2	4	5	2	4	5	6	4	6	7	7
s_9	1	3	3	5	2	4	4	4	2	4	5	5
s_{10}	2	4	4	5	3	5	5	6	3	7	7	7
s_{11}	2	3	4	3	3	6	5	6	4	5	6	7
s_{12}	2	4	5	5	4	6	7	6	5	5	6	6

(a) Perform a complete analysis of variance on these data.
(b) The analysis reveals a nonsignificant three-way interaction. Thus we can concentrate upon two-way interactions, since they are representative of the phenomenon under study. One of these is the $A \times C$ (Task $\times$ Trials) interaction. If you look at the sums within the body of the AC matrix, you will see that the interaction is the result of a steeper learning curve for the task in which the transfer of specific habits was not possible (a_1) than for the task in which such transfer was possible (a_2). You may also notice that both learning curves are approximately linear in form. Verify this observation by determining the significance of the $A \times C_{\text{linear}}$ interaction.
(c) The other significant two-way interaction is the interaction of Task and Cycles (i.e., the $A \times B$ interaction). Look at the AB sums in the AB matrix. One way to describe the interaction is to say that there is little improvement in performance over the three cycles for task a_1, while there is marked improvement for task a_2. Or, viewing the interaction another way, we could say that there is little difference between the two transfer tasks on the first two cycles (b_1 and b_2), but that task a_2 is clearly superior to task a_1 on the third cycle (b_3). Which way we decide to describe the interaction depends upon the point we want to make. For this problem, however, test the significance of the simple main effects of factor A at the three levels of factor B.

PART VI

Designs Intended to Decrease Error Variance

In the analysis of any experiment, whatever the design, the significance of a main effect or an interaction is assessed with reference to an error term. In the behavioral sciences large error terms are common, and anything that can be done to reduce their size directly increases the sensitivity of the experiment in detecting treatment effects. As we noted earlier, the virtue of repeated-measures designs is in the elimination of between-subject differences—i.e., consistent individual differences—from the error term. In Part V we discussed some of the deficiencies of the repeated-measures design, the most important of which is the possibility of Treatment × Subject interactions. These interactions, which may result from carry-over effects or from the differential effects of treatments for different subjects, contribute to the size of the error term and, if of sufficient magnitude, greatly reduce the advantage of the repeated-measures design. Additionally, the presence of Treatment × Subject interactions often leads to heterogeneity of covariance, a condition which results in a positively biased F test. Finally, and most important, differential carry-over effects are reflected in the treatment main effects and interactions. Thus, even if the null hypothesis is rejected, we are still left with the possibility that the treatment means are "distorted" by differential carry-over effects. Under these circumstances, the repeated-measures design should be avoided unless the carry-over effects themselves are the object of study—in spite of its advantages in economy.

There are alternative methods for decreasing the size of the error term, however, which do not suffer from these serious failings. One method, the *analysis of covariance*, which we will consider in Chapter 22, is intended to reduce the error term and increase the sensitivity of an experiment by *statistical* means. Information from a control variable is used to adjust the scores obtained from the actual experiment for chance differences which were present before the start of the differential treatments. Another method, *blocking*, is presented in Chapter 23 and accomplishes a reduction in the error term *experimentally* by introducing subject characteristics as a control factor in the experiment. The variability due to this individual-differences factor or subject-control factor, which would otherwise contribute heavily to error variance, is isolated and removed from the error term.

Blocking introduces no new statistical procedures, while covariance does. Consequently, we need to spend more time with the analysis of covariance in order to develop the rationale for the statistical adjustment and to present the computational formulas with which the adjustment is accomplished. The relative amounts of time spent on the two procedures should not be equated with their relative importance to the researcher. On the contrary, blocking is the preferred adjustment method, as we will argue in the final section of Chapter 23.

chapter twenty-two

ANALYSIS OF COVARIANCE[1]

The primary purpose of the analysis of covariance is to provide an adjustment of the results of an experiment for differences existing among subjects *before* the start of the experiment. That is, scores on a control variable are used (1) to adjust for chance differences among treatment groups and (2) to reduce error variance. The magnitude of these adjustments depends upon the correlation between the control variable and the dependent variable.[2]

THE CONTROL VARIABLE

The main criterion for a control variable is a high correlation with the dependent variable. In most cases, the scores on the control variable are obtained *prior*

[1] Numerical examples illustrating arithmetic operations discussed in this chapter may be found at the end of Part VI (pp. 517–518).

[2] Various terms are used to designate these two sets of scores. Such terms as *control variable*, *concomitant variable*, and *covariate* have been used to designate the measures obtained before the experiment begins, while *criterion variable* and *dependent variable* have been used to designate the response measure obtained during the experiment. In our discussions we will use the terms control variable and dependent variable.

to the initiation of the experimental treatment. There may be a formal pretest of some sort administered to all potential participants in the experiment, or the scores may be available from records of the subjects. Achievement scores, IQ determinations, and grade-point averages are common examples. Occasionally, the scores on the control variable are gathered *after* the experiment is completed. Such a procedure is defensible only when it is certain that the experimental treatment did *not* influence the control scores. For relatively "permanent" subject abilities (e.g., reading ability) this may be a reasonable assumption, but for labile tendencies (e.g., anxiety, ego involvement) it may be an untenable position to take. The analysis of covariance is predicated upon the availability of information that is *independent* of the experimental treatment. Therefore, any determination that is taken following the end of the experiment should be scrutinized carefully.

Just as we should be wary of control scores which come from postexperiment tests, we must question the use of scores which are taken during the course of the experiment. Unless these scores are obtained during a phase of the experiment in which all subjects are precisely treated alike, we will find it difficult to argue that differences on the control variable are independent of the treatment effects. Consider, for example, covariance in two different memory studies, one where it is appropriate and one where it is inappropriate. In the first, we are studying the course of forgetting following a constant number of training trials. In this experiment, suppose five independent groups of subjects are given 10 training trials and are tested after either 2 minutes, 20 minutes, 1 hour, 6 hours, or 24 hours. With a constant amount of training, not all subjects will attain the same level of performance after the 10 training trials. Previous research has shown that degree of learning and delayed recall are positively correlated. Since there will be obvious within-group and between-group differences in degree of learning following the termination of training, the use of these terminal learning scores provides an obvious control variable to be used in conjunction with the recall score in an analysis of covariance. Because all of the subjects were treated identically prior to the administration of the experimental conditions (retention intervals of varying duration), such a procedure would be entirely appropriate, providing, of course, that the assumptions underlying the covariance test are met.

In the other example, suppose independent groups of subjects receive 10 training trials on sets of material that differ in difficulty. Following training, all subjects are to return after 24 hours for a retention test. As in the first case, there will be within-group and between-group differences in degree of learning attained on the last training trial, and these differences are known to correlate highly with the delayed-retention scores. In contrast, however, covariance would *not* be appropriate, because between-group differences reflect *experimental treatment* as well as error variance. It is not possible to adjust for such *systematic* differences by the analysis of covariance. As obvious as this point may be, we continually find examples of this inappropriate use of covariance in the literature.

In certain applications, such as educational research, it is convenient to assign the different experimental treatments to entire classes of school children. It would be rare for these intact groups to be equated on characteristics considered important for performance on the experimental task. Classes in school are usually not equated on such factors as IQ or grade-point average. Typically, useful information is available for each subject prior to the start of the experiment, so that covariance appears to be an attractive means for adjusting differences among groups. Offhand, this use of covariance seems appropriate. Unfortunately, it usually is not. That is, unless the intact groups were constituted randomly originally and treated identically during the period preceding the experiment, we can never be sure that differences among intact groups reflect a freedom from *systematic* bias. It is always possible, for example, that the groups differ on a number of uncontrolled variables for which we have no measure. We avoid this problem in a completely randomized experiment, since uncontrolled variables exert an *unsystematic* influence on the response measure and their influence is reflected in the estimate of error variance.

THE BASIC ANALYSIS

The analysis of covariance consists of a statistical adjustment of the scores on the dependent variable, based upon a knowledge of the corresponding scores on the control variable. There are two basic adjustments: an adjustment for chance differences on the control variable of *subjects* within each treatment group and an adjustment for chance differences for the treatment *groups*. The first adjustment is individual and is based upon the deviation of each subject from his group mean. The second adjustment is constant for all subjects within any given group and is based upon the deviation of each group mean from the overall mean. It will not be necessary to apply the actual adjustments to the individual subjects, however, since they may be accomplished more simply on the sums of squares from the standard analysis.

The particular relationship used in the adjustment comes from the *linear* relationship between scores on the control variable and scores on the dependent variable. This relationship is represented by a best-fitting straight line (called a *linear regression line*) that describes the covariation of the two variables.[3] (Other types of relationships could be used, but this is the one represented in nearly all applications of the analysis of covariance.) A different line is obtained for each treatment group, but the adjustments are made with a regression line that is an *average* of the regression lines for the different treatment groups.

What is accomplished in the analysis is to remove from the variability of the scores on the *dependent variable* any variability that is *predictable* from a knowledge of the linear relationship between the control and dependent

[3] A best-fitting line is one that minimizes the average squared deviation of the data points from the line.

variables. In other words, we perform a statistical analysis on the scores that would have been obtained had the subjects within groups and the groups themselves been *equated on the control variable*. Again, this equation is based upon an important assumption—namely, that the form of the relationship between the two variables is linear and the same for each treatment group.

It is perhaps useful to make more explicit the possible situations which covariance may correct:

1. *Adjustment of error term.* Suppose that the group means on the control variable are *identical*, while subjects differ within the groups. Under these circumstances, covariance will operate to reduce the size of the error term, making any differences among the treatment groups on the *dependent variable* more visible and producing a larger *F*. Of course, the probability of obtaining identical means from the random assignment of subjects to conditions is virtually zero. Thus, in addition to an adjustment of the error term for individual differences on the control variable, covariance will also "correct" for group differences as well.

2. *Adjustment when mean differences on control and dependent variables are in **same** direction.* In this situation, some portion of the differences due to the experimental treatments is the result of differences which existed *before the start of the experiment*. Under these circumstances, any adjustment for these differences will result in a *reduced* mean square for the treatment effects.

3. *Adjustment when mean differences on control and dependent variables are in **opposite** directions.* In this situation, the treatment effects may appear to be minimal on the dependent variable, but the control variable would have predicted a difference between the groups in the *other* direction. Thus, the adjustment will show that the experimental treatments are really *more* effective because they have overcome differences which existed before the start of the experiment.

Logic of the Adjustment

The key to the analysis of covariance is the *linear regression coefficient*. This coefficient specifies the slope of the straight line relating the two variables. This regression line reflects what can be predicted about the scores on the dependent variable from a knowledge about corresponding scores on the control variable. In the analysis of *variance*, deviation scores formed the basic ingredient in our calculations. In the analysis of *covariance*, we are still interested in deviation scores, but this time in the *residual deviations*—variability that is *not* associated with the control variable, at least in the sense that the variability is *free from the linear effect of the control variable.*

Suppose we have before us the scores from a completely randomized, single-factor experiment, with *a* independent groups and *s* subjects in each group. (To be consistent with most other texts, we will refer to scores on the *control variable* with an "*x*" subscript and to scores on the *dependent variable* with a "*y*" subscript. *Adjusted scores* will be designated with a prime.) In terms of deviation scores, the residual deviation (the deviation from the regression line) can be expressed as follows:

$$AS_{ij(y)} - AS'_{ij(y)} = (AS_{ij(y)} - \overline{T}_y) - b_T(AS_{ij(x)} - \overline{T}_x). \tag{22-1}$$

In words, the residual or adjusted deviation for any given subject $(AS_{ij(y)} - AS'_{ij(y)})$ is found by subtracting from his *unadjusted* deviation on the dependent variable $(AS_{ij(y)} - \overline{T}_y)$ his corresponding deviation on the control variable $(AS_{ij(x)} - \overline{T}_x)$, weighted by the regression coefficient (b_T). This latter term represents the slope of a straight line relating the two variables.

Rather than work through some tedious algebra, we will simply indicate that if the quantities specified in Eq. (22-1) are calculated for all of the *as* subjects in the experiment, then are squared and summed, we will have

$$SS_{T(adj.)} = SS_{T(y)} - (b_T)^2(SS_{T(x)}), \tag{22-2}$$

a formula which indicates that it is not necessary to perform adjustments to each score on the dependent variable separately, but that we will be able to deal with the sums of squares directly.[4]

The only new quantity in Eq. (22-2) is, of course, the regression coefficient. This quantity is defined as follows:

$$b_T = \frac{\sum (AS_{ij(x)} - \overline{T}_x)(AS_{ij(y)} - \overline{T}_y)}{\sum (AS_{ij(x)} - \overline{T}_x)^2}. \tag{22-3}$$

We should consider the numerator and denominator terms carefully. The *denominator* is merely the total sum of squares for the *control variable*—the $SS_{T(x)}$. The *numerator* is an analogous quantity, except that it represents the *sum of the products* of the two deviation scores available for each subject, one for the control variable $(AS_{ij(x)} - \overline{T}_x)$ and one for the dependent variable $(AS_{ij(y)} - \overline{T}_y)$. It is convenient to refer to the numerator term (the sum of the products of the total deviation scores) as SP_T. We can now write Eq. (22-3) as

$$b_T = \frac{SP_T}{SS_{T(x)}}. \tag{22-4}$$

The final step in developing a convenient statement of the adjustment is to express the calculations in terms of sums of squares and sums of products. This is easily accomplished by substituting Eq. (22-4) into Eq. (22-2) and simplifying the expression:

$$SS_{T(adj.)} = SS_{T(y)} - \left(\frac{SP_T}{SS_{T(x)}}\right)^2(SS_{T(x)})$$

$$= SS_{T(y)} - \frac{(SP_T)^2}{SS_{T(x)}}. \tag{22-5}$$

Equation (22-5) is the basic formula for the adjusted total sum of squares. We will consider the computational formulas shortly.

[4] Kirk (1968, pp. 458–459) provides the algebraic development of Eq. (22-2).

We can now proceed directly to the analysis of covariance. So far, we have seen that we can remove the linear effect of the control variable from the total sum of squares for the dependent variable. What is represented in this residual quantity is the total sum of squares which is free of the linear effect of the control variable. While we could repeat the steps necessary to produce compact equations such as Eq. (22-5) for the component sources (A and S/A), their explication is not needed in the subsequent discussions. It is sufficient to see how the formulas for the adjusted total sum of squares are developed and to accept the end products for other adjusted sums of squares required of the analysis. In the next section we will consider a set of formulas that will generate the appropriate adjustment for *any* factorial design.

GENERAL COMPUTATIONAL RULES

Although we have discussed the procedures for adjusting the $SS_{T(y)}$ for the linear effect of the control variable, we actually have little use for this quantity in the analysis of covariance. The exposition in the last section is not wasted, however, because the same sorts of manipulations can be offered for the development of formulas for the adjusted sums of squares for other sources of variance. In *all* computations, the adjusted sum of squares is obtained by subtracting a quantity that consists of the sum of squares for the control variable (x), weighted by the square of the linear regression coefficient. This quantity, in turn, can be transformed into something that may be represented as

$$\frac{(SP)^2}{SS_x}.$$

As we will see, all such "corrections" for the linear effect of the control variable have this form, except that the corrections for treatment effects (main effects and interactions) are computed indirectly.

The computational scheme is surprisingly simple. Consider first the adjustment of *error variance*, presented in the upper portion of Table 22-1. Error variance refers to any source of variance which will be used as a denominator in the test of the significance of a treatment effect. It is clear that the correction is identical in form to the one specified in Eq. (22-5) for the total sum of squares. The *df* for the error term are specified in the lower portion of the table. These *df* are the same as those associated with the error term in the corresponding analysis of variance, *minus* 1. The loss of this *df* is due to the restriction that the deviations are to be computed from an average regression line.

As we have indicated already, the calculation of adjusted sums of squares for treatment effects is indirect. The reason is that a "direct" calculation, such as the one presented for the error term, would not produce an adjusted sum of squares which is independent of the adjusted error sum of squares and which is unrelated to the treatment effects (see Kirk, 1968, p. 464). An inspection of Table 22-1 indicates that two quantities are involved in the adjustment: the

TABLE 22-1 *General Computational Formulas for the Analysis of Covariance*

ADJUSTED SUMS OF SQUARES

Source	Adjusted Sum of Squares ($SS_{adj.}$)
Treatment effect	$SS_{effect(adj.)} = SS_{effect(y)} - \left[\dfrac{(SP_{effect} + SP_{error})^2}{SS_{effect(x)} + SS_{error(x)}} - \dfrac{(SP_{error})^2}{SS_{error(x)}} \right]$
Error	$SS_{error(adj.)} = SS_{error(y)} - \dfrac{(SP_{error})^2}{SS_{error(x)}}$

SUMMARY OF THE ANALYSIS

Source	$SS_{adj.}$	df	$MS_{adj.}$	F
Treatment effect	$SS_{effect(adj.)}$	df_{effect}	$\dfrac{SS_{effect(adj.)}}{df_{effect}}$	$\dfrac{MS_{effect(adj.)}}{MS_{error(adj.)}}$
Error	$SS_{error(adj.)}$	$df_{error} - 1$	$\dfrac{SS_{error(adj.)}}{df_{error} - 1}$	

first one combines the sums of squares (or products) for the treatment effect *and* for error, and the second is the correction we will use for the error sum of squares. The df associated with the adjusted sum of squares for treatment effects are identical to those associated with the unadjusted sum of squares. A df is *not* lost in the calculation of these adjusted sums of squares, since the regression lines for the *means* involved in the different treatment effects were not used in the computation of these sums of squares.

The remaining steps in the analysis are summarized in the lower portion of Table 22-1. The F ratio is formed by dividing the adjusted mean square for the treatment effect by the adjusted mean square for error. The significance of the F ratio is evaluated against the tabled valued of F corresponding to the adjusted df's.

The computational scheme outlined in Table 22-1 can be extended to any factorial design. The adjusted mean squares for treatment effects are evaluated by the same error terms (adjusted, of course) which would be used in the usual analysis of variance. It will be noted that over *three times* as much computational effort is required for the analysis of covariance as for the standard analysis of variance. In essence, we must obtain the same set of sums of squares for the scores on the control variable, the scores on the dependent variable, and the products of these two sets of scores. The gain in precision can be considerable, however, and this increased efficiency may justify the extra computational effort.

Assumptions Underlying the Analysis of Covariance

Before we complete this general outline of the analysis of covariance, some mention must be made of the assumptions upon which the analysis is based.[5]

---

[5] We are assuming the fixed-effects model in this chapter. A statistician should be consulted for the appropriate analysis for experiments with random independent variables.

The assumptions underlying the analysis of *variance* continue to be applicable to the adjusted observations in the corresponding analysis of covariance. (Consult the earlier chapters for discussions of these assumptions.) Several other assumptions concern the analysis of covariance in particular. We will consider these assumptions briefly in this section and supply more detail when we discuss actual analyses.

The first assumption specifies an independence of the control variable from any treatment effects. We discussed this fundamental requirement in an earlier section of this chapter. The most common way to guarantee that this assumption is met is to collect the scores on the control variable before the start of the experiment and to assign subjects randomly to the treatment conditions in complete ignorance of these preexperimental scores. If there is any possibility that the treatments may have affected the scores on the control variable, the analysis of covariance is inappropriate.

The next two assumptions concern regression. One of these is the assumption of *linear regression*. More formally, the assumption is that the deviations from regression—i.e., the adjusted or residual scores—are normally and independently distributed in the population, with means of zero and homogeneous variances. (Since these assumptions concerning the distribution of the residuals will generally not hold if the true regression is not linear, it is accurate to refer to them as an assumption of linear regression.) Presumably, if linear regression is used in the analysis while the true regression is of another form (e.g., curvilinear), adjustments will not be of great benefit. More importantly, however, we could question the meaning of the treatment means, which are also adjusted on the assumption of linear regression.

The final assumption specifies *homogeneity of regression* coefficients for the different treatment populations. As we will see, individual within-group regression coefficients are averaged in the analysis, and adjustments are made on the basis of this average regression line. The assumption of homogeneous within-group regression is critical for a meaningful interpretation of the results of the F test in the analysis of covariance. Unfortunately, however, statisticians have not evaluated the consequences of violations of this assumption and so, we cannot offer a practical solution to this problem. This means, therefore, that a test of homogeneity of regression should be conducted *before* the analysis of covariance can be validly interpreted.

THE COMPLETELY RANDOMIZED, SINGLE-FACTOR EXPERIMENT

The simplest design in which the analysis of covariance is applicable is the single-factor experiment with independent groups of subjects. We will describe the analysis of this design in considerable detail, since most of the procedures are easily generalized to more complex designs. We will work through the statistical analysis first and later consider tests of the assumptions underlying the main analysis of covariance.

Computational Formulas

In this design we are assuming that there are a treatment conditions and that s subjects have been randomly assigned to each of the conditions. Each of the subjects provides us with two scores, one from the control variable (x) and the other from the dependent variable (y).

CALCULATION OF SS's AND SP's   It is convenient to consider the analysis of covariance in two major steps. The first step consists of the calculation of basic sums of squares and sums of products for the control and dependent variables. For the single-factor experiment there are two sources of variance in which we are interested: A and S/A. The computational formulas for the sums of squares and the products for these two sources are given in the upper portion of Table 22-2. The formulas for the sums of squares should pose no problem, as they are the standard ones we have been using all along for the calculation of the SS_A and the $SS_{S/A}$. The only additions to the formulas are the x and y subscripts to indicate whether the scores are from the control or dependent variable, respectively.

The formulas for the sums of products may take a while to comprehend. Consider the formula for the calculation of the SP_A. In the numerator of the first term we are asked to multiply each "treatment" sum for the control variable, $A_{i(x)}$, by the corresponding treatment sum for the dependent variable, $A_{i(y)}$. (The treatment subscript, i, is used to stress the fact that the products are

TABLE 22-2   *Computational Formulas for the Single-Factor Analysis of Covariance*

BASIC CALCULATIONS

Source	Control Variable (x)	Cross-Products (xy)	Dependent Variable (y)
A	$\dfrac{\sum (A_x)^2}{s} - \dfrac{(T_x)^2}{as}$	$\dfrac{\sum (A_{i(x)})(A_{i(y)})}{s} - \dfrac{(T_x)(T_y)}{as}$	$\dfrac{\sum (A_y)^2}{s} - \dfrac{(T_y)^2}{as}$
S/A	$\sum (AS_x)^2 - \dfrac{\sum (A_x)^2}{s}$	$\sum (AS_{ij(x)})(AS_{ij(y)}) - \dfrac{\sum (A_{i(x)})(A_{i(y)})}{s}$	$\sum (AS_y)^2 - \dfrac{\sum (A_y)^2}{s}$

ANALYSIS OF COVARIANCE

Source	Adjusted Sum of Squares	df	F
A	$SS_{A(\text{adj.})} = SS_{A(y)} - \left[\dfrac{(SP_A + SP_{S/A})^2}{SS_{A(x)} + SS_{S/A(x)}} - \dfrac{(SP_{S/A})^2}{SS_{S/A(x)}} \right]$	$a - 1$	$\dfrac{MS_{A(\text{adj.})}}{MS_{S/A(\text{adj.})}}$
S/A	$SS_{S/A(\text{adj.})} = SS_{S/A(y)} - \dfrac{(SP_{S/A})^2}{SS_{S/A(x)}}$	$a(s-1) - 1$	

formed with sums from the same levels of factor A.) The single summation sign in the numerator indicates that all of the possible products are summed in this operation. In the numerator of the second term we multiply the grand total of the control scores, T_x, by the grand total of the scores on the dependent variable, T_y. The denominators are the same as those specified for the corresponding quantities in the computational formulas for either sum of square.

The formula for the SP_A can be generated easily from the formula for either the $SS_{A(x)}$ or the $SS_{A(y)}$. We would start, for example, with the formula for the sum of squares, rewriting as follows:

$$SS_{A(x)} = \frac{\sum (A_{i(x)})^2}{s} - \frac{(T_x)^2}{as}$$

$$= \frac{\sum (A_{i(x)})(A_{i(x)})}{s} - \frac{(T_x)(T_x)}{as}.$$

Next, we simply substitute corresponding sums involving the dependent variable (y) for each of the duplicated quantities in the numerator:

$$SP_A = \frac{\sum (A_{i(x)})(A_{i(y)})}{s} - \frac{(T_x)(T_y)}{as}.$$

The only new term appearing in the formula for the $SP_{S/A}$ is the first, which indicates that the two scores for each subject are multiplied and then summed over all of the subjects in the experiment.

ADJUSTED SS'S AND THE ANALYSIS OF COVARIANCE   The second major step in the analysis is the calculation of the adjusted sums of squares and the formation of the F ratio. The computational formulas for the adjusted sums of squares appear in the lower part of Table 22-2 and are obtained from the general formulas given previously in Table 22-1 (p. 483). This translation is made by substituting "A" for "$effect$" and "S/A" for "$error$" in Table 22-1. (You should verify these translations in order to ensure that you understand how the formulas for the general case can be used to generate specific computational formulas.) All of the quantities which are needed for the two adjustments are found in the upper portion of Table 22-2. After the adjusted sums of squares are calculated, the adjusted mean squares are obtained. (This latter step is not indicated in the table, as it is certainly familiar by now.) The final step, of course, is the formation and evaluation of the F ratio. We will now illustrate these calculations with a numerical example.

Numerical Example

For this hypothetical example we have three levels of factor A, with $s = 8$ subjects in each condition. We will assume that the subjects were given a pretest before the start of the experiment and were assigned randomly to the three experimental conditions. Thus, we have no reason to believe that the experimental treatments exerted any influence on the pretest scores. The pairs of AS_{ij} scores are presented in an AS matrix in Table 22-3.

An inspection of the data suggests a positive correlation between the two sets of scores within each of the treatment conditions: the larger the control score, the larger the score on the dependent variable. The presence of any within-group correlation implies that the adjusted error term will be smaller than the unadjusted one. The $A_{i(y)}$ totals indicate a numerical difference among the conditions and the $A_{i(x)}$ totals suggest relative comparability of the three groups on the control variable.

TABLE 22-3 *Numerical Example: Single-Factor Analysis of Covariance*

AS MATRIX

	a_1		a_2		a_3	
x	y	x	y	x	y
10	15	4	6	7	14
6	1	8	13	8	9
5	4	8	5	7	16
8	6	8	18	3	7
9	10	6	9	6	13
4	0	11	7	8	18
9	7	10	15	6	13
12	13	9	15	8	6
Sum: 63	56	64	88	53	96
Mean: 7.88	7.00	8.00	11.00	6.62	12.00

$$T_x = 63 + 64 + 53 = 180; \quad \bar{T}_x = 7.50$$
$$T_y = 56 + 88 + 96 = 240; \quad \bar{T}_y = 10.00$$

The first step is to substitute these data into the computational formulas for the sums of squares and of products given in Table 22-2. As in the preceding chapters, we will perform these operations in two substeps, first calculating the basic terms entering into the computational formulas and then adding and subtracting these terms in the actual determination of the various sums of squares and products. Working first with the scores on the control variable,

$$[T_x] = \frac{(T_x)^2}{as} = \frac{(180)^2}{3(8)} = \frac{32,400}{24} = 1350.00,$$

$$[A_x] = \frac{\sum (A_x)^2}{s} = \frac{(63)^2 + (64)^2 + (53)^2}{8} = \frac{10,874}{8} = 1359.25,$$

$$[AS_x] = \sum (AS_x)^2 = (10)^2 + (6)^2 + \cdots + (6)^2 + (8)^2 = 1464.$$

Identical operations on the scores on the dependent variable produce

$$[T_y] = \frac{(T_y)^2}{as} = \frac{(240)^2}{3(8)} = \frac{57,600}{24} = 2400.00,$$

$$[A_y] = \frac{\sum (A_y)^2}{s} = \frac{(56)^2 + (88)^2 + (96)^2}{8} = \frac{20,096}{8} = 2512.00,$$

$$[AS_y] = \sum (AS_y)^2 = (15)^2 + (1)^2 + \cdots + (13)^2 + (6)^2 = 3010.$$

Finally, we will perform analogous calculations on the cross-products:

$$[T_{xy}] = \frac{(T_x)(T_y)}{as} = \frac{(180)(240)}{3(8)} = \frac{43,200}{24} = 1800.00,$$

$$[A_{xy}] = \frac{\sum (A_{i(x)})(A_{i(y)})}{s} = \frac{(63)(56) + (64)(88) + (53)(96)}{8}$$

$$= \frac{14,248}{8} = 1781.00,$$

$$[AS_{xy}] = \sum (AS_{i(x)})(AS_{i(y)}) = (10)(15) + (6)(1) + \cdots + (6)(13) + (8)(6)$$

$$= 1912.$$

These quantities are combined in the upper portion of Table 22-4 to produce the desired sums of squares and products.

The next step in the analysis is to bring together the appropriate quantities to provide the adjustment for the linear effect of the control variable. The computational formulas for these determinations are given in the bottom portion of Table 22-2. With the calculations already completed in the upper portion of Table 22-4, we have

$$SS_{A(adj.)} = SS_{A(y)} - \left[\frac{(SP_A + SP_{S/A})^2}{SS_{A(x)} + SS_{S/A(x)}} - \frac{(SP_{S/A})^2}{SS_{S/A(x)}} \right]$$

$$= 112.00 - \left[\frac{(-19.00 + 131.00)^2}{9.25 + 104.75} - \frac{(131.00)^2}{104.75} \right]$$

$$= 112.00 - \left(\frac{12,544.00}{114.00} - \frac{17,161.00}{104.75} \right)$$

$$= 112.00 - (110.04 - 163.83) = 165.79$$

and

$$SS_{S/A(adj.)} = SS_{S/A(y)} - \frac{(SP_{S/A})^2}{SS_{S/A(x)}}$$

$$= 498.00 - \frac{(131.00)^2}{104.75}$$

$$= 498.00 - 163.83 = 334.17.$$

These adjusted sums of squares are entered in the summary table presented in the bottom portion of Table 22-4. The calculation of the adjusted df's and the adjusted mean squares is straightforward. The resultant F test indicates a significant value when evaluated against the tabled value of $F(2, 20)$, $p < .025$.

TABLE 22-4   *Single-Factor Analysis of Covariance*

BASIC SUMS OF SQUARES AND PRODUCTS[a]

Source	Control Variable (x)	Cross-Products (xy)	Dependent Variable (y)
A	$[A_x] - [T_x] =$ 9.25	$[A_{xy}] - [T_{xy}] = -19.00$	$[A_y] - [T_y] = 112.00$
S/A	$[AS_x] - [A_x] = 104.75$	$[AS_{xy}] - [A_{xy}] =$ 131.00	$[AS_y] - [A_y] = 498.00$
Total	$[AS_x] - [T_x] = 114.00$	$[AS_{xy}] - [T_{xy}] =$ 112.00	$[AS_y] - [T_y] = 610.00$

SUMMARY OF ANALYSIS

Source	$SS_{adj.}$	df	$MS_{adj.}$	F
A	165.79	2	82.90	4.96*
S/A	334.17	20	16.71	

[a] Bracketed letters represent complete terms in the computational formulas; a particular term is identified by the letter(s) appearing in the numerator.
* $p < .025$

It is instructive to see what this analysis of covariance accomplished. If we calculate the F on the *unadjusted* y scores, we find that the differences among the three means is not significant. That is,

$$F = \frac{SS_{A(y)}/df_A}{SS_{S/A(y)}/df_{S/A}}$$

$$= \frac{112.00/2}{498.00/21} = \frac{56.00}{23.71} = 2.36,$$

a value that lies between the 10 and 25 percent levels of significance. The larger F from the analysis of covariance was the result of *two* changes: (1) a *decrease* in the size of the within-groups mean square, which we expected from the correlation between the two sets of scores, and (2) an *increase* in the size of the main effect of factor A. This latter adjustment "corrects" for chance differences between groups on the control variable. Let's see how this correction increased the SS_A. We have noted that there is a positive correlation within groups; in addition, differences among the groups on the control variable are in a direction *opposite* to the outcome of the experiment. Any adjustment of these chance differences, then, *must increase* the magnitude of the treatment effects. This, of course, is what happened in our numerical example. We will see in the next section how this adjustment is applied to the actual treatment means.

Comparisons Involving Adjusted Means

ADJUSTMENT OF TREATMENT MEANS   If any comparisons are to be conducted among the treatment groups, they must be made with the adjusted treatment means. The adjustments are performed by substituting the means from the control and dependent variables in a linear equation relating the predicted (or adjusted) means to differences among the means on the control variable. This relationship is given by

$$\bar{A}'_{i(y)} = \bar{A}_{i(y)} - b_{S/A}(\bar{A}_{i(x)} - \bar{T}_x),\qquad(22\text{-}6)$$

where $\bar{A}'_{i(y)}$ is the adjusted treatment mean and $b_{S/A}$ is the average within-groups regression coefficient. This latter quantity is given by

$$b_{S/A} = \frac{SP_{S/A}}{SS_{S/A(x)}}.\qquad(22\text{-}7)$$

If we look closely at Eq. (22-6), we see that the adjusted mean of a treatment group, $\bar{A}'_{i(y)}$, is found by subtracting from the observed mean $(\bar{A}_{i(y)})$ a value which takes into consideration the deviation of the group from the overall mean on the covariate—i.e., $(b_{S/A})(\bar{A}_{i(x)} - \bar{T}_x)$. It will be noted that the regression coefficient is based on the linear regression obtained from groups of subjects who are treated alike—i.e., an average or pooled within-groups coefficient. Actually, $b_{S/A}$ is an average that weights each group coefficient by the variability of the groups on the control variable. (We will demonstrate this fact when we consider the regression assumptions.)

Since we will usually want to obtain all of the adjusted means, it is convenient to arrange the application of Eq. (22-6) as a series of steps. This has been done in Table 22-5. The unadjusted treatment means $(\bar{A}_{i(y)})$ are entered in the first row of the table. The *deviation* of each group mean from the total mean on the control variable is given in the second row. The data for these entries are taken from Table 22-3. That is,

$$\bar{A}_{1(x)} - \bar{T}_x = 7.88 - 7.50 = .38,$$
$$\bar{A}_{2(x)} - \bar{T}_x = 8.00 - 7.50 = .50,$$
$$\bar{A}_{3(x)} - \bar{T}_x = 6.62 - 7.50 = -.88.$$

In order to complete the operations specified in the third row, we must calculate the within-groups regression coefficient, $b_{S/A}$. From Eq. (22-7) and using the relevant numbers from Table 22-4, we have

$$b_{S/A} = \frac{SP_{S/A}}{SS_{S/A(x)}} = \frac{131.00}{104.75} = 1.25.$$

Thus,

$$b_{S/A}(\bar{A}_{1(x)} - \bar{T}_x) = (1.25)(.38) = .48,$$
$$b_{S/A}(\bar{A}_{2(x)} - \bar{T}_x) = (1.25)(.50) = .62,$$
$$b_{S/A}(\bar{A}_{3(x)} - \bar{T}_x) = (1.25)(-.88) = -1.10.$$

TABLE 22-5   *Calculation of Adjusted Treatment Means*

Steps		a_1	a_2	a_3
	$\bar{A}_{i(y)}$	7.00	11.00	12.00
	$\bar{A}_{i(x)} - \bar{T}_x$	.38	.50	$-.88$
	$b_{S/A}(\bar{A}_{i(x)} - \bar{T}_x)$	.48	.62	-1.10
$\bar{A}'_{i(y)} = \bar{A}_{i(y)} - b_{S/A}(\bar{A}_{i(x)} - \bar{T}_x)$		6.52	10.38	13.10
	$A'_{i(y)} = s\bar{A}'_{i(y)}$	52.16	83.04	104.80

The adjusted means are finally calculated in the fourth row:

$$\bar{A}'_{1(y)} = 7.00 - .48 = 6.52,$$

$$\bar{A}'_{2(y)} = 11.00 - .62 = 10.38,$$

$$\bar{A}'_{3(y)} = 12.00 - (-1.10) = 13.10.$$

It is clear that the adjustments for the linear effect of the control variable have spread out the treatment means, as we indicated they would in the previous section.

In the final row are given the adjusted treatment *sums* which will prove useful in subsequent analyses. These are obviously obtained by multiplying the adjusted means by the sample size, s. Specifically,

$$A'_{1(y)} = 8(6.52) = 52.16,$$

$$A'_{2(y)} = 8(10.38) = 83.04,$$

$$A'_{3(y)} = 8(13.10) = 104.80.$$

COMPARISONS BETWEEN PAIRS OF MEANS   We may perform any of the comparisons on the adjusted means that we would consider with unadjusted data from a single-factor experiment. These techniques and procedures were discussed in detail in Part II. In all of these single-df comparisons, we calculate the sum of squares for the particular comparison in exactly the same fashion as we would for the analysis of variance, except that we use adjusted treatment sums. For instance, the general formula for this type of comparison is translated as

$$SS_{A_{comp.(adj.)}} = \frac{[\sum (c_i)(A'_{i(y)})]^2}{s[\sum (c_i)^2]}, \tag{22-8}$$

where the c_i terms are the coefficients required to effect the desired comparison. If we want to deal with the adjusted *means* directly, Eq. (22-8) becomes

$$SS_{A_{comp.(adj.)}} = \frac{s[\sum (c_i)(\bar{A}'_{i(y)})]^2}{\sum (c_i)^2}. \tag{22-8a}$$

The main change in the analysis is in the calculation of the error term. In the one-factor analysis of variance, we would use the $MS_{S/A}$, unless there were heterogeneity of variance, in which case we would obtain an error term based on the particular groups involved in the comparison. For the analysis of covariance we must perform an additional operation on the adjusted error term before comparisons among groups are conducted. We will refer to this mean square as the MS'_{error}, which is calculated as follows:

$$MS'_{error} = MS_{S/A(adj.)}\left[1 + \frac{SS_{A(x)}/(a-1)}{SS_{S/A(x)}}\right]. \tag{22-9}$$

An inspection of Eq. (22-9) reveals that the MS'_{error} will always be at least as large as the $MS_{S/A(adj.)}$ and that the size of the adjustment called for is directly related to the differences among the treatment conditions on the *control* variable. Winer (1962, 1971) indicates that Eq. (22-9) is the appropriate error term for nearly all comparisons. The one exception appears with a *planned comparison* involving two groups. To be more specific, some authors [e.g., Winer (1962, p. 592; 1971, p. 779) and Kirk (1968, p. 472)] suggest the following error term for planned comparisons:

$$MS'_{error} = MS_{S/A(adj.)}\left[1 + \frac{SS_{A_{comp.(x)}}}{SS_{S/A(x)}}\right]. \tag{22-10}$$

The error term specified in Eq. (22-10) differs from Eq. (22-9) by the introduction of the sum of squares on the control variable for the two groups being compared, rather than an average of all possible differences.[6] For comparisons tested with either error term, however, the obtained F is evaluated with $df_{num.} = 1$ and $df_{denom.} = df_{error(adj.)}$.

As an example, we will compare the adjusted mean at level a_1 with the combined adjusted means at levels a_2 and a_3. We will conduct this comparison with the adjusted sums listed in Table 22-5. The coefficients for this comparison and the adjusted sums are given below:

	a_1	a_2	a_3
c_i:	2	-1	-1
$A'_{i(y)}$:	52.16	83.04	104.80

The sum of squares for this comparison is obtained from Eq. (22-8):

$$\begin{aligned}
SS_{A_{comp.(adj.)}} &= \frac{[(2)(52.16) + (-1)(83.04) + (-1)(104.80)]^2}{8[(2)^2 + (-1)^2 + (-1)^2]} \\
&= \frac{(-83.52)^2}{8(6)} = \frac{6975.59}{48} = 145.32.
\end{aligned}$$

---

[6] Snedecor (1956, pp. 401–402) indicates that we may use Eq. (22-9) instead of Eq. (22-10) when the $df_{error} > 20$ and when the differences among treatment groups on the control variable are not significant.

Since there is 1 df associated with this comparison, $MS_{A_{comp.(adj.)}} = 145.32$. We will use as the error term for this comparison the quantity given in Eq. (22-9). Substituting into the equation with appropriate values from Table 22-4, we have

$$MS'_{error} = 16.71\left[1 + \frac{9.25/(3-1)}{104.75}\right]$$

$$= 16.71\left[1 + \frac{4.62}{104.75}\right]$$

$$= 16.71(1 + .04) = 17.38.$$

The F ratio for this comparison becomes

$$F = \frac{MS_{A_{comp.(adj.)}}}{MS'_{error}} = \frac{145.32}{17.38} = 8.36$$

and is significant at the 1 percent level—i.e., $F(1, 20) = 8.10, p < .01$.

MULTIPLE COMPARISONS   Multiple comparisons involving pairs of adjusted treatment means pose no difficulty. Once the corrected error term from Eq. (22-9), the MS'_{error}, has been calculated, we proceed exactly as we would in a single-factor analysis of variance. These methods and procedures are discussed in Chapter 8 (see pp. 135–152).

Assumptions Concerning Regression

The two assumptions which will concern us are (1) homogeneity of within-group regression coefficients and (2) linearity of regression. We discussed these assumptions briefly earlier. In this section we will consider in detail the actual tests of these assumptions.

HOMOGENEITY OF REGRESSION   The adjustment for the linear effect of the control variable involves an average within-groups regression coefficient, $b_{S/A}$. A critical assumption of the analysis of covariance is that the individual within-group regression coefficients (b_{S/A_i}), which form the basis of the average, are equal, i.e., homogeneous. This assumption is tested by contrasting two sources of variance: (1) a source reflecting the deviation of the *group* regression coefficients from the *average* regression coefficient, and (2) a source reflecting the deviation of *individual subjects* from their own *group* regression lines. The first source is actually a sort of *between-groups* source of variance, but one involving group regression coefficients rather than group means. We will refer to the sum of squares associated with this source as the *between-regression* sum of squares ($SS_{bet.\,regr.}$). The second source is a sort of *within-groups* source of variance, but one involving the deviation of subjects from their group regression coefficients. We will refer to the sum of squares associated with this source as the *within-groups* regression sum of squares ($SS_{\text{w. regr.}}$).[7]

The computational formulas for these two quantities are given in Table 22-6. The first thing to note is that

$$SS_{\text{bet. regr.}} + SS_{\text{w. regr.}} = SS_{S/A(\text{adj.})}, \tag{22-11}$$

which may be verified by adding the sums of squares in the first two rows of the table. It will also be noted that the two computational formulas together contain three unique terms and that we have dealt with two of these already in the calculation of the adjusted within-groups sum of squares. Thus, there is only one new quantity we need to discuss, which is

$$\sum \left[\frac{(SP_{S/A_i})^2}{SS_{S/A_{i(x)}}} \right].$$

This quantity is, in essence, a within-group adjustment for *each group*, summed over the different treatment groups. More specifically, the quantity within the brackets is the within-group adjustment for any one of the treatment groups—the one at level a_i. The numerator term is the squared sum of products for the ith group and the denominator term is the sum of squares on the control variable for the ith group. The summation sign indicates a pooling of these adjustments over the different treatment groups.

TABLE 22-6   *Test of the Assumption of Homogeneity of Regression*

Source	Sum of Squares	df	F
Between regression	$\sum \left[\dfrac{(SP_{S/A_i})^2}{SS_{S/A_i(x)}} \right] - \dfrac{(SP_{S/A})^2}{SS_{S/A(x)}}$	$a - 1$	$\dfrac{MS_{\text{bet. regr.}}}{MS_{\text{w. regr.}}}$
Within regression	$SS_{S/A(y)} - \sum \left[\dfrac{(SP_{S/A_i})^2}{SS_{S/A_i(x)}} \right]$	$a(s - 2)$	
Adjusted S/A	$SS_{S/A(y)} - \dfrac{(SP_{S/A})^2}{SS_{S/A(x)}}$	$a(s - 1) - 1$	

The df for the different sources of variance are also given in Table 22-6. The df for the source representing the variation among the group regression coefficients—i.e., between-groups regression—is simply one less than the number of coefficients: $df_{\text{bet. regr.}} = a - 1$. The df for the source representing the variation of subjects about their group regression lines—i.e., within-groups regression—equals the number of subjects (s) minus 2, summed over the a treatment groups: $df_{\text{w. regr.}} = a(s - 2)$. An additional df is lost by estimating a different regression coefficient for each group.

The test of the hypothesis that the group regression coefficients are equal is indicated in the last column of the table. The numerator reflects the degree to

---

[7] Most authors refer to the $SS_{\text{bet.regr.}}$ as S_2 and to the $SS_{\text{w.regr.}}$ as S_1.

which the group regression coefficients deviate from each other—i.e., are not "accounted" for by the average coefficient. The denominator reflects the degree to which the separate coefficients fail to predict the actual scores on the dependent variable. When the null hypothesis is true, the expected value of the ratio is approximately 1.0 and the ratio is distributed as F with $df_{num.} = a - 1$ and $df_{denom.} = a(s - 2)$.

We are ready for a numerical example. We have already calculated two of the unique quantities in Table 22-6, namely, the unadjusted within-groups sum of squares and the correction for the linear effect of the control variable. The next step, then, is to calculate the remaining quantity, the sum of the individual group adjustments. The computations are summarized in the upper portion of Table 22-7. For the control sums of squares, we obtain the separate within-group sums of squares with the usual computational formula. That is, for any group,

$$SS_{S/A_i(x)} = \sum_j^s (AS_{ij(x)})^2 - \frac{(A_{i(x)})^2}{s}.$$

Substituting the data from Table 22-3 (p. 487) in this formula,

$$SS_{S/A_1(x)} = \sum (AS_{1j(x)})^2 - \frac{(A_{1(x)})^2}{s}$$

$$= [(10)^2 + (6)^2 + \cdots + (9)^2 + (12)^2] - \frac{(63)^2}{8},$$

$$SS_{S/A_2(x)} = \sum (AS_{2j(x)})^2 - \frac{(A_{2(x)})^2}{s}$$

$$= [(4)^2 + (8)^2 + \cdots + (10)^2 + (9)^2] - \frac{(64)^2}{8},$$

$$SS_{S/A_3(x)} = \sum (AS_{3j(x)})^2 - \frac{(A_{3(x)})^2}{s}$$

$$= [(7)^2 + (8)^2 + \cdots + (6)^2 + (8)^2] - \frac{(53)^2}{8}.$$

The calculations for the corresponding sums of products are given by

$$SP_{S/A_i} = \sum_j^s (AS_{ij(x)})(AS_{ij(y)}) - \frac{(A_{i(x)})(A_{i(y)})}{s}.$$

For the three groups,

$$SP_{S/A_1} = \sum (AS_{1j(x)})(AS_{1j(y)}) - \frac{(A_{1(x)})(A_{1(y)})}{s}$$

$$= [(10)(15) + (6)(1) + \cdots + (9)(7) + (12)(13)] - \frac{(63)(56)}{8},$$

$$SP_{S/A_2} = \sum (AS_{2j(x)})(AS_{2j(y)}) - \frac{(A_{2(x)})(A_{2(y)})}{s}$$

$$= [(4)(6) + (8)(13) + \cdots + (10)(15) + (9)(15)] - \frac{(64)(88)}{8},$$

$$SP_{S/A_3} = \sum (AS_{3j(x)})(AS_{3j(y)}) - \frac{(A_{3(x)})(A_{3(y)})}{s}$$

$$= [(7)(14) + (8)(9) + \cdots + (6)(13) + (8)(6)] - \frac{(53)(96)}{8}.$$

These two sets of calculations are completed in the upper portion of Table 22-7. As a computational check, we can verify that the sum of these component sums of squares equals the respective $SS_{S/A}$. That is,

$$\sum SS_{S/A_i(x)} = 50.88 + 34.00 + 19.88 = 104.76,$$

which agrees within rounding error with the value listed in Table 22-4, $SS_{S/A(x)} = 104.75$. There is a similar check for the sum of products:

$$\sum SP_{S/A_i} = 92.00 + 24.00 + 15.00 = 131.00 = SP_{S/A}.$$

We can now calculate the two component sums of squares:

$$SS_{bet.\,regr.} = \left[\frac{(92.00)^2}{50.88} + \frac{(24.00)^2}{34.00} + \frac{(15.00)^2}{19.88}\right] - \frac{(131.00)^2}{104.75}$$

$$= (166.35 + 16.94 + 11.32) - 163.83 = 30.78,$$

$$SS_{w.\,regr.} = 498.00 - \left[\frac{(92.00)^2}{50.88} + \frac{(24.00)^2}{34.00} + \frac{(15.00)^2}{19.88}\right]$$

$$= 498.00 - (166.35 + 16.94 + 11.32) = 303.39.$$

TABLE 22-7 *Test of the Homogeneity Assumption*

BASIC CALCULATIONS

Source	Control Variable (x)	Cross-Products (xy)
S/A_1	$547 - 496.12 = 50.88$	$533 - 441.00 = 92.00$
S/A_2	$546 - 512.00 = 34.00$	$728 - 704.00 = 24.00$
S/A_3	$371 - 351.12 = 19.88$	$651 - 636.00 = 15.00$

SUMMARY OF THE ANALYSIS

Source	SS	df	MS	F
Between regression	30.78	2	15.39	<1
Within regression	303.39	18	16.86	
S/A(adj.)	334.17	20		

Again, as a computational check,

$$SS_{bet.\,regr.} + SS_{w.\,regr.} = 30.78 + 303.39 = 334.17 = SS_{S/A(adj.)}.$$

These two sums of squares are entered in the bottom portion of Table 22-7.

The df for the deviation among regression coefficients is one less than the number of coefficients: $df_{bet.\,regr.} = a - 1 = 3 - 1 = 2$. The df for the deviation of individual subjects from the group regression lines is given by the equation $df_{w.\,regr.} = a(s - 2) = 3(8 - 2) = 18$. The result of the F test, summarized in the table, indicates that the hypothesis of homogeneity of group regression coefficients is tenable. Some authors [e.g., Kirk (1968)] suggest that we use a significance level much larger than usual, say $\alpha = .10$ or $.25$, in evaluating the significance of this F test. The reasoning behind this recommendation is that since it is in our interest to *accept* the null hypothesis, we should, under these circumstances, worry about committing a type II error. (A type II error, in this case, would consist of failing to recognize an actual violation of a statistical assumption.) A direct way of decreasing the type II error is to increase the α level. In the present example, of course, there is no ambiguity, since $F < 1$.

It is informative to calculate the group regression lines. The regression coefficient for any one of the groups is given by

$$b_{S/A_i} = \frac{SP_{S/A_i}}{SS_{S/A_i(x)}}. \tag{22-12}$$

Substituting in Eq. (22-12), we have

$$b_{S/A_1} = \frac{92.00}{50.88} = 1.81, \qquad b_{S/A_2} = \frac{24.00}{34.00} = .71,$$

$$b_{S/A_3} = \frac{15.00}{19.88} = .75.$$

(The hypothesis we have just tested is that the regression coefficients are equal.) The *average* within-groups coefficient is given by Eq. (22-7):

$$b_{S/A} = \frac{SP_{S/A}}{SS_{S/A(x)}} = \frac{131.00}{104.75} = 1.25.$$

As mentioned earlier, the within-groups coefficient is actually a weighted mean of the individual group coefficients. For this example,

$$b_{S/A} = \frac{(SS_{S/A_1(x)})(b_{S/A_1}) + (SS_{S/A_2(x)})(b_{S/A_2}) + (SS_{S/A_3(x)})(b_{S/A_3})}{SS_{S/A_1(x)} + SS_{S/A_2(x)} + SS_{S/A_3(x)}}.$$

In words, the group coefficients are weighted by the corresponding within-group sum of squares on the control variable, summed, and divided by the sum of the weights. From the values calculated above and from Table 22-7, we find with this alternative formula,

$$b_{S/A} = \frac{(50.88)(1.81) + (34.00)(.71) + (19.88)(.75)}{50.88 + 34.00 + 19.88}$$

$$= \frac{131.14}{104.76} = 1.25.$$

While we are on the subject, another useful index of the relationship between the control and dependent variables is the within-groups *correlation coefficient*. This index is obtained by combining quantities with which we are already familiar:

$$r_{S/A} = \frac{SP_{S/A}}{\sqrt{(SS_{S/A(x)})(SS_{S/A(y)})}}. \tag{22-13}$$

From Table 22-4,

$$r_{S/A} = \frac{131.00}{\sqrt{(104.75)(498.00)}} = \frac{131.00}{228.40} = .57.$$

The precision afforded by covariance is directly related to the magnitude of the within-groups correlation.

LINEARITY OF REGRESSION   The other assumption of covariance is that regression is linear. If the true regression is not linear, we should be worried about our interpretation of the differences among the means which have been adjusted on this basis. We will see shortly how this assumption is tested. For the moment, however, consider the possible actions we might take if the assumption were not met. We could forget about the analysis of covariance. Alternatively, as some authors suggest, we could use a transformation of the actual data which would produce linear regression, but we might then worry about the behavioral meaning of the data thus transformed. Another possibility would be to search for a different form of regression that would fit the data more adequately. Such analyses are available, but they are not discussed in statistics books for psychologists.

The test of the linearity assumption involves the partition of the adjusted sum of squares for the *treatment effects.* What is done is to calculate a sum of squares that reflects the deviation of the unadjusted group means from the between-groups regression line. If these deviations represent more than the operation of error variance, then it is concluded that the correct form of regression (i.e., linear regression) has not been employed.

The test we have just described is relatively simple to conduct. The sum of squares associated with the deviation of the group means from the between-groups regression line is given by

$$SS_{A(y)\text{dev. fr. lin.}} = SS_{A(y)} - \frac{(SP_A)^2}{SS_{A(x)}}. \tag{22-14}$$

(Many authors refer to this quantity as S_3.) In words, we subtract from the *unadjusted* between-groups sum of squares, an adjustment for the linear effect of the group means on the control variable. What is left over, of course, would be the residual variation of the deviations from the between-groups regression line. We have not calculated this quantity before, since the adjustment of the treatment effects was obtained indirectly (see the first row of the lower portion of Table 22-2, p. 485).

As a numerical example, consider the sums of squares and products presented in the upper portion of Table 22-4 (p. 489). Substituting in Eq. (22-14),

$$SS_{A(y)\text{dev. fr. lin.}} = 112.00 - \frac{(-19.00)^2}{9.25}$$

$$= 112.00 - 39.03 = 72.97.$$

For this sum of squares, $df = a - 2$, the additional df being lost in the estimation of the between-groups regression line. The test of the hypothesis that the between-groups regression line is linear is given by

$$F = \frac{MS_{A(y)\text{dev. fr. lin.}}}{MS_{S/A(\text{adj.})}}. \tag{22-15}$$

For this example,

$$F = \frac{72.97/(3-2)}{16.71} = \frac{72.97}{16.71} = 4.37.$$

At $\alpha = .05$, $F(1, 20) = 4.35$. The obtained F of 4.37 is thus significant at the 5 percent level of significance.

COMMENTS   There seems to be complete agreement among statisticians that the assumption of homogeneity of within-group regression coefficients is critical for a proper interpretation of the F test conducted in the main analysis. Because of its importance, this test should be conducted before the analysis of covariance itself is performed. The assumption of linear within-groups regression concerns the legitimacy of using the between-groups regression line to adjust the treatment means if the regression is not linear. As Winer (1962) puts it, "If this regression does not prove to be linear, interpretation of the adjusted means becomes difficult" (p. 588). In view of the ambiguity concerning the assumption of linearity in the analysis of covariance, you should seek the advice of a statistician if you have reason to suspect a violation of this assumption.

Multiple Control Variables

Occasionally, even greater precision may result if additional control variables are included in the analysis. The analysis is not overly complicated with two control variables, although the computational effort is approximately twice that required for the analysis with a single control variable. There is often little gain in precision with the addition of three or more control variables, provided that the first two are reasonably correlated with the dependent variable and uncorrelated with each other.

The adjustment made with two control variables essentially involves the separate adjustments of the $SS_{A(y)}$ and $SS_{S/A(y)}$ for the linear effects of the two control variables. Winer (1962, pp. 618–621; 1971, pp. 809–814) discusses the analysis of a number of control variables, while Kirk (1968, pp. 472–475) provides a worked example of a one-factor analysis of covariance with two control variables.

FACTORIAL DESIGNS

The analysis of covariance can be extended to factorial designs. The formal analyses involve simple adaptations of the rules given in Table 22-1. We do not have room in this book to consider these applications of the rules, although Exercise 3 for Part VI allows you to develop the computational formulas for an $A \times B$ design and to apply them to some actual data. If you are interested in a formal discussion of the covariance analysis of factorial experiments, see Myers (1966, pp. 315–322) or Winer (1962, pp. 595–618; 1971, pp. 781–809).

chapter twenty-three

RANDOMIZED BLOCKS, OTHER ALTERNATIVES, AND EVALUATION OF THE TECHNIQUES

For the designs discussed in Parts II–IV, individual differences are essentially allowed to remain unchecked. We assign subjects to the experimental treatments in a random fashion, so that a poor subject is just as likely to be assigned to a particular condition as is a good subject. Obviously, we do not expect groups of subjects assigned this way to be equivalent on all subject characteristics. Some groups will be favored with the better subjects, some will not. There is no *bias*, however, since each treatment has equal probability of having high- and low-ability subjects.

One way to help the system "work" is to select subjects from the most *homogeneous population* possible. If, in a hypothetical situation, we were able to obtain a pool of perfectly matched subjects and then assigned these subjects randomly to the different conditions, we would feel quite confident that the groups were nearly equivalent at the outset. (There are still other factors that would be responsible for variability in the scores of subjects treated alike, such as variations in the testing environment, in the actual treatments, in the subjects themselves, and so on.) If we could assign subjects to the treatments from a homogeneous pool, there would be another related benefit: a marked reduction in the within-groups mean square. We will pursue this point in some detail, since the latter possibility holds great interest for the researcher.

The first step in accomplishing a reduction in error variance is to find some basis for the selection of subjects for our experiment. That is, we must identify characteristics of subjects which are known to influence the behavior of interest and which may be measured *before* the start of the experiment. We can find examples of such characteristics in most areas of the behavioral sciences. In problem-solving experiments, for instance, we might turn to scores on intelligence tests or to grade-point averages. In psychophysical experiments, differences in sensory acuity might be considered an important matching variable. In educational research, social-class differences is a possibility, while in social psychology, differences in certain attitudes may be used by the investigator.

If we are able to identify important sources of individual differences before the start of the experiment, we can select a homogeneous group of subjects to serve in the study. We would randomly assign these selected subjects to the different treatment conditions. This type of procedure would reduce the within-groups variance by restricting the variation due to a particular subject characteristic that otherwise would be left unchecked in an experiment. We must be concerned, of course, about the potentially limited generalizability such a set of results would offer. That is, the treatment effects obtained with subjects of "average" intelligence or with subjects from middle-income families may not be representative of the effects that would be obtained with subjects from other portions of the general population. To be more specific, there might be an *interaction* between the treatments and the subject characteristic which formed the basis for the selection. Fortunately, it is possible to avoid this difficulty and at the same time to maintain the advantage of homogeneous groupings of subjects.

RANDOMIZED BLOCK DESIGN

The block design provides a solution to this problem of generalization by including more than one block of homogeneous subjects in the experiment. Rather than drawing a single group of subjects from one ability level, the block design includes groups of homogeneous subjects drawn from two or more ability levels. There are several different names for this sort of design—e.g., the *randomized block design*, the *Treatment × Levels design*, and the *stratified design*.

The Design and Analysis

Suppose we have a pool of 60 subjects available for the experiment and that there are $a = 4$ levels of the treatment factor (factor A). If we were conducting a completely randomized, single-factor experiment, we would randomly assign $s = 15$ subjects to each of the four experimental conditions. On the basis of information available to us before the start of the experiment, let us assume that we can classify the 60 subjects into three equal blocks of subjects, each block containing 20 subjects who are relatively homogeneous on the classification factor. The randomized block design is formed by assigning the subjects within blocks to the four experimental conditions, as diagrammed in the upper portion of Table 23-1. (The randomized block design appears on the right and the corresponding single-factor design appears on the left.)

We can view the block design as consisting of three independent experiments, one containing subjects of high ability, say, a second containing subjects of medium ability, and a third containing subjects of low ability. In each case, the subjects within each of these blocks are assigned randomly to the four treatment conditions—hence, the terms "randomized block" or "Treatment × Levels" design. Note that the design was constructed in two steps: first an initial grouping of subjects into blocks, and then the random assignment of subjects within blocks to the different treatments. In essence, the original single-factor experiment has become a two-factor design, factor A being completely crossed with the blocking factor (factor B in this example).

It is instructive to point out that the analysis of covariance utilizes the *same information* as does the randomized block design. That is, scores on a correlated

TABLE 23-1 *Comparison of Blocked and Unblocked Single-Factor Experiments*

COMPLETELY RANDOMIZED DESIGN

Levels of Factor A

a_1	a_2	a_3	a_4
$s = 15$	$s = 15$	$s = 15$	$s = 15$

RANDOMIZED BLOCK DESIGN

Levels of Factor A

Blocks	a_1	a_2	a_3	a_4
b_1	$s = 5$	$s = 5$	$s = 5$	$s = 5$
b_2	$s = 5$	$s = 5$	$s = 5$	$s = 5$
b_3	$s = 5$	$s = 5$	$s = 5$	$s = 5$

SOURCES OF VARIANCE AND df's

Source	df
A	$a - 1 = 3$
S/A	$a(s - 1) = 56$
Total	$as - 1 = 59$

Source	df
A	$a - 1 = 3$
B	$b - 1 = 2$
$A \times B$	$(a - 1)(b - 1) = 6$
S/AB	$ab(s - 1) = 48$
Total	$abs - 1 = 59$

control variable must be available in both cases. An important difference between these approaches is the way in which the control score is used. For the randomized block design the score must be at hand *before* the start of the experiment, and it actually forms the basis for assignment of subjects to the treatment conditions. With covariance, however, subjects are assigned *without regard* for the score on the control variable. Through random assignment of subjects to conditions, each treatment condition will contain a "representative" sample of subjects. Differences among groups as well as within groups on the control variable are attributable to experimental error. The covariance procedure is applied to the data *after* they are collected to adjust for these chance differences among groups on the control variable and to eliminate from the estimate of error variance variability that is predictable from subject variability on the control variable.

The sources of variance and corresponding df's for the two designs are given in the lower portion of the table. As we can see, the analysis of this design requires no new computational procedures. We simply apply the formulas for the analysis of the completely randomized, two-factor experiment. The sums of squares are extracted in the usual way and the error term is based upon a pooling of subjects within specific treatment-block combinations. This general type of design, in which blocking is introduced as an independent variable, may be extended to multifactor designs. All that the presence of blocks does is to increase by one the number of factors represented in the experiment. Thus, an $A \times B$ design becomes a three-factor experiment, $A \times B \times Blocks$, and an $A \times B \times C$ design becomes a four-factor experiment, $A \times B \times C \times Blocks$. The analyses of these experiments follow the general form outlined in Chapter 15 for higher-order factorial experiments.

Blocking and the Within-Groups Mean Square

The use of randomized blocks often results in an experiment that is more sensitive than the corresponding experiment without blocks. The error term in the completely randomized experiment of Table 23-1, $MS_{S/A}$, reflects the variability of subjects from populations in which the blocking factor is allowed to vary unchecked. In contrast, the error term for the randomized block design, $MS_{S/AB}$, reflects the variability of subjects from populations in which variation in the blocking factor is greatly restricted. Additionally, any Treatment × Block interaction, which remains undetected in the completely randomized experiment (except for differences in within-group variances), is isolated and removed from the error term in the randomized block design.

It is informative to see how a grouping of homogeneous subjects results in a reduction in the size of the error term. The error term for any completely randomized design consists of an averaging of the within-group mean squares for the different treatment conditions. Suppose we look at the mean square obtained for the subjects receiving the treatment at level a_1 in a single-factor design and in a randomized block design. Let us assume that there are nine subjects, all of whom are given the same treatment at level a_1, and who, for computational convenience, produce the scores 1, 2, 3, 4, 5, 6, 7, 8, and 9 on the dependent variable. In the single-factor experiment, the variability of these nine scores would constitute the within-group mean square at level a_1. Calculating first the sum of squares for these scores,

$$SS_{S/A_1} = [(1)^2 + (2)^2 + \cdots + (8)^2 + (9)^2] - \frac{(1 + 2 + \cdots + 8 + 9)^2}{9}$$

$$= 285 - \frac{(45)^2}{9} = 285 - 225 = 60.$$

The corresponding mean square is

$$MS_{S/A_1} = \frac{SS_{S/A_1}}{df_{S/A_1}} = \frac{60}{9 - 1} = 7.5.$$

Next, suppose that these nine subjects had been divided into three blocks based on the results of some ideal pretest and that the subjects responsible for the three lowest scores (1, 2, and 3) were placed in block b_1, the subjects producing the next three scores (4, 5, and 6) were placed in block b_2, and the subjects giving the three highest scores (7, 8, and 9) were placed in block b_3. The within-group mean squares will now be based on the subjects within each of the three blocks. That is,

$$SS_{S/AB_{11}} = [(1)^2 + (2)^2 + (3)^2] - \frac{(1 + 2 + 3)^2}{3}$$

$$= 14 - \frac{(6)^2}{3} = 14 - 12 = 2,$$

$$SS_{S/AB_{12}} = [(4)^2 + (5)^2 + (6)^2] - \frac{(4 + 5 + 6)^2}{3}$$

$$= 77 - \frac{(15)^2}{3} = 77 - 75 = 2,$$

$$SS_{S/AB_{13}} = [(7)^2 + (8)^2 + (9)^2] - \frac{(7 + 8 + 9)^2}{3}$$

$$= 194 - \frac{(24)^2}{3} = 194 - 192 = 2.$$

The mean squares are each obtained by dividing the sums of squares by the appropriate df—i.e., $df = 3 - 1 = 2$. Thus,

$$MS_{S/AB_{11}} = \tfrac{2}{2} = 1.0,$$

$$MS_{S/AB_{12}} = \tfrac{2}{2} = 1.0,$$

$$MS_{S/AB_{13}} = \tfrac{2}{2} = 1.0.$$

In order to compare the two designs, we will have to average the mean squares obtained for the three blocks at level a_1. Specifically,

$$MS_{S/A \text{ at } a_1} = \frac{MS_{S/AB_{11}} + MS_{S/AB_{12}} + MS_{S/AB_{13}}}{b}$$

$$= \frac{1 + 1 + 1}{3} = \frac{3}{3} = 1.0.$$

It is obvious, then, that under ideal circumstances, such as those represented in this simple example, grouping of homogeneous subjects results in an average mean square (1.0) that is considerably smaller than that obtained without the grouping (7.5).

Design of Experiments with Blocking

SELECTION OF THE BLOCKING FACTOR   The primary criterion for the selection of a subject characteristic, which will form the basis for the blocking or grouping into homogeneous groups, is a substantial correlation with the response measure (the dependent variable) in the experiment itself. The degree of error-term reduction is directly related to the size of this correlation. Other considerations may come into play, however. For example, there is the ease with which the information about the subjects can be obtained. Some measures may be readily accessible from school records, while others may require the administration of a test or an interview before they are available to the experimenter. Another consideration is theoretical. Some blocking factors may arouse theoretical interest in the prediction of certain interactions of the treatments and the blocking factor, while others may not. Still, if the researcher's main concern is the refinement of the error term, he will pay greatest attention to the first criterion—the correlation between the blocking factor and the behavior under study.

TYPES OF BLOCKING FACTORS   A blocking factor is a different sort of independent variable than the ones we have considered previously. A blocking factor results from *classifying* subjects rather than *manipulating* some feature of the experimental treatment. Glass and Stanley (1970, pp. 492–495) distinguish three types of blocking factors, basing the distinction on the scales of measurement used to sort subjects out on the different factors. We will mention these types of factors briefly.

Quite frequently, we will categorize subjects in terms of an unordered or *nominal* scale. A subdivision into male and female subjects is a common example. Other examples are classifications of subjects according to racial background, religious affiliation, or political party. The use of twins or litter mates as blocks also constitutes matching on an unordered scale. A second type of blocking consists of a stratification based on an *ordinal* scale, where groupings reflect a "greater than" or "lesser than" property. A common example in educational research is a grouping into socioeconomic status, such as low, lower-middle, middle, upper-middle, and high. Finally, the blocking may be based on measures from an *interval* or *ratio* scale. Age, IQ, and scores on all sorts of pretests are examples of this type of blocking.

METHODS OF BLOCKING   We will assume that a blocking factor has been selected and that the scores are available before the start of the experiment. Two questions of immediate concern are (1) the number of blocks into which subjects will be classified and (2) the number of subjects in each block. We can have as many levels of the blocking factor as we wish, provided there are sufficient numbers of subjects in each block to assign *two* to each treatment condition. (We can have *one* subject per condition, but the analysis becomes more complicated.) As we will see subsequently, however, it is possible to make a rational choice concerning the optimal number of blocking levels in any given experiment.

With regard to the second question, most typically we will see equal numbers of subjects assigned to each blocking level and to each treatment condition within these blocks. Suppose we have four treatments in our experiment and we have 60 subjects available for testing. On the basis of IQ scores, say, we could divide these subjects into a number of different categories. Suppose we choose three categories formed by ranking the subjects in terms of IQ and designating the 20 subjects with the highest scores as "high," the 20 with the next highest scores as "medium," and the remaining 20 subjects as "low." The subjects within each block would then be randomly assigned to the four treatments, with the restriction that there would be $s = 5$ subjects in each treatment condition.

There are variants to this procedure, of course.[1] If the blocks contain unequal numbers of subjects, as would be the case if the researcher wanted to preserve the underlying distribution in the population of the blocking factor, the assignment of subjects to conditions should still require equal numbers of subjects in each treatment condition within the blocks. While it may make sense to allow block size to vary, there is usually no reason to weight one treatment more heavily than another by assigning to it a greater proportion of the subjects.

OPTIMAL NUMBER OF LEVELS   We have already asserted that the degree to which blocking results in a reduction of the error term, relative to the completely randomized design, depends upon the magnitude of the correlation between the scores forming the basis of the blocking and the scores on the dependent variable. Not so obvious is the relationship between the efficiency of the design and a number of other factors—(1) the total number of subjects, (2) the number of treatment levels, and (3) the number of ability levels. Although the

---

[1] Lindquist (1953, pp. 127–132) presents a detailed discussion of alternative methods of constituting the levels of the blocking factor.

interrelationships among these various factors are complex, it is possible to summarize them in such a way as to assist us in designing an experiment.

First, we should realize that in a large number of applications, most of these factors are effectively *constant* and cannot be changed. For example, we may have to "live" with the facts that there is a certain correlation between the pretest scores and the dependent variable, that our pool of available subjects may be limited and cannot be increased, and that the number of treatment levels is dictated to a large extent by the purpose of our experiment. What we *can* vary is the *number of blocking levels* that we include in the experiment. Given these restrictions, we want to select the number of levels that will achieve maximum precision.

Feldt (1958) has provided this information in a useful summary table which is duplicated in Table 23-2. For different correlations between the scores on the blocking factor and scores on the dependent variable (.2, .4, .6, and .8), for two numbers of levels of factor A (2 and 5), and for various total sample sizes (20 to 150), the *optimal* numbers of blocks are tabulated. (Values in Table 23-2 have been rounded to the nearest integer; certain entries have been limited by the requirement that $s > 2$ in a treatment-level cell.) For example, suppose we have 50 subjects available for our study and that we have five different treatment conditions. Under these circumstances, the optimal numbers of ability levels will be 2, 4, 5, and 5 for correlations of .2, .4, .6, and .8, respectively.

It will be noted that for some entries in the table it is not possible to obtain equal numbers of subjects for each treatment-level combination. If we have 50 subjects available, for instance, a correlation of .4, and will include five

TABLE 23-2 *Optimal Number of Levels for Selected Experimental Conditions, Assuming Levels Defined by Equal Proportions of the Population* (from Feldt, 1958)[a]

Correlation[b]	Treatment Levels	Total Number of Subjects Available					
		20	30	50	70	100	150
.2	2	2	3	4	5	7	9
	5	1	2	2	3	4	6
.4	2	3	4	6	9	13	17
	5	2	3	4	5	7	10
.6	2	4	6	9	13	17	25
	5	2	3	5	7	9	14
.8	2	5	7	12	17	23	25
	5	2	3	5	7	10	15

[a] By permission of the author and the editor of *Psychometrika*.
[b] Correlation between the pretest and the dependent variable.

levels in the experiment, Table 23-2 indicates that four blocking levels will be optimal. Following this advice, we would have a total of 4(5) = 20 treatment-level combinations. But since there are only 50 subjects to apportion to these combinations, we can elect either to operate with unequal sample sizes and to conduct the analysis with unweighted means or to place equal numbers of subjects in each of the cells. If we made this latter choice, we would set $s = 2$ and use only 40 subjects.

Feldt indicates that we can reasonably approximate combinations not presented in the table by means of linear interpolation for the number of treatment levels and the total number of available subjects. In order to obtain approximations for correlations not presented in the table, we should make the interpolation in terms of the squared correlation coefficient.[2]

Blocking as an Experimental Factor

We have seen how the inclusion of blocks as a factor in an experiment can increase the precision of the experimental design. In this regard, blocking may be thought of as a *control* factor, where its introduction is motivated by a desire to reduce error variance rather than to study the effect of the subject factor per se. Moreover, we attempt to guarantee this precision by selecting a characteristic or ability that is highly correlated with the dependent variable— otherwise, what is the point of selecting a randomized block design? We are certainly interested in the possibility of a Treatment × Block interaction in this sort of experiment, but this is not the main reason for choosing this type of design.

In contrast, there are many applications of this design in which characteristics of subjects become the *object of study* and not merely a means to reduce error variance. We may want, for example, to compare the rates of forgetting of slow and fast learners, or the performance in a conditioning experiment of subjects differing in anxiety, or the relative success of different types of therapy administered to subjects varying in their attitudes towards the treatments. [As we noted in Chapter 9 (pp. 181–182), Gollin (1965) has made a strong case for the use of this sort of design in developmental work.] In experiments where blocks have experimental interest, there is no necessary requirement of a correlation between the pretest (or selection factor) and the dependent variable. In fact, we might not even know whether there is a correlation before the start of the experiment.

When a blocking factor is introduced as the object of study, we sometimes see the variable referred to as a *subject variable* or an *organismic variable*. It has been frequently noted, but not widely appreciated, that the *interpretation* of experiments with subject variables is extremely complicated. The basis for the problem lies in the fact that subject variables are not the result of experimental

[2] See Myers (1966, pp. 145–146) for a detailed explanation of this procedure.

manipulation, but of subject selection or classification. Selecting subjects on one characteristic, such as sex, religious affiliation, or grade-point average, does not guarantee that only these characteristics are varying in the experiment. On the contrary, there may be a large number of other characteristics, which are correlated with the selection factor and which may be responsible for any differences found.

Suppose, for example, that we compared male and female subjects on a number of different problem-solving tasks. The significance of sex as a main effect would provide problems of interpretation, since merely knowing that males and females differ on a collection of problem-solving tasks gives us no insight into either sex differences or problem-solving processes. A significant Task × Sex interaction, however, does offer the possibility of isolating the processes involved in the tasks and contributing to differences between males and females. To find that males are worse than females on one type of problem, equivalent on a second type, and better on a third task might be interpretable. That is, not only will an explanation of this sort of finding have to specify differences in the abilities of males and females, but also how these differences contribute differentially to the different types of problems. In short, we will have to know a great deal about intellectual differences between the sexes as well as the basic problem-solving processes "tapped" by the different types of problems.[3]

Evaluation of the Randomized Block Design

The advantages of the randomized block design are considerable. We may make an experiment more precise by eliminating from the error term sources of variance associated with the blocking factor. Additionally, the design allows an assessment of possible interactions between treatment effects and blocks. If such an interaction is significant, then we will know that the effects of the treatments do not generalize across the abilities or classification of subjects represented in the experiment. If these interactions are not significant, then we have achieved a certain degree of generalizability of the results. Finally, it must be stressed that these advantages are obtained with statistical assumptions which are no more restrictive than those specified for the completely randomized experiments in general. Such is *not* the case for the repeated-measures design, where the homogeneity assumptions are often not met and where potential Treatment × Subject interactions may threaten to cloud the interpretation of treatment effects. Similarly, statistical assumptions underlying the analysis of covariance are quite restrictive. The randomized block design is free from these sorts of difficulties.

Certain disadvantages of blocking must be mentioned also. First, there is the cost of introducing the blocking factor. Second, it may be difficult to find

---

[3] Underwood (1957, pp. 112–125) provides a detailed discussion of the problem of inference associated with this type of situation.

blocking factors that are highly correlated with the dependent variable used in the experiment. Finally, we must be concerned with the possible loss of power when the blocking factor is poorly correlated with the dependent variable. Suppose, for example, that there is no correlation between the pretest and the dependent variable. Under these circumstances, the error term will be based on sets of scores that are just as "heterogeneous" as those in a completely randomized experiment without blocking, and we will suffer a loss in power because there are fewer *df* associated with the error term in the block design than in the one without blocking. This discrepancy in error term *df*'s increases with the number of blocks, the number of treatment levels, and the number of treatment factors. In this regard, Feldt (1958) concludes that it is more efficient to use the *unblocked* design when the correlation between the blocking factor and the dependent variable is *less than .2*. Again, if the assessment of Treatment × Block interactions is the primary purpose of the study, then a low correlation will not affect the decision to use randomized blocks in an experiment.

ALTERNATIVE METHODS

In this and the last chapter we have contrasted two methods—blocking and covariance—which utilize scores on a concomitant or control variable to increase the precision of the experiment. Although these procedures will be evaluated in the next section, we will mention one point in favor of the use of covariance: the impossibility in some applications of forming homogeneous blocks of subjects before the start of the experiment. In this section we will consider two alternative analyses which can be conducted with exactly the same information that is available for the analysis of covariance. The first is what we might call *post-hoc blocking*; the other is the *analysis of difference scores*.

Post-Hoc Blocking

Post-hoc blocking consists of an arrangement of subjects in blocks *after* the experiment has been conducted. Let us assume that scores on a control variable of some sort were taken, but that subjects were assigned randomly to the treatment conditions without regard for the control scores. Instead of conducting an analysis of covariance, suppose we classified all of the subjects into a number of blocks according to their control scores. We will assume that three categories are formed with approximately equal numbers of subjects in each. The subjects in each *treatment* group would now be segregated into the three categories, transforming a single-factor experiment into a Treatment × Block design. Because subjects were assigned at random to the treatment conditions, we would certainly not expect to have equal frequencies of subjects in each block-treatment combination. On the other hand, the frequencies should not be too variable from cell to cell.

The statistical analysis is complicated by the presence of unequal cell frequencies. The appropriate analysis of these data would be one conducted on the *unweighted means*. To be more specific, the block-treatment *means* would be entered in an *AB* matrix and the sums of squares for the treatment sources of variance—*A* (treatments), *B* (blocks), and *A* × *B*—would be based on these means. An illustration in Chapter 17 (see pp. 358–360) provides a relevant example of the analysis. In that example, subjects were divided into blocks of male and female subjects after the conduct of the experiment.

One virtue of post-hoc blocking is a marked reduction in computational effort relative to that required of the corresponding covariance analysis. More important, however, is the freedom of this analysis from the restrictive assumptions associated with the analysis of covariance. Winer (1962) suggests that if the blocking results in sample sizes of 5 or more that this type of blocking "... is generally to be preferred to the analysis of covariance" (p. 594). Another advantage of post-hoc blocking is the possibility of evaluating the significance of any Treatment × Block interaction that may be revealed in this analysis. Again, the example in Chapter 17 illustrates such a situation. The disadvantages are that with small sample sizes, such as $s = 8$ in the original experiment, cell frequencies cannot all be greater than 5 and there is the possibility that some block-treatment cells will have fewer than 2 entries, making it impossible to calculate a within-groups mean square. We also lose the ability to adjust the treatment means for differences on the control variable, but if the assignment of subjects is random, this adjustment in the covariance analysis will usually be small.

Analysis of Difference Scores

With scores on the control and dependent variables available for each subject, it may make sense in some situations to form *difference* scores by subtracting either the score on the dependent variable from the control score or the reverse. That is, the difference might be defined as

$$D_{ij} = AS_{ij(x)} - AS_{ij(y)} \quad \text{or} \quad D_{ij} = AS_{ij(y)} - AS_{ij(x)}.$$

This procedure becomes feasible when the control and dependent variables are of the same nature. In an animal-learning experiment, for example, the dependent variable might be the number of bar presses a rat makes in a given period of time under a specific experimental treatment and the control variable might be the number of bar presses taken at the beginning of the experiment before the introduction of the independent variable. In an experiment on reading comprehension, the dependent variable might be a comprehension score taken after different types of training, while the control score might be a score obtained from a pretest given to all subjects prior to the start of the differential training. In a memory experiment, the control score could be the number of correct responses on the last training trial and the score on the dependent variable the number of responses recalled on a delayed-retention test. In short, for the types of control variables we have in mind it makes sense to talk about a *gain* or a *loss* in performance as a result of the treatments.

Suppose, then, that we have such a situation. Subtracting one score from the other will allow us to perform the statistical analysis on a type of *residual* score directly—on scores where the initial differences among subjects have been removed. In contrast with post-hoc blocking, this procedure *will* result in a correction for chance differences among the groups on the control variable. The statistical analysis of these difference scores is quite simple: we merely treat the scores as separate observations in a completely randomized experiment and conduct the analysis of *variance* appropriate to that design.

Despite these apparent advantages and an obvious simplicity, an analysis of difference scores is a questionable procedure. One of the problems concerns the unrealistic assumption that the within-groups regression coefficient is a particular value, namely, 1.0. (In covariance, the regression coefficient is actually estimated from the data.) The main problem with difference scores, however, is that "change" scores are usually more unreliable than either the original or final scores alone. This happens because any error variance present in the two sets of scores, which is not predicted by linear regression, combines to influence jointly the error variance estimated from the difference scores (Feldt, 1958, p. 348). The result, then, is an increased insensitivity under these circumstances. We will return to this point in the next section.

AN EVALUATION OF THE DIFFERENT PROCEDURES

Two basic procedures for increasing the precision of experiments have been discussed, experimental (blocking and post-hoc blocking) and statistical (covariance and difference measures). The main difference between blocking and the other techniques is that the scores on the control variable form the basis for the assignment of subjects to conditions, while subjects (and the control scores associated with them) are assigned randomly to conditions in the other types of design. The possibility of post-hoc blocking makes it feasible to extend the advantages of the blocking technique to experiments in which blocking cannot be conducted prior to the start of the experiment. We will now evaluate these procedures on a number of criteria.

Precision

Since the main reason for turning to these methods is the hope of increasing precision, mainly in the refinement of the magnitude of the error term, it is reasonable to compare the different approaches on this important criterion.

Feldt (1958) has evaluated three of the methods for increasing precision: blocking, covariance, and difference measures. Post-hoc blocking was not considered. Feldt contrasted *optimal* blocking with the other two methods for a number of different situations. In general, he found that *blocking* is more precise when the correlation is less than .4, while *covariance* is more precise with correlations greater than .6. Since we *rarely* find correlations of this latter magnitude in the behavioral sciences, we will not find a unique advantage of covariance in most applications. In fact, with correlations less than .2 and with small sample sizes, Feldt indicates that neither covariance nor blocking offers much of an advantage over a standard analysis of variance.

Concerning the relative precision of *difference measures*, Feldt states his conclusions explicitly as follows: a comparison of the three methods "... indicates the lower precision of the difference approach. It is also indicated that unless a substantial correlation exists between the control and [dependent] variables the difference approach results in considerably lower precision than that yielded by the completely randomized design" (p. 349).

Assumptions

Covariance requires a number of specialized statistical assumptions, the most stringent of which is the assumption of homogeneous within-group regression. The presence of heterogeneous regression means that subjects who score high on the control variable produce results different from those produced by subjects who score low on the control variable. In terms of the randomized block design, heterogeneity of regression is reflected by the presence of a Treatment × Block interaction. Here, too, a *block* of subjects scoring high on the control variable produces results different from those produced by a block of subjects scoring low on the control variable. Unless we have evidence to the contrary, we usually suspect that such interactions do exist in the behavioral sciences. For this reason, then, blocking is to be preferred for its relative freedom from the statistical assumptions concerning the form of the regression between the control and dependent variables.

There is an additional implication of the covariance assumptions that the researcher must keep in mind. The covariance adjustments, as well as adjustments accomplished by means of difference scores, are based upon the assumption of a specific model of the relationship between the control and dependent variables—namely, the linear regression model. As we have seen, there is the *statistical* consideration of the correctness of this model with the particular data at hand; i.e., there is the assumption that the correct form of regression has been applied. There is the further implication that the statistical model has for any *theoretical* explanations of the data. Specifically, an experimenter must decide whether or not it makes theoretical sense to transform or change his observed data according to this form of adjustment. Should a subject have his score on the dependent variable adjusted by an amount that is directly proportional to his score on the control variable? Or should subjects with high scores be boosted more or less than the linear regression line dictates? Most researchers do not worry about such considerations when they turn to covariance procedures, but they should. Whether we like it or not, the application of covariance implies a commitment to a particular theoretical position on this point. The blocking method, on the other hand, requires no such theoretical commitment.

Assessment of the Treatment × Block Interaction

While the presence of a Treatment × Block interaction can invalidate an analysis of covariance by producing heterogeneous within-group regression, the randomized block design is capable of assessing its presence directly. This is an obvious advantage of the blocking method. If such interactions exist, they should be unearthed and studied. The randomized block design provides one way of accomplishing this goal.

Removal of Bias

Several authors cite as an advantage associated with covariance and difference scores the adjustment of the treatment *means* for differences among groups on the control variable. This adjustment of the means is sometimes described as the removal of a potential *bias* or confounding due to the presence of chance differences among the groups on the control variable. This is an important consideration, but it should also be pointed out that such differences will ordinarily be small when the sample size is reasonably large and the random assignment of subjects to conditions has had an "opportunity" to bring the groups close together prior to the start of the experiment.

But suppose the groups *do* differ widely on the control variable, so much so that these differences are significant when an analysis of variance is performed on them. Our interpretation of such an occurrence is to attribute the differences to the randomization procedure, since we do expect to find significant differences a fixed proportion of the time (i.e., α). Nevertheless, most researchers will still be suspicious of the results of the experiment itself—i.e., the scores on the dependent variable, or at least of the group or groups which apparently are the "deviant" ones. Covariance is a technique designed to adjust for chance differences among the groups, but the adjustment of significant differences is still a cause for concern.

In order to cope with such a situation, experimenters will sometimes attempt to remove the bias through the post-hoc elimination from *all* treatment groups of the subject (or subjects) producing the most deviant score on the control variable. This type of procedure will be successful in reducing the bias only if one or two greatly deviant subjects are in fact responsible for the differences observed among the means; otherwise, the technique will not bring the groups in line. It is assumed with this procedure that the *same* criterion for dropping subjects is being applied to each of the treatment groups. This is why we eliminate the most deviant subject from *each* group. It should be clear, however, that in dropping these subjects, we are assuming that a deviant subject in one group is "equivalent" to a deviant subject in another group—an assumption that may not be reasonable to make.

Perhaps the most appropriate procedure is to replicate or to repeat the experiment with a new set of subjects or, if this is not feasible, to repeat the experiment with only a few of the treatment conditions—the deviant group or groups plus other treatment conditions which will allow the assimilation of the results of the partial replication with those of the original experiment. These additional groups might be control groups or groups which would allow meaningful comparisons to be made in the new experiment. If the performance of these latter groups matches the performance of these same groups in the original experiment, it may be possible to assimilate the results of the two experiments.

In short, any differences among groups that are present before the introduction of the differential treatments are of real concern to the investigator. If he has no control variable, he simply accepts the fact that he will commit a type I error a certain α proportion of the time. If control scores are available, he may decide to turn to the analysis of covariance to adjust for these chance differences among the treatment groups. It is the author's observation that differences on the dependent variable which are removed or, perhaps more critically, are *produced* by the adjustment of the treatment means are viewed with considerable alarm by other researchers. Thus, this advantage of covariance over blocking is not a real one, since any experimental conclusion which is based on relatively large adjustments of the treatment means will receive "suspended judgment" by other researchers in the field.

Summary

The analysis of covariance can be useful in increasing the precision of an experiment. The statistical model underlying its use is highly restrictive and thus not generally applicable. On almost every count, blocking is the method of choice and post-hoc blocking is a second-best technique to increase precision. The use of covariance should be questioned except in the simple and clear cases, while the analysis of difference scores should generally be avoided.

EXERCISES FOR PART VI[1]

1. It occurred to an experimenter that he could increase the precision of an experiment by obtaining information about the subjects which could be used as control scores in an analysis of covariance. Since it was inconvenient to collect this information at the start of the experiment, he did so at the completion of the testing session for each subject. He had 20 subjects available for a single-factor experiment with $a = 4$ treatment conditions. Subjects were assigned randomly to conditions with the restriction of equal sample sizes in each group. The scores on the control and dependent variables for these 20 subjects are presented in the accompanying AS matrix.

AS Matrix

a_1		a_2		a_3		a_4	
x	y	x	y	x	y	x	y
4	13	5	7	3	12	4	13
4	8	3	4	2	4	7	14
6	8	5	10	4	5	7	13
5	6	2	5	1	2	5	8
3	6	3	5	3	3	6	9

(a) Perform an analysis of covariance on these data.

(b) Conduct two analyses of *variance*, one on the control scores and one on the unadjusted scores on the dependent variable. How do you interpret the outcome of the analysis of covariance in light of these two analyses?

2. The subjects for this experiment were assigned randomly to the $a = 3$ different levels of the independent variable. The control scores were obtained prior to the administration of the experimental treatments. The AS matrix is given below.

AS Matrix

a_1		a_2		a_3	
x	y	x	y	x	y
2	11	5	15	2	12
1	8	3	12	2	9
4	8	1	16	5	8
1	9	3	19	1	11
3	7	3	16	3	7
5	9	5	20	1	7

(a) Perform an analysis of covariance on these data.

(b) Do you feel that the experimenter benefited from the introduction of the control variable into the statistical analysis? Be specific.

[1] The answers to the exercises are found in Appendix D.

3. Consider the following factorial design and the scores produced by the $s = 4$ subjects in each of the treatment conditions. The control scores were obtained before the start of the experiment, and the subjects were assigned randomly to the conditions without knowledge of the control scores.

ABS MATRIX

ab_{11}		ab_{12}		ab_{13}		ab_{21}		ab_{22}		ab_{23}		ab_{31}		ab_{32}		ab_{33}	
x	y	x	y	x	y	x	y	x	y	x	y	x	y	x	y	x	y
2	11	5	9	2	12	4	15	6	19	3	8	3	12	2	11	1	10
1	8	5	7	3	7	5	12	4	16	4	9	2	9	3	7	5	9
5	8	1	9	4	6	3	16	3	20	4	7	5	8	4	7	3	7
4	7	3	10	1	11	4	14	5	15	1	10	2	10	3	9	4	11

(a) With the help of Table 22-1 (p. 483), construct the computational formulas necessary to conduct an analysis of covariance with this particular experiment.

(b) Perform an analysis of covariance on these data.

PART VII

Sensitivity of Experimental Designs and Controversial Topics

In this section we will consider a number of topics which warrant extended discussion but did not "fit" conveniently in the earlier chapters. The major topic is the sensitivity of experimental designs (Chapter 24). Although we have discussed this topic previously in a variety of contexts, these discussions have been scattered and directed at specific issues. It is useful, therefore, to summarize their content in a general consideration of the subject. In Chapter 24 we will also talk about the relevance of design sensitivity to such topics as power and the role of replications. The final chapter (Chapter 25) considers a number of procedures which can be reasonably described as "controversial." Primary attention is directed towards the estimate of the *strength* of treatment effects. The remaining sections of the chapter will consist of such topics as the use of data transformations and the pooling of alternative estimates of error variance—which, although only briefly discussed, round out the coverage of analysis of variance techniques for the researcher in the behavioral sciences.

Numerical examples illustrating arithmetic operations discussed in this section may be found at the end of Part VII (p. 561).

chapter twenty-four

SENSITIVITY OF
EXPERIMENTAL DESIGNS

The error term for completely randomized designs is based on the variability of subjects given the same experimental treatment. These estimates for the different groups are then combined to form the within-groups mean square. The presence or absence of a main effect or of an interaction is assessed by means of the F ratio. As we discussed in Part II, for example, the expected value of the numerator of the F ratio, $E(MS_A)$, is the sum of a treatment component and an error component, while the expected value of the denominator term, $E(MS_{S/A})$, contains only the error component. The logic behind the F test is that the F ratio will be greater than 1.0 when there is a treatment effect and approximately equal to 1.0 when there is not.

REDUCTION OF ERROR VARIANCE

Sensitivity and Error Variance

While we have been over this argument before, it is of interest to see how the sensitivity of an experiment is related to the size of the error component. With a treatment effect of a given magnitude, any increase in the size of the error variance reduces the size of the F ratio and lessens our chances of rejecting the null hypothesis; any decrease in error increases these chances. As a concrete example, suppose that in the population the treatment component equals 5 units and that the error component is 2 units. On the average, then, we would expect the F ratio to equal

$$F = \frac{\text{treatment} + \text{error}}{\text{error}} = \frac{5 + 2}{2} = 3.5.$$

If it is possible to reduce error variance, say from 2 to 1, the F ratio will be increased:

$$F = \frac{5 + 1}{1} = 6.0.$$

On the other hand, if we have to work with increased error variance, say from 2 to 5, the ratio will be decreased:

$$F = \frac{5 + 5}{5} = 2.0.$$

It is clear, then, that any procedure which results in a reduction of error variance will increase the sensitivity of the experiment.

There are three major sources of error variance: random variation in the actual treatments, the presence of unanalyzed control factors, and individual differences ("permanent" or "temporary" factors affecting a subject's performance during the course of the experiment). All of these sources reflect themselves in a subject's score on the dependent variable and thus contribute to error variance. Certain steps can be taken to reduce the magnitude of these sources of experimental error, however, and we will mention them briefly. (A detailed treatment of this topic cannot be presented here, as the particular problems are tied to specific research areas. Their solutions, therefore, require a specialized knowledge that is best obtained from the workers in the field.)[1]

Reduction of Treatment Variability

We have noted previously that no experimental treatment is *exactly* alike for every subject in a particular condition. The calibration of the equipment may change from session to session, the experimenter will not be perfectly consistent in the conduct of the experiment, and environmental factors such as noise level, illumination, and temperature will not be identical for each subject. To the extent that these different factors influence the behavior under study, their variation from subject to subject contributes to the estimate of experi-

---

[1] A source that may prove helpful in this regard is a handbook entitled, *Experimental methods and instrumentation in psychology*, edited by Sidowski (1966).

mental error. We should add to this list errors of measurement and of recording that appear randomly.

We can take certain steps to minimize these sources of variability. Carefully calibrated equipment, well-trained experimenters, and special testing rooms help to accomplish this goal. In essence, this solution attempts to hold constant the specific conditions of testing in the experiment. If we are worried about the *generality* of the findings, we might consider introducing these sources as *control variables* in the experiment. That is, instead of keeping the illumination of the testing room at a single value, we can add illumination as an independent variable, the levels of which are factorially combined with the experimental factors. We will still base our estimate of error variance on subjects who are given the same illumination level, and at the same time we will obtain additional information on the presence or absence of an *interaction* of the control factor and the experimental treatments.

Unanalyzed Control Factors

Control factors are introduced into an experiment for a variety of reasons, but primarily for the removal of possible bias (internal validity) and for an increase in the generality of the results (external validity). We discussed these reasons in Chapter 15 (see pp. 313–318). As we noted there, experimenters frequently disregard these control factors in the analysis of their experiments. The issues involved in such a decision were considered in Chapter 15, but the relevance to this discussion is that if these factors are left unanalyzed, any variability associated with them, either as main effects or as interactions, contributes to error variance.

For example, suppose an experimenter plans an experiment which requires far too many subjects for one assistant to run. If he employs more than one assistant, he should make sure that each assistant runs an equal number of subjects in each of the treatment conditions.[2] To do otherwise would introduce a confounding of assistants and treatments into the experiment.

Now, consider the implications if these assistants were differentially successful in eliciting the relevant behavior from subjects (i.e., the children or the animals performed consistently better for one assistant than for another), or if the assistants ran their subjects at different times of day or in different laboratories and these differences affected the performance of their subjects. Just as long as no *interactions* involving assistants appear, the results of the experiment *are* free from bias. We will assume that this is the case. Under these circumstances, the experimenter might be tempted to drop the classification of assistants from his analysis. If he does, the consistent effects of the different assistants on the behavior of their subjects will be thrown back into the analysis as error

---

[2] Each assistant must run at least two subjects in each treatment condition so that the within-groups source of variance can be calculated.

variance (along with the variances due to interactions with assistants). A nonrandom source of variance, which is spread equally over all treatment conditions, does not bias the treatment effects, but it does contribute to experimental error. The obvious solution to such a situation is to include assistants as a control factor in the analysis.

Reduction of Subject Variability

Undoubtedly the major source of error variance in the behavioral sciences is that contributed by individual differences. The fact that subjects differ widely in performance on laboratory tasks means that when they are assigned randomly to the treatment conditions, this variability becomes an important source of error variance. We have studied three general methods designed to reduce this source of variability: the blocking or matching of subjects, the use of repeated measures, and the analysis of covariance.

We discussed blocking in Chapter 23, where we demonstrated that the grouping of subjects into homogeneous blocks serves to reduce experimental error. The reason blocking "works" is that the variability of subjects drawn from a homogeneous pool is less than the variability of subjects drawn from a heterogeneous one. The basic technique consists of the selection of groups of subjects who give evidence of being similar on one or more characteristics that are known to be related to the performance under study. Typically, two or more such blocks are formed, with the between-blocks differences being as large as possible. Subjects from each block are assigned randomly to the treatment conditions. This design achieves a reduction in error variance by restricting the within-groups variability. The design has the further advantage of allowing the determination of the presence or absence of a Treatment × Block interaction.

The repeated-measures design is related to the randomized block design in the sense that matching is nearly perfect because the same subject is observed in more than one of the experimental treatments. In general, the error terms associated with repeated factors are considerably smaller than those obtained with nonrepeated factors. This reduction occurs because consistent individual differences are removed from the estimates of error variance. (See Chapter 19 for a more complete explanation.) There are serious problems with the repeated-measures design, however. Statistically, for example, there are the restrictive assumptions of homogeneous variances and covariances. Whereas we might be able to "handle" the statistical violations by means of corrections or specialized statistics, we have no way of solving the *experimental* problems associated with this type of design. There is the distinct possibility in this design of differential carry-over effects—i.e., the residual effects of earlier conditions combining with and influencing the experimental treatment currently being administered. If such carry-over effects are present, the treatment means will be influenced and the results will be distorted. Ways in which carry-over effects may be eliminated or reduced were discussed in the introduction to Part V. With any repeated-measures design, we must be absolutely sure that these interactions do not distort our conclusions.

Covariance produces a reduction in error variance by adjusting estimates of error *and* of treatment effects for the linear effects of a control variable, a variable that is correlated with the dependent variable chosen for the experiment. If the correlation between the two scores is quite high, say $r = .8$, the increase in sensitivity afforded by covariance can be considerable. As we noted in Chapter 23, however, the correlations generally obtained in the behavioral sciences are not this high, and often they are of insufficient magnitude even to justify the extra computational effort required of the analysis. Moreover, the distinct possibilities of heterogeneity of regression and of nonlinearity often limit the use of the covariance techniques.

POWER AND THE F TEST

Relationship between Type I and Type II Errors

A quantitative index of the sensitivity of an experiment is its *power.* Power refers to the probability of *rejecting* the null hypothesis when an alternative hypothesis is *true.* Said another way, power represents the probability that a statistical test of the null hypothesis will result in the conclusion that the phenomenon under study exists. In this sense, power is interpreted as the probability of making a *correct* decision when the null hypothesis is false.

Power is usually defined in terms of the probability of making a type II error (β). Specifically,

$$\text{power} = 1 - \beta.$$

Thus, the smaller the type II error (β), the greater the power and, therefore, the greater the sensitivity of the test. Most extended treatments of power focus upon simple cases—e.g., the test of the hypothesis that the population mean is different from some hypothetical mean. [Hays (1963, chap. 9) presents an excellent discussion of this sort of example.] Cohen (1969), on the other hand, devotes an entire book to the treatment of power in a variety of applications; his Chapters 1 and 8 are most relevant to our needs.

In the types of analyses with which we are concerned, the statistical hypothesis that is being evaluated is the hypothesis that the treatment effects are zero. We have seen already that our decision to reject or not to reject the null hypothesis on the basis of an obtained value of F may result in an error of inference. If there is *no* treatment effect and we *reject* the null hypothesis, we have made a type I error—we have accepted a false fact. On the other hand, if there *is* a treatment effect and we *fail to reject* the null hypothesis, we have committed a type II error—we have failed to recognize real differences.

These situations are illustrated in Fig. 24-1. The upper panel represents the theoretical distribution of F when the null hypothesis is true—i.e., when there are no treatment effects. The region of rejection, which is specified by the shaded area to the right of the ordinate at F_α, represents the magnitude of the type I error. That is, an F which falls within this region will lead to a rejection of the null hypothesis and thus constitute a type I error. The probability with which this will occur is α. The unshaded area to the left of F_α represents the probability of making a correct inference.

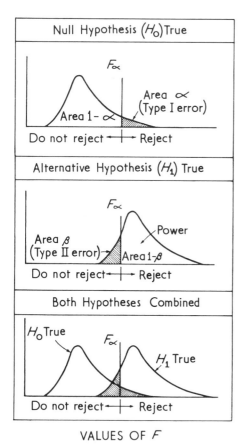

VALUES OF F

Fig. 24-1   Sampling distribution of the F ratio when the null hypothesis is true (top panel) and when the alternative hypothesis is true (middle panel). The two sampling distributions are shown together in the bottom panel.

The middle panel represents the theoretical distribution of F when the alternative hypothesis is true. In order to "locate" this distribution on the baseline, we have to assume a particular alternative hypothesis—i.e., treatment effects of a certain magnitude. (As we noted in Chapter 4, the resulting distribution is not the F distribution, but the *noncentral F* distribution.) The region of rejection is again specified by the area to the right of F_α. It is clear that the critical value of F defining the beginning of the rejection region is the same in these two situations. The reason is that we set F_α with the null hypothesis in mind, and we are now considering the consequences of having set this rejection region when the alternative hypothesis is true. Consider, then, the rejection region—the area to the right of F_α. This area represents the probability of making a correct inference under these circumstances. This probability is the power of the test for this particular alternative hypothesis. The shaded area to the left of F_α (the region of nonrejection) represents the probability of making a type II error (β).

The bottom panel brings together the two separate distributions. The reciprocity of the two types of errors is evident. Any change in the size of the rejection region (the area to the right of F_α) will produce changes in opposite directions for the two types of error. To be more specific, by moving the point of transition (F_α) to the right—i.e., lowering the α level—we decrease the type I error and increase the type II error. By moving F_α to the left—i.e., raising the α level—we increase the type I error and decrease the type II error.

It should be realized that a different display is needed for each particular alternative hypothesis we might consider. To make the point, however, it is sufficient to consider only one alternative hypothesis. The F distribution under the null hypothesis will not change with other alternative hypotheses. What does change is the location of the distribution of noncentral F. With an alternative hypothesis which specifies larger treatment effects than those depicted here, the noncentral F distribution will move to the right. Again, since F_α remains the same, this displacement of the distribution reduces the type II error. Similarly, a reduction in the treatment effects will move the distribution to the left and increase the type II error. In our discussion of power, then, we must be concerned with the relationship between type I and type II errors as well as factors that affect the location of the noncentral F distribution.

Control of Type I and Type II Errors

Obviously, we are able to control the magnitude of type I error through our choice of a rejection region for the F distribution (the α level). The control of the size of the type II error (and power) is usually not this direct. We have already seen the reciprocity between the types of error—any change in the size of the type I error will produce a change in the opposite direction in the type II error. Given this reciprocity, then, one obvious way to decrease a type II error (and to increase power) would be to increase the probability of a type I error.

Unfortunately, we seem to be "stuck" with rigidly set α level, since rarely will we see the α level set at any value greater than .05.

There are several reasons why the type I error has become fixed. First, in the absence of any rational way of deciding the relative seriousness of the two types of errors, we *must* be arbitrary. It may be possible to make these estimates in certain applied fields, however. In the medical sciences, for instance, we might be able to place a numerical value upon the consequences of failing to recognize a new wonder drug (a type II error) and contrast this with the value placed upon the consequences of switching to a new drug that is no better than the original one (a type I error). But in most research areas of the behavioral sciences we are without such guidance. How serious is it if a new hypothesis is not recognized or if an old one is incorrectly rejected? Without explicit values to guide us, we must proceed by conventions. Thus, we fix the type I error at a level that will be acceptable to most researchers—i.e., $\alpha = .05$ or lower—and allow the type II error (and power) be what it has to be. We cannot answer the question of what is an acceptable level of power, since we are usually not in a position to be able to give weight to the relative consequences of the two types of error. If we could agree that a type II error is quite serious and that a type I error is not as serious, we could very reasonably increase the α level. No such agreement as yet exists. (On the other hand, a first step in attempting to evolve a consensus among researchers is to *recognize* that a problem exists and to start thinking about it.)

A second reason why we set the α level at some fixed value is that there are other ways by which we can increase the power of an experiment. Several of these steps may be mentioned:

1. *Sample size.* Power is increased as the number of observations per treatment condition is increased.
2. *Uncontrolled variance.* Power is increased as we eliminate uncontrolled sources of variance. We have already discussed how such a reduction may be accomplished.
3. *Treatment effects.* Power is increased as the size of the treatment effects is increased. This may be accomplished by choosing widely spaced levels of the independent variable or by including conditions which are thought to maximize the appearance of the phenomenon we are studying.

It would certainly be useful to be able to determine the level of power present in an experiment. Consider an experiment in which we have evaluated a source of variance and failed to reject the null hypothesis. Before we abandon this research, we should evaluate the sensitivity of the experiment in detecting the real differences we might have observed. That is, we may suppose that the differences obtained in the experiment represent real differences. We may have failed to reject the null hypothesis because the effect itself is quite small. Under this circumstance, we would probably lose interest in the effect altogether. But we may also have failed to reject the null hypothesis because the experiment was relatively insensitive to differences. If this were the case, most researchers would be reluctant to say anything concerning the "acceptability" of the null hypothesis—because the experiment was simply not sufficiently sensitive to detect differences that are considered important. [In this situation, Hays (1963, pp. 263–266) recommends a *suspension of judgment* rather than a tacit acceptance of the null hypothesis.] A post-hoc determination of power, then, can guide a researcher in his choice of a next step: either to drop the present line of research or to press on with a more sensitive experiment.

There is no question that an understanding of power is important, both in the planning of an experiment and in the interpretation of nonsignificant findings. The practical difficulty is to find a way of determining its value. The major stumbling block is the specification of a reasonable alternative hypothesis. In the context of the analysis of variance, this consists of being able to state *ahead of time* the magnitude of the treatment effects that are expected in the study. We can see why most investigators do not make power estimates before the start of the experiment. How can they specify the magnitude of the treatment effects when all that they can point to is a prediction that there will be a "significant" effect? In most cases, if we knew enough about the phenomenon to be able to state the magnitude of the treatment effects, we would not bother to do the experiment![3]

Suppose we *are* able to make a realistic estimate of the magnitude of the treatment effects. Consider how we might be able to benefit from such a determination. We might examine the sensitivity of the experiment in detecting an acceptable *minimum* size of the treatment effects. One way to do this is to (1) formalize our estimate of the minimum treatment effects with actual numbers, (2) estimate the anticipated error variance for the experiment, and (3) decide upon a level of power that will be acceptable to us. There are no established conventions in selecting a level of power, mainly because most investigators do not attempt to use this information either in the planning of an experiment or in the assessment of the sensitivity of an experiment after it has been conducted.

How much power do we want in an experiment? There are certainly practical limits to the amount of power we can achieve. Since we will probably maintain α at a conventional level, say .05, we will have to rely on other stratagems to effect an increase in power. These have been listed already: an increase in sample size, a reduction in uncontrolled variance, and an increase in the magnitude of the expected treatment effects. Practically speaking, however, the factor we can most easily manipulate is the *sample size*.

Determination of Sample Size

SINGLE-FACTOR CASE   Suppose we *can* estimate the magnitude of the treatment effects, estimate error variance, and attach a probability to our

---

[3] Cohen (1969, p. 349) enumerates a number of ways in which treatment effects can be expressed so that a power analysis may be conducted. Briefly, these range from an actual specification of treatment means and the common population variance to a statement of the relative "size" of the treatment effects.

concern for power. We are now able to determine the sample size needed to attain this degree of sensitivity. (In this discussion we will assume a fixed-effects model.) In order to accomplish this goal, we will have to work with the noncentral F distribution. Three parameters determine this distribution: the degrees of freedom for the numerator and denominator terms of the F ratio and the so-called *noncentrality parameter* (see Winer, 1971, pp. 220–221).

Statisticians have constructed tables which relate the different parameters we have to consider when attempting to determine sample size. These are (1) the minimum treatment effects, (2) the number of treatment levels, (3) the α level, (4) population error variance, and (5) the desired level of power. If we can specify all five factors, we can use tabled power functions. A set of such functions appears in Table C-6 of Appendix C. There are eight different charts in this table. They differ with regard to the *numerator df*. (The charts are numbered consecutively, $df_{num.} = 1$ to 8.) For any one chart, the other four factors are taken into consideration. To be more specific, there are two families of power functions for each chart, one for $\alpha = .05$ and the other for $\alpha = .01$. Except for the first chart, the functions for $\alpha = .05$ appear on the left and those for $\alpha = .01$ appear on the right. For a given α level, power functions are drawn for 11 different values of *denominator df*, $df_{denom.} = 6, 7, 8, 9, 10, 12, 15, 20, 30, 60,$ and ∞. Intermediate values may be interpolated visually. The remaining two factors are power, which appears on the ordinate of the tables as probability, and a parameter, ϕ, which appears on the baseline.[4] For the single-factor case,

$$\phi_A^2 = \frac{s'\left[\sum (\mu_i - \mu)^2\right]/a}{\sigma_{S/A}^2}, \tag{24-1}$$

where the μ_i terms are the population treatment means, μ is the overall population mean, s' is the sample size, and $\sigma_{S/A}^2$ is the pooled within-groups error variance. [We have used s' rather than s to refer to sample size in order to emphasize the fact that different values of s' will be tried in Eq. (24-1) to determine the sample size needed to achieve a given level of power.]

The calculation of appropriate sample sizes is somewhat tedious and involves a trial-and-error operation. What we have to do is to fix the factors we can fix, such as the α level, the number of treatment levels, the estimate of the minimum treatment effects, and the estimate of error variance. Then we try a value of s' and determine the power thus obtained. (Setting s' allows us to calculate ϕ_A and to select the appropriate power function for denominator df.) If the resultant power estimate is unsatisfactory (too low), then we increase the sample size and repeat the operations.

---

[4] Cohen (1969) uses a related index, **f**. See p. 268 of his book for a statement of the relationship between ϕ and **f** or footnote 6 on the next page.

Let us assume that we have decided to include four treatment conditions ($a = 4$) and that the following means represent the expected minimum treatment effects:[5]

Treatment Means	Deviations from μ
$\mu_1 = 16$	$\mu_1 - \mu = 16 - 20 = -4$
$\mu_2 = 21$	$\mu_2 - \mu = 21 - 20 = 1$
$\mu_3 = 23$	$\mu_3 - \mu = 23 - 20 = 3$
$\mu_4 = 20$	$\mu_4 - \mu = 20 - 20 = 0$

Assume next that an accurate estimate of error variance is available, namely, $\sigma_{S/A}^2 = 20$. From this information we can solve for ϕ_A by using Eq. (24-1):

$$\phi_A^2 = \frac{s'[(-4)^2 + (1)^2 + (3)^2 + (0)^2]/4}{20}$$

$$= \frac{s'(26)/4}{20} = \frac{s'(6.5)}{20} = .325s'.$$

Solving for ϕ_A,

$$\phi_A = \sqrt{\phi_A^2} = \sqrt{.325s'} = .57\sqrt{s'}.$$

With ϕ_A expressed in this form, we can vary sample size and determine when we have obtained enough power.

First we will have to decide upon acceptable levels for α and for power. For the example, assume that $\alpha = .05$ and that the desired power $= .80$. We will now see what happens when we set the sample size at $s' = 5$. With this value,

$$\phi_A = .57\sqrt{s'} = .57\sqrt{5} = .57(2.24) = 1.28.$$

Turning to the third power chart in Table C-6 of Appendix C ($df_{num.} = 3$), we locate the function at $\alpha = .05$ for $df_{denom.} = a(s' - 1) = 4(5 - 1) = 16$. (We will use the function for $df = 15$.) We next move along this power function until we find the point at which $\phi = 1.28$ and then read off the power on the ordinate. In this case, power equals approximately .45.[6] Since we are striving

---

[5] In this example, we estimated each mean individually. It might make more sense in some applications to specify the minimum *distance* between pairs of means. For instance, we might say that we want the means to be separated by at least 4 units. The corresponding deviations would then be -6, -2, 2, and 6. It is not necessary, of course, to "space" the treatment means equally as we have done. Any pattern which is most parsimonious with the expected outcome of the experiment can be used. Cohen (1969, pp. 269–273) proposes that researchers narrow their choice to a selection from among three patterns that differ in degree of variability represented.

[6] Cohen (1969, pp. 282–347) presents these power charts in tabular form. To use his tables, we must convert ϕ to $\mathbf{f}$. This is simple, since

$$\mathbf{f} = \frac{\phi}{\sqrt{s'}} = \frac{.57\sqrt{s'}}{\sqrt{s'}} = .57.$$

Turning to his Table 8.3.14 (pp. 308–309), we find that with a sample size of $s' = 5$ and $\mathbf{f} = .57$, power is a little less than .50. For a closer approximation, Cohen suggests linear interpolation.

for a probability of .80, we must greatly increase the sample size. If we let $s' = 10$,

$$\phi_A = .57\sqrt{10} = .57(3.16) = 1.80.$$

To find out which power function to use this time, we will again have to calculate the $df_{\text{denom.}}$. In this case, $df = a(s' - 1) = 4(10 - 1) = 36$. Shifting to the function at $df = 30$, we find that the power associated with $\phi = 1.80$ is approximately .82. (If we had greatly overshot the desired level of power, we could have reduced the sample size somewhat.)

A more direct way of calculating sample size has been provided by Feldt and Mahmoud (1958) and by Cohen (1969). The former offers charts which list *sample size* on the ordinate, ϕ' on the baseline, and functions of different power in the body of the chart. All that is necessary is to calculate ϕ' (where $\phi' = \phi/\sqrt{s'}$), to decide upon a probability for power and for α, and then to locate the sample size necessary to meet these conditions. Winer has provided these charts instead of the power functions in 1962 (pp. 657–658) and together with power functions in 1971 (pp. 879–880). Note, however, that these charts are useful only if the desired sample size is greater than 10. Cohen (pp. 374–382) presents tables which are more extensive than those of Feldt and Mahmoud. All that is necessary to use Cohen's tables is to calculate $\mathbf{f}$ (where $\mathbf{f} = \phi/\sqrt{s'}$) and then to enter the appropriate table directly. [For a description of this procedure and a numerical example, see Cohen (1969, pp. 383–384).]

THE GENERAL CASE   These determinations can be extended to factorial designs. The same basic procedure is involved; the major change is in the calculation of ϕ. These extensions are given comprehensive treatment by Cohen (1969, pp. 357–373) and by Guenther (1964, e.g., pp. 47–49, 107–108, and 128–129). It is possible to adapt a formula Guenther presents in his discussion of power analyses in three-factor designs [p. 128, Formula (5.96)] for use with the general case. Specifically,

$$\phi^2_{\text{effect}} = \frac{(\text{est. obsn.})\left[\sum (\text{dev.})^2\right]/(df_{\text{effect}} + 1)}{\sigma^2_{\text{error}}}, \tag{24-2}$$

where (est. obsn.) refers to the number of observations that will contribute to each basic deviation score, $\sum (\text{dev.})^2$ represents the basic population deviation scores constituting the treatment effects in question, df_{effect} are the df associated with the treatment effects based on *sample* values, and σ^2_{error} is the population error variance.

As an example of the application of Eq. (24-2), consider the formulas constructed for the $A \times B$ design in Table 24-1. The basic deviation scores for each factorial effect are listed in the second column of the table. These deviations come from the formal statement of the structural model we enumerated in Eq. (16-1) (p. 330). Deviations for higher-order factorials can be generated from corresponding df statements. For the $A \times B \times C$ interaction, for example,

$$df_{A \times B \times C} = (a - 1)(b - 1)(c - 1)$$
$$= abc - ab - ac - bc + a + b + c - 1,$$

and the deviation is $(\mu_{ijk} - \mu_{ij} - \mu_{ik} - \mu_{jk} + \mu_i + \mu_j + \mu_k - \mu)$. In the third column appear what are called the "estimated observations," the observations upon which estimates of these deviations would be based in the actual experiment. For the main effect of factor A, bs' observations are available to estimate the deviation for any given mean; for the main effect of factor B, as' observations are available; and for the interaction, s' observations are available. The formulas for ϕ^2_{effect} are completed in the final column of the table.

TABLE 24-1   *Values of ϕ^2_{effect} in the $A \times B$ Design (Both Factors Fixed)*

Source	Dev.	Est. Obsn.	ϕ^2_{effect}
A	α_i	bs'	$\dfrac{bs'[\sum (\alpha_i)^2]/a}{\sigma^2_{S/AB}}$
B	β_j	as'	$\dfrac{as'[\sum (\beta_j)^2]/b}{\sigma^2_{S/AB}}$
$A \times B$	$(\alpha\beta)_{ij}$	s'	$\dfrac{s'[\sum (\alpha\beta_{ij})^2]/[(a - 1)(b - 1) + 1]}{\sigma^2_{S/AB}}$

Note: $\alpha_i = \mu_i - \mu$, $\beta_j = \mu_j - \mu$, $(\alpha\beta)_{ij} = \mu_{ij} - \mu_i - \mu_j + \mu$.

Consider the three completed formulas. In determining the sample size to be used in any given experiment, we will vary s', since the levels of factors A and B (a and b, respectively) are determined by the nature of the experimental questions we want to ask and thus are presumably fixed at this stage of the planning. If we are interested in achieving a certain power for all three factorial effects, the final sample size will be determined by the *largest* estimate of s'. Generally, the largest estimate will come from the *interaction*. The reason is that power is in part a function of the actual number of observations contributing to the different means; because of the nature of the factorial design, fewer observations contribute to the cell means (i.e., the interaction) than to either set of marginal means (i.e., the main effects). Thus, if we are interested primarily in interaction, which often we will be with a factorial design, then we only need to work with the corresponding relevant formula in our estimation of sample size.

COMMENTS   The obvious difficulty in attempting to use power functions in the planning of an experiment is the problem of estimating the treatment effects and the population error variance. An author of a statistics text can make up these values, since there is no experimental reality facing him. The researcher, in contrast, has to *do* the experiment and suffer the consequences if he has overestimated or underestimated either of these values. In some instances, we can use past research to guide us in obtaining these estimates. Experiments conducted under relatively standard conditions, with subjects drawn from roughly the same population, offer a remarkably stable estimate of error variance.[7]

The selection of the minimum treatment effects is the other stumbling block. Again, previous research may provide a hint as to what sorts of effects we might expect from a certain type of manipulation. In applied work, the situation is often clearer because actual dollar costs may be attached to the appearance of treatment differences of a certain magnitude. Frequently, however, an investigator is testing a theory, and the *size* of the treatment effects associated with the prediction is not very important—the experimenter wants to detect a difference, but he cannot specify its size. Obviously there will be a point at which an investigator will discard a theory if the prediction results in extremely small treatment effects. Nevertheless, if one theory predicts a particular outcome while alternative theories do not, the evaluation of this differential prediction may be of critical importance, and the size of the actual treatment effects of little interest per se.

Post-Hoc Determinations of Power and Sample Size

DETERMINATION OF POWER   We have indicated that a power analysis performed *after* an experiment has been conducted can provide useful information about any conclusions we may draw from the results of the statistical analyses. If, for example, an *F* test is *not* significant, are we to take it as "proof" that treatment effects are completely absent (the null hypothesis is true) or that the effects are too small in relation to the sensitivity of the experiment to be detected in the analysis? Suppose we find that a comparison, which was not significant in the statistical analysis, is associated with a low level of power, say .20. Such a situation indicates that the experimental test is relatively insensitive and implies that we really do not have strong evidence *in favor of* the null hypothesis. On the other hand, suppose a high level of power is present, say .80 or .90. In this case we do have a relatively sensitive experiment and, consequently, we feel more comfortable in concluding that treatment effects are probably not present in this particular comparison. In short, an experiment with high power provides strong support for our decision not to reject the null hypothesis, while an experiment with low power provides little support for either the null or the alternative hypotheses.[8]

---

[7] If such estimates are simply not available, we can use an alternative method of estimating sample size described by Kirk (1968, pp. 109–110) which does not use σ^2_{error} in the determination.

[8] It can be argued, however, that the null hypothesis is rarely true in the behavioral sciences; the administration of differential treatments is bound to produce some effect, no matter how small. What we are implying, then, is that a failure to reject the null hypothesis under conditions of high power is equivalent to "accepting" the null hypothesis.

The computational formulas presented in the last section are based upon population values and, as such, are free from contamination by experimental error. Estimates based upon sample values—the outcome of actual experiments —obviously are not. Consequently, there will be some changes in the power analysis. The revised computational formula for the single-factor experiment is given by

$$\hat{\phi}_A^2 = \frac{(a - 1)(MS_A - MS_{S/A})/a}{MS_{S/A}}. \tag{24-3}$$

(The caret indicates a population estimate.) The quantity in the denominator of Eq. (24-3), $MS_{S/A}$, provides an estimate of $\sigma_{S/A}^2$. The quantity in the numerator represents in part an estimate of the basic deviation scores, $\sum(\alpha_i)^2 = \sum(\mu_i - \mu)^2$. The detailed algebraic steps followed to arrive at Eq. (24-3) are not intuitively obvious, although they are not difficult. [For an enumeration of these steps, see Kirk (1968, p. 108).]

As an example, consider an experiment in which $a = 3$, $s = 3$, $MS_A = 12.20$, and $MS_{S/A} = 2.45$. The F test reveals $F(2, 6) = 12.20/2.45 = 4.98$, $.05 < p < .10$. Using Eq. (24-3), we first calculate

$$\hat{\phi}_A^2 = \frac{(3 - 1)(12.20 - 2.45)/3}{2.45}$$

$$= \frac{2(9.75)/3}{2.45} = \frac{6.50}{2.45} = 2.65;$$

then

$$\hat{\phi}_A = \sqrt{2.65} = 1.63.$$

If we consult the second power chart ($df_{\text{num.}} = 2$) at $\alpha = .05$, $df_{\text{denom.}} = 6$, and $\phi = 1.63$, we find power to be approximately .48.

How has this analysis aided us in interpreting the nonsignificant F test? We have found that even with an experiment of moderate power, the null hypothesis is not rejected. This finding might suggest that the experimental manipulations represented in this study are not reasonably effective and that our time might better be spent in a different approach to the problem under investigation. If, on the other hand, the power analysis indicated a much lower value, e.g., .30, we might consider pushing ahead with a replication study, perhaps incorporating refinements in the design (including a larger sample size) to achieve an experiment of greater sensitivity.

Post-hoc determinations of power presumably can be extended to the main effects and interactions of factorial experiments. As with the single-factor design, power analyses are complicated by the fact that estimates of treatment effects must be obtained from the data of the experiments themselves. We will consider a generalized formula for $\hat{\phi}_{\text{effect}}^2$ in the next section, when we discuss the determination of sample size from the data of a pilot experiment.

ESTIMATION OF SAMPLE SIZE FROM PILOT DATA We have speculated that possibly researchers do not use power estimates when planning an experiment because of their inability to make reasonable estimates of the expected treatment effects and of the population error variance. A pilot experiment, which is followed by a major experimental effort, provides a practical solution to this difficulty. We might conduct a preliminary experiment, identical to the main experiment, except that a smaller sample of subjects is run. If we can accept the sample means as reasonably stable estimates of the population means and the error mean square as an adequate estimate of population error variance, we are in a position to make a rough estimate of the *critical* sample size—i.e., the sample size necessary to produce sufficient power to detect treatment effects at least as large as those obtained in the pilot study. After we conduct the new experiment and assess the significance of the comparisons, we can feel confident that we have finally achieved some balance between type I and type II errors. That is, we have made a rational choice of sample size by selecting a value that will result in a certain level of power, given the appearance of treatment effects of a specified magnitude and the same error variance.

We will consider the single-factor design first and then follow this simplest design with a discussion of the general case. Before we begin, however, it should be noted that none of the standard statistics texts for psychologists discusses the estimation of sample size from pilot data. The formulas to be presented are what appear to the author to be a natural extension of Eqs. (24-2) and (24-3). While they may not provide unbiased estimates of ϕ^2_{effect}, they should give us estimates of sample sizes which are still useful in planning the experiment. With this caution in mind, we will now turn to the problem at hand.

If you refer back to Eq. (24-3), which was used to obtain a post-hoc determination of power in a single-factor experiment, you will note that sample size does not appear. We can modify the formula so that we are able to introduce different sample sizes and determine the approximate power associated with them. What we will do is estimate the sum of the squared deviation scores *first* and then introduce this estimate into a formula in which sample size can be varied. For the single-factor design,

$$\sum (\hat{\alpha}_i)^2 = \frac{a-1}{s}(MS_A - MS_{S/A}) \tag{24-4}$$

and

$$\hat{\phi}^2_A = \frac{s'\left[\sum (\hat{\alpha}_i)^2\right]/a}{MS_{S/A}}. \tag{24-4a}$$

In Eq. (24-4), which provides an estimate of the sum of the squared deviation scores, s refers to the sample size in the *pilot* experiment, while in Eq. (24-4a) s' refers to the different sample sizes that will be tried in an attempt to find a value producing the desired level of power.

As an illustration, we will continue with the example considered in the last section, where $a = 3$, $s = 3$, $MS_A = 12.20$, and $MS_{S/A} = 2.45$. Substituting in Eq. (24-4), we find

$$\sum (\hat{\alpha}_i)^2 = \frac{3-1}{3}(12.20 - 2.45) = \frac{2}{3}(9.75) = 6.50$$

Continuing with Eq. (24-4a),

$$\hat{\phi}_A^2 = \frac{s'(6.50)/3}{2.45} = \frac{s'(2.17)}{2.45} = .89\,s'$$

and

$$\hat{\phi}_A = \sqrt{.89\,s'} = .94\sqrt{s'}.$$

Suppose we want to set power at .90 or greater, with $\alpha = .05$. With $s' = 6$, $df_{\text{denom.}} = 3(6-1) = 15$,

$$\hat{\phi}_A = .94\sqrt{6} = (.94)(2.45) = 2.30,$$

and an inspection of the second chart in Table C-6 of Appendix C indicates that power is quite close to .90.

A general formula based on this approach to the problem is possible:

$$\sum (\widehat{\text{dev.}})^2 = \frac{df_{\text{effect}}}{(\text{no. obsn.})}(MS_{\text{effect}} - MS_{\text{error}}) \tag{24-5}$$

and

$$\hat{\phi}^2_{\text{effect}} = \frac{(\text{est. obsn.})[\sum (\widehat{\text{dev.}})^2]/(df_{\text{effect}} + 1)}{MS_{\text{error}}}. \tag{24-5a}$$

[The similarity of Eq. (24-5a) to Eq. (24-2), (p. 532), where population values are used, is obvious.] In the last section we discussed the post-hoc determination of power. These two equations can be used for this purpose, although a simpler

TABLE 24-2   *Values of $\hat{\phi}^2_{\text{effect}}$ in the $A \times B$ Design (Both Factors Fixed)*

Source	$\sum (\widehat{\text{dev.}})^2$	Est. Obsn.	$\hat{\phi}^2_{\text{effect}}$
A	$\dfrac{(a-1)}{bs}(MS_A - MS_{S/AB})$	bs'	$\dfrac{bs'[\sum (\hat{\alpha}_i)^2]/a}{MS_{S/AB}}$
B	$\dfrac{(b-1)}{as}(MS_B - MS_{S/AB})$	as'	$\dfrac{as'[\sum (\hat{\beta}_j)^2]/b}{MS_{S/AB}}$
$A \times B$	$\dfrac{(a-1)(b-1)}{s}(MS_{A \times B} - MS_{S/AB})$	s'	$\dfrac{s'[\sum (\widehat{\alpha\beta}_{ij})^2]/[(a-1)(b-1)+1]}{MS_{S/AB}}$

Note: $\hat{\alpha}_i = \hat{\mu}_i - \hat{\mu}$, $\hat{\beta}_j = \hat{\mu}_j - \hat{\mu}$, $(\widehat{\alpha\beta})_{ij} = \hat{\mu}_{ij} - \hat{\mu}_i - \hat{\mu}_j + \hat{\mu}$.

formula is possible:

$$\hat{\phi}^2_{effect} = \frac{(df_{effect})(MS_{effect} - MS_{error})/(df_{effect} + 1)}{MS_{error}}. \tag{24-6}$$

The adaptation of Eqs. (24-5) and (24-5a) to the $A \times B$ design is presented in Table 24-2. Again, s' refers to the *estimated* sample size while s refers to the sample size of the *pilot study*. As an example, we will use the data from the two-factor experiment summarized in Table 10-5 (p. 201). This is a 3×2 factorial, with $s = 4$ subjects. As an illustration of the calculations, we will work with the main effect of factor A. Other relevant values needed for the two equations are $MS_A = 56.00$ and $MS_{S/AB} = 18.33$. From Table 24-2,

$$\sum(\widehat{dev.})^2 = \frac{(a - 1)}{bs}(MS_A - MS_{S/AB})$$

$$= \frac{(3 - 1)}{2(4)}(56.00 - 18.33)$$

$$= \frac{2}{8}(37.67) = 9.42$$

Substituting in Eq. (24-5a),

$$\hat{\phi}^2_A = \frac{bs\left[\sum(\widehat{dev.})^2\right]/a}{MS_{S/AB}}$$

$$= \frac{2(s')(9.42)/3}{18.33}$$

$$= \frac{6.28s'}{18.33} = .34s',$$

$$\hat{\phi}_A = \sqrt{.34s'} = .58\sqrt{s'}.$$

If power is set at .80, then we will need a sample size of approximately $s' = 10$. That is, $df_{denom.} = ab(s' - 1) = 3(2)(10 - 1) = 54$,

$$\hat{\phi}_A = .58\sqrt{10} = (.58)(3.16) = 1.83$$

and the second power chart at $\alpha = .05$ indicates approximately .80.

An alternative method might be used in which we base our estimate of the population deviation scores on the sample means alone. What this entails is to assume, for the purpose of estimating sample size, that the treatment effects in the population are *exactly equal* to the corresponding deviations of the sample means in the pilot study. Such a procedure is relatively simple and apparently straightforward. On the other hand, we realize that the assumption is incorrect and can only lead to an overestimation of the population treatment effects and, consequently, to an *underestimation* of the sample size.[9] Of course, we may only need an approximate estimate of sample size, and this procedure may prove to be useful in the planning of a piece of research.

As an example, we will return to the data we used above. From Table 10-5, the relevant group means and deviations from $\bar{T}$ for the main effect of factor A are as follows:

Group Means	Deviations from $\bar{T}$
$\hat{\mu}_1 = \bar{A}_1 = 7.00$	$\hat{\mu}_1 - \hat{\mu} = \bar{A}_1 - \bar{T} = 7.00 - 10.00 = -3.00$
$\hat{\mu}_2 = \bar{A}_2 = 11.00$	$\hat{\mu}_2 - \hat{\mu} = \bar{A}_2 - \bar{T} = 11.00 - 10.00 = 1.00$
$\hat{\mu}_3 = \bar{A}_3 = 12.00$	$\hat{\mu}_3 - \hat{\mu} = \bar{A}_3 - \bar{T} = 12.00 - 10.00 = 2.00$

You will note that estimates of population treatment effects are based on the sample means without correction. First, we calculate

$$\sum (\widehat{dev.})^2 = \sum (\hat{\alpha}_i)^2 = (-3.00)^2 + (1.00)^2 + (2.00)^2$$
$$= 14.00.$$

Substituting in Eq. (24-5a),

$$\hat{\phi}_A^2 = \frac{bs'[\sum (\widehat{dev.})^2]/a}{MS_{S/AB}}$$

$$= \frac{2(s')(14.00)/3}{18.33} = \frac{(9.33)s'}{18.33} = .51s',$$

$$\hat{\phi}_A = \sqrt{.51s'} = .71\sqrt{s'}.$$

If we try $s' = 7$,

$$\hat{\phi}_A = .71\sqrt{7} = (.71)(2.65) = 1.88.$$

Entering this value in Table C-6 at $df_{num.} = 2$, $df_{denom.} = ab(s' - 1) = 3(2)(7 - 1) = 36$, and $\alpha = .05$, we find that power is approximately .80.

You will recall that we obtained an estimate of sample size for this source using a procedure which takes into consideration the inflation of sample treatment effects by experimental error. With Eq. (24-5) providing the "undistorted" estimate of $\sum (\alpha_i)^2$, we found that a sample size of 10 was needed to achieve a power of .80. There is a moderate difference in the magnitudes of these two estimates (7 and 10). In general, the size of this discrepancy will increase with the relative size of the MS_{error}. The implication is obvious: if we are concerned about the power of our experiment in detecting treatment effects at least as large as those observed in the pilot study, then we should use the "best" estimate we can obtain. This is the estimate provided by Eq. (24-5).

[9] The overestimation of population treatment effects results from the fact that sample means reflect treatment effects *and* experimental error.

COMMENTS   It must be emphasized that the procedures we have discussed in this section are approximate and, to the author's knowledge, have not been "validated" by statisticians. On the other hand, a researcher is turning to these procedures to aid him in setting his sample size in a rational manner. Even if they are biased in a statistical sense, the estimates of sample size and power should not be too far off.

Another way of looking at the problem of sensitivity is to realize that in most, if not all, of the experiments we conduct, the null hypothesis is *false*. That is, when we treat groups of subjects differently, they will behave differently. Sometimes the differences in behavior will be small, but they are probably still present. With this conviction, one could reasonably advocate the strategy of choosing a sample size just as large as the researcher can "afford" in the sense of time, energy, and other resources. If it is important to recognize the presence of a particular source of treatment effects, then we must design an experiment which is sufficiently sensitive to detect these effects. This is not the strategy recommended in applied fields, where it is possible to work out the monetary value of minimum treatment effects. There, a researcher is usually not free to study treatments that fall below this economically motivated minimum. In contrast, researchers in the nonapplied fields turn to the experiment as a means for increasing their knowledge concerning a particular aspect of behavior. They are motivated more by the theoretical implications of a given finding and not whether it is "large" or "small." We will pursue this point in the next chapter.

Summary

A consideration of power should be a necessary step in the planning of any experiment. An estimate of power, no matter how approximate it may be, gives us some degree of control of the type II error. If we are unable to make a reasonable guess concerning the magnitude of the treatment effects or of the error variance, a practical procedure is the two-step approach outlined in the last section—a miniature experiment or pilot study that will provide us with these estimates. From this information we can make rational decisions concerning the power we need in our experiment. Perhaps we will find that the cost of adding subjects is just too great and that this solution is not feasible.

We might consider increasing power by other means—for example, exercising greater control in the administration of the experiment, choosing levels that will maximize the treatment effects, selecting a more sensitive design (such as the repeated-measures and stratified designs), or introducing a control variable that will allow a covariance analysis. Statisticians have provided us with a sizable pool of designs and analyses, but it is up to us to use them wisely and effectively. Certainly, however, there are points other than power to consider in the planning of an experiment. For example, we might not be able to turn to a repeated-measures design for *experimental* reasons. In this case, the promise of increased power is overruled by the dictates of the specific research area.

It is interesting to note that researchers often implicitly take power into consideration when they design an experiment. This occurs when an investigator has worked in a particular field for some time and has evolved a "feeling" for the general sensitivity of his experimental designs. Under these circumstances, he may take the position that most of the phenomena in which he is interested will be detected with a sample size of, say, $s = 16$. He will not be concerned with treatment effects that are not detected, given the level of sensitivity he expects in his research. Of course, when a manipulation is of *critical* interest to him he will immediately drop this attitude and take whatever steps he can to assess the presence of treatment effects.

POWER AND INDEPENDENT REPLICATION

Suppose we administer the same experiment a number of times and that each time we fail to reject the null hypothesis. Suppose further, however, that the *same pattern* of results is obtained in each of the replications. The separate F tests do not take into consideration the *consistency* of the data obtained in these independent experiments. Just how likely is it that we would obtain the same pattern each time on the basis of chance? This question points up the fact that few experiments are conducted in isolation and that an independent replication, even if not significant, means something more than the significance of the single F test implies.

So much for the feeling of "confidence" in a particular outcome that successive replications of the same finding bring. We will first discuss why such replications come about and then how we can test the significance of a particular pattern of results in a series of independent experiments.

Reasons for Independent Replications

We will distinguish between two types of replications, those that are planned as part of the experimental design and those that are not, and we will consider examples of each.

Why would an experimenter choose to incorporate a number of replications into his experimental design? For one reason, he may only be able to administer the experiment to a small number of subjects at a time. In animal-learning experiments, for example, each animal is given extensive training, often lasting for weeks. The same may be true for experiments in education, where the "treatments" consist of different methods of teaching applied over a school term. The length of these experiments may make it impossible to run more than a fraction of the subjects at a time. There may be other limitations in addition to time, such as limited space in which to house the animals during the experiment and limited equipment. The experimeter tries to include in each replication an equal number of subjects so that any general differences from one replication to the next will be spread equally over the treatment conditions. For another reason, the investigator might want to associate with replications such factors as the experimenter's administering the treatments to the subjects, the testing rooms, the "batch" of animals sent by the supplier, the time of day (or year), the school system, and so on. Any and all factors which can vary between replications are held constant for the subjects tested *within* the replication. The object in this arrangement of the testing is to make between-replication differences as great as possible and to hold these factors constant within the replications.

Such a procedure offers gains of two types. The first removes from the error term sources of variability which, without this arrangement, would have been left uncontrolled. The second takes account of the possibility that the treatment effects may actually differ from replication to replication. Here the interest is in testing for the presence of an interaction of replication with treatments rather than for a reduction in the size of the error term.[10]

Not all replications are of the sort we described in the last two paragraphs. An experimenter may decide to repeat his experiment (or someone else's) to see whether he obtains the same set of results. Alternatively, he may find that he has duplicated a number of treatment conditions in a series of experiments directed at entirely different problems. Or he may want to compare the results of experiments conducted in different laboratories. In these various cases, he will have two or more treatment conditions, which are present in several independent experiments, and the question that interests him is whether the results are consistent from experiment to experiment or whether there is an interaction of the treatments with the experiments.

Statistical Analysis

The most common way of analyzing a replicated experiment is to treat replications as an independent factor and to analyze the results accordingly.[11] We will illustrate the analysis with a numerical example. The data come from a series of actual experiments.[12] (The results of one experiment were changed slightly to provide a more interesting illustration.) Four experiments were conducted over several years in which two basic conditions were always represented. We will call these conditions simply a_1 and a_2. There were $s = 16$ subjects in each condition and in all of the experiments. There were many differences from experiment to experiment, but these two conditions represented the same two treatments each time. The data necessary to perform the analysis

---

[10] There is a useful discussion of this type of design in Lindquist (1953, pp. 190–202).

[11] Winer discusses the statistical analysis we will present (1962, pp. 213–216; 1971, pp. 391–394); he also introduces a different sort of procedure which is applicable for replications in which *two* treatment conditions are compared (1962, pp. 43–45; 1971, pp. 49–50). The virtue of the latter procedure, which is really a special case, is that estimates of error variance are not pooled over replications as they are in the former approach.

[12] Keppel, Bonge, Strand, and Parker (1971).

of the factorial as well as separate F tests for each experiment are presented in Table 24-3.

We can see from the means presented in the second column of the table that the performance at a_1 is consistently higher than that at a_2. In no case, however, is the F for this comparison significant. To illustrate the calculations, consider the data from Exp. 1:

$$SS_A = \frac{\sum (A)^2}{s} - \frac{(T)^2}{as}$$

$$= \frac{(149)^2 + (135)^2}{16} - \frac{(284)^2}{2(16)}$$

$$= \frac{40,426}{16} - \frac{80,656}{32}$$

$$= 2526.62 - 2520.50$$

$$= 6.12$$

and

$$SS_{S/A} = \sum (AS)^2 - \frac{\sum (A)^2}{s}$$

$$= 2601 - \frac{(149)^2 + (135)^2}{16}$$

$$= 2601 - \frac{40,426}{16}$$

$$= 2601 - 2526.62$$

$$= 74.38.$$

The MS_A is found by dividing the SS_A by $df = a - 1 = 1$, while the $MS_{S/A}$ is found by dividing the $SS_{S/A}$ by $df = a(s - 1) = 2(16 - 1) = 30$. The results

TABLE 24-3 *The Results of Four Independent Replications*

Experiment	Treatment Means		Treatment Sums	$\sum (AS)^2$	$MS_A/MS_{S/A} = F$
	$\bar{A}_1$	$\bar{A}_2$	$A_1 + A_2 = T$		
1	9.31	8.44	149 + 135 = 284	2601	6.12/2.48 = 2.47***
2	10.81	10.12	173 + 162 = 335	3613	3.78/3.41 = 1.11*
3	11.06	10.44	177 + 167 = 344	3760	3.12/1.96 = 1.59**
4	9.56	8.38	153 + 134 = 287	2801	11.28/7.19 = 1.57**
		Sum:	652 + 598 = 1250	12,775	

* $p = .30$, ** $p < .25$, *** $p < .20$.

of these divisions are presented in the final column of the table. The other F ratios are obtained in the same fashion.

It is clear that each experiment, taken by itself, does not provide encouraging evidence that the two treatment conditions produce different effects. The consistency of the "effect" over four independent attempts, however, suggests that there may in fact be a small treatment effect. In an attempt to capitalize on this consistency, we will combine the different replications in a single analysis. One approach might be to collapse across experiments and simply conduct an analysis of the single-factor design resulting from this combination. Such a procedure would clearly increase the overall sample size and, hence, the power of the experimental test. On the other hand, pooling subjects, who were treated alike but who were tested at different times, may grossly inflate the size of the error term and obscure the trend in the data we are trying to illuminate. An alternative approach, which allows the removal of variability between experiments from the error term, is to treat experiments (or replications) as an additional factor in the analysis of the data.

We will use the data in Table 24-3 to illustrate this analysis. It will be recalled that each of the four experiments contained two treatment conditions. Thus, if we treat replications as a factor, we will have a 2 × 4 factorial. The two-way data matrix is presented in the third column of the table. (Entries within the matrix are AB sums, column marginal totals are the A sums, and row marginal totals are B sums.) The basic calculations are as follows:

$$[T] = \frac{(T)^2}{abs} = \frac{(1250)^2}{2(4)(16)} = \frac{1,562,500}{128} = 12,207.03,$$

$$[A] = \frac{\sum (A)^2}{bs} = \frac{(652)^2 + (598)^2}{4(16)}$$

$$= \frac{782,708}{64} = 12,229.81,$$

$$[B] = \frac{\sum (B)^2}{as} = \frac{(284)^2 + (335)^2 + (344)^2 + (287)^2}{2(16)}$$

$$= \frac{393,586}{32} = 12,299.56,$$

$$[AB] = \frac{\sum (AB)^2}{s} = \frac{(149)^2 + (173)^2 + \cdots + (167)^2 + (134)^2}{16}$$

$$= \frac{197,182}{16} = 12,323.88,$$

$$[ABS] = \sum (ABS)^2 = 2601 + 3613 + 3760 + 2801$$

$$= 12,775.$$

TABLE 24-4   *Numerical Example: A × Replication Design*

Source	Calculations[a]	SS	df	MS	F
A	$[A] - [T] =$	22.78	1	22.78	6.06*
Replication (B)	$[B] - [T] =$	92.53	3	30.84	8.20**
A × B	$[AB] - [A] - [B] + [T] =$	1.54	3	.51	< 1
S/AB	$[ABS] - [AB] =$	451.12	120	3.76	
Total	$[ABS] - [T] =$	567.97	127		

[a] Bracketed letters represent complete terms in the computational formulas; a particular term is identified by the letter(s) appearing in the numerator.
* $p < .025$
** $p < .01$.

These basic quantities are combined in Table 24-4 to produce the necessary sums of squares. The remainder of the analysis is also summarized in the table. It will be noted that the two main effects, factor A and "replication," are significant, but that the interaction is clearly not. This analysis, therefore, picked up the consistency of the effect observed in the four experiments. The effect is significant because of the increased power and the consistency of the effect from experiment to experiment. The significance of "replication" indicates that there were real differences among the four experiments. If we had lumped together the data from all four experiments, this variation plus the interaction sum of squares would have been included in the error term.

Comments

One difficulty with the analysis just outlined is the very real possibility of the heterogeneity of the within-groups variances from experiment to experiment. Consider the four $MS_{S/A}$ terms listed in Table 24-3 for the separate experiments—there is a sizable range from 1.96 in Exp. 3 to 7.19 in Exp. 4. These experiments were conducted over a period of several years, each new experiment representing a number of important refinements of the experimental procedures. The degree of heterogeneity observed in analyses of replicated experiments depends, obviously, on the nature of the different replications. If the replications are planned and the testing conditions from replication to replication relatively constant, then there will very likely be homogeneity. On the other hand, if the replications consist of experiments conducted in different laboratories, the degree of heterogeneity will undoubtedly be greater than that observed in the present case.

What can we do about this problem? We could turn to the empirical studies concerning the effect on the distribution of F when heterogeneity is present and conclude that the tabled values of F are relatively accurate for our purposes. Of course, this is a different sort of situation from those examined in these empirical studies. Cochran and Cox (1957) point out that between-experiment heterogeneity may produce a positive bias in the test of the Treatment $\times$ Replication interaction and a decrease in sensitivity. They conclude their discussion, however, by still recommending this analysis (p. 555). There is nothing to stop us from drawing tentative conclusions from this sort of analysis. The analysis does give us some indication of consistency of results (or the lack of it) in a number of independent replications. If there are serious violations of the assumptions underlying the F test and if the F's are of borderline significance, the advice of a statistician should be sought.

A final comment concerns the general importance of replication studies in our experimental work. While I have argued that we should be especially careful to avoid type II errors, the plea was ended with a request for replication. That is, we should be sensitive to the implications of F ratios which are significant at $p = .10$ or $.20$ and not ruthlessly discard a finding because it fails to surpass the conventional 5 percent level of significance. If we do the latter, the finding may be lost and its implications not pursued. If we do the former, however, we temporarily suspend judgment concerning the correctness of the null hypothesis and await further information. This further information will usually take the form of an independent replication, one that we hope will be sensitive in detecting this particular difference.

A number of psychologists of the author's acquaintance have expressed the opinion that the independent replication of a significant difference in several experiments is more convincing than a significant difference in a single experiment. Implicit in this statement is the belief that when a particular pattern of results is duplicated in spite of the many changes occurring from replication to replication, it must represent a relatively "robust" phenomenon. A significant finding in a single experiment may always be the result of a set of fortuitous circumstances, favoring some conditions over others, producing the particular pattern observed. We will never be sure of the falseness of this hypothesis until we do replicate the finding two or more times. (Of course, it is still possible that the consistent results were the result of chance, but the probability that this will occur in several independent replications is quite small indeed.) Before the replications are conducted, we will still base our theories on the results of *single* experiments, knowing full well that the statistical machinery brought to play in the analysis of a single experiment is an attempt to assess the future replicability of a particular phenomenon. The ultimate test of any significant finding *is* its repeatability, and it is to this end that the Treatment $\times$ Replication design serves an important function. As Fisher (1951) puts it, ". . . we may say that a phenomenon is experimentally demonstrable when we know how to conduct an experiment which will rarely fail to give us a statistically significant result" (p. 14).

chapter twenty-five

CONTROVERSIAL TOPICS

In this chapter we will consider three topics which are relevant to the analyses we have described in the preceding chapters but for which there is no consistent agreement as to their usefulness (or appropriateness). The first, estimates of the strength of treatment effects, is closely related to points raised in Chapter 24: should we not be guided more by the principle of *size* of a treatment effect than by a concern for the *power* of an experiment in detecting treatment effects of often *small* magnitude? The second topic deals with the rationale behind transforming scores obtained in an experiment into a new metric. Finally, we will discuss a procedure designed to increase power by pooling additional estimates of error variance which are revealed during the conduct of a preliminary analysis of the data.

MAGNITUDE OF TREATMENT EFFECTS

Prediction is a primary goal of science. One index of our ability to predict behavior is the degree to which we can "force" it around with our experimental manipulations. Said another way, the importance of an experimental manipulation is demonstrated by the degree to which we can account for the total variability among subjects by isolating the experimental effects. It would be useful to have an index of the efficacy of experimental treatments. Such an index could guide us in our decision to follow or not to follow a certain direction in our research. It would point to manipulations that eventually must be included in any comprehensive theory of the behavior we are studying. In applied research, the importance of experimental treatments can be translated into dollars-and-cents language.

Many investigators already use one such index—the significance level associated with a given F test. Unfortunately, however, this index is simply not appropriate. All too frequently, we find researchers comparing a difference which is significant at $p < .00001$ with one which is significant at $p < .05$ and concluding that the first comparison represents an impressive degree of prediction, while the second comparison commands only passing interest. The truth of the matter is that this sort of statement gives us *no* information as to the *strength* or *magnitude* of the association between the experimental manipulations, on the one hand, and the resultant behavior, on the other. We have already seen the reason for this: it is the direct relationship between power and sample size. *Any* difference in the population can be made significant at any level of significance provided the sample size is made large enough.

Suppose we approach this important point from another direction. Consider two experiments, one with a sample size of 5 and the other with a sample size of 20, in which both experiments produce an F that is significant at $p = .05$. Which set of results would be most impressive, the one with the small sample size or the one with the large sample size? Rosenthal and Gaito (1963) report that many researchers will choose the experiment with the *larger* sample size, when in fact the experiment with the *smaller* sample size would be correct. In view of the fact that power and sample size are positively correlated, we simply cannot use significance level alone as an index of the strength of an experimental effect. What we need is an index that is (1) responsive to the strength of the association between an experimental manipulation and changes in behavior and (2) independent of sample size.

An Index of Association

Hays (1963, pp. 323–333, 381–384) is largely responsible for introducing to psychologists an index which attempts to provide just such an estimate. The index, *omega squared* (ω^2), is essentially a correlation ratio contrasting the variability due to the experimental manipulations to the total variability in the experiment.[1] For the single-factor case,

$$\hat{\omega}_A^2 = \frac{\hat{\sigma}_A^2}{\hat{\sigma}_T^2} = \frac{\hat{\sigma}_A^2}{\hat{\sigma}_A^2 + \hat{\sigma}_{S/A}^2}. \tag{25-1}$$

[1] Alternative measures have been proposed (see Fleiss, 1969, p. 273).

The index is the ratio of an estimate of the population treatment variance ($\hat{\sigma}_A^2$) to an estimate of the population total variance ($\hat{\sigma}_T^2$), and it reflects the proportional amount of variability *accounted* for by the experimental treatment—the stronger the experiment effect, the larger the index.[2]

While the formula for $\hat{\omega}_A^2$ given in Eq. (25-1) is uncomplicated, the formulas for the calculation of the two population estimates are not. For the completely randomized designs and the fixed-effects model, a relatively simple formula can still be given. When random factors are introduced or repeated measures are involved, however, the estimations become complex. For this reason, therefore, we will consider the computational formulas only for the first case. (We will also assume equal sample size.) Vaughan and Corballis (1969) present a readable discussion of the remaining cases just mentioned.

The approach we will take is to write the formulas which will provide estimates of the different variance components. In the completely randomized designs, these components consist of the main effects, the interactions, and the within-groups sources of variance. The estimate of any treatment effect is given by

$$\hat{\sigma}_{\text{effect}}^2 = \frac{(df_{\text{effect}})(MS_{\text{effect}} - MS_{wg})}{N}, \tag{25-2}$$

where the MS_{wg} refers to the within-groups mean square, and N refers to the total number of observations in the experiment. The difference between MS_{effect} and MS_{wg} results in just the sort of estimate we want:[3]

$$E(MS_{\text{effect}}) = \text{(treatment component)} + \text{(error component)},$$

$$E(MS_{wg}) = \text{(error component)},$$

and

$$E(MS_{\text{effect}} - MS_{wg}) = E(MS_{\text{effect}}) - E(MS_{wg})$$

$$= \text{(treatment component)}.$$

The other operations specified in Eq. (25-2)—the multiplication by df_{effect} and the division by N—are needed to transform these sample values into population estimates.[4] The estimate for the within-groups variance is straightforward:

$$\hat{\sigma}_{wg}^2 = MS_{wg}. \tag{25-3}$$

To obtain the formulas for the single-factor design, we simply substitute in Eqs. (25-2) and (25-3):

$$\hat{\sigma}_A^2 = \frac{(a - 1)(MS_A - MS_{S/A})}{as} \tag{25-4}$$

---

[2] Marascuilo (1971, pp. 364–365) describes this index as "explained variance."

[3] You will notice, of course, the similarity between Eq. (25-2), which estimates the treatment variance component, and Eq. (24-5) (p. 537), which estimates the deviations upon which the variance component is based.

[4] See Vaughan and Corballis (1969, p. 206) for an explanation of these corrections.

and

$$\hat{\sigma}^2_{S/A} = MS_{S/A}, \tag{25-5}$$

respectively. To find $\hat{\omega}^2_A$, we substitute these two estimates in Eq. (25-1).

As an example, consider the summary of a single-factor experiment, with $a = 3$ and $s = 8$, presented in the upper half of Table 25-1. The obtained F is significant, $p < .01$. All of the necessary ingredients are available in the table. Specifically,

$$\hat{\sigma}^2_A = \frac{(3 - 1)(116.66 - 17.90)}{3(8)}$$

$$= \frac{2(98.76)}{24}$$

$$= \frac{197.52}{24} = 8.23,$$

$$\hat{\sigma}^2_{S/A} = 17.90.$$

Substituting these values in Eq. (25-1), we have

$$\hat{\omega}^2_A = \frac{8.23}{8.23 + 17.90}$$

$$= \frac{8.23}{26.13}$$

$$= .315.$$

What this value indicates is that approximately 31 percent of the total variance is accounted for by the experimental treatments.

TABLE 25-1 *Summary Tables for Two Experiments*

Source	SS	df	MS	F
A	233.33	2	116.66	6.52*
S/A	376.00	21	17.90	
Total	609.33	23		
A	233.33	2	116.66	6.52*
S/A	1557.30	87	17.90	
Total	1790.63	89		

*$p < .01$.

The basic analysis for a second example is presented in the bottom half of the table. In this case, the identical results were obtained (the same MS_A, $MS_{S/A}$, and F), but the sample size is considerably larger ($s = 30$) than in the first case ($s = 8$). With the second set of data,

$$\hat{\sigma}_A^2 = \frac{(3 - 1)(116.66 - 17.90)}{3(30)}$$

$$= \frac{2(98.76)}{90}$$

$$= \frac{197.52}{90} = 2.19,$$

$$\hat{\sigma}_{S/A}^2 = 17.90,$$

$$\hat{\omega}_A^2 = \frac{2.19}{2.19 + 17.90} = \frac{2.19}{20.09} = .109.$$

Under this altered situation, we are accounting only for about 11 percent of the total variance—a much less impressive achievement. It will be noted that these two examples illustrate the situation with which we began the discussion of omega squared: with other factors held constant, a stronger treatment effect is associated with the experiment having the *smaller* sample size.

ALTERNATIVE FORMULAS   Simpler formulas are available, but they lose some of the intuitive appeal of the set of formulas given in Eqs. (25-1), (25-2), and (25-3). Consider, for example, the computational formula given by Hays (1963, p. 382) and others:

$$\hat{\omega}_A^2 = \frac{SS_A - (a - 1)(MS_{S/A})}{SS_T + MS_{S/A}}. \tag{25-6a}$$

It is difficult to see in Eq. (25-6a) the basic definition of $\hat{\omega}_A^2$ specified in Eq. (25-1). An even simpler formula is preferred by Fleiss (1969). His are written in terms of the F ratio. For example,

$$\hat{\omega}_A^2 = \frac{(a - 1)(F - 1)}{(a - 1)(F - 1) + as}. \tag{25-6b}$$

The advantage of Eq. (25-6b) is its convenience in calculating $\hat{\omega}_A^2$ from research reports where mean squares and sums of squares are not presented.

To illustrate the equivalence of the various equations, we will return to the experiment appearing in the upper portion of Table 25-1. With Eq. (25-6a),

$$\hat{\omega}_A^2 = \frac{233.33 - (3 - 1)(17.90)}{609.33 + 17.90} = \frac{197.53}{627.23} = .315,$$

while with Eq. (25-6b),

$$\hat{\omega}_A^2 = \frac{(3-1)(6.52-1)}{(3-1)(6.52-1)+3(8)} = \frac{2(5.52)}{2(5.52)+24} = \frac{11.04}{35.04} = .315.$$

These two values are the same and are equal to the value obtained with Eq. (25-1).

General Formulas

It is a simple matter to generate a formula for the general case. We have already specified the formulas which provide estimates of the population variance components in Eqs. (25-2) and (25-3). The general definition of $\hat{\omega}_{\text{effect}}^2$ suggested by Hays (1963, pp. 406–407) and others (e.g., Winer, 1971, pp. 428–430) can be expressed as follows:

$$\hat{\omega}_{\text{effect}}^2 = \frac{\hat{\sigma}_{\text{effect}}^2}{\hat{\sigma}_T^2}, \tag{25-7}$$

where $\hat{\sigma}_T^2$ consists of the sum of the variance estimates for all factorial effects and error. In a two-factor design, for example,

$$\hat{\omega}_{\text{effect}}^2 = \frac{\hat{\sigma}_{\text{effect}}^2}{\hat{\sigma}_T^2} = \frac{\hat{\sigma}_{\text{effect}}^2}{\hat{\sigma}_A^2 + \hat{\sigma}_B^2 + \hat{\sigma}_{A \times B}^2 + \hat{\sigma}_{S/AB}^2}. \tag{25-8}$$

The factorial components are estimated from Eq. (25-2):

$$\hat{\sigma}_{\text{effect}}^2 = \frac{(df_{\text{effect}})(MS_{\text{effect}} - MS_{\text{wg}})}{N},$$

$$\hat{\sigma}_A^2 = \frac{(a-1)(MS_A - MS_{S/AB})}{abs},$$

$$\hat{\sigma}_B^2 = \frac{(b-1)(MS_B - MS_{S/AB})}{abs},$$

$$\hat{\sigma}_{A \times B}^2 = \frac{[(a-1)(b-1)](MS_{A \times B} - MS_{S/AB})}{abs},$$

while the error component is obtained from Eq. (25-3):

$$\hat{\sigma}_{S/AB}^2 = MS_{S/AB}.$$

Depending upon the estimate needed, these quantities are substituted in Eq. (25-8).

An alternative general formula is computationally simpler than the approach just outlined. We can obtain exactly the same estimates from

$$\hat{\omega}_{\text{effect}}^2 = \frac{SS_{\text{effect}} - (df_{\text{effect}})(MS_{\text{wg}})}{SS_T + MS_{\text{wg}}}. \tag{25-9}$$

Using Eq. (25-9) to estimate $\omega^2_{A \times B}$ in a two-factor experiment, we have

$$\hat{\omega}^2_{A \times B} = \frac{SS_{A \times B} - (a - 1)(b - 1)(MS_{S/AB})}{SS_T + MS_{S/AB}}.$$

A serious objection can be raised concerning the appropriateness of these general formulas. Consider Eq. (25-7) for a moment. This formula relates the estimate of the population treatment component to the sum of *all* of the components specified under the model. This means that a particular omega squared, say $\hat{\omega}^2_A$, will be defined *differently* for each type of design. For instance,

$$\hat{\omega}^2_A = \frac{\hat{\sigma}^2_A}{\hat{\sigma}^2_A + \hat{\sigma}^2_{S/A}} \quad \text{and} \quad \frac{\hat{\sigma}^2_A}{\hat{\sigma}^2_A + \hat{\sigma}^2_B + \hat{\sigma}^2_{A \times B} + \hat{\sigma}^2_{S/AB}}$$

in the one- and two-factor designs, respectively. Depending upon the nature of the design, therefore, the same manipulation will result in different omega squares, even when the variance component estimated for that manipulation is *identical* in these designs.

A reasonable solution to this problem would seem to lie in a different definition of omega squared, always relating the treatment component to the sum of only *two* components, the treatment component and the error component.[5] In symbols,

$$\hat{\omega}^2_{\text{effect}} = \frac{\hat{\sigma}^2_{\text{effect}}}{\hat{\sigma}^2_{\text{effect}} + \hat{\sigma}^2_{\text{wg}}}. \tag{25-10}$$

As applied to one-, two-, and three-factor designs, for example,

$$\hat{\omega}^2_A = \frac{\hat{\sigma}^2_A}{\hat{\sigma}^2_A + \hat{\sigma}^2_{S/A}}, \quad \frac{\hat{\sigma}^2_A}{\hat{\sigma}^2_A + \hat{\sigma}^2_{S/AB}}, \quad \text{and} \quad \frac{\hat{\sigma}^2_A}{\hat{\sigma}^2_A + \hat{\sigma}^2_{S/ABC}},$$

respectively. This example illustrates that Eq. (25-10) provides a meaningful way of comparing estimates of the influence of a particular manipulation which is not dependent upon the complexity of the underlying design. For this reason, Eq. (25-10) is to be preferred over Eqs. (25-8) and (25-9).

Strength of a Comparison

In addition to a concern for an estimate of the strength of treatment effects, we may often find it profitable to consider the strength of certain comparisons which in part contribute to the overall treatment effects. The $\hat{\omega}^2_{\text{effect}}$, defined in Eq. (25-1), merely provides an estimate of the strength of the *average* or "omnibus" treatment effects—nothing is said about the relative contribution of orthogonal contrasts. Levin (1967) makes this point by describing a single-factor experiment with $a = 6$ levels in which $\hat{\omega}^2_A$ was found to equal .37. Of this

---

[5] Cohen (1969, pp. 359–360) offers the same suggestion in a different, but related context.

37 percent, the variability accounted for by the experimental treatment, "over 85 percent of the total 'explained variation' resulted from the superiority of one of the experimental groups to all the others" (p. 676).

A more revealing procedure than a calculation of this "omnibus" $\hat{\omega}^2_{\text{effect}}$ would be to obtain an estimate of omega squared for *meaningful comparisons*. Vaughan and Corballis (1969, pp. 210–211) indicate how this is accomplished. In the single-factor case, for example, a ratio is obtained of the estimated population variance due to the comparison of interest relative to the estimated population variance due to the experimental treatments:

$$\hat{\omega}^2_{A_{\text{comp.}}} = \frac{\hat{\sigma}^2_{A_{\text{comp.}}}}{\hat{\sigma}^2_A}$$

$$= \frac{MS_{A_{\text{comp.}}} - MS_{S/A}}{(a - 1)(MS_A - MS_{S/A})}. \tag{25-11}$$

Comments

The presence of a significant F test gives us some assurance that a *statistical association* (predictability between the treatment groupings and the scores on the dependent variable) exists. The size of the F itself does not reflect the degree of this statistical association unambiguously. Omega squared provides this information and thus supplements any inference to be drawn from the outcome of the experiment.[6] In addition, even with a nonsignificant F, it is still possible to obtain a sizable omega squared. This sort of situation would occur with an experiment of low power.

There is no question that both statistics, the significance level of an F test and $\hat{\omega}^2$, contribute to a complete understanding of the outcome of the statistical test. Moreover, it is clear that we should be looking for treatments that produce large estimates of statistical association. We have also seen that $\hat{\omega}^2$ may provide useful information when a statistical test is not significant. On the other hand, if we based *all* of our actions on the size of $\hat{\omega}^2$ alone, we would be making a mistake. Just as with power, we have the problem of deciding upon an *acceptable* level in this case of omega squared. Often a small statistical association may be sufficient to justify the introduction of a change suggested by the treatment conditions.

It is also important to note that the adaptation of the correlation ratio into omega squared hides a serious shortcoming—namely, that within certain limits

---

[6] Vaughan and Corballis (1969) indicate in a footnote that some authors have pointed out that the estimate of ω^2_{effect} is likely to be biased. They conclude, however, that "the risk of bias may not be a serious objection to the use of [omega squared], particularly if large samples are used, and if one adopts the view that even a biased estimate is better than none" (p. 205).

the size of omega squared is in fact under the control of the experimenter.[7] That is, since he selects the actual treatments appearing in his experiment, he can influence the size of the treatment component and, consequently, $\hat{\omega}^2$. (Only with random independent variables do we find a situation in which the levels included in the experiment are not directly determined by the researcher.) A small omega squared, then, could mean relatively small treatment effects, which is what its advocates maintain, or it could mean an unfortunate choice of levels. Only when a researcher is convinced that he has represented the full extent of the independent variable in his experiment can he obtain unambiguous information from the estimate of omega squared.

We can also question the general usefulness of omega squared. The index can be especially informative when an investigator begins work in a new and previously unanalyzed research area. His first strategy of research may be to search for independent variables that seem to produce large effects. It is exactly for this sort of enterprise that omega squared provides an important research tool for the investigator. In applied areas of research also, omega squared can be used to isolate manipulations which produce economically interesting results. At other times, however, the size of omega squared will be of little interest. Consider how this might come about. Initial explorations in a research area can often be characterized as reflecting relatively large treatment effects. In fact, it is usually the size of the new finding that draws researchers into these new fields. Subsequent research will usually not be concerned with the original finding, however, but with a refinement of the discovery into component parts, each being responsive to a different collection of experimental manipulations. As theories develop to account for these findings and for the interrelationships among the components, a researcher eventually finds that he is no longer working with large effects, but with small ones representing manipulations that are theoretically interesting. Under these circumstances, even small differences—as indexed by omega squared—may provide a decision between two competing theoretical explanations. Thus, we could say that one indication of a "healthy" and productive area of research is a preponderance of experiments with relatively *small* omega squares!

In short, then, a researcher uses just as many indices as he can to help him in his interpretation of an experimental outcome. In addition to the results of statistical tests and of estimates of omega squared and of power, additional analyses are conducted to shed some light on the meaning of particular outcomes of an experiment. These analyses may involve the original response measure or supplemental ones also obtainable from the response protocols of the subjects. They may include the plotting of the means and other graphical devices. Of critical concern, of course, is an understanding of the implications of the

[7] I wish to thank my colleague, Dr. Rheem F. Jarrett, for pointing out this objection and allowing me to read an unpublished paper he has prepared ("A note on the use of omega squared when *Y* is not a homogeneous random variable") examining this and other objections to omega squared.

different statistical indices, so that we may use them to advance knowledge in our chosen fields of research.

DATA TRANSFORMATIONS

A transformation refers to a translation of the scores obtained on the dependent variable to a set of new numbers. The translation is specified by means of some systematic relationship between the original scale and the transformed scale. In discussions of this topic, authors usually refer to the fact that scales of measurement are purely arbitrary. Thus, we should not be shocked by any change in the scale of measurement. Most response measures represent a simple coding of an observable event, such as a counting of the number of correct responses or the clocking of the time required by an animal to run down an alley. These straightforward transformations of the observed behavior lose little of the original event. We usually do not stray very far from response measures that seem to reflect directly the behavior under study. Occasionally, however, a theory may specify the use of a certain transformation, but as yet these situations are rare. We tend to use the same measures that others use so that we can achieve some degree of communication among investigators.

Reasons for Performing Transformations

Transformations commonly found in the literature include the translation of basic scores involving number of correct responses or errors into percentages, or of scores consisting of elapsed "clock" time into speed scores or reciprocal time scores, or of scores into less understandable quantities such as square roots and logarithms. Let us now consider why these data transformations are undertaken in the first place.

Sometimes a conversion of the original response measure into a new derived one will result in a quantity that provides a more useful description of the behavior under study. In a learning experiment, for example, a researcher might be interested in the rate at which overt errors are made during the course of the training. Under these circumstances, he might choose to translate the numbers of overt errors into a percentage score, in which the errors are related to the number of "opportunities" the learner has to make them. This way the fast learner, who has fewer "opportunities" to actually make overt errors, would be equated in a sense with the slow learner, who has more such "opportunities." Another example is the translation of running times into a more general "speed" score reflecting the distance traveled per unit of time. This measure makes it possible to compare experiments with apparatus of different size and dimension. In both of these cases, the transformations are applied to the original data of the experiment to produce a more useful and perhaps less ambiguous measure of the behavior under study.

A second reason researchers use a transformation is to "correct" a violation of the assumptions underlying the statistical analysis. Two basic assumptions of the completely randomized designs are those of within-group normality and the homogeneity of the within-group variances. If a set of data is found to violate either or both of these assumptions, a transformation may be found to produce *transformed data* that *will* satisfy the assumptions. Transformations designed to "correct" violations of these sorts are being used increasingly less frequently in the behavioral sciences. The main reason for the reduction in this use of transformations is the demonstration that even serious violations of these two assumptions do not materially affect the evaluation of F ratios obtained from such experiments. (See pp. 74–76 for a discussion of this point.) For repeated-measures designs, on the other hand, some authors recommend the use of a transformation to reduce heterogeneity of covariance. Similarly, it is often suggested that transformations be applied to the scores in a covariance analysis to remove heterogeneity or nonlinearity of regression. The use of transformations for repeated-measures and covariance designs is complicated, and any prospective user of transformations for these purposes should consult with a statistician.

A third use of transformations is to minimize the contribution of deviant subjects to the results of an experiment. In studies where performance must reach a criterion of excellence before the experiment is terminated, it is common to find an occasional subject who takes an inordinate number of trials to attain this criterion. (Statisticians often refer to such an individual as an *outlier*.) Including the subject in the data analysis will weight his performance disproportionately to the other subjects in his treatment condition. One way of dealing with the problem is to exclude the deviant subject from the experiment entirely. The main objection to such a procedure is the possible introduction of a potential bias in the assignment of subjects to conditions. To avoid this, or at least to reduce the bias, the researcher might exclude the most deviant subject from *each* condition—in a sense, extending the bias to all of the conditions.[8] An alternative procedure is to use a transformation designed to reduce the influence of deviant scores. A logarithmic transformation or a square-root transformation is often recommended for such purposes.

A final use of transformations is for theoretical reasons. Occasionally, a theory may specify the use of a particular transformation. It is conceivable, for example, that one theory of memory might consider forgetting in terms of the *amount* that is lost—i.e., a difference score based on a performance estimate obtained at the end of learning and at recall taken after a period of time. Another theory might view forgetting in terms of *percentages*—i.e., the percentage lost relative to the amount originally learned. The loss score does not deviate far from the original data, while the percentage measure is a transformed or *derived* score. Both types of measures have been used in the study of forgetting.

[8] Winer (1971, pp. 51–54) discusses several procedures by which this is sometimes accomplished, such as *trimming* and *winsorization*.

The point of this discussion, however, is to show that the two measures will not necessarily lead to the same conclusion.

Suppose that at the end of learning one subject gave 4 correct responses and another gave 8 correct responses. In addition, suppose that both subjects showed a loss of 2 responses over a 24-hour period. By the first measure (the amount lost) we would conclude that the two subjects showed *equal forgetting* over the retention interval. On the other hand, a different picture emerges with the percentage measure. That is, the first subject shows $(2/4) \times 100 = 50$ percent forgetting, while the second subject shows $(2/8) \times 100 = 25$ percent forgetting. Depending upon the theory, then, different conclusions would be drawn from this simple set of data.

A response measure is chosen to reflect the behavior of the subjects in an experiment as faithfully as possible. A reader can "get back" to the original observations if the data have not been transformed. This usually cannot be done with data that have been transformed. While it is obvious that we can "untransform" individual scores for subjects back to the original response measure, this cannot be done with the *means* of the transformed scores. Thus, there should be compelling, theoretical reasons for the introduction of a data transformation in an experiment.

An Example of a Transformation

Most data transformations accomplish their intended function without changing the basic conclusions drawn from an experiment. However, they do result in a change of the means as well as a change in the individual scores. Most authors recommend the use of *monotonic* transformations, ones that preserve the rank order of the scores involved. But even these will change the relationship among the means. To borrow a dramatic example from Myers (1966, p. 65), consider the following scores:

	a_1	a_2
	4	25
	64	36
Mean:	34.0	30.5

For these scores, the mean at level a_1 is higher than the mean at level a_2. But suppose we apply the common square-root transformation to these data, in which case each score is subjected to the following transformation: $AS' = \sqrt{AS}$. Consider what happens when this transformation is applied to these four scores:

	a_1		a_2	
AS	$AS' = \sqrt{AS}$	AS	$AS' = \sqrt{AS}$
4	2	25	5
64	8	36	6
Mean: 34.0	5.0	30.5	5.5

The outcome of the experiment is exactly *reversed*.

Summary

It should be obvious that the decision to use a transformation of the data is a complicated business. A researcher should know exactly why he wants to transform his data. If it is to satisfy assumptions of normality and homogeneity of within-cell variances, then he might as well save himself the trouble, since the F test is robust with regard to these violations. If it is to simplify the statistical model, he should seek competent statistical advice. The justification of a data transformation is in the hands of the *user*. Readers of research reports are entitled to know whether or not the outcome of the experiment was materially affected by the transformation. Whether we like it or not, our analysis and our conclusions are based on the data actually entering into the analysis. If the scores are not transformed, then our conclusions involve the means of the original scores. If the scores are transformed, then our conclusions are restricted to the *transformed means*. For further information about transformations, see Kirk (1968, pp. 63–67), Myers (1966, pp. 64–66), and Winer (1962, pp. 218–222; 1971, pp. 397–402).

POOLING IN THE ANALYSIS OF VARIANCE

The appropriate error term for the factorial design with independent groups is the within-groups mean squares. The reason is that with the fixed-effects model, each treatment mean square on the average is thought to be the sum of two components, a treatment component and an error component. The question sometimes arises about what we should do, if anything, when there is reason to believe that certain treatment components are not present in the phenomenon we are studying. Suppose that we conduct a three-way factorial and have strong reason to believe, on the basis of previous research, that there will be no three-way interaction. If we trust the previous research, we should not include the three-way interaction in our statistical model. Under this revised model, there would then be *two* independent estimates of error variance, the $MS_{S/ABC}$ and the $MS_{A \times B \times C}$. If these two mean squares are independent estimates of the same quantity, we can average them in order to obtain a more stable estimate of error variance. This sort of averaging, or *pooling* as it is called, consists of the combination of the respective sums of squares which are then divided by the sum of the corresponding degrees of freedom. In this example,

$$MS_{\text{error (pooled)}} = \frac{SS_{A \times B \times C} + SS_{S/ABC}}{df_{A \times B \times C} + df_{S/ABC}}.$$

The advantages of pooling are the greater power afforded by the increase in denominator df and the greater stability of the estimate of error variance.

Pooling is a complicated procedure, however, and there is no agreement as to whether it should be done or not—and, if it is to be done, under what circumstances. The safest and most conservative position is that rarely in the real world will there be the complete absence of a treatment effect and that pooling of any sort constitutes an improper procedure. If we pool on the basis of previous work done in the area, we may obscure interactions that really do exist—they may not have been detected in the earlier research because of a lack of power. When this happens, we may introduce a *negative* bias to the F test, since we would be using an error term that is too large—i.e., includes *more* than error variance.

An alternative procedure is to base our decision about pooling on the results of a *preliminary test* of the statistical model. To be more specific, it has been suggested that we run through the complete analysis and consider pooling those sources of variance that fail to be rejected at $p < .25$ or greater. The difficulty here is that the subsequent analysis represents a post-hoc analysis, and there are difficulties in determining the sampling distribution that is appropriate to this situation.[9]

Authors do not agree that the question of the appropriateness of pooling has been fully and completely answered by the statisticians (nor should it!). As long as we include a sufficiently large sample size, it seems clear that pooling will not be useful. (The gain in power afforded by the pooling of df's is minimal once $df_{\text{wg}} > 20$.) The real dangers of pooling are that we might prematurely "reject" a source of variance because of an insensitive experiment and that we may be capitalizing on chance factors by pooling nonsignificant sources of variance after the data are in. Until statisticians fully understand the consequences of pooling, we should remain advocates of the "never-pool" rule. Scheffé (1959, p. 126) offers this recommendation in clear and unambiguous terms:

> A common but questionable practice is to pool into the error SS all interaction SS's found to be not significant at some chosen level. This would be justified ... if the corresponding interactions were known to be absent—but in that case there

---

[9] As a final complication, it is not entirely clear what sorts of situations are conducive to pooling and what sorts are not. Winer (1962), for example, indicates that preliminary tests "... are particularly appropriate when one is dealing with experiments in which interactions between fixed and random factors or interactions between random factors are potential in the model" (p. 202).

would be no point in testing for their presence!... Not very much is known about the operating characteristics of these procedures, and it seems best to try to avoid such pooling by designing the experiment so that there will be a sufficient number of "*df* for error" in the error *SS* selected in the design.

EXERCISES FOR PART VII[10]

1. Suppose an experimenter is planning an experiment with $a = 5$ different treatments. While it is difficult to specify expected outcomes in terms of actual means, it is sometimes possible to make predictions in terms of pairs of conditions. Suppose he assumes the following population data: $\mu_1 = \mu_2$, $\mu_3 - \mu_2 = 4$, $\mu_4 - \mu_3 = 2$, and $\mu_4 - \mu_5 = 1$. On the basis of past research, he is willing to assume the population error variance to be 15. What sample size will he need to achieve power of .80 at $\alpha = .05$? [*Hint*: A set of means fitting this pattern can be constructed by assuming an arbitrary number for one of the means and solving for the others.]

2. The statistical results of four independent replications of the same experiment are presented in Table 24-3 (p. 543). On the basis of the results of the first experiment, which we will assume was a pilot study, determine the sample size needed in a new experiment that will have a power of .90 in detecting a difference as large as the one obtained here. Set $\alpha = .05$. (Note: Experiment 1 in Table 24-3 has $s = 16$ subjects in each of the two conditions.)

3. A 5×3 factorial experiment is conducted with independent groups of $s = 5$ subjects in each condition. The $MS_{A \times B} = 17.50$ and the $MS_{S/AB} = 12.25$. The resulting $F(8, 60) = 1.43$, $p > .05$. Perform a post-hoc power analysis with this information.

4. Table 4-2 (p. 56) summarizes the analysis of a single-factor experiment.
   (a) Estimate the magnitude of the treatment effects using the formulas written in terms of estimated variance components—i.e., Eqs. (25-1), (25-4), and (25-5).
   (b) Estimate the same quantity by means of the two alternative formulas, Eqs. (25-6a) and (25-6b).

5. The analysis of a two-factor design is summarized in Table 11-1 (p. 215). Estimate the omega squared for each of the factorial effects.

[10] The answers to these problems are found in Appendix D.

chapter twenty-six

CONCLUDING REMARKS

We have come to the end of the formal presentation. It might be fruitful, at this time, to indicate where we are in our discussion of the design and analysis of experiments. In the process of doing so, we will consider briefly directions that the reader might take to increase his understanding of the general area of study.

We have focused entirely upon a particular approach to statistical analysis—namely, hypothesis testing by means of analysis of variance techniques. The justification for this emphasis is that these are the procedures used by most of the researchers in the experimental areas of the behavioral sciences. As a consequence, we have paid no attention to problems of *estimation* per se. Our discussions of estimation in Chapters 24 and 25 were centered around the use of point estimates in the testing of statistical hypotheses. We did not worry about interval estimation or properties of estimators—all important problems in any complete consideration of statistical inference. On the other hand, this emphasis upon hypothesis testing does in fact reflect current practices in psychology and its overwhelming prevalence in the research journals. The case can be made, however, for an intelligent use of both estimation and of hypothesis testing. Myers (1966, chap. 2) provides a useful discussion of these two procedures and of their relative merits. You may also be interested in the supplementary readings listed at the end of his chapter (p. 37).

A second area we have not considered is the *multivariate analysis of variance*, an analysis in which more than one dependent variable is incorporated into the experimental design. Multivariate procedures are finding application in research areas where a number of dependent variables, which are not too highly intercorrelated, have been identified and are of interest to study jointly. Most of these analyses are extremely time-consuming with a desk calculator and are best accomplished on a computer. A widely cited introduction to multivariate procedures is a book by Anderson (1958). Winer has introduced a discussion of multivariate analysis of variance in the second edition of his useful book (1971, pp. 232–240).

Finally, we have given no mention to *nonparametric or distribution-free statistics*. The interest in nonparametric statistics is twofold: (1) their freedom from assumptions about the distribution of the scores in the population and (2) their simplicity, especially when compared with the analysis of variance. On the negative side, however, nonparametric statistics are not as flexible with regard to the types of hypotheses that may be tested as is the analysis of variance. In addition, they are not as powerful and provide less information from the data when the assumptions underlying the analysis of variance are met. Moreover, nonparametric procedures have not been developed for the higher-order factorial designs that are so widely represented in the current experimental literature. If you want to pursue the topic, various excellent discussions are available. Both Kirk (1968, pp. 491–503) and Winer (1962, pp. 622–629; 1971, pp. 848–855), for example, provide brief discussions. Siegel (1956) has written a popular book on the subject and at least two more recent books have appeared: Bradley (1968) and Edgington (1969).

Just what constitutes an *understanding* of the material covered in this book is controversial, and any answer is bound to be highly individualistic. You have been exposed to what might be described as an *experimenter's* approach to the design and analysis of experiments. In the writer's opinion, then, you have been given the basic ingredients necessary for a *working* knowledge of statistical analysis. The major objection to the approach taken in this book is the failure to consider in any detail the mathematical and statistical support for the analyses presented in the different chapters. By way of reply, it should be noted that there already are some excellent advanced books, written for psychologists, which develop statistical analysis from exactly this point of view. These treatments, which we have referred to repeatedly in the present book, are readily available if you decide that you want to increase your statistical knowledge in this regard.

Perhaps a more important region toward which one's future study should point is that of *experimental design*. A study of general principles of experimental design is useful in forcing us to examine our methods and procedures with a highly critical eye. Two brief, but excellent, sources may be recommended, an article by Campbell and Stanley, which originally appeared as a chapter in a book (1963), but has been reprinted as a separate monograph (1966), and a book by Underwood (1957) in which Chapters 4 and 5 are particularly relevant. Another useful book, *Unobstrusive Measures*, by Webb, Campbell, Schwartz, and Sechrest (1966), discusses the role of experimentation in changing the actual behavior under study.

General discussions, however, whether focused on experimental design or on the statistical analysis of experiments, are only a first step: they still must be applied by the researcher in the laboratory. The success of any research attempt will depend in part upon the skill with which he accomplishes this translation.

appendix a

ORTHOGONALITY OF SOURCES
OF VARIANCE

At various points we have asserted that the sources of variance normally extracted in the analysis of single- and multifactor designs—the main effects, interactions, and error terms—are mutually orthogonal. It is possible to demonstrate the orthogonality of these sources of variance, but the demonstration is complicated and a little tedious. We will include such an illustration, nevertheless, because students frequently express an interest in the problem, and their understanding of the analysis of variance seems enhanced when it is presented to them. The general plan of this appendix will be to devise a set of coefficients which are orthogonal and which reflect the sources of variance being extracted. These coefficients will then be applied to actual treatment sums to produce corresponding sums of squares. Finally, the sums of squares associated with each set of coefficients will be added together to produce values that are numerically equivalent to the sums of squares obtained for the same sources of variance with the usual computational formulas.

Comparisons and Orthogonality—A Review

The notion of comparisons (or contrasts) was first introduced in Chapter 6. Briefly, a comparison is produced by applying weights (or coefficients) to the different treatment sums and then calculating the sums of squares associated with the comparison. More specifically, a comparison must satisfy the requirement that

$$\sum (c_i) = 0, \qquad (A\text{-}1)$$

where the c_i terms are the coefficients for a particular comparison. Suppose we have four groups in a single-factor experiment and we want to make the following comparisons: (1) the group at a_1 versus the group at a_3, (2) the group at a_2 versus the group at a_4, and (3) the average of the groups at a_1 and a_3 versus the average of the groups at a_2 and a_4. These comparisons are reflected by the coefficients of combination (c_i) listed for each group:

	Levels of Factor A			
	a_1	a_2	a_3	a_4
Sums:	A_1	A_2	A_3	A_4
Comparison 1:	1	0	-1	0
Comparison 2:	0	1	0	-1
Comparison 3:	1	-1	1	-1

The requirement specified in Eq. (A-1) is met with each of these comparisons.

Two comparisons are orthogonal if the sum of the products of corresponding coefficients equals zero.[1] In symbols,

$$\sum (c_i)(c_i') = 0,$$

where c_i represents the coefficients for one comparison and c_i' represents the corresponding coefficients for the other comparison. The three comparisons listed above are mutually orthogonal:

(1) vs. (2): $(1)(0) + (0)(1) + (-1)(0) + (0)(-1) = 0,$

(1) vs. (3): $(1)(1) + (0)(-1) + (-1)(1) + (0)(-1) = 0,$

(2) vs. (3): $(0)(1) + (1)(-1) + (0)(1) + (-1)(-1) = 0.$

We will consider a numerical example in which there are $s = 4$ subjects in each of the four groups. The sums for these groups are presented in the first r w of Table A-1. The three sets of coefficients are entered in the next three rows. The computational formula for the sum of squares associated with

---

[1] This statement is technically true only if the observations upon which the comparisons are based come from normal populations. But even if normality is not present, the comparisons are *uncorrelated*, provided the treatment populations are independent.

a comparison is given by

$$SS_{A_{comp.}} = \frac{[\sum (c_i)(A_i)]^2}{s[\sum (c_i)^2]}. \qquad (A\text{-}2)$$

TABLE A-1 *Orthogonal Comparisons among Four Treatment Conditions*

	a_1	a_2	a_3	a_4	$\sum (c_i)(A_i)$	$\sum (c_i)^2$
Sum:	20	12	28	40		
Comp. 1:	1	0	-1	0	-8	2
Comp. 2:	0	1	0	-1	-28	2
Comp. 3:	1	-1	1	-1	-4	4

The quantity within the brackets in the numerator consists of the sum of the weighted treatment totals. These sums are listed to the right of the coefficients for each of the three comparisons. As an example, the sum of the weighted totals for comparison 3 is found as follows:

$$\sum (c_{3i})(A_i) = (1)(20) + (-1)(12) + (1)(28) + (-1)(40)$$
$$= 20 - 12 + 28 - 40 = -4.$$

Substituting in Eq. (A-2), we find the following sums of squares:

$$SS_{A_{comp.\ 1}} = \frac{[\sum (c_{1i})(A_i)]^2}{s[\sum (c_{1i})^2]}$$
$$= \frac{(-8)^2}{4(2)} = \frac{64}{8} = 8.0,$$

$$SS_{A_{comp.\ 2}} = \frac{[\sum (c_{2i})(A_i)]^2}{s[\sum (c_{2i})^2]}$$
$$= \frac{(-28)^2}{4(2)} = \frac{784}{8} = 98.0,$$

$$SS_{A_{comp.\ 3}} = \frac{[\sum (c_{3i})(A_i)]^2}{s[\sum (c_{3i})^2]}$$
$$= \frac{(-4)^2}{4(4)} = \frac{16}{16} = 1.0.$$

As noted in Chapter 7, the SS_A can be partitioned into a set of orthogonal comparisons, the number of which is equal to the df_A—i.e., $a - 1$. To show this property with the present data, we must calculate the SS_A:

$$SS_A = \frac{\sum (A)^2}{s} - \frac{(T)^2}{as}$$

$$= \frac{(20)^2 + (12)^2 + (28)^2 + (40)^2}{4} - \frac{(20 + 12 + 28 + 40)^2}{4(4)}$$

$$= \frac{2928}{4} - \frac{10,000}{16}$$

$$= 732.0 - 625.0 = 107.0.$$

As verification of the additivity property,

$$SS_A = \sum SS_{A_{comp.}},$$

$$107.0 = 8.0 + 98.0 + 1.0 = 107.0.$$

This breakdown of the SS_A into a set of orthogonal comparisons illustrates the meaning of degrees of freedom: the number of degrees of freedom specifies the number of *orthogonal comparisons* that may be constructed from a given set of data. We are now ready to use this property and Eqs. (A-1) and (A-2) to show that the SS_A and the $SS_{S/A}$ are themselves orthogonal.

Orthogonality of the SS_A and the $SS_{S/A}$ in the Single-Factor Design

It was stated in Part II that the total variability among subjects (SS_T) may be partitioned into two orthogonal sources, the SS_A and the $SS_{S/A}$. We will demonstrate that this is true by dividing the total sum of squares into $as - 1$ orthogonal comparisons, $a - 1$ of which will reflect collectively the SS_A, and $a(s - 1)$ of which will reflect the $SS_{S/A}$. If all these comparisons are mutually orthogonal, then we will have demonstrated that *two subsets* of the comparisons, the SS_A and the $SS_{S/A}$, are orthogonal also.

For this illustration we will use the individual scores as our basic entry. In the single-factor experiment these are designated as AS_{ij}. These scores have been listed at the top of Table A-2. There are four AS scores ($s = 4$) for each treatment condition, and a total of $as = 4(4) = 16$ scores are listed across the table. The first step is to write a complete set of coefficients representing orthogonal comparisons, one comparison for each of the total number of df available in the experiment: $df_T = as - 1 = 4(4) - 1 = 15$. This has been accomplished in the 15 rows below the actual scores.

Consider, initially, the first three comparisons and the coefficients presented in the table. It will be noted that these comparisons are the numerical equivalents of the three comparisons listed in Table A-1. Comparison 1, for example, combines the four scores at level a_1 and contrasts them with the four scores at level a_3. This is exactly what is specified in Table A-1, except that we are operating on the treatment sums; i.e., the four AS scores have been combined already. The next two comparisons in Table A-2 correspond to comparisons 2 and 3 in Table A-1. Thus, if we apply the formula for the sum of squares to these data, we will extract the same quantities from Table A-2 as we were able to extract from Table A-1. A formula for a comparison, modified to this situation, is given by

$$SS_{AS_{comp.}} = \frac{[\sum (c_{ij})(AS_{ij})]^2}{\sum (c_{ij})^2},$$ (A-3)

where c_{ij} represents the coefficients for the jth subject in one of the ith treatment conditions. Since we are dealing with single AS scores, s does not appear as a multiplier in the denominator of Eq. (A-3). The sums of the weighted AS scores for these three comparisons are given to the right of the coefficients. Substituting in Eq. (A-3),

$$SS_{AS_{comp. 1}} = \frac{[\sum (c_{1ij})(AS_{ij})]^2}{\sum (c_{1ij})^2} = \frac{(-8)^2}{8} = \frac{64}{8} = 8.0,$$

$$SS_{AS_{comp. 2}} = \frac{[\sum (c_{2ij})(AS_{ij})]^2}{\sum (c_{2ij})^2} = \frac{(-28)^2}{8} = \frac{784}{8} = 98.0,$$

$$SS_{AS_{comp. 3}} = \frac{[\sum (c_{3ij})(AS_{ij})]^2}{\sum (c_{3ij})^2} = \frac{(-4)^2}{16} = \frac{16}{16} = 1.0.$$

These sums of squares are identical to those obtained from the treatment sums and Eq. (A-2), and, as we have seen, collectively they constitute the SS_A.

We will now construct a set of orthogonal comparisons that will permit the calculation of the within-groups sum of squares. Consider the coefficients constituting the next three orthogonal comparisons in Table A-2. As we will see, these comparisons are mutually orthogonal to one another and to comparisons 1–3. Also, they only involve the four AS scores at level a_1; the coefficients are zero for all other scores. Orthogonality may be verified quite easily. The three sets of cross-products involving the within-group comparisons at a_1 all sum to zero:

Comp. 4 vs. 5:

$$(1)(1) + (1)(-1) + (-1)(0) + (-1)(0) + (0)(0) + \cdots + (0)(0) = 0,$$

Comp. 4 vs. 6:

$$(1)(0) + (1)(0) + (-1)(1) + (-1)(-1) + (0)(0) + \cdots + (0)(0) = 0,$$

Comp. 5 vs. 6:

$$(1)(0) + (-1)(0) + (0)(1) + (0)(-1) + (0)(0) + \cdots + (0)(0) = 0.$$

The choice of this set of coefficients was entirely arbitrary. Any set would have sufficed. (This point is illustrated by the use of different sets of coefficients

A-2 A Complete Set of Orthogonal Comparisons for the Single-Factor Design

	a_1				a_2				a_3				a_4					
	AS_{11}	AS_{12}	AS_{13}	AS_{14}	AS_{21}	AS_{22}	AS_{23}	AS_{24}	AS_{31}	AS_{32}	AS_{33}	AS_{34}	AS_{41}	AS_{42}	AS_{43}	AS_{44}	$\sum(c_{ij})(AS_{ij})$	$\sum(c_{ij})^2$
Score:	3	5	7	5	1	3	6	2	8	6	5	9	10	9	14	7		
Comp. 1	1	1	1	1	0	0	0	0	−1	−1	−1	−1	0	0	0	0	−8	8
Comp. 2	0	0	0	0	1	1	1	1	0	0	0	0	−1	−1	−1	−1	−28	8
Comp. 3	1	1	1	1	−1	−1	−1	−1	1	1	1	1	−1	−1	−1	−1	−4	16
Comp. 4	1	1	−1	−1	0	0	0	0	0	0	0	0	0	0	0	0	−4	4
Comp. 5	1	−1	0	0	0	0	0	0	0	0	0	0	0	0	0	0	−2	2
Comp. 6	0	0	1	−1	0	0	0	0	0	0	0	0	0	0	0	0	2	2
Comp. 7	0	0	0	0	3	−1	−1	−1	0	0	0	0	0	0	0	0	−8	12
Comp. 8	0	0	0	0	0	−1	2	−1	0	0	0	0	0	0	0	0	7	6
Comp. 9	0	0	0	0	0	1	0	−1	0	0	0	0	0	0	0	0	1	2
Comp. 10	0	0	0	0	0	0	0	0	−1	−1	3	−1	0	0	0	0	−8	12
Comp. 11	0	0	0	0	0	0	0	0	−1	2	0	−1	0	0	0	0	−5	6
Comp. 12	0	0	0	0	0	0	0	0	1	0	0	−1	0	0	0	0	−1	2
Comp. 13	0	0	0	0	0	0	0	0	0	0	0	0	1	1	−1	−1	−2	4
Comp. 14	0	0	0	0	0	0	0	0	0	0	0	0	1	−1	1	−1	8	4
Comp. 15	0	0	0	0	0	0	0	0	0	0	0	0	1	−1	−1	1	−6	4

for the remaining within-group sums of squares.) You should be able to see that these three comparisons are orthogonal to comparisons 1–3, since they will be multiplied in each case by a constant, $+1$ for comparison 1, 0 for comparison 2, and $+1$ for comparison 3.

The remaining sets of three comparisons each extract the within-group sums of squares for levels a_2, a_3, and a_4. These comparisons, too, are orthogonal to all other comparisons in the table. Thus, we have constructed a total of 15 orthogonal comparisons, completely using up the degrees of freedom that are available. No additional orthogonal comparisons are possible.

Before we calculate the within-group sums of squares, we should consider the form that these four sets of coefficients take. For each set, the coefficients "operate" only on the scores constituting the variation that is being calculated. We have already noted that the comparisons contributing to the within-group sum of squares for a_1 contain nonzero coefficients for the AS scores appearing at that level and zero coefficients for all others. The comparisons at a_2 contain nonzero coefficients for scores at that level and zero coefficients for all others. The same is true at a_3 and a_4. The arrangement clearly indicates that the within-groups sum of squares, which is obtained by pooling the separate within-group sums of squares, is produced by a *nested* factor—i.e., subjects who are nested within the levels of factor A. That is, any set of orthogonal comparisons which makes up one of the within-group sums of squares involves the variability of the scores at that level of factor A only.

We will now obtain the separate within-group sums of squares and from these the pooled within-groups sum of squares, $SS_{S/A}$. The sums of the weighted AS scores appear on the righthand side of the table. Applying Eq. (A-3) to the comparisons listed for level a_1, we have

$$SS_{AS_{comp.\,4}} = \frac{(-4)^2}{4} = \frac{16}{4} = 4.0,$$

$$SS_{AS_{comp.\,5}} = \frac{(-2)^2}{2} = \frac{4}{2} = 2.0,$$

$$SS_{AS_{comp.\,6}} = \frac{(2)^2}{2} = \frac{4}{2} = 2.0.$$

Calculated in the usual manner, the within-group sum of squares is given by

$$SS_{S/A_1} = \sum (AS_{1j})^2 - \frac{(A_1)^2}{s}$$

$$= [(3)^2 + (5)^2 + (7)^2 + (5)^2] - \frac{(3 + 5 + 7 + 5)^2}{4}$$

$$= 108.0 - 100.0 = 8.0.$$

This value, 8.0, is identical to the value obtained by summing the sums of squares for the three orthogonal comparisons:

$$\sum SS_{AS_{comp.}} = 4.0 + 2.0 + 2.0 = 8.0.$$

The sums of squares for the orthogonal comparisons, the within-group sums of squares, and the verification of additivity for the remaining three levels of factor A are as follows. For a_2:

$$SS_{AS_{comp.7}} = \frac{(-8)^2}{12} = \frac{64}{12} = 5.3,$$

$$SS_{AS_{comp.8}} = \frac{(7)^2}{6} = \frac{49}{6} = 8.2,$$

$$SS_{AS_{comp.9}} = \frac{(1)^2}{2} = \frac{1}{2} = .5;$$

$$SS_{S/A_2} = \sum (AS_{2j})^2 - \frac{(A_2)^2}{s}$$

$$= [(1)^2 + (3)^2 + (6)^2 + (2)^2] - \frac{(1 + 3 + 6 + 2)^2}{4}$$

$$= 50.0 - 36.0 = 14.0;$$

$$\sum SS_{AS_{comp.}} = 5.3 + 8.2 + .5 = 14.0.$$

Next, for a_3, we have

$$SS_{AS_{comp.10}} = \frac{(-8)^2}{12} = \frac{64}{12} = 5.3,$$

$$SS_{AS_{comp.11}} = \frac{(-5)^2}{6} = \frac{25}{6} = 4.2,$$

$$SS_{AS_{comp.12}} = \frac{(-1)^2}{2} = \frac{1}{2} = .5;$$

$$SS_{S/A_3} = \sum (AS_{3j})^2 - \frac{(A_3)^2}{s}$$

$$= [(8)^2 + (6)^2 + (5)^2 + (9)^2] - \frac{(8 + 6 + 5 + 9)^2}{4}$$

$$= 206.0 - 196.0 = 10.0;$$

$$\sum SS_{AS_{comp.}} = 5.3 + 4.2 + .5 = 10.0.$$

Finally, for a_4:

$$SS_{AS_{comp.\ 13}} = \frac{(-2)^2}{4} = \frac{4}{4} = 1.0,$$

$$SS_{AS_{comp.\ 14}} = \frac{(8)^2}{4} = \frac{64}{4} = 16.0,$$

$$SS_{AS_{comp.\ 15}} = \frac{(-6)^2}{4} = \frac{36}{4} = 9.0;$$

$$SS_{S/A_4} = \sum (AS_{4j})^2 - \frac{(A_4)^2}{s}$$

$$= [(10)^2 + (9)^2 + (14)^2 + (7)^2] - \frac{(10 + 9 + 14 + 7)^2}{4}$$

$$= 426.0 - 400.0 = 26.0;$$

$$\sum SS_{AS_{comp.}} = 1.0 + 16.0 + 9.0 = 26.0.$$

The remaining step in this illustration is to show that the sum of the four within-group sums of squares equals the $SS_{S/A}$. Calculating this latter quantity directly,

$$SS_{S/A} = \sum (AS)^2 - \frac{\sum (A)^2}{s}$$

$$= [(3)^2 + (5)^2 + \cdots + (14)^2 + (7)^2] - \frac{(20)^2 + (12)^2 + (28)^2 + (40)^2}{4}$$

$$= 790 - \frac{2928}{4}$$

$$= 790 - 732.0 = 58.0.$$

This value is also found when the individual within-group sums of squares are combined:

$$\sum SS_{S/A_i} = 8.0 + 14.0 + 10.0 + 26.0 = 58.0.$$

SUMMARY   We have seen that it is possible to construct a set of comparisons that contains as many orthogonal comparisons as there are degrees of freedom. Moreover, these comparisons may be selected to reflect sources of variance that are of interest—namely, comparisons contributing to the between-groups sum of squares (SS_A) and comparisons contributing to the within-groups sum of squares ($SS_{S/A}$). Since the comparisons constituting these two quantities are mutually orthogonal, these two sums of squares are orthogonal as well.

Orthogonality of Main Effects and Interaction in the Two-Factor Design

We will now consider an $A \times B$ design and demonstrate that the three sums of squares normally isolated in the analysis—the SS_A, the SS_B, and the $SS_{A \times B}$—are orthogonal. We will do this by writing a different comparison for each degree of freedom associated with the variability of the ab treatment means (i.e., $df = ab - 1$), which are mutually orthogonal and reflect the variation being extracted in the usual analysis. We will concern ourselves only with the between-groups variability in this example. (We could also show that the two main effects and the interaction are orthogonal to the within-groups sum of squares, $SS_{S/AB}$, by the procedures followed in the last section.) The design is a 4×3 factorial, and the data come from an experiment that we analyzed in Chapter 11 (see Table 11-1, p. 215). The 12 treatment sums and the coefficients for a set of $ab - 1 = 4(3) - 1 = 11$ orthogonal comparisons are presented in Table A-3. (In this example, there are $s = 3$ subjects in each treatment condition.) The orthogonality of these comparisons can be verified by summing the cross-products of corresponding coefficients for all possible pairs of comparisons.

The first three comparisons represent a set of contrasts which, when summed, will equal the SS_A. It will be noted that for each of these comparisons, the same patterns of coefficients operating on the four levels of factor A are repeated at each of the three levels of factor B. In comparison 1, for example, the basic pattern is $+3, -1, -1, -1$, while in comparison 2 the pattern is $0, -1, +2, -1$, and in comparison 3 it is $0, +1, 0, -1$. Since the patterns are repeated at each level of factor B, we are in essence collapsing across the B classification and obtaining sums of squares reflecting only the variation among the A means.

The next two comparisons involve the variation among the B means. In this case, the same patterns of coefficients operating on the levels of factor B are repeated at each of the four levels of factor A. For comparison 4 the pattern is $+2, -1, -1$; for comparison 5 the pattern is $0, +1, -1$. The repetition of these patterns at each level of factor A results in a collapsing across the A classification and a set of contrasts involving the B means.

The final set of coefficients represents components of the $A \times B$ interaction. Each of these six comparisons is "sensitive" to a different component of the interaction. In comparison 6, for instance, we are contrasting the combined groups at a_1 and a_2 with the combined groups at a_3 and a_4. However, the particular comparison at level b_1 $(+1, +1, -1, -1)$ is exactly *reversed* at level b_3 $(-1, -1, +1, +1)$. What we are asking in this comparison is whether or not the comparison at b_1 is *equal* to the comparison at b_3. This may be seen by writing the comparison as

$$(+1, +1, -1, -1) - (+1, +1, -1, -1),$$

which is algebraically equivalent to the coefficients presented in the table.

TABLE A-3 *A Complete Set of Orthogonal Comparisons Involving Treatment Conditions in the Two-Way Factorial*

	b_1				b_2				b_3					
	AB_{11}	AB_{21}	AB_{31}	AB_{41}	AB_{12}	AB_{22}	AB_{32}	AB_{42}	AB_{13}	AB_{23}	AB_{33}	AB_{43}	$\sum (c_{ij})(AB_{ij})$	$\sum (c_{ij})^2$
Sum:	18	20	17	19	21	21	24	22	18	30	34	32		
Comp. 1	3	−1	−1	−1	3	−1	−1	−1	3	−1	−1	−1	−48	36
Comp. 2	0	−1	2	−1	0	−1	2	−1	0	−1	2	−1	6	18
Comp. 3	0	1	0	−1	0	1	0	−1	0	1	0	−1	−2	6
Comp. 4	2	2	2	2	−1	−1	−1	−1	−1	−1	−1	−1	−54	24
Comp. 5	0	0	0	0	1	1	1	1	−1	−1	−1	−1	−26	8
Comp. 6	1	1	−1	−1	0	0	0	0	−1	−1	1	1	20	8
Comp. 7	−1	−1	1	1	2	2	−2	−2	−1	−1	1	1	8	24
Comp. 8	−1	−1	0	0	0	0	0	0	−1	−1	0	0	10	4
Comp. 9	−1	1	0	0	2	−2	0	0	−1	1	0	0	14	12
Comp. 10	0	0	1	−1	0	0	0	0	0	0	−1	1	−4	4
Comp. 11	0	0	−1	1	0	0	2	−2	0	0	−1	1	4	12

If the *same* difference between the two combined means appears at b_1 and b_3, then an interaction is *not* present with this particular component of the $A \times B$ interaction. On the other hand, if the differences are *not* equal at the two levels of factor B, then an interaction *is* present. Each of the remaining components of the $A \times B$ interaction follows this sort of pattern.

We will now compute the two main effects and the interaction by means of these orthogonal comparisons. The computational formula for these comparisons is given by

$$SS_{AB_{comp.}} = \frac{[\sum (c_{ij})(AB_{ij})]^2}{s[\sum (c_{ij})^2]},$$
(A-4)

where c_{ij} represents the coefficients associated with the ab treatment conditions. The sums of the products obtained by multiplying the coefficients and the treatment sums and the sums of the squared coefficients appear in Table A-3 to the right of the coefficients.

Using Eq. (A-4) and the data in the last two columns of Table A-3, we can now calculate the three sums of squares which collectively constitute the SS_A. Specifically,

$$SS_{AB_{comp.\ 1}} = \frac{[\sum (c_{1ij})(AB_{ij})]^2}{s[\sum (c_{1ij})^2]} = \frac{(-48)^2}{3(36)} = \frac{2304}{108} = 21.33,$$

$$SS_{AB_{comp.\ 2}} = \frac{[\sum (c_{2ij})(AB_{ij})]^2}{s[\sum (c_{2ij})^2]} = \frac{(6)^2}{3(18)} = \frac{36}{54} = .67,$$

$$SS_{AB_{comp.\ 3}} = \frac{[\sum (c_{3ij})(AB_{ij})]^2}{s[\sum (c_{3ij})^2]} = \frac{(-2)^2}{3(6)} = \frac{4}{18} = .22.$$

From the analysis presented in Table 11-1,

$$SS_A = 22.22,$$

which is what we obtain when we sum the SS's found with the first three comparisons:

$$21.33 + .67 + .22 = 22.22.$$

Turning next to the two comparisons for SS_B,

$$SS_{AB_{comp.\ 4}} = \frac{[\sum (c_{4ij})(AB_{ij})]^2}{s[\sum (c_{4ij})^2]} = \frac{(-54)^2}{3(24)} = \frac{2916}{72} = 40.50,$$

$$SS_{AB_{comp.\ 5}} = \frac{[\sum (c_{5ij})(AB_{ij})]^2}{s[\sum (c_{5ij})^2]} = \frac{(-26)^2}{3(8)} = \frac{676}{24} = 28.17.$$

The sum of these two SS's,

$$40.50 + 28.17 = 68.67,$$

equals the quantity obtained in the original analysis:

$$SS_B = 68.67.$$

The SS's for the final set of comparisons collectively add up to the $SS_{A \times B}$. To show this,

$$SS_{AB_{comp.\ 6}} = \frac{[\sum(c_{6ij})(AB_{ij})]^2}{s[\sum(c_{6ij})^2]} = \frac{(20)^2}{3(8)} = \frac{400}{24} = 16.67,$$

$$SS_{AB_{comp.\ 7}} = \frac{[\sum(c_{7ij})(AB_{ij})]^2}{s[\sum(c_{7ij})^2]} = \frac{(8)^2}{3(24)} = \frac{64}{72} = .89,$$

$$SS_{AB_{comp.\ 8}} = \frac{[\sum(c_{8ij})(AB_{ij})]^2}{s[\sum(c_{8ij})^2]} = \frac{(10)^2}{3(4)} = \frac{100}{12} = 8.33,$$

$$SS_{AB_{comp.\ 9}} = \frac{[\sum(c_{9ij})(AB_{ij})]^2}{s[\sum(c_{9ij})^2]} = \frac{(14)^2}{3(12)} = \frac{196}{36} = 5.44,$$

$$SS_{AB_{comp.\ 10}} = \frac{[\sum(c_{10ij})(AB_{ij})]^2}{s[\sum(c_{10ij})^2]} = \frac{(-4)^2}{3(4)} = \frac{16}{12} = 1.33,$$

$$SS_{AB_{comp.\ 11}} = \frac{[\sum(c_{11ij})(AB_{ij})]^2}{s[\sum(c_{11ij})^2]} = \frac{(4)^2}{3(12)} = \frac{16}{36} = .44.$$

The sum of these six comparisons,

$$16.67 + .89 + \cdots + 1.33 + .44 = 33.10,$$

agrees with the value obtained in Table 11-1 except for rounding error:

$$SS_{A \times B} = 33.11.$$

Summary

A similar demonstration may be conducted for more complicated designs, but the point has been made with the examples considered here. When we use orthogonal comparisons in an *actual* analysis, we do not make up just *any* set of comparisons. Instead, we consider comparisons that make *meaningful* contrasts among the treatment conditions. In so doing, we would probably not even want to construct a complete set of orthogonal comparisons. In an interaction, for example, we might only be interested in one or two of the orthogonal components—not the complete set. The purpose of these demonstrations, of course, was not the extraction of meaningful comparisons. Specifically, they were presented to show that the different sources of variance, into which we usually partition the total sums of squares (in the single-factor case) and the between-groups sum of squares (in the two-factor case), do in fact represent independent pieces of information.

appendix b

CALCULATION OF ORTHOGONAL
POLYNOMIAL COEFFICIENTS

In Chapter 7 we discussed the analysis of experiments in which the independent variable represents a quantitative dimension (see pp. 113–132). The analysis consisted of a division of the SS_A into orthogonal components of trend. The sums of squares associated with each trend component were calculated by substituting the treatment sums (A_i) and the orthogonal polynomial coefficients (c_i) in the general formula for a comparison, Eq. (6-6). Each set of coefficients reflects a different type of trend in its pure form—linear, quadratic, cubic, and so on. As long as the levels of the independent variable are equally spaced, we can obtain the orthogonal polynomial coefficients from tables, such as Table C-2 of Appendix C. However, as we noted in Chapter 7, often we will *not* want to use equally spaced intervals in an experiment. Nevertheless, trend analyses are still possible with data obtained from such experiments. The only troublesome feature is that the sets of orthogonal polynomial coefficients must be calculated for the *specific spacings* represented in each individual experiment.

The sets of coefficients are calculated in a series of steps. We start with the linear coefficients, using information about the spacing of the levels of the independent variable and the general property of comparisons—namely, that the coefficients sum to zero—to allow the determination of a single unknown in the formulas. The quadratic coefficients are calculated next. The computational effort is more involved, as there are now *two* unknowns for which solutions must be found. The information needed for these determinations comes from the spacing of the levels, the general property of comparisons, and the requirement of orthogonality of comparisons—i.e., that the sum of pairs of corresponding coefficients equals zero.

We will construct sets of coefficients for two examples in this appendix, one with *equal* spacing, so that we can compare our handiwork with the tabled values, and one with *unequal* spacing. The general procedure that we will follow assumes equal sample sizes for the various treatment groups.

Equal Spacing on the Independent Variable

LINEAR COEFFICIENTS   In our first example we will assume that the independent variable is represented by four points with values of 2, 4, 6, and 8. We will start our calculations with the linear coefficients. We begin with the following formula representing any one of the linear coefficients:

$$\alpha_1 + X_i,$$

where α_1 is a constant and X_i stands for the numerical values of the *independent variable*. Next, we write this expression out for each of the four levels. This has been done in column 2 of Table B-1. (Some authors recommend that the X_i values be reduced to smaller multiples, X_i'. In the present case, X_i' would be 1, 2, 3, and 4. The reason for this suggestion is to reduce the magnitude of the numbers which are encountered in the calculations, especially with the higher-degree coefficients.)

TABLE B-1 *Calculation of Linear Coefficients (Equal Intervals)*

(1) X_i	(2) $\alpha_1 + X_i$	(3) Substitution	(4) c_{1i}
2	$\alpha_1 + 2$	$-5 + 2 =$	-3
4	$\alpha_1 + 4$	$-5 + 4 =$	-1
6	$\alpha_1 + 6$	$-5 + 6 =$	1
8	$\alpha_1 + 8$	$-5 + 8 =$	3

We now have the four coefficients represented by numbers and one unknown, α_1. We can solve for the unknown by employing the general requirement of a set of coefficients that they sum to zero [Eq. (6-4)]. That is, we will add the four coefficients and set the sum equal to zero. This will give us one equation and one unknown—sufficient information to permit us to solve for α_1. From Eq. (6-4),

$$\sum c_i = 0.$$

Substituting the four coefficients in Table B-1 in this equation, we have

$$(\alpha_1 + 2) + (\alpha_1 + 4) + (\alpha_1 + 6) + (\alpha_1 + 8) = 0,$$

$$4\alpha_1 + 20 = 0.$$

Solving for α_1,

$$4\alpha_1 = -20$$

$$\alpha_1 = -\tfrac{20}{4} = -5.$$

If we now substitute $\alpha_1 = -5$ in the formulas representing the four coefficients, we will obtain numerical values for the linear coefficients (c_{1i}). These substitutions are shown in column 3, and the final coefficients are given in column 4. As a check, we can verify that the coefficients sum to zero [Eq. (6-4)] and that the coefficients form a straight line when plotted against the independent variable.

QUADRATIC COEFFICIENTS   In order to calculate the quadratic coefficients, we begin with a formula representing one of these coefficients:

$$\alpha_2 + (\beta_2)(X_i) + (X_i)^2,$$

where α_2 and β_2 are constants and X_i refers to the values of the independent variable. These formulas are written for each coefficient in column 2 of Table B-2. Again, we can apply Eq. (6-4) and set the sum of the four coefficients to zero. That is,

$$(\alpha_2 + 2\beta_2 + 4) + (\alpha_2 + 4\beta_2 + 16) + (\alpha_2 + 6\beta_2 + 36) + (\alpha_2 + 8\beta_2 + 64) = 0,$$

$$4\alpha_2 + 20\beta_2 + 120 = 0. \tag{B-1}$$

This time, however, we have *one* equation and *two* unknowns, α_2 and β_2, which is not sufficient information to allow us to solve for the unknowns. We need

TABLE B-2   *Calculation of Quadratic Coefficients (Equal Intervals)*

(1) X_i	(2) $\alpha_2 + (\beta_2)(X_i) + (X_i)^2$	(3) c_{1i}	(4) $(c_{1i})(c_{2i})$	(5) Substitution	(6) c_{2i}
2	$\alpha_2 + 2\beta_2 + 4$	-3	$-3\alpha_2 - 6\beta_2 - 12$	$20 - 20 + 4 =$	4
4	$\alpha_2 + 4\beta_2 + 16$	-1	$-1\alpha_2 - 4\beta_2 - 16$	$20 - 40 + 16 =$	-4
6	$\alpha_2 + 6\beta_2 + 36$	1	$1\alpha_2 + 6\beta_2 + 36$	$20 - 60 + 36 =$	-4
8	$\alpha_2 + 8\beta_2 + 64$	3	$3\alpha_2 + 24\beta_2 + 192$	$20 - 80 + 64 =$	4

another equation involving these constants. This equation comes from the additional requirement of these coefficients that the set must be *independent* of the set of linear coefficients we have constructed already. This property is stated in Eq. (7-1):

$$\sum (c_i)(c_i') = 0.$$

We will now see how we can use this requirement to help in the determination of the two unknowns.

We apply Eq. (7-1) using the linear coefficients from Table B-1 (c_{1i}) and the formulas for the quadratic coefficients from Table B-2 (c_{2i}). The linear coefficients are entered in column 3 of Table B-2, and the products of corresponding coefficients—$(c_{1i})(c_{2i})$ or (column 2) × (column 3)—are given in column 4. From Eq. (7-1), then,

$$\sum (c_{1i})(c_{2i}) = 0.$$

Performing this summation on the products in column 4 of the table, we have

$$(-3\alpha_2 - 6\beta_2 - 12) + (-\alpha_2 - 4\beta_2 - 16)$$
$$+ (\alpha_2 + 6\beta_2 + 36) + (3\alpha_2 + 24\beta_2 + 192) = 0,$$
$$0\alpha_2 + 20\beta_2 + 200 = 0.$$

We can now solve for β_2:

$$20\beta_2 = -200$$
$$\beta_2 = -\tfrac{200}{20} = -10.$$

The other unknown, α_2, is obtained by substituting in Eq. (B-1) and solving for α_2:

$$4\alpha_2 + 20\beta_2 + 120 = 0,$$
$$4\alpha_2 + 20(-10) + 120 = 0,$$
$$4\alpha_2 - 200 + 120 = 0,$$
$$4\alpha_2 = 200 - 120 = 80,$$
$$\alpha_2 = \tfrac{80}{4} = 20.$$

The final steps involve the substitution of the values of the two unknowns into the original formulas (column 2) and the completion of the arithmetic. These two operations are enumerated in columns 5 and 6, respectively, of Table B-2. It will be noted that these coefficients are all multiples of 4. We can divide each coefficient by 4 and not change the nature of the comparison represented by the coefficients (see pp. 100–101 for a justification of this procedure.) The coefficients become

$$1, \quad -1, \quad -1, \quad \text{and} \quad 1.$$

We can compare the linear and quadratic coefficients we have just constructed with those listed in Table C-2 of Appendix C. They are identical.

Unequal Spacing on the Independent Variable

LINEAR COEFFICIENTS   In this example, suppose we decide to choose the levels of a particular independent variable over a wide range and to take cognizance of the fact that the basic functional relationship may be negatively accelerated—i.e., that changes will become progressively smaller as we increase the value of the independent variable. This is the justification for choosing the six values that appear in column 1 of Table B-3—smaller intervals at the lower end of the continuum to pick up the large changes expected in this portion of the function. In column 2, we write the linear coefficients in the form

$$\alpha_1 + X_i.$$

TABLE B-3   *Calculation of Linear Coefficients (Unequal Intervals)*

(1) X_i	(2) $\alpha_1 + X_i$	(3) Substitution	(4) c_{1i}
1	$\alpha_1 + \ 1$	$-26 + \ 1 =$	-25
5	$\alpha_1 + \ 5$	$-26 + \ 5 =$	-21
10	$\alpha_1 + 10$	$-26 + 10 =$	-16
20	$\alpha_1 + 20$	$-26 + 20 =$	-6
40	$\alpha_1 + 40$	$-26 + 40 =$	14
80	$\alpha_1 + 80$	$-26 + 80 =$	54

Then we set the sum of these equations to zero and solve for α_1:

$$\sum c_{1i} = 0,$$

$$(\alpha_1 + 1) + (\alpha_1 + 5) + \cdots + (\alpha_1 + 40) + (\alpha_1 + 80) = 0,$$

$$6\alpha_1 + 156 = 0.$$

Solving for α_1,

$$6\alpha_1 = -156$$

$$\alpha_1 = -\tfrac{156}{6} = -26.$$

We can now substitute this value for α_1 in the original formulas (column 2) and solve for the linear coefficients. These two steps are enumerated in columns 3 and 4 of the table, respectively.

QUADRATIC COEFFICIENTS   The quadratic coefficients are calculated in the same manner as they were for equal intervals. In column 2 of Table B-4 are listed the formulas for the six quadratic coefficients. If we sum the coefficients in column 2 and set this sum to zero, we obtain an equation with two unknowns; that is,

$$\sum c_{2i} = 0,$$

$$(\alpha_2 + \beta_2 + 1) + (\alpha_2 + 5\beta_2 + 25) + \cdots$$

$$+ (\alpha_2 + 40\beta_2 + 1600) + (\alpha_2 + 80\beta_2 + 6400) = 0,$$

$$6\alpha_2 + 156\beta_2 + 8526 = 0. \tag{B-2}$$

In order to solve for the two unknowns, we need a second equation. This equation is obtained from the orthogonality requirement of the linear and quadratic coefficients. The linear coefficients from Table B-3 are entered in column 3, and the products of the linear and quadratic coefficients—$(c_{1i})(c_{2i})$ or (column 2) × (column 3)—are enumerated in column 4 of Table B-4. Setting the sum of these products to zero guarantees orthogonality—i.e., Eq. (7-1). Specifically, we have

$$(-25\alpha_2 - 25\beta_2 - 25) + (-21\alpha_2 - 105\beta_2 - 525) + \cdots$$

$$+ (14\alpha_2 + 560\beta_2 + 22{,}400) + (54\alpha_2 + 4320\beta_2 + 345{,}600) = 0,$$

$$0\alpha_2 + 4470\beta_2 + 363{,}450 = 0.$$

Solving for β_2,

$$4470\beta_2 = -363{,}450,$$

$$\beta_2 = -\frac{363{,}450}{4470} = -81.309.$$

If we substitute in Eq. (B-2), we can solve for α_2:

$$6\alpha_2 + 156\beta_2 + 8526 = 0,$$

$$6\alpha_2 + 156(-81.309) + 8526 = 0,$$

$$6\alpha_2 - 12{,}684.204 + 8526 = 0,$$

$$6\alpha_2 = 12{,}684.204 - 8526 = 4158.204,$$

$$\alpha_2 = \frac{4158.204}{6} = 693.034.$$

The values for the two unknowns are now substituted in the formulas listed in column 2 and the quadratic coefficients are obtained by the appropriate additions and subtractions. This is accomplished in the last two columns of Table B-4.

COMPUTATIONAL CHECKS   It is generally a good idea to check the sets of coefficients for their presumed properties: (1) Plot the sets to see that the appropriate trend component is present. (2) Check to see that the sums of

TABLE B-4 Calculation of Quadratic Coefficients (Unequal Intervals)

(1) X_i	(2) $\alpha_2 + (\beta_2)(X_i) + (X_i)^2$	(3) c_{1i}	(4) $(c_{1i})(c_{2i})$	(5) Substitution	(6) c_{2i}
1	$\alpha_2 + 1\beta_2 + 1$	-25	$-25\alpha_2 - 25\beta_2 - 25$	$693.034 - 81.309 + 1 =$	612.725
5	$\alpha_2 + 5\beta_2 + 25$	-21	$-21\alpha_2 - 105\beta_2 - 525$	$693.034 - 406.545 + 25 =$	311.489
10	$\alpha_2 + 10\beta_2 + 100$	-16	$-16\alpha_2 - 160\beta_2 - 1600$	$693.034 - 813.090 + 100 =$	-20.056
20	$\alpha_2 + 20\beta_2 + 400$	-6	$-6\alpha_2 - 120\beta_2 - 2400$	$693.034 - 1626.180 + 400 =$	-533.146
40	$\alpha_2 + 40\beta_2 + 1600$	14	$14\alpha_2 + 560\beta_2 + 22{,}400$	$693.034 - 3252.360 + 1600 =$	-959.326
80	$\alpha_2 + 80\beta_2 + 6400$	54	$54\alpha_2 + 4320\beta_2 + 345{,}600$	$693.034 - 6504.720 + 6400 =$	588.314

the coefficients equal zero. (3) Check for orthogonality by summing the products of the coefficients.

We should expect some rounding error when we are dealing with fractional coefficients. For both sets of coefficients, the requirement is met that the sums of the coefficients equal zero. That is,

Linear: $\qquad\qquad\qquad\qquad\qquad -25 - 21 - 16 - 6 + 14 + 54 = 0,$

Quadratic: $\quad 612.725 + 311.489 - 20.056 - 533.146 - 959.326 + 588.314 = 0.$

The result of the test for orthogonality is not zero, however. More specifically,

$$(-25)(612.725) + (-21)(311.489) + (-16)(-20.056)$$
$$+ (-6)(-533.146) + (14)(-959.326) + (54)(588.314) \overset{?}{=} 0,$$
$$-15,318.125 - 6541.269 + 320.896 + 3198.876$$
$$-13,430.564 + 31,768.956 = -1.230.$$

Considering the size of the quadratic coefficients, however, this discrepancy due to rounding error should make little difference in the calculation of the $SS_{A_{\text{quadratic}}}$.

Computation of Higher-Degree Coefficients

The calculation of the higher-degree orthogonal polynomial coefficients is accomplished in the same manner as the quadratic coefficients in our two examples:

1. Apply the general formula for the coefficients to each value of X_i. The formula for the cubic coefficients is

$$\alpha_3 + (\beta_3)(X_i) + (\gamma_3)(X_i)^2 + (X_i)^3,$$

and for the quartic coefficient is

$$\alpha_4 + (\beta_4)(X_i) + (\gamma_4)(X_i)^2 + (\delta_4)(X_i)^3 + (X_i)^4.$$

2. Set the sum of these formulas equal to zero [Eq. (6-4)]. This step gives us one equation and several unknowns.

3. Additional equations involving these unknowns are obtained by ensuring that the requirement of orthogonality holds [Eq. (7-1)] for each of the sets of coefficients constructed for the lower-degree components. For the cubic coefficients there are two equations (linear × cubic and quadratic × cubic), and for the quartic coefficients there are three (linear × quartic, quadratic × quartic, and cubic × quartic).

4. Solve for the different unknowns by using the sets of equations obtained in steps 2 and 3. There will be sufficient information to allow the solution of the unknowns; e.g., for the cubic coefficients there will be three equations and three unknowns, and for the quartic coefficients there will be four equations and four unknowns.

5. Substitute the constants into the original formulas for the coefficients (step 1) to obtain the desired coefficients.

EXERCISES FOR APPENDIX B[1]

1. An experiment is conducted in which the effect on the recall of a list of words is studied as a function of the number of trials on a second list of unrelated words. There are three basic groups, one group receiving one trial on the second list, another receiving five trials on the second list, and a third receiving 20 trials. There are $s = 20$ subjects in treatment condition. The following set of data was obtained:

Number of Trials:	1 Trial	5 Trials	20 Trials
Treatment Sums (A_i):	241	170	130

In addition, $\sum (AS)^2 = 5545$.

(a) Conduct a one-way analysis of variance on these data.

(b) Conduct a trend analysis, constructing your own orthogonal polynomial coefficients. Construct the two sets of coefficients by the procedure outlined in the appendix. (Note: Although you could obtain the quadratic sum of squares by subtraction, don't!)

---

[1] The answer to this problem is found in Appendix D.

appendix c

STATISTICAL TABLES

TABLE C-1 *Critical Values of the F Distribution*

df for denom.	α	df for numerator																	
		1	2	3	4	5	6	7	8	9	10	12	15	20	24	30	40	60	∞
3	.25	2.02	2.28	2.36	2.39	2.41	2.42	2.43	2.44	2.44	2.44	2.45	2.46	2.46	2.46	2.47	2.47	2.47	2.47
	.10	5.54	5.46	5.39	5.34	5.31	5.28	5.27	5.25	5.24	5.23	5.22	5.20	5.18	5.18	5.17	5.16	5.15	5.13
	.05	10.1	9.55	9.28	9.12	9.01	8.94	8.89	8.85	8.81	8.79	8.74	8.70	8.66	8.64	8.62	8.59	8.57	8.53
	.025	17.4	16.0	15.4	15.1	14.9	14.7	14.6	14.5	14.5	14.4	14.3	14.2	14.2	14.1	14.1	14.0	14.0	13.9
	.01	34.1	30.8	29.5	28.7	28.2	27.9	27.7	27.5	27.4	27.2	27.0	26.9	26.7	26.6	26.5	26.4	26.3	26.1
	.001	167	148	141	137	135	133	132	131	130	129	128	127	126	126	125	125	124	124
4	.25	1.81	2.00	2.05	2.06	2.07	2.08	2.08	2.08	2.08	2.08	2.08	2.08	2.08	2.08	2.08	2.08	2.08	2.08
	.10	4.54	4.32	4.19	4.11	4.05	4.01	3.98	3.95	3.94	3.92	3.90	3.87	3.84	3.83	3.82	3.80	3.79	3.76
	.05	7.71	6.94	6.59	6.39	6.26	6.16	6.09	6.04	6.00	5.96	5.91	5.86	5.80	5.77	5.75	5.72	5.69	5.63
	.025	12.2	10.6	9.98	9.60	9.36	9.20	9.07	8.98	8.90	8.84	8.75	8.66	8.56	8.51	8.46	8.41	8.36	8.26
	.01	21.2	18.0	16.7	16.0	15.5	15.2	15.0	14.8	14.7	14.6	14.4	14.2	14.0	13.9	13.8	13.8	13.6	13.5
	.001	74.1	61.2	56.2	53.4	51.7	50.5	49.7	49.0	48.5	48.0	47.4	46.8	46.1	45.8	45.4	45.1	44.8	44.0
5	.25	1.69	1.85	1.88	1.89	1.89	1.89	1.89	1.89	1.89	1.89	1.89	1.89	1.88	1.88	1.88	1.88	1.87	1.87
	.10	4.06	3.78	3.62	3.52	3.45	3.40	3.37	3.34	3.32	3.30	3.27	3.24	3.21	3.19	3.17	3.16	3.14	3.10
	.05	6.61	5.79	5.41	5.19	5.05	4.95	4.88	4.82	4.77	4.74	4.68	4.62	4.56	4.53	4.50	4.46	4.43	4.36
	.025	10.0	8.43	7.76	7.39	7.15	6.98	6.85	6.76	6.68	6.62	6.52	6.43	6.33	6.28	6.23	6.18	6.12	6.02
	.01	16.3	13.3	12.1	11.4	11.0	10.7	10.5	10.3	10.2	10.0	9.89	9.72	9.55	9.47	9.38	9.29	9.20	9.02
	.001	47.2	37.1	33.2	31.1	29.8	28.8	28.2	27.6	27.2	26.9	26.4	25.9	25.4	25.1	24.9	24.6	24.3	23.8
6	.25	1.62	1.76	1.78	1.79	1.79	1.78	1.78	1.78	1.77	1.77	1.77	1.76	1.76	1.75	1.75	1.75	1.74	1.74
	.10	3.78	3.46	3.29	3.18	3.11	3.05	3.01	2.98	2.96	2.94	2.90	2.87	2.84	2.82	2.80	2.78	2.76	2.72
	.05	5.99	5.14	4.76	4.53	4.39	4.28	4.21	4.15	4.10	4.06	4.00	3.94	3.87	3.84	3.81	3.77	3.74	3.67
	.025	8.81	7.26	6.60	6.23	5.99	5.82	5.70	5.60	5.52	5.46	5.37	5.27	5.17	5.12	5.07	5.01	4.96	4.85
	.01	13.8	10.9	9.78	9.15	8.75	8.47	8.26	8.10	7.98	7.87	7.72	7.56	7.40	7.31	7.23	7.14	7.06	6.88
	.001	35.5	27.0	23.7	21.9	20.8	20.0	19.5	19.0	18.7	18.4	18.0	17.6	17.1	16.9	16.7	16.4	16.2	15.8

TABLE C-1 (*Cont.*)

df for denom.	α	\multicolumn{18}{c}{df for numerator}

df for denom.	α	1	2	3	4	5	6	7	8	9	10	12	15	20	24	30	40	60	∞
7	.25	1.57	1.70	1.72	1.72	1.71	1.71	1.70	1.70	1.69	1.69	1.68	1.68	1.67	1.67	1.66	1.66	1.65	1.65
	.10	3.59	3.26	3.07	2.96	2.88	2.83	2.78	2.75	2.72	2.70	2.67	2.63	2.59	2.58	2.56	2.54	2.51	2.47
	.05	**5.59**	**4.74**	**4.35**	**4.12**	**3.97**	**3.87**	**3.79**	**3.73**	**3.68**	**3.64**	**3.57**	**3.51**	**3.44**	**3.41**	**3.38**	**3.34**	**3.30**	**3.23**
	.025	8.07	6.54	5.89	5.52	5.29	5.12	4.99	4.90	4.82	4.76	4.67	4.57	4.47	4.42	4.36	4.31	4.25	4.14
	.01	**12.2**	**9.55**	**8.45**	**7.85**	**7.46**	**7.19**	**6.99**	**6.84**	**6.72**	**6.62**	**6.47**	**6.31**	**6.16**	**6.07**	**5.99**	**5.91**	**5.82**	**5.65**
	.001	29.2	21.7	18.8	17.2	16.2	15.5	15.0	14.6	14.3	14.1	13.7	13.3	12.9	12.7	12.5	12.3	12.1	11.7
8	.25	1.54	1.66	1.67	1.66	1.66	1.65	1.64	1.64	1.63	1.63	1.62	1.62	1.61	1.60	1.60	1.59	1.59	1.58
	.10	3.46	3.11	2.92	2.81	2.73	2.67	2.62	2.59	2.56	2.54	2.50	2.46	2.42	2.40	2.38	2.36	2.34	2.29
	.05	**5.32**	**4.46**	**4.07**	**3.84**	**3.69**	**3.58**	**3.50**	**3.44**	**3.39**	**3.35**	**3.28**	**3.22**	**3.15**	**3.12**	**3.08**	**3.04**	**3.01**	**2.93**
	.025	7.57	6.06	5.42	5.05	4.82	4.65	4.53	4.43	4.36	4.30	4.20	4.10	4.00	3.95	3.89	3.84	3.78	3.67
	.01	**11.3**	**8.65**	**7.59**	**7.01**	**6.63**	**6.37**	**6.18**	**6.03**	**5.91**	**5.81**	**5.67**	**5.52**	**5.36**	**5.28**	**5.20**	**5.12**	**5.03**	**4.86**
	.001	25.4	18.5	15.8	14.4	13.5	12.9	12.4	12.0	11.8	11.5	11.2	10.8	10.5	10.3	10.1	9.92	9.73	9.33
9	.25	1.51	1.62	1.63	1.63	1.62	1.61	1.60	1.60	1.59	1.59	1.58	1.57	1.56	1.56	1.55	1.54	1.54	1.53
	.10	3.36	3.01	2.81	2.69	2.61	2.55	2.51	2.47	2.44	2.42	2.38	2.34	2.30	2.28	2.25	2.23	2.21	2.16
	.05	**5.12**	**4.26**	**3.86**	**3.63**	**3.48**	**3.37**	**3.29**	**3.23**	**3.18**	**3.14**	**3.07**	**3.01**	**2.94**	**2.90**	**2.86**	**2.83**	**2.79**	**2.71**
	.025	7.21	5.71	5.08	4.72	4.48	4.32	4.20	4.10	4.03	3.96	3.87	3.77	3.67	3.61	3.56	3.51	3.45	3.33
	.01	**10.6**	**8.02**	**6.99**	**6.42**	**6.06**	**5.80**	**5.61**	**5.47**	**5.35**	**5.26**	**5.11**	**4.96**	**4.81**	**4.73**	**4.65**	**4.57**	**4.48**	**4.31**
	.001	22.9	16.4	13.9	12.6	11.7	11.1	10.7	10.4	10.1	9.89	9.57	9.24	8.90	8.72	8.55	8.37	8.19	7.81
10	.25	1.49	1.60	1.60	1.59	1.59	1.58	1.57	1.56	1.56	1.55	1.54	1.53	1.52	1.52	1.51	1.51	1.50	1.48
	.10	3.29	2.92	2.73	2.61	2.52	2.46	2.41	2.38	2.35	2.32	2.28	2.24	2.20	2.18	2.16	2.13	2.11	2.06
	.05	**4.96**	**4.10**	**3.71**	**3.48**	**3.33**	**3.22**	**3.14**	**3.07**	**3.02**	**2.98**	**2.91**	**2.85**	**2.77**	**2.74**	**2.70**	**2.66**	**2.62**	**2.54**
	.025	6.94	5.46	4.83	4.47	4.24	4.07	3.95	3.85	3.78	3.72	3.62	3.52	3.42	3.37	3.31	3.26	3.20	3.08
	.01	**10.0**	**7.56**	**6.55**	**5.99**	**5.64**	**5.39**	**5.20**	**5.06**	**4.94**	**4.85**	**4.71**	**4.56**	**4.41**	**4.33**	**4.25**	**4.17**	**4.08**	**3.91**
	.001	21.0	14.9	12.6	11.3	10.5	9.92	9.52	9.20	8.96	8.75	8.45	8.13	7.80	7.64	7.47	7.30	7.12	6.76

TABLE C-1 (*Cont.*)

df for numerator

df for denom.	α	1	2	3	4	5	6	7	8	9	10	12	15	20	24	30	40	60	∞
11	.25	1.47	1.58	1.58	1.57	1.56	1.55	1.54	1.53	1.53	1.52	1.51	1.50	1.49	1.49	1.48	1.47	1.47	1.45
	.10	3.23	2.86	2.66	2.54	2.45	2.39	2.34	2.30	2.27	2.25	2.21	2.17	2.12	2.10	2.08	2.05	2.03	1.97
	.05	**4.84**	**3.98**	**3.59**	**3.36**	**3.20**	**3.09**	**3.01**	**2.95**	**2.90**	**2.85**	**2.79**	**2.72**	**2.65**	**2.61**	**2.57**	**2.53**	**2.49**	**2.40**
	.025	6.72	5.26	4.63	4.28	4.04	3.88	3.76	3.66	3.59	3.53	3.43	3.33	3.23	3.17	3.12	3.06	3.00	2.88
	.01	**9.65**	**7.21**	**6.22**	**5.67**	**5.32**	**5.07**	**4.89**	**4.74**	**4.63**	**4.54**	**4.40**	**4.25**	**4.10**	**4.02**	**3.94**	**3.86**	**3.78**	**3.60**
	.001	19.7	13.8	11.6	10.4	9.58	9.05	8.66	8.35	8.12	7.92	7.63	7.32	7.01	6.85	6.68	6.52	6.35	6.00
12	.25	1.46	1.56	1.56	1.55	1.54	1.53	1.52	1.51	1.51	1.50	1.49	1.48	1.47	1.46	1.45	1.45	1.44	1.42
	.10	3.18	2.81	2.61	2.48	2.39	2.33	2.28	2.24	2.21	2.19	2.15	2.10	2.06	2.04	2.01	1.99	1.96	1.90
	.05	**4.75**	**3.89**	**3.49**	**3.26**	**3.11**	**3.00**	**2.91**	**2.85**	**2.80**	**2.75**	**2.69**	**2.62**	**2.54**	**2.51**	**2.47**	**2.43**	**2.38**	**2.30**
	.025	6.55	5.10	4.47	4.12	3.89	3.73	3.61	3.51	3.44	3.37	3.28	3.18	3.07	3.02	2.96	2.91	2.85	2.72
	.01	**9.33**	**6.93**	**5.95**	**5.41**	**5.06**	**4.82**	**4.64**	**4.50**	**4.39**	**4.30**	**4.16**	**4.01**	**3.86**	**3.78**	**3.70**	**3.62**	**3.54**	**3.36**
	.001	18.6	13.0	10.8	9.63	8.89	8.38	8.00	7.71	7.48	7.29	7.00	6.71	6.40	6.25	6.09	5.93	5.76	5.42
13	.25	1.45	1.55	1.55	1.53	1.52	1.51	1.50	1.49	1.49	1.48	1.47	1.46	1.45	1.44	1.43	1.42	1.42	1.40
	.10	3.14	2.76	2.56	2.43	2.35	2.28	2.23	2.20	2.16	2.14	2.10	2.05	2.01	1.98	1.96	1.93	1.90	1.85
	.05	**4.67**	**3.81**	**3.41**	**3.18**	**3.03**	**2.92**	**2.83**	**2.77**	**2.71**	**2.67**	**2.60**	**2.53**	**2.46**	**2.42**	**2.38**	**2.34**	**2.30**	**2.21**
	.025	6.41	4.97	4.35	4.00	3.77	3.60	3.48	3.39	3.31	3.25	3.15	3.05	2.95	2.89	2.84	2.78	2.72	2.60
	.01	**9.07**	**6.70**	**5.74**	**5.21**	**4.86**	**4.62**	**4.44**	**4.30**	**4.19**	**4.10**	**3.96**	**3.82**	**3.66**	**3.59**	**3.51**	**3.43**	**3.34**	**3.17**
	.001	17.8	12.3	10.2	9.07	8.35	7.86	7.49	7.21	6.98	6.80	6.52	6.23	5.93	5.78	5.63	5.47	5.30	4.97
14	.25	1.44	1.53	1.53	1.52	1.51	1.50	1.49	1.48	1.47	1.46	1.45	1.44	1.43	1.42	1.41	1.41	1.40	1.38
	.10	3.10	2.73	2.52	2.39	2.31	2.24	2.19	2.15	2.12	2.10	2.05	2.01	1.96	1.94	1.91	1.89	1.86	1.80
	.05	**4.60**	**3.74**	**3.34**	**3.11**	**2.96**	**2.85**	**2.76**	**2.70**	**2.65**	**2.60**	**2.53**	**2.46**	**2.39**	**2.35**	**2.31**	**2.27**	**2.22**	**2.13**
	.025	6.30	4.86	4.24	3.89	3.66	3.50	3.38	3.29	3.21	3.15	3.05	2.95	2.84	2.79	2.73	2.67	2.61	2.49
	.01	**8.86**	**6.51**	**5.56**	**5.04**	**4.69**	**4.46**	**4.28**	**4.14**	**4.03**	**3.94**	**3.80**	**3.66**	**3.51**	**3.43**	**3.35**	**3.27**	**3.18**	**3.00**
	.001	17.1	11.8	9.73	8.62	7.92	7.43	7.08	6.80	6.58	6.40	6.13	5.85	5.56	5.41	5.25	5.10	4.94	4.60

TABLE C-1 *(Cont.)*

df for denom.	α	\multicolumn{18}{c}{df for numerator}

df for denom.	α	1	2	3	4	5	6	7	8	9	10	12	15	20	24	30	40	60	∞
15	.25	1.43	1.52	1.52	1.51	1.49	1.48	1.47	1.46	1.46	1.45	1.44	1.43	1.41	1.41	1.40	1.39	1.38	1.36
	.10	3.07	2.70	2.49	2.36	2.27	2.21	2.16	2.12	2.09	2.06	2.02	1.97	1.92	1.90	1.87	1.85	1.82	1.76
	.05	**4.54**	**3.68**	**3.29**	**3.06**	**2.90**	**2.79**	**2.71**	**2.64**	**2.59**	**2.54**	**2.48**	**2.40**	**2.33**	**2.29**	**2.25**	**2.20**	**2.16**	**2.07**
	.025	6.20	4.77	4.15	3.80	3.58	3.41	3.29	3.20	3.12	3.06	2.96	2.86	2.76	2.70	2.64	2.59	2.52	2.40
	.01	**8.68**	**6.36**	**5.42**	**4.89**	**4.56**	**4.32**	**4.14**	**4.00**	**3.89**	**3.80**	**3.67**	**3.52**	**3.37**	**3.29**	**3.21**	**3.13**	**3.05**	**2.87**
	.001	16.6	11.3	9.34	8.25	7.57	7.09	6.74	6.47	6.26	6.08	5.81	5.54	5.25	5.10	4.95	4.80	4.64	4.31
16	.25	1.42	1.51	1.51	1.50	1.48	1.47	1.46	1.45	1.44	1.44	1.43	1.41	1.40	1.39	1.38	1.37	1.36	1.34
	.10	3.05	2.67	2.46	2.33	2.24	2.18	2.13	2.09	2.06	2.03	1.99	1.94	1.89	1.87	1.84	1.81	1.78	1.72
	.05	**4.49**	**3.63**	**3.24**	**3.01**	**2.85**	**2.74**	**2.66**	**2.59**	**2.54**	**2.49**	**2.42**	**2.35**	**2.28**	**2.24**	**2.19**	**2.15**	**2.11**	**2.01**
	.025	6.12	4.69	4.08	3.73	3.50	3.34	3.22	3.12	3.05	2.99	2.89	2.79	2.68	2.63	2.57	2.51	2.45	2.32
	.01	**8.53**	**6.23**	**5.29**	**4.77**	**4.44**	**4.20**	**4.03**	**3.89**	**3.78**	**3.69**	**3.55**	**3.41**	**3.26**	**3.18**	**3.10**	**3.02**	**2.93**	**2.75**
	.001	16.1	11.0	9.00	7.94	7.27	6.81	6.46	6.19	5.98	5.81	5.55	5.27	4.99	4.85	4.70	4.54	4.39	4.06
17	.25	1.42	1.51	1.50	1.49	1.47	1.46	1.45	1.44	1.43	1.43	1.41	1.40	1.39	1.38	1.37	1.36	1.35	1.33
	.10	3.03	2.64	2.44	2.31	2.22	2.15	2.10	2.06	2.03	2.00	1.96	1.91	1.86	1.84	1.81	1.78	1.75	1.69
	.05	**4.45**	**3.59**	**3.20**	**2.96**	**2.81**	**2.70**	**2.61**	**2.55**	**2.49**	**2.45**	**2.38**	**2.31**	**2.23**	**2.19**	**2.15**	**2.10**	**2.06**	**1.96**
	.025	6.04	4.62	4.01	3.66	3.44	3.28	3.16	3.06	2.98	2.92	2.82	2.72	2.62	2.56	2.50	2.44	2.38	2.25
	.01	**8.40**	**6.11**	**5.18**	**4.67**	**4.34**	**4.10**	**3.93**	**3.79**	**3.68**	**3.59**	**3.46**	**3.31**	**3.16**	**3.08**	**3.00**	**2.92**	**2.83**	**2.65**
	.001	15.7	10.7	8.73	7.68	7.02	6.56	6.22	5.96	5.75	5.58	5.32	5.05	4.78	4.63	4.48	4.33	4.18	3.85
18	.25	1.41	1.50	1.49	1.48	1.46	1.45	1.44	1.43	1.42	1.42	1.40	1.39	1.38	1.37	1.36	1.35	1.34	1.32
	.10	3.01	2.62	2.42	2.29	2.20	2.13	2.08	2.04	2.00	1.98	1.93	1.89	1.84	1.81	1.78	1.75	1.72	1.66
	.05	**4.41**	**3.55**	**3.16**	**2.93**	**2.77**	**2.66**	**2.58**	**2.51**	**2.46**	**2.41**	**2.34**	**2.27**	**2.19**	**2.15**	**2.11**	**2.06**	**2.02**	**1.92**
	.025	5.98	4.56	3.95	3.61	3.38	3.22	3.10	3.01	2.93	2.87	2.77	2.67	2.56	2.50	2.44	2.38	2.32	2.19
	.01	**8.29**	**6.01**	**5.09**	**4.58**	**4.25**	**4.01**	**3.84**	**3.71**	**3.60**	**3.51**	**3.37**	**3.23**	**3.08**	**3.00**	**2.92**	**2.84**	**2.75**	**2.57**
	.001	15.4	10.4	8.49	7.46	6.81	6.35	6.02	5.76	5.56	5.39	5.13	4.87	4.59	4.45	4.30	4.15	4.00	3.67

TABLE C-1 (*Cont.*)

df for denom.	α	df for numerator																	
		1	2	3	4	5	6	7	8	9	10	12	15	20	24	30	40	60	∞
19	.25	1.41	1.49	1.49	1.47	1.46	1.44	1.43	1.42	1.41	1.41	1.40	1.38	1.37	1.36	1.35	1.34	1.33	1.30
	.10	2.99	2.61	2.40	2.27	2.18	2.11	2.06	2.02	1.98	1.96	1.91	1.86	1.81	1.79	1.76	1.73	1.70	1.63
	.05	4.38	3.52	3.13	2.90	2.74	2.63	2.54	2.48	2.42	2.38	2.31	2.23	2.16	2.11	2.07	2.03	1.98	1.88
	.025	5.92	4.51	3.90	3.56	3.33	3.17	3.05	2.96	2.88	2.82	2.72	2.62	2.51	2.45	2.39	2.33	2.27	2.13
	.01	8.18	5.93	5.01	4.50	4.17	3.94	3.77	3.63	3.52	3.43	3.30	3.15	3.00	2.92	2.84	2.76	2.67	2.49
	.001	15.1	10.2	8.28	7.26	6.62	6.18	5.85	5.59	5.39	5.22	4.97	4.70	4.43	4.29	4.14	3.99	3.84	3.51
20	.25	1.40	1.49	1.48	1.47	1.45	1.44	1.43	1.42	1.41	1.40	1.39	1.37	1.36	1.35	1.34	1.33	1.32	1.29
	.10	2.97	2.59	2.38	2.25	2.16	2.09	2.04	2.00	1.96	1.94	1.89	1.84	1.79	1.77	1.74	1.71	1.68	1.61
	.05	4.35	3.49	3.10	2.87	2.71	2.60	2.51	2.45	2.39	2.35	2.28	2.20	2.12	2.08	2.04	1.99	1.95	1.84
	.025	5.87	4.46	3.86	3.51	3.29	3.13	3.01	2.91	2.84	2.77	2.68	2.57	2.46	2.41	2.35	2.29	2.22	2.09
	.01	8.10	5.85	4.94	4.43	4.10	3.87	3.70	3.56	3.46	3.37	3.23	3.09	2.94	2.86	2.78	2.69	2.61	2.42
	.001	14.8	9.95	8.10	7.10	6.46	6.02	5.69	5.44	5.24	5.08	4.82	4.56	4.29	4.15	4.00	3.86	3.70	3.38
22	.25	1.40	1.48	1.47	1.45	1.44	1.42	1.41	1.40	1.39	1.39	1.37	1.36	1.34	1.33	1.32	1.31	1.30	1.28
	.10	2.95	2.56	2.35	2.22	2.13	2.06	2.01	1.97	1.93	1.90	1.86	1.81	1.76	1.73	1.70	1.67	1.64	1.57
	.05	4.30	3.44	3.05	2.82	2.66	2.55	2.46	2.40	2.34	2.30	2.23	2.15	2.07	2.03	1.98	1.94	1.89	1.78
	.025	5.79	4.38	3.78	3.44	3.22	3.05	2.93	2.84	2.76	2.70	2.60	2.50	2.39	2.33	2.27	2.21	2.14	2.00
	.01	7.95	5.72	4.82	4.31	3.99	3.76	3.59	3.45	3.35	3.26	3.12	2.98	2.83	2.75	2.67	2.58	2.50	2.31
	.001	14.4	9.61	7.80	6.81	6.19	5.76	5.44	5.19	4.99	4.83	4.58	4.33	4.06	3.92	3.78	3.63	3.48	3.15
24	.25	1.39	1.47	1.46	1.44	1.43	1.41	1.40	1.39	1.38	1.38	1.36	1.35	1.33	1.32	1.31	1.30	1.29	1.26
	.10	2.93	2.54	2.33	2.19	2.10	2.04	1.98	1.94	1.91	1.88	1.83	1.78	1.73	1.70	1.67	1.64	1.61	1.53
	.05	4.26	3.40	3.01	2.78	2.62	2.51	2.42	2.36	2.30	2.25	2.18	2.11	2.03	1.98	1.94	1.89	1.84	1.73
	.025	5.72	4.32	3.72	3.38	3.15	2.99	2.87	2.78	2.70	2.64	2.54	2.44	2.33	2.27	2.21	2.15	2.08	1.94
	.01	7.82	5.61	4.72	4.22	3.90	3.67	3.50	3.36	3.26	3.17	3.03	2.89	2.74	2.66	2.58	2.49	2.40	2.21
	.001	14.0	9.34	7.55	6.59	5.98	5.55	5.23	4.99	4.80	4.64	4.39	4.14	3.87	3.74	3.59	3.45	3.29	2.97

TABLE C-1 (*Cont.*)

df for denom.	α	\(df\) for numerator 1	2	3	4	5	6	7	8	9	10	12	15	20	24	30	40	60	∞
26	.25	1.38	1.46	1.45	1.44	1.42	1.41	1.39	1.38	1.37	1.37	1.35	1.34	1.32	1.31	1.30	1.29	1.28	1.25
	.10	2.91	2.52	2.31	2.17	2.08	2.01	1.96	1.92	1.88	1.86	1.81	1.76	1.71	1.68	1.65	1.61	1.58	1.50
	.05	4.23	3.37	2.98	2.74	2.59	2.47	2.39	2.32	2.27	2.22	2.15	2.07	1.99	1.95	1.90	1.85	1.80	1.69
	.025	5.66	4.27	3.67	3.33	3.10	2.94	2.82	2.73	2.65	2.59	2.49	2.39	2.28	2.22	2.16	2.09	2.03	1.88
	.01	7.72	5.53	4.64	4.14	3.82	3.59	3.42	3.29	3.18	3.09	2.96	2.81	2.66	2.58	2.50	2.42	2.33	2.13
	.001	13.7	9.12	7.36	6.41	5.80	5.38	5.07	4.83	4.64	4.48	4.24	3.99	3.72	3.59	3.44	3.30	3.15	2.82
28	.25	1.38	1.46	1.45	1.43	1.41	1.40	1.39	1.38	1.37	1.36	1.34	1.33	1.31	1.30	1.29	1.28	1.27	1.24
	.10	2.89	2.50	2.29	2.16	2.06	2.00	1.94	1.90	1.87	1.84	1.79	1.74	1.69	1.66	1.63	1.59	1.56	1.48
	.05	4.20	3.34	2.95	2.71	2.56	2.45	2.36	2.29	2.24	2.19	2.12	2.04	1.96	1.91	1.87	1.82	1.77	1.65
	.025	5.61	4.22	3.63	3.29	3.06	2.90	2.78	2.69	2.61	2.55	2.45	2.34	2.23	2.17	2.11	2.05	1.98	1.83
	.01	7.64	5.45	4.57	4.07	3.75	3.53	3.36	3.23	3.12	3.03	2.90	2.75	2.60	2.52	2.44	2.35	2.26	2.06
	.001	13.5	8.93	7.19	6.25	5.66	5.24	4.93	4.69	4.50	4.35	4.11	3.86	3.60	3.46	3.32	3.18	3.02	2.69
30	.25	1.38	1.45	1.44	1.42	1.41	1.39	1.38	1.37	1.36	1.35	1.34	1.32	1.30	1.29	1.28	1.27	1.26	1.23
	.10	2.88	2.49	2.28	2.14	2.05	1.98	1.93	1.88	1.85	1.82	1.77	1.72	1.67	1.64	1.61	1.57	1.54	1.46
	.05	4.17	3.32	2.92	2.69	2.53	2.42	2.33	2.27	2.21	2.16	2.09	2.01	1.93	1.89	1.84	1.79	1.74	1.62
	.025	5.57	4.18	3.59	3.25	3.03	2.87	2.75	2.65	2.57	2.51	2.41	2.31	2.20	2.14	2.07	2.01	1.94	1.79
	.01	7.56	5.39	4.51	4.02	3.70	3.47	3.30	3.17	3.07	2.98	2.84	2.70	2.55	2.47	2.39	2.30	2.21	2.01
	.001	13.3	8.77	7.05	6.12	5.53	5.12	4.82	4.58	4.39	4.24	4.00	3.75	3.49	3.36	3.22	3.07	2.92	2.59
40	.25	1.36	1.44	1.42	1.40	1.39	1.37	1.36	1.35	1.34	1.33	1.31	1.30	1.28	1.26	1.25	1.24	1.22	1.19
	.10	2.84	2.44	2.23	2.09	2.00	1.93	1.87	1.83	1.79	1.76	1.71	1.66	1.61	1.57	1.54	1.51	1.47	1.38
	.05	4.08	3.23	2.84	2.61	2.45	2.34	2.25	2.18	2.12	2.08	2.00	1.92	1.84	1.79	1.74	1.69	1.64	1.51
	.025	5.42	4.05	3.46	3.13	2.90	2.74	2.62	2.53	2.45	2.39	2.29	2.18	2.07	2.01	1.94	1.88	1.80	1.64
	.01	7.31	5.18	4.31	3.83	3.51	3.29	3.12	2.99	2.89	2.80	2.66	2.52	2.37	2.29	2.20	2.11	2.02	1.80
	.001	12.6	8.25	6.60	5.70	5.13	4.73	4.44	4.21	4.02	3.87	3.64	3.40	3.15	3.01	2.87	2.73	2.57	2.23

TABLE C-1 (*Cont.*)

										df for numerator									
df for denom.	α	1	2	3	4	5	6	7	8	9	10	12	15	20	24	30	40	60	∞
60	.25	1.35	1.42	1.41	1.38	1.37	1.35	1.33	1.32	1.31	1.30	1.29	1.27	1.25	1.24	1.22	1.21	1.19	1.15
	.10	2.79	2.39	2.18	2.04	1.95	1.87	1.82	1.77	1.74	1.71	1.66	1.60	1.54	1.51	1.48	1.44	1.40	1.29
	.05	4.00	3.15	2.76	2.53	2.37	2.25	2.17	2.10	2.04	1.99	1.92	1.84	1.75	1.70	1.65	1.59	1.53	1.39
	.025	5.29	3.93	3.34	3.01	2.79	2.63	2.51	2.41	2.33	2.27	2.17	2.06	1.94	1.88	1.82	1.74	1.67	1.48
	.01	7.08	4.98	4.13	3.65	3.34	3.12	2.95	2.82	2.72	2.63	2.50	2.35	2.20	2.12	2.03	1.94	1.84	1.60
	.001	12.0	7.76	6.17	5.31	4.76	4.37	4.09	3.87	3.69	3.54	3.31	3.08	2.83	2.69	2.55	2.41	2.25	1.89
120	.25	1.34	1.40	1.39	1.37	1.35	1.33	1.31	1.30	1.29	1.28	1.26	1.24	1.22	1.21	1.19	1.18	1.16	1.10
	.10	2.75	2.35	2.13	1.99	1.90	1.82	1.77	1.72	1.68	1.65	1.60	1.55	1.48	1.45	1.41	1.37	1.32	1.19
	.05	3.92	3.07	2.68	2.45	2.29	2.17	2.09	2.02	1.96	1.91	1.83	1.75	1.66	1.61	1.55	1.50	1.43	1.25
	.025	5.15	3.80	3.23	2.89	2.67	2.52	2.39	2.30	2.22	2.16	2.05	1.94	1.82	1.76	1.69	1.61	1.53	1.31
	.01	6.85	4.79	3.95	3.48	3.17	2.96	2.79	2.66	2.56	2.47	2.34	2.19	2.03	1.95	1.86	1.76	1.66	1.38
	.001	11.4	7.32	5.79	4.95	4.42	4.04	3.77	3.55	3.38	3.24	3.02	2.78	2.53	2.40	2.26	2.11	1.95	1.54
∞	.25	1.32	1.39	1.37	1.35	1.33	1.31	1.29	1.28	1.27	1.25	1.24	1.22	1.19	1.18	1.16	1.14	1.12	1.00
	.10	2.71	2.30	2.08	1.94	1.85	1.77	1.72	1.67	1.63	1.60	1.55	1.49	1.42	1.38	1.34	1.30	1.24	1.00
	.05	3.84	3.00	2.60	2.37	2.21	2.10	2.01	1.94	1.88	1.83	1.75	1.67	1.57	1.52	1.46	1.39	1.32	1.00
	.025	5.02	3.69	3.12	2.79	2.57	2.41	2.29	2.19	2.11	2.05	1.94	1.83	1.71	1.64	1.57	1.48	1.39	1.00
	.01	6.63	4.61	3.78	3.32	3.02	2.80	2.64	2.51	2.41	2.32	2.18	2.04	1.88	1.79	1.70	1.59	1.47	1.00
	.001	10.8	6.91	5.42	4.62	4.10	3.74	3.47	3.27	3.10	2.96	2.74	2.51	2.27	2.13	1.99	1.84	1.66	1.00

This table is abridged from Table 18 in *Biometrika tables for statisticians*, 2nd ed., vol. 1. (New York: Cambridge University Press, 1958), edited by E. S. Pearson and H. O. Hartley, by permission of the *Biometrika* Trustees.

TABLE C-2   *Coefficients of Orthogonal Polynomials*

k levels	Polynomial	Coefficients										$\sum (c_i)^2$
3	Linear	−1	0	1								2
	Quadratic	1	−2	1								6
4	Linear	−3	−1	1	3							20
	Quadratic	1	−1	−1	1							4
	Cubic	−1	3	−3	1							20
5	Linear	−2	−1	0	1	2						10
	Quadratic	2	−1	−2	−1	2						14
	Cubic	−1	2	0	−2	1						10
	Quartic	1	−4	6	−4	1						70
6	Linear	−5	−3	−1	1	3	5					70
	Quadratic	5	−1	−4	−4	−1	5					84
	Cubic	−5	7	4	−4	−7	5					180
	Quartic	1	−3	2	2	−3	1					28
	Quintic	−1	5	−10	10	−5	1					252
7	Linear	−3	−2	−1	0	1	2	3				28
	Quadratic	5	0	−3	−4	−3	0	5				84
	Cubic	−1	1	1	0	−1	−1	1				6
	Quartic	3	−7	1	6	1	−7	3				154
	Quintic	−1	4	−5	0	5	−4	1				84
8	Linear	−7	−5	−3	−1	1	3	5	7			168
	Quadratic	7	1	−3	−5	−5	−3	1	7			168
	Cubic	−7	5	7	3	−3	−7	−5	7			264
	Quartic	7	−13	−3	9	9	−3	−13	7			616
	Quintic	−7	23	−17	−15	15	17	−23	7			2184
9	Linear	−4	−3	−2	−1	0	1	2	3	4		60
	Quadratic	28	7	−8	−17	−20	−17	−8	7	28		2772
	Cubic	−14	7	13	9	0	−9	−13	−7	14		990
	Quartic	14	−21	−11	9	18	9	−11	−21	14		2002
	Quintic	−4	11	−4	−9	0	9	4	−11	4		468
10	Linear	−9	−7	−5	−3	−1	1	3	5	7	9	330
	Quadratic	6	2	−1	−3	−4	−4	−3	−1	2	6	132
	Cubic	−42	14	35	31	12	−12	−31	−35	−14	42	8580
	Quartic	18	−22	−17	3	18	18	3	−17	−22	18	2860
	Quintic	−6	14	−1	−11	−6	6	11	1	−14	6	780

This table is abridged from Table 23 in R. A. Fisher and F. Yates, *Statistical tables for biological, agricultural and medical research* (Edinburgh: Oliver and Boyd Ltd., 1963), by permission of the authors and publishers.

TABLE C-3 *Critical Values of the Studentized Range Statistic*

df_{error}	α	\multicolumn{10}{c}{r = number of means or number of steps between ordered means}
		2	3	4	5	6	7	8	9	10	11
5	.05	3.64	4.60	5.22	5.67	6.03	6.33	6.58	6.80	6.99	7.17
	.01	5.70	6.98	7.80	8.42	8.91	9.32	9.67	9.97	10.24	10.48
6	.05	3.46	4.34	4.90	5.30	5.63	5.90	6.12	6.32	6.49	6.65
	.01	5.24	6.33	7.03	7.56	7.97	8.32	8.61	8.87	9.10	9.30
7	.05	3.34	4.16	4.68	5.06	5.36	5.61	5.82	6.00	6.16	6.30
	.01	4.95	5.92	6.54	7.01	7.37	7.68	7.94	8.17	8.37	8.55
8	.05	3.26	4.04	4.53	4.89	5.17	5.40	5.60	5.77	5.92	6.05
	.01	4.75	5.64	6.20	6.62	6.96	7.24	7.47	7.68	7.86	8.03
9	.05	3.20	3.95	4.41	4.76	5.02	5.24	5.43	5.59	5.74	5.87
	.01	4.60	5.43	5.96	6.35	6.66	6.91	7.13	7.33	7.49	7.65
10	.05	3.15	3.88	4.33	4.65	4.91	5.12	5.30	5.46	5.60	5.72
	.01	4.48	5.27	5.77	6.14	6.43	6.67	6.87	7.05	7.21	7.36
11	.05	3.11	3.82	4.26	4.57	4.82	5.03	5.20	5.35	5.49	5.61
	.01	4.39	5.15	5.62	5.97	6.25	6.48	6.67	6.84	6.99	7.13
12	.05	3.08	3.77	4.20	4.51	4.75	4.95	5.12	5.27	5.39	5.51
	.01	4.32	5.05	5.50	5.84	6.10	6.32	6.51	6.67	6.81	6.94
13	.05	3.06	3.73	4.15	4.45	4.69	4.88	5.05	5.19	5.32	5.43
	.01	4.26	4.96	5.40	5.73	5.98	6.19	6.37	6.53	6.67	6.79
14	.05	3.03	3.70	4.11	4.41	4.64	4.83	4.99	5.13	5.25	5.36
	.01	4.21	4.89	5.32	5.63	5.88	6.08	6.26	6.41	6.54	6.66
15	.05	3.01	3.67	4.08	4.37	4.59	4.78	4.94	5.08	5.20	5.31
	.01	4.17	4.84	5.25	5.56	5.80	5.99	6.16	6.31	6.44	6.55
16	.05	3.00	3.65	4.05	4.33	4.56	4.74	4.90	5.03	5.15	5.26
	.01	4.13	4.79	5.19	5.49	5.72	5.92	6.08	6.22	6.35	6.46
17	.05	2.98	3.63	4.02	4.30	4.52	4.70	4.86	4.99	5.11	5.21
	.01	4.10	4.74	5.14	5.43	5.66	5.85	6.01	6.15	6.27	6.38
18	.05	2.97	3.61	4.00	4.28	4.49	4.67	4.82	4.96	5.07	5.17
	.01	4.07	4.70	5.09	5.38	5.60	5.79	5.94	6.08	6.20	6.31
19	.05	2.96	3.59	3.98	4.25	4.47	4.65	4.79	4.92	5.04	5.14
	.01	4.05	4.67	5.05	5.33	5.55	5.73	5.89	6.02	6.14	6.25
20	.05	2.95	3.58	3.96	4.23	4.45	4.62	4.77	4.90	5.01	5.11
	.01	4.02	4.64	5.02	5.29	5.51	5.69	5.84	5.97	6.09	6.19
24	.05	2.92	3.53	3.90	4.17	4.37	4.54	4.68	4.81	4.92	5.01
	.01	3.96	4.55	4.91	5.17	5.37	5.54	5.69	5.81	5.92	6.02
30	.05	2.89	3.49	3.85	4.10	4.30	4.46	4.60	4.72	4.82	4.92
	.01	3.89	4.45	4.80	5.05	5.24	5.40	5.54	5.65	5.76	5.85
40	.05	2.86	3.44	3.79	4.04	4.23	4.39	4.52	4.63	4.73	4.82
	.01	3.82	4.37	4.70	4.93	5.11	5.26	5.39	5.50	5.60	5.69

TABLE C-3 (*Contd.*)

r = *number of means or number of steps between ordered means*

12	13	14	15	16	17	18	19	20	α	df_{error}
7.32	7.47	7.60	7.72	7.83	7.93	8.03	8.12	8.21	.05	5
10.70	10.89	11.08	11.24	11.40	11.55	11.68	11.81	11.93	.01	
6.79	6.92	7.03	7.14	7.24	7.34	7.43	7.51	7.59	.05	6
9.48	9.65	9.81	9.95	10.08	10.21	10.32	10.43	10.54	.01	
6.43	6.55	6.66	6.76	6.85	6.94	7.02	7.10	7.17	.05	7
8.71	8.86	9.00	9.12	9.24	9.35	9.46	9.55	9.65	.01	
6.18	6.29	6.39	6.48	6.57	6.65	6.73	6.80	6.87	.05	8
8.18	8.31	8.44	8.55	8.66	8.76	8.85	8.94	9.03	.01	
5.98	6.09	6.19	6.28	6.36	6.44	6.51	6.58	6.64	.05	9
7.78	7.91	8.03	8.13	8.23	8.33	8.41	8.49	8.57	.01	
5.83	5.93	6.03	6.11	6.19	6.27	6.34	6.40	6.47	.05	10
7.49	7.60	7.71	7.81	7.91	7.99	8.08	8.15	8.23	.01	
5.71	5.81	5.90	5.98	6.06	6.13	6.20	6.27	6.33	.05	11
7.25	7.36	7.46	7.56	7.65	7.73	7.81	7.88	7.95	.01	
5.61	5.71	5.80	5.88	5.95	6.02	6.09	6.15	6.21	.05	12
7.06	7.17	7.26	7.36	7.44	7.52	7.59	7.66	7.73	.01	
5.53	5.63	5.71	5.79	5.86	5.93	5.99	6.05	6.11	.05	13
6.90	7.01	7.10	7.19	7.27	7.35	7.42	7.48	7.55	.01	
5.46	5.55	5.64	5.71	5.79	5.85	5.91	5.97	6.03	.05	14
6.77	6.87	6.96	7.05	7.13	7.20	7.27	7.33	7.39	.01	
5.40	5.49	5.57	5.65	5.72	5.78	5.85	5.90	5.96	.05	15
6.66	6.76	6.84	6.93	7.00	7.07	7.14	7.20	7.26	.01	
5.35	5.44	5.52	5.59	5.66	5.73	5.79	5.84	5.90	.05	16
6.56	6.66	6.74	8.82	6.90	6.97	7.03	7.09	7.15	.01	
5.31	5.39	5.47	5.54	5.61	5.67	5.73	5.79	5.84	.05	17
6.48	6.57	6.66	6.73	6.81	6.87	6.94	7.00	7.05	.01	
5.27	5.35	5.43	5.50	5.57	5.63	5.69	5.74	5.79	.05	18
6.41	6.50	6.58	6.65	6.73	6.79	6.85	6.91	6.97	.01	
5.23	5.31	5.39	5.46	5.53	5.59	5.65	5.70	5.75	.05	19
6.34	6.43	6.51	6.58	6.65	6.72	6.78	6.84	6.89	.01	
5.20	5.28	5.36	5.43	5.49	5.55	5.61	5.66	5.71	.05	20
6.28	6.37	6.45	6.52	6.59	6.65	6.71	6.77	6.82	.01	
5.10	5.18	5.25	5.32	5.38	5.44	5.49	5.55	5.59	.05	24
6.11	6.19	6.26	6.33	6.39	6.45	6.51	6.56	6.61	.01	
5.00	5.08	5.15	5.21	5.27	5.33	5.38	5.43	5.47	.05	30
5.93	6.01	6.08	6.14	6.20	6.26	6.31	6.36	6.41	.01	
4.90	4.98	5.04	5.11	5.16	5.22	5.27	5.31	5.36	.05	40
5.76	5.83	5.90	5.96	6.02	6.07	6.12	6.16	6.21	.01	

TABLE C-3   (*Cont.*)

		r = number of means or number of steps between ordered means									
df_{error}	α	2	3	4	5	6	7	8	9	10	11
60	.05	2.83	3.40	3.74	3.98	4.16	4.31	4.44	4.55	4.65	4.73
	.01	3.76	4.28	4.59	4.82	4.99	5.13	5.25	5.36	5.45	5.53
120	.05	2.80	3.36	3.68	3.92	4.10	4.24	4.36	4.47	4.56	4.64
	.01	3.70	4.20	4.50	4.71	4.87	5.01	5.12	5.21	5.30	5.37
∞	.05	2.77	3.31	3.63	3.86	4.03	4.17	4.29	4.39	4.47	4.55
	.01	3.64	4.12	4.40	4.60	4.76	4.88	4.99	5.08	5.16	5.23

TABLE C-3 (*Cont.*)

					r = number of means or number of steps between ordered means					
12	13	14	15	16	17	18	19	20	α	df_{error}
4.81	4.88	4.94	5.00	5.06	5.11	5.15	5.20	5.24	.05	60
5.60	5.67	5.73	5.78	5.84	5.89	5.93	5.97	6.01	.01	
4.71	4.78	4.84	4.90	4.95	5.00	5.04	5.09	5.13	.05	120
5.44	5.50	5.56	5.61	5.66	5.71	5.75	5.79	5.83	.01	
4.62	4.68	4.74	4.80	4.85	4.89	4.93	4.97	5.01	.05	∞
5.29	5.35	5.40	5.45	5.49	5.54	5.57	5.61	5.65	.01	

TABLE C-4 *Critical Values of the Dunn Multiple Comparison Test*

Number of Comparisons (C)	α	df_{error}											
		5	7	10	12	15	20	24	30	40	60	120	∞
2	.05	3.17	2.84	2.64	2.56	2.49	2.42	2.39	2.36	2.33	2.30	2.27	2.24
	.01	4.78	4.03	3.58	3.43	3.29	3.16	3.09	3.03	2.97	2.92	2.86	2.81
3	.05	3.54	3.13	2.87	2.78	2.69	2.61	2.58	2.54	2.50	2.47	2.43	2.39
	.01	5.25	4.36	3.83	3.65	3.48	3.33	3.26	3.19	3.12	3.06	2.99	2.94
4	.05	3.81	3.34	3.04	2.94	2.84	2.75	2.70	2.66	2.62	2.58	2.54	2.50
	.01	5.60	4.59	4.01	3.80	3.62	3.46	3.38	3.30	3.23	3.16	3.09	3.02
5	.05	4.04	3.50	3.17	3.06	2.95	2.85	2.80	2.75	2.71	2.66	2.62	2.58
	.01	5.89	4.78	4.15	3.93	3.74	3.55	3.47	3.39	3.31	3.24	3.16	3.09
6	.05	4.22	3.64	3.28	3.15	3.04	2.93	2.88	2.83	2.78	2.73	2.68	2.64
	.01	6.15	4.95	4.27	4.04	3.82	3.63	3.54	3.46	3.38	3.30	3.22	3.15
7	.05	4.38	3.76	3.37	3.24	3.11	3.00	2.94	2.89	2.84	2.79	2.74	2.69
	.01	6.36	5.09	4.37	4.13	3.90	3.70	3.61	3.52	3.43	3.34	3.27	3.19
8	.05	4.53	3.86	3.45	3.31	3.18	3.06	3.00	2.94	2.89	2.84	2.79	2.74
	.01	6.56	5.21	4.45	4.20	3.97	3.76	3.66	3.57	3.48	3.39	3.31	3.23
9	.05	4.66	3.95	3.52	3.37	3.24	3.11	3.05	2.99	2.93	2.88	2.83	2.77
	.01	6.70	5.31	4.53	4.26	4.02	3.80	3.70	3.61	3.51	3.42	3.34	3.26
10	.05	4.78	4.03	3.58	3.43	3.29	3.16	3.09	3.03	2.97	2.92	2.86	2.81
	.01	6.86	5.40	4.59	4.32	4.07	3.85	3.74	3.65	3.55	3.46	3.37	3.29
15	.05	5.25	4.36	3.83	3.65	3.48	3.33	3.26	3.19	3.12	3.06	2.99	2.94
	.01	7.51	5.79	4.86	4.56	4.29	4.03	3.91	3.80	3.70	3.59	3.50	3.40
20	.05	5.60	4.59	4.01	3.80	3.62	3.46	3.38	3.30	3.23	3.16	3.09	3.02
	.01	8.00	6.08	5.06	4.73	4.42	4.15	4.04	3.90	3.79	3.69	3.58	3.48
25	.05	5.89	4.78	4.15	3.93	3.74	3.55	3.47	3.39	3.31	3.24	3.16	3.09
	.01	8.37	6.30	5.20	4.86	4.53	4.25	4.1*	3.98	3.88	3.76	3.64	3.54
30	.05	6.15	4.95	4.27	4.04	3.82	3.63	3.54	3.46	3.38	3.30	3.22	3.15
	.01	8.68	6.49	5.33	4.95	4.61	4.33	4.2*	4.13	3.93	3.81	3.69	3.59
35	.05	6.36	5.09	4.37	4.13	3.90	3.70	3.61	3.52	3.43	3.34	3.27	3.19
	.01	8.95	6.67	5.44	5.04	4.71	4.39	4.3*	4.26	3.97	3.84	3.73	3.63
40	.05	6.56	5.21	4.45	4.20	3.97	3.76	3.66	3.57	3.48	3.39	3.31	3.23
	.01	9.19	6.83	5.52	5.12	4.78	4.46	4.3*	4.1*	4.01	3.89	3.77	3.66
45	.05	6.70	5.31	4.53	4.26	4.02	3.80	3.70	3.61	3.51	3.42	3.34	3.26
	.01	9.41	6.93	5.60	5.20	4.84	4.52	4.3*	4.2*	4·1*	3.93	3.80	3.69
50	.05	6.86	5.40	4.59	4.32	4.07	3.85	3.74	3.65	3.55	3.46	3.37	3.29
	.01	9.68	7.06	5.70	5.27	4.90	4.56	4.4*	4.2*	4.1*	3.97	3.83	3.72
100	.05	8.00	6.08	5.06	4.73	4.42	4.15	4.04	3.90	3.79	3.69	3.58	3.48
	.01	11.04	7.80	6.20	5.70	5.20	4.80	4.7*	4.4*	4.5*		4.00	3.89
250	.05	9.68	7.06	5.70	5.27	4.90	4.56	4.4*	4.2*	4.1*	3.97	3.83	3.72
	.01	13.26	8.83	6.9*	6.3*	5.8*	5.2*	5.0*	4.9*	4.8*			4.11

This table is reproduced from O. J. Dunn, Multiple comparisons among means, *Journal of the American Statistical Association*, 1961, **56**, 52–64, by permission of the author and the editor.
* Obtained by graphical interpolation.

TABLE C-5 *Critical Values of the Dunnett Test for Comparing Treatment Means with a Control*

ONE-TAILED COMPARISONS

k = number of treatment means, including control

df_{error}	α	2	3	4	5	6	7	8	9	10
5	.05	2.02	2.44	2.68	2.85	2.98	3.08	3.16	3.24	3.30
	.01	3.37	3.90	4.21	4.43	4.60	4.73	4.85	4.94	5.03
6	.05	1.94	2.34	2.56	2.71	2.83	2.92	3.00	3.07	3.12
	.01	3.14	3.61	3.88	4.07	4.21	4.33	4.43	4.51	4.59
7	.05	1.89	2.27	2.48	2.62	2.73	2.82	2.89	2.95	3.01
	.01	3.00	3.42	3.66	3.83	3.96	4.07	4.15	4.23	4.30
8	.05	1.86	2.22	2.42	2.55	2.66	2.74	2.81	2.87	2.92
	.01	2.90	3.29	3.51	3.67	3.79	3.88	3.96	4.03	4.09
9	.05	1.83	2.18	2.37	2.50	2.60	2.68	2.75	2.81	2.86
	.01	2.82	3.19	3.40	3.55	3.66	3.75	3.82	3.89	3.94
10	.05	1.81	2.15	2.34	2.47	2.56	2.64	2.70	2.76	2.81
	.01	2.76	3.11	3.31	3.45	3.56	3.64	3.71	3.78	3.83
11	.05	1.80	2.13	2.31	2.44	2.53	2.60	2.67	2.72	2.77
	.01	2.72	3.06	3.25	3.38	3.48	3.56	3.63	3.69	3.74
12	.05	1.78	2.11	2.29	2.41	2.50	2.58	2.64	2.69	2.74
	.01	2.68	3.01	3.19	3.32	3.42	3.50	3.56	3.62	3.67
13	.05	1.77	2.09	2.27	2.39	2.48	2.55	2.61	2.66	2.71
	.01	2.65	2.97	3.15	3.27	3.37	3.44	3.51	3.56	3.61
14	.05	1.76	2.08	2.25	2.37	2.46	2.53	2.59	2.64	2.69
	.01	2.62	2.94	3.11	3.23	3.32	3.40	3.46	3.51	3.56
15	.05	1.75	2.07	2.24	2.36	2.44	2.51	2.57	2.62	2.67
	.01	2.60	2.91	3.08	3.20	3.29	3.36	3.42	3.47	3.52
16	.05	1.75	2.06	2.23	2.34	2.43	2.50	2.56	2.61	2.65
	.01	2.58	2.88	3.05	3.17	3.26	3.33	3.39	3.44	3.48
17	.05	1.74	2.05	2.22	2.33	2.42	2.49	2.54	2.59	2.64
	.01	2.57	2.86	3.03	3.14	3.23	3.30	3.36	3.41	3.45
18	.05	1.73	2.04	2.21	2.32	2.41	2.48	2.53	2.58	2.62
	.01	2.55	2.84	3.01	3.12	3.21	3.27	3.33	3.38	3.42
19	.05	1.73	2.03	2.20	2.31	2.40	2.47	2.52	2.57	2.61
	.01	2.54	2.83	2.99	3.10	3.18	3.25	3.31	3.36	3.40
20	.05	1.72	2.03	2.19	2.30	2.39	2.46	2.51	2.56	2.60
	.01	2.53	2.81	2.97	3.08	3.17	3.23	3.29	3.34	3.38
24	.05	1.71	2.01	2.17	2.28	2.36	2.43	2.48	2.53	2.57
	.01	2.49	2.77	2.92	3.03	3.11	3.17	3.22	3.27	3.31
30	.05	1.70	1.99	2.15	2.25	2.33	2.40	2.45	2.50	2.54
	.01	2.46	2.72	2.87	2.97	3.05	3.11	3.16	3.21	3.24

TABLE C-5 (Cont.)

df_{error}	α	\multicolumn{9}{c}{k = number of treatment means, including control}
		2	3	4	5	6	7	8	9	10
40	.05	1.68	1.97	2.13	2.23	2.31	2.37	2.42	2.47	2.51
	.01	2.42	2.68	2.82	2.92	2.99	3.05	3.10	3.14	3.18
60	.05	1.67	1.95	2.10	2.21	2.28	2.35	2.39	2.44	2.48
	.01	2.39	2.64	2.78	2.87	2.94	3.00	3.04	3.08	3.12
120	.05	1.66	1.93	2.08	2.18	2.26	2.32	2.37	2.41	2.45
	.01	2.36	2.60	2.73	2.82	2.89	2.94	2.99	3.03	3.06
∞	.05	1.64	1.92	2.06	2.16	2.23	2.29	2.34	2.38	2.42
	.01	2.33	2.56	2.68	2.77	2.84	2.89	2.93	2.97	3.00

This table is reproduced from C. W. Dunnett, A multiple comparison procedure for comparing several treatments with a control, *Journal of the American Statistical Association*, 1955, **50**, 1096–1121, by permission of the author and the editor.

TWO-TAILED COMPARISONS

df_{error}	α	\multicolumn{9}{c}{k = number of treatment means, including control}
		2	3	4	5	6	7	8	9	10
5	.05	2.57	3.03	3.29	3.48	3.62	3.73	3.82	3.90	3.97
	.01	4.03	4.63	4.98	5.22	5.41	5.56	5.69	5.80	5.89
6	.05	2.45	2.86	3.10	3.26	3.39	3.49	3.57	3.64	3.71
	.01	3.71	4.21	4.51	4.71	4.87	5.00	5.10	5.20	5.28
7	.05	2.36	2.75	2.97	3.12	3.24	3.33	3.41	3.47	3.53
	.01	3.50	3.95	4.21	4.39	4.53	4.64	4.74	4.82	4.89
8	.05	2.31	2.67	2.88	3.02	3.13	3.22	3.29	3.35	3.41
	.01	3.36	3.77	4.00	4.17	4.29	4.40	4.48	4.56	4.62
9	.05	2.26	2.61	2.81	2.95	3.05	3.14	3.20	3.26	3.32
	.01	3.25	3.63	3.85	4.01	4.12	4.22	4.30	4.37	4.43
10	.05	2.23	2.57	2.76	2.89	2.99	3.07	3.14	3.19	3.24
	.01	3.17	3.53	3.74	3.88	3.99	4.08	4.16	4.22	4.28
11	.05	2.20	2.53	2.72	2.84	2.94	3.02	3.08	3.14	3.19
	.01	3.11	3.45	3.65	3.79	3.89	3.98	4.05	4.11	4.16
12	.05	2.18	2.50	2.68	2.81	2.90	2.98	3.04	3.09	3.14
	.01	3.05	3.39	3.58	3.71	3.81	3.89	3.96	4.02	4.07
13	.05	2.16	2.48	2.65	2.78	2.87	2.94	3.00	3.06	3.10
	.01	3.01	3.33	3.52	3.65	3.74	3.82	3.89	3.94	3.99
14	.05	2.14	2.46	2.63	2.75	2.84	2.91	2.97	3.02	3.07
	.01	2.98	3.29	3.47	3.59	3.69	3.76	3.83	3.88	3.93
15	.05	2.13	2.44	2.61	2.73	2.82	2.89	2.95	3.00	3.04
	.01	2.95	3.25	3.43	3.55	3.64	3.71	3.78	3.83	3.88

TABLE C-5 (*Cont.*)

df_{error}	α	$k = $ number of treatment means, including control								
		2	3	4	5	6	7	8	9	10
16	.05	2.12	2.42	2.59	2.71	2.80	2.87	2.92	2.97	3.02
	.01	2.92	3.22	3.39	3.51	3.60	3.67	3.73	3.78	3.83
17	.05	2.11	2.41	2.58	2.69	2.78	2.85	2.90	2.95	3.00
	.01	2.90	3.19	3.36	3.47	3.56	3.63	3.69	3.74	3.79
18	.05	2.10	2.40	2.56	2.68	2.76	2.83	2.89	2.94	2.98
	.01	2.88	3.17	3.33	3.44	3.53	3.60	3.66	3.71	3.75
19	.05	2.09	2.39	2.55	2.66	2.75	2.81	2.87	2.92	2.96
	.01	2.86	3.15	3.31	3.42	3.50	3.57	3.63	3.68	3.72
20	.05	2.09	2.38	2.54	2.65	2.73	2.80	2.86	2.90	2.95
	.01	2.85	3.13	3.29	3.40	3.48	3.55	3.60	3.65	3.69
24	.05	2.06	2.35	2.51	2.61	2.70	2.76	2.81	2.86	2.90
	.01	2.80	3.07	3.22	3.32	3.40	3.47	3.52	3.57	3.61
30	.05	2.04	2.32	2.47	2.58	2.66	2.72	2.77	2.82	2.86
	.01	2.75	3.01	3.15	3.25	3.33	3.39	3.44	3.49	3.52
40	.05	2.02	2.29	2.44	2.54	2.62	2.68	2.73	2.77	2.81
	.01	2.70	2.95	3.09	3.19	3.26	3.32	3.37	3.41	3.44
60	.05	2.00	2.27	2.41	2.51	2.58	2.64	2.69	2.73	2.77
	.01	2.66	2.90	3.03	3.12	3.19	3.25	3.29	3.33	3.37
120	.05	1.98	2.24	2.38	2.47	2.55	2.60	2.65	2.69	2.73
	.01	2.62	2.85	2.97	3.06	3.12	3.18	3.22	3.26	3.29
∞	.05	1.96	2.21	2.35	2.44	2.51	2.57	2.61	2.65	2.69
	.01	2.58	2.79	2.92	3.00	3.06	3.11	3.15	3.19	3.22

This table is abridged from C. W. Dunnett, New tables for multiple comparisons with a control, *Biometrics*, 1964, **20**, 482–491, by permission of the author and the editor.

TABLE C-6   *Power Functions for Analysis of Variance (Fixed-Effects Model)*

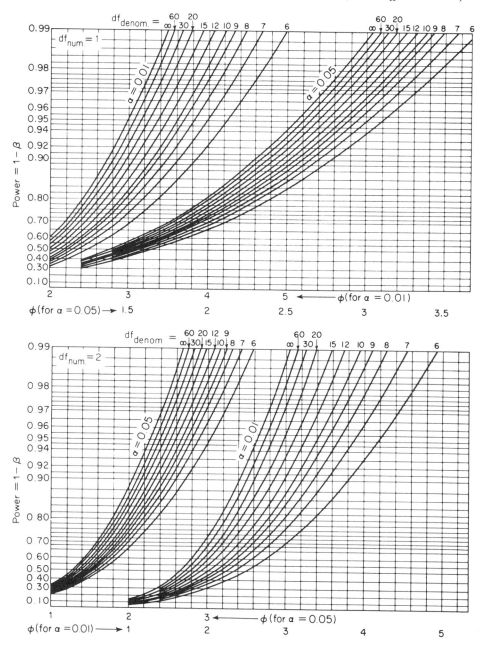

These charts are reproduced from E. S. Pearson and H. O. Hartley, Charts of the power function for analysis of variance tests, derived from the non-central *F* distribution, *Biometrika*, 1951, **38**, 112–130, by permission of the *Biometrika* Trustees.

TABLE C-6 (*Cont.*)

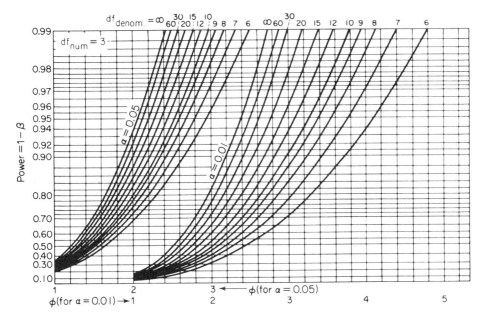

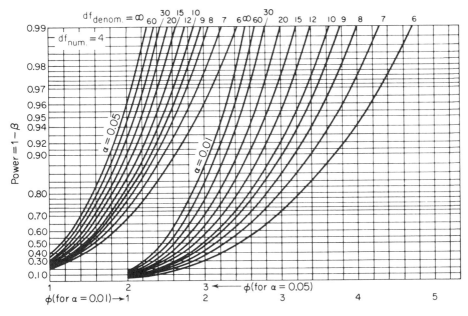

TABLE C-6 *(Cont.)*

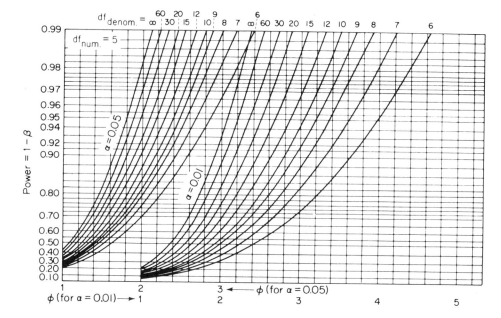

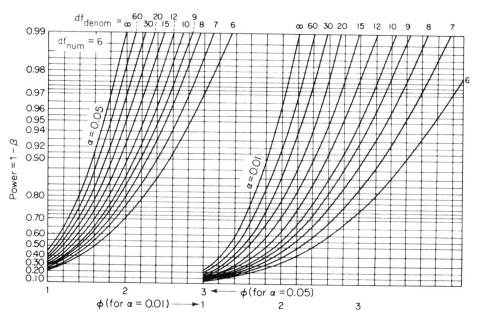

TABLE C-6 *(Cont.)*

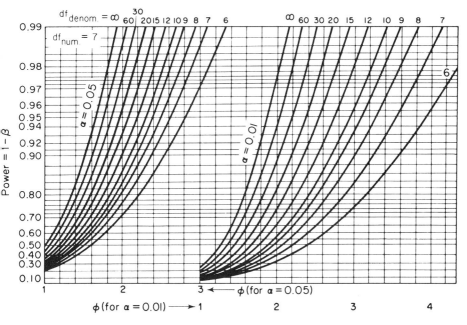

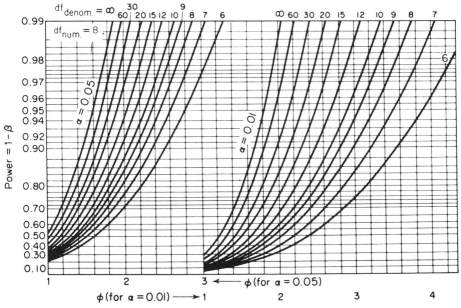

appendix d

ANSWERS TO PROBLEMS
AND EXERCISES

PART II

1. (a) $F(4, 30) = 2.69$, $p = .05$.

  (b) $F(1, 120) = 11.4$, $p = .001$.

  (c) $df_{num.} = a - 1 = 7 - 1 = 6$; $df_{denom.} = a(s - 1) = 7(5 - 1) = 7(4) = 28$; $F(6, 28) = 2.00$, $p = .10$.

  (d) $df_{num.} = a - 1 = 3 - 1 = 2$; $df_{denom.} = a(s - 1) = 3(9 - 1) = 3(8) = 24$; $F(2, 24) = 1.47$, $p = .25$.

2.

Source	Calculations	SS	df	MS	F
A	$374.00 - 365.07 =$	8.93	2	4.46	< 1
S/A	$518 - 374.00 =$	144.00	12	12.00	
Total	$518 - 365.07 =$	152.93			

3. (a)

AS Matrix: Transformed Scores, $Z_{ij} = |AS_{ij} - A_i|$

a_1	a_2	a_3	a_4	a_5
5	1	5	2	3
1	2	4	0	4
0	2	3	3	4
1	5	2	5	2
0	4	2	3	3
2	1	3	2	0
2	1	5	2	2
1	3	1	5	6
2	1	4	2	1
2	2	1	0	1

We now conduct an analysis of variance on these transformed scores:

Source	Calculations	SS	df	MS	F
A	$289.20 - 278.48 =$	10.72	4	2.68	1.09
S/A	$400 - 289.20 =$	110.80	45	2.46	
Total	$400 - 278.48 =$	121.52	49		

The results of the Levene test indicate that the variances are homogeneous.

(b)

Source	Calculations	SS	df	MS	F
A	$3930.00 - 3698.00 =$	232.00	4	58.00	6.52*
S/A	$4330 - 3930.00 =$	400.00	45	8.89	
Total	$4330 - 3698.00 =$	632.00	49		

* $p < .01$.

4. (a)

Source	Calculations	SS	df	MS	F
A	$640.00 - 563.33 =$	76.67	5	15.33	3.14*
S/A	$757 - 640.00 =$	117.00	24	4.88	
Total	$757 - 563.33 =$	193.67	29		

* $p < .05$.

(b) The formula for any one of the within-group variances ($\hat{\sigma}_i^2$) may be written in a more convenient form for this analysis:

$$\hat{\sigma}_i^2 = \frac{SS_{S/A_i}}{df_{S/A_i}} = \frac{\sum_{j}^{s}(AS_{ij})^2 - \dfrac{(A_i)^2}{s}}{s - 1} = \frac{s\left[\sum_{j}^{s}(AS_{ij})^2\right] - (A_i)^2}{s(s - 1)}.$$

This form of the equation eliminates rounding error and is ideal for use with desk calculators. That is, most calculators allow the multiplication of the quantity $s\left[\sum_j^s (AS_{ij})^2\right]$, and then the *negative* squaring of the quantity A_i; negative squaring accomplishes the required subtraction of $(A_i)^2$ from $s\left[\sum_j^s (AS_{ij})^2\right]$. The necessary sums are given in the second and third columns of the following table:

Groups	A_i	$\sum_j^s (AS_{ij})^2$	$s\left[\sum_j^s (AS_{ij})^2\right] - (A_i)^2$	$\hat{\sigma}_i^2$
a_1	15	65	100	5.00
a_2	10	35	75	3.75
a_3	25	130	25	1.25
a_4	35	275	150	7.50
a_5	25	150	125	6.25
a_6	20	102	110	5.50

To illustrate one of the calculations, the variance at a_6,

$$s\left[\sum (AS_{6j})^2\right] - (A_6)^2 = 5(102) - (20)^2 = 510 - 400 = 110,$$

$$\hat{\sigma}_6^2 = \frac{110}{5(4)} = \frac{110}{20} = 5.50.$$

The average variance is found by summing the individual within-group variances obtained in the preceding calculations and dividing by the number of variances:

$$\hat{\sigma}_{S/A}^2 = \frac{\sum \hat{\sigma}_i^2}{a} = \frac{29.25}{6} = 4.88.$$

This average variance is identical to the $MS_{S/A}$ calculated in part (a) of this question. The equality indicates that the within-groups mean square is an average of the separate within-group variances.

5. (a)

Source	Calculations	SS	df	MS	F
A	$5117.25 - 4651.25 =$	466.00	4	116.50	3.15*
S/A			15	37.00	

$* p < .05.$

(b)

COEFFICIENTS AND WEIGHTED TOTALS

	a_1	a_2	a_3	a_4	a_5	$\sum (c_i)(A_i)$	$\sum (c_i)^2$
A_i:	60	55	32	66	92		
Comp. 1:	4	-1	-1	-1	-1	-5	20
Comp. 2:	0	1	1	-1	-1	-71	4
Comp. 3:	0	1	-1	0	0	23	2
Comp. 4:	0	0	0	1	-1	-26	2

(c) (Comp. 1) × (Comp. 2):

$$(4)(0) + (-1)(1) + (-1)(1) + (-1)(-1) + (-1)(-1) = 0,$$

(Comp. 1) × (Comp. 3):

$$(4)(0) + (-1)(1) + (-1)(-1) + (-1)(0) + (-1)(0) = 0,$$

. . .

(Comp. 3) × (Comp. 4):

$$(0)(0) + (1)(0) + (-1)(0) + (0)(1) + (0)(-1) = 0.$$

(d) Substituting the values in the table into Eq. (6-6), we have

$$SS_{A_{comp.\ 1}} = \frac{(-5)^2}{4(20)}, \qquad SS_{A_{comp.\ 2}} = \frac{(-71)^2}{4(4)},$$

$$SS_{A_{comp.\ 3}} = \frac{(23)^2}{4(2)}, \qquad SS_{A_{comp.\ 4}} = \frac{(-26)^2}{4(2)}.$$

The remainder of the analysis is summarized as follows:

Source	SS	df	MS	F
A	(466.0000)	(4)		
Comp. 1	.3125	1	.3125	<1
Comp. 2	315.0625	1	315.0625	8.52*
Comp. 3	66.1250	1	66.1250	1.79
Comp. 4	84.5000	1	84.5000	2.28
S/A		15	37.00	

* $p < .025$.

The analysis indicates that the main outcome of the experiment was a difference between the two drugs.

6. For the overall between-groups sum of squares, $SS_A = 25.00$. It is up to you to construct your set of five orthogonal comparisons and the sums of squares associated with each and to show that the sum of these different sums of squares equals the SS_A.

7. This problem has various answers. One solution is as follows:

	a_1	a_2	a_3	a_4	a_5
			(a)		
Comp. 3	0	1	1	0	-2
Comp. 4	0	1	-1	0	0
			(b)		
Comp. 3	0	0	-1	-1	2
Comp. 4	-1	4	-1	-1	-1

(c)

Comp. 3	1	0	−1	−1	1
Comp. 4	−1	4	−1	−1	−1

(d)

Comp. 3	1	−1	0	0	0
Comp. 4	0	0	1	0	−1

8. (a)

Source	Calculations	SS	df	MS	F
A	1208.62 − 1092.02 =	116.60	4	29.15	13.37*
S/A	1285 − 1208.62 =	76.38	35	2.18	
Total	1285 − 1092.02 =	192.98	39		

* $p < .01$.

(b) The formulas for the four component SS's and the summary of the analysis appear below.

$$SS_{A_{\text{linear}}} = \frac{(-12)^2}{8(10)}, \qquad SS_{A_{\text{quadratic}}} = \frac{(-10)^2}{8(14)},$$

$$SS_{A_{\text{cubic}}} = \frac{(94)^2}{8(10)}, \qquad SS_{A_{\text{quartic}}} = \frac{(44)^2}{8(70)}.$$

Source	SS	df	MS	F
A	(116.60)	(4)		
Linear	1.80	1	1.80	<1
Quadratic	.89	1	.89	<1
Cubic	110.45	1	110.45	50.67*
Quartic	3.46	1	3.46	1.59
S/A	76.38	35	2.18	
Total	192.98	39		

* $p < .01$.

9. (a)

Source	Calculations	SS	df	MS	F
A	122,754.43 − 112,770.88 =	9983.55	7	1426.22	24.32*
S/A			48	58.65	

* $p < .01$.

(b) The critical ranges for increasing values of r for the Newman-Keuls test are as follows: $CR_{\text{N-K}} = 57.94, 69.69, 76.79, 81.85, 85.70, 88.94, 91.58$; the critical range for the Tukey test is $CR_T = 91.58$. (Note: Since $df_{S/A} = 48$ does not appear in the tables, we used the next lower entry, $df_{S/A} = 40$.) The tabular summary of the two tests is given first:

	a_7	a_6	a_3	a_1	a_2	a_4	a_5	a_8
A_i:	123	227	307	316	333	373	398	436
$A_7 = 123$	—	$104^{a,b}$	$184^{a,b}$	$193^{a,b}$	$210^{a,b}$	$250^{a,b}$	$275^{a,b}$	$313^{a,b}$
$A_6 = 227$		—	80^a	89^a	$106^{a,b}$	$146^{a,b}$	$171^{a,b}$	$209^{a,b}$
$A_3 = 307$			—	9	26	66	91^a	$129^{a,b}$
$A_1 = 316$				—	17	57	82^a	$120^{a,b}$
$A_2 = 333$					—	40	65	$103^{a,b}$
$A_4 = 373$						—	25	63
$A_5 = 398$							—	38
$A_8 = 436$								—

[a] $p < .05$, Newman-Keuls test.
[b] $p < .05$, Tukey test.

Graphically, the results can be represented as follows

Treatment Sums

	A_7	A_6	A_3	A_1	A_2	A_4	A_5	A_8

Newman-Keuls test:

Tukey test:

10. (a)

Source	Calculations	SS	df	MS	F
A	$28,463.88 - 27,789.03 =$	674.85	7	96.41	3.35*
S/A			120	28.75	

* $p < .01$.

(b) Critical C-E difference $= 2.65\sqrt{2(16)(28.75)} = 80.37$. Thus,

	E_1	E_2	E_3	E_4	E_5	E_6	E_7
C-E:	19	48	10	98*	76	84*	91*

* $p < .05$.

(c) $CR_S = \sqrt{7(2.09)}\sqrt{2(16)(28.75)} = 116.02$. None of the differences is significant, which demonstrates the marked advantage of specifying a restricted set of comparisons with multiple-comparison techniques.

PART III

1. (a) no interaction present; (b) no interaction present; (c–f) interactions present.

2. The within-group mean squares $(MS_{S/AB_{ij}})$ are given below:

	a_1	a_2	a_3
b_1	10.00	22.67	15.33
b_2	15.33	30.00	16.67

As an example of the calculations,

$$SS_{S/AB_{11}} = \sum (ABS_{11k})^2 - \frac{(AB_{11})^2}{s}$$

$$= [(1)^2 + (4)^2 + (0)^2 + (7)^2] - \frac{(12)^2}{4}$$

$$= 66 - 36.00 = 30.00$$

and

$$MS_{S/AB_{11}} = \frac{SS_{S/AB_{11}}}{s - 1} = \frac{30.00}{4 - 1} = \frac{30.00}{3} = 10.00.$$

Finally,

$$\frac{\sum MS_{S/AB_{ij}}}{ab} = \frac{10.00 + 15.33 + \cdots + 15.33 + 16.67}{3(2)}$$

$$= \frac{110.00}{6} = 18.33 = MS_{S/AB}.$$

3. (a)

Source	Calculations	SS	df	MS	F
A	$12{,}892.00 - 12{,}701.01 =$	190.99	4	47.75	7.70**
B	$13{,}125.20 - [T] =$	424.19	2	212.10	34.21**
$A \times B$	$13{,}454.00 - [A] - [B] + [T] =$	137.81	8	17.23	2.78*
S/AB	$13{,}826 - [AB] =$	372.00	60	6.20	
Total	$[ABS] - [T] =$	1124.99	74		

$* \, p < .025.$
$** \, p < .01.$

(b) First, we test the significance of the linear component:

$$SS_{A_{linear} \times B} = \frac{(118)^2 + (25)^2 + (19)^2}{5(10)} - \frac{(162)^2}{3(5)(10)}$$

$$= 298.20 - 174.96 = 123.24,$$

$$df_{A_{linear} \times B} = b - 1 = 2,$$

$$F = \frac{MS_{A_{linear} \times B}}{MS_{S/AB}} = \frac{123.24/2}{6.20} = 9.94, \ p < .01.$$

Next, we test the significance of the *residual* component:

$$SS_{A_{residual} \times B} = SS_{A \times B} - SS_{A_{linear} \times B} = 137.81 - 123.24 = 14.57,$$

$$df_{A_{residual} \times B} = df_{A \times B} - df_{A_{linear} \times B} = 8 - 2 = 6,$$

$$F = \frac{MS_{A_{residual} \times B}}{MS_{S/AB}} = \frac{14.57/6}{6.20} = \frac{2.43}{6.20} < 1.$$

Since the residual source is not significant, we stop extracting trend components and conclude that the $A \times B$ interaction is largely the result of the interaction of the linear trends at the different levels of factor B.

3. (c)

$$SS_{A_{linear} \, at \, b_1} = \frac{(118)^2}{5(10)}, \qquad SS_{A_{linear} \, at \, b_2} = \frac{(25)^2}{5(10)},$$

$$SS_{A_{linear} \, at \, b_3} = \frac{(19)^2}{5(10)}$$

Source	SS	df	MS	F
A_{linear} at b_1	278.48	1	278.48	44.92*
A_{linear} at b_2	12.50	1	12.50	2.02
A_{linear} at b_3	7.22	1	7.22	1.16
S/AB		60	6.20	

* $p < .01$.

4. (a)

Source	Calculations	SS	df	MS	F
A	$4525.13 - 4440.20 =$	84.93	2	42.46	11.51*
B	$4510.56 - [T] =$	70.36	4	17.59	4.77*
$A \times B$	$4766.33 - [A] - [B] + [T] =$	170.84	8	21.36	5.79*
S/AB	$4877 - [AB] =$	110.67	30	3.69	
Total	$[ABS] - [T] =$	436.80	44		

* $p < .01$.

(b)

Source	Calculations	SS	df	MS	F
B at a_1	$1165.33 - 1161.60 =$	3.73	4	.93	<1
B at a_2	$2345.33 - 2112.27 =$	233.06	4	58.26	15.79*
B at a_3	$1255.67 - 1251.27 =$	4.40	4	1.10	<1
S/AB			30	3.69	

* $p < .01$.

As a check: $\sum SS_{B\,at\,a_i} = 241.19$ and $SS_{A \times B} + SS_B = 241.20$.

(c) The critical range for the Scheffé test is $CR_S = \sqrt{4(2.69)}\sqrt{2(3)(3.69)} = 15.43$. The results of the test are summarized two ways:

	ab_{24}	ab_{21}	ab_{25}	ab_{22}	ab_{23}		AB_{24}	AB_{21}	AB_{25}	AB_{22}	AB_{23}
AB_{2j}:	24	25	31	43	55						
$AB_{24} = 24$	—	1	7	19*	31*						
$AB_{21} = 25$		—	6	18*	30*						
$AB_{25} = 31$			—	12	24*						
$AB_{22} = 43$				—	12						
$AB_{23} = 55$					—						

* $p < .05$, Scheffé test.

(d) (1) $CR_T = q(3, 30)\sqrt{bs(MS_{S/AB})} = 3.49\sqrt{5(3)(3.69)} = 25.97$.

(2) $CR_T = q(5, 30)\sqrt{as(MS_{S/AB})} = 4.10\sqrt{3(3)(3.69)} = 23.62$.

(3) $CR_T = q(3, 30)\sqrt{s(MS_{S/AB})} = 3.49\sqrt{3(3.69)} = 11.62$.

(4) $CR_T = q(15, 30)\sqrt{s(MS_{S/AB})} = 5.21\sqrt{3(3.69)} = 17.35$.

(5) In order to hold the EW error rate at .05 for all of the comparisons, we divide the EW error rate by the number of levels for factor B and use this new error rate for comparisons at any one of these levels. Specifically, set $\alpha = (\alpha_{EW})/b = .05/5 = .01$ and

$$CR_T = q(3, 30)\sqrt{s(MS_{S/AB})} = 4.45\sqrt{3(3.69)} = 14.82.$$

You will note the difference in the critical ranges for (4) and (5), reflecting the restriction of multiple comparisons to meaningful groupings of the cell means.

5. (a)

Source	Calculations	SS	df	MS	F
A	$1617.55 - 1402.81 =$	214.74	3	71.58	3.11*
B	$1480.82 - [T] =$	78.01	1	78.01	3.39
$A \times B$	$1704.30 - [A] - [B] + [T] =$	8.74	3	2.91	<1
S/AB	$3361 - [AB] =$	1656.70	72	23.01	
Total	$[ABS] - [T] =$	1958.19	79		

* $p < .05$.

(b) Coefficients and weighted totals:

	a_1	a_2	a_3	a_4	$\sum (c_i)(A_i)$	$\sum (c_i)^2$
A_i:	66	45	91	133		
Comp. 1:	1	0	-1	0	-25	2
Comp. 2:	-1	3	-1	-1	-155	12
Comp. 3:	-1	0	-1	2	109	6

Orthogonality:

(Comp. 1) × (Comp. 2): $(1)(-1) + (0)(3) + (-1)(-1) + (0)(-1) = 0,$

(Comp. 1) × (Comp. 3): $(1)(-1) + (0)(0) + (-1)(-1) + (0)(2) = 0,$

(Comp. 2) × (Comp. 3): $(-1)(-1) + (3)(0) + (-1)(-1) + (-1)(2) = 0.$

$$SS_{A_{\text{comp. 1}}} = \frac{(-25)^2}{2(10)(2)}, \qquad SS_{A_{\text{comp. 2}}} = \frac{(-155)^2}{2(10)(12)},$$

$$SS_{A_{\text{comp. 3}}} = \frac{(-109)^2}{2(10)(6)},$$

Source	SS	df	MS	F
A	(214.74)	(3)		
Comp. 1	15.62	1	15.62	<1
Comp. 2	100.10	1	100.10	4.35*
Comp. 3	99.01	1	99.01	4.30*
S/A		72	23.01	

* $p < .05$.

6. First, convert the means to sums and calculate the treatment SS's. The resultant AB matrix is given below:

	a_1	a_2	a_3	Sum
b_1	44	48	40	132
b_2	12	40	56	108
Sum	56	88	96	240

Since we are given the value of F for the interaction source of variance, we can solve for the $MS_{S/AB}$. That is,

$$F = \frac{MS_{A \times B}}{MS_{S/AB}} = 3.93,$$

$$MS_{S/AB} = \frac{MS_{A \times B}}{3.93} = \frac{72.00}{3.93} = 18.32.$$

With this value, we can calculate the F's for the two main effects and the $SS_{S/AB}$. These quantities are presented in the following summary table:

Source	Calculations	SS	df	MS	F
A	2512.00 − 2400.00 =	112.00	2	56.00	3.06*
B	2424.00 − [T] =	24.00	1	24.00	1.31
A × B	2680.00 − [A] − [B] + [T] =	144.00	2	72.00	3.93**
S/AB			18	18.32	

* $p < .10$.
** $p < .05$.

7. (a)

Source	Calculations	SS
A	745.00 − 722.50 =	22.50
B	785.00 − [T] =	62.50
A × B	930.00 − [A] − [B] + [T] =	122.50

(b) Coefficients and weighted totals:

	ab_{11}	ab_{12}	ab_{21}	ab_{22}	$\sum (c_{ij})(AB_{ij})$	$\sum (c_{ij})^2$
AB_{ij}:	30	40	80	20		
A:	1	1	−1	−1	−30	4
B:	1	−1	1	−1	50	4
A × B:	1	−1	−1	1	−70	4

$$SS_A = \frac{(-30)^2}{10(4)} = 22.50, \qquad SS_B = \frac{(50)^2}{10(4)} = 62.50,$$

$$SS_{A \times B} = \frac{(-70)^2}{10(4)} = 122.50.$$

8. (a)

Source	Calculations	SS	df	MS	F
A	5218.40 − 5198.40 =	20.00	3	6.67	2.16*
B	5428.80 − [T] =	230.40	1	230.40	74.56***
A × B	5483.20 − [A] − [B] + [T] =	34.40	3	11.47	3.71**
S/AB	5582 − [AB] =	98.80	32	3.09	
Total	[ABS] − [T] =	383.60	39		

* $p < .25$
** $p < .05$.
*** $p < .01$.

(b) For Comp. 1—coefficients and weighted sums:

	a_1	a_2	a_3	a_4	Sum of Weighted Totals
Comp. 1:	3	-1	-1	-1	
AB_{i1}:	70	72	65	69	4
AB_{i2}:	32	48	53	47	-52
A_i:	102	120	118	116	-48

$$SS_{A_{comp. 1} \times B} = \frac{(4)^2 + (-52)^2}{5(12)} - \frac{(-48)^2}{2(5)(12)}$$

$$= 45.33 - 19.20 = 26.13.$$

For Comp. 2, we will treat the three *incentive* conditions as a separate experiment. That is, from the modified AB matrix given below, we calculate the $SS_{A_{comp. 2}}$:

	a_2	a_3	a_4	Sum
b_1	72	65	69	206
b_2	48	53	47	148
Sum	120	118	116	354

$$SS_{A_{comp. 2} \times B} = \frac{(72)^2 + (48)^2 + \cdots + (69)^2 + (47)^2}{5} - \frac{(120)^2 + (118)^2 + (116)^2}{2(5)}$$

$$- \frac{(206)^2 + (148)^2}{3(5)} + \frac{(354)^2}{3(2)(5)}$$

$$= 4298.40 - 4178.00 - 4289.33 + 4177.20 = 8.27.$$

We could, of course, have obtained this same quantity by subtraction:

$$SS_{A_{comp. 2} \times B} = SS_{A \times B} - SS_{A_{comp. 1} \times B}$$

$$= 34.40 - 26.13 = 8.27.$$

9. The two sets of interaction coefficients (d_{ij}) are given below:

$A_{comp. 2} \times B_{comp. 1}$

Coefficients $(B_{comp. 1})$	Coefficients $(A_{comp. 2})$				
	1	-1	0	0	0
1	1	-1	0	0	0
-1	-1	1	0	0	0
0	0	0	0	0	0

$A_{comp. 2} \times B_{comp. 2}$

Coefficients $(B_{comp. 2})$	Coefficients $(A_{comp. 2})$				
	1	-1	0	0	0
0	0	0	0	0	0
1	1	-1	0	0	0
-1	-1	1	0	0	0

Applying these coefficients to the data presented in Table 12-7 (p. 243), we obtain

$$SS_{A_{comp.\ 2} \times B_{comp.\ 1}} = \frac{[(1)(21) + (-1)(75) + \cdots + (0)(69) + (0)(46)]^2}{5[(1)^2 + (-1)^2 + \cdots + (0)^2 + (0)^2]}$$

$$= \frac{(18)^2}{5(4)} = 16.20$$

and

$$SS_{A_{comp.\ 2} \times B_{comp.\ 2}} = \frac{[(0)(21) + (1)(75) + \cdots + (0)(69) + (0)(46)]^2}{5[(0)^2 + (1)^2 + \cdots + (0)^2 + (0)^2]}$$

$$= \frac{(-44)^2}{5(4)} = 96.80.$$

PART IV

1.

	Three-Way Interactions	Two-Way Interactions	Main Effects
Example 1:	No	None	A
Example 2:	No	None	A and B
Example 3:	No	None	A, B, and C
Example 4:	No	$A \times B$	None
Example 5:	No	$A \times B$	C^a
Example 6:	No	$B \times C$	A^a
Example 7:	No	$A \times B$ and $A \times C$	—
Example 8:	Yes	—	—
Example 9:	Yes	—	—
Example 10:	Yes	—	—

^{a} This main effect is interpretable, since it does not enter the two-way interaction.

2. (a)

(a)

c_1	a_1	a_2
b_1	30	20
b_2	30	20

c_2	a_1	a_2
b_1	30	20
b_2	30	20

(b)

c_1	a_1	a_2
b_1	30	20
b_2	40	30

c_2	a_1	a_2
b_1	25	15
b_2	35	25

(c)

c_1	a_1	a_2
b_1	30	20
b_2	20	30

c_2	a_1	a_2
b_1	30	20
b_2	20	30

(d)

c_1	a_1	a_2
b_1	30	20
b_2	20	30

c_2	a_1	a_2
b_1	40	30
b_2	30	40

(e)

	c_1			c_2	
	a_1	a_2		a_1	a_2
b_1	30	20	b_1	20	30
b_2	20	30	b_2	30	20

(f)

	c_1			c_2	
	a_1	a_2		a_1	a_2
b_1	30	20	b_1	10	20
b_2	20	30	b_2	20	10

3. (a)

Source	Calculations	SS	df	MS	F
A	$2540.75 - 2222.22 =$	318.53	2	159.26	91.01**
B	$2431.25 - [T] =$	209.03	2	104.52	59.73**
C	$2242.28 - [T] =$	20.06	1	20.06	11.46**
$A \times B$	$2762.00 - [A] - [B] + [T] =$	12.22	4	3.06	1.75
$A \times C$	$2575.83 - [A] - [C] + [T] =$	15.02	2	7.51	4.29*
$B \times C$	$2456.00 - [B] - [C] + [T] =$	4.69	2	2.34	1.34
$A \times B \times C$	$2815.50 - [AB] - [AC] - [BC]$				
	$+ [A] + [B] + [C] - [T] =$	13.73	4	3.43	1.96
S/ABC	$2910 - [ABC] =$	94.50	54	1.75	
Total	$[ABCS] - [T] =$	687.78	71		

* $p < .05$.
** $p < .01$.

(b)

Source	Calculations	SS	df	MS	F
C at a_1	$301.42 - 301.04 =$	.38	1	.38	<1
C at a_2	$555.33 - 522.67 =$	32.66	1	32.66	18.66*
C at a_3	$1719.08 - 1717.04 =$	2.04	1	2.04	1.17
S/ABC			54	1.75	

* $p < .01$.

As a check, $\sum SS_{C \text{ at } a_i} = 35.08$ and $SS_{A \times C} + SS_C = 35.08$.

(c)

	b_1	b_2	b_3	$\sum (c_j)(B_j)$	$\sum (c_j)^2$
B_j:	190	115	95		
Comp. 1:	-1	2	-1	-55	6
Comp. 2:	1	0	-1	95	2

$$SS_{B_{\text{comp. 1}}} = \frac{(-55)^2}{3(2)(4)(6)} \quad \text{and} \quad SS_{B_{\text{comp. 2}}} = \frac{(95)^2}{3(2)(4)(2)}.$$

Source	SS	df	MS	F
B	(209.03)	(2)		
Comp. 1	21.01	1	21.01	12.01*
Comp. 2	188.02	1	188.02	107.44*
S/ABC		54	1.75	

*$p < .01$.

As a check, $\sum SS_{B_{comp.}} = 209.03 = SS_B$.

4. (a)

Source	Calculations	SS	df	MS	F
A	$8643.40 - 8534.53 =$	108.87	3	36.29	19.51*
B	$8851.40 - [T] =$	316.87	2	158.44	85.18*
C	$8624.67 - [T] =$	90.14	1	90.14	48.46*
A × B	$9006.60 - [A] - [B] + [T] =$	46.33	6	7.72	4.15*
A × C	$8765.33 - [A] - [C] + [T] =$	31.79	3	10.60	5.70*
B × C	$9076.40 - [B] - [C] + [T] =$	134.86	2	67.43	36.25*
A × B × C	$9311.60 - [AB] - [AC] - [BC]$				
	$+ [A] + [B] + [C] - [T] =$	48.21	6	8.04	4.32*
S/ABC	$9490 - [ABC] =$	178.40	96	1.86	
Total	$[ABCS] - [T] =$	955.47	119		

*$p < .01$.

(b) For these simple interactions, it is most convenient to form AB matrices at each level of factor C:

AB Matrix at Level c_1

	a_1	a_2	a_3	a_4	Sum
b_1	35	46	49	55	185
b_2	42	51	55	62	210
b_3	29	40	45	49	163
Sum	106	137	149	166	558

AB Matrix at Level c_2

	a_1	a_2	a_3	a_3	Sum
b_1	37	49	56	65	207
b_2	40	38	44	42	164
b_3	27	23	19	14	83
Sum	104	110	119	121	454

$$SS_{A \times B \, at \, c_1} = \frac{(35)^2 + (42)^2 + \cdots + (62)^2 + (49)^2}{5} - \frac{(106)^2 + (137)^2 + (149)^2 + (166)^2}{3(5)}$$

$$- \frac{(185)^2 + (210)^2 + (163)^2}{4(5)} + \frac{(558)^2}{4(3)(5)}$$

$$= 5373.60 - 5317.47 - 5244.70 + 5189.40 = .83,$$

$$SS_{A \times B \, at \, c_2} = \frac{(37)^2 + (40)^2 + \cdots + (42)^2 + (14)^2}{5} - \frac{(104)^2 + (110)^2 + (119)^2 + (121)^2}{3(5)}$$

$$- \frac{(207)^2 + (164)^2 + (83)^2}{4(5)} + \frac{(454)^2}{4(3)(5)}$$

$$= 3938.00 - 3447.87 - 3831.70 + 3435.27 = 93.70.$$

Source	SS	df	MS	F
$A \times B$ at c_1	.83	6	.14	< 1
$A \times B$ at c_2	93.70	6	15.62	8.40*
S/ABC		96	1.86	

* $p < .01$.

As a check,

$$\sum SS_{A \times B \text{ at } c_k} = 94.53 \quad \text{and} \quad SS_{A \times B \times C} + SS_{A \times B} = 94.54.$$

(c) The first task is to calculate the linear component of the three-way interaction. To do this, we will have to form three matrices from which we will extract the needed sums of weighted (linear) totals:

ABC MATRIX (LINEAR)

c_1

	a_1	a_2	a_3	a_4	Sum of Weighted Totals
c_{1i}:	-3	-1	1	3	
ABC_{i11}:	35	46	49	55	63
ABC_{i21}:	42	51	55	62	64
ABC_{i31}:	29	40	45	49	65

c_2

	a_1	a_2	a_3	a_4	Sum of Weighted Totals
c_{1i}:	-3	-1	1	3	
ABC_{i12}:	37	49	56	65	91
ABC_{i22}:	40	38	44	42	12
ABC_{i32}:	27	23	19	14	-43

AB MATRIX (LINEAR)

	a_1	a_2	a_3	a_4	Sum of Weighted Totals
c_{1i}:	-3	-1	1	3	
AB_{i1}:	72	95	105	120	154
AB_{i2}:	82	89	99	104	76
AB_{i3}:	56	63	64	63	22
A_i:	210	247	268	287	252

AC MATRIX (LINEAR)

	a_1	a_2	a_3	a_4	Sum of Weighted Totals
c_{1i}:	-3	-1	1	3	
AC_{i1}:	106	137	149	166	192
AC_{i2}:	104	110	119	121	60
A_i:	210	247	268	287	252

Solving now for the linear component in all sources of variance involving factor A, we have

$$SS_{A_{\text{linear}}} = \frac{(252)^2}{3(2)(5)(20)} = 105.84,$$

$$SS_{A_{\text{linear}} \times B} = \frac{(154)^2 + (76)^2 + (22)^2}{2(5)(20)} - SS_{A_{\text{linear}}} = 44.04,$$

$$SS_{A_{\text{linear}} \times C} = \frac{(192)^2 + (60)^2}{3(5)(20)} - SS_{A_{\text{linear}}} = 29.04,$$

$$SS_{A_{\text{linear}} \times B \times C} = \frac{(63)^2 + (64)^2 + \cdots + (12)^2 + (-43)^2}{5(20)} - SS_{A_{\text{linear}} \times B}$$

$$- SS_{A_{\text{linear}} \times C} - SS_{A_{\text{linear}}} = 46.72.$$

Since $df_{A_{\text{linear}} \times B \times C} = (b-1)(c-1) = 2$, then

$$F = \frac{MS_{A_{\text{linear}} \times B \times C}}{MS_{S/ABC}} = \frac{46.72/2}{1.86} = 12.56, \ p < .01.$$

Inasmuch as we had no a priori hypothesis concerning trend, we will test the significance of the residual source of variance. That is,

$$SS_{A_{\text{residual}} \times B \times C} = SS_{A \times B \times C} - SS_{A_{\text{linear}} \times B \times C}$$
$$= 48.21 - 46.72 = 1.49,$$

$$df_{A_{\text{residual}} \times B \times C} = df_{A \times B \times C} - df_{A_{\text{linear}} \times B \times C} = 6 - 2 = 4,$$

$$F = \frac{MS_{A_{\text{residual}} \times B \times C}}{MS_{S/ABC}} = \frac{1.49/4}{1.86} = \frac{.37}{1.86} < 1.$$

Thus, we stop extracting trend components of the triple interaction and conclude that the interaction is localized in the linear component.

5. (a) Main effects: A, B, C, D, and E; two-way interactions: $A \times B$, $A \times C$, $A \times D$, $A \times E$, $B \times C$, $B \times D$, $B \times E$, $C \times D$, $C \times E$, and $D \times E$; three-way interactions: $A \times B \times C$, $A \times B \times D$, $A \times B \times E$, $A \times C \times D$, $A \times C \times E$, $A \times D \times E$, $B \times C \times D$, $B \times C \times E$, $B \times D \times E$, and $C \times D \times E$; four-way interactions: $A \times B \times C \times D$, $A \times B \times C \times E$, $A \times B \times D \times E$, $A \times C \times D \times E$, and $B \times C \times D \times E$; and five-way interaction: $A \times B \times C \times D \times E$.

   Generality is tested with any interaction involving both control and experimental factors.

(b) (1) From $df_{A \times B} = (a-1)(b-1)$,

$$SS_{A \times B} = \frac{\sum (AB)^2}{cdes} - \frac{\sum (A)^2}{bcdes} - \frac{\sum (B)^2}{acdes} + \frac{(T)^2}{abcdes}.$$

(2) From $df_{B \times D} = (b-1)(d-1)$,

$$SS_{B \times D} = \frac{\sum (BD)^2}{aces} - \frac{\sum (B)^2}{acdes} - \frac{\sum (D)^2}{abces} + \frac{(T)^2}{abcdes}.$$

(3) From $df_{B \times C \times E} = (b-1)(c-1)(e-1)$,

$$SS_{B \times C \times E} = \frac{\sum (BCE)^2}{ads} - \frac{\sum (BC)^2}{ades} - \frac{\sum (BE)^2}{acds} - \frac{\sum (CE)^2}{abds}$$
$$+ \frac{\sum (B)^2}{acdes} + \frac{\sum (C)^2}{abdes} + \frac{\sum (E)^2}{abcds} - \frac{(T)^2}{abcdes}.$$

(4) From $df_{S/ABCDE} = abcde(s-1)$,

$$SS_{S/ABCDE} = \sum (ABCDES)^2 - \frac{\sum (ABCDE)^2}{s}.$$

6. (a) From $df_{B_{\text{comp.}}} = b'$,

$$SS_{B_{\text{comp.}}} = \frac{\left[\sum_{j}^{b} (c_j)(B_j) \right]^2}{acdes\left[\sum (c_j)^2 \right]}.$$

(b) From $df_{A \times B_{\text{comp.}}} = (df_A)(df_{B_{\text{comp.}}}) = (a-1)(b')$,

$$SS_{A \times B_{\text{comp.}}} = \frac{\sum\limits_{i}^{a}\left[\sum\limits_{j}^{b}(c_j)(AB_{ij})\right]^2}{cdes\left[\sum(c_j)^2\right]} - \frac{\left[\sum\limits_{j}^{b}(c_j)(B_j)\right]^2}{acdes\left[\sum(c_j)^2\right]}.$$

(c) From $df_{B_{\text{comp. at }ac_{ik}}} = (df_{B_{\text{comp.}}})(ac_{ik}) = (b')(ac_{ik})$,

$$SS_{B_{\text{comp. at }ac_{ik}}} = \frac{\left[\sum\limits_{j}^{b}(c_j)(ABC_{ijk})\right]^2}{des\left[\sum(c_j)^2\right]}.$$

7. (a) From $df_{A \times C \times D\text{ at }b_j} = (df_A)(df_C)(df_D)(b_j) = (a-1)(c-1)(d-1)(b_j)$,

$$SS_{A \times C \times D\text{ at }b_j} = \frac{\sum\limits_{i}^{a}\sum\limits_{k}^{c}\sum\limits_{l}^{d}(ABCD_{ijkl})^2}{s} - \frac{\sum\limits_{i}^{a}\sum\limits_{k}^{c}(ABC_{ijk})^2}{ds} - \frac{\sum\limits_{i}^{a}\sum\limits_{l}^{d}(ABD_{ijl})^2}{cs}$$

$$- \frac{\sum\limits_{k}^{c}\sum\limits_{l}^{d}(BCD_{jkl})^2}{as} + \frac{\sum\limits_{i}^{a}(AB_{ij})^2}{cds}$$

$$+ \frac{\sum\limits_{k}^{c}(BC_{jk})^2}{ads} + \frac{\sum\limits_{l}^{d}(BD_{jl})^2}{acs} - \frac{(B_j)^2}{acds}.$$

(b) From $df_{A \times D\text{ at }bc_{jk}} = (df_A)(df_D)(bc_{jk}) = (a-1)(d-1)(bc_{jk})$,

$$SS_{A \times D\text{ at }bc_{jk}} = \frac{\sum\limits_{i}^{a}\sum\limits_{l}^{d}(ABCD_{ijkl})^2}{s} - \frac{\sum\limits_{i}^{a}(ABC_{ijk})^2}{ds}$$

$$- \frac{\sum\limits_{l}^{d}(BCD_{jkl})^2}{as} + \frac{(BC_{jk})^2}{ads}.$$

8.

Sources	(a) Factors A, C, and D Fixed; Factor B Random	(b) Factors B and D Fixed; Factors A and C Random
A	$A \times b$	$a \times c$
B	Wg	None
C	$b \times C$	$a \times c$
D	$b \times D$	None
$A \times B$	Wg	$a \times B \times c$
$A \times C$	$A \times b \times C$	Wg
$A \times D$	$A \times b \times D$	$a \times c \times D$
$B \times C$	Wg	$a \times B \times c$
$B \times D$	Wg	None
$C \times D$	$b \times C \times D$	$a \times c \times D$
$A \times B \times C$	Wg	Wg
$A \times B \times D$	Wg	$a \times B \times c \times D$
$A \times C \times D$	$A \times b \times C \times D$	Wg
$B \times C \times D$	Wg	$a \times B \times c \times D$
$A \times B \times C \times D$	Wg	Wg
$S/ABCD$ (Wg)	—	—

9.

Source	Calculations	SS	df	MS	F
A	$(13.79)(156.19 - 145.44)$ $= (13.79)(10.75) = 148.24$	148.24	3	49.41	5.62*
S/A	$2751 - 2276.23 = 474.77$	474.77	54	8.79	

* $p < .01$.

10. (a)

Source	Calculations	SS	df	MS	F
A	$(7.96)(1369.13 - 1339.56)$ $= (7.96)(29.57) = 235.38$	235.38	2	117.69	29.57*
B	$(7.96)(1356.36 - T')$ $= (7.96)(16.80) = 133.73$	133.73	2	66.86	16.80*
A × B	$(7.96)(1425.10 - A' - B' + T')$ $= (7.96)(39.17) = 311.79$	311.79	4	77.95	19.59*
S/AB	$15,834 - 15,511.62 = 322.38$	322.38	81	3.98	

* $p < .01$.

(b) Computational formula:

$$SS_{B \, at \, a_i} = \tilde{s}\left[\sum_j^b (\overline{AB}_{ij})^2 - \frac{(A_i')^2}{b} \right].$$

Source	Calculations	SS	df	MS	F
B at a_1	$(7.96)(282.50 - 278.98)$ $= (7.96)(3.52) = 28.02$	28.02	2	14.01	3.52*
B at a_2	$(7.96)(542.51 - 532.00)$ $= (7.96)(10.51) = 83.66$	83.66	2	41.83	10.51**
B at a_3	$(7.96)(600.09 - 558.15)$ $= (7.96)(41.94) = 333.84$	333.84	2	166.92	41.94**
S/AB			81	3.98	

* $p < .05$.
** $p < .01$.

11. (a) Basic experimental design:

(1) From the design explicated above, we can see that factor C is nested in the different combinations of the levels of factors A and B, i.e., C/AB.

(2)

Source	Error Term
A	$A \times b$
b	c/Ab
c/Ab	s/Abc
$A \times b$	c/Ab
s/Abc	—

(b) Basic experimental design:

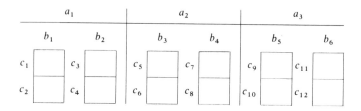

(1) Factor C continues to be nested as before (i.e., C/AB), while factor B is now nested in A (B/A). That is, the school systems receiving one book are different from the systems receiving the other two books.

(2)

Source	Error Term
A	b/A
b/A	c/Ab
c/Ab	s/Abc
s/Abc	—

(c) For both examples, factor B is now fixed. Thus,

Example (a)		Example (b)	
Source	Error Term	Source	Error Term
A	c/AB	A	c/AB
B	c/AB	B/A	c/AB
c/AB	s/ABc	c/AB	s/ABc
$A \times B$	c/AB	s/ABc	—
s/ABc	—		

12. In this analysis, we will treat the nested factor (Problems) two ways: (1) as a pooled source of variance and (2) as two separate sources, one at level a_1 and the other at level a_2. The latter would seem to be more appropriate since it is more informative to examine problems of the same type than to lose this information in pooling.

Source	Calculations	SS	df	MS	F
Task (A)	$1582.20 - 1560.60 =$ 21.60		1	21.60	4.24*
Feedback (B)	$1687.30 - [T] =$ 126.70		2	63.35	12.42**
$A \times B$	$1765.60 - [A] - [B] + [T] =$ 56.70		2	28.35	5.56**
Problems (C/A)	$2142.00 - [A] = (559.80)$		(8)	(69.98)	(13.72)**
C/A_1	$1226.17 - 974.70 =$ 251.47		4	62.87	12.33**
C/A_2	$915.83 - 607.50 =$ 308.33		4	77.08	15.11**
$B \times C/A$	$2356.00 - [AB] - [AC] + [A] = (30.60)$		(16)	(1.91)	(<1)
$B \times C/A_1$	$1427.50 - 1148.30 - 1226.17 + 974.70 =$ 27.73		8	3.47	<1
$B \times C/A_2$	$928.50 - 617.30 - 915.83 + 607.50 =$ 2.87		8	.36	<1
S/ABC	$2509 - [ABC] =$ 153.00		30	5.10	
Total	$[ABCS] - [T] =$ 948.40		59		

* $p < .05$.
** $p < .01$.

PART V

1.

Source	Calculations	SS	df	MS	F
A	$1208.62 - 1092.02 =$ 116.60		4	29.15	16.28*
S	$1118.20 - [T] =$ 26.18		7	3.74	
$A \times S$	$1285 - [A] - [S] + [T] =$ 50.20		28	1.79	
Total	$[AS] - [T] =$ 192.98		39		

* $p < .01$.

2. Applying the quadratic coefficients $(2, -1, -2, -1, 2)$ to the numbers in the AS matrix, we find

$$SS_{A_{\text{quadratic}}} = \frac{(-107)^2}{8(14)},$$

$$SS_{A_{\text{quadratic}} \times S} = \frac{(-8)^2 + (-19)^2 + \cdots + (-13)^2 + (-15)^2}{14} - \frac{(-107)^2}{8(14)}.$$

Source	SS	df	MS	F
$A_{quadratic}$	102.22	1	102.22	47.77*
$A_{quadratic} \times S$	14.99	7	2.14	

* $p < .01$.

A rough test for a curvilinear trend is afforded by comparing the mean for the condition in the middle of the stimulus dimension with the means for the conditions at the two ends. The coefficients for this comparison $(1, 0, -2, 0, 1)$ are applied in the usual fashion.

3.

$$F = \frac{(8-1)(12)^2}{8(76) - (12)^2} = \frac{1008}{464} = 2.17.$$

4.

Source	Calculations	SS	df	MS	F
A	$5450.10 - 5360.03 =$	90.07	2	45.04	4.21*
S	$5479.83 - [T] =$	119.80	4	29.95	
$A \times S$	$5655.50 - [A] - [S] + [T] =$	85.60	8	10.70	
B	$5367.53 - [T] =$	7.50	1	7.50	<1
$B \times S$	$5639.00 - [B] - [S] + [T] =$	151.67	4	37.92	
$A \times B$	$5462.60 - [A] - [B] + [T] =$	5.00	2	2.50	<1
$A \times B \times S$	$6009 - [AB] - [AS] - [BS]$ $+ [A] + [B] + [S] - [T] =$	189.33	8	23.67	
Total	$[ABS] - [T] =$	648.97	29		

* $p < .10$.

5.

Source	Calculations	SS	df	MS	F
A	$37,710.88 - 37,296.75 =$	414.13	2	207.06	6.17*
S/A	$38,013.00 - [A] =$	302.12	9	33.57	
B	$38,449.17 - [T] =$	1152.42	3	384.14	114.67**
$A \times B$	$38,993.50 - [A] - [B] + [T] =$	130.20	6	21.70	6.48**
$B \times S/A$	$39,386 - [AB] - [AS] + [A] =$	90.38	27	3.35	
Total	$[ABS] - [T] =$	2089.25	47		

* $p < .05$.
** $p < .01$.

6. (a)

Source	Calculations	SS	df	MS	F
B		(1152.42)	(3)		
Linear		1066.82	1	1066.82	233.44**
Quadratic		85.33	1	85.33	36.31**
Cubic		.27	1	.27	<1
A × B		(130.20)	(6)		
Linear	1164.68 − 1066.82 =	97.86	2	48.93	10.71**
Quadratic	109.88 − 85.33 =	24.55	2	12.28	5.23*
Cubic	8.08 − .27 =	7.81	2	3.90	1.25
B × S/A		(90.38)	(27)		
Linear	1205.80 − 1164.68 =	41.12	9	4.57	
Quadratic	131.00 − 109.88 =	21.12	9	2.35	
Cubic	36.20 − 8.08 =	28.12	9	3.12	

* $p < .05$.
** $p < .01$.

(b) For this analysis, we will compute separate error terms for each of the simple main effects.

Source	Calculations	SS	df	MS	F
A at b_1	4924.25 − 4920.75 =	3.50	2	1.75	<1
A at b_2	8874.00 − 8748.00 =	126.00	2	63.00	4.81*
A at b_3	12,056.25 − 11,844.08 =	212.17	2	106.08	12.44**
A at b_4	13,139.00 − 12,936.33 =	202.67	2	101.34	13.21**
S/A at b_1	5053 − 4924.25 =	128.75	9	14.31	
S/A at b_2	8992 − 8874.00 =	118.00	9	13.11	
S/A at b_3	12,133 − 12,056.25 =	76.75	9	8.53	
S/A at b_4	13,208 − 13,139.00 =	69.00	9	7.67	

* $p < .05$.
** $p < .01$.

We can apply two computational checks: (1) $\sum SS_{A \text{ at } b_j} = 544.34$ and $SS_{A \times B} + SS_A = 544.33$; and (2) $\sum SS_{S/A \text{ at } b_j} = 392.50$ and $SS_{B \times S/A} + SS_{S/A} = 392.50$.

7. From $df_{B_{\text{comp.}} \times S} = (df_{B_{\text{comp.}}})(df_S) = (b')(s - 1)$,

$$SS_{B_{\text{comp.}} \times S} = \frac{\sum\limits_{k}^{s} \left[\sum\limits_{j}^{b} (c_j)(BS_{jk}) \right]^2}{a \left[\sum (c_j)^2 \right]} - \frac{\left[\sum\limits_{j}^{b} (c_j)(B_j) \right]^2}{as \left[\sum (c_j)^2 \right]}.$$

(b) From $df_{A \times B_{comp.} \times S} = (df_A)(df_{B_{comp.}})(df_S) = (a - 1)(b')(s - 1)$,

$$SS_{A \times B_{comp.} \times S} = \frac{\sum_i^a \sum_k^s \left[\sum_j^b (c_j)(ABS_{ijk}) \right]^2}{\sum (c_j)^2} - \frac{\sum_i^a \left[\sum_j^b (c_j)(AB_{ij}) \right]^2}{s\left[\sum (c_j)^2 \right]}$$
$$- \frac{\sum_k^s \left[\sum_j^b (c_j)(BS_{jk}) \right]^2}{a\left[\sum (c_j)^2 \right]} + \frac{\left[\sum_j^b (c_j)(B_j) \right]^2}{as\left[\sum (c_j)^2 \right]}.$$

8.

Treatment Source	Error Term	Treatment Source	Error Term
NO REPEATED FACTORS		TWO REPEATED FACTORS	
A	S/A	$B \times C$	$B \times C \times S/A$
		$A \times B \times C$	$B \times C \times S/A$
ONE REPEATED FACTOR		$B \times D$	$B \times D \times S/A$
B	$B \times S/A$	$A \times B \times D$	$B \times D \times S/A$
$A \times B$	$B \times S/A$		
		$C \times D$	$C \times D \times S/A$
C	$C \times S/A$	$A \times C \times D$	$C \times D \times S/A$
$A \times C$	$C \times S/A$		
		THREE REPEATED FACTORS	
D	$D \times S/A$		
$A \times D$	$D \times S/A$	$B \times C \times D$ $B \times C \times D \times S/A$	
		$A \times B \times C \times D$ $B \times C \times D \times S/A$	

(Note: From this outline of the analysis, you should be able to write the df statements for each source of variance and to generate the corresponding computational formulas from these statements.)

9.

Source	Calculations	SS	df	MS	F
A	$2306.47 - 2305.63 =$	.84	1	.84	<1
B	$2306.07 - [T] =$	.44	3	.15	<1
$A \times B$	$2320.80 - [A] - [B] + [T] =$	13.89	3	4.63	<1
S/AB	$2424.80 - [AB] =$	104.00	16	6.50	
C	$2737.75 - [T] =$	432.12	4	108.03	109.12^*
$A \times C$	$2740.33 - [A] - [C] + [T] =$	1.74	4	.44	<1
$B \times C$	$2751.00 - [B] - [C] + [T] =$	12.81	12	1.07	1.08
$A \times B \times C$	$2784.67 - [AB] - [AC] - [BC]$				
	$+ [A] + [B] + [C] - [T] =$	17.20	12	1.43	1.44
$C \times S/AB$	$2952 - [ABC] - [ABS] + [AB] =$	63.33	64	.99	
Total	$[ABCS] - [T] =$	646.37	119		

$^* p < .01.$

10. (a)

Source	Calculations	SS	df	MS	F
A	$3017.01 - 3015.84 =$	1.17	1	1.17	<1
S/A	$3057.08 - [A] =$	40.07	10	4.01	
B	$3047.27 - [T] =$	31.43	2	15.72	17.09*
$A \times B$	$3064.88 - [A] - [B] + [T] =$	16.44	2	8.22	8.93*
$B \times S/A$	$3123.25 - [AB] - [AS] + [A] =$	18.30	20	.92	
C	$3260.36 - [T] =$	244.52	3	81.51	169.81*
$A \times C$	$3271.94 - [A] - [C] + [T] =$	10.41	3	3.47	7.23*
$C \times S/A$	$3326.33 - [AC] - [AS] + [A] =$	14.32	30	.48	
$B \times C$	$3292.75 - [B] - [C] + [T] =$	.96	6	.16	<1
$A \times B \times C$	$3321.17 - [AB] - [AC] - [BC]$				
	$+ [A] + [B] + [C] - [T] =$	.40	6	.07	<1
$B \times C \times S/A$	$3419 - [ABC] - [ABS] - [ACS]$				
	$+ [AB] + [AC] + [AS] - [A] =$	25.14	60	.42	
Total	$[ABCS] - [T] =$	403.16	143		

$* p < .01.$

(b) In this analysis, we will be working with the AC and ACS matrices. The computational formulas for the analysis are easily derived from the df statements. From

$$df_{A \times C_{comp.}} = (df_A)(df_{C_{comp.}}) = (a - 1)(c'),$$

$$SS_{A \times C_{linear}} = \frac{\sum\limits_{i}^{a}\left[\sum\limits_{k}^{c}(c_{1k})(AC_{ik})\right]^2}{bs\left[\sum(c_{1k})^2\right]} - \frac{\left[\sum\limits_{k}^{c}(c_{1k})(C_k)\right]^2}{abs\left[\sum(c_{1k})^2\right]}$$

$$= \frac{(247)^2 + (164)^2}{3(6)(20)} - \frac{(411)^2}{2(3)(6)(20)}.$$

From $df_{C_{comp.} \times S/A} = (df_{C_{comp.}})(df_S)(a) = (c')(s - 1)(a),$

$$SS_{C_{linear} \times S/A} = \frac{\sum\limits_{i}^{a}\sum\limits_{l}^{s}\left[\sum\limits_{k}^{c}(c_{1k})(ACS_{ikl})\right]^2}{b\left[\sum(c_{1k})^2\right]} - \frac{\sum\limits_{i}^{a}\left[\sum\limits_{k}^{c}(c_{1k})(AC_{ik})\right]^2}{bs\left[\sum(c_{1k})^2\right]}$$

$$= \frac{(45)^2 + (40)^2 + \cdots + (22)^2 + (21)^2}{3(20)} - \frac{(247)^2 + (164)^2}{3(6)(20)}.$$

Source	Calculations	SS	df	MS	F
$A \times C_{linear}$	$244.18 - 234.61 =$	9.57	1	9.57	24.54*
$C_{linear} \times S/A$	$248.08 - 244.18 =$	3.90	10	.39	

$* p < .01.$

(c) For this analysis, we can think of the data as coming from an $A \times (B \times S)$ design. The only modification we need is an adjustment of the denominator term to reflect the appropriate number of observations upon which each ABS_{ikl} and AB_{ij} sum is based. More specifically: from $df_{A \text{ at } b_j} = (df_A)(b_j) = (a - 1)(b_j)$,

$$SS_{A \text{ at } b_j} = \frac{\sum\limits_{i}^{a} (AB_{ij})^2}{cs} - \frac{(B_j)^2}{acs},$$

and from $df_{S/A \text{ at } b_j} = (df_S)(a)(b_j) = (s - 1)(a)(b_j)$,

$$SS_{S/A \text{ at } b_j} = \frac{\sum\limits_{i}^{a} \sum\limits_{l}^{s} (ABS_{ijl})^2}{c} - \frac{\sum\limits_{i}^{a} (AB_{ij})^2}{cs}.$$

Source	Calculations	SS	df	MS	F
A at b_1	$747.71 - 744.19 =$	3.52	1	3.52	1.76
A at b_2	$1083.00 - 1083.00 =$	0.00	1	0.00	<1
A at b_3	$1234.17 - 1220.08 =$	14.09	1	14.09	8.64*
S/A at b_1	$767.75 - 747.71 =$	20.04	10	2.00	
S/A at b_2	$1105.00 - 1083.00 =$	22.00	10	2.20	
S/A at b_3	$1250.50 - 1234.17 =$	16.33	10	1.63	

* $p < .025$.

There are two computational checks: (1) $\sum SS_{A \text{ at } b_j} = 17.61$ and $SS_{A \times B} + SS_A = 17.61$; and (2) $\sum SS_{S/A \text{ at } b_j} = 58.37$ and $SS_{B \times S/A} + SS_{S/A} = 58.37$.

PART VI

1. (a)

Source	Calculations	$SS_{adj.}$	df	$MS_{adj.}$	F
A	$112.15 - (112.98 - 19.48) =$	18.65	3	6.22	<1
S/A	$147.60 - 19.48 =$	128.12	15	8.54	

(b)

CONTROL VARIABLE

Source	Calculations	SS	df	MS	F
A	$363.60 - 336.20 =$	27.40	3	9.13	6.01*
S/A	$388 - [A_x] =$	24.40	16	1.52	
Total	$[AS_x] - [T_x] =$	51.80	19		

* $p < .01$.

Dependent Variable

Source	Calculations	SS	df	MS	F
A	1313.40 − 1201.25 = 112.15		3	37.38	4.05*
S/A	1461 − [A_y] = 147.60		16	9.22	
Total	[AS_y] − [T_y] = 259.75		19		

*$p < .05$.

The analysis of covariance actually *eliminated* differences revealed by the analysis of the uncorrected scores. This happened in part because of a sizable positive between-groups correlation. Considering the way in which the control scores were obtained—i.e., *after* the experiment—there is reason to believe that the differences between the groups on the control variable reflect the differential experimental treatments. Covariance is probably not appropriate in this situation.

2. (a)

Source	Calculations	$SS_{adj.}$	df	$MS_{adj.}$	F
A	225.33 − (13.92 − .05) = 211.46		2	105.73	20.37*
S/A	72.67 − .05 = 72.62		14	5.19	

* $p < .01$.

(b) It is obvious that little or no adjustment was applied to the within-groups error term. This fact clearly indicates that no precision was gained from the introduction of a control variable into the analysis. This lack of gain is reflected in the near-zero within-groups correlation between the control and dependent variables. That is,

$$r_{S/A} = \frac{-1.33}{\sqrt{(36.00)(72.67)}} = -.03.$$

3. (a) The computational formulas are found in Table D-1. Table D-2 gives an even more detailed specification of the calculations of the different sums of squares and products.

(b)

Source	Calculations	$SS_{adj.}$	df	$MS_{adj.}$	F
A	160.06 − (.65 − 21.66) = 181.07		2	90.54	30.48*
B	45.39 − (8.61 − 21.66) = 58.44		2	29.22	9.84*
A × B	124.44 − (6.44 − 21.66) = 139.66		4	34.92	11.76*
S/AB	99.00 − 21.66 = 77.34		26	2.97	

*$p < .01$.

TABLE D-1 *Analysis of Covariance: $A \times B$ Design*

Source	Adjusted Sum of Squares	df	F
A	$SS_{A(y)} - \left[\dfrac{(SP_A + SP_{S/AB})^2}{SS_{A(x)} + SS_{S/AB(x)}} - \dfrac{(SP_{S/AB})^2}{SS_{S/AB(x)}} \right]$	$a - 1$	$\dfrac{MS_{A(\text{adj.})}}{MS_{S/AB(\text{adj.})}}$
B	$SS_{B(y)} - \left[\dfrac{(SP_B + SP_{S/AB})^2}{SS_{B(x)} + SS_{S/AB(x)}} - \dfrac{(SP_{S/AB})^2}{SS_{S/AB(x)}} \right]$	$b - 1$	$\dfrac{MS_{B(\text{adj.})}}{MS_{S/AB(\text{adj.})}}$
$A \times B$	$SS_{(A \times B)(y)} - \left[\dfrac{(SP_{(A \times B)} + SP_{S/AB})^2}{SS_{(A \times B)(x)} + SS_{S/AB(x)}} - \dfrac{(SP_{S/AB})^2}{SS_{S/AB(x)}} \right]$	$(a - 1)(b - 1)$	$\dfrac{MS_{(A \times B)(\text{adj.})}}{MS_{S/AB(\text{adj.})}}$
S/AB	$SS_{S/AB(y)} - \dfrac{(SP_{S/AB})^2}{SS_{S/AB(x)}}$	$ab(s - 1) - 1$	

TABLE D-2 *Sums of Squares and Products: Two-Factor Analysis of Covariance*[a]

Source	Control Variable (x)	Cross-Products (xy)	Dependent Variable (y)
A	$\sum\dfrac{(A_x)^2}{bs} - \dfrac{(T_x)^2}{abs}$	$\sum\dfrac{(A_{i(x)})(A_{i(y)})}{bs} - \dfrac{(T_x)(T_y)}{abs}$	$\sum\dfrac{(A_y)^2}{bs} - \dfrac{(T_y)^2}{abs}$
B	$\sum\dfrac{(B_x)^2}{as} - [T_x]$	$\sum\dfrac{(B_{j(x)})(B_{j(y)})}{as} - [T_{xy}]$	$\sum\dfrac{(B_y)^2}{as} - [T_y]$
A × B	$\sum\dfrac{(AB_x)^2}{s} - [A_x] - [B_x] + [T_x]$	$\sum\dfrac{(AB_{ij(x)})(AB_{ij(y)})}{s} - [A_{xy}] - [B_{xy}] + [T_{xy}]$	$\sum\dfrac{(AB_y)^2}{s} - [A_y] - [B_y] + [T_y]$
S/AB	$\sum(ABS_x)^2 - [AB_x]$	$\sum(ABS_{ijk(x)})(ABS_{ijk(y)}) - [AB_{xy}]$	$\sum(ABS_y)^2 - [AB_y]$
Total	$[ABS_x] - [T_x]$	$[ABS_{xy}] - [T_{xy}]$	$[ABS_y] - [T_y]$

[a] Bracketed letters represent complete terms in the computational formulas; a particular term is identified by the letter(s) appearing in the numerator.

PART VII

1. If we let $\mu_1 = 10$, $\mu_2 = 10$, $\mu_3 = 14$, $\mu_4 = 16$, and $\mu_5 = 15$; $\mu = \sum \mu_i/a = 65/5 = 13$.
Then,

$$\sum (\alpha_i)^2 = (10 - 13)^2 + (10 - 13)^2 + (14 - 13)^2 + (16 - 13)^2 + (15 - 13)^2$$
$$= 32.$$

From Eq. (24-1),

$$\phi_A^2 = \frac{s'(32)/5}{15} = .43s' ; \phi_A = \sqrt{.43s'} = .66\sqrt{s'}.$$

If we try $s' = 7$, we find $\phi_A = (.66)(2.65) = 1.75$, $df_{denom.} = 5(7 - 1) = 30$, and power $= .83$. Any smaller sample size gives power $< .80$.

2. From Eq. (24-5),

$$\sum (\widehat{dev.})^2 = \frac{2 - 1}{16} (6.12 - 2.48) = .23 ;$$

and from Eq. (24-5a),

$$\hat{\phi}_A^2 = \frac{s'(.23)/2}{2.48} = .048s' ; \hat{\phi}_A = \sqrt{.048s'} = .22\sqrt{s'}.$$

If we try $s' = 110$, we find $\hat{\phi}_A = (.22)(10.49) = 2.31$, $df_{denom.} = 2(110 - 1) = 218$, and power $= .90$.

3. From Eq. (24-6),

$$\hat{\phi}_{A \times B}^2 = \frac{(4)(2)(17.50 - 12.25)/9}{12.25} = .38$$

or from Eq. (24-5),

$$\sum (\widehat{\alpha\beta_{ij}})^2 = \frac{4(2)}{5}(17.50 - 12.25) = 8.40,$$

and from Eq. (24-5a),

$$\hat{\phi}_{A \times B}^2 = \frac{5(8.40)/9}{12.25} = .38.$$

From Chart 8 in Table C-6, $df_{denom.} = 60$, $\alpha = .05$, $\hat{\phi}_{A \times B} = .62$; power is off the chart (less than .50).

4. (a) $\hat{\sigma}_A^2 = \frac{2(105.00 - 14.17)}{3(5)} = 12.11$, $\hat{\sigma}_{S/A}^2 = 14.17$, and

$$\hat{\omega}_A^2 = \frac{12.11}{12.11 + 14.17} = .46.$$

(b) From Eq. (25-6a),

$$\hat{\omega}_A^2 = \frac{210.00 - (2)(14.17)}{380.00 + 14.17} = .46,$$

and from Eq. (25-6b),

$$\hat{\omega}_A^2 = \frac{2(7.41 - 1)}{2(7.41 - 1) + 3(5)} = .46.$$

5. $\hat{\sigma}_A^2 = \dfrac{3(7.41 - 2.12)}{4(3)(3)} = .44, \quad \hat{\sigma}_B^2 = \dfrac{2(34.34 - 2.12)}{4(3)(3)} = 1.79,$

$$\hat{\sigma}_{A \times B}^2 = \frac{6(5.52 - 2.12)}{4(3)(3)} = .57, \quad \text{and} \quad \hat{\sigma}_{S/AB}^2 = 2.12;$$

$$\hat{\omega}_A^2 = \frac{.44}{.44 + 2.12} = .17, \quad \hat{\omega}_B^2 = \frac{1.79}{1.79 + 2.12} = .46,$$

$$\hat{\omega}_{A \times B}^2 = \frac{.57}{.57 + 2.12} = .21.$$

If you used Eq. (25-8), the three values would be .09, .36, and .12, respectively.

APPENDIX B

1. (a)

Source	Calculations	SS	df	MS	F
A	5194.05 − 4878.02 =	316.03	2	158.02	25.65*
S/A	5545 − [A] =	350.95	57	6.16	
Total	[AS] − [T] =	666.98	59		

* $p < .01$.

(b)

	a_1	a_2	a_3		
A_i:	241	170	130	$\sum (c_i)(A_i)$	$\sum (c_i)^2$
c_{1i}:	−7.67	−3.67	11.33	−999.47	200.67
c_{2i}:	28.43	−35.97	7.53	1715.63	2158.81

$$SS_{A_{\text{linear}}} = \frac{(-999.47)^2}{20(200.67)} \quad \text{and} \quad SS_{A_{\text{quadratic}}} = \frac{(1715.63)^2}{20(2158.81)}$$

Source	SS	df	MS	F
A	(316.03)	(2)	•	
Linear	248.90	1	248.90	40.41*
Quadratic	68.17	1	68.17	11.07*
S/A		57	6.16	

* $p < .01$.

(Note: $\sum SS_{A_{\text{comp}}} = 317.07$ and $SS_A = 316.03$; the discrepancy is the rounding error introduced in the calculation of the coefficients.)

REFERENCES

ANDERSON, T. W. *Introduction to multivariate statistical analysis.* New York: Wiley, 1958.

BAKAN, D. The test of significance in psychological research. *Psychological Bulletin*, 1966, **66**, 423–437.

BAKER, B. O., HARDYCK, C. D., & PETRINOVICH, L. F. Weak measurements vs. strong statistics: an empirical critique of S. S. Stevens' proscriptions on statistics. *Educational and Psychological Measurement*, 1966, **26**, 291–309.

BONEAU, C. A. The effects of violations of assumptions underlying the *t* test. *Psychological Bulletin*, 1960, **57**, 49–64.

BOX, G. E. P. Non-normality and tests on variance. *Biometrika*, 1953, **40**, 318–335.

BOX, G. E. P. Some theorems on quadratic forms applied in the study of analysis of variance problems. I. Effect of inequality of variance in the one-way classification. *Annals of Mathematical Statistics*, 1954, **25**, 290–302.

BRADLEY, J. V. *Distribution-free statistical tests.* Englewood Cliffs, N.J.: Prentice-Hall, 1968.

CAMPBELL, D. T., & STANLEY, J. C. Experimental and quasi-experimental designs for research on teaching. In N. L. Gage (Ed.), *Handbook of research on teaching*. Skokie, Ill.: Rand McNally, 1963. Pp. 171–246.

CAMPBELL, D. T., & STANLEY, J. C. *Experimental and quasi-experimental designs for research*. Skokie, Ill.: Rand McNally, 1966.

COCHRAN, W. G., & COX, G. M. *Experimental designs*. (2nd ed.) New York: Wiley, 1957.

COHEN, J. *Statistical power analysis for the behavioral sciences*. New York: Academic Press, 1969.

COLLIER, R. O., JR., BAKER, F. B., MANDEVILLE, G. K., & HAYES, T. F. Estimates of test size for several test procedures based on conventional variance ratios in the repeated measures design. *Psychometrika*, 1967, **32**, 339–353.

CORNFIELD, J., & TUKEY, J. W. Average values of mean squares in factorials. *Annals of Mathematical Statistics*, 1956, **27**, 907–949.

COTTON, J. W., JENSEN, G. D., & LEWIS, D. J. Spontaneous recovery interval as a factor in reacquisition of T maze behavior. *Journal of Experimental Psychology*, 1962, **63**, 555–562.

DIXON, W. J., & MASSEY, F. J., JR. *Introduction to statistical analysis*. (2nd ed.) New York: McGraw-Hill, 1957.

DUNCAN, D. B. Multiple range and multiple *F* tests. *Biometrics*, 1955, **11**, 1–42.

DUNN, O. J. Multiple comparisons among means. *Journal of the American Statistical Association*, 1961, **56**, 52–64.

DUNNETT, C. W. A multiple comparison procedure for comparing several treatments with a control. *Journal of the American Statistical Association*, 1955, **50**, 1096–1121.

DUNNETT, C. W. New tables for multiple comparisons with a control. *Biometrics*, 1964, **20**, 482–491.

EDGINGTON, E. S. *Statistical inference: the distribution-free approach*. New York: McGraw-Hill, 1969.

EDWARDS, A. L. *Experimental design in psychological research*. (3rd ed.) New York: Holt, Rinehart and Winston, 1968.

FELDT, L. S. A comparison of the precision of three experimental designs employing a concomitant variable. *Psychometrika*, 1958, **23**, 335–353.

FELDT, L. S., & MAHMOUD, M. W. Power function charts for specification of sample size in analysis of variance. *Psychometrika*, 1958, **23**, 201–210.

FISHER, R. A. *The design of experiments*. (6th ed.) Edinburgh: Oliver and Boyd, 1951.

FISHER, R. A., & YATES, F. *Statistical tables for biological, agricultural and medical research*. (4th ed.) Edinburgh: Oliver and Boyd, 1953.

FLEISS, J. L. Estimating the magnitude of experimental effects. *Psychological Bulletin*, 1969, **72**, 273–276.

GAITO, J. Unequal intervals and unequal *n* in trend analyses. *Psychological Bulletin*, 1965, **63**, 125–127.

GARDNER, R. A. On box score methodology as illustrated by three reviews of overtraining reversal effects. *Psychological Bulletin*, 1966, **66**, 416–418.

GLASS, G. V. Testing homogeneity of variances. *American Educational Research Journal*, 1966, **3**, 187–190.

GLASS, G. V., & STANLEY, J. C. *Statistical methods in education and psychology*. Englewood Cliffs, N.J.: Prentice-Hall, 1970.

GOLLIN, E. S. A developmental approach to learning and cognition. In L. P. Lipsitt & C. C. Spiker (Eds.), *Advances in child development and behavior*, vol. II. New York: Academic Press, 1965. Pp. 159–186.

GRANT, D. A. Analysis-of-variance tests in the analysis and comparison of curves. *Psychological Bulletin*, 1956, **53**, 141–154.

GRANT, D. A. Testing the null hypothesis and the strategy and tactics of investigating theoretical models. *Psychological Review*, 1962, **69**, 54–61.

GREENHOUSE, S. W., & GEISSER, S. On methods in the analysis of profile data. *Psychometrika*, 1959, **24**, 95–112.

GUENTHER, W. C. *Analysis of variance*. Englewood Cliffs, N.J.: Prentice-Hall, 1964.

HARTER, H. L. Error rates and sample sizes for range tests in multiple comparisons. *Biometrics*, 1957, **13**, 511–536.

HAYS, W. L. *Statistics for psychologists*. New York: Holt, Rinehart and Winston, 1963.

HOPKINS, K. D., & CHADBOURN, R. A. A schema for proper utilization of multiple comparisons in research and a case study. *American Educational Research Journal*, 1967, **4**, 407–412.

KEPPEL, G., BONGE, D., STRAND, B. Z., & PARKER, J. Direct and indirect interference in the recall of paired associates. *Journal of Experimental Psychology*, 1971, **88**, 414–422.

KEPPEL, G., POSTMAN, L., & ZAVORTINK, B. Studies of learning to learn: VIII. The influence of massive amounts of training upon the learning and retention of paired-associate lists. *Journal of Verbal Learning and Verbal Behavior*, 1968, **7**, 790–796.

KIRK, R. E. *Experimental design: procedures for the behavioral sciences*. Monterey, Calif.: Brooks/Cole, 1968.

LASHLEY, K. S. *Brain mechanisms and intelligence: a quantitative study of injuries to the brain*. Chicago: University of Chicago Press, 1929.

LEVENE, H. Robust tests for equality of variances. In I. Olkins (Ed.), *Contributions to probability and statistics*. Stanford, Calif.: Stanford University Press, 1960. Pp. 278–292.

LEVIN, J. R. Misinterpreting the significance of "explained variation." *American Psychologist*, 1967, **22**, 675–676.

LEWIS, D. *Quantitative methods in psychology*. New York: McGraw-Hill, 1960.

LINDQUIST, E. F. *Design and analysis of experiments in psychology and education*. Boston: Houghton Mifflin, 1953.

MARASCUILO, L. A. *Statistical methods for behavioral science research*. New York: McGraw-Hill, 1971.

MARASCUILO, L. A., & LEVIN, J. R. Appropriate post hoc comparisons for interaction and nested hypotheses in analysis of variance designs: the elimination of Type IV errors. *American Educational Research Journal*, 1970, **7**, 397–421.

Moses, L. E., & Oakford, R. V. *Tables of random permutations.* Stanford, Calif.: Stanford University Press, 1963.

Myers, J. L. *Fundamentals of experimental design.* Boston: Allyn and Bacon, 1966.

Norton, D. W. An empirical investigation of some effects of non-normality and heterogeneity of the *F*-distribution. Unpublished doctoral dissertation, State University of Iowa, 1952.

Pearson, E. S., & Hartley, H. O. Charts of the power function for analysis of variance tests, derived from the non-central *F* distribution. *Biometrika*, 1951, **38**, 112–130.

Pearson, E. S., & Hartley, H. O. (Eds.) *Biometrika tables for statisticians.* New York: Cambridge University Press, 1958.

Petrinovich, L. F., & Hardyck, C. D. Error rates for multiple comparison methods: some evidence concerning the frequency of erroneous conclusions. *Psychological Bulletin*, 1969, **71**, 43–54.

Postman, L. Studies of learning to learn: II. Changes in transfer as a function of practice. *Journal of Verbal Learning and Verbal Behavior*, 1964, **3**, 437–447.

Postman, L., & Keppel, G. Retroactive inhibition in free recall. *Journal of Experimental Psychology*, 1967, **74**, 203–211.

RAND Corporation. *A million random digits with 100,000 normal deviates.* New York: Free Press, 1955.

Rosenthal, R., & Gaito, J. The interpretation of levels of significance by psychological researchers. *Journal of Psychology*, 1963, **55**, 33–38.

Scheffé, H. A method for judging all possible contrasts in the analysis of variance. *Biometrika*, 1953, **40**, 87–104.

Scheffé, H. *The analysis of variance.* New York: Wiley, 1959.

Sidowski, J. B. (Ed.) *Experimental methods and instrumentation in psychology.* New York: McGraw-Hill, 1966.

Siegel, S. *Nonparametric statistics for the behavioral sciences.* New York: McGraw-Hill, 1956.

Slobin, D. I. Grammatical transformations and sentence comprehension in childhood and adulthood. *Journal of Verbal Learning and Verbal Behavior*, 1966, **5**, 219–227.

Snedecor, G. W. *Statistical methods.* (5th ed.) Ames, Iowa: Iowa State University Press, 1956.

Tukey, J. W. The problem of multiple comparisons. Unpublished manuscript, Princeton University, 1953.

Underwood, B. J. *Psychological research.* New York: Appleton-Century-Crofts, 1957.

Underwood, B. J. Ten years of massed practice on distributed practice. *Psychological Review*, 1961, **68**, 229–247.

Underwood, B. J., & Richardson, J. The influence of meaningfulness, intralist similarity, and serial position on retention. *Journal of Experimental Psychology*, 1956, **52**, 119–126.

Vaughan, G. M., & Corballis, M. C. Beyond tests of significance: estimating strength of effects in selected ANOVA designs. *Psychological Bulletin*, 1969, **72**, 204–213.

Wagenaar, W. A. Note on the construction of digram-balanced Latin squares. *Psychological Bulletin*, 1969, **72**, 384–386.

WALKER, H. M., & LEV, J. *Statistical inference.* New York: Holt, 1953.

WALLACE, W. P., & UNDERWOOD, B. J. Implicit responses and the role of intralist similarity in verbal learning by normal and retarded subjects. *Journal of Educational Psychology,* 1964, **55**, 362–370.

WEBB, E. J., CAMPBELL, D. T., SCHWARTZ, R. D., & SECHREST, L. *Unobtrusive measures: nonreactive research in the social sciences.* Chicago: Rand McNally, 1966.

WINER, B. J. *Statistical principles in experimental design.* New York: McGraw-Hill, 1962.

WINER, B. J. *Statistical principles in experimental design.* (2nd ed.) New York: McGraw-Hill, 1971.

YOUSEF, Z. I. Association and integration in serial learning. *American Journal of Psychology,* 1967, **80**, 355–362.

AUTHOR INDEX

650

SUBJECT INDEX